Engraved by T. B. Welch from a Painting by E. G. Leutze.

HUGH LAWSON WHITE

A MEMOIR OF HUGH LAWSON WHITE,

JUDGE OF THE SUPREME COURT OF TENNESSEE, MEMBER OF THE SENATE OF THE UNITED STATES, ETC., ETC.

WITH SELECTIONS FROM HIS

SPEECHES AND CORRESPONDENCE.

EDITED BY

NANCY N. SCOTT,

ONE OF HIS DESCENDANTS.

PHILADELPHIA

J. B. LIPPINCOTT, & Co.

1856.

W. H. Tinson, Stereotyper.
24 Beekman St., New York.

TO

MRS. MARY M. OVERTON,

THE ONLY SURVIVING SISTER OF HUGH LAWSON WHITE "THE JUST,"

This Memorial

OF HIS PURE LIFE AND WORTHY DEEDS,

THE IRREPRESSIBLE OUTPOURING OF A YEARNING SPIRIT, WRITTEN

WITH A HOPE THAT IT MAY CONTRIBUTE TO

A RIGHT ESTIMATE OF THE MAN,

BUT WITH THE CONVICTION THAT A MUCH MORE PERFECT AND LOFTY TRIBUTE IS JUSTLY HIS DUE,

IS RESPECTFULLY AND LOVINGLY DEDICATED BY

THE WRITER.

PREFACE.

This book has many imperfections. It is not compiled by an experienced writer, nor has it been prepared with the advantages of position or reputation. It is simply a tribute to the memory of one beloved and departed; the offering of that almost idolatry which is found only in the breasts of those few who by nature are nearest and dearest to man. Only the merits of earnestness and devotion can therefore be claimed for it.

The writer has endeavored to retire from view; to accomplish the present purpose in the most unobtrusive manner, by a narrative brief and plain, interspersed with such letters, speeches, and other documents, as may best illustrate the relations of Judge White to the great men and measures of the times, and the high and honorable position—honorable to himself, his state, and his country—which he held in the hearts and councils of his countrymen.

CONTENTS.

CHAPTER I.

PAGE

Ancestry—Gen. James White—Mary Lawson his Wife, ... 1

CHAPTER II.

Childhood—Youth—Studies—Expedition against the Indians—Private Secretaryship, ... 8

CHAPTER III.

Lawyer and Judge—Other Public Appointments, ... 15

CHAPTER IV.

State Legislator—Controversy with Mr. Grundy—Duelling, . . . 19

CHAPTER V.

Wilderness Journey to Gen. Jackson, ... 24

CHAPTER VI.

A Financier—Presidency of Bank of Tennessee, ... 28

CHAPTER VII.

Commissioner under Treaty with Spain—Second Commissionership, . . . 33

CHAPTER VIII.

Senate—Panama Mission—Federal Judiciary Apportionment, . . . 36

CHAPTER IX.

Senate—Internal Improvements—United States Bank, ... 70

CHAPTER X.

Senate—Indian Tribes—"Force Bill"—Executive Patronage—Expunging Resolutions, ... 153

CHAPTER XI.

PAGE

Senate—Abolition—Public Land Distribution—Sub-Treasury Bill—Appearance—Business habits—Surname, ... 197

CHAPTER XII.

First Political Position—Subsequent Change—Letter from Mr. Polk—Public Confidence in Judge White—His Singular Position, . . . 245

CHAPTER XIII.

Relations to Messrs. Grundy, Polk, Johnson, and Catron—Correspondence with Polk and Johnson—Judge White and the Presidency, . . . 253

CHAPTER XIV.

His relations to Gen. Jackson, ... 265

CHAPTER XV.

Canvass with Mr. Van Buren—Letter from Mr. Clay, ... 327

CHAPTER XVI.

Retirement from Public Life—Legislative Instructions—Resignation of Senatorship, ... 369

CHAPTER XVII.

Dinner at Washington—Speeches of Messrs. Preston, White, Corwin, Evans, Habersham, and Biddle, ... 395

CHAPTER XVIII.

Journey Home—Flattering Reception, ... 409

CHAPTER XIX.

His Family—Afflictions—Letter to Dr. Coffin, ... 413

CHAPTER XX.

His Death—Public Meetings—Proceedings of the Bar of Tennessee, . 420

Conclusion, ... 437
Appendix, ... 449

MEMOIR

OF

HUGH LAWSON WHITE

CHAPTER I.

ANCESTRY.

One mile above Knoxville, on the banks of the Holston River there stood, until within the last two years, a house worthy of remembrance as the home of two eminent Tennesseans; Hugh Lawson White, the subject of this memoir, and his father, General James White. The daguerreotype of the old building is before me. All over the great West there are thousands like it—the shelters, palaces, and castles of the hardy pioneer; his first forest home, the scene and centre of freedom, energy, courage, privation, truly and peculiarly American; the altar of his first triumphs over the subdued wilderness; often the humble birth-place of talent and genius, and of ambition high, noble, swift, and strong, such as rarely or never before sprung into existence.

A front view of the old edifice displays two square sections, "pens," or separate apartments, of unequal size, each a story and-a-half high, built of logs coarsely hewn, the interstices of which are stuffed with clay, and with an outer covering of boards. Between these two rooms stands a heavy stone chimney, furnishing a fire-place in each. A rude piazza extends across the whole front, its roof some distance below the eaves of the house, and supported by six slender sawed posts. The whole stands upon wooden blocks or underpinning; one small window is visible, while a simple step-ladder in one corner of the piazza is the stairway to the half story above.

In this house lived the father of Hugh Lawson White, and here he brought up his family, during that trying period when East Tennessee was a wilderness of wild beasts and fiercer savages. General James White was, in many respects, a remarkable man. He was of Irish descent, and during his earlier years was an inhabitant and citizen of North Carolina, where he married, and where his son Hugh was born. He served his country faithfully in the Revolutionary war; afterwards removed with his family to Fort Chiswell, in Virginia, and, finally, in 1781, emigrated to Knox county, Tennessee, where he erected for himself the humble home just described, on the banks of the beautiful Holston. For himself—but also for a home and resting-place for every weary wanderer. From his hospitable door none were ever sent empty away; and the more needy the applicant, the more certain was he of enjoying a full measure of hospitality.

Here his characteristic decision, energy, and philanthropy made him a leader among the few but determined spirits with whom his lot was cast. The privations and dangers to which all new settlers are exposed, seemed only to nerve him to greater exertions. The wild and boundless forests, their inhabitants, whether savage beasts of prey, or yet more savage red men, their enmities, their snares, their secret and open attacks, all failed to intimidate him. With his fellow-emigrants, he determined that the fertile valleys and rugged hills, the blue mountains and sparkling streams of East Tennessee should become the paradise of the white man.

But enlarged and comprehensive as were his views and plans, and brilliant as were his anticipations, yet when in 1792, he founded the good town of Knoxville, he certainly could not have foreseen that within fifty years there would stand in the place of the gloomy forest, a large and populous city, with its many spires pointing to heaven, much less the triumphs of modern science. Little did he dream of the gallant steamers that were to plough the clear blue waters where then was seen only the Indian's bark canoe, or the rude raft of the trader. Little did he dream of the iron horse, rushing with wind-like speed along his fiery way, through the valleys and over the hills. Nor could he even anticipate that almost within the half century there would be erected, not a hundred yards from the site of his own humble cabin, a manufactory of the very window-glass which he considered not only a useless superfluity, but a harmful luxury.

During his forty years' residence in Tennessee, Gen. White occupied almost every post of distinction in the gift of the people. He was a member of the convention chosen in 1785, for ratifying or altering the proposed Constitution of the State of Franklin; and preserved the independence and integrity of his character through the stormy scenes of its sessions. He was elected to the first Territorial Assembly at Knoxville, in 1794; and, while serving in that body, introduced a bill creating a literary institution; which measure was the origin of Greenville College. Statesmen, judges, lawyers, clergymen, men eminent in every variety of public station in Tennessee, date the beginning of their career in learning from the day when, often as rude, awkward, penniless boys, they first turned their hesitating steps toward the modest tower and white spire of that institution, which gleamed so long with the light of science and religion over that beautiful landscape. Its memory now alone remains, inseparably blended, however, with that of the good men who gave it a name and power in the land.

General White was also a member of the convention which framed the Constitution of the State of Tennessee—a legislative body whose disinterestedness is without parallel in our national history. By act of Assembly, each member was entitled to two dollars and a half *per diem* for services, and as much for every thirty miles of travel in going and coming. The convention first reduced this compensation nearly fifty *per cent.*, and then, to show their disregard for mere pecuniary reward, voted unanimously to receive nothing.

He was also, at a subsequent period, a member and speaker of the State Senate. In 1812, although now an old man, he again proffered his services to his country, in order to maintain the independence which in his youth he had assisted to establish. He was chosen Brigadier-General by the militia of Tennessee, and distinguished himself in the Creek War.

General White was admirably fitted by physical and mental constitution, for the times and circumstances in which he was placed. Strong, hardy and active in person, intrepid, cool and hopeful, he was ever ready to encounter any hardship or to brave any peril. On the 26th of June, 1791, Zeigler's Station, near Bledsoe's Lick, the rude defence for several families, was attacked by a large party of Creek Indians and burnt. Zeigler himself, who was intoxicated, and could not make his escape, was consumed in the flames; his three little daughters, together with Mrs. Wilson, General White's half-sister, were taken prisoners, and were afterwards ransomed by him. But his niece, Miss Wilson, only nine years old, was hurried away by the savages, although twice redeemed from them. General White determined to make a third effort to liberate her; and accordingly made the long journey alone on horseback, reached the Indian encampment in safety, a third time paid ransom for his niece, and feeling assured that all was now satisfactorily arranged, set out on his return home; his little charge, in the primitive style of those days, seated on his horse behind him. But his self-gratulation was short. He was soon overtaken by a friendly Indian, who told him that the treacherous Creeks, already repenting their bargain, had determined to way-lay and kill him; and offered to guide him by a different route from that first contemplated. General White gratefully accepted his assistance, and was soon beyond the reach of his enemies; while his savage ally returned to his companions, who, still in ambush, impatiently awaited the approach of their victims. When assured of their escape, they gave way to rage and disappointment; and were only appeased by the adroitness of the fellow, who told them that the General was a good man, and therefore the Great Spirit had caused him and his horse to pass invisible.

At another time, on his noble grey, rifle in hand, he leaped, unconscious of danger, directly over an Indian who was concealed behind a fallen tree with the express design of killing him. Apparently it was only Providential interposition that saved him.

General White's bravery and military skill were fully tested during the hostilities of 1793, with the Creek and Cherokee Indians; and particularly, while he was colonel of militia in the "Hamilton District," composed of Jefferson and Knox counties, by the coolness and tact displayed in the arrangements made by him to oppose an Indian invasion. This attack was contemplated by a force of savages nearly fifteen hundred in number, three-fourths Creeks, who intended to invade the settlements on the Holston, and to destroy Knoxville. The excuse for this attack, on the part of the savages was the cruelty practised by Major Beard on Hanging Maw, a Cherokee, and the murder of his wife, and of several other Cherokees. In the absence of Gov. Blount, Beard had been despatched by Secretary Smith, with fifty-six men, in pursuit of a party of Indians who had murdered a white family within sixteen miles of Knoxville; with instructions not to cross the Tennessee river, nor to invade the Indian settlements. He, however, violated these orders, and a failure by a court-martial to inflict punishment for this violation, and thereby to satisfy the revengeful spirit of the red men, was the ostensible reason for the meditated invasion. The Spaniards having become allies of the hostile Creeks and Cherokees, had furnished them with ammunition for the occasion. As continual ravages by the Indians had long demanded active measures for the defence of the frontier, which the General Government, despite many and increasing complaints, neglected to take, the whites now at last determined to defend themselves against the constant inroads of the treacherous foe. The dauntless heroism exhibited subsequently, as well as upon the particular occasion now mentioned, is commemorated in an address delivered by Rev. Thos. W. Humes, on the fiftieth anniversary of the settlement of Knoxville.

"Their entire number," he says, speaking of the Indian forces, "has been variously estimated from nine to fifteen hundred, but was most probably about the latter. Knoxville, the object of plunder and ruin by this formidable band, and which the news of its coming had reached, could at that time muster but forty fighting men; but these forty were no cravens, to fly at the approach of danger, even though it presented itself in the terrible shape in which it then menaced them. Here were their homes, their families, their all; and with an alacrity and zeal worthy of the crisis, they prepared to defend their firesides. A knowledge of Indian cunning, with other reasons, induced them to conclude that the approach of the savages to the town would not be made by the main western road, but in a more northern and circuitous direction; and they determined to meet them on the ridge, over which the road to Clinton now passes, about a mile and a half from town, and there, by a skilful arrangement of their little company, attack their line of march, and, if possible, alarm and intimidate them. Leaving the two oldest of their number to mould bullets in the block-house, which stood on the spot now occupied by the Mansion House, and which contained three hundred guns belonging to the United States, the other thirty-eight proceeded, under the command of Col. James White, to station themselves on the north side of the ridge we have mentioned, with an interval of twenty feet between each man. Orders were given to reserve their fire until the Indians were brought within the range of every gun, when at a given signal, they were to pour in upon them a well-directed volley, and, before the savages could recover from their surprise, secure their own retreat to the block-house, and there, with their wives, mothers, and children around them, sell their lives at a fearful price, or scatter from the port-holes a shower of leaden hail among the besiegers that would drive them from their banquet of blood." Fortunately, neither of these contingencies awaited them. The Indians were so delayed by their own dissensions, that they were unable to reach Knoxville before daylight, and, therefore, abandoned the attack. This fact, however, detracts nothing from the cool and dauntless courage, and skilful and deliberate arrangements with which the citizens prepared for the attack. The Rev. Mr. Foster, whose quaint pen has recorded the event, has declared, that "an incident fraught with so much magnanimity in the early fortunes of Knoxville, should not be blotted from the records of her fame. It is an incident on which the memory of her sons will linger without tiring, when the din of party shall be hushed, and its strife forgotten. Those men of former days were made of sterner stuff than to shrink from danger at the call of duty. And it will be left to a future historian to do justice to that little band of thirty-eight citizens, who flinched not from the deliberate exposure of their persons in the open field, within the calculated gun-shot of fifteen hundred of the fleetest running and boldest savages."

General White endeared himself to all about him by the noble charity which he showered with bounteous hand upon the poor and needy; a charity of which many instances are yet remembered. In that day grist-mills were few and far between. The General owned two; and when grain was scarce throughout the country, he often refused to sell to purchasers, that he might give to those too poor to buy. More than once he loaned money without expectation of being repaid. When warned by his son, on one such occasion, that he might lose the amount thus advanced, he answered, "That is the very reason that I let him have it. If he were rich, he would need neither money nor friends. It is for the very reason that he is poor that no one will help him." The practical Christianity of this reply, and of such conduct, might well be adopted as a rule of action in our own times.

While expressing his pleasure at the rising prospects of the village he had founded, now the city of Knoxville, and in general at the happiness which he had been able to bestow upon others, he was told by his daughter that it might be well for him to remember the old proverb, that "Charity begins at home;" and that he would have nothing left to give his children. "My children," he answered, "are independent. I love to aid those who really need assistance." Such sentiments are frequently enunciated; but we rarely find them carried out in action so literally as they were by General White.

He was by religious profession a Presbyterian; and a true and devout Christian. His family altar was faithfully served. It was one of his peculiarities that all the children were required to sing. On one occasion he noticed that a grandson who was present failed to observe this rule. "Why don't you sing, James?" said the old gentleman. "I can't, sir," was the reply. "Well, try;" insisted his grandfather. James *did* try, but the result was a succession of sounds so hideous, that he was ever after excused from participating in that portion of the service.

It would not be proper to close this brief sketch without some notice of Mary Lawson, General White's noble and devoted wife. She was slight and delicate in figure, but firm and decided in character. Like her husband, she was a devout and consistent Christian, and a steady Presbyterian; and possessed of more than ordinary intellectual powers. She had courage equal to any endurance, and proved indeed a helpmeet for her husband in the many severe vicissitudes of their experience. Often, when the Indians were prowling in the vicinity, and her husband was absent, she stood sentinel over her own home, rifle in hand. Often she spent whole nights in moulding bullets; and she was habituated to similar hardships.

General White was married in 1770. His wife died before him, and he soon followed. They are united in a world far different from this, but for which, the trials of this were a fitting preparation.

CHAPTER II.

CHILDHOOD—YOUTH—STUDIES.

Hugh Lawson White, eldest son and second child of Gen. James White and Mary Lawson his wife, was born in Iredell county, North Carolina, October 30th, 1773. At the age of eight, he emigrated with his parents to Tennessee. From a combination of circumstances, these two States were more intimately blended and incorporated than any other two in the Union. At this period, Congress had not accepted the act of the Legislature of North Carolina, ceding to the United States her Western Territory, to assist in liquidating the heavy national debt incurred in the achievement of National Independence; and the interests and feelings of the inhabitants of the two commonwealths consequently yet remained the same. North Carolina, however, failed to make adequate provision for the defence of the frontier and the protection of the Western settlers, and they were accordingly obliged to organize themselves and devise means of securing the safety of themselves and families.

In the seasons of loneliness and peril incident to a life in the almost unbroken wilderness, while their father was absent on military duty, Hugh and his brothers were the only sentinels to watch, and to warn their noble mother when the savages approached their dwelling for plunder. And well and faithfully was the task performed. The family were often obliged to take refuge in the fort, upon which occasions Hugh always acted in the capacity of guide. This sometimes had to be done when the night was so dark that the person of the young leader was wholly invisible. At such times he was accustomed to mount a white horse and go before them, that by distinguishing the color of the animal they might be able to follow to a place of comparative safety. After the treaty of 1791, while the Indians still continued their depredations, stealing horses and cattle, and murdering the helpless victims that fell into their power, travellers frequently turned aside from the fatigues and dangers of their journey to enjoy the hospitalities of General White's house. Their horses, which were belled and turned loose to graze, sometimes wandered to a distance; when their owners often hired young Hugh and his brothers to seek them. In doing this he ran great risks; and in such youthful enterprises and exposures he learned and proved, even in early boyhood, the dauntless courage which so strongly characterized him in after life.

Of the luxuries of civilization the family of General White, as well as their neighbors, were wholly deprived. Added to the other discomforts of their situation was the difficulty of obtaining bread; there being at that time but a single "tub-mill" in the neighborhood. It was Hugh's business to act in the capacity of mill-boy, which he regularly did, despite the constant danger from lurking savages. And after his return home, he often found way-faring guests enough to dispose of all his meal; whereupon, he and the rest of the family would make their repast of pounded hominy and milk.

It will easily be seen that the circumstances of a youth passed amid such scenes must have precluded young White from the enjoyment even of such opportunities of study as are now offered to all. In the wild regions where he lived, refined and extensive scholarship was hardly known; and existed, if at all, in the persons of some few whose acquirements were elsewhere made. He attended such schools as the country afforded, during the winter, laboring industriously upon his father's farm through the remainder of the year. In this manner he might acquire a knowledge of those studies which were necessary to qualify him for the competent discharge of the plainest practical duties of life, but nothing more. And if afterwards he rose to distinction, his success in so doing is one more example of the success of noble ambition, and honorable and unfaltering exertions victorious over surroundings the most unfavorable and disheartening. Though hundreds of miles from any college, he applied himself, at the age of fifteen, to the study of the ancient languages, under the tuition of Rev. Samuel Carrick, with some assistance from Mr. (afterwards Judge) Roane, both gentlemen and scholars of eminence.

But these literary pursuits were soon and sadly interrupted. Indian hostilities still continued. The inconveniences and sufferings to which the settlements were exposed by savage depredations, were extreme. Almost daily, reports were brought into the stronger settlements of the murder and scalping of men and lads, of the brutal abuse of women and children. The burning of Cavat's Station in 1793, and the cruelties inflicted upon the settlers at that point by Double Head, the Creek chief, and his followers, while on their way to attack Knoxville (of the failure of which enterprise an account was above given), so effectually aroused the apprehensions and indignation of the whites, that a force of seven hundred volunteers was immediately raised for the pursuit and punishment of the marauders. At such a time, it was impossible for Hugh L. White to sit quietly over his books, congenial as literary pursuits were to his tastes and disposition. With native generosity and bravery, he abandoned his studies, and at the age of nineteen volunteered as a private soldier in the Indian campaign.

Of the battle of Etowah, at which young White did good service, the following account is extracted from Ramsey's Annals of Tennessee:

"Finding no Indians to attack at Estimaula, Sevier took up his line of march in the direction of Etowah, with the Coosa on the right. Near the confluence of these streams, and immediately below, was the Indian town, Etowah. The river of the same name had to be crossed before the town could be attacked. Firing was heard in the direction of the town; and apprehending a general attack, Sevier judiciously ordered a halt, and sent forward a detachment from the main body against the town. By mistake of Carey and Findleston, the guides, the party was led to a ferry half a mile below the fording-places, and immediately opposite the town. A few of the foremost plunged into the stream and were soon in swimming water, and pushing their way to the opposite bank. The main body, however, discovering the mistake, wheeled to the left, and rode rapidly up the river to the ford, where they crossed with the design of riding down to the town, and attacking it without delay.

"The Indians, having previously obtained information of Sevier's approach, had made excavations in the bank of the river nearest their town, each of them large enough for one man to lie with his gun poised, and with a leisurely aim to shoot our men as soon as they came in sight. In these, the warriors were safely entrenched; but perceiving the movement of horsemen down the river, and suspecting some other project was devised against their town, they quitted precipitately their places of ambush, crossed the river, and hurried down on its other side to defend it.

"A fortunate mistake of the pilots thus drew this formidable party out of its intrenchments, exposed it in the open field, and left to the invaders a safe passage through that bank of the river so recently lined with armed men. But for this mistake, the horsemen could not have escaped a most deadly fire, and in all probability, a summary defeat. But the method of fighting was now entirely changed. The crossing by the horsemen was too quickly done to allow the Indians to regain their hiding-places; their ranks were scattered, and the main body of them hemmed in between the assailants and the river. This done, the men dismounted, betook themselves to trees, and poured in a deadly fire upon the enemy. They resisted bravely, under the lead of the King Fisher, one of their most distinguished braves. He made a daring sally within a few yards of where one of the party, Hugh L. White, was standing, and the action was becoming sharp and spirited, when White and a few comrades near him, levelling their rifles, this formidable champion fell, and his warriors immediately fled.*

"The town was set on fire late in the evening, and the troops encamped near it. During the night they were attacked by the Indians. McNutt and Grant were standing as sentinels in an exposed point of the encampment. The Indians approached stealthily upon them, and each of them fired. Grant was shot through the body, but ultimately recovered.

"After the engagement the Indians made good their escape into the secret passes of the adjoining country. The army, after the town was burned, rescued from the places in which they were obliged to conceal themselves, Col. Kelly and the five horsemen who had swam their horses at the lower crossing.

"Sevier having accomplished thus much of the object of the expedition, desired to extend his conquests to Indian towns still lower down the country. The guides informed him there was but one accessible path by which the army could reach these distant villages, and that it could be passed only under disadvantageous circumstances. Little hope remained of meeting the enemy in such numbers as to inflict upon the perpetrators of the mischief at Cavat's suitable punishment for their atrocities. They had been expelled from the frontier, the heart of their country had been penetrated, their warriors defeated and baffled, and their towns and crops burnt up and destroyed. Orders for the return march were given, and the army soon reached their homes in safety. This was Gen. Sevier's last military service."

"The troops employed in this expedition"—we quote from Rev. Mr. Hume's address, above referred to—"were refused payment, on the ground that it was undertaken without authority from the President, and in violation of instructions from the Department of War to Governor Blount, forbidding offensive operations against the Indians. In 1796, Hugh L. White, who served in the campaign, petitioned Congress for remuneration, with the view of establishing a precedent that might apply to all his fellow-soldiers. In January, 1797, Andrew

* Judge White shot the King Fisher. Yet such was his instinctive horror at the idea of destroying human life, that he could never endure to have the deed mentioned; and explicitly forbid Dr. Ramsey, the historian, so to state the fact in his "Annals."

Jackson, from the Committee of the House of Representatives, to which the petition was referred, reported in favor of a provision by law for the payment of the troops."

That this was not the only occasion upon which Hugh L. White displayed a lofty and honorable bravery in the defence of his country, we have the following testimony from the narrative of the same events, by one conversant with the history of those times of peril and suffering.

"It was about the year 1793 that a large body of Indians came into the settlements on Holston, murdered a family, and carried off all the plunder which fell within their reach. A force was immediately raised to pursue them. Hugh L. White, then a youth under twenty, made one of the party. The battle was fought on the banks of a river whose current was rapid, and its crossing difficult. The Indians took advantage of this position, and attacked the white men as they passed the stream; one detachment of the latter having rushed forward, rose the steep ascent, and were in the midst of the enemy at once, when an obstinate conflict ensued; whilst the other party waited under the bank to form, where they continued until the battle was fought and won—until the war-whoops ceased to be heard, and until the report of the rifle died away in the distance; then they formed a most excellent line, presented an unbroken front, marched boldly up, and deliberately took possession of all the plunder, to the last beaver-skin. When the fighting-men returned from the pursuit, White, who had been from the start amongst the foremost of them, found that one of these bank-men, in his eagerness for the spoils of victory, had taken possession of his wallet of provisions, which had got lost in the scuffle. But he demanded that as his own right, and made him give it up." Upon this unimportant occasion, as often afterwards in more critical contingencies, young White, though he scorned to strive for, or to appropriate, any share of the spoil, contended obstinately and uncompromisingly for the full extent of the rights involved.

During this expedition, while the Tennessee troops were encamped at Estimaula, on the Coosa River, a little adventure occurred, which gave quite unexpected evidence of the dexterous strength contained in the slender frame of our young soldier. Colonel Blair, of the Washington District, had given to Colonel Christy, of the Hamilton District, a sort of challenge, after the old Scriptural fashion of Abner's suggestion to Joab. "Let the young men arise and play before us." He said, in other words, that a certain man in his regiment could "whip any other man on the ground." With this, of course, a wrestling-match was arranged; and Colonel Christy appointed to the championship, on his part, Hugh L. White, who was by far the most delicate-looking man in the regiment. The challenger made his appearance; his gigantic stature and brawny frame inspiring the stoutest with awe; the combatants laid aside their coats, and entered the ring; both regiments being quite confident that the victory was safe for the "biggest bones." But, to the astonishment of all, the slender White, after a long and doubtful struggle, overthrew his burly antagonist, and retired with his laurels, amidst the shouts of the whole multitude.

At the age of twenty, Hugh L. White was appointed Private Secretary to Governor Blount; for his strong and elastic intellect, his habits of laborious application, and his determined practice of doing well and thoroughly whatever he undertook, had already rendered him conspicuous for talent and ability. Mr. Blount, in addition to the office of Territorial Governor, held the important and responsible post of Superintendent of Indian Affairs; which devolved upon him the management of all negotiations and transactions with, and concerning the Cherokee, Creek, Choctaw, and Chickasaw tribes. The duties of these two stations were arduous and complicated in the extreme; requiring the most wise, patient, and skilful management. The Federal authorities restricted the Territorial Government to purely defensive warfare; and the settlements were but scantily provided with able-bodied men. The Indian nations, however, were strong in numbers and in physical power. Naturally ferocious and relentless, their savage passions were, moreover, continually nourished and stimulated by the contrivances of Spanish and British traders, interested against the quiet and prosperity of the white settlers. In each tribe there was a minority which faithfully adhered to the United States. This circumstance produced continual dissensions and disputes among themselves, for the adjustment of which resort was had to Governor Blount. In all the intricate and critical duties of this active service, as well as in the accompanying heavy official correspondence with individuals and public functionaries, the young Secretary so faithfully and efficiently aided the Governor, as to secure to himself the life-long confidence and affection of that eminent man, as well as the esteem of his fellow-citizens of the Territory.

Having thus borne himself with gallantry and honor during the war, young White, at its close, determined to pursue a course of mathematical study at Philadelphia, under the supervision of Professor Patterson. But here a temporary difficulty arose. General White, his father, although possessed of extensive and valuable landed property, was never, owing to his excessive liberality, a man of wealth, and could not, at the time, command the means necessary to accomplish the laudable desire of his son. It is due to the generosity of General White's son-in-law, Colonel Charles McClung, to say that, in this strait, he kindly came forward and advanced the money necessary to complete the education of his brother-in-law.

In 1795, Hugh L. White left Philadelphia for Lancaster, Pennsylvania, where he engaged with great zeal and energy in the study of the law, under the instructions of James Hopkins, an eminent counsel of that place. As a proof of his continued attachment to the people of Pennsylvania, after a lapse of thirty-two years, it may not be inappropriate to quote here an extract from a speech made at a dinner given to him in Knoxville, in 1827:

"I ask but one favor more, and that is, that you join me in a sentiment, in relation to a people, who, next to those of my own and native State, I most esteem; amongst whom I have spent a small portion of my early life, which I reflect upon with much satisfaction, because it was spent inoffensively and pleasantly, if not profitably. I offer you—'*The people of Pennsylvania.* Modest and unpretending; too enlightened to be misled, and too virtuous to be seduced from Republican principles.'"

CHAPTER III.

LAWYER AND JUDGE.

Having completed the usual course of preparatory study, Mr. White returned to Knoxville, and in 1796 assumed a station at the Tennessee bar, with favorable prospects; and very soon, if his contemporaries may be credited, rose to a place which he maintained for years, at the head of his profession.

After he had passed away from the busy scenes of time, one who knew him well, and was himself distinguished for more than ordinary talents, wrote in the following terms of his powers, both as a lawyer and a judge—

"Judge Hugh L. White," he says, "was a remarkable man—remarkable for his eccentricities, and for the very high order of his moral and mental endowments. He had but little taste and care for polite scholarship and general literature. His great superiority was, not in his moral integrity, which was equal to the very best any where to be found, for many first-rate moralists there are to equal anybody. His great eminence—the especial gift of God, and inherited directly from his mother, Mary Lawson, consisted in all those peculiar points of intellect, which made the lawyer and the judge. In this order of mental endowments he had not five equals in America, and perhaps but two superiors—John Marshall and John Haywood. The superiority of these two men over him, was the result only of circumstances. Like John Marshall, Hugh L. White was a great lawyer and a great judge, even without reading and without books. Naturally enough for him, he despised a 'case lawyer,' and still more, a mere *case judge*."

During the following five years, he devoted himself assiduously to his studies and his business; steadily increasing and extending his reputation for honesty, industry, and ability. The whole results of the professional efforts of those five years, eternity only can disclose; but time has already developed enough to demonstrate that Hugh L. White is entitled to an overflowing measure of the purest and loftiest fame which the noblest professional exertions of the lawyer can give—the fame of powerful benevolence—of earnestly and effectively promoting the welfare of his fellow-men. There are none who are conversant with his own history, and with the history of East Tennessee, who cannot remember many irrefutable testimonies to his praise—tears of gratitude, shed by wives whose husbands his powerful arguments have saved from the hangman's rope, and blessings of children whose fathers have been preserved from the brand of blood-guiltiness. There are men even now living, whose powerful frames will heave with mighty emotion when they speak of him, who now rests so quietly from his labors; not only because as a lawyer he argued their cases, but because as a kind and sympathizing friend he lifted them from depths of degradation and crime, and with words of kindly counsel, as well as by his own pure and lofty example, encouraged them to "go, and sin no more."

The noble powers of his vigorous and elastic intellect, and the whole exertions of an uncommon faculty of steady and laborious application, were scrupulously devoted to the interests of his clients. His invariable punctuality to every engagement, and his faithfulness in the discharge of every responsibility gave him so strong an additional hold upon the esteem and confidence of the community, that it would have been difficult to empannel a jury not already strongly inclined in his favor. This predisposition was always corroborated by his straightforward contempt for any advantages derivable from legal quibbles, even in advance of the weight of his argumentation, and the influence of the fervent earnestness with which he plead his cause.

At the end of this short term of practice, Mr. White's legal acquirements and abilities had given him such a professional reputation, that, in 1801, at the early age of twenty-eight, he was elected Judge of the Superior Court, then the highest judicial tribunal in the State. Concentrated and successful assiduity in the study of his profession had already, however, prepared him to perform with credit the important functions of this high station. Possessed of an eminently legal mind, he had equal or superior moral endowments. In the practice of law he had ever applied the principles of justice; and had to an uncommon extent escaped the one-sided habits of thought, and incapacity of balancing both sides of a question, which is the common fate of the mere attorney.

While on the bench, his intercourse with the members of the bar was marked by the kindliness and genuine courtesy which characterized him in every relation in life. He assumed no personal nor official superiority, nor exhibited any favoritism or preference, unless such names could be applied to a constant readiness to aid and encourage the younger lawyers, and to afford them every fair opportunity of getting into notice and business.

In 1809, Judge White was appointed District Attorney of the United States, but soon resigned the office; for the reason, stated in a letter to James Madison, then Secretary of State, that he found it impossible to attend at once to the duties of the office, and to others which he considered paramount; and that by the constitution of the State, he should, by acceptance of the Attorneyship, be precluded from taking the seat in the Legislature, to which he had been re-elected.

In the same year the judiciary of Tennessee was organized anew, and a supreme court established, in which, although not a candidate for the office, he was appointed to preside. He held this station six years; during which time he was continually associated with the most eminent men in Tennessee, and by the able and impartial discharge of his duties, gave universal satisfaction. The perspicuity, accuracy, and uncompromising honesty of his opinions raised him into such high and universal estimation, that his final resignation of his seat was received with great and unmingled regret.

At the close of his appointment as Spanish Commissioner, in 1824, he was again unanimously appointed by the legislature, Judge of the Supreme Court of Errors and Appeals of the State of Tennessee, but declined the appointment, alleging in his letter of declinature to Governor Carroll, his feeble health, and the fact that his acceptance would compel a number of clients to seek new counsel; thus, in his opinion, causing them more injury than would be compensated by his acceptance, with no fairer prospect of ability for the discharge of the duties of the office. This declinature is an honorable instance of self-sacrifice and devotion to the interests of his fellow-men.

On more than one occasion Judge White was offered a seat on the bench of the Supreme Court of the United States by President Jackson; but this appointment he steadily refused. This refusal may be considered fortunate, in saving Judge White from coming under any real or fancied obligations to the dominant political party, and more especially, as being the means of preserving a noble example of purity and high-minded disinterestedness where it certainly was needed—in the field of political action.

2

A single short anecdote, relating to this portion of Judge White's public life, will naturally conclude this chapter. A law student, living at a considerable distance, had come to Knoxville for a license. Having heard much of the professional learning and ability of Judge White, he proceeded to his residence, and with great trepidation inquired for him; thinking possibly that the judge would receive him "with his ermine on," and with an imposing display of official pomp. Being told that the Judge was at his farm, he went in search of him; and discovering an individual very busily engaged in ploughing, inquired for Judge White. "I am the man, sir," was the answer. "I wish to obtain a law license," said the young man; "and have come to be examined." "Well, sir," replied the Judge, "if you will be good enough to come down into the shade, I will attend to the business with great pleasure." So the Judge fastened his horse, selected a shady seat, invited the aspirant to another, subjected him forthwith to a searching examination, found him well qualified, invited him to partake of the hospitalities of his house, made out the required license, and returned to his plough-handle.

CHAPTER IV.

A STATE LEGISLATOR.

In 1807, Judge White was elected a member of the State Senate; and re-elected in 1809. So acceptably did he perform the duties of this position, that he was a third time, in 1817, requested to resume it, which he consented to do, and was elected by a vote nearly unanimous. During the session of 1807, he compiled the present state system of Land Laws, and procured their enactment; a service for which all Tennesseans who remember the destructive frauds and violent and bitter controversies which were frequently attendant upon the old system, must still feel grateful. On this occasion he delivered his first political speech, which was acknowledged to be a production of great power and cogency. In 1817, he took charge of a bill introduced by Mr. Trimble, a member from Davidson county, taxing very heavily any banking institution which should attempt to do business in the State without a charter from it. The object of this bill, which was generally approved, and indeed passed almost unanimously, was to prevent the Directors of the United States Bank from establishing a branch bank in the State. We shall here proceed to narrate, though out of their strict order in time, certain subsequent occurrences relating to this bill, for the sake of the connection, and to exemplify the State patriotism and disinterestedness with which Judge White could advocate the undefended cause of the absent, notwithstanding his dissent from their political opinions, and disapproval of their course: and that without sacrificing his own consistency or beliefs. Four months before the passage of this bill in the State Legislature, an application had been made for the establishment in Nashville of a branch of the United States Bank, which was signed by sixty of the most influential citizens of the town and its vicinity. At the head of this list stood the name of the Hon. Felix Grundy. In the face of this petition however the bill passed, to the entire satisfaction of a large majority of the people of the State, so far at least as could be

* He received *every* vote but one in Knox county.

judged from the cordiality with which their representatives were received by them, and the number of them afterwards re-elected.

This act of this body was prominently noticed in the Senate Chamber of the United States, as late as April 20th, 1838, when the Adminis tration, influenced greatly in its general policy by General Jackson, was making powerful efforts to carry through its favorite scheme, the passage of "A bill to prevent the issuing and circulation of the bills, notes, and securities of corporations, created by Congress, which have expired." During the discussion Mr. Benton read a letter from General Jackson, dated Nov. 29th, 1837, in which, to manifest his utter aversion to the banking system, he denominated these sixty gentlemen, many of them his own friends and honest supporters, and some of them determined to stand by and defend his administration at all hazards, an "aristocratic few," attempting to carry their own ends, in defiance of the State authority. When subsequently Mr. Grundy in particular, and perhaps others of these gentlemen, apparently forgetful of having ever borne any part in the movement, thus so severely condemned by General Jackson, made war upon the whole banking system—"war," in Mr. Grundy's strong and emphatic language, "to the knife, and the knife to the hilt"—Judge White, though the main instrument in the passage of the law, in opposition to the wishes of the sixty, hearing them thus denounced upon the floor of the Senate, spoke in their defence. Although Mr. Grundy offered not a word of apology or explanation for them or for himself, Judge White exculpated them from the serious charge of attempting that which was expressly prohibited by the laws of their State, by showing that their petition was prepared and presented before the enactment of the law for taxing foreign banks doing business in Tennessee. During this debate, Judge White showed that General Jackson, in 1818, while that law was in full force, in anticipation of the establishment of this bank at Nashville, signed recommendations of two gentlemen, one for President, and the other for Cashier; thus lending to the scheme the sanction of his name, and even, in order that it might have its full weight, appending his former official title of "Major General, Southern Division"; to which, as Judge White insisted, he then had no right. During this forcible exposition of the varying and inconstant courses of men in high positions, Judge White also read a document transmitted to the President and Directors of the United States Bank at Philadelphia, dated in 1818, containing the proceedings of a town meeting at Nashville, and likewise a letter from the

Nashville committee of sixty, headed by Mr. Grundy, in which this same legislature is most contemptuously spoken of; from each of which documents we make an extract. The town meeting

Resolved—"That it is the sense of this meeting, that the State law passed by the legislature of this State, in taxing banks to be established in this State by an authority other than the laws of this State, while the banks established by the authority of the State are not taxed, is *impolitic and unconstitutional.*"

The committee in their letter say:

"In making this statement to you, we are influenced by what we believe a duty we owe to the character of Tennessee. For she has not been less uniform in her political principle, and inviolable attachment to the general government, than distinguished for her alacrity and prowess in defending the honor of the Union. And lest persons at a distance should suppose from her legislature having inconsiderably raised the arm of hostility against a great fiscal establishment of the general government, that her character was not to be confided in, we seize with pleasure every opportunity to show to the world that such conclusion is erroneous."

There was also a private letter from Judge Grundy to this same bank at Philadelphia (which Judge Grundy admitted to Judge White, while in the presence of Col. Benton and others, to be a true copy); which Judge White read on the floor of the Senate, as follows:

NASHVILLE, February 14, 1818.

"DEAR SIR: From a knowledge that some acquaintance must have been formed between you and myself at Washington, many of my neighbors have frequently solicited me to forward to you a list of the names of fit persons to whom to confide the management of a branch bank of the United States at this place. I have heretofore declined it, nor should I at any time have said anything on the subject, had it not been for the puerile attempt of our last Legislature to prevent an establishment of a branch here altogether. The motives which gave birth to that measure were selfish, the policy contracted, and the views of such men cannot be liberal and impartial. Any number, from seven to thirteen, might be selected from the following, and the choice could not be a bad one. Jenkin Whitesides, *Andrew Hays*, Randall McGavocke, *John P. Erwin*, *Thomas H. Fletcher*, *James Stewart*, Felix Robertson, Robert Weakly, Elihu S. Hall, Alfred Balch, *William Carroll*, *Thomas Hill*, George W. Gibbs, Robert C. Foster, *Samuel Zelford*.

"Those *printed in italics* are merchants; the others, substantial freeholders, and men of intelligence. A board of managers selected from them would, in my opinion, conduct the affairs of the institution with ability and integrity. Although you and the directors have a discretion as to number, between seven and thirteen, I would submit to you the propriety of the largest number. It may have an effect in keeping down that spirit of opposition which has hitherto manifested itself.

"I have no fears that any attempt will be made to enforce the Tennessee law. Should there be, it will be re-visited with effect here, no concern need be felt on that subject. Should there be no impropriety in it, I should like to know when you will put the institution in operation here? and it would seem to me that some persons should be authorized beforehand to provide a house, &c. You will excuse me for the freedom of my suggestions. If unnecessary, they are harmless."

Your obedient servant,

FELIX GRUNDY.

WM. JONES, ESQ., *President U. S. Bank, Philadelphia.*

"P. S.—Although this is addressed to you only, I have no objection to its being seen by any of the directors.

F. G."

Judge White then added, "This letter was written in 1818. It remained a *secret* in the hands, and for the guidance of, a directory of a powerful monied institution, from the time of its receipt, till 1835, without any one of those calumniated in it, having any suspicion that among their acquaintances there could be found a man, capable of thus *stabbing their reputation in the dark.* It was brought to light by the investigating committee, and from the time I first saw it, until now, I have never been able to think favorably of its author. The man who could thus treat me *might deceive me once,* but he never will a second time, unless, perchance, he should hereafter do some act, which comports with the character of an honorable man." Mr. Grundy was forced to make a rejoinder, which embraced a confession of having done all Judge White had charged him with doing—even to speaking, writing, reporting, and memorializing in favor of a U. S. Bank and of a branch institution at Nashville. In the following June Mr. Grundy replied to Judge White's remarks, which he affected to repel with disdain and scorn, and attributed them to the predominance of prejudice and passion in the bosom of the latter. Judge White replied with much spirit and effect to Mr. Grundy's defence. "He hoped never to see the day when he would be obliged to take six weeks to prepare and con over an answer to any speech; he regretted sincerely to know that his colleague had grown so deaf of late, as not to have heard the whole of his remarks. But," asked Judge White, "what is the substance of his reply, so long in coming? Does he controvert a single fact? Does he attack a single position? Does he meet a single argument of mine? Take his reply now and at the time my speech was delivered, and can you find in either, a single fact alleged by me, denied or controverted? No, sir! no discipline, no drilling can bring him to deny anything advanced. I will not take back a word (continued Judge W.); nothing but the character of this place prevents me from saying more: and my colleague has permission to believe that I have spoken out of the Senate, what I have spoken here."

To this thorough exposition no reply was possible, and none was made.

In the session of the Tennessee legislature of 1817, Judge White drafted an act for the prevention of duelling, which effectually preserved that State from becoming the scene of this horrible and senseless mode of indulging personal enmity. He held in utter abhorrence this wicked and desperate practice of setting at naught one's own life, the life of an antagonist, and the peace and happiness of the many interested on either side. His whole private and public life may attest his high sense of honor; but he would never admit that duelling is the proper means for its defence when assailed. He maintained that it required far greater courage to refuse to fight, in the face of the so-called "laws of honor" than to fight; and avowed himself deficient in that sort of courage which was requisite either to rush unbidden into the presence of his God before the appointed time, and without having finished the work assigned to him on earth, or to consign his fellow-creatures to a like destiny. His views upon this subject made a lasting impression throughout the length and breadth of the State. In East Tennessee, where he was best known, and exerted the most profound influence, an aversion to duelling is proverbial. Men ever ready to defend their rights, to protect the defenceless from all aggressions, or at an hour's warning to go forth armed at their country's call, shun the reputation of the duellist, and the crime of the duel.

These measures, important and meritorious as they were, are only a few, selected from the many important services rendered by Judge White to his own State while a member of her legislature; although it is impossible in this place to do more than barely make allusion to the remainder.

CHAPTER V.

PATRIOTIC EPISODE—WILDERNESS JOURNEY TO GENERAL JACKSON.

In the spring of 1812, an Indian styling himself "The Prophet," belonging to the Northern tribe of Shawnees, who, partly instigated by the British, were making preparations for a war against the United States, despatched his brother Tecumseh to the Creek Indians, inhabiting the tract of country between the Chattahoochee and Tombigbee rivers, and extending from the Tennessee river to the Florida line, for the purpose of enlisting the Southern tribes in the same enterprise. After repeated conferences, Tecumseh succeeded in infusing into the minds of several of their most influential leaders a feeling of deadly hostility towards the whites. These chiefs, in turn, by their intrigues and harangues, at length aroused an insatiate desire for warfare in the majority of the nation. They resolved upon instant hostilities; and savage incursions of the usual sudden and devastating nature ensued. Whole families were horribly butchered. All the frontier of Georgia and Southern Tennessee, at once became the scene of frightful outrages; and this cruel warfare was waged, not only against the whites, but also against such of the Creeks as were disposed to preserve their friendship with them. Many peaceable Indians were thus driven to take refuge with such settlers as they might have formerly befriended, or with whom they might otherwise have amicable relations.

The treacherous massacre of Fort Mimms, which took place August 30th, 1812, awoke a universal feeling of horror and violent resentment throughout Tennessee. Her legislature, which convened a few days afterwards, passed an act authorizing the Executive, in conformity with instructions previously received from the Secretary of War, to call into the field three thousand five hundred volunteers, and to commence a vigorous campaign against the enemy. To guard against all contingencies, two hundred thousand dollars were voted for their support. General Jackson, who was supposed to be better qualified than any other man in the State, having been appointed by the Governor to the command of the Second Division of Tennessee Militia, and having received orders for immediate action, hastened to carry them into effect. He accordingly set out early in October and was soon encamped on the borders of the enemy's country.

Rumors of General Jackson's near approach to the Creek Nation, and of the strong probability that he would be opposed by a considerable body of Creeks, arrived almost daily at Knoxville. Then it was reported that he was surrounded with serious difficulties; that his brave men were contending not only with the sons of the forest, but with famine and want, even to the extremity of sustaining life on "roots and acorns." Hoping to be able to render some relief to his countrymen in their distressed and destitute condition, Judge White left the bench, and with two other companions, the Honorable Luke Lea, and Honorable Thomas L. Williams, started for the wilderness. After several days and nights of perilous adventure, they reached the encampment of the East Tennessee troops, at Fort Armstrong on the Coosa, on the 13th of November. Here they learned from General Cocke that owing to some disaffection among his troops, no junction had been formed between the East and West Tennessee divisions, that for want of a messenger no communication had passed between them, and that General Jackson did not even know the reasons which led to General White's return from Turkey-town.* Judge White expressed great anxiety for the fate of the West Tennessee division, and fear that they might be cut off, or very materially injured, for the want of that support which had been expected from the East Tennessee troops; and offered to be the bearer of any despatches General Cocke might choose to send. He accordingly left on the

* It is proper here to advert to the charges or insinuations of insubordination, or other sinister motives, which were made by General Jackson's biographers, at and since this time, against General White, for joining General Cocke, instead of continuing on to join Jackson at Fort Strother, at the time alluded to in the text. The truth of the case was this: General White, having been ordered by Jackson to join him, undertook to put his force in motion from Turkeytown, for that purpose; but discovered that the men would not obey such orders, but would return to General Cocke, instead, for the reason, alleged by them, that they and their horses would incur an imminent risk of starvation in the advance. This was not an unreasonable fear; it is well known that General Jackson's forces at that very time were almost entirely disorganized from lack of provisions. Under these circumstances General Cocke decided to recall General White. He was influenced hereto, also, by the consideration that after this junction, the superior *morale* of the troops under his own command would enable him to compel White's men to march anywhither; and by the fact that the delay would enable him to procure supplies. Instead of being sent to Jackson, therefore, General White was detached in another direction, against the Hillabee Towns, where he did good service. Such being the case, the blame, if any, must rest with the rank and file and subordinate officers of General White's detachment, for refusing to encounter what they supposed would be serious danger of starvation; and not with their commander, who could not compel the services of unwilling militia.

morning of the 14th November, with both verbal and written despatches, and reached General Jackson's encampment on the 18th, at 12 o'clock. After consultation with General Jackson as to the best means of relieving him from his embarrassed situation, he returned to Fort Armstrong with important despatches from General Jackson to General Cocke, and remained until General White's detachment returned from the Creek Nation, and a junction was formed on the 8th December, between the two divisions at Fort Strother. It was then determined that he should return through the wilderness to Tennessee, and exert his influence in raising volunteers, and procuring provisions for the distressed and famishing army.

He appealed directly to the patriotism of his brother-in-law, Colonel John Williams, commander of the 39th regiment, who, having raised a force of 600 men, had enlisted in the regular army, and was making preparations for an expedition to New Orleans. He told Colonel Williams that he had been commissioned by General Jackson, to represent to him "his condition as very deplorable, that his men had all abandoned him except his life-guard, and unless he came to his aid, the country would be overrun by savages, the inhabitants become victims of every species of cruelty, and the reputation of their State forever blasted."

But Judge White's exertions did not end here. He remained with Colonel Williams nearly all night, using every means in his power to impress upon his mind the necessity of relieving Jackson's force. His importunities finally prevailed.* Colonel Williams acquiesced in his wishes; wrote to the War Department, stating his intention to proceed to General Jackson's head-quarters, instead of to the South according to his previous instructions; and upon learning that his plans were approved by the government, at once marched for the former destination, and arrived with his troops, February 6th, 1814.

On the 14th, they marched in quest of the enemy, and reached the village of Tohopeka on the 27th, where they found a strong force of Indians, a thousand or twelve hundred in number, awaiting their approach; upon which there ensued the most desperate engagement of the whole war, the bloody Battle of the Horse-Shoe.†

The intrepidity and firmness of the 39th regiment, the skill

* Colonel Williams said that Judge White's arguments and persuasions used to him at this time, were altogether superior to anything he ever heard from him at the Bar.

† General Jackson, in expressing his gratitude to Col. W., after the engagement, remarked, "Sir, you have placed me on the road to high military fame."

of their commander, Colonel Williams, the aid of the friendly Indians under Colonel Gideon Morgan, and of Captain Russell's company of spies, decided the hard-fought battle; which gave a death-blow to the hopes of the enemy, and brought the war to a successful termination.

While absent on this expedition, Judge White missed several terms of his court. By the laws of Tennessee the Judges were paid only in proportion to duty performed. The legislature, however, in consideration of the services he had rendered to General Jackson, passed a resolution that there should be no deduction from his salary. But he declined the gift; refusing to receive more than that for which he had rendered actual service. He said that "his country was in distress; that the aid he had rendered was without the hope of reward. and that he would receive none."

CHAPTER VI.

A FINANCIER.

Before resigning his seat on the Supreme Bench in 1815, Judge White was elected President of the Bank of Tennessee. Fortunately for him, his early habits of labor and activity had so strengthened his constitution, which was naturally delicate, as to enable him to endure an immense amount of bodily and mental fatigue. In order fully to discharge his numerous and important duties, he was at this time accustomed to rise early, take breakfast by candle-light, and be in town at his post, by dawn of day, usually riding to and from his duties. He was fond of horseback exercise, and always rode fine horses, and with great ease and grace. His command over them was extraordinary. One morning while acting as supreme judge, he was riding into town from the eastern entrance (all who are acquainted with the location of Knoxville, know something of the hilly ascent). Near what was then denominated the "Spout Spring," he came across a man driving a wagon, very heavily loaded. It was during the winter season; the roads heavy, the hill very steep, and the driver not very well skilled in the management of his horses, which seemed much more inclined to descend than to ascend the elevation. Many persons were collected on either side of the street, whose object seemed to be rather to observe, than to render aid. Judge White sat for some minutes on his horse, closely scanning the operations. He finally dismounted, and offering his assistance, took the lines, mounted the saddle-horse, and by his skill as a driver, quickly carried the load and horses to the top of the slippery hill.

His high qualifications as a financier were fully established by the success of the bank; "such was the wisdom of his management, that its paper was always equal to specie, as it was 'lifted' with silver and gold when presented for payment; indeed, it was the only instance for several years of a bank paying specie in the Western country.

The stock of this bank never depreciated, but was always equal to any bank stock in the Union."

In July, 1827, Judge White resigned the office of President as well as Director of the bank; his reasons for this course are given in a letter to the directors of the bank, June 30th, 1827. We need not insert them here. It is, however, proper to substitute the following statement of the Directors in reference to this transaction, which is found in the Register of July 18th, 1827:

"The Bank of Tennessee commenced its operations on the 30th day of November, 1812. Hugh L. White has been the President thereof ever since. He has repeatedly and earnestly desired, that he might not be elected either a Director or the President, but the stockholders have uniformly been desirous to retain him and avail themselves of his services. From the 30th day of Nov., 1812, to the 10th day of January, 1815, he received no salary or compensation whatever for his services. On the 9th day of January, 1815, the stockholders allowed him an annual salary of one thousand dollars, which continued till the 1st of January, 1820, at which time it was increased to fifteen hundred dollars per annum.

"On the 31st of March, 1821, he was appointed a Commissioner under the Florida Treaty with Spain, which appointment he continued to hold until the 9th day of June, 1824, a little upwards of three years. When the Commission was not in session, his attention was devoted to the business of the bank; and although this was the case, he uniformly refused to receive any salary for his services, and never has received one cent for any services he rendered the bank between the 31st of March, 1821, and the 1st day of July, 1824. About the last of October, 1825, he was elected Senator of the U. S.; and since his election, he has uniformly given his attention to the business of the bank when he was not necessarily absent, and during the whole of this time, that is from the 31st Dec., 1825, to this date, has received from the bank for his services, only the sum of three hundred and seventy-five dollars, equal, barely, to one quarter's salary. From the first organization of the bank to this time, it has uniformly relied upon him, for all the legal advice the Directors needed, which he has uniformly given, for which he has never demanded or received one cent in compensation. Any suits to which the bank was a party, when the business could be done at Knoxville, he has attended to as a lawyer, for which he has never asked or received one cent.

"He is not a borrower of money from the bank to the amount of one dollar, and is an endorser on one note only, and that for barely three hundred dollars.

"The bank has uniformly had the use of his private funds for nothing. He has, in many instances, taken journeys upon the business of the bank, when a confidential person was necessary, and in no instance has he received any compensation whatever for any such services.

"Given under our hands at Knoxville, the 27th day of June, 1827:

LUKE LEA, *Cashier.*	JOHN CROZIER,
WILLIAM PARK, *Ex-Cashier.*	JOHN HILLSMAN,
ANDREW MCMILLAN, H. A. M. WHITE, } *Late Clerks.*	JAMES PARK,
	DAVID CAMPBELL,
	CALVIN MORGAN,
	ROBT. KING,
	JAMES DARDIS, } *Directors.*

JOSEPH C. STRONG, *Former Director.*"

This home testimony, from neighbours and men of standing, well acquainted with the circumstances of the case, and from different political parties, is entirely reliable; and its statements strikingly illustrate the lofty purity of Judge White, and his unselfish devotion to the interests of his fellow-citizens. We have here the case of a man who performed the onerous and responsible duties of a leading Bank officer three years for nothing; three years more for nothing also, but this time while the salary of fifteen hundred dollars only awaited acceptance; for a year and a half more, for three months' salary; who declined to receive such sums, not on the ground that he had not done the work, but for the unprecedented reason that he had been in the receipt of contemporary income for public services rendered during the same period; who, under these circumstances, having also transacted the law business of the bank without fee or reward, obtained accommodation from it not even to the extent of a single cent, raised no money by its help, nor, except as endorser upon one single small note, aided others to do so. Such indifference to pecuniary gains usually esteemed perfectly legitimate, and at the same time such active and untiring efficiency in the discharge of these unpaid duties, is very rare in this or any country. Whether such conduct be considered a lofty exertion of virtue, or, as by Judge White himself, the mere performance of ordinary duty, it is not here assumed to decide. But in either event, its rarity at least is the same: and that alone entitles it to a careful record.

To show that Judge White's character in this respect was appreciated abroad as well as at home, are given a few words from the United States Telegraph, published about the time of his resignation of the Presidency of the Bank:

"Few men in any age have possessed more of that incorruptible integrity which places public men above private scandal. We venture to assert that no other man who has been so long associated with any monied institution in the country, can deserve as much as the officers of this bank have said of Judge White. We take pleasure in recording this evidence of his Roman virtues."

One or two anecdotes, kindly furnished by Dr. Ramsey, the well-known historian of Tennessee, will further illustrate the home reputation and influence of Judge White, as a safe and reliable financier.

"When in 1836 the books for the subscription of stock in our great railroad enterprise were first opened in Knoxville, we who were appointed commissioners for that purpose, experienced great difficulty in obtaining subscriptions. We found few willing to adventure anything; some objecting to the whole scheme as wild, visionary, and impracticable. On the evening of the last day of subscription Judge White was sent for. We exhibited to him our meagre list of subscribers, and the inadequate amount of stock. He made a few sensible remarks on the subject, and added that elsewhere, when citizens had not the money on hand unemployed, they used their credit. He proposed the formation of an association of twenty, of which he would himself be one, to subscribe to the enterprise. The association was at once formed, nineteen of us joined him, with him subscribing $200,000, and thus securing the charter at the very end of the time to which the commissioners were limited by law. His example and influence thus saved the charter."

When the Bank of the State of Tennessee was chartered (I believe in 1813) some one was needed to go to the East to have the necessary engravings—plates &c., prepared to put the bank in operation. The task was then herculean—there were no stages—much less steamboats and railroad cars. The long journey was to be performed on horseback. Younger men shrunk from the undertaking. His professional duties at home scarcely allowed him to leave the State. But mounting his horse he rode to the Eastern cities—had the engravings made—the bills struck—looked into the forms of financiering which were then all unknown in the West—and with the whole machinery of the first Bank of Tennessee about his person and in his portmanteau, he returned to Knoxville in so short a space of time, that the expedition was considered quite a remarkable adventure.

I may as well here add one word of his *financial ability*. At that time gold and silver were the only circulating money in the State, banking in the West was in its infancy; and to put a State institution into successful operation among a people strangers to a paper currency and prejudiced against the credit system, required fiscal talents of the first order. But his strong common sense, his far-seeing discernment and his unquestioned probity succeeded in overcoming the seemingly insurmountable difficulties which he encountered. The parent bank he managed in person at Knoxville, established several branches elsewhere, and a sounder currency no State was blessed with while he managed its finances.

The following is an instance of the careful punctuality with which Judge White superintended even minute details of Bank management.

Believing that "example is better than precept," and being a man of few words, Judge White generally acted instead of talking. While he was president of the Bank of Tennessee, he accompanied his daughters to a ball, given in Knoxville. Luke Lea, who was cashier at the time, and a single gentleman, was also present. When the hour for dispersing came, the Judge went to Mr. Lea (whom he found at the card table, with a number of other gentlemen, engaged in a game of whist), and said, "If you are not going to leave this place, give me the key of the bank, and I will act as guard myself." Mr. Lea answered that he would go immediately to his post, and remain there. The Judge, after seeing his daughters home (two miles in the country), fearing Mr. Lea might become so absorbed as to neglect or become forgetful of his duty, mounted his horse, and returned to town. He went first to the bank, but finding no one there, he repaired to the ball-room, and there found Mr. Lea still at the card table. Without saying one word, he stepped forward and demanded the key. Against this Mr. Lea remonstrated, but the Judge was inexorable. He could not be induced to abandon his intention of remaining all night, which he actually did.

Mr. Lea, who became distinguished for business habits, and for great uprightness and integrity of character, says this was the most effectual rebuke he ever had. It was a lesson he never forgot.

CHAPTER VII.

SERVICES UNDER THE GENERAL GOVERNMENT, AS COMMISSIONER UNDER THE TREATY WITH SPAIN.

WHEN Florida was ceded to the United States in 1819, the latter agreed to exonerate the Spanish Government from all future claims on account of depredations committed during the war of 1812 by Spanish subjects upon property of her citizens; and likewise that those citizens should be indemnified to the amount of the purchase money ($5,000,000) for all loss or injury originating from the doings of foreign cruisers, agents, consuls, or tribunals, in the Spanish territory, which might be imputable to the Spanish government. It was to ascertain the amount of valid claims under this treaty, that Judge White, Hon. Littleton W. Tazewell of Virginia, and Governor King of Maine, were appointed Commissioners by President Monroe, in 1821.

In 1820, from too close application to business, Judge White's health had begun to decline; and it was feared that he must inevitably become a victim of the dreadful disease which afterwards proved such a terrible scourge in his family. He therefore changed in some measure his habits of living, partly gave up business and retired to his farm, where by his remarkable energy of will, in planning and pursuing a course of judicious exercise, he succeeded in regaining sufficient strength for undertaking the laborious task assigned him by this commission. During this temporary relief from the pressure of his many cares, he was in the habit of walking or riding over his farm, once every day. During one of these excursions, an incident occurred, trivial in itself, but not without results of some personal importance to him. One morning, while visiting his plantation two miles distant from his residence, he had occasion to walk a log which lay across a creek. The weather was very cold, and the log covered with ice. His foot slipped and he was plunged into the stream, which was of sufficient depth completely to immerse him. His clothes immediately became frozen, and in this condition he rode home, changed his dress, and went to bed without delay. All were apprehensive, that, in his delicate state of health, this accident would prove fatal. But the excitement threw him into a profuse perspiration, and having slept, he arose as well as usual. He was ever of opinion that this circumstance cured him, for from that time forward his health began to improve.

Although Judge White held many important trusts in his own State, and was known there as a profound jurist and able statesman, yet he had never held office under the general government until he received this appointment under the treaty with Spain. Some idea may be had of the arduous duties of the position he had now assumed, when it is recollected that the commission only lasted for the short space of three years, and that the whole immense amount of claims had to be received, examined, and decided upon, according to the principles of justice, the laws of nations and the stipulations of the treaty between the high contracting parties.* The Intelligencer says: "The praise of ability, assiduity, and devotion to business will be conceded to this board; and it is admitted that the President could not have made a more judicious choice of persons to execute this arduous trust."

In reference to the manner in which that trust was executed, Mr. Tazewell thus expresses himself in a letter to the writer, dated Nov. 15th, 1853:

"The duties of this commission proved to be very burdensome; much more so than either of us had anticipated. Many reasons combined to induce us to endeavor to complete it within the three years prescribed by the statute as the term for the continuance of the commission. To enable us to accomplish this work with more facility to ourselves, we took lodgings in the same boarding-house, to the end that our conferences might be more conveniently held; and labored at our task indefatigably until it was finished. It would not become me to say how the duties of the commission were discharged. But it is due to Judge White to state that whatever of good may have been done by it, ought to be ascribed mainly to his patience, industry and excellent judgment."

During these three years, Judge W. lived on terms of great intimacy with Mr. Tazewell, and contracted a strong friendship for that thorough lawyer and profound thinker. This friendship was warmly

* The Hon. Daniel Webster is said to have received $75,000 for prosecuting claims before this Board.

reciprocated. Says Mr. Tazewell: "When we parted in Washington after the close of the Florida commission, in 1824, it was in the painful belief that we should not probably ever meet again. In this, however, we were mistaken. The death of one of the Senators of Virginia in the Congress of the United States produced a vacancy in that office. To fill that vacancy I was elected by the legislature of this State; and I returned to my old lodgings in Washington, in the latter end of 1824, to enter upon the duties of this new station.'

"Judge W. was not a member of the Senate when I first entered that body. But the next year, 1825, Gen. Jackson, then one of the Senators of the State of Tennessee, resigned his seat, and Judge W. was elected as his successor, and his votes while in that body prove that he was a Republican of the 'most straitest sect.' And this evidence was amply confirmed, by every sentiment I ever heard him utter, whether in private or public." At the close of the session of 1831-32 they parted—Mr. Tazewell having resigned his seat in the Senate; and although Judge White continued in that body eight years afterwards, they never met again. It was during one of the recesses of Congress that the hand of affliction was laid heavily upon them both. Each lost a grown-up son; and their meeting at the commencement of the next session is described by one who witnessed it as very affecting, neither being capable of utterance, but both giving vent to their feelings in floods of tears.

If any further evidence is needed of the high estimation in which the legal ability and statesmanship of Judge W. were held, it appears in the selection of himself and Judge Burnett of Ohio, on the 19th Nov., 1822, by the Government of Kentucky, as Commissioners to adjust the military land claims of Virginia. The Commissioners appointed on the part of Virginia, were Benj. W. Leigh and Wm. Gaston of North Carolina. His association with such men in the discharge of such highly responsible duties, is a sufficient proof of his great reputation for solid and reliable sagacity and integrity, as well as of professional acquirements.

CHAPTER VIII.

SENATORIAL CAREER—PANAMA MISSION—FEDERAL JUDICIARY.

THUS far, Judge White has been presented to the reader chiefly as a local jurist and politician. He will now appear as an actor in more important and interesting scenes; in which his life and acts are interwoven with national interests, and become portions of national history. Nor can his character be adequately estimated without a full view of the manner in which he discharged the duties of his elevated station in the National Legislature.

When General Jackson resigned his seat in the Senate of the United States, in 1825, Judge White, being then fifty-two years of age, was elected for the remainder of his term, and continued to fill the place until 1840, being thrice elected not only by a unanimous vote, but without having solicited the office. Even at his entrance upon the duties of his position he brought much weight of character into our national councils, acquired by the punctual and faithful discharge of all the responsibilities which had before that time been imposed upon him, by unyielding integrity, and by his well-known sound and safe habits of investigation, decision and action.

The fifteen years of Judge White's senatorship belong to a period of more stormy and thrilling interest than any in American political history, since the adoption of the Constitution; a period of party reorganization, and reform and re-direction of public policy, effected and opposed, amidst the most reckless and impassioned political warfare. During all the mighty conflicts of principles and opinions, interests, parties and men, which made the Senate during Jackson's administration a chosen arena for the combats of intellectual giants; during the memorable conflicts upon the Mission to Panama, Internal Improvements; during the great struggle to establish Mr. Clay's "American System," the critical battle with Nullification, the desperate contest with the United States Bank, and also during all the collateral and contemporary minor debates that crowded every session, Judge

White was often upon the floor, and in every struggle sustained his part fearlessly, honorably and well. He was a disciple of the old Republican school; of the school of Jefferson and of Jackson, and in accordance with the views of the statesmen of that school he discussed all the questions of the day; and whatever external differences he may have had with others of his own political belief, to the declared principles of that belief he adhered firmly and consistently to the last.

In 1826, during the administration of John Quincy Adams, was introduced the question, now almost forgotten, of the Panama Mission. This was debated in Congress, upon motions to send accredited Ministers from the Government of the United States to a proposed Convention of the Republics of North and South America, to be holden upon the Isthmus of Panama. This Convention, was to discuss and determine, if possible, commercial and international principles and courses of action in a free and liberal manner, such as was befitting the joint action of free nations. Its objects were noble, and such as temporarily to enlist an overwhelming popular feeling in favor of the mission. The purposes for which it was claimed that the United States should participate in the Congress were represented to be

1. To establish liberal international commercial regulations.
2. To determine and agree upon a doctrine of maritime neutrality.
3. To establish the doctrine that "free ships make free goods."
4. To establish the "Monroe doctrine," so called; of preventing European interference with American national action.
5. To advance religious liberty.
6. To conciliate the good will of our American co-nations, by accepting their invitation and aiding in their deliberations.

This was an administration measure, and was opposed by the great mass of the opposition, then already organized as the Democratic party. Judge White, as an opposition speaker, delivered against it on the 26th of March, 1826, a speech which discussed the general principles brought up in the course of the debate (which was secret, although afterwards allowed to be published); and which was pronounced "the ablest exposition of the powers of government made during the whole discussion."

After showing that the question was whether the Senate should *advise* this mission, and also that the not advising it ought not to give offence to the nations inviting it, Judge White said, speaking upon the report of the committee of the Senate, adversely to the Mission:

Mr. President: Were I to be advised by my feelings I should remain silent, but when I reflect upon the relation in which I stand to the report now under consideration, a sense of duty compels me to submit to the Senate some of the views which my mind has taken of this subject.

The only question is, the *expediency* of the Mission to Panama. The President has distinctly asked of us an opinion upon this question.

Our advice is to be given as freemen, not as slaves. In this course we serve the Executive, maintain the dignity and independence of the Senate, and promote the best interests of the United States. If the mission should not be advised, we give no cause of offence to the Spanish American States. The evidences heretofore given of our friendship for them, in acknowledging their independence, and interposing our good offices to effect it, ought to shield us against any suspicion of unfriendly feelings towards them, at present. The President will likewise comply with the only promise made to those who have tendered the invitation, his acceptance of it having been *conditional* "if the Senate advise," &c.

The subject is then fairly before us, for the exercise of our best judgment, without a fear that any promise of the Executive will be violated, should the Senate disagree with him in opinion: but even if this were not so, we could not without a shameful dereliction of duty, offer anything, as our advice, but the result of our best judgment.

The first reflection upon this subject, is produced by its novelty. Since the acknowledgment of our independence, it has no precedent in our history. This ought to beget caution and circumspection.

If this mission should be advised, a new era will have commenced in the history of our foreign relations. Peace with, and good-will towards all nations, entangling alliances with none; has been our cardinal policy, in the time past. It was recommended by the Father of our Country—repeated, and practised upon, by his *republican* successors. When given, we were few in number, comparatively poor, and insignificant, in the scale of nations; now, we are twelve millions; rich in men, in means and in character. Our prosperity has surpassed the most extravagant calculations of the most sanguine amongst us.

In our late contest with the most powerful nation in the civilized world, unaided by, and unallied to, any other nation, we furnished conclusive evidence, both upon the ocean and upon the land, that we are able and willing to defend the rich inheritance derived from our ancestors.

The sincerity of our conduct in our intercourse with other nations, and a careful abstinence from all interference in their concerns, united to our determined and successful resistance to lawless encroachments upon our rights, have given us a proud name throughout the nations of the earth. Happy at home, and respected abroad, why should we change the policy by which these blessings have been obtained?

We ought not to advise it, except to obtain some *lasting and important benefit for the United States*, *certainly* attainable in *this* mode, probably to be attained in no other; but never from sympathy for others, from a desire to serve them, or from a desire of gratifying national vanity.

We are then naturally led to inquire into the objects expected to be obtained, and the probability of accomplishing them in this mode.

Here we cannot fail to perceive how difficult it appears to have been, for those who gave the invitations, to fix upon any subject for discussion, which they believed of sufficient importance to the United States, to induce them to accept those invitations; hence, both the Minister from Columbia, and from Mexico, introduce the idea of subjects "which the Congress may give rise to," &c.

How can the Senate advise the President to send Ministers to discuss unknown subjects? to accomplish objects which no person can designate? and in relation to which it is impossible to say whether their attainment would comport with the honor and interest of the United States, or not? Suppose those giving these invitations had specified no subject whatever for discussion, but had asked the attendance of our Ministers, to discuss, and come to an agreement, upon such subjects as the Congress might give rise to; is there any one member of the Senate, that would advise a mission upon such an invitation? Would it not be thought both useless and hazardous?

To these questions it would seem to me there can be but one answer. Fond would he be of the creation of officers, and heedless of the honor and interest of his country, who would advise the appointment of Ministers to a foreign country, to attend a Congress for the purpose of seeing whether a subject could be produced that might be proper for an agreement with the United States. I will not degrade the Senate by supposing there is any such man among us, and will proceed with this investigation, as if no allusion had been made to any unknown subject, which could neither be designated, nor described.

The first subject mentioned is, the resistance or opposition to be made to the interference of any neutral nation in the war of Independence, &c.

This appears to be a point of *primary importance*, in the estimation of all concerned. Let us calmly and dispassionately reflect upon it. Six of the former Spanish American Colonies have declared themselves independent of Spain, and to maintain this independence, have put at hazard their lives and their fortunes. Spain asserts that they are still parts of her dominions, that she has the right to govern them, and that, cost what it may, she will reduce them to subjection. The decision of this issue is submitted to the God of battles. These six colonies have become six States, and are belligerent on one side, and Spain on the other. Heretofore these States have exerted their strength separately without any regular alliance with each other, although they have had a common enemy to contend with. The belief, that it would conduce to their common interest, and best secure that independence for which all are contending, has induced five of them to enter into treaties, by which they are bound to make common cause against Spain, and by their united efforts, to compel her to acknowledge the independence of each. To produce union in council, and concord in action and design among the new States, they have devised the Congress at Panama. It is to be perpetual. Its primary and leading object is belligerent. Its secondary and inferior objects and duties are peaceful. The first subject, then, which will claim the attention of this Congress, is some plan, by which the independence of each State, will not only be maintained, but secured.

A fear has been entertained, that some European power, now neutral in this war, will be induced to unite with Spain, and lend her assistance to reduce these States to the condition of colonies. They wish to provide against such an event, and in giving these invitations, they state, that they have a pledge from the President, and that there is an accord between them and the Cabinet at Washington; that if any neutral power does take part with Spain, the United States will take part with them; and wish the attendance of our Ministers with a view to discuss the subject, and come to an agreement in relation to it, by which it will be stipulated, what contingent each party shall furnish when the *casus fœderis* shall occur; and they say, that in the meantime this agreement or convention may be kept *secret*.

Mr. President, I object to sending ministers for the purpose of discussing and coming to any agreement or convention upon this subject. It is not true, as far as I am advised, that the United States stand pledged to take part in this war in any event whatever. Nothing can bind us to go to war with any nation, but a declaration made in the proper form, and by the proper department of this Government. The Executive cannot declare war, but I admit he may pursue a course of policy which will justify other nations in making war upon us. Congress has taken no step, has done no act, has passed no law, by which we are bound to unite with these new States in their war of independence, upon any contingency whatever. The Executive had no power to bind the United States by any *pledge* he could give. But what has he done? The groundwork of this pretended pledge, it seems, is found in President Monroe's Message of December 1823. It contains no pledge—it is a general declaration to his own Congress, of the sentiment which would be felt if any neutral should interfere on the side of Spain. Notwithstanding that declaration, the United States were still at liberty, consistently with their honor, to take part with the new States, or omit to do so, as the wisdom of Congress might judge best, when any neutral power did take part with Spain. This declaration had a good effect. Not wishing to give offence to the United States, it may have prevented some of the European States from taking part with Spain. The new States have had the full benefit of this declaration. Thus the matter appears to have rested, till the close of Mr. Monroe's Administration. Since the new Administration came into power, it seems, that upon the appearance of a French fleet in our seas, some of the new States called upon the Executive to redeem the pledge which had been given. Upon this application, in place of correcting the mistake upon the subject, it would appear from the documents with which we are furnished, the Administration admitted that which I do not see was the fact, that a pledge had been given, and directed Mr. Brown, our Minister in France to ask an explanation, &c. Upon this point, however, I think we are still in the dark; we have no copy of the application from the new States, nor of our answer to them. These documents would have shown how far our new Administration have gone towards compelling us to take part in this war. It is very singular, that after all the calls for information which the Senate have been compelled to make, upon this important business, there is still a want of documents, that would probably be useful. But if we are at liberty to judge from the correspondence between Mr. Poinsett and the Mexican Minister, and from Mr. Secretary's letter to Mr. Poinsett, it does really seem that the Executive has admitted to Mexico, that we have given a pledge, which we may be called on to redeem, whenever the contingency shall occur.* Of this pledge, the people of these States are yet uninformed. I feel persuaded they have no idea we stand pledged upon any contingency to embark in the war with these new States, whether it may comport with our interest or not. This is an inadvertence which cannot be corrected too soon. If we send Ministers and an agreement is entered into, then indeed, will the United States be *pledged*. We now know the object. We see the predicament in which we are placed, and with this knowledge, if Congress can be induced to give its sanction to this measure, and this pledge of the Executive is refined into an agreement, by which the United States shall be bound to furnish men, money, ships, &c., in aid of the new States, whenever any power, now neutral, may choose to take part with Spain, then, indeed, shall I think this nation has given a pledge,

* Mr. Poinsett's letter to Mr. Clay, 28th September, 1825:

"To these observations I replied, that against the power of Spain they had given sufficient proof that they required no assistance, and the United States had *pledged* themselves not to permit any other power to interfere with their independence or form of government; and that as in the event of such an attempt being made by the powers of Europe, we would be *compelled to take the most active and efficient part and to bear the brunt of the contest*, it was not just that we should be placed on a less favorable footing, than the other republics of America, whose existence we were ready to *support* at such hazards."

one that it may cost us too much to redeem, when the *casus fœderis* shall happen.

But, sir, how is it that we are told our neutral character is not to be compromitted? that we are not to enter into any alliance? to engage in nothing importing hostility to any other nation? Are we to be led away from the substance of things by mere names? Are we to have so much faith as to induce us to disregard the plainest evidence that can be furnished? I hope not. What is the substance of this proposition? These new States say, the President has given a pledge to take a part in the war now waged, if any neutral nation shall take part with Spain; and that the Cabinet at Washington has done the like: but, as this is only a *general pledge*, and they do not know exactly what assistance they are to receive, they wish the United States to send Ministers to Panama, empowered to discuss this subject, and come to a *definite agreement* upon it, by which it may be distinctly known what contingent the United States are to furnish, when the *casus fœderis* happens, and that all this matter shall be kept secret.

Suppose we do send Ministers, for such a purpose, to a Congress composed entirely of belligerents on one side, is it not a violation of our neutrality? What is our situation? We profess friendship for both the parties to this war, and that we are not disposed to aid either. Is it no departure from the professions to send our Ministers? Can any gentleman doubt upon this point? Recollect that this Congress is *created* and assembled avowedly for the purpose of discussing *war* measures, settling *plans*, and devising *means*, by which Spain shall be compelled to acknowledge their independence, and by which that independence can be best secured.

With this knowledge, and for the purpose of entering upon the discussion, and making an agreement, by which we will be bound, upon a certain contingency, to aid the party with whom we make the agreement we send our Ministers. Can we be called indifferent? Countenancing neither, to the prejudice of the other? Surely not. What is the answer to this argument? The only one as yet attempted is by the gentleman from Rhode Island, that if two nations are at war, it is no breach of neutrality in a third Power to send a Minister to both, or either. This is very true, and yet it proves nothing, as it relates to the question now in dispute. For peaceful purposes—for any purpose unconnected with the *war*—the third power may send a Minister, may discuss, may treat upon any *peaceful* subject; but, does this prove that you may send a Minister to the Court of one *belligerent* to discuss *belligerent questions*, to advise one party what steps he is to take in the *war*, whether it is most prudent to strike his adversary at a given time, or in a given quarter? Surely not. And yet this is the very point which gentlemen on the other side must maintain. This part of the subject has been placed by the gentleman from South Carolina on ground which cannot be shaken. His argument has not been answered. It never will be, while there is a distinction between truth and the reverse.

Mr. President, I go one step farther, and insist, if you do send Ministers, and they discuss this subject, and enter into the proposed agreement, so far as you have power over the matter, your neutrality is not only broken, but you are in a state of war, and that with any and every power that is now neutral, and may hereafter elect to take a part with Spain. This is a dilemma from which we cannot escape, without disgrace. Send Ministers, make the agreement—and the question of peace, or war, is not *with us;* and, at any moment afterwards, any European or even an American nation can put you at war, whether it may suit your interest or not.

I object to sending Ministers for the discussion of any such subject, or for the accomplishment of any such object. Even if we believed that such a state of things would probably be produced, as to make it proper for us to take a part in this war, I would still be opposed to any agreement by which we will become bound to do so. It is impossible now to foresee what may best comport with the interest of the United States at any subsequent period; and they ought to be left free to act, unfettered by any agreement whatever, as their interest or honor may require, when some other power does actually interfere.

It is vain to say, we are not to take a part in any belligerent question; that our neutrality is not to be violated; that we are not to engage in anything importing hostility to any other power, while this proposition is presented to us. One of the Ministers who gave the invitation classes the subject to be discussed into *belligerent* and *peaceful*, and states that the United States are not expected to take any part in the *first;* but, in the last, they are, and in *this class*, he specifies this very subject. Does this make it peaceful? Surely not. It is belligerent. I admit it is not an *absolute* stipulation to take part in the war, and, therefore, some may feel justified in saying it does not import hostility; yet, it is undoubtedly an agreement to take part upon the happening of a certain contingency. It will import hostility upon a certain condition, which contingency or condition is not within the control of the United States.

After remarking upon the failure to transmit to the Senate certain information in regard to the feelings of the European cabinets in relation to any attempt to wrest Cuba from Spain, Judge White proceeded with observations by no means unimportant or unseasonable in their bearing upon subjects at this very day exciting a lively interest in the public mind. He said, on this point:

These colonies (Cuba and Porto Rico) are convenient to the new (South American) States; which having expelled their enemies from their own territory, will probably stimulate a portion of the inhabitants of those Islands to rebel, to declare themselves independent of Spain, and by uniting their forces with those revolted subjects, endeavor to put down the Spanish authorities in those Islands. What consequences are likely to flow from such a measure? Russia probably, and France almost certainly, would then immediately take part *with Spain*, in the war. From the documents, we have evidence that they would have strong inducements to interpose immediately. It is their wish that Spain should retain her dominion over those Islands, because then that balance would be kept up in the seas where those Islands are situate which those powers think ought to be preserved.*

Again: all monarchs, and these in particular, would feel an interest to check this spirit of revolt; if not put down, none of them would feel safe; and while aiding Spain, they would be rendering more secure their own dominions. To lend assistance would be esteemed by them a principle of self-defence. Lastly, these new States have told us, even now, they suspect that France is secretly furnishing Spain the means of continuing the war. Spain tells you France is her friend—that "in six troubles she has stood by her, and that, in the seventh, she will not forsake her;" and from the connection between these powers, at home, it is rendered extremely probable, that the opinions entertained, both by the new States and Spain, as to the policy of France, will turn out to be correct. Suppose, then, you sanction this mission, your Ministers discuss this subject, come to an agreement upon it, stipulate that if any neutral power interferes on the part of Spain, that the United States will take part with the new States, and Russia and France do thus take part with Spain, the *casus fœderis* will then have happened, and the United States, in connection with the Spanish American States, will thus become one party in the war, and Spain, Russia, and France the other, and how or when it will terminate, no man can foresee.

In this state of things what is to become of our own important interests, our commerce for example, to secure which we seem so anxious? Great Britain is ever attentive to her own interest, watching the course

* "She is, however, in the mean while, pleased to hope, that the United States, becoming every day more convinced of the evils and dangers that would result to Cuba and Porto Rico from a change of Government, being satisfied, as Mr. Clay has said in his dispatch, with the commercial legislation of these two Islands, and deriving an additional motive of security from the honorable resolution of Spain not to grant to them, any longer, letters of marque, will use their influence in defeating, as far as may be in their power, every enterprise against these Islands, in securing to the rights of his Catholic Majesty constant and proper respect in maintaining the *only state of things that can preserve a just balance of power in the Sea of the Antilles, prevent shocking examples*, and, as the Cabinet at Washington has remarked, secure to the general peace salutary guaranties."—Count Nesselrode to Mr. Middleton, 20th Aug. 1825.

of events, and turning them to the advantage of her own subjects. Even now, some fear she is at this Congress, not as a party but as a listener, and will gain some advantage by our delay: how would she probably act? She would take no part in the war. She would be neutral, the United States belligerent; and what then becomes of your commerce? It will be engrossed by your neighbor, who has been attending to her own interest, while you have been seeking distinction by neglecting your own concerns, and attending to those of other nations.

But, sir, if in this I mistake the course of Great Britain, and she should elect to take a part in the war, it would probably be on the side of Spain, and then we should have our difficulties increased to the full extent of her means and resources.

To this view of the case, I beg the attention of the gentleman from Rhode Island, and respectfully ask an application of the rule of "probabilities," and then let him say whether this Congress is so harmless. and whether, in his judgment, we have nothing to apprehend?

There are other views of this subject which render it inexpedient to sanction this measure.

This agreement or treaty is to be kept secret. By the frame of our Government, treaties are to be the supreme law; would it be discreet to have a treaty, by which the United States may be involved, *concealed* from the People? It is their Government, it is their interests, that are at stake, and nothing material ought to be secreted from them.

Again, such an arrangement would be inconsistent with our character for candor. We owe it to ourselves to do no act, to make no agreement, that we ought to be unwilling to avow.

The very circumstance of a desire to *conceal* is a proof that the project is inconsistent with our professed neutrality, and would be justly offensive to Spain and to other nations.

After showing that it was inconsistent with the dignity of the United States to stipulate with other nations, according to that article of the Panama programme, which provided for mutual agreement that no contracting State should suffer European colonies to be planted within its borders, Judge White proceeded to another subject, also absorbingly interesting at this day, as follows:

Mr. President: I pass to the next subject specified. It is to discuss and agree upon the means to be employed for the *entire abolition* of the *slave trade*. Of all subjects that could be thought of, none would be found more unfortunate than this. It was hoped, that, after rejecting the convention with Columbia upon this subject, the Senate would have no more of it from foreigners. If slavery is an affliction, all the Southern and Western States have it, and with it, their peculiar modes of thinking upon all subjects connected with it. In these new States, some of them have put it down in their fundamental law, "that whoever owns a slave shall cease to be a citizen." Is it then fit that the United States should disturb the quiet of the Southern and Western States, by a discussion and argument with the new States, upon any subject connected with slavery? I think not. Can it be the desire of any prominent politician in the United States, to divide us into parties upon the subject of *Slavery?* I hope not. Let us then cease to talk of slavery in this House; let us cease to negotiate upon any subject connected with it. The United States have by their own laws put an end to the slave trade so far as their citizens, or their vessels, are concerned in it—more than this, they ought not to attempt. Let other nations discharge their duty as well, and the slave trade, so called, will be abolished.

One word more upon this point, Mr. President, and I will dismiss it. If there be any gentlemen in the United States, who seriously wish to see an end of slavery, let them cease talking and writing, to induce the Federal Government to take up the subject, because, by the course now pursued by some, they are postponing a measure, whose accomplishment they profess a wish to hasten. Whenever the States in which slavery exists, feel it as an evil too intolerable, move towards its removal at home, and apply through their Legislatures to this Government for aid to abolish it, then, and not sooner, we may discuss it within these walls.

We are invited to attend and settle "the basis of our relations to Hayti," and *others*, that may be in like circumstances, &c.

Will gentlemen tell us whether a Representative from Hayti is invited to attend this Congress? It appears to me that it will be very unfair to settle this question, when that Government is unrepresented. It is therefore most probable, her Minister is to be there likewise. Reflect, Mr. President, upon the population of that country, and upon that of a portion of our own, as well as upon the peculiar modes of thinking in Spanish America, and then let honorable gentlemen say whether they think this will be a fit subject for discussion. It is a question which the South American statesmen must settle for themselves and by themselves. Our situation, in relation to this subject, is so peculiarly delicate, that I cannot suppose any real friend to the Union, would propose that it should be settled at the Congress of Panama. The suggestion of such a project may be readily excused in a foreigner, but in an American citizen it would be inexcusable.

Upon the proposition to establish an American system, Judge White remarked, with solid and profound wisdom:

The Minister from Central America proposes, that at this Congress an American Continental System shall be got up, as Europe has one.

Let us bestow a few thoughts upon this subject, and see to what it tends. In Europe, the object of their system is to make common cause to support monarchs on their thrones.

The contrary would be, to make common cause to secure in America a Republican form of government to each nation. Our fundamental principle is, that every nation ought to be permitted to have just such a form of government as the people of that nation may think best suited to their condition, and best calculated to secure their lives, liberty, and property, and that, in settling their forms of government, no other nation has any right to interfere.

We find fault with the European system, and with the Holy Alliance, because it is their object to fix monarchy upon the people of the respective States, whether the majorities in those States are pleased with such governments or not. Are we then to combine with other States, to compel each one to preserve a republican form of government, whether they will it or not? We believe, and I flatter myself truly believe, that ours is the best plan of government which has yet been devised; but, if it is the best for the people of these United States, does it thence follow that it would be the best for every other nation?

Ours is the best for an intelligent and virtuous people; but it does not thence follow, that it would be best for an ignorant and vicious people. The people of each country ought to understand their own character better than the people of any other country; and they ought to be the exclusive judges of what plan of government is best suited to their peculiar character and condition, and any interference by the people of any other country, to force upon them a form of government which they do not themselves choose, is an act of tyranny and oppression. The whole project, then, is wrong in principle and therefore ought not to meet our sanction.

Again, we are only in the course of experiment at home. Whether our plan is as perfect as it ought to be, is at this moment a subject of discussion over the way. We are endeavoring to improve it, and hope to render it so perfect that we shall be pleased with it for ever: yet, even we may change our minds upon that subject, and if we do, we shall claim the right of changing our government likewise. Let us then not be too hasty. Are we sure our politicians are well acquainted with the character of our own people upon all points? It would be unreasonable to suppose them intimately acquainted with every peculiarity of character in each of the Spanish American States. Without this knowledge, we are not in a situation to form an opinion on this subject. Their true character is yet to be developed. The war must be finished first. A foreign enemy may have kept them in a state of internal peace. Remove the idea of this foreign enemy, and we cannot foresee how soon discord and bloodshed may ensue among themselves. Even the other day, in one of these States, we saw considerable resistance made to some of their laws. Let us then afford time for a thorough development of character, before we identify our fate with theirs to too great an extent, upon this, or any other point. But, again, in Europe, they have a continental system, and therefore we are to get up a countervailing one in America. We are to have a system opposed to a system; the friends of each endeavoring to make proselytes; in what will this course terminate? In warm words, if not in blows. It leads to discord and war. We have extensive commercial intercourse with the powers of Europe, as well as with those of the new States. Our interest consists in peace and friendship with all; let us not rashly adopt a course calculated to disturb our harmony with either. To preserve our own liberty; to better the condition of our own citizens; will furnish sufficient employment for our own most enlightened public servants, and let us not suffer any one, from a vain desire to fill an uncommon number of pages in our own future history, to influence us to such an interference in the concerns of others, as will put in jeopardy those of our own people.

After examining the other proposed objects of the mission, Judge White proceeds to exhibit the danger from such uncontrolled powers of appointment as would seem to exist in the Executive, if the nominations were to be confirmed.

Another point, however, is not to be lost sight of. I have, Mr. President, upon this argument, been endeavoring to maintain, that this mission is inexpedient. Upon one of the incidental questions which we have heretofore partially discussed, I had the honor of making to the Senate, some observations upon a question first suggested by a gentleman from Kentucky, and afterwards enlarged upon by the gentleman from Virginia. It is this—is there in truth, any vacant office to fill with the persons now nominated? I have insisted there is not, that we have begun this business at the wrong end. In our government we can have but two sources from which offices can be created. The one is the Constitution, the other statutes made by Congress. These offices are not created by the one, or by the other. By the Constitution, the President, by and with the advice and consent of the Senate, can appoint ambassadors, and other public ministers, &c.

Under this provision, the President has the power, with the advice and consent of the Senate, to appoint an ambassador, or any other public agent, recognized by, and known to the laws of civilized nations; but as to all other offices, they must be *created* by some statute of the United States, before any person is nominated to fill them. The sole question upon this point, then, is, are such ministers as those now proposed, known to, and recognized by the law of nations? I deny that they are. The

Congress is created by treaties, among the Spanish American States. It is contended by gentlemen on the other side, that it has no attribute of sovereignty attached to it—if this be so, then you cannot, by the law of nations, send any ministers to transact business with such a body. If you do send them, it must be in virtue of some treaty, or by virtue of some statute of the United States. In this instance, there is neither the one nor the other. Therefore, there is no office as yet created, and until one is created, neither the President alone, nor he, with the advice of the Senate, can, consistently with the Constitution, proceed to fill it.

The fair way to have taken the sense of the nation upon the expediency of this mission would have been to have consulted Congress, in their *legislative* capacity, on the propriety of the mission, by asking an appropriation to defray the expenses of it, and stating the objects expected to be obtained by it. The subject would then have come fairly before the representatives of the nation, who would have discussed and decided upon its expediency with *open* doors. If affirmatively decided, the offices would have been created by statute, and then the President could have nominated characters, which he deemed suitable to fill them, and upon these nominations, the Senate would have acted in their executive capacity, and advised the President whether, in their opinion, these men were or were not, suitable persons to fill these offices. But here the order of things is reversed—the Senate has been called upon to discuss and settle the expediency of this mission, upon mere *nominations* to office, and if the nominations should be confirmed, then we are to pass a law in the shape of an appropriation bill, by which, the offices will, for the first time, be *created.* The injustice of this course, to the minority on this question, and to the nation, is obvious. Upon the nominations we have been constrained to act with *closed doors*, the nation has no knowledge of the facts upon which our opinions rest, nor of the reasons in support of those opinions. Little do they suspect that principles of such vital importance are involved in this decision.

I have again mentioned this point, not intending to argue it the second time. I mention it because, if a majority—thus irregularly, I might say—in my opinion, unconstitutionally—determine that this mission is expedient, I must and will, entertaining the opinion I now do, vote against any man, who has been, or can be nominated, because I will not agree to fill any office which I do not believe has the sanction of either the Constitution or law of the United States for its *creation.*

The result of the discussion was that the nominees of the President, Messrs. John Sergeant, of Pennsylvania, and Richard C. Anderson, of Kentucky, were confirmed, by a vote of 24 to 20. But they were never sent upon their errand, for the Congress was never held. And the effervescence of popular interest in the scheme rapidly dying

4

away, the "sober second thought" of the people resulted in a general acquiescence in the sound and moderate views of Judge White and his fellow opponents to the mission.

At the time of Judge White's entrance into the Senate there was, and had for some time existed, throughout the Western States, a very just cause of complaint, in the unfair apportionment of the United States Judiciary Districts. In nine of the Western States, the decisions in the United States Courts were rendered, either by a District Judge alone, or with very little and cursory assistance from the Circuit Judge; a state of things which caused the administration of justice in those States to be both slower and more erroneous than in the remaining fifteen, by reason of the action of a single judge, and of the necessary shortness and infrequency of the terms in each circuit. Upon Judge White's first entrance into Congress, his attention was given to this subject. With great difficulty a bill passed the House of Representatives, creating three additional circuits, and requiring three additional judges of the Supreme Court. It was sent to the Senate, and then to the Judiciary Committee, who amended it in two particulars; making it the duty of the three additional judges to *reside in the new circuits*, and secondly, changing the distribution of the different States from that proposed in the original bill. These amendments passed the Senate by a very large majority. Of the ten Senators from the five States of Kentucky, Ohio, Indiana, Illinois, and Missouri, only three were in favor of the distribution made in the bill from the House. That body, however, refused to agree to either of the Senate amendments, the Senate adhered to both, and thus the bill was lost. Judge White voted with the majority. His former position at the bar, and on the bench, enabled him to appreciate the wants of the Western country in this particular, and he did not slumber over them. At the next session, he again brought the subject before Congress in a speech, showing the inequality as to the administration of justice under which the Western States had been laboring, and arguing that the evil ought to be remedied; and used his endeavors to have it acted on, but for want of time the subject was then postponed.

Judge White's remarks on this subject, furnish a clear analysis of the wants of the West in the particular under consideration, and intelligent views of the operation of residence or non-residence upon the professional ability and success of a judge; and contain so many suggestions of permanent value upon the practical duties of the judicial office, as to justify the insertion of portions of his speech, delivered April 11, 1826, that is, during that one of the two sessions above referred to, in which the Senate and House failed to agree upon a bill to meet the wants of the West in the required reformation of the courts.

Judge White said:

If it could be shown that the remedy proposed to obviate the inconveniences complained of in those sections of country, would be injurious to the whole Union, he ought not to expect, or to wish, that their special inconveniences should be removed to the injury of the whole community. The subject on which we are about to legislate is, in my mind, one of infinite importance. We are about to pass an act in relation to a department of the government which every man feels and ought to understand. It is in vain we enact good laws unless they are well administered. It is that department of government which operates directly on the persons and property of individuals who happen to be citizens of the United States, so far as the jurisdiction is local, or so far as it relates to the internal concerns of the citizens of the respective States. So far as it may operate on general principles it is still more important—therefore have I heard with great attention everything that has been urged by gentlemen who are opposed to it, and I shall still be glad to hear all further objections that can be urged.

We cannot judge whether the alteration will be beneficial or injurious, without first making ourselves acquainted with the inconveniences which are supposed to exist. Till we are acquainted with the disease we cannot tell what will be a suitable remedy. I think I can, if favored with the attention of the Senate, if not already satisfied on that point, satisfy them that the disease lies much deeper than the gentleman from Rhode Island seems to suppose. I paid great attention to the argument, and he seems to think, so far as I can understand it, that the main grievance which we are called on to remedy, is the *delay* which takes place in the Supreme Court of the United States. He has not even, in his excellent argument, given the most distant glance at the situation of that section of the country which is on the other side of the mountains, to see what the local inconveniences are, and whether the remedy he proposes would be a suitable one or not. The grievances which do exist in the country, are, as I think, of two kinds; one, in the manner in which the business is conducted in the respective States; the other, that which exists in the Supreme Court itself; and this latter does not consist so much in the delay, as in the incorrectness of the decisions where the questions depend upon the municipal laws of the respective States.

These are the grievances which exist, and which it is the object of this bill to remedy. First, by extending to nine States the circuit system, which is applicable to, and practised beneficially in, the other fifteen States; and secondly, to increase on the bench of the Supreme Court a knowledge of the local laws; those are its leading objects. These nine States, when we look to them, we find thus circumstanced: Six of them have never had, either nominally or in fact, the benefit of a circuit judge, three of these States had nominally, and to a very limited extent, the benefit of the attendance of a judge of the Supreme Court from the year 1809 up to this time. I say they have had it nominally, but not so, in point of fact. When the judge of the seventh circuit was in the vigor of life, and in the enjoyment of perfect health, it was his duty to attend and hold circuit courts in the districts of East and West Tennessee, of Kentucky and Ohio, and from the necessity he was under of leaving one court in time to arrive at the next, in his circuit, an opportunity was not afforded him of disposing of the causes on either docket. For example, he would have suits enough in West Tennessee to require a session of two months, but at the end of three or four weeks he was compelled to be in Kentucky, distant two hundred miles, and so on; and thus it happened, either that the district judges must continue the courts after his departure, or the causes must remain undecided. In important suits, parties would not be willing to trust the opinion of the district judge alone, and he would willingly yield to applications for delay, until he could have the assistance of the judge of the Supreme Court, and thus the business must be either long delayed, or in most instances decided in the circuit courts of those three States, by the district judge alone. For several of the last years of Judge Todd's life, his want of health put it out of his power to attend his circuit courts, and thus it has happened that the business in Tennessee, Kentucky and Ohio, has accumulated to an unreasonable extent, and those States have, in truth, been no better provided with an opportunity of obtaining a due administration of justice in their Federal Courts, than the other six Western States; and how is it with regard to *them?* *They* have never had the benefit of the circuit system, even nominally. They have each a district judge, who does all the duties which other district judges perform, and who is vested with the jurisdiction which circuit courts possess in the other States. So far as relates to the grievances which exist in the country, we are safe in considering the whole nine States to be practically in the same situation. When we come to look at the laws which vest the courts with jurisdiction, we find that a large portion of the jurisdiction which is to be exercised in those nine States, is of that description which falls within the jurisdiction of a circuit court, and not within the jurisdiction of a district court. A district court, as such, can have no jurisdiction of suits between A and B, whether citizens of the United States, or of different States. Some attempts have been made to get them to entertain jurisdiction of the suits between citizens of different States, when the matter in dispute is of more value than twenty, and of less than five hundred dollars, but so far as I know, they have been unsuccessful.

As it relates to a great portion of the jurisdiction which is to be exercised in those nine States, the Senate must see at once, it is of that class of cases which belongs to the circuit courts in the other States. What is the situation of these other States? They have, in point of fact, as well as in point of law, a circuit court, composed of one judge of the Supreme Court, and the district judge. When a suit is brought, and the matter in dispute exceeds the sum of two thousand dollars, upon the trial, the parties have the benefit of the opinions of two men, which will in most instances be satisfactory: but if not, the unsuccessful party can remove it to the Supreme Court and there have the judgment revised, and if wrong reversed. If the matter in dispute is less than two thousand dollars, and the judges disagree in opinion upon any point, either party can have that point certified to the Supreme Court, then revised, and the judgment of the circuit court rendered in conformity with the opinion of the Supreme Court. In all criminal cases the defendant has the like advantage. How is it in those nine States? In no case, either civil or criminal, can the parties in the circuit court have any opinion but that of the district judge, which in every criminal case, and in every civil one where the matter in dispute is of less value than two thousand dollars, is final and conclusive whether right or wrong; and in all other civil causes, although an erroneous judgment may be revised in the Supreme Court, it is at an expense and trouble which would often be avoided if two judges sat in the circuit court.

The gentleman from New Hampshire said yesterday, we of the West would not compare wealth with those in the East; all true enough; and therefore there are many causes where the matter in dispute does not amount to two thousand dollars, and still it is very material to the parties that they should be correctly decided. It is certainly not just that a man should be punished as a criminal under an erroneous judgment, or that he should lose his all by the like means, while those living under the same government are protected in their persons and property because more wealthy. We are one people living under a government common to us all, and each State has a right to expect from the Federal Government, that a like provision will be made for her citizens, with that made for the citizens of the other States. This has not been done, and as we are to be one people, we have a right to expect it will be no longer delayed.

Fifteen of the States of this Union have more than double the chance for a correct exposition of your laws that the other nine have; these nine complain of this inequality, and the only wonder is, that their complaints have not been more loud and frequent against this crying injustice.

Tennessee was admitted into this Union upon an *equal footing with the original States*, and so have the other Western States been. These States feel that this promised equality has not been extended to them; as sovereign States, they insist that their citizens must be placed in a situation where their persons and property shall be equally as safe in the Federal Courts, as the citizens of any other State are in their persons and property. With nothing less than this will they be contented. But it is said the proper time is not come; we are used as well as others have been used. I should be glad to know when the time will arrive?

Tennessee is thirty years old, Kentucky is older. Ohio came into the Union in 1803, Louisiana in 1812, Indiana in 1816, Illinois in 1816, Missouri in 1821, Mississippi in 1817, Alabama several years ago. Will the gentleman tell us when we shall have arrived at such mature age, as to entitle us to the same benefits of the Federal judiciary that are enjoyed by the other States? Sometimes they are willing to recognize us as at years of discretion, to put their dearest interests in our keeping. Personal services, money, anything we have, we are disposed to render freely our full share of, according to our abilities. We are willing to do our duty; and I call upon the Senate to say whether they do their duty to us, if they do not put the administration of justice on the same footing in the Western States, as it is in the others. Is not the life of a man in any one of those nine States, worth as much to society as it would be, if he were a constituent of the gentleman from New Hampshire or Rhode Island? Is it not reasonable to afford the same man as good a chance for justice in the States where he now lives as he would have if he lived in any other? Is that opportunity furnished? No, Sir, it is not.

It was intimated we had not applied in time. Why did we not apply at the time we were admitted into the Union? We did apply, and you promised us, and we now respectfully ask a compliance with that promise. Had we been of the original States, should we not have had the benefit we now ask you to extend to us? Surely we should; therefore, do not put us off with less now.

It may be said there is not much in all this; the wrong is on a limited scale, because the State Courts do the mass of the business. When the people are called to account for crimes, they are called before State Courts, to answer for offences against the State, and not for those against the United States. If gentlemen will think a little they will see the case is not so. We have heard a good deal respecting Indians latterly; there is a portion of the territory within the limits of the Western States, where the Indian title is not extinguished, and when that is the case, every offence committed by a white citizen against an Indian on the Indian side of the line, is a subject of Federal and not of State jurisdiction, according to our laws; so likewise of crimes committed by Indians on citizens. Trials for crimes under this branch of your laws are not unfrequent, and no matter whether the accused is a white, or a red man, a fair opportunity for a correct exposition and application of the laws ought to be furnished. Against the Indians, prejudices invariably exist; they are ignorant, not only of our laws and forms of proceedings, but of our language also; and common humanity requires that at least the same measure of justice should be meted them, as to a white citizen. I have witnessed several of those trials, and have no doubt they were conducted with perfect integrity; yet the legal correctness of some might well be doubted. The criminal business then which has existed and may exist in the courts in some of these States is not so limited as those at a distance might incline to believe.

But, sir, we are told that the accumulation of business in some of these courts, in the three States, is produced by temporary causes that are passing away, and that there is no necessity for any alteration in the system on that account: that one circuit judge can do all the business in those three States. It is not to pass away so rapidly as the gentlemen suppose. I do not doubt the correctness of the statement of any gentleman living in any one of those States; he knows what the business is; therefore I do not choose to doubt the correctness of what was advanced by the gentleman from Kentucky. I have before me a certificate from the clerk of the district and circuit court of Kentucky, and at the session of November last, the number of causes on the two dockets combined were nine hundred and fifty. As very little business is to be done in this district court, much the greater portion must be on the circuit court docket of that State. How is it in Tennessee? You have the statement of the gentleman who belongs to the Western part, and altogether it may be estimated at two hundred. But it is not the number of causes which proves the necessity of a circuit judge, and an extension of the system this necessity is produced, more by the kind of causes that are to be decided, than by their number. These causes are generally in their own nature, especially those brought into the Federal Court of Tennessee, of the most litigated description. Many of them relate to lands; foreigners claim titles to them, and assert them in the Federal Courts. It is necessary to go back and examine what was the condition of the country forty years ago, and you get into a set of difficulties, from which nothing can extricate you, but a patient, laborious and protracted investigation. They necessarily consume a great deal of time, first in ascertaining the facts before a jury who are to decide the cause, and next in investigating the legal principles which are to govern that decision. To investigate and decide one of those causes, has sometimes taken two weeks; suppose only one hundred causes on the docket, I ask, if it would not be more necessary to extend the judicial system through a country like that, than to a place where there was five hundred on the docket, of which thirty or forty might be disposed of in a day. If we were to be governed by the mere number of causes we should make a most important mistake as relates to this matter. Many disputes in Tennessee relate to land, the titles tc which are founded on the act of 1777 in North Carolina, or the act of 1783, or those acts to which these two have given birth, and in investigating matters of fact, it is necessary to go back and ascertain what were the names of different places at different times, from those periods up to this time; the whole country was a wilderness, and every man who had a claim under these laws had a right to select a piece of land within a certain boundary, of from four to five hundred miles one way, and one hundred miles the other. We had not only to investigate our titles derived from the State of North Carolina, but in some instances those issued by Virginia and perhaps Kentucky, likewise, as disputes respecting boundary with those States once existed, upon adjusting which provision is made to secure individual rights.

We have amongst our own citizens those who claim under Virginia grants, under Kentucky grants, under North Carolina grants, and under those issued by the State of Tennessee. Wherever there is any dispute respecting any of these conflicting titles, they may go into the Federal Court, although the parties may be citizens of the same State. You are extinguishing the Indian title as fast as those people are willing to sell; and, wherever you do, the settlements will keep pace with the extinguishment of title. In Tennessee there is a very large district of country, granted to individuals under the law of North Carolina in 1783, which, until a very short time ago, the United States had secured to the Indians by treaty; that country is now settling, and every man has to look for the land for which he obtained his patent. Many of these conflict, and whenever they do, and a foreigner happens to be the owner of one of these titles, the consequence is, that the cause goes into the Federal Court. So long as this process of extinguishing the Indian title, and settling the country, is going on, it is in vain for gentlemen to say that those disputes are produced by temporary causes, or that they are passing away; they cannot pass away until your settlements are completed.

Do we not all know that, in 1794, and onward for several years, a great rage for speculation existed, in Philadelphia, New York and the Eastern States; that immense quantities of Western lands were bought up by foreigners, or citizens of other States? Considerable quantities were purchased in Tennessee. These companies have found it convenient to part with their titles to various individuals, and those claimants who have got titles in this manner, living in other States, when they come forward to assert their titles, now that the Indian title is extinguished, assert them in the Federal Courts.

But, the gentleman says, you have Federal Courts, and the people must have confidence in them, because, if they had not, they would sue in the State Courts. Will the Senate reflect, for a moment, on the idea suggested, and they will easily see some of the difficulties under which we labor. The titles to the land must be settled by the laws of the State in which the land lies. A citizen of another State, or a foreigner, claims title to a tract in Tennessee; he finds a man in possession under a conflicting title. This foreigner can sue either in the Federal or State Courts, at his election. He submits his title to counsel, who advises him that, according to the decisions of the State Courts, the man in possession has the better title. The foreigner orders suit in the Federal Court; there is but one judge, and he, living in the State, will likely follow the State decisions, and give judgment in favor of the defendant. The plaintiff takes a writ of error, and carries the cause to the Supreme Court, before a set of judges, who neither know or have they the means of knowing, the local laws, or the true reasons of the decision; and, for want of this information, judgment is reversed, and thus the plaintiff becomes the owner of a piece of property which he otherwise would not have acquired. Plaintiffs often commence suit in the Federal Courts expressly for the sake of gaining an advantage over their adversaries, which they could not get in any other tribunal whatever. And yet, this is the argument relied on to show that Federal justice is well administered to us.

What, sir, is the situation of the other States, Louisiania for example? These are British, Spanish, and French grants; so also, in Mississippi and Missouri. All these may go, and mostly do go, into the Federal Courts, principally for the sake of having these cases removed into the Supreme Court of the United States, if such a decision is not given as is satisfactory to the plaintiff. So far as Tennessee is concerned, those who act under the belief that our business has accumulated from temporary causes, are in the main mistaken: to a limited extent, no doubt, they are correct. I believe if our circuit had been one of reasonable extent, and we had the benefit of our circuit judge the number of suits on our docket would have been much less. Where a man has a cause which he thinks he ought to gain, if the law is well understood, he will not agree to have that cause tried before any one man, when there is another of a higher legal character. It is a very unpleasant thing to have to settle disputes between man and man, and when it comes to the last stage, there are few men who would not like to be eased of a portion of the responsibility of the decision. If a reasonable excuse can be made to defer it to another time the district judge will fall in with it, because his associate will then be with him, and he will have the benefit of his opinion, and be better satisfied, if they agree, that he is right, than if there was none with him, and if he should disagree in opinion with him, by certifying that there was a difference of opinion, it could be carried into the Supreme Court, and no mischief would arise. It is to their credit that they have this disposition. I do not make unnecessary complaints against the district judge of the State in which I live. He is entitled to as much character as any other judicial officer on the score of integrity; and if he ever does make mistakes, which, I think, is but seldom, it is in endeavoring to attain that which he thinks the justice of particular cases. The people of Tennessee have as much right as the people of any other State in the Union, to have the opinions of two men who will concur, as to which is right in their disputes. It is vain to tell me we are placed on an equal footing with the other States, while they have one measure of justice meted to their citizens and the citizens of Tennessee have a different measure meted to them. I would rather you should lop off one of our Senators, or three of our Representatives—reduce us as to the power we have in the Executive and Legislative business of this government, but when you come to the practical operations of this government, that are to take away a man's life, liberty or property, let our citizens have an equal opportunity for the administration of justice, with any portion of the good people of the United States.

During the last session this subject was before you and was put off by saying, we have not had time to examine it, and at the next session, we will all lay our shoulders to the wheel and accomplish this particular task. And, sir, where are we now? About the 12th of April they took up this subject in the other house, the committee made a report, the subject was examined and amply discussed, and they passed a bill in substance similar to the one on your table. The same subject was referred to the Judiciary Committee of this body, who concurred in a similar report; and after the bill from the other house was brought here, it was referred to them, and they reported it, with an amendment, which is not calculated to change very materially the principles of the bill. Every gentleman has matured his judgment on this subject, and, if he does not like the present proposition, let him give us his system in its stead. But now the worthy gentleman from New Hampshire comes forward with a general proposition to refer the bill to the Judiciary Committee, to see whether they cannot contrive, in some way or other, to relieve our local distress and inconvenience, without adding any member to the Supreme Court. I put it to the gentleman himself, and to every member of the Senate, whether, if they have solid objections to this bill, if they are able to digest a system which they think better suited to put us on an equality with the rest of the Union; whether they do not owe it to their own justice, to their own character, to their own high standing, to have brought forward a distinct proposition, containing another system that would have placed us in a similar condition with the other States of the Union? It is very easy to raise objections; but you can never test the merits of this bill, compared with any other plan, until you have the other in detail likewise. Suppose sir, that a majority of this Senate should believe that the number of judges ought to be seven, and they send it back to the committee to find out how the United States are to be divided into seven circuits; they try it every way. They cannot fix on any plan that is not liable to stronger objections than the present bill —what then? Are we to have no relief? If the gentleman who made this proposition had given us something like a detailed plan for his seven judges, and compared that plan with this, then there would have been something to test the principle he has so ably advocated on this occasion. It is a principle which seems plausible within itself; but when you come to detail it, to reduce it to practical operation, it is found to be one which, when compared to the situation of the United States, cannot be used. I think we have cause to complain when we find that, after this matter has been postponed for eight or ten years, and the lapse of time which has taken place during the present session, those who are opposed to it say they are disposed to do what is just towards us, but find fault without submitting any plan which might keep up hopes that we are not to be always in the situation in which we are now placed.

The gentleman from Rhode Island I understand exactly. He wishes to get back to the good old system of 1801, because he thinks it is better than any other which can be devised. I do not intend for him anything which I say upon the subject of unkindness, they are all intended for the gentleman from New Hampshire, who sends us so many good wishes, of which I wish to see the fruits.

As to the circuit court part of the system, every one must be satisfied that we are not on an equal footing with the other States. Increase, then, the number of judges to such an extent as to enable us, with reasonable circuits, to have the services of some one or other of the judges of the Supreme Court. This is the remedy, and then shall we be on an equal footing with the others. Let no gentleman object to this system because we cannot furnish good materials for judges; if they cannot be found in that part of the country, we will receive, thankfully, the addition of talent from any quarter of the Union. That luminary which gives us light rises in the East and passes to the West. I suppose it is the same with genius and talent: let us then go to the morning, and draw from the fountain-head of talent as much as will answer the wants of the West, and give us the benefit of it. I wish justice administered. I indulge in no prejudices. From the East they have sent us out those who have made us valuable officers, whom I should be sorry to part with. I wish them to remain with us as citizens of our State, and if the present system should be adopted, the President should see fit to find the materials to fill the offices in the East, let him make the experiment, and if it turns out that they are qualified, I shall never be disposed to be very clamorous on that subject.

The gentlemen from Rhode Island and New Hampshire seem to think, that on this system, if it should pass, no benefit to us can result as to an increase of knowledge of local laws on the bench of the Supreme

Court. In this I disagree with the gentlemen. Take a man from Rhode Island, and I think it likely he is as ignorant of the laws of Tennessee as I am of those of Rhode Island; place him on the Supreme Court bench, and let him be compelled to hold our circuit courts, and reside among us, and I think that in the course of one year he will be better qualified to decide our causes than any judge in the Supreme Court in the present organization will be in forty years. He sets out ignorant of our local laws—but he is acquainted with his own profession; he is associated at once with the district judge, who is intimately acquainted with the local laws; he meets with that which he never met with in the Supreme Court; he meets with the most intelligent of the profession in that county where he goes to do business. They have their own materials, their own books; they have had leisure to make preparations for every cause; they have looked into every act of Assembly which relates to the subject, into every record, into every case found which has any relation to the subject, and this judge, so called on to dispense justice, after he has heard the arguments on both sides, and has conferred with the district judge, will be very likely to decide correctly even in the first instance—for six weeks or two months his court may continue—daily, causes depending on the local laws are under discussion; his leisure moments are spent in conversation relative to those local laws; at the end of his first term will he not have acquired more knowledge of the local laws than on the bench of the Supreme Court during his life? In the Supreme Court one cause, depending on those local laws, may be argued during a term, without the necessary books, without much preparation, by those ill informed of those laws; it is decided: and perhaps for twelve months no other cause, depending on those same laws, comes before the court. The subject is then taken up as a new one; and thus he may go on from year to year, without any improvement in a knowledge of local law. Take a man of good natural capacity—a scientific, well-bred lawyer, compel him to reside in the circuit; he immediately acquires a knowledge of the local laws of the States in his circuit because he must continue his mind upon a succession of similar causes, until he has disposed of perhaps fifty or one hundred without having it distracted by an attention to any other. He soon acquires a knowledge of the laws as a system, which is not to be forgotten. But upon the bench of the Supreme Court, he has no such advantage; and it would be strange if he did not go off almost as ignorant of local laws as he came on it.

Now, whether it be seven or ten, or of whatever number it may be, I insist that it is a valuable feature in our system, and one that I would not part with any more than I would with that most valuable political privilege, of trial by jury; that the man who is ultimately to decide the cause must be in a situation to have a reasonable opportunity of becoming acquainted with the laws that are to form the ground of that decision.

Says the gentleman, by what mystery is it that you are going to communicate the information which that one judge has obtained, to the other nine? The moment a cause is brought into the Supreme Court, instead of their having to grope about without knowing how, or where to find the necessary statutes and authorities, they make common stock of all the knowledge they have acquired, and the judge who has made himself acquainted with the local laws, applicable to the case in question, brings to their view at once, not only the statutes, but all the authorities he has had access to, in relation to the same question, and when these materials are spread before them, then, sir, they are prepared to come to a correct determination. There is no mystery in this? Each is not to lock up within his own breast all the information he has acquired upon legal subjects, and let his brethren be groping about in darkness. They talk freely on legal subjects amongst themselves, they make joint-stock of their knowledge, they apply their natural talents, and then, sir, they bring out such a result as they think will be according to the justice and law of the case. The moment you give me one judge on the bench of the Supreme Court that has a knowledge of the laws of the country in which I live, the Supreme Court is placed in a situation that it can dispense justice between man and man in Tennessee; but till that is done, it is as much a matter of accident, as anything else, that justice should be done, I have no complaint to make against the judges of the Supreme Court, nor have I any eulogies to pronounce on them. In some causes that have come from Tennessee to the Supreme Court, I think their decisions erroneous; I have the same opinion as it relates to some other States. But in the situation in which they have been placed, I am surprised they have not been oftener wrong. It is the lot of human beings to err when they have the best means of information, and it would be strange if they did not err, when you compel them to act without the necessary means of information. There was one case in which their decision was in opposition to all the decisions of the State Courts, in which they applied old principles that were inapplicable to our local laws, and thereby reversed the decision of the district judge doing duty as a circuit judge, and sent the cause back to be retried; upon the second trial, a more enlarged view of the case was given in a bill of exceptions, and the cause again brought to the Supreme Court, and they a second time reversed the judgment of the circuit court, and took great pains to explain away what seemed to be the ground of the first decision, thereby using their endeavors to ward off the mischief likely to flow from the first opinion. I mention these things, not as a ground on which to censure any man who is on that bench; I have as much confidence in them as any man who has no more acquaintance with them, and who is as little capable of forming opinions relative to their decisions. Still, I am constrained to believe, that not only in the case alluded to, but in some others, they have not correctly expounded our municipal laws, and that mischiefs have been produced; and that more must inevitably be produced, if that court is not placed on a different footing from that on which it now stands.

Had we not better pass the bill on the table, than throw everything into a state of confusion by the reference? Had we not better refuse the gentleman's proposition? If you agree to it, when is there to be an end? The gentleman from New York stated that there were grievances under which we labored, but that he did not deem them to be so great as to justify all the clamor that had been raised in that part of the country. I think he has not yet got to the bottom of our grievances, unless—

[Mr. Van Buren rose to explain; he had stated on the part of Tennessee, that there had been no complaint—their memorials were such as they ought to have been—they stated their grievances fairly and fully, and left it to the wisdom of Congress to apply the remedy. But he had stated that complaints had been made elsewhere.]

Mr. White resumed. I am very glad to receive the explanation. It gave me pain to think our complaints should be censured from so respectable a quarter, and I am relieved to find I misunderstood the gentleman. By the bill upon your table, we can be relieved; without some change, the causes of complaint must continue. The gentleman from New Hampshire finds fault with the bill, and chalks out no plan. The gentleman from Rhode Island excepts to the bill, and refers to a substitute. What is his remedy? He wishes the judges of the Supreme Court to form an appellate court, and to be relieved from all circuit duties, and to have a separate set of judges, called circuit judges, to try all causes in the respective circuits. Indeed, sir, I should think (to use his own language) he would give us a remedy worse than the disease, and I believe that no man that has reflected well on this subject, and is a friend to the Supreme Court of the United States, will ever put its high character in jeopardy by any such system. As an American I am proud of the character it now sustains. It is not only a blessing upon the whole to the nation, but some of its members are a credit to the age in which we live. And how did they become so? Not by being shut up in Washington, in New York, or in Rhode Island, but by letting them have a fair opportunity to become acquainted, not only with those things which are to be got out of books, but with those things which are going on in that society of which they are members. Let me not be told that I wish to send the judges out popularity hunting—to drink a dram with this ignorant man, or to take his breakfast with another; but I say, send the judges of the Supreme Court, to administer and dispense justice in the respective States in the presence of the citizens of those States, of the counsel that attend the bar and the jury; let them hear the witnesses that depose as to the facts of the case.

While the judge in his circuit dispenses justice, he watches, with all possible care, the conduct of the counsel, the course of the testimony, and sees its practical application to the particular transactions of men; at the same time that he is dispensing justice, he is keeping up an essential part of his education; he is keeping up his personal knowledge of human nature, he sees its workings as it is;—and of all the places on earth where a man can be placed to acquire a knowledge of human nature, the best is a court of justice, when the jury is to decide a matter of fact, and *viva voce* testimony is given, to inform them on it. Put the question down in the most careful state you can, in a bill of exceptions, and an appellate court never can have the same impression made on their minds, that they would have had, if they had seen and heard the same testimony delivered to a jury. Do you believe there would have been the improvement there has been in the doctrine of evidence during the last hundred years, if those who established these rules had possessed no practical knowledge acquired at *nisi prius* or elsewhere? How long is it since the distinction has been drawn between a competent and a credible witness? But lock these judges up in Westminster Hall, or in Rhode Island, or in New York, or Washington, and you take them from the source of information, and what becomes of them? If I wished to lessen their standing in society, and to destroy public confidence in them, to put them in such a situation that, instead of doing justice between man and man, they should become a curse to the country, I would adopt the system recommended by the gentleman from Rhode Island.

Again sir: it is a great object in the administration of justice to keep mankind satisfied. If I could spare the property, I would almost as soon lose a portion of mine, by the decision of a man in whom I had entire confidence, as to gain by the judgment of one that I believed decided in my favor, he thinking that his own decision was wrong; because in such case, I would feel that neither my person or property was safe. Take the judges of the Supreme Court from all circuit duties, and you make them strangers to society; they will have no acquaintance with any portion of the profession, except the very few who may practice at their bar; let them then decide some favorite statute of some of your large sovereign States to be unconstitutional, and it will be found that they have not enough of character to sustain them. But keep each of them in the discharge of circuit duties, and they are all forced into society; in their respective circuits, they become personally and intimately known to most of the respectable men in those circuits; to clerks, marshals, jurors, witnesses, lawyers, bystanders, and if they have integrity and talents to fit them for their high station, it becomes known, and felt by the mass of society; who are witnesses of their usefulness: then let them decide such a statute to be unconstitutional (and so they ought to do, if such be the fact), and then see how well public opinion will sustain them. The moment the decision is complained of, the inquiry by every man will be, did the judge with whom I am acquainted, concur in that decision? and if answered in the affirmative, he will immediately say, the decision must be right, he is honest and enlightened, and would not have concurred unless the judgment was correct.

Again, you put a man of middle life upon the Bench well qualified for his station; make the court stationary; take from the judge all circuit duties: and, if he live to reasonable age, he will most probably die unqualified for his office. How will the judges fill up the intervals of time between the sessions of the Supreme Court? It is answered by reading. I put it to every practical, well-informed lawyer to say, whether it would not be more profitably employed in holding circuit courts. Take any one legal subject, and let the judge be in search of information upon it, and, I say he will, in my opinion, acquire more by hearing arguments upon it, for *one* day in the week, than he will by reading the *whole* week; and that which he has thus acquired, will remain with him for life.

Again. Take from them circuit duties, and a main stimulus to exertion is destroyed; the mind is, for a considerable portion of life, improved by use, one exertion prepares it for another, and by repeated efforts, it acquires a vigor and force not to be otherwise acquired. Make the judges stationary, and they will soon content themselves with moderate labors, their reading will be alone; none to help them to compare and examine ideas collected from books, they will have no precise object in view: but keep them to the circuits, and then they will have every inducement to exertion; their conduct will be in the view of the world; the causes openly argued; the opinions of the judge are formed for present use, must be accompanied by his reasons to support them, delivered in presence of jury, witnesses, parties, counsel, and by-standers; if wrong, he will be called upon to re-examine them on motion for a new trial, when their errors will be openly exposed, and refuted. He will therefore, have every inducement to continued and unremitted exertion; and this exertion will daily increase his capacity for usefulness.

On the plan proposed by this bill, you make the judges men of vigorous minds, well stored with useful knowledge, capable of forming and continually, not only forming, but actually expressing opinions for themselves.

On that proposed by the gentleman from Rhode Island, you will soon have your judges, bookworms, if you choose, without any practical knowledge; their minds enervated for want of use, neither habituated to form, nor to express opinions for themselves, acting seldom or never on *individual* responsibility; always in the presence only of the comparatively few, who may be attendant on the Supreme Court. By this plan, they will soon lose that manly independence so beneficial to society, and become mere drivellers, drones, ready to lean upon any associate, ambitious of distinction, and admirably fitted for any unworthy purposes to which a designing Executive may wish to apply them.

It is said that another misfortune from the proposed plan will be, that it will add to the existing grievance in the Supreme Court—delay. At the first view, there certainly appeared something very plausible in this objection; but, upon mature consideration, I think the business will rather be expedited by this additional number of justices, than otherwise.

How is the delay to be increased? Because, say gentlemen, each judge must make himself acquainted with the contents of the record, and it will take ten men longer to do so than seven.

This difficulty is in a good degree removed, if we suppose the judges will make such arrangement as that one shall read the record, and the other nine listen to him while reading it; upon this plan, ten will become acquainted with its contents in as short a time as seven But suppose some delay to be occasioned from this cause, it is more than counterbalanced by positive advantages by an increase of the number of judges.

Have ten judges of the Supreme Court performing the duties of circuit judges, and you bring to the Bench of the Supreme Court in a short time, an intimate knowledge of the municipal laws of the respective States; when one of those causes depending for its decision upon any of those local laws shall be brought into the Supreme Court, the court will at once be able to refer to all the statutes and decisions which ought to govern their judgment; when as now they are frequently at a loss to procure either the one or the other; and it consumes much time and requires great labor to procure those materials, from which, alone, a correct opinion can be formed; and often it must happen, that decisions are given without the benefit of all the information from these sources which they ought to have.

Suppose a case to be decided upon the local laws of a State, and the State desirous to have fixed the construction of a doubtful statute; but no book of reports containing those decisions to exist—how can the Supreme Court acquire the necessary information? Only through the industry and research of the counsel employed. They may and often will report them differently, and leave the court in great doubt. But pass this bill, and one at least of the members of the Supreme Court will, on his circuit, have acquired a knowledge of those decisions, and can give correct information to his brethren.

But, sir, it has been urged that by increasing the number of judges, you increase the number of causes in the Supreme Court, and of course must delay the decisions there. To this argument I answer, first, it is not likely the fact will turn out to be as supposed: in all suits exceeding the value of two thousand dollars writs of error can now be brought; if a judge of the Supreme Court is associated with the district judge on the trial below, and they concur in opinion, most frequently both parties will be satisfied, and no writ of error will be brought; whereas now, when the causes are decided below, by one man, and he a district judge, writs of error will be almost invariably brought if there is the least room for a doubt. It is therefore most probable the number of writs of error will be diminished in all those cases to which I have alluded.

But it is said now, no criminal case can be brought to the Supreme Court, nor can any civil one, when the matter in dispute is of less value than two thousand dollars; because as the decisions will be by the district judge alone, there can be no certificate of a division of opinion, by which means only such cases can be brought to the Supreme Court.

I must regret that such an argument should be used to defeat this bill. It conforms to the rule by which tyrants govern. The substance of it is, that it is better that a man in one of those nine Western States, should be hanged or lose his property by the erroneous decision of the single judge, than that a suitor from any other of the fifteen States should have his suit delayed in the Supreme Court, by increasing the number of causes upon its docket.

This argument cannot be tolerated; all are to be equally obedient to the same laws; all must be protected by them. The main object of government, and one of its first duties is, to protect the innocent at the same time that it punishes the guilty. The citizens of one State are not to be unjustly punished, that those of another may have a speedy revision of their causes in the Supreme Court. The citizens of each are entitled to the same measure of justice, and an equal chance for a correct administration of it must be furnished to all. Will it be allowed that a citizen of Tennessee must submit to injustice, for no better reason than to enable a citizen of New York, or Rhode Island, to have his cause speedily decided in the Supreme Court? It is hoped not.

Something was said about the weight of population, and that the proposed bill would give to the West more judges than their relative numbers would entitle them to.

Mr. President, I have not felt the force of any argument used upon this point. Before the judicial system of the United States is extended, there must be States, those States must have citizens living in them; and those citizens must have suits, or a reasonable prospect for suits of Federal jurisdiction to be decided, and whenever these things occur, your system, applicable to the other States, ought to be extended to embrace them.

Take a State composed of a number of counties, some of them thickly populated, others with a population more sparse; what would be thought of a legislature which, in devising a judicial system, would make one system for those counties of dense, another for those of thin population? Would they act wisely or justly when they directed the courts in counties thinly settled, to be held by a single justice of the peace whose decision should be *final;* and the courts in the counties thickly settled, to be holden by a justice of the peace and a judge of the Supreme Court; and that in all cases where they disagreed, no judgment should be entered until a Supreme Court, composed of seven men should be consulted? All would concur in pronouncing such a course unwise and unjust; yet the very argument now used goes to justify such a system.

Upon this branch of the subject I hope it will be seen that, if this bill passes, the confidence reposed in the decisions of the circuit courts, will tend to diminish rather than increase appeals; that the increased knowledge of local laws on the Supreme Bench will facilitate the decisions there, in place of delaying them; but that, if some delay should be produced, it is far better that should be submitted to, than that nine States should be compelled to live under a judicial system less favorable to the administration of justice than that which is afforded to the other fifteen.

There is another point of view in which this matter ought to be considered, when we are considering and comparing the utility of the bill upon your table, with the system of 1801, which the gentleman from Rhode Island desires to re-establish as a substitute for it.

That which this bill proposes is a mere extension of the judicial system, as it now exists, and has existed in fifteen of the States for many years. Its utility has been tested by experience, and its provisions have been generally approved. If the bill passes, no change even in the nine States, will be affected by which society can be disturbed; the courts will sit at the same time in the respective circuits; the business will be conducted upon the same plan heretofore adopted; the only sensible alteration will be that, instead of *one* man upon the bench when the courts sit, there will be two. We are creatures of habit, and any radical change in a judicial system, by which the settled habits of the people are disturbed, or changed, is not likely to succeed, even if the new would, in the end, be better than the old; it is not likely that the new will be tolerated long enough to give it a fair experiment, unless the old has been found glaringly defective. In this instance this is not the case—the old has been tested and approved, and if now changed, as the gentleman wishes, the people will compel us to change *back* to that which this bill proposes.

It has been said that the system of 1801 did not go into operation, it was unpopular on account of those who proposed and adopted it, and therefore, put down without a fair experiment. Be it so; and it is a proof of the correctness of my argument. The old system, that which we wish now to extend, had been adopted in 1789; its utility had been proved; without necessity a new experiment was made by the act of 1801, not called for by any existing grievance; the people would not submit to it;

they put it down, and with it, or rather before it, those who had brought it into existence. You now wish to re-instate that system to relieve the West. From that very quarter came the attack upon it. It was commenced by Breckenridge, of Kentucky, and it was repealed. It is a mistake to suppose it never went into operation; we had the circuit system in operation, for a short time, both in Kentucky and Tennessee, the only two Western States then in existence. No time was lost in putting it in operation anywhere, and but little lost in commencing the struggle by which it was put down, and that of 1789 re-instated. Let us not repeat the experiment. We need not flatter ourselves it will be better received now than it was then. The system then approved, is that which is still approved; pass this bill, and thereby extend its benefits to the nine Western States. By this means you will keep the people happy and contented: but, disturb their settled habits, uselessly make the radical change which gentlemen desire, and a struggle is again commenced, which will produce great discontent, and end in the overthrow of the new system and the re-establishment of that which is now known and approved.

The alteration effected by this bill will be, that the Supreme Court will be composed of ten in place of seven. Gentlemen say they would rather reduce, than increase the number of judges—six, say they; and then, as circumstances will permit, until the number which composes it shall be only four. Seven is the favorite number in religious matters, and four in legal matters, according to the opinion of gentlemen on the other side. And why fix upon the number of four? Because, in Great Britain, four is the number which comprises their highest courts.

Mr. President, we have borrowed many of our most valuable ideas upon legal subjects from Great Britain; but care must be taken not to copy too far. That country is of small extent, an island; a judge in any one part of it has it perfectly in his power to acquire a knowledge of the general laws applicable to the whole, and also of the particular customs applicable to any particular part. That is not our situation in the United States—our country is of immense extent; even judges of the Supreme Court ought to be well acquainted with the general laws of nations; your conventional laws; with the Constitution and laws of the United States, and with the Constitution and laws of twenty-four distinct and independent States, varying from each other in many important particulars. The same system which has been found well adapted to the one country, may be entirely unsuited to the other. Four judges would be more likely to bring all necessary legal knowledge into the Court of King's Bench, in England, than ten will be to bring all the legal knowledge necessary to the bench of the Supreme Court. The situation and circumstances of our own country must be carefully attended to, otherwise we shall do great mischief by borrowing from others, and adopting systems not suited to the extent of our territory, to the circumstances, and situation, and habits of our citizens, nor to the various and multiplied peculiarities in our Federal and State laws. From no country upon earth can we expect a model which will suit us for a judiciary. Our country, and everything in it, is upon a more extended scale; and our judiciary must be adapted to our own situation and circumstances. The politician, who will be useful in the United States, must permit his mind to comprehend the various interests of the different sections of country; the habits, customs, and pursuits of the people in different quarters—even their prejudices, if you choose—and from all these considerations, enact his laws upon such principles as will secure the interests of the whole. He who will not permit his mind so far to expand as to embrace the whole extent of his own country, will always be in danger of inflicting injury, while he intends to afford protection. Let us then pass this bill; make our system co-extensive with the country; adapt it to the wishes and expectations of society; place every State on an equal footing in fact, with every other: we will then have made an effort upon this subject from which we have reason to anticipate much good. Should it, contrary to our expectations and wishes, be productive of mischief, the fifteen States which now have an efficient system, can have no just cause of complaint. The situation of all will be equal; the inconvenience will be common to all. We have a right to expect and therefore do expect, this risk will be encountered in an attempt to do justice to all.

CHAPTER IX.

SENATORIAL CAREER—INTERNAL IMPROVEMENTS—U. S. BANK.

DURING the period from the session of 1825–6 to that of 1831–2, Judge White delivered few speeches of any considerable length. Indeed, during his whole life, he spoke unfrequently; saying so much as would explain his reasons for voting, where necessary, or briefly presenting his views upon any subject of sufficient importance.

In the days of President Jackson, the question of Internal Improvements was one as yet not fully investigated. There was in many sections of the country, a strong feeling, based upon the evident profits to accrue from such improvements, in favor of the extension of aid to them by the general government; and the question was, moreover, warmly urged by the opposition, probably not without a view of embarrassing the administration, by forcing it either to appropriate vast sums for the purpose, and so to incur the odium of extravagance, or to defeat all such appropriations, and so to incur dislike in the sections of country asking them. Judge White never sanctioned the doctrine of Internal Improvements by the federal government. He believed that no power was expressly granted by the Constitution to the federal government to engage in the business of Internal Improvements *as a system.* On the contrary, it was his opinion that the extensive power of making roads and canals through States, be longed exclusively to the States, and should never be surrendered to the central government; that although in a state of war, or for purposes of war, the United States possessed the power to make a road through any State, as, in a case of necessity they might also, under the power to "establish post roads," construct a road, such powers were only to be exercised in extraordinary cases. And, aside from this decision upon the ground of unconstitutionality, the power in question would, he believed, be dangerous from its capacity of being abused. It would place an immense patronage in the hands of the federal Executive, and might thus be most destructively wielded whenever the Executive should choose, in purchasing friends at elections or other critical periods.

As a good summary of his opinion on this and some other subjects, and likewise for the sake of exhibiting by its latter paragraphs the principles avowed by the party which elected General Jackson, which were deserted by them at their convenience, when expediency seemed to call for tergiversation; and for consistent adherence to which principles, and for the consequent necessary severance from the remainder of his former friends, they poured out upon him during the last years of his life, such floods of unfounded reproach, we here insert the larger part of a speech delivered by Judge White to his constituents at Knoxville, April 5th, 1827, at a dinner there given by them to him, in acknowledgment of his services in the Senate.

GENTLEMEN:—

I should be worse than insensible, if I did not feel very grateful for the kind sentiments just expressed. Next to being conscious of good intention, is the approbation of those who have reposed confidence in me; and, especially, that portion of them, who have been witnesses of my conduct from youth to manhood, and from middle age to the decline of life. For this testimony in my favor, I tender you my most grateful acknowledgments. It is due, however, to myself to say, that I feel humbled under the conviction that it has not been in my power to render any service to my country, in my present station, at all equal to those your kind partiality has been pleased to ascribe to me. Had I been fully aware of the difficulties I would have to encounter, and of the afflictions I was doomed to suffer, I believe I should have shrunk from the task assigned me by the Legislature; but, having voluntarily undertaken it, no domestic afflictions, no public calumny, could make me seriously doubt for one moment the course I ought to pursue. I must remain at my post fearlessly, and without faltering discharge my duty, trusting to the intelligence of my countrymen to refute calumny, and to my neighbors, by acts of personal kindness, to soften private afflictions.

Happily, associated with those who espouse different sides of all doubtful political questions, every way better qualified to discuss them than myself, I have been, in most instances, relieved from taking much part in public debate, and have been content to listen patiently, and vote according to what I considered the best interests of the country. It would be presumptuous in me to suppose I have not sometimes erred; but, I can safely say, never intentionally. Too unimportant to be often singled out by name as an object of abuse, I have still come in for a share in the presses in the employ of the administration, under the general appellation of "the unprincipled faction of the Senate." This charge, so far as it applies to me, no matter by whom stated, I have no hesitation in pronouncing an unfounded calumny; and as it may relate to others, with whom I have acted, I believe it to be equally destitute of truth. So far as it has related to every measure calculated to cause the affairs of the United States to be conducted upon the principles to which we have been accustomed during the republican administrations, there has been little variety of opinion since I have been in Congress: and, in every instance, as it relates to such measures, the Administration has had the most prompt and efficient aid from those who, in the coalition prints, have been denominated "the unprincipled faction." Indeed, when elected to the Senate, I never dreamed that the General Assembly of Tennessee expected me to go dressed in the uniform either of those opposed to the Administration, or of the Administration itself—I was sent in the uniform of my country, and to vote, as in my judgment, would most promote *its interest*, and this duty, I feel conscious, I have discharged in the best manner I knew how. So far from expecting *that* was to happen, which has come to pass during the pendency of the last Presidential election (although I always had a decided preference), I believed the government would be administered upon republican principles, let which of the candidates might prevail, and, until after my election to the Senate, had seen no good reason to change that opinion.

The President's message to Congress, at the commencement of the first session, since I was a member, took me by surprise. I saw in it a claim of powers for the federal government, more extravagant than had ever been made in the days of federalism—a claim which I believed every sound American federalist, as well as every republican, ought to be equally prompt in condemning. This was soon followed by a message to the Senate, on the mission to Panama, in which was claimed for the Executive, powers which, if yielded, would leave to the Senate nothing on the subject of foreign missions worth preserving.

From my entrance into the bustle of life, I had been in the habit of thinking, that those who denied to the federal government, all power, except that which is granted in *express* terms, or which is *necessary* to carry into effect some power expressly granted, expounded the Constitution more correctly than that sect who wish to confer power by implication, who believe the federal government ought to protect the people "against their worst enemies—themselves;" because they have "not virtue and intelligence sufficient for self-government;" I could not, therefore, do otherwise than oppose the Executive in those extravagant pretensions. This celebrated mission to Panama, it appeared to me, was inconsistent with our former policy, with the wholesome advice given us by the Father of his Country, and uselessly putting at hazard the liberty and happiness of the people of the United States. My best wishes, as well as yours, were with those who were struggling for the right to govern themselves; but these wishes could not induce me to sanction a policy, which, according to my best judgment, put at hazard the true interest of our own citizens, for the wild notion of being esteemed the friends and upholders of liberty throughout the civilized world. We might, I thought, better employ ourselves in strengthening our own Union—a union, which, if perpetuated, will furnish adequate employ for all our patriots and statesmen, without extending the sphere of our duties to embrace other nations, to whom we are under no special obligations.

If doubts were entertained in the first instance, whether it was not intended to make some agreement with these Spanish American States, by which our fate would, in some respects, be identified with theirs, those doubts were very much increased when the President openly came out, and endeavored to satisfy the American people, that the advice of Washington against "entangling alliances" had no application to republics on our own continent. But I pass from a topic which has been long since amply discussed, and in relation to which at this day, there cannot well be more than one opinion.

In comparatively modern days, a subject has been got up, concerning which, I will venture a very few remarks. I allude to internal improvements by the *federal government.* The most I have found it my duty heretofore to say upon that subject was, that where the road or canal was to pass *through a State*, I doubted the power of the federal government, and while I thus doubted, I would not vote in favor of an appropriation for such an object. In relation to roads or canals through a territory, the case was different.

Whether the federal government possesses the power to engage in the business of internal improvement *as a system*, is a question of very grave import. This is neither the time nor place to engage in the discussion of such a question. Thus much, however, I frankly state as my opinion; that I cannot find any such power *expressly* granted in the Constitution of the United States, nor do I believe it at all *necessary* to give effect to any power that is expressly granted by that instrument. Still, it may be true, that in a state of war, and for the purposes of war, the United States may have power to make a road through any State. So, likewise it may be true in a case of necessity under the power "to establish post roads" that they may have power to construct a road: but if they have such power in these extraordinary cases, I think it is not true, that they possess the power to embark in the business of constructing roads and canals through the respective States when and where they choose in defiance of the will of the States. I am the decided friend of internal improvements, but I am friendly to them when made by the power which, consistently with the Constitution, can make them. No man, I think, can reasonably doubt but that each of the States has the power to make as many roads and canals as they please, within their own limits, and that they will exercise this power in every instance where the interest of their citizens require it, I cannot doubt.

I think not only that the United States do not possess this extensive power, but farther, that it ought never to be surrendered to them.

Already it is alarming to contemplate the patronage of the federal government when acting within the sphere of Constitutional power: grant it this additional power, and, in my opinion, it will be useless to talk of State rights, or the people's rights; they will exist in name, only, or at most, at the *will* of the federal government. Of all powers this would be wielded most destructively whenever the federal executive might choose. At present, offices, the hope of offices, or the use of the people's own money, placed at the disposal of the executive, are the common means of corrupting one class of the community, who may be relied upon, to mislead and deceive another: but with this power, whole sections of country might be operated upon directly. At present, the executive can only *purchase friends* by retail; then, they could engage in the *wholesale* business. We are not altogether destitute of experience upon this subject. A few years ago, I think in 1824, Congress passed an act authorizing the President to have such routes surveyed, for roads and canals, as would be considered *national* in relation to commerce, to post roads, or to military roads, and to enable him to give effect to this law, has at each session since, appropriated large sums of money, to defray the expense of the engineer corps engaged in the business. And how has this law been practised upon? It has been in many instances abused and perverted from its meaning. If there is any one road that would be considered more national than any other, it would be one from Washington to New Orleans. Accordingly, one was to be surveyed, and three routes were proposed for a road between those points. One to go through the capital of each of the Southern States—another to go along the foot of the mountains on their southern side, and the third to cross the Blue Ridge not far from Washington and come along the valley through this quarter of the country, and so on to New Orleans. Engineers were ordered to view these routes, and ascertain the advantages and disadvantages relating to each, that it might be decided which of the three should be preferred. The surveys of the southern and middle routes were made by three engineers; and when the one, in which we are interested, called the northern, was to be examined, only two of the three could be spared, and they were ordered to hurry on by the nearest practicable course; and so it is, that they travelled at a gait which enabled them to come with nearly as much speed as travellers on ordinary business, not feeling themselves at liberty to deviate to the right hand or the left from the most direct route, to make any examination whatever. It is true, that they were necessarily detained in this place a few days, waiting the arrival of a gentleman now present, who had been appointed to accompany them through this State. Here, they were requested by myself and others, to view the several routes which had been spoken of through Tennessee, but the answer was, their orders did not permit them to deviate from the most direct route, for the sake of examining any other. Upon a report after *such a survey*, the northern route is to come in competition with the other two, and to have its advantages and disadvantages, compared with those of the others; and after all this haste, no route is yet located. All three are taught to expect the road, and at the same time that a friend of the Administration here is trying to satisfy you, that, if you will be friendly to those in power, and vote for them and their friends, they will deal kindly with you, and cause the road to be located on your route, exactly the same language may be employed by their advocates on each of the other routes, and thus, by keeping those three routes in the market, it is hoped that the mass of the people, from the extreme of the *northern* route, to the *Atlantic* may be influenced the whole distance from Washington to New Orleans. The like practices are pursuing elsewhere. In Maine, a State which has more sea coast than, perhaps, any in the Union, in the course of the past year, engineers were kept well employed in surveying routes for roads and canals—their elections were going on, and to get a good senator in Congress, it was necessary to have good members of assembly, and so it is, that Mr. Holmes has been engineered out and another put in his place, who, it may be hoped, will not be "an unprincipled factionist."

In Virginia, towards Greenbrier, routes were also carefully attended to, and surveyed, and Mr. Randolph is disposed of. In one of the other districts of Virginia, the people were becoming restless, their representative was likely to be considered a coalitionist, and an opposition candidate was talked of: but application is made for a part of the engineer corps to survey a little *eight-mile* route for a canal in the neighborhood, where you must bring water twelve miles to feed it, and the executive promptly attended to the call; a detachment of engineers was sent, the route surveyed and the people soothed because all this was effected through the representative, who is on good terms with the Administration, who are every ready to attend to such applications. I cannot upon this subject do better than to refer such as have not read it, to Mr. Rives's speech at the last session. He shows, practically, what use may be made; nay more, what is made, of this power, by the federal executive.

In the midst of all this waste, although repeatedly applied to, they had no spare engineers to survey any route for a road or canal for Tennessee or for Alabama. Have patience my friends, our elections are to come on in August, a detachment will be here in due season. Tennessee needs good members of Congress and members of Assembly, as well as other States, and the executive will have *its* business attended to here even if something is neglected elsewhere. This is a power so capable of being abused, already so much abused, so destructive of the purity of elections, that I cannot think the federal government either does, or ought to possess it. After what I have said, it is necessary, to prevent misconception, that I should add, it is not my intention to throw out a hint against any gentleman in the engineer corps. I have never heard aught to their prejudice; I presume they are well qualified for the stations they respectively fill, and I have in no one instance heard of any of them interfering in the elections, or political concerns of the country. The influence of which I complain is of a different description—the very fact of having routes surveyed for these roads and canals is calculated, and I believe intended, to excite expectations in different quarters of the country, that the present rulers are kindly disposed, and that they will, if continued in power, cause roads and canals to be made where it is not intended to make them, and where, if made, they would be of little or no importance.

Should, however, a majority of Congress determine on making a road from Washington to New Orleans, which, to say the least, I doubt their power to do, I have no question, but the northern route, that which leads through this section of country, ought for many reasons to be preferred, to either of the other two; and I think we have much cause to complain, that the engineers were not permitted to give to it as thorough an examination, as they did to those others.

The tariff, as it is called, was much talked of during the last winter, and a bill passed the House of Representatives, the object of which was to increase very considerably, the duty upon woollens, not of the highest price. It was not discussed or acted upon in the Senate for want of time. I have never heard any public discussion of the question relative to taxes imposed on foreign merchandise, with a view to protect and encourage the manufacture of similar fabrics, in the United States. To give protection to a certain extent, I have never doubted the power of the federal government; but this, like every other power, ought always to be exercised for the good of the whole; and under my present impression I never would impose a tax upon a *foreign* article, which *as a nation*, we could conveniently do without, where I saw, or had reason to believe, it would increase the price of the article throughout an extensive section of country and none were to be benefited by it but a few capitalists who would be thereby levying a tax upon a considerable portion of the community for their individual benefit. I should like to see domestic manufactures flourish; but would never wish to see them brought into existence or nourished in one section of country at the expense and positive loss of another.

In some quarters of the United States, I see the last Congress is complained of, because they passed but few laws. For my own part, I believe if the necessary laws are passed to enable the United States to perform promptly their appropriate functions, and to meet punctually their just engagements, it ought never to be cause of regret, that there is little legislation. As to our internal concerns, they are better understood and acted upon in the respective States than they can ever be in Congress. Indeed, there are but few internal concerns with which Congress can properly intermeddle. It is mainly to regulate our foreign concerns, that the federal government was created, and it ought never to be the policy of those who wish well to the United States to increase the action of the federal government; because, as you increase its action you increase the expenditure of money, and as there are but few of the States in which legitimate objects of expenditure can be found, it will operate most injuriously that large sums should be drawn from *all* equally and expended among few. Although it is true but few laws were enacted at the late session; yet, some of great importance were acted upon finally; the bankrupt bill, long and ably debated, was finally negatived, a provision for a naval school was also a good deal discussed and finally negatived; as well as many others which it were useless to allude to at this time.

There is one other subject upon which it is natural to expect I should say something, and I do it the more willingly, as this may be the only occasion offered at present, where I can see many of my fellow citizens under circumstances in which it would be proper to say anything publicly; and there is no usage of which I am aware to justify printed communications to them. I allude to the next election for President. It is said by the Administration and their friends that there is nothing of principle involved in it, that it is a mere question among men, whether A or B shall be preferred. In my conception, there cannot well be a statement more incorrect. The present incumbent is placed in the highest office known to our law, agreeably to the forms *of the Constitution*, in direct opposition to the *known will* of a majority of the people of the United States, and this, through the active agency of the man, who *now fills* the most honorable station in his cabinet. Thus placed by their own management (hard words are useless) in berths which give them the control of the whole executive patronage of the United States, they believe the judicious use of the patronage, thus placed in their power, is sufficient to procure as many partisans as will secure the re-election of the present incumbent for the next term, and then, according to "safe precedent," a suitable successor, and so on, perpetually. The true question is, whether the people are sufficiently virtuous and enlightened to govern themselves. If they are, they will at the time pointed out in the Constitution, by their votes, displace the present incumbent, and thus give a lesson not to be misunderstood, one which will teach every aspirant for office, that the *will of the people* shall not be disobeyed with impunity, that they are not yet so uninformed and corrupt, as to be bought up with their own money and their own offices, in sufficient numbers to enslave the majority.

Every effort of which the opposition Congress was capable, was made to have the Constitution so amended, as to permit the people, in person, in their respective districts, to vote for the man of their choice, and thus prevent them from being defrauded by the faithlessness of their agents, but this proposition was strenuously resisted and ultimately failed.

That the people are the sovereigns, is our theory; that their will, as to who shall fill their offices when fairly expressed, must be obeyed; yet some States in the last election were misrepresented and the representatives, in defiance of the known will of their constituents, and in opposition to solemn public pledges, gave their votes to the present incumbent; the only punishment which the people could inflict upon these faithless representatives was to dismiss them from further employ at the next election. This they have done, and yet, with this mark of the people's displeasure imprinted upon them, if I am correctly informed, some of them have lately been remunerated by the executive with offices, conferred as a reward for their treachery. As this course is pursued, let the people put forth their own strength, and let the President feel that *their will* is to be consulted, and not that of any set of political jugglers whatever. Let them dismiss him from public employ, who, with their offices and their money, would defraud them of their most invaluable privilege, that of having those to serve them, whom the majority wills should do so.

If this ill-gotten power is sufficient, if offices actually given, and the hope of offices hereafter expected; if money already given, and that hereafter expected, are sufficient to procure partisans, who have management enough to mislead a majority, there is an end of free government; it exists in name only. That is the experiment now making, that is the issue made up and to be tried at the next election. Let every man take his side—in such cases there can be but two parties, and all who are not disposed to come forth in vindication of the people's right and capacity to govern themselves, are with the coalition, who would fix upon us, that which is worse than monarchy itself, and yet leave us the name of a republic.

On the subject of Internal Improvements, Judge White afterwards writes to a political personal friend and correspondent, March 31st, 1830:

Your favor giving an account of the meeting in Knoxville, on the subject of the Buffalo and New Orleans Road came safely to hand. . . . The result* is creditable to the integrity and intelligence of Knox County. The temptation to transgress the constitutional bounds is very strong . . . I lament that my friend R. should not control his temper. Knives and pistols are *silencing*, though seldom *convincing* arguments. They ought never to be tolerated in a country civilized and free.

* An expression of opinion against the propriety of building the Road (which would have crossed Tennessee) by federal aid.

This last digressive paragraph is in consonance with the writer's well-known and lofty sentiments upon the barbarian custom of single combat.

He writes again, sarcastically, on the same Road Bill, under date April 2d, 1830:

A thought upon this road:—If we are really to sell out our principles for pay, or if it be intended through the medium of Internal Improvements to give us a due share of public disbursements, how is it that we are to have only a dirt road at fifteen hundred dollars a mile? Why not give us a Macadamized turnpike or a railroad? I view it as an indignity to my country and my constituents. Give us as good as is given to others, or give us nothing, say I. I am against the *power* to make the road; but I would infinitely rather vote for a decent one, such as is made for others, than for one made on this *dirt-dabbing* plan.

Again, to the same, in relation to the well-known Maysville and Lexington Road, May 21st, 1830:

Several bills have been introduced, and some of them passed, requiring the United States to subscribe for stock in companies created by *State Laws* to make Roads or Canals. One of them, to wit, for making a road from Maysville to Lexington, in Kentucky, is now before the President for his signature. Great doubts are entertained as to what he will do with it. Some think he will sign, others that he will not. Without *knowing* anything, I hope for the last. The common impression is, that our opponents have had a settled plan to appropriate so much money as to prevent the President from paying the National Debt: and it is a matter of regret that some of our political friends have acted with them, under a hope that their own particular counties could in a partnership scramble obtain some local advantage.

I hope much from the integrity, firmness and intelligence of the President. If he yields to this corrupting branch of federal patronage, I shall consider the country ruined.

The Bank of the United States was chartered in 1816. It was made the receptacle of the public moneys of the United States; and by means of this powerful substantial aid in connection with the numerous branches throughout the Union, and by the skilful use of certain exclusive privileges, it soon became the centre and fountain of a vast and constantly increasing circulation of paper-money. Judge White looked upon this rapid extension as a dangerous stimulus to business, and as hazarding the public good by encouraging extravagant speculation. This was a serious evil; but another which he dreaded more, was the power which the bank or any similar institution might exercise in controlling elections. He opposed the bank from principle; as he would oppose any measure or establishment which would place it in the power of politicians, or capitalists, or combinations of both, to exert any undue influence upon the use of the elective franchise. He had been long and intimately connected with banks, was well versed in their nature, operations and tendencies; and early and accurately augured the revulsions of 1819–'20, as well as those which followed up to 1834, as natural results of the operations of the United States Bank.

It has been shown that while a member of the Tennessee Legislature, in 1827, he opposed the establishment of a branch of this institution in that State. At a still earlier period, when the bill containing the original charter of the central bank was before the House of of Representatives at Washington, Wm. G. Blount, then representative from Judge White's district (who had been his ward, and an inmate of his family), sent him a printed copy of the bill, asking his opinion of it. Judge White wrote to him, giving a decided opinion against it. Mr. Blount alone voted against the bill, of all the Tennessee delegation.

Judge White went into the Senate in 1825, entertaining the opinion that the charter was both unconstitutional and impolitic; and upon that opinion he uniformly acted. When the bill for the renewal of the charter was brought before Congress in 1832, he opposed it in a speech of some length, which was characterized by the public prints as the ablest argument on the subject made during the session. What state of feeling prevailed at Washington, between the friends and enemies of the bank, may be inferred from a letter of Judge White's, dated Feb. 22d, 1832; just one day before Mr. Clayton's motion to appoint a committee for investigating the affairs of the bank.

Judge White says:

Everything here is in a bustle. Nothing out of which mischief can be made is suffered to slumber. Ill blood is produced by almost every event; and a great disposition is manifested by some to appeal to the trial by battle. Newspapers have, as yet, answered to let off the superabundant steam. As the weather grows warmer, passions will rise higher, and, I think, depletion *by the drawing of blood*, will, before long, become indispensable to restore that courtesy which never ought to be lost sight of by those entrusted by society with the promotion of its highest interest. No man can tell when or with whom he is to be involved. I will do all that a prudent man ought to do to avoid difficulties, but should it be my lot to have them forced upon me, my reliance is, that Providence will guide me through them in safety.

Judge White's speech, delivered on the 7th and 8th of June, 1832, of the same year, on the question of the engrossment and third reading of the bill to renew the charter of the bank, was as follows:

Mr. President—I am pleased with the manner in which the discussion of this important subject has been commenced and continued thus far; and, although it is my intention to express my own sentiments with that freedom which belongs to my place, and with the frankness of one who has no opinion to conceal, yet I should be sorry if, in the remarks I am about to submit, I should unnecessarily say anything calculated to change the tone of the debate.

Whether the charter of the existing Bank of the United States ought to be renewed, is a question which should not be blended with another great question, and that is, whether the high duties to be performed by the federal government can be discharged without the aid of a bank of some description.*

To the existing company the United States should, in good faith, discharge every obligation they have contracted; up to this time they have done so; and if they shall not put in operation any other bank until the existing charter expires, and in other respects comply with existing stipulations, in the meantime, no violation of their faith can be charged to them.

The present stockholders, so far as they are citizens, will have had a complete monopoly for twenty years, and would, in my opinion, have less claim to become subscribers to any other bank to be created by the federal government, than other citizens who have been excluded from all banking privileges, in time past. Foreigners, who, at present, are stockholders, have no claims whatever upon us. This charter was always exceptionable, on account of the United States being a stockholder. By owning stock they become the partner of a few private citizens, and give them the benefit of the character, resources, and influence of the whole, thus enabling a favored few to make profits out of the whole, for their own exclusive benefit; this is wrong in principle. Ours is a government founded on equality, and ought never to be so conducted as to give a few

* I do not wish it to be understood, as my opinion, that a bank, chartered by Congress, may not be necessary to insure the correct management of the fiscal concerns of the federal government. On the contrary, I think it very probable, that, upon the expiration of the present charter, one may be devised, consistent with the Constitution, giving to the United States all the benefits which a bank can confer, and guard against the evils feared from the bill now under consideration.—*Note by Judge White.*

an advantage over the whole. Although it may be said, all had an equal opportunity to subscribe originally, and therefore those who did not, cannot now complain; yet, when we come to the question we are now considering, that of giving a new charter, this answer loses all its force; because now we select a few by name, become connected with them, and exclude all others from any participation for an additional fifteen years. If we now renew this charter, because the present stockholders have been the partners of the United States for twenty years, the argument for a second renewal will become stronger at the end of the next fifteen, and thus we shall have created permanently a privileged class of society, who will have the sanction, influence, and resources of the government afforded them to make money at the expense of the rest of society. But of all partnerships, this would be the most exceptionable. The United States own seven millions of stock, foreigners, we know, own eight millions; how much more in the names of citizens we cannot tell, and the residue is owned by others, and these different interests are to be combined in one act of incorporation, and to be partners in banking for fifteen years. This ought not to be done, when our citizens have spare capital, which they are anxious to invest in such stock.

There might be some apology for this course, if we were destitute of capital and needed foreign aid; but this we know is not the case—our own surplus capital, seeking safe and profitable investments, is the cause of our present political discontents. During the European wars, which commenced soon after the formation of the present Constitution, by the employment of our own capital, in navigation and commerce, great additions were made to it. The French decrees and British orders in council produced our restrictive measures, and terminated in the declaration of war in 1812. This war caused much of the capital, previously employed in navigation and commerce, to seek employment at home. It was invested in manufactures, and upon the return of peace it asked and obtained from Congress protection from foreign competition. This protection occasioned new investments, and these new applications for additional protection, at different periods, up to the present time. We have no scarcity of American capital—it is fully equal to all our wants. Why then should we renew this charter, and give exclusive privileges to foreigners, when our citizens are anxious to invest their money in the bank, and are offering to Congress terms *more* favorable, than are secured to us by this bill? It is said this bank has restored specie payments, collected your revenue, paid it out, paid your pensioners, and equalized exchange.

Sir, it is the character of the United States, of which this bank has had the exclusive use, it is the funds of the United States, of which the bank has had complete control, it is the influence of our character, and our money, that restored specie payments, and enabled the bank to continue them in spite of bad management.

The collection of your revenue has not cost the bank one cent. It has only done for you, what any bank would gladly do for an individual. It has received your money on deposit, when carried to its vaults at your expense. It has received your custom-house, and other bonds for collection. It voluntarily paid, and received the money when due. If not paid, it put the bonds into the hands of your law officer, and he has made the collections, at your expense, and then deposited the money in the bank. Your drafts upon the bank have been paid, when and where presented, and well they might, because you had your money deposited, in every place where there was either a principal or a branch bank. This, in place of a disadvantage, must have been a source of profit to the bank, because upon your funds it could draw, and re-draw bills in favor of individuals, and secure premiums to itself.

By the laws, the bank was not bound to pay, nor did it pay, as is believed, pensioners, except in States where there was either the principal or a branch bank. The only trouble was to pay the pensioners when they applied at the bank and take receipts. This service any bank would gladly have performed for the benefit of the deposit, till pay-day should arrive.

As to the uniformity of our currency, every man knows that the notes of this bank are not, in every quarter of the country, as good as the specie. A branch note payable at Nashville or New Orleans, is necessarily at a discount, in Maine or New York; and as to the domestic exchange, it is always in favor of the bank, so as to enable it to receive a premium upon a bill, or draft, when it sells one, and obtain a discount when it purchases.

Much credit has been claimed for the able administration of the affairs of the bank. Gentlemen ought to remember that this praise has been claimed on a scale too extensive. For a portion of the time, since this bank has been in operation, it has been managed as badly as any institution ever was, under either Federal or State authority. It was literally bankrupt by bad management. By good fortune, at a lucky moment, the services of Mr. Cheves were procured, at the head of the institution; his talents, his business habits, his stern integrity, and, above all, his unyielding firmness, gave to its concerns a direction, which saved it from open and notorious bankruptcy, and enabled it, gradually, by the *whole pecuniary assistance* the United States could afford, to recover its character, and afterwards sustain its credit. These transactions it has not been thought necessary to preserve, by placing them in the same volume with the affairs relating to our banks, and with which we have each been furnished; but we ought, nevertheless, to recollect them, and ought to remember, also, that there is no certainty, but the affairs of this institution may again be under the direction of those equally as incompetent, or faithless, as any that have preceded them.

The bank now has, and at the end of the charter will have, its transactions widely spread over an immense territory. It will have many debts to pay, and many to collect. Until it commences winding up, those who have transactions with it will not generally speak out, according to the truth. While it is discounting, and accommodating, it will be popular; but when the hour for final payment shall have arrived, then we will hear of the mismanagement, if any exists; then we will find out the bad debts, and how, and for what contracted. Every thing now looks well upon paper. We see that the bank has in circulation upwards of twenty millions of dollars, in notes. The sum due for deposits is large; all these debts are to be paid, and with what? With the funds in possession, and the proceeds of debts due. No man living can tell, until the time of collection, how many of these debts are due from solvent men. Whenever that time shall have arrived, the country at large, and Congress, can find out whether this bank has been managed well or ill, with fidelity or not. Nay, more, we can then see, and know, whether such a bank, in its operations, is beneficial or injurious to society.

Every merchant, long in business, knows, that if he has done a business upon credit, he must, at the end of every ten or fifteen years, change his style, and commence a new concern, for the purpose of being able to wind up his old concern—he must collect his debts, and pay those to whom he is indebted. In no other way can he tell, certainly, whether his business has been profitable or otherwise. If this be true, in mercantile concerns, how much more so is it in the case of such a bank as this?

By suffering this charter to expire, a flood of light would be shed upon this subject, which would be of great use to society, and which would enable Congress to know whether a bank ought to be again chartered, and what ought to be the modification and improvement in the charter to be granted.

Again. If we were disposed to renew the present charter, it is too soon to do so. It has almost four years yet to run, and then two years are allowed for collections. By renewing now, we put the corporation four years, unnecessarily, beyond our control. The main security we have for the good behavior of the bank, is, that at the termination of the charter, a renewal will be refused, unless its concerns shall have been faithfully managed. Why, then, should we give up this security, so long in advance? All our offices of trust are based upon the principle, that the person employed shall come, as frequently as convenience will permit, to the power which gave him employ, that his capacity and fidelity may be judged of; and, if found deficient in either, then a better man may be chosen in his stead. The principle is the same here, and yet this immense moneyed institution is to be made an exception, and *four* years in advance, its charter is to be renewed.

The reason assigned for this is entirely unsatisfactory. It has been said, if the directors had the charter renewed, they can not only continue, but extend their business. If not renewed now, they must begin to collect their debts, &c. A little reflection will satisfy us, that there is not much force in this argument. It has always been urged, in favor of this bank, that the paper, in which it deals, is *business* paper. If this be true, what does it want with time to wind up? A owes B five thousand dollars, for which he gives his note, payable in ninety, or any other number of days. B wishes to use the money presently; he carries the note to the bank, endorses it, and has it discounted. When this note falls due, A is notified that it belongs the bank; he goes and pays it, and there is an end of the transaction. If this be the description of paper, in which the bank deals, it does not need any time for winding up. All that need be done is, to omit discounting when the charter expires, and the debts come in of course. But if a considerable portion of the business of the bank is done upon *accommodation* paper, no time ought to be granted. It is unsafe to the bank, ruinous to society, and should be discountenanced.

The man who opens a standing accommodation with the bank, and relies upon renewing his note, periodically, by paying the discounts, be his business what it may, will generally be taken by surprise, when called on to pay the principal, will be ruined himself, and very often his endorsers with him.

I fear very many of the debts due to this bank are substantially founded upon accommodation paper. Look at the case from New York, disclosed in the report of the committee of the other house—the debt was contracted with the bank in 1831, payable by installments, the last of which was only due in the fall of 1836, six months after the charter is to expire. Does any one pretend, this was anything but accommodation paper? I speak not of the purity of this transaction, but suppose it to be, as the friends of this institution represent it, and then say, I think such transactions with banks can never be considered real business transactions, but must fall within the class called accommodations.

Examine the documents upon our desks, and see the items of domestic bills. I am strongly impressed with the opinion, if examined, they are substantially accommodation paper of the most ruinous kind. On the 1st of April, 1831, they amounted to $14,725,923. On the 1st December, of the same year, they amounted to $14,853,530, with but little variation, as to amount in the meantime. This would scarcely have happened for so long a period, unless they were in substance accommodations. I will take the liberty of suggesting, how some of these domestic bills are probably brought into existence, and continued—I will take for my illustration, what may be the operations of the branch in my own State.

A merchant needs an addition to his capital; he procures endorsers, and obtains a discount for sixty days. When his note falls due he discounts another, and by paying in the discount, and applying the nett proceeds of the last note, to the discharge of the first, he lifts it. When the second falls due, he is called upon for actual payment—this he cannot make, but offers a bill upon his commission merchant, in New Orleans, payable in four months; this is received by the bank, taking off the discount and charging one or two per cent.; or whatever else is the difference of exchange, between Nashville and New Orleans. To obtain endorsers for these notes, a guarantee for the bill of exchange, and to procure acceptance of the bill, the borrower has to pay to each of the persons concerned, probably two per cent. His reliance for lifting the bill when due, is the proceeds of a crop, which he hopes to raise, and ship to New Orleans, in time to meet the demand. If he is disappointed in whole, or in part, when the bill falls due, it is lifted by re-drawing upon Nashville, at the same heavy expense, incurred in the first instance, and thus in the shape of domestic bills drawn first one way, and then the other, the accommodation is continued as long as the man's means of paying discounts, rates of exchange, and other charges continue; and then he fails, and when he does, if a merchant, every farmer, to whom he is indebted, will probably lose his debt, and if the debtor was a farmer, he will probably lose his plantation, or his slaves, besides injuring his endorser. I have no knowledge of any transactions such as I have described; but they may, and I fear do exist, if not at the Nashville branch, at some others. If such there are, they are injurious to the country, and ought to be checked.

By permitting the question of renewal to remain for the present, we shall obtain information upon the subject, and three years hence can better determine, whether the operations of the bank are friendly to the community or not.

The stockholders have weakened very much their claims to the renewal of the charter, by some of their transactions in time past. I allude now to the issuing and circulating checks, or drafts, for twenty dollars and under, in place of notes of the same denominations. I consider this as a plain *evasion* of the charter, and under very peculiar circumstances. When this charter was granted in 1816, the community suffered on account of two difficulties, relating to the paper of the State banks. First, if the notes in circulation were genuine, they were not as good as the sum called for, because the banks issuing them did not redeem them by paying specie. Second, the State banks were so numerous, that when a note was found in circulation, in many instances, no man could tell whether is was genuine or a counterfeit. The Bank of the United States was intended, and expected to remove both these difficulties. It was to pay specie, and thereby put down all State banks, which did *not* pay likewise. The fundamental articles require that every note issued, and put in circulation, should be signed by the president and cashier of the principal bank. By having the signatures of only these two officers it was supposed that their hand-writing would soon become familiar to every man of business, who would thus readily distinguish the genuine from the counterfeit. In the course of a few years, the directors applied to Congress for permission to designate two other persons to sign small notes, as it was physically impossible for the president and cashier to sign the number required. Congress refused to grant this request--a second, third, and if I mistake not, fourth application of the like kind was made, and refused; at all events not granted. After this, in the year 1826 or '27, the directors searched in the charter, for what is called a *new combination* of their powers, and these drafts were devised, to be used as substitutes for small notes. These drafts are, in form, bills of exchange, bearing the signatures of the presidents of the respective branches, addressed to the cashier of the principal bank and requiring him to pay upon demand, the amount specified. The circulation of them as a substitute for notes, is a plain violation of the charter. It takes from society, without the consent of Congress, that security against *counterfeits*, which was given by the charter. We must not, in examining this point, confound two things which are separate and distinct. Whether the bank is bound to *pay* these drafts, when presented at the principal bank, is one question which I answer in the affirmative. But whether these drafts furnish the uniformity of paper currency, the same security against counterfeits, which the notes would do, is a very different question, which I answer in the negative. There are now how many branches? Seventeen is it? I have not counted. No, says Mr. Benton, twenty-five. Well then; the holder of one of those drafts runs twenty-five times as many risks of having counterfeit paper put on him, as Congress intended he should run. This, I say ought not to have been, and still I have all respect for the learned counsel, who were consulted, and who I doubt not are entitled to all the respect and character which society has awarded to them. It cannot escape notice, that the stress of the opinion, is placed upon a point, upon which I think there can be no doubt, the liability of the bank to pay, and the other point, the want of *uniformity* in *signatures* to the paper currency is almost entirely overlooked. My respect for those counsel I know, and for the character of the one I am unacquainted with, constrains me to think, if the true question had been directly put to them, they would have given such opinions as I now insist conform to the true construction of the charter.

For a moment let us examine the excuse set up for this evasion—"That the president and cashier were not able to sign a sufficient number of notes." Be it so; and what ought they to have done? Surely not to have issued these checks, they ought to have signed as many notes as they could, and to have used specie, when they had not a sufficiency of notes. This would have conformed to the charter, been very acceptable to the public, and have been in furtherance of the great object in establishing the bank, that of restoring to society a specie currency. Besides, it would have been actually testing the utility of the excellent experiment spoken of by the Senator from Massachusetts, Mr. Webster, that of ceasing to circulate any notes as low as twenty dollars, and using in their place, a specie circulation.

It appears to me that the use made of these checks, is highly injurious on another ground. The effect of such a circulation in the South and West, is to remove from those sections of country the whole of the specie, which can be collected there, and leave us nothing but a paper currency composed of those checks.

I assume it as a fact, that every one of those drafts or checks, is upon its face, made payable by the cashier of the principal bank. They are, therefore, payable in Philadelphia, and payment cannot be legally demanded in the first instance, at any other place. What then is to be the inevitable result? The specie must be withdrawn from the branches, which circulate these checks, and taken to Philadelphia, and be there in readiness to lift them, when they arrive. So far as common people are concerned, this will never happen. No man will ever travel from Louisiana, Tennessee, or Kentucky, to Philadelphia with a note of five, ten, or twenty dollars, to demand the specie for it. He would save money by putting it in the fire, in preference. As matter of accommodation, as long as the specie would hold out, the branches would no doubt give specie for them, but that must soon fail, and then the holders will be told, we have sent the money to Philadelphia, to lift them, whither you must go. We have at present hardly any small notes in circulation; nothing but these checks. I do not believe I have seen a single note for five or ten dollars in Tennessee for the last two years. No inconvenience has as yet been experienced, because you can get the specie for one of them, in any merchant's shop you step into: but this must soon cease: the specie will by the circulation of such paper be all withdrawn, and you will have a paper medium, and no specie within any *reasonable distance.* The very process of which I am now speaking, is, and has been going on; the documents upon our table prove it. In a letter under date of 24th December, 1831, from the cashier of the principal bank, to the cashier of the New Orleans branch, found at page 516 of the report of the minority of the committee, we find this language: "On every account we should, from present appearance, desire to be reinforced by all the means which you can throw into our hands, and would therefore recommend, that your local discounts should be prudently and gradually reduced—a course, which circumstances with you evidently favor; and that you should extend your operations in a corresponding degree in exchange, and afford us large supplies of specie to meet *your circulation*, as it comes in at the North." Can any one doubt what this means? It is the same thing as if he had said, your circulation, these checks, are payable at the North, *here;* send us on large supplies of specie with which *to pay them.*

At page 205, of the report of the majority of the committee, we see the actual operation, as it is going on. In 1831, the amount of specie sent from the branches to the principal bank was $3,628,853 76. In 1830, it was $3,653,202 13. In 1829, it was $2,673,115 97. In 1828, it was $2,055,756 78, and in 1827, it was $1,787,049 18. This is the year in which the checks first began to be used, instead of notes, as a circulating medium. To me it is obvious, that by continuing their use, and withdrawing the specie, we shall have nothing but paper, near the branches of the West and South.

It may be asked what benefit the bank can derive from this process? The answer is obvious. They can extend their discounts, and make *more money*. In 1827, when they began to issue them, their notes in circulation were upwards of $18,000,000. Since then, they have extended to from twenty to twenty-four millions of dollars. The bank can safely put in circulation, *far from the place of payment*, a much *larger* amount of these drafts than they could of notes made payable where they were issued. I cannot but consider what has been done in this respect, an evasion of the charter, highly injurious to society, and done under circumstances calculated to take from the bank all claim to a renewal of the charter. The honorable chairman of the committee, which reported this bill, has told us, that the committee did not feel called upon to investigate how the bank had been conducted. Because, says he, if a public officer abuses his trust, that is no reason why you should abolish the office, etc.; and added, he had no doubt, if they had inquired, it would have been found, that the bank had been faithfully and ably conducted.

While I admit, that if a public officer abuses his trust, that is no reason why you should abolish the office, then the remedy would be to turn out the faithless officer, and put a better man into the office necessary for the public interest, I deny entirely the analogy of this case. Here I say, if the directors have abused their trust, and the stockholders, after knowing the fact, continue them in office, the charter ought to be rescinded; at all events, it ought not to be renewed, when it expires.

I urge these considerations against renewing this charter *at any time*, and especially at the present time, in addition to other conclusive reasons, urged a few days ago, by the Senator from Missouri (Col. Benton), and which I shall not repeat.

The great questions still remain to be considered:

1st. Is it proper, at any time for Congress to incorporate a banking company, vesting it with the powers which this bill confers?

I am free to declare, that in preference to vesting such powers in any company whatever, powers which may be used to such pernicious purposes, even if I believed I had the power to do so, I would trust the well-doing of this government, and the people, to a specie currency alone, and to such facilities as banks incorporated by the respective States may be able to afford.

It will operate as a conductor, to carry off all the circulating medium from those sections of country, principally agricultural, where few or no stockholders reside; and place it down to be used in those sections of country where stockholders may be found. Take, for example, the operation of the branch bank at Nashville. It is now doing a business of from four to five millions of dollars—suppose it to be four and a half millions. The common interest upon that sum would equal two hundred and seventy thousand dollars per annum. All these profits are made from those living convenient enough to the bank to be its customers. At the end of each six months, they are taken and distributed among the stockholders. In Tennessee we have only three or four stockholders, owning some *two* or *three* hundred shares. Nearly the whole of this sum must therefore be taken *from that State*, and paid over to persons residing in *other* States, and in *Great Britain*. This operation is to be continued from year to year, so long as the charter lasts; and ere long, will, as I think, withdraw from our use the whole circulating medium we possess. The same effect must be produced in every other State, similarly circumstanced. What benefit does the bank confer equivalent to this loss? In most cases I think none. Banks are generally of no use in countries highly agricultural. They are of use to those engaged in commerce, whose business is increased by anticipating their funds, who handle money freely, and can be punctual. The farmer whose profits are small, and long coming into possession, is generally injured by the bank, from which he obtains an accommodation. The longer he borrows the worse he gets, and after paying interest for several years, it too frequently happens he is compelled to sell his home, to liquidate the debt thus contracted.

Suppose it to be a merchant who borrows with a view to aid his capital. Where he has so many to compete with, who have capital sufficient of their own on which to do business, it will seldom happen that a bank accommodation will enable him to succeed; most usually it gives him a false credit, which he will use in purchasing produce upon credit, by promising something more than the cash price: eventually he fails, the bank may collect its debt, either from the drawer, or his endorser, but the farmer loses the debt due for his produce. The bank may give the appearance of prosperity to the country, it may enable people to purchase or improve lots in a town, or to build houses on farms in the country; but this appearance will, in the end, be found deceptive. These houses and lots, and these plantations, thus improved, will generally change owners, and all the benefit the borrower will receive will be the honor of having had an account with the Bank of the United States which has stripped him of his possessions, and thus prepared him to seek a new home.

Believing, therefore, that a charter such as this, authorizing two branches if the directors choose, to be established in each State, without the consent of the legislature, may, and will, prove a means of impoverishing the citizens of many States for the benefit of others, I cannot, and will not vote for this bill.

It is idle to insist that we must have this bank to enable the farmers to sell their surplus produce. Take away the bank to-morrow, and every man who has produce for sale will find, if it is in demand, that those who wish to purchase will send their agents, *with funds*, into the market, who will purchase and make prompt payment, as was the case before the bank was established. When there is no demand for the produce, no one will purchase, whether there is or is not a bank. With the immense capital furnished this bank, all concentrated in, and controlled by the same persons, backed by the deposits, the name and influence of the United States, this bank will have the power at any time it chooses to exert it, to take to itself *all the active capital of the State banks*, in all places not very highly commercial; therefore it may, and probably will, be the place, at which all men of business and influence, in the Union, will do their business, and obtain their accommodations.

Is it to have power to establish as many as two branches in each State, without the consent of the State, and to withdraw them at pleasure?

The directors of the principal bank appoint whom they please as directors of the respective branches, and can change them at pleasure. Seven directors at the principal bank constitute a board, and four of them will form a majority.

Already it has its operations throughout the whole country, presently they will be extended into every corner of society.

Suppose the directors to wish their charter changed, so as to suspend specie payments, or any other alteration made; or suppose them to wish a tariff changed, the price of the public lands made higher or lower, or any other public measure carried, can they not control the Congressional and *State* elections whenever they choose? Yes, less than one half-dozen men, seated in the principal bank in Philadelphia, will have the power, if they choose to exercise it, to have the same story in praise, or dispraise, of any man, or set of men, put in circulation in every neighborhood, in every State in the Union, at any hour of any day in the year, they please; and what makes this power the more terrific is, that no one injured will be able to find out the source from which the injury originates. Thus any man may be put in or out of office at the will of this bank, and of course any measure carried or defeated, as these directors may think will best answer their purposes.

Again, suppose a man elected President of the United States, not disposed to promote the public good, but to pursue his individual interest, and that of his friends, at the public expense, and to have an understanding with the directors of the bank, that so long as he or his friends should continue in office, the interest of the bank should be promoted. Could he ever be displaced? I fear not. When you array all the patronage of the federal executive, and all the influence of this moneyed institution on one side, and have nothing to oppose to it but the ill-arranged and unorganized action of the common people, the country may well tremble for the result. We have now exhibited a curious spectacle to the American people; the President a candidate for re-election, and daring to speak his opinions in opposition to this institution: it is what I never expected to witness; and let the approaching election terminate as it may, the youngest amongst us will not live long enough, in my opinion, to witness the like again. In all time to come, the President and directors of the bank, will, as I fear, think alike and act in concert, on all subjects interesting to either, and doing so on the days of election, will be an over-match for any influence which can be brought to bear against them.

I have heard some intelligent men say, we would gain but little by putting down this bank, because, then the public deposits must be made in the State banks; and through that medium, there would be as much danger of influence as from this bank. Sure I am, those gentlemen had not sufficiently reflected on this subject or they would have perceived the immense difference in the cases. Glance at them, for a moment. If you place the deposits in State banks, your whole funds will be divided among so many as to afford but little temptation to any one. Suppose one or two to be tempted, by these deposits, to interfere improperly in politics, the rest would remain sound, and little or no mischief could ensue. The number to be misled is so great, and so divided, that, having no common connection with each other there is little or nothing to apprehend. But in the case of the Bank of the United States, it must withstand the temptation of your *whole funds*, because the same institution is to have your *whole deposits*. Again—procuring the coöperation of a majority of the directors of *one single board* accomplishes everything; they would manage their respective branches, and the branches their customers, throughout the whole community. The number to be approached and misled by the executive is so limited, that there is infinitely more to apprehend in the latter than in the former case.

Should it ever again be our misfortune to be involved in a war with any foreign power, will not this bank compel you to make peace, whenever it chooses, upon any terms it may dictate.

It will have command of the whole active capital employed in *any banks*. Without money, we cannot successfully prosecute any war. How could these funds be procured? There is no provision in this bill, or the original act, by which the bank is bound to loan the government one dollar. It is prohibited from loaning more than five hundred thousand dollars, without an act of Congress to authorize it. But if an act should be passed, requiring a loan, there is no obligation on the bank, to advance a cent, even of *your own seven millions*, vested in stock. Suppose this bank to have existed during the late war with Great Britain, and the stock to have been owned by British subjects, and by our own citizens, who thought it so unjust, that they esteemed it immoral to thank the Author of all good for our victories—does any man believe we could have procured a loan from this bank? No, sir. You could not have procured enough money to have loaded a musket, or to purchase a ration.

This bank now has, and will continue to have, under this charter, a complete control over the whole circulating medium, in the United States. At its will, money will be plenty, or scarce. The value, therefore, of every man's property, is in its power; it may be enhanced or depressed at pleasure. Should the directors, or their friends, have property to sell, they can make money abundant, and secure an extravagant price. Should they wish to purchase, they need only limit the discount, press debtors for payment, make money scarce, and purchase at their own prices.

They will have a monopoly, in bills of exchange, both foreign and domestic, and can regulate exchanges, to suit the interest of the bank. They can make premiums high, or low, to suit them, or they can in any week change the rates, in most cases, so as to purchase at discounts, when they had, a few days before, been selling for an advance.

Mr. President, is it sound policy? Is it consistent with the freedom of election? Is it just to the rest of the community, to create or continue, any corporation, vested with such powers? Surely not. By the abuse of them, liberty may be endangered, if not destroyed, and our property sacrificed.

It is not a sufficient answer to these arguments to say, none of these mischiefs have happened; the directors are men of integrity and high character; therefore, all is safe. I say no. There is no certainty how long the management of this bank may be in the hands of the present directors. To-morrow we may have dishonest directors; those who will pursue their own interest, and that of the stockholders, regardless of the public welfare; and we are safe only when no powers are given which can be used to the prejudice of society.

Mr. President, there is one other question on this bill, which is surely worth consideration: I mean, the power of Congress to incorporate this bank. The Honorable Chairman of the Committee has told us, this question "is gone by," "is settled." It may be so, with some; with me, it is otherwise. I have been taught, that "a frequent recurrence to fundamental principles is essential to liberty." Why shall we recur to them, if we are to give up our own opinions, and make the opinions of other men the rule of our conduct. Acts of the legislature, containing general rules, must be expounded, and applied to individual cases, by the decisions of courts of justice. After a settled train of judicial decision, on any contested point, those decisions expounding the statute, in courts, are as much esteemed the rule for future decision, as the statute itself. But this is not so, in any legislative body. I admit, everywhere, if a man is called upon to act, and after exercising his best judgment he is in doubt how he ought to act, when he can find what other enlightened men, acting under the same obligations with himself, have done, in the like cases, he ought, as a reasonable man, to conclude, he will most probably be correct, if he follows in their footsteps. But if, after examining the subject fully, he is convinced that they were mistaken, I deny that he is justified in following others in error. How, then, can it be said this question of power is gone by, is settled, not to be thought upon, nor talked about. Sir, it is not settled. It is a vexed question. This power has always been contested, from the formation of the Constitution to this moment. In Congress, in courts, in society, it now is, and ever has been, disputed. In 1791, when the old Bank of the United States was chartered, the power was denied, by those who aided in framing the Constitution. The argument Mr. Madison then made, has never, as I think, been satisfactorily answered. But a majority of Congress affirmed the existence of the power, and acted upon it. General Washington consulted his cabinet, and they were equally divided, two and two. The judicial decisions affirmed the power, and when that charter was about to expire, an application was made to renew it. What did Congress then do? Did it conceive the question was gone by, settled, and that nothing was to be done but to follow on? No, sir. The power was given, contested, and *negatived.* Here, then, is precedent the other way. Thus the matter rested, till during the war; there was then an attempt to get up a bank, *and it failed.* After the war, at the session of 1815-16, this bank was chartered. But the power was contested; and those about to use it were emphatically told, that in 1811, they had *themselves* determined, they did not possess the power.

The judicial decisions have affirmed the power, confirmed by this charter, as they did that confirmed by the act of 1791; but the opponents of this bank cannot now be told, that this question is settled, with any more propriety, than those were so told in 1811, when then the question of re-charter occurred. Indeed I have always thought the granting the charter in 1816, ought to weigh very little. The time was unfriendly to correct constitutional opinions, as to *federal powers.* The war was just ended; those who had struggled through it, had their minds toned for an exercise of federal powers, at which they would have hesitated in time of peace. Only the year before, 1814 and 1815, they had a project for a great paper bank, which was on the eve of passing. Would they have dreamed of such a power, in time of peace? I think not. The giving this charter, then, in 1816, ought not to weigh much on the question of power. It was an act of *necessity*, in the opinion of a majority, and they were spurred up to the exercise of this power, by the contest through which the country had just passed.

Under all these circumstances, I think, I treat with no disrespect, the opinions of enlightened men, who have affirmed this power to be in Congress, when I say my mind has arrived at a different conclusion, and that I feel bound to act upon the best judgment I have been enabled to form myself.

If then, we are yet at liberty to examine the Constitution, and to form an opinion, whether we have the power to create such a bank as this, may not those opposed to it ask, respectfully, of its advocates, to point to that clause which confers this power?

We all know what the answer to such request must be, that no such power is given in express terms, but it is necessary that Congress should exert this power, otherwise effect cannot be given to other important powers, which we are obliged to exercise for the public good.

We ask what they are, and one gentleman says—Congress is authorized to levy and collect taxes, and provide for the common defence and general welfare.

Another, that Congress has the power "to coin money and fix its value and the value of foreign coin, and to regulate the standard of weights and measures," and this gives a complete power over the whole monetary system of the United States.

A third, that the power to coin money, emit bills of credit, and to make anything but gold and silver a tender in payment of debts is expressly taken from the States; and, that therefore, Congress must have the power now claimed, &c. These positions have each been separately examined, and, as I think proved, in argument, to be untenable.

In 1791, Mr. Madison's argument in the House of Representatives, and Mr. Jefferson's opinion in the Cabinet, placed this in a stronger light than anything I could say would do, and on their arguments I very much rely. In 1811, the arguments of other statesmen enforced their doctrine, in a manner I can never hope to imitate; and I do not propose to fatigue the Senate, by repeating the arguments which they have used, and which, in my opinion, have never been satisfactorily answered.

But, sir, I may be permitted to ask, if we infer the power to create a bank such as this is, what power may not be inferred? The United States have a power to declare war—to have an army and navy. We cannot make a successful war, unless preparations are made in time of peace. Arms and ammunition are essentially necessary—why not incorporate a company to make arms, to smelt lead, and to make gunpowder? Clothing and blankets are necessary for your troops—why not incorporate companies to manufacture them? Provisions are essentially necessary to feed the troops—why not incorporate companies to procure lands, to raise grain, and to rear stock? The power to incorporate companies for these purposes could be presumed with better reason than the power to incorporate a bank.

We are to presume that we have a power to incorporate stockholders for a bank; because a bank is a *necessary* and *proper* means to collect, to keep safe, and pay out the revenue. Is it not fair to say, if you create a bank for such purposes, we ought to confine its operations to *these duties?* But when once created by implication, instead of confining it to these duties, we confer upon it other important primary powers, and the performance of these *governmental duties* are the *least part of its business;* mere incidental matters, hardly worth notice. We presume the power to make the bank, and having made it, presume we have the power to keep its paper pure, and therefore presume we can pass laws to hang or imprison those who counterfeit its notes, and the human mind can hardly fix any limits to the presumed powers, which may be created from the first construction.

In my opinion a very erroneous impression has got abroad, founded upon the supposition, that *bank notes are currency.* The Constitution of the United States never contemplated any currency as *legal* but a *metallic* currency. No other is *constitutional*, nor can any other be made legal.

The United States have a power to *coin* money, and to fix the value thereof, and to fix the value of *foreign* coin, and to regulate the standard of weights and measures.

No State shall have power to coin money, emit bills of credit, or make anything but gold and silver a tender in payment of debts.

From these sections some have argued, the Constitution intended to give Congress the power *over the whole currency.*

I agree to this position, and think such was the intention of those who framed the Constitution; but the question recurs, of what was that currency to *consist?* I say not of *paper* of any description. It was to consist of *metals*, and those metals were to be *coined* in the United States, and their values *fixed by law*, or they must be coined in some other country, and their value fixed *here* by *our laws*, and by the same power made *current.* I admit the currency we *actually* have is mostly notes, either of the Bank of the United States or of some of the State banks; but I deny that this paper is any more a *legal* currency within the meaning of the Constitution, than a negotiable promissory note or a bill of exchange would be. Bank notes are used by society, instead of gold and silver, for convenience, by *common consent*—having no constitutional or legal foundation whatever as a standard of value, nor can any such effect be given to them by either federal or State government; all must agree that the States have no power to make a man take bank notes in payment of a debt. I put this question, Can the federal government do so? I say *no.* Congress have no such power. Taking such power from the States, does not necessarily confer it upon the federal government, because the United States have an express power to make *metals* currency, and nothing is said about a paper currency.

I admit Congress has the power to compel their own officers to receive bank notes or anything else they choose, in discharge of debts, due to the United States, but deny that they have any power to compel A to receive from B any description of paper whatever, in discharge of a debt due to him. What then becomes of this power to create a bank, because we have the power to regulate the *currency*, when that currency is to be, according to the Constitution, nothing but *specie?* It vanishes.

Under the articles of confederation, an express power had been given to Congress to emit bills of credit. This power had been liberally used; too much so, as was believed, for the benefit of society. In framing the present Constitution, the convention determined to guard against the exercise of any such power in future, either by the State or federal government. Therefore, by express words, they took from the *States* the power to emit bills of credit; and amended the draft of the Constitution submitted to them, which confined the power to emit bills of credit, by striking those words out. (Journal of Convention, pp. 75 and 256.) Thus by taking from the *States* this power, and *refusing* to give it to Congress, they believed society was secured in a *metallic currency*, and guarded against everything else.

We have the express testimony of Mr. Madison, a member of the convention, of Mr. Martin, another member of the same body, and of Mr. Jefferson, a member of President Washington's cabinet, that in the convention there was an attempt to give Congress the power to *incorporate a bank*, and *it was refused.*

The journal containing the proceedings of that body is now published; and we find that, on three several occasions, an attempt was actually made to give to Congress the power to pass acts of *incorporation*, and it was uniformly *refused.*

It seems, therefore, clear to me that the convention did not intend to give the power, now claimed, to Congress; and that we have no right to vest ourselves with such a power by construction.

In my mind, there are many provisions in this charter violative of the Constitution. The United States themselves cannot purchase and hold lands in any State, without the consent of such State; yet this charter authorizes this corporation composed in part of aliens and of the United States to do so. The friends of this bill have solemnly refused to insert a provision, by which the States can impose any tax upon the capital employed within their limits, although such States will be bound to protect the persons in the employ of, and the property belonging to, this institution.

The bill gives a monopoly to this company for fifteen years, which is not only odious, but against the genius of the Constitution.

It confers upon this corporation the power of regulating the currency of the country, which is an attribute of sovereignty that Congress has no power to transfer to our citizens, much less to foreigners.

The whole emoluments of this bank will go to these stockholders; they have had, and are still to have, all your public money, on which to do business; and by a vote of this body they are to pay *no interest* whatever for the use of these funds. We thus take the money of all for the benefit of a *few*.

But it is said, we are benefited by a sound currency in peace and in war, and by having an institution to which we can have access for loans, in cases of emergency.

How is this matter? When we had the quasi war with France, in 1798–9, we had a bank, and yet had to borrow from individuals at an interest of eight per centum. In case of another war, we cannot obtain loans from this bank, unless specie payments are suspended. Look at its condition, after it has been in operation fifteen or sixteen years in time of peace. It now has notes out for upwards of twenty millions of dollars, owes large deposits, and has from seven to eight millions of dollars only in specie. In case of war, suppose you wish to borrow ten, twenty, or fifty millions of dollars, could it loan you, and continue to pay specie? It could not; you must again have paper money or no money. Your bank could not hold out six months and pay specie.

During the last war, when every resource was likely to fail, a bank was thought of, and what kind of a one was it to be? *A paper bank.* So will this be—if we have a war, and are obliged to borrow a hundred millions of dollars.

Who abused the rags of State during the war? The enemies of the United States, not this government.

The government sanctioned the suspension of specie payments. It was then patriotic to aid the government; without a suspension of specie payments, these loans could not be made. Without these rags, we could not feed, clothe, or pay a single soldier. Paper money carried us through the War of Independence; paper money got us through the last war; and if we have another war of much duration, we will have paper money the third time. But as soon as peace returns, we will do as we have done in time past, work ourselves into *hard money*, into a *sound currency*.

Sir, if we are to have this bank with these extraordinary, and, as I think, unwarranted powers, it may bear down all before it; like other institutions, it will use its powers for the benefit of the stockholders. It has been said, Corporations have no souls. If this one does not injure society it will be an exception; it must have more soul and better feelings than belongs to mortals. We need not fret about the Tariff, or the price of public lands; let it unite its influence with other capitalists, and all can be managed as they choose. Look at the inducements it has to do so. It is to have all your public money on deposit, *without interest.* The higher our taxes, the larger the deposits; the more the deposits, the greater will be the profits of the bank. For the last several years, the United States deposits have averaged from *six* to *eight* millions of dollars. The bank will have an interest in not having them less. If the directors act correctly under such strong temptations, they will be justly entitled to higher eulogiums than any their warmest friends have yet pronounced.

That Judge White's private sentiments were similar to these spoken opinions, if such proof were needful, would appear from the following letter to an intimate friend in Tennessee, written about this time:

The Bank bill is before the House of Representatives. It will without doubt be passed there, and there is much speculation as to what the President will do. I do not profess to know more than others of his opinion on the subject, but am as certain that he will put his veto upon it, should it be presented to him in the shape it left the Senate, as I can be of any future act that depends upon the will of one man.

We will then see whether the bank will or will not endeavor to control the election of the next President. If it does, I hope it will open the eyes of the public, and enable every man to see the danger of such a moneyed corporation, with such immense powers, and large funds in a free country.

From the newspapers it appears that Mr. Baring, one of our foreign stockholders, is spoken of as a probable member of the new ministry in Great Britain. It is a curious spectacle that an American Congress should be incorporating a company, in which foreigners own eight millions of stock, the United States themselves seven millions, and private citizens twenty millions, and that at the very same time, in Great Britain, a whig ministry should be turned out, and in the formation of a new *tory ministry*, one of the foreign stockholders in this *American* company should be likely to be selected as a member.

Much as I like money and good company, I should blush to see my name on the list of American stockholders, but that is only because I do not feel that my God did me injustice in not causing me to be born a nobleman.

The bill passed; and as was anticipated, the President vetoed it. This measure Judge White did not fail to foresee. He writes to a friend, dated June 18th, 1832:

The Bank bill is in the House. I have no doubt it will pass.

The President will be as certain to put his veto upon it as that it is presented to him at the present session in its present shape. I, of course, speak my own opinion, without pretending to know more than is known to every one who has read the public documents; but I calculate upon his course with as much certainty as I can upon that of any man whom I have neither inclination nor power to control.

My calculation is, that he will veto the bill; and that the bank will endeavor to defeat his election; and that that attempt will open the eyes of the people as to their danger, and that they will put down the bank entirely. If they (the bank) should take the veto and still support the President, it will be their strongest recommendation to favorable notice at a subsequent day; but this I am sure they will not do.

My arguments against it are written and with the printer to be published in pamphlet. A job printer is publishing them. I will not degrade myself by any intercourse on the subject with the editors of the principal papers here, considering the manner in which they have conducted.

P. S. You may wash up the types,*——it will be a more angry and bitter political contest than you have either witnessed or heard of.

Again, dated July 2d, 1832. he says, of the reported plans of the friends of the bank:

The chit-chat is, that if the President vetoes the bill, enough of members opposed to the bank will for one cause or another be absent, to let the bank have two thirds in each House to pass the bill, the veto notwithstanding. I hope these insinuations are without any foundation in truth. It seems to me that such a course would, and ought to excite public feeling to a higher pitch than usual.

July 10th he writes from the Senate Chamber, to the same correspondent:

The Senate have this moment received a message from the President, returning the bill to continue for fifteen years the charter of the Bank of the United States, with his objections to its passage. It is a lengthy and plain document. To-morrow at 11 o'clock the Senate will proceed to reconsider the subject. If the Senate is full, and the members retain their former opinions, this bank falls for the present.

Upon the receipt of the veto message in the Senate, Mr. Webster

* His correspondent was editor of a newspaper in Tennessee.

opened the debate, commenting upon the President's objections, and arguing again in favor of the bill. Judge White replied, fully sustaining the course of the President upon this important occasion.

Judge White's remarks, delivered July 11th, 1832, were as follows:

Mr. President:—Pressed as we are for time, I must crave the indulgence of the Senate, while I attempt some answer to the matters urged by the senator from Massachusetts to the message accompanying the bill, now to be re-considered.

I rejoice that for once we have a document from the present Chief Magistrate, acknowledged by the opposition to be frank, plain, and susceptible of only one interpretation. Heretofore, the common complaint from that quarter has been that his important communications were so worded, as to be interpreted one way in one section of the country, and a different way in another. Here it is admitted we have a document so worded, as to be understood every where alike. The honorable senator thinks this frankness on the part of the Chief Magistrate ought to be met in a corresponding spirit, by those who differ from him in opinion. Approving of this course, I shall endeavor to be equally as explicit, in what I propose to say in answer to his argument.

The senator thinks if the charter of this bank is not renewed, ruin to the country is to be the consequence, because the bank must wind up all its concerns. This is nothing but the old argument used in 1811, when the then existing bank applied for a renewal of its charter. Distress to the community, and ruin to the country were predicted by the advocates of the bank. The predictions were not verified. The capital employed in the bank was not annihilated. It still existed, and in loans to individuals, or in some other shape, it was applied to the uses of the community. Debtors sought, and obtained accommodations elsewhere; as the notes of that bank were withdrawn from circulation, their places were supplied by specie, or the paper of local institutions, and little or no inconvenience was experienced; and such will be the case again, should the charter of this bank be allowed to expire in 1836. Debtors, worthy of credit, will obtain accommodations from either individuals or other banks, and discharge their dues to this, and as the notes of this bank disappear, their places will be supplied by specie, or the paper of other banks, and the mass of the community will, in a short time, hardly be sensible that the operation of winding up has been performed. We have been told, that in the Valley of Mississippi alone, there is due to this bank, thirty millions of dollars. Twenty millions for loans made, and ten millions for domestic bills of exchange. That the press occasioned by the collection of this debt, will be too severe to be borne. The charter has almost *four* years yet to run, and then two years are allowed for collections, making nearly six years. How often have we been told, during this session, of the general prosperity of the country, and especially that part of it in the Valley of the Mississippi. If these statements have any resemblance to the truth, it ought to be entirely within the power of these debtors, in five or six years, to adjust and pay whatever they may owe. I must repeat what I said on a former occasion: If these debts are *real* transactions, the adjustment of them will be a simple operation. The paper evidencing these debts will be *paid at maturity*, and let the bank be careful not to discount when the charter is near expiring, and the whole object will be accomplished. If the transactions are not real, but fictitious, and the paper discounted has assumed the appearance of business paper for the purpose of obtaining permanent loans, in other words, standing accommodations, the sooner the truth is known the better to all concerned. The community has a deep interest in this matter; false credit, given to individuals by false appearances, is an injury to society, and of no actual benefit to individuals, and the sooner such transactions are brought to a close, all the better—the fewer will be the number of sufferers.

If I am not very much mistaken, this opinion was, some years ago, advanced, in a report from a Secretary of the Treasury, whose opinions upon such a subject are entitled to the highest respect. But, sir, if when this bank has been in operation only fifteen or sixteen years, the debts have become so numerous, and so large, that we must, on these accounts, renew the charter, I must be allowed to ask, what will be the state of things at the end of thirty-five years? Will they not be much worse? Most certainly they will. What, then, do gentlemen mean? Do they intend that this charter shall become perpetual?—that this company, foreigners and all, shall have this monopoly for ever? If this be not their intention, I must ask the senator from Massachusetts to tell us, at what time the institution can be wound up, with less inconvenience than at the expiration of the present charter. When will the debtors of the Valley of the Mississippi be better able to pay, than when this charter expires? If the argument of the senator proves anything, it proves that this corporation ought to exist *for ever*. Is any gentleman willing to avow this? I am decidedly opposed to it. Pay-day for these debtors must arrive some time; and it appears to me that the affairs of this bank, probably, would be closed with less inconvenience to the community at the expiration of this charter, than they can be fifteen years afterwards.

The senator says, the President alleges that the application to renew the charter is premature, and thinks we ought not to be chided by him for acting on the subject, as he had directed the attention of the nation, and of Congress, to this subject, in his message of 1829, and in two succeeding messages.

Mr. President, to me it is obvious, that the notice taken of the bank in those messages, was not to recommend to Congress to act upon the subject, at either of the sessions when those messages were delivered, but as the subject was esteemed of vital interest to the community, to turn the attention of all to it, at an early period; so that opinions might be well matured upon it, when the charter was about to expire, and when it would become necessary to act upon it.

But if Congress ought now to act upon it, because the subject is brought before us by those messages, why was it not acted on at the sessions when these messages were delivered? Why not at the session in 1829? The senator has answered the question with frankness. He has told us it is material it should be known before the Presidential election, whether the President would sign the act renewing the charter or not, because if he would *not*, he ought to be *turned out*, and another put in his place, who will, and as the election is to take place the succeeding fall, application for the renewal could not be longer delayed.

I thank the senator for the candid avowal, that unless the President will sign such a charter as will suit the directors, they intend to interfere *in the election*, and endeavor to displace him. With the same candor I state, that after this declaration, this charter shall never be renewed with my consent.

Let us look at this matter as it is. Immediately before the election, the directors apply for a charter which they think the President at any other time will not sign, for the *express purpose of compelling him to sign contrary to his judgment*, or to encounter all their hostility, in the canvass and at the polls. Suppose this attempt to have succeeded, and the President, through fear of his election, had signed this charter, although he conscientiously believes it will be destructive of the liberty of the people, who have elected him to preside over them, and preserve their liberties, so far as in his power. What next? Why, whenever the charter is likely to expire hereafter, they will come as they do now, *on the eve of the election*, and compel the Chief Magistrate to sign such a charter as they may dictate on pain of being turned out and disgraced. Would it not be far better to gratify this moneyed aristocracy, to the whole extent at once, and renew their charter for ever? The temptation to a periodical interference in our elections would then be taken away.

Sir, if under these circumstances the charter is renewed, the elective franchise is *destroyed*, and the liberties and prosperity of the people are delivered over to this moneyed institution, to be disposed of at their discretion. Against this I enter my solemn protest.

The honorable senator next adverts to what the President says on the constitutionality of this act, and animadverts on what is stated in relation to there being two precedents in Congress, where this power is asserted, and two in which it is denied, and then asserts that since the year 1791, when the first bank was chartered, Congress has never denied this power.

Mr. President, it appears to me that whether the President can show any recorded vote denying this power, or not, the senator ought not to be too severe upon the executive for this mistake, if it be one. When a renewal of the charter was applied for in 1811, its constitutionality was argued, and ably argued, by those opposed to it, and the application was rejected. The bank then applied for time to wind up its business, the petition was referred to a committee, who reported against the application, alleging that it was *unconstitutional*, and this report was concurred in. Afterwards, in 1815, when a bank charter was under consideration in the House of Representatives, *a member from Massachusetts, in his place*, then acting under the same high obligations which the President acts under, arguing against the charter, stated expressly, that the renewal of the charter had been refused because it was *unconstitutional.* The President, without doubt, has read this argument, and seen this resolution, and if he reposed confidence in these statements, and was thereby misled, which I suppose he was not, I submit to the honorable senator whether, under such circumstances he would not have been entitled to milder treatment, from him, than he has received.

The attention of the Senate has been next called to that part of the message, found in page 6, in which the decisions of the Supreme Court are spoken of.

The honorable senator argues that the Constitution has constituted the Supreme Court a tribunal to decide great constitutional questions, such as this, and that when they have done so, the question is put at rest, and every other department of the government must acquiesce. This doctrine I deny. The Constitution vests "the judicial power in a Supreme Court and in such inferior courts as Congress may from time to time ordain and establish." Whenever a suit is commenced and prosecuted in the Courts of the United States of which they have jurisdiction, and such suit is decided by the Supreme Court, as that is the court of the last resort, its decision is final and conclusive *between the parties.* But as an authority, it does not bind either the Congress, or the President of the United States. If either of these co-ordinate departments is afterwards called upon to perform an official act, and conscientiously believes the performance of that act will be a violation of the Constitution, they are not bound to perform it, but on the contrary are as much at liberty to decline acting, as if no such decision had been made. In examining the extent of their constitutional power, the opinion of so enlightened a tribunal as our Supreme Court has been, and I hope ever will be, will always be entitled to great weight, and without doubt, either Congress or the President would always be disposed, in a doubtful case, to think its decisions correct;—but I hope neither will ever view them as authority binding upon them. They ought to examine the extent of their constitutional powers for themselves; and when they have had access to all the sources of information within their reach, and given to everything its due weight; if they are satisfied the Constitution has not given a power to do the act required, I insist they ought to refrain from doing it.

Suppose the House of Representatives to have passed an act on a given subject for a number of successive sessions, and from want of time the Senate had not acted on it, and the constitutionality of such an act to come before the Senate, would any member think those opinions of the House, authorities by which he was bound? Certainly not. They would have due weight, and be respectfully considered, but disregarded in the decision made by the Senate, if shown to be incorrect. In principle there can be no difference between such cases and the judicial decisions. Suppose the President to recommend ever so often the passage of an act, which he may think constitutional, would the Senate, the House of Representatives, or the Courts, feel themselves bound by his opinions? I think not. Each co-ordinate department, within its appropriate sphere of action, must judge of its own powers, when called upon to do its official duties, and if either blindly follows the others, without forming an opinion for itself, an essential check against the exercise of unconstitutional power is destroyed. A mistake by Congress in passing an act inconsistent with the Constitution, followed by a like mistake by the Supreme Court, in deciding such act to be constitutional, might be attended with the most fatal consequences. Let each department judge for itself, and we are safe. If different interpretations are put upon the Constitution, by the different departments, the people are the tribunal to settle the dispute. Each of the departments is the agent of the people, doing their business according to the powers conferred, and when there is a disagreement, as to the extent of these powers, the people themselves, through the ballot-boxes, must settle it. The senator, if I heard him correctly, has said that the President has asserted that the Supreme Court has no power to decide upon the constitutionality of an act of Congress. The gentleman has not attended to the message with his usual accuracy. No such opinion is advanced, but the contrary one; that each department within its appropriate sphere of action, has the right to judge for itself, and is not bound by the opinion of both, or either of the others; and this I incline to think is the correct constitutional view of the subject. The honorable senator thinks the President entirely mistaken when he supposes Congress cannot deprive itself of some of its legislative powers. Let us for a few minutes attend to the view of this part of the subject presented by the message and then examine its correctness.

The Congress is vested with exclusive legislative powers over the District of Columbia. It therefore has an undoubted power to establish, within the district, as many banks with as much capital to each as it chooses. By this charter it is stipulated that Congress shall *not establish* any bank within the district, nor shall it increase the capital of existing banks. This, the President thinks, is unconstitutional. By this agreement the present Congress, and its successors, are deprived of the powers of establishing any bank, no matter how pressingly the public interest may require one. Congress by this agreement will have stripped itself of all power to legislate upon a subject during the existence of the charter, when the Constitution had vested the most ample power. Is this constitutional? Ought we to be bound by such an agreement for fifteen or twenty years, and permit the best interests of society to be sacrificed for the want of a power which the Constitution has conferred, but which we have bartered away? The message supposes we are not at liberty to dispose of our legislative powers in this manner, and therefore, this act is unconstitutional. This is certainly a very important point. If we make such an agreement we ought to be bound by it, and yet, I think, cases might occur, in which we ought not to be, nor would we, be bound by any such agreement. The public safety, the public interest might long before the expiration of the charter imperiously demand the establishment of one or more banks within the district, and I do not believe we can constitutionally deprive ourselves or our successors of the power to do so.*

The senator insists, that in many cases, we derive our powers not from

* The doctrine in 6th Wheaton, 593, I think fully sustains the message upon this point. It is as follows:

"In the year 1797, the Legislature of Maryland, among other powers given the Corporation of Georgetown, enacted, that they shall have full power and authority to make *such by-laws and ordinances, for the graduation and levelling of the streets, lanes, and alleys within the jurisdiction of the same town, as they may judge necessary for the benefit thereof.*"

In pursuance of this authority, the Corporation, in May, 1799, passed an Ordinance for the graduation of certain streets. The first section appoints Commissioners, and authorizes them to make the *graduation and level* of the streets.

The second section is in these words: "And be it ordained, that the said level and graduation, when signed by the Commissioners, or a majority of them, and returned to the clerk of this Corporation, shall be for ever thereafter considered as the true graduation of the streets so graduated, and be *binding upon this Corporation*, and all other persons whatever, and be for ever thereafter regarded in making improvements upon said streets."

A man named Gosler, owned lots upon one of the streets, and made improvements thereon, according to the graduation made and returned to the clerk of the Corporation. In September 1816, the Corporation passed another Ordinance, *directing* the *level and graduation* of the street to be *altered*. And the Commissioners appointed being *about to cut down the street*, by Gosler's House, he filed a bill to enjoin them from doing so.

In the Supreme Court, one question made, was, whether the Corporation had, by the Ordinance of 1799, put it out of their power to legislate on the levelling and graduation of the streets; and the Court says, "When a Government enters into a contract, there is no doubt of its power to bind itself to any extent not prohibited by *its Constitution*. A corporation can make such contracts only, as are allowed by the acts of incorporation. The power of this body to make a contract, which should so operate as to bind its legislative capacities for ever thereafter, and *disable* it from enacting a *by-law*, which the Legislature *enables* it to enact, may well be questioned. We rather think, that the Corporation *cannot abridge its own legislative power.*"

express grants, but by construction, and asks how we acquire power to pass laws to hang those who rob the mail. He says it might be argued that fine and imprisonment would be sufficiently severe.

To this I answer, that when an express power is granted to Congress to accomplish a given object, and no means for its accomplishment are pointed out, then we must, by construction, have the necessary and appropriate means. In case of the mail-robber, we have the power to hang, because we have an undoubted power to carry the mail and deliver its contents safely, and unless those who violate it can be punished criminally, this granted power cannot be carried into effect; and as putting to death the man who will break open the mail and steal its contents is a necessary and appropriate means for preventing such acts, Congress has the power to thus punish. But this will not furnish a precedent for exercising the power to confer upon a bank created, ostensibly, for public and financial purposes, a set of powers and privileges not in the least necessary or proper for enabling it to perform any of the duties to be required of it by the government.

The honorable senator has wearied himself a good deal with a criticism upon the word "monopoly." He says it is used, at least, twenty times in this message, and never correctly. That the act only confers exclusive privileges, and the word monopoly means the sole power of trading

Mr. President, I do think upon this great subject the minds of statesmen may be more profitably employed, than in close criticisms upon the definition of particular words; but I am content to take the senator's definition and insist it is appropriately used. The charter does grant the sole power of banking for fifteen years to this company. They, therefore, have the sole power of trading in the manner pointed out in that charter for the period of its duration. To make it a monopoly, the company need not have the exclusive right of trading in *everything;* the sole right to carry on a particular branch of business, is sufficient, and as this company is to have sole, or exclusive right, it appears to me the word is properly used. The honorable senator fears much mischief may follow from the objections urged against foreigners owning stock in the bank, unless something shall be done to remove these erroneous impressions. He says we are interested in encouraging them to make loans for public purposes to the general and State governments, and that heretofore it has been our policy to encourage them to hold property among us.

Mr. President, this never has been our policy as to lands; the respective States have, and ought ever to have, the exclusive right to determine who shall hold lands within their limits. It has generally been, and probably ever will be, their policy to prevent aliens from acquiring freeholds within their limits. This policy of theirs, we have no constitutional right to interfere with. As to our public stocks, I think with the senator, foreigners may well make loans to the government, or purchase stock owned by our citizens. Much benefit may result from this, and we have no injury to fear. As to our public stocks, foreigners owning them, can have no agency whatever in creating them or managing them. At the end of each quarter, the government pays the stipulated interest, and at the time agreed on, discharges the principal. The holder of the stock, by no act of his can make his profits more or less. But the case is not so as to bank stock. Although the foreigner can neither vote nor be a director, yet he can in many instances have an indirect influence on the operations of the bank, and by regulating exchanges favorably for the bank and injuriously for our citizens, can increase the profits of the establishment, and thus benefit himself. Will any gentleman say he is of opinion that the Barings, who own a million of stock, can have no influence on the profits to be made by this institution? I think not.

Some of the views then in this message, of the manner in which this stock may, and probably will, be managed by our citizens and foreigners, are very forcible as they strike my mind.

Under the old charter the *bank* could not be taxed by the State governments according to the decision of the Supreme Court, but citizen stockholders might be taxed by the States in which they reside, for the stock which they hold. The assessors in Connecticut applied to the bank in that State for the names of the stockholders residing there. The names were not furnished, and the like application was made to the president of the principal bank, who, by the advice of counsel, returned a very polite answer, declining to give the names, as the bank could not lend their aid, to enforce penalties against their stockholders. To remedy this mischief under the renewed charter, provision is made that the names of the citizen stockholders shall be furnished. The President thinks that under this renewed charter, the construction will be that the bank cannot be *taxed*, therefore, you cannot tax foreigners: but that citizens may be taxed for the stock they own, therefore this stock will be worth one per cent. per annum more, to the foreigner, than to the citizen. That, with this inducement, foreigners will purchase out all the stock except enough to be left in the hands of a few citizens who will thus have a power every year to elect themselves directors. That this company thus formed of a few citizens, and foreign stockholders will manage the institution for their own particular benefit in time of peace, and that in time of war it will possess a power dangerous to the government itself. The honorable senator says the message frequently repeats, that the institution may be "dangerous" to our liberty, dangerous to our prosperity, &c., but that he can see nothing dangerous in it.

Mr. President, we must remember that in case of war, this bank, if in existence, must be our main dependence for raising money, and yet there is no provision by which it is bound to loan us one cent. Now suppose it to have existed during the last war, and the stock to have been owned by British subjects and a few of our own citizens, and those citizens to have belonged to that sect in politics who were seeking to change our federal rulers—who thought it wicked to thank God for our victories upon either land or water—who had sent an embassy to this city to request the then President to resign. Does any man believe the Administration could have procured the loan of one cent? Those politicians, I am willing to suppose, were acting honestly—that they believed the war impolitic, unjust, and wicked; so much so that they would not aid it with their good wishes. Does any one suppose that they would not have held it treason against good morals, to have loaned pecuniary aid? Surely they would. We must then have been without money, and without the means of obtaining any. Peace must have been made, and upon any terms, dictated by the bank or by the enemy.

I put then the questions to the Senate, to the senator from Massachusetts, to answer me, if they can see no danger in this state of things?

The honorable senator next recurs to that part of the message which speaks of the bonus. The President supposes that this is proof upon the face of the act, that more power and greater privileges are conferred than were necessary for the performance of the public business to be done by the bank. The senator thinks this small affair is within a nut-shell, and that shell not worth cracking. That any one capable of taking the view of a statesman would have seen that the other powers were necessary to make a bank of any use for public or private purposes.

Mr. President, I have endeavored to expand my mind so as to take this enlarged view of the subject, and what I find is, that the advocates of this bank, upon the plea that the bank is necessary for the fiscal concerns of the government, wish, by construction, to acquire the power to create a bank, and having thus possessed themselves of the power, wish to use it, so as to confer powers not in any degree necessary for a bank to possess, to enable it to do all which the government may wish to have done: but through which the stockholders may enrich themselves and their friends, and acquire an influence greater than the government itself, and control all our political concerns, in such manner, as to gratify their ambition and promote their interests to any extent they may wish. In short, it appears to me, that in creating the bank, the pretence is, through it to do the public business, and as soon as created, the public business is a mere insignificant incident, and private emolument without limit, is the main object.

But it is said, we have the President's project for a bank. It is to be one without money, without credit, and to do no business.

Others, before the honorable senator, have supposed the President to mean any sort of bank, that could be most easily turned into ridicule. I do not know when the honorable member has seen the project of which he speaks. I have never seen or heard of any such thing from the President.

The senator seems to suppose the President's fears upon the subject of the States not being allowed to impose a tax entirely too great.

How stands this matter? The Supreme Court has decided that the States cannot tax the bank. This charter imposes no condition upon the bank that it shall pay any tax to any State, and provides a mode by which resident stockholders may be taxed for their stock. What then will be the construction under this renewed charter? No man can doubt it. As no provision is made, no tax can be collected. I hold that in every State where a branch is situated—as the State laws must protect the persons who manage the affairs of this corporation, and must protect the property within their limits, it is strictly just that a reasonable tax should be paid for this protection.

All this might have been easily provided for. Although Congress cannot confer upon a State the power of taxation, it certainly can impose a *condition* upon this corporation, that it shall pay a tax or the charter be forfeited. As no such condition is imposed, the States must lose the tax, under the decision of the Supreme Court. I take the liberty of saying further, that the reasoning in that case, if correct and carried out, will produce a class of persons exempt from taxation that would be highly inconvenient. The principle established is, that the bank is necessary for the federal government. That the State government is an adversary power, and if allowed the power to tax, could tax so heavily as to exclude the bank and branches from the States. Carry out the same principle, and you must exempt from State taxation the houses and the property, of every other federal officer of every grade. If the bank is necessary to the United States in an individual State, and that State cannot tax it, because it may, by taxing, exclude it, I ask, are not federal judges necessary—marshals, clerks, collectors, and a host of officers? Why shall the States tax them or their property? They may be taxed out of the States by this adversary power, and, therefore, they must be freed from taxation. I am not prepared to yield my assent to a doctrine leading to such a result. The President must be right in wishing to preserve for the States all the powers of taxation, which they have not in express terms surrendered in the Constitution; these are few. He says, imports and exports. The objects of taxation are only limited by their discretion—persons, and property of every description, real and personal, corporeal and incorporeal, with the exception mentioned, are, and of right ought to be, liable to State taxation; yet, under the charter, they will be deprived of it for want of some such provision as it was attempted to introduce here, and was rejected.

The honorable member has alluded to that part of the message which speaks of the investigation of the bank being unwillingly yielded, and at the same time, he says, as it does not allude to this branch of the legislature, we cannot notice it.

Sir, is not the statement true? Was not the creation of a committee opposed? The bank had its agents here no doubt. Gentlemen of the House, confiding in the statements of the agents, thought the investigation useless, therefore they opposed it. It *was* unwillingly yielded. Who is blamed for this in the message? Not the House—not the members of the House—let any candid mind examine the whole paragraph, and he must see, it is those who applied for a renewal of the charter, and persisted in the application after this limited and unsatisfactory examination. The honorable senator thinks the message is unfortunate, in ascribing to the patriots of the Revolution the spirit of compromise, which ought not to be imitated. Mr. President, if the message did read as the senator has read it, it would have been substantially correct. The leading patriots of the Revolution, were the leading men in framing and adopting the Constitution; and, it is the spirit of compromise, which these men manifested in adopting the Constitution, which we are called upon to imitate—not that displayed during the Revolution in fighting the enemy—but the paragraph was misread by the senator, no doubt unintentionally, and furnishes no color, when correctly read, for the criticism we have heard upon it.

It has been argued, that it is strange the message should intimate that the executive ought to have been called upon for a draft of the project of a bank. I submit, Mr. President, that it is not at all strange. In every instance, heretofore, the bank projects have proceeded from the treasury, and so they ought. Although the bank established in General Washington's day may have been the best that could be devised, as things then were; yet, the increase of population—numerous changes in almost every thing—might make it a very unsuitable plan at this time. The Secretary of the Treasury, whose duty it is to watch the finances of the country, and the operations of the bank, could better judge of the details proper for a bill, than any other officer; and now, as in time past, ought to have been consulted.

Mr. President:—In submitting this message, one of the highest duties of the Chief Magistrate has been performed. Under peculiar and trying circumstances, he has given his sentiments, plainly, and frankly, as he believed his duty required.

When the excitement of the time in which we act, shall have passed away, and the historian and biographer shall be employed in giving his account of the acts of our most distinguished public men, and comes to the name of Andrew Jackson, when he shall have recounted all the great and good deeds done by this man, in the course of a long and eventful life, and the circumstances under which this message was communicated, shall have been stated, the conclusion will be, that, in doing this, he has shown a willingness to risk more to promote the happiness of his fellow-men, and to secure their liberties, than by the doing of any other act whatever.

That the arguments above set forth were conclusive, may be inferred from the circumstance that Webster, having made the first speech, after being responded to by Judge White, refused to close the debate. Judge White writes next day.

The veto message on the subject of re-chartering the bank was taken up for consideration in the Senate yesterday. Mr. Webster opened the debate. He openly avowed that this time was selected for applying for a renewal of the charter, that the opinion of the executive be known, to the end that if adverse to the bank, he might be displaced at the approaching election. This declaration was followed up and affirmed by Ewing, Holmes, and Clayton, who all spoke on the same side yesterday.

It is no longer a question of doubt, whether the bank is disposed to interfere in the approaching election. We have it openly avowed in the Senate by the advocates of the charter. Those who are opposed to the renewal of the charter, have sustained, and will continue to sustain, as well as they can, the opinion of the President upon the subject.

No one has spoken in support of the message except your humble correspondent. What he said is so inaccurately reported in the Intelligencer of the morning, that he will be compelled to write out before he leaves Washington, what he actually did say.

In 1833, when by order of President Jackson, the public deposits were removed from the United States Bank, and placed in certain State Banks, in consequence of which measure the country was plunged from a condition of unprecedented prosperity into sudden and wide-spread adversity, Mr. Webster, as a means of relief to the commercial community, moved in the Senate, in the latter half of the session of 1834, for leave to bring in a bill to extend the charter of the bank for six years, from and after March 3d, 1836. He accompanied the application by a speech of great ability, and was followed by Mr. Calhoun, Mr. Wright, and Mr. Benton, each presenting his own views on the subject. Judge White considered the opportunity a suitable one for the statement of some of his own opinions relating to the bank, its management, the conduct of the Secretary of the Treasury in removing the deposits, and that of the President in removing Mr. Duane.

Mr. White's speech, delivered March 24, 1834, was as follows:

Mr. President: When a subject of so much importance is under consideration; when topics are discussed which produce a diversity of opinion, not only as to the powers conferred upon the federal government, but also, as to the manner in which the powers certainly conferred, are distributed among the several departments; and when our decision may vitally affect, as well the fiscal concerns of the government, as the pecuniary interests of all classes of the community, I am unwilling to record my vote until I shall have given some of the reasons, at least, which lead to them.

I am pleased that the honorable senator from Massachusetts has asked leave to introduce this bill; not because I approve of it, but because it offers something practical, which we can discuss, consider, and decide.

If the bill proposed contained any principle, which, under any modification, I believed we had a power to enact into a law, I would most willingly extend the usual courtesy of granting leave to introduce it. although I might disapprove all its details; but, in my judgment, its object is to do that which, by the Constitution, we have no power to do.

The sole object is, to extend the charter of the present Bank of the United States, under certain modifications, for the term of six years after the 3d of March, 1836, when the existing charter will expire.

It is said the country is distressed in consequence of the derangement of our currency, and the object of this bill is to relieve that distress, by extending the charter. If leave is granted to introduce the bill, the hope will be indulged, that in due season the bill will be passed into a law, and the relief desired be thus afforded. We ought not, in my opinion, even by our silence, to encourage any expectation, or hope, which we do not intend to make good.

Entertaining the opinions which I do, in relation to this bank, I cannot silently acquiesce in the introduction of this bill, without creating expectations which, so far as is in my power, I should certainly disappoint; therefore, I hope, when I deny the leave asked, my conduct may not be attributed to a willingness to act otherwise than courteously, toward the honorable senator who has submitted the motion.

I hold that, by the Constitution of the United States, Congress has *no power* to *create* a bank, and having no power to create it, we have no power to *continue* it beyond the period limited for its termination.

I wish the Senate not to be alarmed, from a belief that I am about to weary their patience, or exhaust my own strength, by an elaborate argument to prove the truth of this position.

I am well aware that this question has been repeatedly and ably discussed, in Congress, and before our highest judicial tribunals, and that many of the most enlightened and pure men we have ever had in public employ, have affirmed the existence of this power; yet, I consider the question unsettled. The power has always been questioned and disputed;

it never has been yielded. The decisions are not binding as authorities, when Congress is called upon to exercise the power. If we are certain we do not possess it, or it is doubtful whether we do, it ought not to be exercised.

Those who affirm the existence of this power, do not pretend that in the Constitution it is expressly granted, but rely upon that clause of the 8th section, 1st article, which provides that "Congress shall have power to pass all laws *necessary* and *proper* to carry into effect the powers expressly granted." They next say that, by the 5th paragraph of the same section, Congress has an express grant of power "to coin money, and to fix the value thereof, and the value of foreign coin, and to regulate the standard of weights and measures." Hence, they argue that it was the intention to vest in Congress the whole power over the monetary system of the United States, and that this cannot be done without giving a power to incorporate a bank. I admit it was intended to vest the whole power in Congress, over our *money*, our *currency*, but deny that there is any necessity for a bank to give effect to this power.

By the 10th section, 1st article, it is said, "no State shall coin money, emit bills of credit, make anything but gold and silver a tender in payment of debts; pass any bill of attainder, *ex post facto* law, or law impairing the obligation of contracts." Before the formation of this Constitution, much injury was supposed to have resulted from the power which the individual States possessed and exercised, of emitting bills of credit; therefore, this power is taken from the States, by *express* words. The federal government has no power but that which is *expressly* given, as is said in the tenth amendment to the Constitution. There is no power given, in any part of that instrument, to *emit* bills of credit. Since the adoption of this Constitution, the power to emit bills of credit is *extinct* in the United States. The State governments cannot exercise it, because it is *expressly* taken away; the federal government cannot exercise it, because it is *not given* to it; therefore this evil of a *paper currency* is effectually cured. Before the adoption of this Constitution the States had a power to make articles of produce, or merchandise, a tender in payment of debts. This power, in some of the States, had been exercised. It is also extinguished under the present Constitution.

Formerly, there was a want of *uniformity* in the value of the same piece of money, in the different States: in some, a dollar was four shillings and eightpence; in another, six shillings; in others, seven and sixpence; and in some others, eight shillings. This was an evil cured by this Constitution. Congress has the power to "coin money and *fix its value*, and the *value* of foreign coin;" and the power to coin money, *in future*, is denied to the States. Thus, uniformity in value is produced: a dollar in one State, is a dollar, and no more, in every other. Weights and measures were, and might be varied in different States. The power to regulate the *standard* of weights and measures is given to Congress: when exercised, uniformity in each State is produced; a bushel of wheat must be of the same quantity, and an hundred pounds of hemp or tobacco, must be of the same weight, in each State.

By these different provisions, the whole people of the United States were intended to be secured, in a *uniform currency*, a uniform standard of weights and measures, and the same provisions contain a prohibition against making anything but gold and silver a tender in payment of debts, and a denial of any power to pass a law to *impair* the obligation of contracts.

What species of currency then, I ask, was intended? *Metallic* and nothing else. Money *coined*, and the *value fixed*, under the authority of Congress, or foreign *coin*, the value of which is fixed by the same power. Will any gentleman state, that in his opinion, either Congress, or a State legislature, has a power, under our Constitution, to make one individual receive from another anything but a *metallic currency*, in discharge of a debt due?

The opinion that Congress has no power to create a bank, is, as I think, very much strengthened, when we reflect where the convention sat, when it sat, and what was going on in relation to banks.

The Bank of North America commenced business in January, 1782, in Philadelphia. It had a double authority, as was supposed, for so doing --from Congress, and from the legislature of Pennsylvania. In 1785, it had become so odious, that several counties petitioned the legislature to repeal the charter. These petitions were referred to a committee, who made a report, upon which, an act did pass, repealing the charter, without giving the corporators any form of trial whatever. This gave rise to a most violent controversy, in the course of which there were many publications. The bank still continued its business, under the power it had derived from Congress. In 1786, an attempt was made in the legislature, to repeal the repealing act, but this attempt was successfully resisted by the democrats of that day, headed by Finley and Smilie, and the confusion continued till the next year, when a limited charter for *fourteen* years was granted. Thus we find at the very time the convention sat, and in the very place it sat, the practical operations of the bank of that day, were considered decidedly hostile to the liberty and independence of the country. Is it then probable that it was intended to vest a power in Congress to create any institution capable of so much mischief?

I have looked into the petitions presented to the legislature, and the report of the committee, to ascertain the objections upon which the repealing act was founded, and have been so forcibly struck with the similarity of the reasons then urged, with those since relied upon, that I must ask the indulgence of the Senate, while I read the report, a copy of which is before me, in these words: "That it is the opinion of this committee, that the said bank, as at present established, is in every view incompatible with the public safety; that in the present state of our trade, the said bank has a direct tendency to banish a great part of the specie from the country, so as to produce a scarcity of money, and to collect into the hands of the stockholders of the said bank, almost the whole of the money which remains amongst us. That the accumulation of enormous wealth, in the hands of a society who claim perpetual duration, will necessarily produce a degree of influence and power, which cannot be intrusted in the hands of any set of men whatsoever, without endangering the public safety. That the said bank, in its corporate capacity, is empowered to hold estates, to the amount of ten millions of dollars, and by the tenor of the present charter, is to exist for ever, without being obliged to yield any emolument to the government, or to be at all dependent upon it. That the great profits of the bank, which will daily increase, as money grows scarcer, and which already far exceed the profits of European banks, have tempted foreigners to vest their money in this bank, and thus to draw from us large sums of interest.

"That foreigners will, doubtless, be more and more induced to become stockholders, until the time may arrive, when this enormous engine of power may become subject to *foreign influence;* this country may be agitated with the politics of European courts, and the good people of America reduced, once more, to a state of subordination and dependence upon some one or other of the European powers. That at last, even if it were confined to the hands of Americans, it would be totally destructive of that *equality*, which ought to prevail in a republic. We have nothing in our free and equal government, capable of balancing the influence the bank must create; and we see nothing, which, in the course of a few years, can prevent the directors of the bank from governing Pennsylvania. Already we have felt its influence, directly interfering in the measures of the legislature. Already the House of Assembly, the representatives of the people, have been threatened, that the credit of our paper currency will be blasted by the bank; and if this growing evil continues, we fear the time is not very distant when the bank will be able to dictate to the legislature, what laws to pass, and what to forbear."

Much has been said of the President's opinions upon the subject of banks, and his ideas respecting the dangers to be apprehended from the operations of this bank. He appears to be maintaining the same doctrines maintained by the republican people of Pennsylvania in 1785, 1786, and 1787; and, as I verily believe, the same doctrines intended to be incorporated into the Constitution, and made perpetual by it.

It seems to be thought by the honorable senator from South Carolina [Mr. Calhoun], that although we cannot establish a bank to make *money*, we may, to have a currency, which will control the currency of State banks. I find no warrant in the Constitution for any such distinction. [Here Mr. Calhoun interrupted Mr. White, and said he had taken a distinction between doing and undoing.] Mr. W. continued, and said, I hope the honorable senator will believe me when I say nothing is farther from my wish than to misrepresent his arguments. I can have no motive to do so. The distinction between doing and undoing can have no influence on my argument. This bill attempts to *do something*, not to *undo*. Its object is to continue this charter *six years longer*. This is an exertion of the same *kind* of power which was exerted in passing the charter for twenty years, in 1816. This power is not given by the Constitution. The honorable senator thinks the wise course is, to look at the circumstances in which we are placed, and adapt our measures to our situation. This is all true when we possess the power to act; but here the first consideration is, Have we the power? if we have not, it is vain to consider how that ought to be *used* which we do not possess. The present charter has yet two years to run: if the object of this bill were now to *repeal* it, then the doctrine of the honorable senator would be applicable. With him I would look to the circumstances in which we are placed, and although I might believe the act of 1816, incorporating the bank, to be unconstitutional, yet as the stockholders and society had acquired interests under the act, I would not offend the *moral sense* of the community by voting for the *repeal;* besides, I would reflect that these rights were subjects of judicial cognizance, and if a mistake were made here, as to our powers, the courts would protect the rights of individuals; but the object of this bill is not to repeal, it is to *extend*. It is not to take anything from the bank, but to continue its powers six years longer, as the bill now is; twelve years, as the senator from South Carolina thinks it ought to be. I deny the power to do this. The case of Louisiana, referred to by the honorable senator from Virginia [Mr. Leigh], and which the senator from South Carolina thinks so happy an illustration of his doctrine, with great deference, I must say, does not appear to me to have any application.

Mr. Jefferson, it is said, entertained an opinion that Louisiana could not, consistently with the Constitution, be purchased and added to the Union. It was purchased, has been formed into a State, and admitted on an equal footing with the other States; and gentlemen ask, will you now exclude her because it was unconstitutional to admit her? I answer, no. I would look to the existing state of things, and take no step—let them remain as I found them. But suppose it had been possible to have admitted her upon trial for six years, to see how she would behave in the Union, and when those six years had elapsed, there was an application to admit her permanently, then we would have an analogous case, and, I say. the constitutional question would be as much open as it was when she was admitted for the six years. [Here Mr. Leigh interrupted Mr. White, and said, he desired to know what would be done when Arkansas applied for admission, and he would, with as much pleasure receive the information from the senator of Tennessee as from any other gentleman.] Mr. W. continued: In answer to the interrogatory put by the honorable senator from Virginia, I can only say, that when Arkansas does apply to be admitted as a member State, if any gentleman shall think it unconstitutional to admit her, we will then examine and decide the question.

Mr. President: I can find no warrant in the Constitution, for a distinction between *money* and *currency*. That *circulating medium* which is to be the standard by which the seller and buyer of property are to ascertain its value, is *metallic*, to be *coined*, and its value *fixed* by Congress; or *foreign coin*, the value of which is fixed by the same power. Nothing else is *money*, nothing else is *currency*, by the Constitution.

By the first clause of the 8th section of the 1st article of the Constitution, a power is vested in Congress, "to lay and collect taxes, imposts, duties, and excises, to pay the debts, and provide for the common defence and general welfare of the United States." It is argued by those who maintain the power to incorporate a bank, that it is necessary and proper to have one, as an agent to collect the taxes, to keep them safely, and to pay the debts due by the government, in the different sections of the country. I think a Bank of the United States would be *convenient* for these purposes, but deny that one is *necessary*.

Mr. President, if there were no bank, either State or federal, in the Union, our taxes could be collected, the money safely kept and paid out, according to the provisions of law, by the appointment of natural persons. Now we may employ them in preference to banks, if we choose. There cannot, therefore, be a *necessity* to create a bank for such purpose; and if we infer the power to make the bank, because it would be a matter of *convenience*, where can any limit be fixed to implied powers? I cannot fix any. But suppose a bank to be necessary and proper as a fiscal agent, there are State banks—why not employ them? It is said that, as these banks are not created by Congress, we cannot have any control over them. This I deny; we will have all the control over them which we ought to have. The custom of the United States, as *depositors*, will always be sufficient to ensure fidelity in collection, safe-keeping, and disbursements of your money; and these are the only uses we have for such agents. Whenever it is believed one is about to act in bad faith, dismiss it. This we will always have a power to do; and a fear that this power will be exercised, will procure fidelity. Your power will always be sufficient for every salutary purpose: seldom, if ever, sufficient to be productive of mischief. Suppose a bank employed in each State, over which we have no control, except what our deposits would give: there would then be twenty-four banks, governed by directors, created under the authority of the respective States; accountable to them; and each independent of every other. How could the United States procure a concert of action among them, for any unworthy purpose? Corrupting one would be no advantage in attaining the object. All must be corrupted, the moment the attempt was made—and one honest man found in any one board, the whole plan would be exposed, and its authors held up to public contempt and scorn. A bank, created by the United States, accountable to them, having the use of *all your money*, and managed by a *majority* of a board, composed of *seven* men, is in a very different situation. The pecuniary influence you would have, would be much greater --the number of men necessary to corrupt, would be so small, that the danger of improper influence is increased to an alarming extent.

But it is said the very admission that Congress may employ State banks, as fiscal agents, is an admission of the power to create a bank, for the same purpose. This, I think, is not so. You may wish an artificial person to perform a particular service for you—you may find artificial persons already made, that can perform these services—there cannot therefore be any *necessity* that you should create one, simply that you may employ him in preference.

What is the real difficulty and struggle here? It is not that we create a bank to have a fiscal agent. No. The real struggle is to keep in existence a commercial bank, for commercial purposes. It is dismissed by the excutive from its fiscal agency, and yet it continues, endowed with powers sufficient to embarrass all commercial transactions.

The truth is, that upon a supposed necessity for a bank as a fiscal agent, one was created in 1816, endowed with powers for the most extensive commercial uses, and instead of the duties of a fiscal agent being its main, or principal business, its leading, its general, its profitable, and almost constant employ is unconnected with this agency, and its business is devoted, almost exclusively, to other purposes. The business of a fiscal agent dwindles into a mere by-business, entirely *incidental*; so much so, that when these duties are taken from it, we find it possessed of powers and capacities, almost without limit, for good or for evil, so far as the moneyed affairs of the country are concerned. This I conceive is a practice under the Constitution, unsupported by a fair construction of it. I think with the honorable senator from South Carolina, that these powers are *trust* powers, and ought to be so exerted, as to attain the object in vesting the trust. Now if it be true, that we have a constitutional power to create a bank, for the purpose of *collecting* the public money, *keeping it safe*, and *paying it out*, at the points desired, it gives no power to create a bank, for the purposes of *issuing bank notes*, and granting accommodations to those concerned in trade and commerce, to any extent the wants or wishes of society may require.

Again. If it is *necessary* and *proper* to incorporate a bank, as a *fiscal agent*, which I do not admit, there can be no power to establish such a bank as this. We can neither wish, nor expect a bank of issues, and of calculation; all we can possibly need will be a bank of discount and deposit, and that of small capital. Such a bank would be perfectly able to make our collections, preserve, and pay out the public moneys; and in addition to the discharge of these duties, such a bank could, and would most effectually *check excessive issues* of paper by the *State banks*; it could also grant discounts to a reasonable extent to commercial men, or others; and likewise by drafts, on the different branches, in different sections of country, could furnish the means of remittance, to any extent that would be reasonably required.

Indeed, one on a scale still more limited, would answer every fiscal purpose. A bank of *deposit* and *transfer* is all that the government could have occasion for. How then it is possible we can fairly deduce a power to establish a bank, and vest in the corporation the immense powers which this charter confers, I am unable to discover; therefore, I will not consent to use a power which I do not think we possess, to prolong the existence of such an institution, for a day, a year, or for any other term whatever. Holding these opinions, I am not among the number of those who can ever be embarrassed by the question, whether the United States Bank ought to be placed in Chesnut street or in Wall street.

Mr. President, if we had the power to create a bank, I insist it is bad policy to exercise it as is now proposed.

The objections to extending this charter are, in my opinion, stronger than they were to incorporating the bank originally. The theory of our government is perfect equality. Make all safe in every thing to which they have a just right, and give no one an advantage, *by law*, over any other. This we ought, as far as we can, to carry out in practice. When the act of incorporation was passed, there was an apparent equality, at least, because every citizen had an equal opportunity of subscribing for stock, but if we extend the charter the value of the stock is immediately increased, and the present stockholders have, by law, a privilege extended to them, in *exclusion* of every other person.

But, sir, if I am mistaken in everything I have said, I still contend the charter ought not to be prolonged. The immediate benefit to be derived from the passage of this bill is a relief to a distressed community. To form a proper estimate of the remedy, we ought to have some opinion of the extent of the disease, and of the causes which have produced it.

I am not among the number of those, who deny that there is any pecuniary distress. That there is, in many parts of the country, a want of money, and considerable sacrifices because it cannot be obtained, I verily believe. These sufferings have not yet reached the particular country which I in part represent: but as all others, as well as my immediate constituents, are to be affected by my votes, I consider it as much my duty to relieve the distresses of others, if in my power, as it would be to relieve the distresses of those I immediately represent. I will add, that there does not live in the United States, the human being, whose condition I would not gladly make better. What has led to these pecuniary wants, is a question, on which there has been some variety of opinion. I think it very obvious, that the operations of the Bank of the United States have been the principal cause. She has not only refrained from granting the usual accommodations to men in business, but she has been operating the wrong way; she has been curtailing her discounts; this has compelled State banks to do so likewise. Money then is made much scarcer than formerly. The demand for it is increased. Under the tariff laws, cash is now to be paid in some instances where credit had formerly been given. In other cases where long credits had been given, short credits are now allowed. The long credits and the short credits have been falling due at the same time. The bank has caused bills to be purchased payable in the large cities, to a greater amount than formerly. These different causes have created an increased demand for money, and the common means of obtaining it are withdrawn. To these ought to be added the doubt and uncertainty, as to the result of our legislation, which prevents men of business from adapting their proceedings to any settled course.

The result of the whole is, the business part of the community need more money than formerly, and can obtain less. I believe there is suffering and distress, and if this bank is to wind up, this suffering must, at some period, be increased. If we admit, which I think we ought not, that the withdrawal of the deposits made some curtailment of her business necessary, on the part of the bank, I do not believe we ought to doubt but they have been carried farther than was necessary. One thing, I think, has been clearly shown, by the honorable senator from Missouri: that is, that no additional curtailments to make the bank safe, can be necessary.

This bank then is the main cause of this suffering and this distress, and to relieve them we are asked to extend its powers for six years longer. Heretofore it has pursued its *own* interest; will it not do so again? If its interest prompts to liberal accommodations, they will be granted, and circulating medium will be plenty. If its objects can be better accomplished by withdrawing accommodations, and lessening the circulating medium, that course will be pursued, and our pecuniary sufferings and distresses will again return. I have no confidence in such a remedy; it will probably be worse than the present disease.

How would the bank employ its vast means, during the prolonged time? I think just in such manner as would most promote its own interest, without any special regard to the interest of the community.

All persons, natural or artificial, dread dissolution. The natural person will cling to existence as long as possible; he will lay hold of anything within his reach, by which he can preserve himself for an hour, a day, or a week; just so with this corporation; it will use its whole power to procure a renewal of the charter, after the lapse of the six years. It will use its means to increase the number of its friends, and to put its opponents in a situation not to thwart its views. It will extend its business whenever, and wherever, such a course will aid its prospects; it will contract its issues, and curtail its discounts, whenever and wherever opposition to its plans can be put down, by oppression. I have no idea that the directors now, or at any other time, have engaged in any scheme of oppression, because they delight in inflicting an injury upon any one. Corporations, it is said, have no souls, but they are managed by those who have, and by those who will be attentive to their own interests, and will use their powers to promote them. Prolong this charter, and your control is gone; the bank will act as it may think best; it will, and must, mingle in your politics; its permanency will depend on displacing enemies from power, and supplying their places by the promotion of friends. No means will be left untried, to accomplish this object. That it should interfere in politics, is inherent in the charter itself. It is a partnership between the government and individuals. It is a *mixture* of political power with money, and in every controversy in which the corporation can have an interest the bank will interfere in elections, on the one side or the other. The principles contained in the charter lead necessarily to this result, and we need expect nothing else. The very object of extending for six years is, to relieve the community presently, and in the meantime, to see whether this bank shall be continued afterwards, or some other substituted. How then can we doubt its course, during this period? It will extend its business first, and contract it afterwards, if success is likely to be attained by such a course.

If its business is ever to cease, why not at the end of the present charter? It is admitted the resources of the country never were greater than now. There is no reason to believe debtors will ever be more able to pay. We have had distress and suffering for five or six months; if the charter is prolonged, this must be gone over again six years hence, and there is no reason to think we shall be better able to meet the demands of the bank then, than now. The remedy for present distress, is only a palliative; the cause of the disease will remain in the system; it will be acquiring strength for six years, and then break out with increased violence, and the injury and ruin will be on a more extensive scale.

We can only form an opinion of what the bank will do in future, by reflecting on what it has done in time past.

In December, 1829, the Chief Magistrate made his first communication to Congress, showing that he was disinclined to a renewal of the charter; this was followed up in his messages of 1830 and 1831. These communications he was bound in duty to make, if he believed the public good would be promoted by an expression of his opinions, to the national legislature. The bank, ever attentive to its own interest, in 1831 began a rapid extension of its business, and early in 1832, had increased its accommodations to the amount of twenty-eight millions of dollars, as its opponents say, and as is admitted by itself, to upwards of seventeen millions. The Presidential elections took place in the fall, 1832. To me it appears plain that this extension was intended to make as many friends, as acts of kindness could make. The accommodations are now reduced from seventy millions to about fifty-four millions. Why this decrease? The expansion, or contraction, must have been too great. The pretence is, that the state of the country required the increase, when there was an extension, and that accommoda tions were curtailed, when the state of business justified the reduction. We all know that there is an error in this statement. There was no such change in the business of the country, as to justify this change in the policy of the bank. Friends were to be made by extending wide the wings of the net, with a full knowledge that when the birds were coaxed in, and those wings contracted, the fluttering would commence, and an escape from the toils would be sought by almost any means.

The increase and decrease, were made with a view to the interest of the stockholders, without regard to the effect upon the customer, or upon society.

The bank went into operation the first day of January, 1817; one of the leading objects in granting its charter was, through its operations, to reduce the extravagant dealings with State banks; to *restore* and *preserve* a *sound* currency to the country. The directors well knew this, yet they acted with a single eye to what they conceived the interest of the bank, and its friends; in place of *checking* it *stimulated* overtrading. Instead of restoring and preserving a sound currency, it adopted measures which in 1818 and 1819, placed it in the power of the State banks, in Philadelphia, to take from it every single dollar and leave it still in debt to them upwards of one hundred and twenty-four thousand dollars. Mr. Cheves took charge of the bank, and as President, pursued a policy, which in seventy days placed the bank in a state of security, but the curtailments were so rapid, and the withdrawal of the circulating medium so great, as to ruin society, compel other banks to suspend specie payment, and again afflict the community with a depreciated currency.

Liberal accommodations, and extensive issues, had given an appearance of wealth, to those worth little, or nothing. Property commanded enormous prices, as this bank had made money plenty; but the counter current commenced, and in 1819, a scene of wide-spread ruin was presented. The bank made money scarce; the price of property fell to almost nothing; those who had been apparently wealthy, were found to be bankrupts, and hardly any man had wherewithal to pay his debts.

An individual had, when money was plenty, purchased a house and lot, for *ten thousand* dollars; he paid six thousand, was sued for the balance; the house and lot sold at *fifteen hundred* dollars; and thus, he sunk in the single bargain, eight thousand five hundred dollars.

In the principal cities and towns, thousands of individuals were thrown out of employ, the whole business of the country was deranged, scenes of misery and distress were produced, to which the present distress and pressure bear but little resemblance. This state of things was produced, because the directors managed the bank with a view to their *own interest*, and that of their *friends*, disregarding the interest of that *community* from which they had acquired their power. May they not do so again? Have we not reason to fear they will, if the charter is prolonged?

[Here Mr. White gave way for a motion to adjourn.]

Mr. White resumed as follows, next day:—

Mr. President: Before I resume the discussion in which I was yesterday engaged, when the Senate adjourned, I must beg permission to call the attention of this body, for the first time since I have been honored with a seat here, to a newspaper paragraph, in which my name has been introduced. I know that my standing here is too humble, and my opinions of too little value, to make it necessary for me, on common occasions, to contradict any statement coupled with my name; but considering the excitement which now prevails in some sections of the country, and the desire repeatedly expressed, for the adoption of some measure, by Congress, to relieve the community from the distresses which it is said they experienced, I think it improper to permit any statement to remain uncontradicted, which is calculated to excite expectations, which, so far as in my power, will not be fully realized.

The publication to which I allude, purports to be a correspondence with the New York Journal of Commerce, and is in the following words:

"Washington, March 19, 1834.

"At length, we may discern one faint glimmer of light in our political prospect. Mr. Calhoun has devised a plan for a new national bank on principles which wholly avoid the constitutional scruples of the Southern representatives, and which will be generally acceptable. The plan has been submitted to a number of senators of different parties, and has been decidedly approved, particularly by those senators who are opposed on constitutional grounds to the re-charter of the present bank, and who are at the same time averse to General Jackson's experiment upon the currency. It is also unequivocally approved, it is said, by Messrs. Grundy and White, who are friendly to the President."

Mr. President, what I have now to say, in relation to the matter mentioned in this letter, is, that I have no knowledge of *any plan for a bank*, to be submitted by the honorable senator from South Carolina; that I know nothing of that gentleman's opinion on the subject of a United States Bank, except what I have collected from the public speeches delivered here. The last of those speeches was not delivered until after the date of this letter. Out of this place in this chamber, I have not heard from him one word during this session, on the subject of any bank whatever. Therefore, the whole statement in this letter, so far as my name is connected with it, is erroneous, and has not the shadow of truth for its foundation. I have shown this letter to my colleague, whose name is also mentioned; he has read it, and I am not only authorized, but requested by him to say, that the same statement which I make as to myself, is equally true as it relates to him.

When the Senate adjourned on yesterday, I was considering the effects on society, in the year 1819, of the proceedings of the Bank of the United States, from the time it went into operation.

The distresses then experienced, and those now felt, are the fruits of the charter granted in 1816. The patriots of that day, found the country flooded with a depreciated paper medium, put in circulation by State banks, and unfortunately, as I think, sought to remedy the evil by the establishment of a bank. As the United States were to have the entire *moneyed* power, by the Constitution, and as the States had established banks, it was believed the United States might establish one also, to regulate the currency. Instead of this, if the collection of the revenue, and all debts due to the government, had been enforced in money, the moral sense of the community, the fertility of our soil, and the industry of the people, would soon have given us a sound circulating medium. State banks, which had the means, would soon have been compelled to resume, and continue, specie payments, and those which were unable to do so, must have stopped business. The duties upon foreign importations alone, were from forty to fifty millions of dollars. With the power of government exerted in the proper direction, a sound currency must have been procured, within a very short period. But bank notes, though not money, were considered *currency*, and with a view to check and control a depreciated State currency, it was supposed the United States had a power to establish a bank, which should give a sound currency itself, and compel State banks to do likewise. This word "*currency*" I cannot find in the Constitution. Constitutionally speaking, nothing but *money* is currency, and nothing can be money which is not metallic. Bank notes issued under the authority of the federal or State governments, are not currency; they are not money, nor can they be made so. They are nothing but *credits* used by common consent, to pass as substitutes for money. Promissory notes, negotiable and negotiated, or bills of exchange, are as much entitled to the appellation, of currency, as bank notes are. If bank notes are currency, what will be said of the notes of the bank of the late Stephen Girard? What of the notes of the bank of my countrymen, Yeatman, Woods, and Co.? These bank notes are as *current* as the notes of the Bank of the United States. A man may set out at New Orleans, and travel on to Philadelphia, and he will find these notes *current* the whole route; yet no charter for a bank was ever granted, by any government, to either of those gentlemen. These notes are nothing but credits; they pass in place of money, by common consent, and so do the other bank notes. The only thing that gives them currency is the *confidence*, that whenever the holder wishes money for them, and will apply for it, at the place specified for payment, the makers will be found able and willing to *pay* the *specie*, and lift them. Nothing can prevent them from depreciation but this confidence.

Mr. President, I know of whom I speak, and I know among them are men, who have the highest claims to our confidence, which purity of motive and strength of intellect can give; yet I must be permitted to say, I think the distinction then taken, and acted upon, by granting this charter, between *money* and *currency*, has no warrant in the Constitution. I think the bank then created in consequence of that distinction, an excrescence, which has grown out of an erroneous construction. This bank is a political cancer, the roots and fibres of which have ramified themselves through all society, and we might as well hope to tear from the human body, the cancer there formed, as to expect to remove from the body politic, this bank, without causing pain and suffering.

It is due, I think, to this subject, that we should permit our minds to recur to the situation in which we were placed, as to our currency, when this act of incorporation was passed, and the causes which led to the state of things which then existed. War had been declared in 1812, without any pecuniary preparation, to meet the extraordinary calls which the prosecuting of the war could not fail to produce. So far from this, the conduct of some of the European powers had driven our government into a series of restrictive measures, which so much embarrassed our commercial operations, as to produce distresses and complaints, which were laid before Congress in the strongest terms. Out of Congress, these measures were reprobated in terms of great bitterness. The measures of the then Administration, were represented as ruinous to the commerce of the country; it was said we were truckling to a foreign power; that there was no mode of maintaining the honor of the country, but by a declaration of war, and that the Administration was so pusillanimous, it could not be kicked into a war.

Congress believed there was just cause, and therefore did declare war against Great Britian. Money was necessary; the treasury had it not; it must be procured by loans; the opponents of the Administration employed themselves assiduously, no doubt many of them from very proper motives, to produce an indisposition in all who had money, to grant those loans. The politicians, the presses, even the pulpits, endeavored to impress the public with the opinion that it was immoral, and wicked, to furnish funds to prosecute a war so unjust, and which had been declared, as they insisted, from motives most unworthy. This course of the opposition, stimulated the advocates of the Administration to exert every nerve, to procure the necessary funds. Individuals and banks made loans to the full extent of all their means. The banks were soon led to believe that it was a test of patriotism to be liberal in their advances. They were urged, nay almost begged, by the Administration, to take up loans. The consequence was, that the banks extended their loans to *government*, and to individuals, beyond the limits which their specie would justify. Let it never be forgotten, that without the paper of these banks, a barrel of flour, a load of ammunition, or even a flint, could not be purchased for your army or navy. Peace was restored in 1815; it found some of the banks already not paying specie; many others soon afterwards suspended such payments also. This, so far from being discountenanced by the government, was most certainly winked at, if not expressly approved.

A depreciation in the value of the notes of these banks was the necessary consequence of suspending specie payments, and the same political party, which declared the war, still constituted the majority, and endeavored to devise some plan to restore a sound currency to the country. The plan devised was the instrumentality of this bank. The object was *not gain* to the stockholders, but the high purpose of *regulating the currency*, through the power of this agent. The government had five directors, and the stockholders twenty, and at the head of the directory, was placed a man of high respectability—one of so much character, that if I mistake not, at one period during the war, he acted as the head of three of the executive departments at the same time.

The bank commenced its operations, and instead of aiming, by a prudent, steady, and wise policy, to attain the object for which it was created, it united with the State banks, in extending accommodations to individuals, and in increasing the issues of bank paper to a most unreasonable extent. Specie payments were resumed, it is true. Branches of this bank were established in several of the States: those established in the West, with which I had the only acquaintance, were not furnished with one dollar of actual capital. The cashier was sent to establish a branch, furnished with drafts for the public moneys deposited in the State banks, and with a power to collect the floating capital in the country, by drawing upon the banks in the Eastern cities. In place, then, of aiding State banks to continue specie payments, when resumed, this very bank withdrew the means of enabling them to do so. In place of inducing them to curtail, by prudent means, their issues, already too great, they were encouraged to increase their circulation still more. The immense amount of money in circulation gave an artificial value to everything. Overtrading was carried to such an extent, that all idea of the true standing and credit of men, in society, was lost sight of. Cities were improved, and villages sprung up, as if by enchantment; each little town was furnished with more merchants than were sufficient to have done the business of the whole country in which it was situated. This artificial state of things could not last. As soon as there was a demand for specie, the counter-current commenced. The United States Bank began a rapid curtailment, to save itself from open bankruptcy; it broke up State banks and individual customers. The State banks broke up their customers; many of them were forced to suspend again specie payments, and a depreciated currency was imposed upon the community. Some of the State banks never afterwards resumed specie payments; and a sound currency was not again restored to the country until from 1824 to 1826. Where, in 1817 and 1818 there appeared nothing but wealth, prosperity, and comfort, in 1819, 1820, and for some time after, there was one scene of pressure, distress, bankruptcy, and ruin. And all this grew out of the incorporation of this bank, and transferring to it the power of *regulating the currency.* The country was flooded with a paper currency when it suited the bank to make property high; and the whole circulating medium was withdrawn, when it was the interest of the bank to reduce property in value. What assurance can we have that the operations of this bank will not, again, be directed to individual gain, should the charter be prolonged?

This bank was vested with its extensive powers for high governmental purposes. It is admitted that the State banks, generally, are completely in its power, and under its control. All these immense powers have been, in some instances, used for the purposes of individual gain, at the expense of the community. Society at large is unsafe while it is in the power of a board of directors of this bank to fix what value they please upon property, by making the common standard of value, the circulating medium, *plenty* or *scarce.*

Mr. President, the conduct of this bank well justified the Secretary of the Treasury in using the power given him by the 16th section of the act of incorporation, if he thought it *sound policy* to withdraw the public deposit.

I will not weary the Senate by travelling over the whole of the reasons he has assigned for the removal, but will only advert briefly to some which, to my mind, would be satisfactory.

The bank, as the fiscal agent, violated the trust reposed in it, by not paying the three per cent. stock as directed.

A summary of the leading facts shows this to have been the case: The administration determined to pay a portion of this stock, at a given time; the bank was furnished with the necessary funds, and instructed to make the payment. Instead of complying with these instructions, it negotiated with the owners of the stock, to induce them not to apply for payment at the time specified, but to delay the application for some eight or twelve months, and promised that it, the bank, would pay the accruing interest. I contend this was a violation of duty, for which the agent should have been dismissed. An individual owes another a sum of money, bearing interest; he determines to pay the debt, and lift the bond: he furnishes his agent with the necessary funds, and instructs him to make the payment at a given period. The agent disobeys his instructions, and promises the creditor that if he will hold the bond twelve months longer, he will pay the interest. What ought the principal to do in such case? I say, dismiss the agent. And it should have been done in this case, with the less hesitation, because here the agent sought its own interest, at the time the instructions were violated. The uses, to which the bank applied the money, yielded a profit of six per cent. And the stock bore an interest of only three; so that the bank would pocket the difference.

Again. As I have already stated, this bank was established for the high purposes of *restoring a sound currency* to the community, and *keeping it sound.* The Secretary tells us in his report, that it commenced rapid curtailments in the month of August, and continued them up to the first of October; that these curtailments compelled the State banks to curtail likewise; that the deposits of public moneys enabled it to accumulate large balances against the State banks, and for those balances it was drawing the specie; that a continuance of this system a short time longer, would have compelled the State banks to have suspended specie payments, and visited the trading part of the community with bankruptcy and ruin. This state of facts, the truth of which I see no reason to doubt, furnished two satisfactory causes for changing the deposits.

Again. One object of vesting this corporation with these extravagant powers, *in trust*, was about to be violated. These powers were exerted in such a manner, as to compel a suspension of specie payments, which would inevitably have led to a depreciated currency. This was a *breach of the trust*, and the Secretary had a right to ward off the mischief, by withdrawing the public funds, which were the instruments employed by

9

the bank, for the accomplishment of its purpose. Upon principle, it seems to me the Secretary had a right to exercise his power to *maintain* a sound currency, and it has been abundantly shown that Mr. Crawford, when Secretary, often exerted the like power to accomplish the same object. But it has been argued that Mr. Crawford did not claim this power by virtue of this 16th section, but by virtue of the joint resolution, adopted during the same session. To this argument by our opponents, I submit two answers. 1st. It is a mistake to suppose that Mr. Crawford did not claim this power in virtue of the 16th section. Some of his letters referred to by other gentlemen, show expressly, as I think, that this power was claimed and exercised in virtue of this very section. 2d. If I am mistaken in this, and the power was exercised in virtue of the resolution, the same power is still continued to the present Secretary. The resolution is not temporary, but permanent. It is *unlimited as to time.* It authorizes the Secretary to adopt such measures as he may judge necessary, to procure a sound currency. Of what use would it be to enable banks to resume specie payments, and afford a sound currency, unless such payments are continued. The same means, therefore, which could lawfully be employed to *procure* a sound currency, may lawfully be used to *continue* such a currency. If, then, Mr. Crawford could rightfully *transfer* the public moneys to State banks, to enable them to *establish* a sound currency, so could Mr. Taney to enable them to *maintain it.*

Again. If I am mistaken in this, from the same facts another reason is furnished, which justifies the removal. It is admitted, by those who put the most limited construction upon the powers of the Secretary, that he may and ought to remove the public moneys whenever they are *unsafe.* They say the power of removal is a *trust*, and to be so used as to *preserve* the fund. Suppose this principle correct, for the sake of the argument. The Secretary informs us, that the bank was pursuing a course in the commercial cities, which, if not checked, would have compelled the State banks to suspend specie payments, and have placed in a state of bankruptcy, the commercial community in those cities. These same merchants were the *debtors* of the government upon bond, for duties constantly falling due; these bonds when taken are always deposited with the bank for collection; the government has the same interest in its debtor continuing *able* to pay a bond thus deposited, that it has in preserving the money from loss, after it has been paid. Upon the principles assumed then, by honorable gentlemen who have argued on the other side, it seems to me the Secretary might well remove the deposits, if by doing so, it would protect the *debtors* of the government from that oppression practised by the bank, which would have ended in their bankruptcy, and have defeated the payment of the bonds already in possession of the bank for collection.

I contend, also, that the bank violated the spirit of the 9th fundamental rule, contained in the 11th section of its charter, which is in these words: "The said corporation shall not, directly or indirectly, deal or trade in anything except bills of exchange, gold or silver bullion, or in the sale of goods, really and truly pledged, for money lent, and not redeemed in due time," &c.

The bank is charged with having interfered in elections, and with having used its *corporate funds*, for the sake of defraying the expenses of publications intended to influence public opinion. The bank admits it has expended various sums to protect itself against unfounded accusations, and to enlighten public opinion as to the nature and operations of the bank. By looking into the bank statements it will be found, that before the present Chief Magistrate came into office, the expense account for printing, was only a few hundred dollars per annum. In the two years, 1831 and 1832, the expense account for "speeches in Congress, and other miscellaneous publications," was upwards of forty-one thousand dollars. In the last of those years was the presidential election. There can be no mistake as to facts; in this case they are shown, and openly admitted by the bank. The justification it sets up is, that it was attacked by the President, and that it had a right to defend itself. The resolutions of the board show, that the directors authorized the president of the bank to expend money without limitation, for such purpose. Now I am willing to admit that a corporation may defend itself, by publishing a contradiction, or giving an explanation of any charge made against it by any person whatever; but there I say it must stop. It has no right, by any expenditure of its *corporate funds*, to enlighten, or regulate public opinion on the science of banking.

How does the bank say the President attacked it? In his different messages to Congress. These communications it was his duty to make if they contained his sentiments, and he believed it for the public interest that these opinions should be made known to the national legislature; and against such communications, the corporation had no right to make publications, or cause them to be made by others. If the bank is useful to the public, if its operations are beneficial to the community, that community and its public agents will advocate its utility. The individuals composing the corporation, have the rights, and are allowed the same powers, through the press, or by other means, to defend their interests, that other individuals have, but they have not the *additional* right, to use their corporate funds for the same purposes. This would give the corporation such an advantage over individuals, as to bear them down, by the mere force of money. The corporation has no right to use a dollar for any purpose not specified in the charter, or necessary to give effect to some purpose specified. The matters, in which the corporation may trade, or deal, are specified. All others are forbidden. It has no right to deal in "speeches," in "addresses" to State Legislatures, or in "miscellaneous publications." If it has a right to *expend* money in purchasing them, it has a right to make money by *selling* them. Why not set up a bookstore? The principle is the same. Nay, worse. The real object is, *to trade in public opinion.* Not to buy "golden opinions," but to procure opinions by the use of gold.

Honorable senators who argue on the other side, say the bank can have no influence in elections, that there is a prejudice against moneyed institutions, and that, in a canvass, they would rather have the bank against, than for them. I think very differently. A bank can, and often has a controlling influence, and the more dangerous, because it is often unseen; and if ever I should be engaged in a contest for popular favor, I would feel much more safe with the friendship, than with the enmity of the bank.

The honorable senator from Georgia who has so ably and so eloquently sustained the course of the Administration, thinks the bank can never influence public opinion, and adduces the result of the last presidential election, as a proof of the correctness of this opinion. Mr. President, I admit the bank did interfere in the last election for President; that it spared no pains or expense, to influence the public opinion against the present Chief Magistrate, and I admit he was elected by an overwhelming majority; but I deny that this was any proof that the bank has no influence, on ordinary occasions, where men of common standing, and ordinary services, are competitors. The popularity of the successful candidate, is not of the ordinary kind—it does not rest on the common foundation. His public services commenced when he was yet a boy. At the close of the Revolution, he was an orphan, without relatives, but not unknown, or without friends. His services and his conduct had already attracted the attention of some. With his manhood commenced a series of public services and employments, which have been continued throughout a long life, and one for usefulness, having hardly any parallel. From these services, the *roots* of his popularity struck deep, and extended far among the people of the United States. They were watered by the sweat of many toils, they were strengthened by numerous and imminent perils, until finally, on the plains of New Orleans, he was presented in an aspect, and his character proclaimed to the world in peals of thunder, accompanied by blazes of lightning, that at the same time astonished, and drew tears of joy from the eyes of patriots within these walls. These services embedded him in the hearts of his countrymen, and enthroned him in their affections. They fixed the conviction in public opinion, that he possessed a strength of mind, which the eloquence of Demosthenes cannot mislead; an integrity, which the wealth of Crœsus cannot corrupt, and a firmness, which the daring boldness of Catiline cannot intimidate. Tell me not, then, that the result of this election is a proof that the bank can have no influence. In this instance, all ages and sexes knew and appreciated the services of the successful candidate. You can hardly find a boy twelve years of age, who cannot tell you something of them. But let a canvass commence, in which the bank feels an interest; let the competitors be men whose character and worth are only known to few public men with whom they may have been associated, and we may witness a very different result.

Honorable senators cannot perceive how the bank, through the use of money can influence public measures. Mr. President, "Money is the root of all evil." Men desire it, because it stands in place of everything else. With it, we can decorate our own persons, and gratify the wishes of our families. With it, we can, as we think, procure almost every temporal comfort. While we are men, it is vain to talk of us as though we were angels. I can imagine many cases, in which the use of money might have a decided influence on the conduct of men esteemed virtuous and enlightened. I have no fear of the influence of this bank, because it will go, or send others to buy votes, among the mass of the people, by giving five dollars to one, ten dollars to another, or twenty to a third. No sir. My apprehensions from its influence are of a different description. Two years ago, this bank applied for a renewal of its charter; you [Mr. King, of Alabama, in the chair], and I, both opposed it. We voted against it, and used our best exertions to defeat it. It now seeks a restoration of the deposits, and an extension of its charter. We came here determined to vote against it, upon all points, and such we believe to be the sentiments, and wishes of those we represent. Shortly after our arrival, you are informed that your crop of cotton has fallen far short of what you expected, and that its price is much lower than you anticipated. You had contracted a debt, say for ten thousand dollars, which you had directed your manager to pay from the proceeds of this crop. He informs you the crop has failed; that your creditor needs, and must have his money. (I beg your pardon for using your name for my illustration, take my own.) Here I am, without any more means than will bear current expenses, and here I must stay until the business of the public is finished. What is to be done? I must borrow if I can, but from whom? Local banks have extended as far as they dare go, I need not apply to them. The United States Bank has means, and could accommodate, but I think it will not; it knows I have done, and will continue to do, all I can to disappoint its wishes. I make my case known to my friends—they advise me to apply to this bank; that it does not proceed upon the selfish and illiberal principles attributed to it. I prepare my note, my friends endorse it, and I make my application. The officers tell me they can spare the money very conveniently; that they know the debt would be good, but if the loan was made, it might not in the end be an accommodation; that the bank is struggling for its existence, against all the influence the executive can bring to bear—already have the public deposits been removed; there is no certainty they will be restored, and if they are, unless the charter is prolonged, they must be arranging their concerns for its determination; therefore, if they make the loan, they can give no assurance how long they can continue the accommodation; that they know I have been opposed to the bank, *upon principle*, and expect me to continue so, but that circumstance can make no difference; that it would give them as much pleasure to accommodate me, as if I were a friend to the institution, provided they could do so. My credit is in jeopardy—I need, and must have the money; I determine to take it, and run the risk of being in some way enabled to repay it, when called upon. With the money, I return with a light heart to my lodging, and enclose it to my correspondent at home, with instructions to lift my bond. My mind dwells upon the transaction, and I begin to conclude after all, this bank is not so bad as it has been represented: its conduct has at all events been more liberal to me than I had any reason to expect. I come to the Senate the next day, and listen attentively to the arguments adduced to prove, that the President, in removing these deposits, has violated the public faith; that he has violated the chartered rights of this corporation; that he has usurped a power not vested in him by the Constitution or laws, and that if such conduct receives no rebuke, the government will be changed, and all power concentrated in the hands of *one man*, who will be a tyrant or a despot. These arguments make a deep impression; I reflect upon them: they acquire additional force, and I am sure they would have been satisfactory to my constituents, if they could have heard them; more especially as the question of "Bank or no Bank," is not involved. The question is, "*Constitution or no Constitution*," "Liberty or Slavery." My mind settles down in favor of restoring the deposits; I so vote, and the deposits are restored. What next? The State banks have extended their loans, on the strength of these deposits, which are now to be withdrawn. These accommodations must be rapidly curtailed; these curtailments produce bankruptcies, and unmeasured distress in society: the funds necessary to protect these banks, against the Bank of the United States, are taken from them, and placed in the hands of an enraged rival; through these funds large balances are immediately accumulated against them; the specie is all withdrawn from some one, and it is compelled to suspend specie payments: this creates a "panic," which produces a run upon all, and ends in a general suspension of specie payments. Here is a new state of things; a depreciated local currency. If we have bank notes at all, they ought to be of that description, that five dollars *here*, will be five dollars *everywhere* in the Union; neither I nor my constituents, will be content to handle as money, rags and trash, with a pocket full of which a man could not pay for his breakfast. Up comes the great question for *renewing or elongating* the charter of this bank; "Bank or no Bank," and what am I now to do? This is precisely similar to the state of things which existed in 1816. As a statesman, I must adapt my legislation to the circumstances in which I find my country. In the like circumstances, men of the strongest intellect, most cultivated minds, purest patriotism, and unsullied characters, gave up their constitutional scruples, and for the sake of purifying the "currency," established this bank; for the like reasons I will lay down my old opinions, and vote to continue it. The session closes, and before I go home, I call at the bank to make some arrangement relative to my loan, until I can return at the next session, and pay the debt. The officers tell me things have taken a direction, which they did not anticipate; fortunately public agents have seen the public interest, in its true light; the bank has had its charter enlarged; its business will be continued, and must of necessity require the services of some professional man, as its legal adviser and attorney, that it will be considered a favor if I will accept my note as a retaining fee. Thus the matter ends. Now, who will venture in the case supposed, to charge me with corruption, and yet does not every one *feel*, and *see* that money was the cause of all these operations through which the mind passed? We must take man as he is; if properly constituted, acts of kindness will have their influence upon him, and none can certainly say, to what extent they may carry him. Who can be unmoved, while his "enemy is heaping coals of fire upon his head," by doing him acts of kindness, which add to his comforts? Few, if any, who are composed of the common materials.

Mr. President: It appears to me that the Secretary of the Treasury, for the reasons which I have stated, as well as for those which have been stated by others, and which I have no inclination to repeat, had the power to remove the public moneys from the Bank of the United States, and place them in other banks for safe-keeping; and that the conduct of the bank justifies the exercise of that power. But, when he came to form an opinion whether it was *good policy to exercise it*, or not, a question was presented, upon which the warmest friends of the Administration, and the sternest opposers of the bank, might *well* and *honestly* entertain *various opinions*. The immense powers of this bank —its great capacity to do good, or inflict evils upon this community, and the unyielding determination it had manifested to procure a renewal of its charter, if possible, might well make the prudent, the timid, if you choose, decline its exercise. But the deposits have been removed, and with me the question now is, is it good policy to restore them. I say no. I am opposed to prolonging the charter of this bank; I wish its concerns closed when the charter expires. It is said the country is distressed. I believe it. The deposits have been removed into State banks, and accommodations have been extended on the strength of these deposits. If the deposits are restored these accommodations must be withdrawn. This will make the confusion greater, and add to the distresses. The United States Bank is under no necessity, as has been clearly demonstrated by the senator from Missouri, to curtail its accommodations any farther at present. If the deposits are restored, the bank will be under no obligations to grant any increased accommodations on account of them: if it does, they must be limited in amount, and for short periods. If the bank is to be wound up it must collect its debts, and pay what it owes. By restoring the deposits, you put the State banks in the power of this bank to destroy them, and to compel them to suspend specie payments at will. This power, I fear, would be exerted, if it were believed that that was the most certain mode in which to procure a renewed charter.

The honorable senator from Massachusetts thinks the deposits ought to be restored, and the bank rechartered, and that this is an effectual plan to relieve a distressed community. With the opinions he entertains, his policy is sound. He is correct throughout, and consistent. If I believed as he does, that we had power to charter a bank, and that this bank was an essential agent for the government, and its operations a blessing to the community, I would go with him and say, the deposits ought not to have been removed; they ought to be restored; the bank rechartered, and society put at rest. But, believing we have no such power (and if we had, that it ought not to be exercised), to restore these deposits, would, I think, aggravate existing distresses, and make "confusion worse confounded."

Mr. President, it has been urged, that if there has been any impropriety in the conduct of the bank, such conduct will find a justification in the conduct of the Chief Magistrate; that he has been guilty of an usurpation of power; that his course has been tyrannical; that he has violated chartered rights, the Constitution of his country, and the public faith. These are high charges, made with great freedom, and maintained by distinguished ability. I am not among the number of those who find fault with this course, on the part of those opposed to the Administration. Our liberty depends on the freedom with which we examine the conduct of those in high offices. If the charges are not well founded, making them cannot do harm to those against whom they are made; and if well founded, society is benefitted by having their misdeeds publicly exposed. The whole of these charges rest upon the supposition that the President has *assumed* and *exercised* powers, with which he was not vested by the Constitution or laws of the United States.

We are here naturally led to inquire, what has he done, and what is the *nature* or character of the power he has exercised.

He has removed one Secretary of the Treasury and appointed another. He called upon the directors of the Bank of the United States, which, with the advice and consent of the Senate, he had appointed, to report to him the manner in which the business of that institution had been conducted and was being conducted. After he received their report, he determined that the public moneys to be collected after the 1st October last, should not be deposited in that bank, but placed in other banks for *safe-keeping*, until called for to satisfy appropriations made by Congress. The whole power then, which the President has undertaken to exercise, is neither more nor less than this, that he, as the Chief Magistrate, has the power to *construe* the Constitution and laws of the United States, to endeavor to ascertain their true meaning, and then carry that meaning into effect, so far as depends upon his own action, or the action of those inferior officers appointed to aid him in the discharge of his executive duties. It appears evident to me that he possesses this power, and that his whole duties consist in exercising such powers. He, therefore, has not assumed or taken upon himself to exercise any power, which, in its nature, he did not possess. In its exercise he may be mistaken; he may think the framers of the Constitution or law meant one thing, when they intended another; but this would only be an error in judgment, if unintentional, or an abuse of power, if designed: in neither case would it be an *assumption* of unauthorized power. In what manner then did he exert this power? He sought the necessary information to enable him and the Secretary of the Treasury to form a correct opinion, whether the power given to the Secretary, in the 16th section of the act incorporating the bank, to remove the public deposits, ought to be exerted or not. When this information was obtained, he came to the conclusion that the public interest required that they should be removed. The then Secretary of the Treasury came to the conclusion that the deposits ought *not* to be removed, and that as he was the officer appointed by the act to give the order, he was constituted the *sole judge*, and that the President had no power to control him. He, therefore, refused to give the *order*, and refused to *resign:* the President dismissed him, and appointed another, who agreed with him in opinion, and ordered the deposits to be removed. Had the President a constitutional power to do this? I have no doubt he possessed the power. By the first section of the second article of the Constitution, the executive power is vested in the President of the United States. In every government there are *two* general classes of power; one to *make* the law, the other to *execute* it.

By our Constitution this latter class is subdivided into judicial and executive. We, therefore, have three great departments:

1. Congress, to make laws, with the aid of the President, upon all subjects confided, by the Constitution, to the general government.

2. The judiciary, to expound and enforce, or execute the laws confided to that department.

3. And the executive power, which is vested in the President, and comprehends the whole executive power given by the Constitution, and not expressely conferred somewhere else.

The whole judicial power is vested in a Supreme Court, and such inferior courts as Congress may, from time to time, ordain and establish. The Treasury department belongs to the executive department, by the Constitution. It has no connection with the power of making laws, therefore, belongs not to the legislative department. It belongs not to the Supreme, or to any inferior court, therefore, is no part of the judiciary. The only remaining department is the executive, to which it must belong.

It appears evident to me, that the framers of the Constitution intended that the executive power should be vested in one head, who would be bound not only to discharge, faithfully, all his *own personal duties*, but likewise should be clothed with the necessary powers to *compel* the inferior officers in the *executive* department, to perform theirs likewise. The President is bound to see that the laws are faithfully executed. This gives him no power over the judiciary. The courts have their appropriate duties confided to them by the laws and the Constitution, and discharge them independently of the executive. But all executive officers falling within the executive department, he has, and must have, a power to control. The heads of departments are appointed by him; they can only be displaced by him, or by impeachment and conviction. If the Secretary of the Treasury should put an improper construction upon a revenue law, and would neither give up his construction, nor retire, he might defeat the collection of the whole revenue before Congress would be in session, unless the President had the power of removing him. In this very case, suppose the President had believed the whole of the money in the bank would be wasted before the session of Congress, and had called upon the Secretary to remove them, and he had refused, saying, he conscientiously believed there was no danger, and the President had yielded, from a belief that he had no power to remove him in such a case, and the money had been all wasted. Would any gentleman justify the President. I think not? When they conscientiously disagree, one must yield, or retire, and that should be the subordinate; otherwise we have no executive government, of any practical utility. There is one thing in which I think Mr. Duane was right, and that is in not giving the order for removal, unless he had been convinced his opinion against the removal was wrong; but his error, as I think, consisted in not withdrawing from the department. While he believed a proper case was not made for the removal, and that a public injury would be done by the removal, no consideration ought to have induced him to sign an order for such a purpose. But if the President believed they ought to be removed, and that a great public injury would result from permitting them to remain, and his Secretary would neither give the order nor retire, I think he had the power to remove him.

But, Mr. President, although I think the Chief Magistrate does possess this power, yet I believe it is one to be exercised with great caution, and only in cases where he is clearly convinced the public interests demand its exercise. This point has been so fully examined, and ably maintained by gentlemen who have preceded me, that I will no longer dwell upon it.

Had the President a right to call upon the government directors, and to receive reports from them, of the manner in which the business of the bank had been conducted? Some honorable members have denied that he had. On a former occasion, I stated my doubts as to their construction of the charter. Since then, I have examined it with more attention, and am satisfied their limited construction is inaccurate. I will, as briefly as I can, state the reasons which have led to the opinion I entertain.

In our examination of the act incorporating this bank, we ought never to forget, that the very objects of its creation were high national ones. To *restore* and *preserve* a sound circulating medium to the community, and to act as fiscal agent, in receiving and paying out the public moneys. To accomplish these important objects, there are to be twenty-five directors to manage the institution; five of these were to be appointed by the President, by and with the advice and consent of the Senate. These directors are to hold their appointments for one year, and until others are appointed; and an express power is given to the President to *remove* the five government directors, within the year, if he believes the public interest requires it. By the 1st section, the United States are to subscribe for *seventy thousand shares*, equal to seven millions of dollars, which is one fifth of the whole capital. By the 7th section of the act, the stockholders are vested with a power to make such by-laws, rules, and regulations, for the government of the corporation, and for the management of its affairs, as to them may seem proper, not inconsistent with the Constitution or laws. In the making of these by-laws, ordinances, rules, and regulations, the United States were to have *no voice*, *no vote*. By the 5th rule in the 11th section, it is provided that a number of stockholders, not less than sixty, who together shall be proprietors of one thousand shares, or upwards, shall have the power at any time, to call a general meeting of the stockholders, for purposes relative to the institution, giving at least, ten weeks' notice, in two public newspapers of the place where the bank is seated, and specifying in each notice, the object or objects of such meeting. By this provision, sixty stockholders owning one thousand shares, can call a general meeting whenever they have reason to fear their business is mismanaged. They can call *their directors* to account *and examine into their whole proceedings*, and make any alterations or regulations they think their interests may require. At this general meeting, the United States are *unrepresented;* they have *no voice;* they have *no vote*, they have *no person to attend*, either to receive, or to give any information, although they own *seventy thousand shares*, worth *seven millions.* Is it possible for us to suppose the executive branch of the government was intended to be *excluded* from *all knowledge* of the manner in which the institution was conducted; that the United States, owning *one-fifth* of the whole stock, should have no voice in *making laws* for the government of the directors, and no means of knowing whether they *conformed* their conduct to the laws or not; more especially that they should have no means of knowing whether the policy prescribed and pursued, was likely to carry into effect the high governmental purpose of preserving a sound currency? I cannot think it possible. Such a construction I must be permitted to say, with great deference, would, in my judgment, be a *severe reflection* upon the enlightened men who passed this act.

But if we admit, which I think we ought, that they intended the five government directors should have an *equal* agency with any other *equal* number of directors, in the management of the affairs of the bank, and that they should be *bound* at any time, when called upon by the executive, representing the United States, *their constituents*, to report to him exactly the same information, which the private stockholders at a general meeting might *demand* of *their directors*, then every thing is consistent and reasonable.

My construction is, I think, very much strengthened, by the provisions in the 23d section, which enacts "that it shall at all times be lawful for a committee of either house of Congress, appointed for that purpose, to inspect the books, and examine into the proceedings of the corporation hereby enacted, and to report whether the provisions of this charter have been by the same violated or not; and whenever any committee, as aforesaid, shall find and report, *or the President of the United States shall have reason to believe*, that the charter has been violated, it may be lawful for Congress to direct, or the President to order, a *scire facias* to be sued out," &c. It must, I think, strike every one reading this section, with great force, that complete power is given to Congress to acquire the most precise information, to enable it to judge whether the charter has been so far violated, as to make the issuing a *scire facias* necessary. In the same section a power is given to the President, to direct a *scire facias*, if *he has reason to believe* the charter is violated. From what source is he to acquire a knowledge of facts upon which to found his opinion? Not the report of the committee. Congress is to act upon it, if any person. It would be absurd to suppose that it was intended Congress should procure the information, and not to order any *scire facias*, and that the President should *upon the same report*, direct one to be issued. Congress was to act upon the report of its own committee; the President to give his *direction* upon information derived from some other source, and that source is *the report of the directors* whom he had appointed, and had a power to remove, for faithless or unwise conduct. This construction is farther confirmed when we see in the same section, that in the *scire facias* the facts which it is supposed have constituted a violation of the charter, must be set down so *precisely*, that an issue can be taken upon them, and tried by a jury. What has been alleged in favor of the opposite construction? Nothing, except that it is said, the five government directors shall, with the other twenty, manage and direct the bank. To single out a single expression or paragraph, and fix the meaning from that alone, is not the sound rule of interpretation; we must take the whole act, compare one part with another, and fix the meaning from the context. Or what is still more correct; we must ascertain the spirit and meaning of the act, and give it such interpretation as will give effect to the will of the lawgiver. If my construction needs farther aid, its correctness is proved beyond question, by the debates when the act was under consideration. Those who opposed that provision in the charter which allows directors to be appointed, insisted the provision should be stricken out, because these directors would be "*spies*," and informers. The friends to the provision say it ought to be retained, because we want these directors as "sentinels on the watch tower," to give information. By what rule then is it that we are to say the executive has violated the charter, in calling for these reports, or the directors for having made them? By none heretofore recognized as a sound one. The true rule is, to ascertain what the legislature intended when they were enacting the law, and then say, that is its construction now. My view of this subject is rendered still more certain by the opinion of a distinguished gentleman from New York, who was at the head of a most respectable committee of the House of Representatives, in November, 1818. They had given this charter, and the proceedings of the directors under it, a laborious examination, and had maturely considered the whole subject. One paragraph, in their report, connected with a proposition of Mr. Spencer, the chairman, shortly afterwards, shows conclusively, his opinion upon this point. The report is in these words: "Two by-laws of the bank, seem to your committee to deserve notice; one of them that no discounts shall be made without the consent of three-fourths of the directors present," and another, "that no director shall, without especial authority, be permitted to inspect the cash account of any person with the bank. These by-laws appear to render nugatory the provisions of the charter authorizing the appointment by the government of one-fifth of the whole number of directors, and are different from the provisions, in that respect, by the former Bank of the United States, although most of the local banks in Philadelphia have similar regulations. Should a state of things exist, in which the stockholders should deem their interest hostile to that of the nation, such provisions as these stated would render the government directors *mere spectators* of the proceedings of the board."

The proposition afterwards submitted by Mr. Spencer, contained various matters, intended as amendments of the charter; the 5th is in these words: "That no by-law of the said corporation, shall *exclude the directors* appointed by the government, from a *full knowledge* of all the concerns of the bank, and of the accounts of every person dealing with it; and that the assent of at least one public director, shall be necessary to allow any discount, and to render valid every act of the board of directors."

By the report, it is obvious the draughtsman and a majority of the committee, at least, were of opinion that the government directors were *bound to report* whatever information they could acquire. Mr. Spencer believed that the by-laws restricted them too much, and that they ought to have access to every account in the bank, as well as the *private accounts* of individuals, as the general accounts. Why enlarge the field in which these directors were to collect information, unless they were at liberty to communicate all they could collect when required? Thus then, it seems to me, the context, the spirit and meaning of the charter, compel us to conclude, Congress intended the government directors should make reports. The friends and enemies of the charter agreed that that was the intention, at the time the act was on its passage, and such has been considered its construction ever since, until this controversy. If the contrary is now settled to be its meaning, and the directors are not at liberty to communicate any information; if the whole proceedings of the board, and all the operations of this great moneyed institution, in which the government has so much at hazard, and which can so materially affect every interest in the community, are to be kept profound *secrets*, then I must be permitted to believe it is too odious, and too dangerous, to be tolerated one moment longer than we are now compelled to allow it to exist.

Mr. President, I have now discharged a duty, far from pleasing to myself. It was due to those who sent me, as well as to others, that from my place in this body, I should state the reasons upon which I expect to rest my votes. Having done so, I will only add my acknowledgments to the Senate, for their patient attention, after the subject had been so long, and so ably discussed, as to have left no hope that anything I could say, would be matter of interest either here or elsewhere.

The following letter, dated the day before the delivery of the speech, is of some importance as showing Judge White's sentiments as to the obligation resting upon him in regard to it. The expression of his sentiments was a delicate task, but one which his constituents expected him to perform; and he acquitted himself satisfactorily to those with whom he acted, and in such a manner as to give no just cause of offence to those who differed from him in opinion. He commences with some very sound reflections suggested by a dissension among some of his friends in Tennessee:

The majority of men are selfish; and whenever their plans for wealth or honor are not seconded by others, their hostility is sure to manifest itself; but by bearing with them, such hostility will only last until they see that the object of their wrath has again the power of giving them assistance. Then, simulated friendship again returns, and all is well. The life of a useful public man is necessarily one of sacrifices of interest and feelings. By these sacrifices alone can he live down the daily slanders with which he is loaded.

On to-morrow, if I live and am favored with tolerable health, I intend to express some of the opinions I entertain, on the topics* so long and so ably discussed. In the extensive field, hardly a head is left for the gleaner; but if I say nothing, the motives of my silence may be misrepresented; therefore something must be said.

I have felt embarrassed, and still do, by the following circumstance. Last summer the President asked my opinion as to the removal of the deposits. I thought, with the information I then had, it was bad policy, and so told him. Although this correspondence was confidential, my letter was shown to his cabinet, and to others. Thus you see the unpleasant situation in which I am placed, by acting with that frankness towards, and friendship which I hope ever to feel for, the Chief Magistrate. Thus situated, I thought silence best became me. Now, we have arrived at a point where, in my opinion, silence would be censurable. I must therefore present my opinions as they are honestly entertained, regardless of all consequences.

He adds, with terse sincerity, in reply to a suggestion that his name should be used for the presidential candidacy in the election of 1836:

There are in my mind two reasons why my friends ought not to think of using my name as you suggest. 1st. The public do not wish it. 2d. I do not.

Condy Raguet, the well-known financial writer, addressed to Judge White, March 28, 1834, the following dexterous letter, which refers to the subject of the bank, and likewise, though very indistinctly, in the final paragraph, to the same plan of making Judge White a presidential candidate in the election of 1836:

Dear Sir: The high opinion I entertain of your public character and private integrity induces me to address you this letter. Being one of the

* Topics connected with the Bank.

very few individuals north of the Potomac who entertain a conscientious conviction of the unconstitutionality of a federal bank, I feel a deep concern lest the course which public opinion seems to be taking, may bring about a state of things far more disastrous than has yet been anticipated. I allude to the mania for the incorporation of State banks with immense capitals, founded solely upon the expectation of having the control of the public money. These banks, if they should be chartered in various States, might by combinations be rendered as dangerous to the peace of the country as any single federal bank; and it seems to me that all who are opposed upon principle to the extension of paper machinery, should use their influence in preventing it.

Taking it for granted that there is not the most remote probability of the renewal of the charter of the present bank for *any* length of time, long or short, or of the incorporation of a new one, during the term of service of the present executive, and believing that the future happiness of the country demands that the government should be wholly separated from the banking system *in all its forms*, I have turned the subject over in my mind, and have placed on paper the result of my reflections, written as I would have worded an editorial article. This sketch I enclose for your perusal. If you think that it contains any suggestions which can be made useful, it is at your service. If not, be pleased to return it to me, and allow me to say that as I have no right to intrude my opinions upon you in such a way as to appear to invite yours, it will give me no umbrage if you do so without a word of comment. The question at issue is one upon which honest men widely differ, and as I do not know your sentiments in relation to it, I cannot be charged with rudeness in making known to you mine. I consider the country to be in a fearful state, and would be glad to see some friend of the Administration upon whose virtue and principles I could rely, bring forward some measure for relief.

I am, dear sir,
With sentiments of much respect,
Your ob't serv't,
CONDY RAGUET.

P. S.—After writing the above, and before the letter was sealed, a respectable gentleman whom I happened to see, made the following remark. "There are two parties here, one of which would do anything to put down General Jackson, and the other anything to sustain him. But there is a third party, and a very large one, who care not a straw about who is President, but who anxiously desire to see some measure of relief for the country, let it operate against, or in favor of, whom it may." This is no doubt true; and the man who should propose in Congress and carry through a measure calculated to conciliate all parties, by yielding something to each, would merit, and would receive, the applause of the whole people."

This letter Judge White answered, April 6, 1834, with a noble and complete statement of absolute political independence, and a manly avowal of consciousness of the comparatively uninfluential station which such independence must always necessitate; and with a clear and vigorous summary of his opinions on the points of the bank question, as follows:

DEAR SIR: Your letter dated 29th ult., and the project which accompanied it, reached me in due course of the mail. Other duties have prevented my answer at an earlier day. I feel gratified that my course has been such as to be approved by one whom I think so well qualified to form correct opinions in everything which relates to the fundamental principles of our government.

Nothing could give me more pleasure than to be the instrument of doing something which would be of lasting benefit to the people whose interests are liable to be affected by my public conduct. But I feel too little confidence in my own abilities, and am sure that my hold upon public opinion is too slender, to permit the hope that this can ever be effected by venturing to become a leader. I do not carry on political or friendly correspondence with any man living: I have a cordial dislike for everything like contrivance, by which to put or keep any man or set of men in power. Thus you will see my course is too *individual* for me to be useful on a large scale. My whole aim and ambition is to fix in my own mind the political principles which in my own opinion best accord with the Constitution, and then to give them such practical effect as will be productive of the most good.

Upon the great questions which now so agitate the public mind, I have employed myself industriously, with an anxious desire to come to correct conclusions, and I give you the results with that candor which I hope belongs to my character.

I do not believe the Constitution of the United States vests in Congress any power to charter a bank, nor do I think the precedents which have been furnished are binding as authorities upon this or any future Congress.

I do not believe the present Congress has any more power to prolong this charter for even a year, than that of 1816 had to grant it for twenty years.

If Congress had the power to incorporate a bank, I do not think it ought to be exercised. Money in large masses ought to be dreaded, and the fewer hands it is placed in the more it is to be dreaded. If continued, the executive and the bank, in time, must and and will unite their influence; and when they do, they will endanger our liberties.

I think the President had the power to *remove* the Secretary of the

Treasury, if he conscientiously believed a serious injury would be the consequence of his not using the power given him to change the place of depositing the public moneys.

I believe the conduct of the bank had been such as to justify the Secretary in the exercise of the power given in the bank charter.

I hold that although the Secretary had the power, and the conduct of the bank well justified its exercise, yet there was another great question remaining to be decided, and that was, the *effect* the change of the deposits would have upon society; and if the Secretary conscientiously believed it would be injurious, he did right to refuse to give an order for the removal; and the willingness of the President to take the responsibility *would not have excused him* for doing what he believed to be wrong. But if the President had formed a different opinion, the Secretary ought to have resigned.

Although I think the President possesses the power of removal on account of a difference of opinion with an executive officer, yet I think it ought not to be exercised except in a case where the executive officer is clearly wrong.

The deposits having been removed, even if it is admitted to have been impolitic to have done so, I hold it would be bad policy now to restore them, unless the bank is to be rechartered.

Against those concerned in the direction of the Bank of the United States, I certainly have no cause of personal dislike, but the contrary. Still, I fear any extension of time to close their concerns would be assiduously employed to procure a recharter. We cannot bind such a corporation by any regulations upon paper, any more than Samson could have been bound by a thread of sewing-silk. An attentive examination of its proceedings has satisfied me that such construction will be put upon any recharter, as will best promote the interests of the stockholders.

Your plan is, in my judgment, greatly preferable to any which I have heard suggested, and I do not discern any objection to it, but my strong conviction that the time allowed for winding up would be employed for the purpose of procuring a new charter, as exceptionable as that which they now have.

I am, however, so much struck with the power of what you advance, that I am unwilling to return the project unless you say I must do so.

Although I have no wish to conceal any of my opinions, yet I have such an instinctive dread of appearing in the public prints, that I beg you to consider this letter for yourself.

In order to the completeness of this view of Judge White's arguments upon the question of the bank, are here inserted, somewhat in advance of their proper succession in time, his remarks delivered in the Senate, April 20th, 1838. The charter of the bank had expired in 1836. It was allowed two years after that time, in which to wind up its concern. In 1838, a bill was reported by the judiciary committee, to prevent the re-issuing of its notes. Judge White, with consistent adherence to his republican sentiments, opposed the bill, as asking an extravagant and unnecessary exertion of power, in a case where there already existed an adequate remedy. He said:

Mr. President: I do not wish that the reasons for the vote which I intend to give on this bill should be misunderstood, and therefore I now address you.

The evil to be remedied by its passage is the reissuing the notes of the late Bank of the United States, chartered by Congress in 1816. The penalty to be inflicted is that of fine and imprisonment. I deny that Congress has the power to pass such a bill.

Let us examine, for a moment, the principles contended for by its friends.

1st. My honorable colleague has deduced the power from the second section of the third article of the Constitution, which says, that the courts of the United States shall have jurisdiction in all cases arising under the Constitution or laws of the United States, &c.

This clause was never intended to designate the cases in which *Congress should legislate*, but the cases which the *judiciary might decide.*

All cases in which we legislate, whether we have the Constitutional power or not, the judiciary may have cognizance of. If, because the judiciary have this jurisdiction in *all* cases, Congress may also legislate in *all* cases, there is an end of all limitation to the powers of the federal government.

This is a more extravagant claim of power than I have ever known to be set up by any class of politicians.

2d. His next recourse is to that clause in the Constitution which gives to Congress the power "to coin money and to regulate the value of it," &c.

From this clause he has argued that Congress has the whole power over the coin, and, if these notes are permitted to circulate, they will put out of circulation an equal amount of coin, therefore, Congress has the power to legislate them out of circulation. I deny the soundness of this argument.

It is true Congress has the sole power over the *coin*, but it is not true that they have, on that account, absolute power over all *credits*, which the States or the people may choose to circulate as *substitutes for coin.* They cannot pass any law which will make it unlawful for one man to circulate the promissory negotiable note of another, as a substitute for coin. Nor can they prohibit the circulation of notes issued by the banks chartered by any of the States.

The circulation of checks or notes on State banks displaces the specie to the same amount, and if this argument of my colleague were sound, this whole circulation could, at any time, be prohibited by Congress.

This claim of power is, in itself, so extravagant, that few have heretofore ventured to assert it. In my opinion, it comes with a bad grace from those claiming to be States right men, or Republicans of the Jeffersonian school.

3d. His last resource, to establish this power, is a recurrence to that clause in the Constitution which gives Congress the power to pass all laws, necessary and proper, to carry into effect any of the powers before vested in them.

This argument of my colleague carries us back, and places us upon the broad old federal doctrine, "that Congress may do any thing which they believe is for the general welfare."

The republican doctrine is, that this clause in the Constitution, instead of vesting in Congress any power on any *new subject*, was intended as a limitation upon powers already granted. Without this clause, Congress would have been compelled, in many cases, to take power by implication, or by construction, otherwise they could not attain many of the objects over which express powers to legislate had been granted to them. To cut off all pretence for assuming powers by implication, this clause was inserted, and express power conferred to pass all laws *necessary and proper* to give effect to the attainment of those objects, in relation to which express powers had been granted.

I cannot but think, that he who now insists on the reverse, and still calls himself a Republican of the Jeffersonian school, mistakes the class of politicians to which he belongs. Certain I am, he and I do not belong to the same class, because I will not take from this clause the power to act on any new or independent subject whatever. I can only take power from it to use the *means necessary* and *appropriate* to effectuate some object, in relation to which an express power to legislate is given.

The honorable senator from New Jersey, who addressed us yesterday, has had recourse to judicial determinations, to prove that Congress possesses the power to pass this bill.

It appeared to me that those authorities only went to establish, that where Congress has the power to *create* an institution, they have the power to regulate it or destroy it.

If this doctrine is sound, the argument leaves me exactly where it found me, because I am one of that unfortunate class of politicians who do *not believe* Congress had the *power to create* this corporation.

The honorable senator from Alabama, farthest from me (Mr. Clay), supposes we have the power to pass this bill, because the notes thus improperly put in circulation, the United States are morally bound to pay.

I deny that the United States ever were, or ever can be, either legally or morally bound to pay a single note issued by that bank.

The bank was called by our name, we were stockholders to the amount of seven millions of dollars, and we were no farther bound to the payment of the debts of that bank than any individual owning the same amount of stock, and the very moment we sold the stock we were not interested in the bank to the amount of one cent.

The cases put by the senator to illustrate his argument, prove that the name of this bank has misled him.

He says, if a man forges a note or obligation upon the Treasurer of the United States, he could be punished for forgery, &c.

Suppose I yield that he could, why would he be thus punishable by an act of Congress? It would be because the Treasurer is an officer of the United States, and because, if the forged note or obligation were genuine, the United States must pay the money out of the Treasury.

The persons this bill intends to punish, are not our officers, our agents, or our trustees; nor are the United States, either legally or morally, bound to pay one dollar to redeem these notes.

The notes, if re-issued, are thus dealt with, by the officers, the agents, or trustees of the bank, in which we have no interest whatever, the United States having sold the whole amount of their stock to the bank chartered by Pennsylvania.

I think if the honorable senator will re-consider the opinions he has advanced, and give them an application to the facts as they really exist, he will be satisfied he is maintaining a doctrine too extravagant to be seriously insisted on by any one.

The argument of the honorable senator from Connecticut (Mr. Niles), is by far more plausible than anything I have heard.

It is this in substance, that we cannot now inquire whether Congress had the power to charter this bank or not. It was chartered, these notes were made in virtue of a power conferred by the charter, and it is our duty to see that society is not defrauded by means of our creation.

If there were no other means of checking the mischief but by our legislation, the necessity of the case would make a man strain hard to find some source from which he could have power to compel those who are trustees to cancel those notes as fast as they are lifted by them.

But there is no sort of necessity for our legislation to check this mischief.

How are the facts?

By the charter of 1816, the bank had twenty years, within which to do business; they expired on the 3d March, 1836. The bank was to have two additional years within which to wind up its concerns; they expired the 3d March, 1838.

Before the expiration of the twenty years, the State of Pennsylvania gave to the stockholders, with the exception of the United States, a new charter, and the old stockholders transferred to this new bank all their funds in trust to wind up their concerns; in other words, in trust to collect all the debts due to the old bank, and to pay all the debts it owed.

Now I am very clear in the opinion that whenever the trustee, with the funds of the old bank, lifted any of its notes, it was a duty to cancel them, and if, instead of doing so, the trustee re-issued them, it was a breach of trust, and upon an application to a court of chancery, by any one having an interest, I have no doubt a decree would be made to restrain the re-issue, and to compel the trustee to cancel the notes as fast as lifted *with the trust funds.*

Where then is the necessity for Congress to exert the power to check a mischief for which there is a clear, unembarrassed, and adequate remedy? There can be none as I think. There certainly is none to protect any interest of the United States. They never had any interest in this new bank, and they have none in the old, because under an act of Congress our seven millions of stock were sold to the new bank, receipted for, and as fast as the installments have fallen due, according to the contract, they have been punctually paid.

There, therefore, as it seems to me, can be no necessity or propriety in deriving the power claimed from the necessity of the case, and there is the more danger in deriving any power from such source, because every honest mind is easily misled by it, as the exercise of the power is to attain an object honest and praiseworthy.

But, Mr. President, are not all those who assume this ground, and think we have no power to charter a bank, assuming a most dangerous and deceptive ground?

I cannot but think so, and with great deference I say, it has appeared to me, we are likely to commit error by not separating in our minds things which ought to be kept distinct.

The new bank and the old bear the same name. The stockholders, with the exception of the United States, are the same in both banks. The principal officers in the old are the prominent officers in the new. Hence I have thought we are inclined to view the officers in this State bank as our officers, exercising an authority derived from the United States, when in truth and in fact they derive their power and authority under a State law, and are neither our officers, our trustees, nor our agents. Their whole power and authority over the affairs of the old bank are derived from the *contract* between the old and the new banks, by which the latter became the trustee of the former.

Is it possible that Congress can derive any power to legislate on this point on the ground of this contract?

Suppose Pennsylvania had never granted this new charter, and the stockholders of the old bank had made just such a contract with the bank of Virginia in virtue of which this latter bank became the trustee, and there was an allegation that this trustee was re-issuing some of the notes instead of cancelling them. Is any gentleman prepared to maintain that Congress could pass a law to send the trustee to jail, or to have him mulcted in a fine?

Upon principle there is no distinction between the cases.

The claim of power rests upon the ground that as we *inferred* the power to *create* the bank, when in truth we had no such power, we may assume any other power we choose to check our own mischief.

I deny this doctrine entirely, and insist that by our *own legislation* we can never *enlarge* our own powers.

Here we have created a bank. Will any gentleman affirm that an express power to charter a bank is given in the Constitution? No gentleman can so allege. Even those who claim such a power for Congress have never pretended there is any *express* grant of power. All agree it is a power that must be *inferred* for the sake of carrying out some other express grant of power.

Some have said we have express power to lay and collect taxes, and a bank is necessary as a fiscal agent.

Others that we have a power to coin money, and, therefore Congress has power over the whole currency, and to keep that sound, a bank is essential.

While those who deny any such power have denominated it "a *vagrant*, crawling over the Constitution in search of a soft place on which to make a comfortable settlement."

If we pass this bill, in my judgment, we first assume, by implication, that Congress had the power to charter the bank, and then we *infer* that Congress can impose whatever pains and penalties it pleases, even unto death, to compel the cancelling of the notes.

These powers, I think, we do not possess, and, therefore, I will not exercise them. I will adhere to what I think the old republican doctrine:

1st. Show an express grant of power to do the principal matter, and then

2d. That the means you wish to employ are the *necessary* and *proper* means to be used, and I am ready to act; if I doubt, reasonably, I ought not to act.

Is there any gentleman who hears me who can say there is no reasonable doubt in this case?

After all, if we pass this bill, how is any one to find out what notes were re-issued? There will be no mark put upon them.

We can only believe some have been re-issued, because we see, at an after day, more are in circulation than there were on a former one: but what identical notes they were, society can have no means of knowing.

I now have one or two in my pocket, but I have no knowledge when or how they were put in circulation, nor had I any means of ascertaining. All I know is that they came to my hands fairly.

Other gentlemen, who condemn my rule of construing the Constitution, may find a satisfactory source from which to derive their power to pass this bill; if so, let them pass it. All I wish, is, that the principles on which I act may be understood.

CHAPTER X.

SENATORIAL CAREER—INDIAN TRIBES—EXECUTIVE PATRONAGE—EXPUNGING RESOLUTIONS.

THE condition of the Indian tribes was the principal subject which attracted Judge White's attention, and commanded his most earnest efforts. The history of this race has been one of curious and stirring interest to every reflecting mind, and must awaken sympathy in every feeling heart. Comparatively few years have passed, since they were sole masters of this glorious land, erecting their wigwams at pleasure, and ranging free and untrammelled throughout their vast hunting-grounds. By a rapid and singular, but sure process, those tribes which had occupied our extreme Northern territory were nearly wasted away, or quite exterminated, by the white man, in his lust for gain. Nor was the work to stop here. The same influences were beginning to be felt by our Southern and Western tribes. The heart of every philanthropist recoiled from the view of the future prospects of this miserable race; and a desire to preserve and elevate them gave rise at an early day to the benevolent design of colonizing them in the vast territory west of the Mississippi. The scheme was originated by that profound and organizing statesman, Thomas Jefferson, and had been pursued or attempted without much success by subsequent administrations. It was anew submitted to Congress in the session of 1829–'30, and after a most laborious examination and discussion was sanctioned by that body. Judge White was at that time chairman of the committee on Indian Affairs. Although he had in early life been engaged in warfare against them, and although he had looked with horror upon the scenes of their savage barbarity, he could not calmly witness their extinction.

His feelings were all enlisted in the measures for ameliorating their condition. His plans contemplated not merely their preservation from the utter annihilation which so evidently menaced them, but their instruction in the arts of civilization, and the communication to them of the saving influences of Christianity. When the bill providing for their colonization was brought before the Senate, though overborne by heavy domestic affliction, with his characteristic devotion to the interests of others, he rose superior to his private griefs, aroused all his energies, and poured forth his soul in a fervid plea for the appropriation to them of a permanent home. The measure was carried by that powerful effort, and probably no act of his life ever gave him more pleasure. His interest in the Indian was deep and abiding. Its fervor was undiminished to the last hour of his life. "Almost in my last interview with him," says the Rev. Dr. Foot, "he spoke with inimitable tenderness of their having been rescued from gradual extinction—of their prospect in the colony—of his expectation that civilization and Christianity would now prevail amongst them, and as he described the elevation to which he believed them destined to arrive, the tears fell from his eyes, and his whole countenance told his delight in anticipating their prosperity."

Feb. 22, 1830, Judge White, as chairman of the Committee on Indian Affairs, made a report upon the business in their charge, which we insert, as follows:

Everything which relates to those Indian tribes or nations with which we have political relations, *created* or *regulated* by treaties, is becoming, every year, more and more interesting; especially those relating to such as reside within any of the States of the Union, or of the territories belonging to it. The matters communicated by the President, in his message, relative to the Cherokees, are of the most delicate and interesting character, whether considered in relation to the United States, to the States of Georgia and Alabama, or to the Cherokee nation. The committee have employed themselves assiduously in their investigation, with an anxious wish to avail themselves of all the information within their reach, and desirous to recommend something to the Senate, which, if productive of no positive good, will at least have the merit of not farther embarrassing questions already sufficiently complicated.

With this nation, the United States have formed a number of treaties, commencing as early as the year 1785, and ending in the year 1819. At the formation of the first, the Indians occupied portions of territory within the chartered limits of the States of North Carolina, South Carolina, and Georgia. Since that period, North Carolina ceded a part of her territory, on which a portion of these Indians resided, to the United States; and that territory, *according to the terms of the deed of cession*, has been since formed into the State of Tennessee. South Carolina and

Georgia amicably settled the boundary between them; and by an agreement between the United States and Georgia, dated in the year 1802, the United States acquired the title to a portion of territory, out of which the State of Alabama, and the greater part of the State of Mississippi, have been since formed. And now, it so happens, that a part of the Cherokees still reside within the States of North Carolina and Georgia, according to their *present* boundaries, as well as within the limits of Tennessee and of Alabama. Latterly, Georgia, in the exercise, as she supposes, of her sovereign powers, has extended her laws over the whole of the State, and subjected the Indians to her jurisdiction. Meantime, the Cherokees have formed a civil government of their own, entirely independent of any State, claiming to have a right to do so in virtue of their original title to the lands on which they reside, and relying, likewise, upon the guarantee of their country, in several of their treaties formed with the United States. They have called upon the executive to make good this guarantee, by preventing the operation of the laws of either Georgia or Alabama, within those limits secured to them by the said treaties. To this application, the President has replied, that he has no power to check the operation of the laws of those States, within their respective limits; that the Constitution of the United States forbids the formation of any new State within the limits of an old one, without its consent; therefore, the Cherokees cannot be recognized as a separate State, within those limits where they now reside; and that, if they choose to remain *there*, they shall be protected in doing so, but that they must submit to the laws of the respective States, at the same time they are protected by them, and earnestly recommends to them to consent to exchange the territory where they now reside, for one west of the Mississippi, owned by the United States, and not yet included within the bounds of any State or territory, where they can be again united with that portion of their nation which has already emigrated, and where the United States can, and will, make them forever secure from any interruption from the whites, or from any other nation or people whatever.

To this proposition the Indians have given an absolute refusal, still insisting on a fulfillment of their treaty stipulations.

The laws of Georgia will commence their operation in the month of June next. It is easy to foresee the painful consequences which will probably follow, from laws operating over the same territory, at one and the same time, and flowing from jurisdictions or sovereigns, *independent* of each other.

The evil will not stop here; already we are advised that Mississippi has passed a law, incorporating her Indian population with her citizens; that Alabama has extended her laws over the Creek Indians within her limits; and, before long, we may anticipate that the like policy will be pursued by several other States.

From the information before the committee, no hope need be entertained that either of these States will change their policy, and repeal those laws; a period has arrived when the United States have a duty to perform, which must be discharged, in *good faith*, to the States concerned, to the Indians, and with a *sacred regard* to their own high character.

In the view which the committee have of this subject, they believe it would be unnecessary, if not improper, for them to offer any opinion upon the points in dispute between the contending parties, because there can be no reason to suppose any additional enactments by Congress are necessary to put it in the power of the executive to make good the *guaranties* contained in the treaties, if, in his judgment, they ought to have the construction for which the Cherokees insist, and his duty, according to the constitution, would authorize him to oppose the operation of the State laws.

In 1802, Congress passed an act to regulate trade and intercourse with the Indians, the provisions of which, connected with the treaties, are sufficiently broad to authorize the executive to give effect to every stipulation, which it is the duty of the United States to perform.

The failure to comply with the wishes of the Cherokees, as it appears to the committee, proceeded not from a defect in the law, but because in the opinion of the executive, *constitutional* objections exist, which it is not in the power of Congress to remove, by any law which they could enact.

The difficulties which have actually occurred, were foreseen some years since, and successive Administrations seem to have been anxiously endeavoring to avoid them; and the only remedy suggested by any, appears to have been, to provide a country west of the Mississippi, beyond the limits of any State or organized territory; to have it laid off and divided into as many districts as would accommodate *all the Indians* residing within any of the States or territories; to have those districts so described, by natural or artificial marks, that each could be known from every other; and then, by fair and peaceable means, to induce the Indians to exchange the lands *where they live*, for some of those thus described, and to emigrate. Suitable country, as is believed, has been procured, but, owing to some cause or other, the districts have not, as yet, been laid off, and properly described. Exchanges, however, to a considerable extent, have been made, and, consequent emigrations from various tribes have taken place. A portion of the Cherokees, equal, as is believed, to from one third to one half of the whole, has actually removed to, and settled in, a country well suited to their wants and wishes, west of the Mississippi. There is good reason to believe that many more would have removed before this time, except for various causes, which, as yet, the United States have not been able to overcome. The principal one is, the idea of a separate and independent State of their own, where they now live. This is the work, principally, of comparatively a few, who are either white men connected with the nations by marriage, or of those of mixed blood, born in the nation, who are well educated and intelligent, who have acquired considerable property, and, through the annuities paid by the United States, and by other means, are yearly adding to it. This class of people, it is believed, do not altogether equal one hundred in number. A very small portion of full-blooded Indians can be named, who are in the like circumstances, or who have much agency in their public affairs.

Those who are in public employ have an influence almost unbounded over the nation. They fill all the offices created by their laws, and have the entire management of the funds derived from every source. The rest of the nation may be divided into two classes. The one, owning some small property, and having settlements of their own, upon which they make a sufficiency to support themselves and their families, and but little surplus. Those of the other, comprehending, as is believed, the mass of the population, are as poor and degraded as can well be imagined. They may be said to live without hope of better circumstances; they have almost no property, and seem destitute of the means or prospect of acquiring any. There is very little game in their country. They are without industry, without information, unlettered, and subsisting chiefly upon what they can beg, and upon the birds and fish they can procure. A stranger who travels along a leading road through the nation, or makes but a short stay in it, will form a very erroneous opinion of the condition of the great mass of the population. He has intercourse only with those of the first or second class before mentioned, and forms his opinions of all, from the condition of those with whom he associates. It may then be asked, why do these people refuse to emigrate? The answer is, those who have influence over them use every means in their power to prevent them. They misrepresent the country offered, west of the Mississippi. They use persuasion while it answers the purpose, and threats, when persuasion is likely to fail. The committee are well satisfied, that every humane and benevolent individual, who is anxious for the welfare of the great body of the Cherokees, *and is correctly informed of their true condition*, must feel desirous for their removal, provided it can be effected with their *consent*.

Other strong inducements for this desire, must be found in the condition to which they are now brought, by the collision between them and the laws of the States in which they reside.

Although the committee, for the reasons before given, consider it unnecessary, if not improper, in them, to offer any opinion upon the validity of the conflicting claims of the parties; yet, it may not be without its use to call the attention of the Senate to some of the leading facts, and main points, upon which the controversy has depended, and must hereafter depend.

The title of the Cherokees must rest upon their original right of occupancy, and upon the treaties formed with the United States.

As to the first, "their title by occupancy," the answer would be, when the country was discovered, they were savages; and that this discovery, of itself, gave a right to form settlements, and to exclude all other civilized nations. That is conferred upon the nation of the discoverer and settler, the right to acquire the usufructuary interest which the natives had. It would be added, that, at a very early period, the Cherokees formed a treaty with Great Britain, by which they gave up their independence, and put themselves under the protection of his Britannic Majesty. That they took a part with the British Crown in the war of the Revolution. That the American arms were employed against them, and they conquered, when Independence was acknowledged, and the treaty of peace made with Great Britain. That this conquest conferred upon the respective *States*, within whose limits they were, all the rights, and gave them all the powers which the Crown had, *prior* to the Revolution. That this right still continued in the States, and never was yielded to the United States. That, in securing these rights, they severally exercised these powers, from the year 1776 up to the year 1785, in such manner, as, in their sovereign will, they believed to be wise and just, without any control from the United States.

That, although, in the Articles of Confederation, there is a power given to the United States to make treaties with Indians residing *out* of their limits, yet there is, in the ninth article, an express saving to *each State*, of all its legislative rights, *within its chartered limits.*

As to the second point, the political condition of the Indians, as established by treaties between them and the United States. The first and only treaty with the Cherokees, during the Articles of Confederation, was concluded in November, 1785.

By that treaty, a boundary is established, which allots to the Indians a great extent of country, within the acknowledged limits of both North Carolina and Georgia, and over which those States had actually legislated; had previously authorized by law the sales of land therein; a considerable quantity had in fact been sold to individuals, and the consideration money paid to the State.

Against this treaty both Georgia and North Carolina entered their *solemn protests*, it being, as they alleged, in violation of their *legislative rights.*

Not very long after this treaty, the Cherokees waged a war against the citizens of those States, which continued until some short time prior to the treaty of Holston, concluded in the year 1791.

This was the first treaty made with those Indians under the authority of the present Constitution of the United States, and by it a new boundary is agreed upon, by which the limits before allotted to the Indians are reduced to a smaller compass.

By the seventh article, "*the United States solemnly guarantee to the Cherokee nation all their lands not hereby ceded.*"

On the seventh day of February, 1792, an additional article to this last-mentioned treaty is agreed upon, by which an addition of five hundred dollars is made to the annuity stipulated in the former treaty.

In June, 1794, another treaty is made between the parties, by which the provisions of the treaty of 1791 are revived, an addition made to their annuity, and provision for running and marking the boundary line.

In October, 1798, an additional treaty is concluded, by which *former treaties are revived*, the boundary of Indian lands curtailed by another cession to the United States, for an additional compensation.

In October, 1804, another treaty is concluded, by which more land is ceded by the Indians, for a consideration agreed upon and specified in the treaty.

In October, 1805, two treaties are made, by which the Indians cede an additional quantity of land.

On the seventh day of January, 1806, another treaty is concluded, in which more land is ceded to the United States; and in September, 1807, an explanation is agreed upon of the boundary line intended in the treaty last mentioned.

On the twenty-second day of March, 1816, another treaty is concluded, by which the Indians relinquish their title to lands in South Carolina, for which the United States engage South Carolina will make payment; and on the same day another treaty is made, in which the Indians relinquish to the United States their claim to more lands, and agree to allow the use of the water courses in their remaining country, and also to permit roads to be made through the same.

On the fourteenth of September, 1816, another treaty is made, by which an additional quantity of land is ceded to the United States.

On the eighth day of July, 1817, another treaty is concluded, by which an exchange of lands is agreed on, and a plan for dividing the Cherokees settled: one part to remain east of the Mississippi; another to emigrate west of the Mississippi, to a country designated in the treaty; and those who might happen to fall within the territory ceded, to have *an election to become citizens of the United States*, and each head of an Indian family to have a reservation of six hundred and forty acres of land, to include his improvements.

And on the twenty-seventh of February, 1819, another treaty is concluded, intended to be in execution of the stipulations contained in that of 1817, in several particulars, and in which an additional tract of country is ceded to the United States.

These, as the committee believe, are all the treaties between the United States and the Cherokee nation on the *east side* of the Mississippi, and within the limits of any of the United States.

In several of them there are stipulations for *roads, the navigation of rivers, and the establishment of ferries, within the bounds reserved by the Cherokees to themselves*, and guaranteed to them by the United States.

In virtue of these treaties, the Cherokees contend they have a valid and complete title to the lands of which they are in possession; and that they have a right to establish such government, as, in their own opinion, is best suited to their condition; and that such government is *independent* of any of the States within the limits of which any portions of their territory may happen to be; and that the United States stand *solemnly pledged* to *protect* them in the *peaceable enjoyment* of it, against all the world.

On the other side, the States may admit, that, if the *political condition* of the Cherokees was to be considered, as it related to the *rights* and *powers* of the *United States only*, then it is true they are, and ought to be, a community *sovereign*, in all respects—those only excepted in which they had by the treaties expressly *surrendered* their independence; and still contend that Georgia was a sovereign and independent State, from the fourth day of July, 1776, a period *anterior* to the Union of the States, under either the Articles of Confederation, or of the present Constitution. That, as a sovereign State, she had a right to govern every human being within her limits, according to her own will, and to dispose of all the vacant lands, when, to whom, and for what consideration, she pleased. That she is still in the possession of all those rights and powers, excepting only such as she has expressly surrendered. That she never has surrendered to the United States, either by a treaty, or by any other means, the power to dispose of her vacant territory, or to authorize the establishment of a government within her limits, without her consent. So far from it, that the ninth article of the Confederation forbids any violation of her legislative rights, and expressly provides that no State shall be deprived of territory for the benefit of the United States; and that the third section of the fourth article of the Constitution expressly says: *No new State* shall be formed within the limits of one or more of the *old*, without their consent. And the tenth amendment of the Constitution declares, that even "private property shall not be taken for public use, without making just compensation." That, if private property cannot be taken *without compensation*, the conclusion is very strong, that it was not intended to give a power to take the property which belonged to a *sovereign State*, under any circumstances whatever. That she never did give her consent to this disposition of either her jurisdiction or of her territory; so far from it, she entered her *solemn protest* against the *first treaty* formed in the year 1785, as violative of her rights, and that no inference can be drawn, to her disadvantage, from her silence, or from anything she may have said in relation to any subsequent treaty; because in each of them a change was made, by which a portion of her territory and jurisdiction was restored to her, and thus her condition rendered better than it was under the treaty of 1785, against which she had protested.

She may further insist, that the second section of the second article of the Constitution, which gives to the President, with the advice and consent of two-thirds of the Senate, power to make treaties, has no application to Indians within the chartered limits of any of the States; nor the eighth section of the first article, which gives Congress power to regulate commerce with the Indian tribes. That if Indians can be treated with, it must be those only who reside *out* of *the limits* of the States, and those with whom commerce may be regulated must be similarly situated; otherwise, that part of the second section of the first article, which forbids the enumeration of Indians residing within the States, and "not taxed," will be without any appropriate meaning. That although the United States may have contracted *obligations* with the Cherokee nation, yet they had *previously* contracted those equally as *solemn* with *each of the States*. That in the fourth section of the fourth article of the Constitution, the following pledge is given: "The United States shall *solemnly guarantee to every State in this Union* a republican form of Government, and shall protect each of them against invasion, and, on application of the Legislature, or of the Executive (when the Legislature cannot be convened), against *domestic violence*."

She may ask, how can Georgia have a "republican form of government," co-extensive with her limits, unless a majority of her citizens are permitted to prescribe rules, to which *all must conform?* How will the United States have made good the "guarantee against *domestic violence*," if they permit a portion of the population *within her limits* to establish a government, contrary to her will, with authority to prescribe rules inconsistent with those prescribed by herself? She may add, that it was in the confidence that this "solemn guarantee" would be sacredly kept, that she consented to *give up* any portion of her sovereignty, and become a member of the Union.

In addition, she may urge, that in 1802, upwards of twenty-seven years ago, she made a contract with the United States, by which they became bound to purchase any claim which the Cherokee nation, or any other, might set up to lands within her limits, as soon as such purchase could be made upon reasonable terms. That, for this stipulation, she paid at the time a valuable consideration, in lands which she conveyed. That, after waiting thus long, and seeing for several years past, the prospect of a compliance on the part of the United States decreasing, she had determined to exert her own sovereign powers, over her *whole* territory, in such manner as she believes will be *just* to her whole population. That the object of this agreement was to obtain a benefit for herself, within her reserved limits, and that, if she should fail to receive the benefit she expected, she will take care not to suffer her condition to be made worse.

That she is yet sovereign, within her own limits, to every extent she was when she became a member of the Union, except so far as she expressly surrendered her sovereignty by the *terms* of the Constitution. That, although she is determined to use her power within her limits, yet she owes it to her own character so to exert it as most to promote the happiness of every rational being who may remain subject to her control, no matter what may be his color, or in what language he may make known his wants.

Alabama and Mississippi may say they were a part of the State of Georgia, up to the time of the compact and cession, in 1802, and that they have been erected upon parts of the territory then ceded to the United States; and that, with the exception of the difference, produced by not owning the soil within their limits, they are entitled to the benefit of every argument which Georgia could urge in this controversy.

Should these arguments, or any others, in favor of the States, have the effect of proving that the United States have not the *power* to comply with the stipulations contained in their treaties with the Cherokees, on account of *prior* and *superior* obligations which they had contracted, it could not, in the opinion of the committee, take anything from that character for integrity and good faith, to which they are so justly entitled. None could suspect that the obligation was contracted with a design to mislead or to deceive; and while the United States are both able and willing to make a full and adequate compensation for all that may be lost for want of a *specific performance* of their agreement, their faith is preserved as inviolate as it would be if *all their stipulations were specifically complied with.* Should the Indians continue determined to reside where they now are, and become subject to the laws of the respective States in which they reside, no difficulty can occur, as your committee see no reason to apprehend that either of the States have it in contemplation to force them to abandon the country in which they dwell; but, if they determine to remain, and continue to insist on a separate and independent government, and refuse obedience to the laws of the States, the consequences which must inevitably ensue, are such as the humane and benevolent cannot reflect upon without feelings of the deepest sorrow and distress.

If, on the contrary, they should consent to exchange their present places of residence for a country west of the Mississippi, it is in the power of the United States to furnish one suited, as the committee believe, to their wants and condition, where they can be secured against the intrusion of any other people; where, under the protection of the United States, and with their *aid*, they can pursue their plan of civilization, and, ere long, be in the peaceable enjoyment of a civil government of their own choice, and where Christian and philanthropist can have ample scope for their labors of love and benevolence.

Your committee are of opinion, that ample means should be placed, by Congress, in the power of the President of the United States, to authorize and enable him to have the country west of the Mississippi, out of the limits of all the States, laid off into as many districts as may be deemed necessary for the residence of the Indians, now within the respective States, with which the United States have treaties; to have those districts accurately described; and also, to make exchanges and purchases with such tribes, or parts of them, as may choose to remove; to give aid in the removal, and to contribute, for a season, to their support, at their new places of residence. For which purposes, the committee ask leave to report a bill.

A BILL

To provide for an exchange of lands with the Indians residing in any of the States or Territories, and for their removal west of the river Mississippi.

Be it enacted by the Senate and House of Representatives of the United States of America in Congress assembled, That it shall and may be lawful for the President of the United States, to cause so much of any territory belonging to the United States, west of the river Mississippi, not included in any State, and to which the Indian title has been extinguished, as he may judge necessary, to be divided into a suitable number of districts for the reception of such tribes or nations of Indians as may choose to exchange the lands where they now reside, and remove there, and to cause each of said districts to be so described by natural or artificial marks, as to be easily distinguished from every other.

SEC. 2. *And be it further enacted*, That it shall and may be lawful for the President to exchange any or all of such districts, so to be laid off and described, with any tribe or nation of Indians now residing within the limits of any of the States or territories, and with which the United States have existing treaties, for the whole, or any part or portion of the territory claimed and occupied by such tribe or nation, within the bounds of any one, or more, of the States or territories.

SEC. 3. *And be it further enacted*, That, in the making of any such exchange, or exchanges, it shall and may be lawful for the President solemnly to assure the tribe or nation with which the exchange is made, that the United States will forever secure and guarantee to them, and their heirs or successors, the country so exchanged with them, and that, if they prefer it, the United States will cause a patent or grant to be made and executed to them for the same: *Provided always*, That such lands shall revert to the United States, if the Indians become extinct, or abandon the same.

Sec. 4. *And be it further enacted*, That if, upon any of the lands now occupied by the Indians, and to be exchanged for, there should be such improvements as add value to the land claimed by any individual or individuals of such tribes or nations, it shall and may be lawful for the President to cause such value to be ascertained, by appraisement or otherwise, and to cause such ascertained value to be paid to the person or persons claiming such improvements.

Sec. 5. *And be it further enacted*, That, upon the making of any such exchange as is contemplated by this act, it shall and may be lawful for the President to cause such aid and assistance to be furnished to the emigrants, as may be necessary and proper to enable them to remove to, and settle in, the country for which they may have exchanged; and also, to give them such aid and assistance as may be necessary for their support and subsistence for the first year after their removal.

Sec. 6. *And be it further enacted*, That it shall and may be lawful for the President to cause such tribe or nation to be protected, at their new residence, against all interruption or disturbance from any other tribe or nation of Indians, or from any other person or persons whatever.

Sec. 7. *And be it further enacted*, That it shall and may be lawful for the President to have the same superintendence and care over any tribe or nation in the country to which they may remove, as contemplated by this act, that he is now authorized to have over them at their present places of residence.

Sec. 8. *And be it further enacted*, That for the purpose of giving effect to the provisions of this act, the sum of   dollars is hereby appropriated, to be paid out of any money in the Treasury, not otherwise appropriated.

Still continuing to take his accustomed interest in the concerns of the Indians, Judge White, in relation to the so-called "Cherokee Memorial," presented by Mr. Clay, spoke as follows, Feb. 4th, 1835;

In presenting the memorial and resolutions, the Hon. Senator has gone into a discussion of the powers of the States, and the manner in which those powers have been exerted over the Indians.

I do not believe any benefit is likely to result to the people of the United States, or to the Indians, from such discussions; but as the subject has been introduced, it is due to the States, that, at least, some of the grounds upon which they have acted, should be brought to the notice of the Senate.

What was the condition of the Indians, *within the limits of the States* at the close of the revolutionary war?

The people of the United States declared their independence, and the revolutionary war in maintenance of that declaration, terminated in a treaty of peace in 1783. The limits and bounds of the States are described in that treaty. Each of the States, within its territorial limits, believed it was free, sovereign, and independent, and that a majority had a right to prescribe whatever rules they pleased for the government of every person, of every age, sex, and color, within their acknowledged boundaries.

Each of these States believe they still possess all these powers, except so far as they have *expressly* granted to the Federal Government, for the good of the whole.

The articles of confederation gave to the Federal government power to regulate trade and intercourse with the Indians, but contain an express proviso that Congress shall not interfere with the territorial rights of the States.

The first treaty with the Cherokees was made in 1785, and although the articles referred to were then in force, the lands allotted to the Indians included a large portion of the *territory* of North Carolina.

That State was not inattentive to her rights. She had an agent present when the treaty was negotiated, and he there entered the solemn protest of his State, more than once, against this exercise of federal power. These protests are still on record, and can yet be produced at any time the Senate may desire.

The next treaty with the Cherokees was after the present constitution was adopted.

In the mean time, North Carolina had been urged to cede her western lands to the United States, and one motive for this was, that the United States would be the better enabled to regulate her affairs with the Cherokees, it being then believed, they all, or nearly all, lived on these lands.

In 1789, North Carolina, yielding to these solicitations, made the cession.

The vacant lands, after satisfying all existing claims against North Carolina, were the property of the United States, who also had the sole power of legislation. The United States thus *owning* the vacant soil, and having the *entire sovereignty and jurisdiction*, and still believing the Cherokees resident upon this territory, made the treaty of Holston in 1791.

After arguing upon the boundary between the Whites and the Indians, there is one express guarantee to the Indians of their lands. This, if my memory serves me, is the *first* guarantee to these Indians. This guarantee was inserted not by the mere motion of our Commissioner, but by the express instructions of President Washington. The reason of this is obvious to me. General Washington believed, at that day, the country guaranteed to the Indians was a tract over which the United States alone had the sovereignty and jurisdiction, and that they were the owners of the soil; that neither the sovereign nor territorial rights of any State were invaded by such a stipulation, and that it would be the means of preventing future encroachments upon the Indians.

We now know by our own executive journal, kept secret until a few years past, that when the first agreements with the Indians were made, after the adoption of the constitution, the President himself doubted whether they ought to go through the forms prescribed for treaties; he sent a message to the Senate; it doubted, but eventually seemed to have acted upon the opinion, that the formal sanction of two-thirds of the Senators present, required to ratify treaties, would be a safe rule, as to these compacts or agreements, which course has been pursued ever since.

A further illustration of General Washington's views as to the rights of States, may be given by his conduct in relation to lands within the limits of New York, which were attempted to be secured to Indians by treaty. He condemned this course on the part of the agent, and made it the subject of a special letter on record.

The tract of country, ceded by North Carolina to the United States, in 1789, and which was a territory in 1791, when the Holston treaty was made, continued to be a territory till February, 1796, when the residents framed the constitution, and afterwards were admitted into the Union.

In the treaties with Cherokees, subsequent to that period (and there were many of them, as has been correctly said by the honorable senator from Kentucky) the United States seemed te have lost sight of the distinction between their powers over a country, of which they had both the right of *soil* and *jurisdiction*, and one where the *States* had the right of soil and jurisdiction, and to have continued the guarantee as inserted in the treaty of 1791.

The States, however, do not acquiesce in this exercise of federal power. The same opinion entertained by North Carolina, in 1785, is adhered to now. They maintain that they are sovereign and independent communities, within the whole of their chartered limits, upon all points, where they have not transferred their powers to the federal government.

They maintain that these agreements with a portion of their own population are not treaties, within the meaning of the Constitution; and they deny that they have ever vested in the federal government the power by treaty, or otherwise, with any portion of the people within their limits, no matter whether French, German, or Indians, to take from the State one acre of its territory, and transfer it to any other people whatever.

They maintain that each State has the right, independently of the federal and all other governments, to enact such laws for the government of their whole population, as, in the wisdom of their own legislatures, may seem best suited to the interest of all; and that in the exercise of this power, none, out of their limits, has the right to interfere.

If the States are right in the operation of these powers, it must clearly follow that they alone have the power to judge whether their laws are adapted to the condition and wants of the people.

Whether the States are correct in the assertion and maintenance of these rights and powers or not, they think they are, and many others think with them. They have acted upon them, and will continue to do so, as I firmly believe. Georgia has extended her laws over the whole limits. Tennessee has, to some purposes, done the same thing, and so have North Carolina and Alabama.

How, then, are these States to be induced to rescind or repeal those laws? Suppose the United States apply to them for the repeal; they will answer, their laws are approved by their people, they had the power to enact them, and they will not repeal them. What then? Are the United States to apply force to compel the repeal? If they do, and such force is met by an opposing force from the States, we then have presented to our view the most horrid of all spectacles. Armed strife between brothers, and in the midst of it, what becomes of the Red men for whose rights this war is waged? They are swept from this state of existence. When the war terminates, there will be no Indians to be protected by the United States, or by those States individually.

The time has arrived when we must all speak out plainly as we think. These people, if they remain where they are, must submit to the laws of the respective States. They cannot exist in the States as a separate and distinct community, governed by their own customs and laws. Some of them are civilized and enlightened; they will make useful and respectable members of the community. They may still remain where they are if they choose. But this is not the condition of the mass of the Indian population. They are poor, ignorant, and uninformed.

Residing where they now do, certain misery and ruin await them. If they will remove beyond the Mississippi, out of our States and organized territories, they may be preserved. Then they may progress in that civilization which has commenced; they can, as freemen, have a government of their own choice; their interests can be promoted, and their rights protected, by the United States, without collision with any State. Who now doubts that it is their interest to do so? Few men can doubt it, who will take pains to acquire correct information, and then duly consider the subject. I believe the time has nearly arrived, and will certainly soon have arrived, when there will be but one opinion upon this subject throughout the country.

The policy of inducing our Indians to remove west of the Mississippi, did not originate with this administration. As early, at all events, as 1804, it was the policy of Mr. Jefferson. It has been the policy of every succeeding administration; and during the last administration, it had, in the then Secretary of War, one of its ablest advocates. The great distinction between this and prior administrations consists in the present having succeeded to a much greater extent in carrying into effect, what all, from the time of Mr. Jefferson, desired to accomplish.

The honorable Senator from Kentucky thinks, as the State of Georgia has shut her courts against those people, we ought to open those of the United States to them. And if we can, let me ask, Mr. President, of what practical benefit will such a provision be? Useless. Encourage a poor Indian, living surrounded by Whites, unfriendly to him, to commence suit in the federal circuit court, and then follow it here to the Supreme court, to assert his title to 160 or to 640 acres of land, and by the time the cause is decided, he and his family will starve to death.

Instead of this, let us encourage them by all the means in our power, to remove. Every day they remain, the means of the United States to furnish them comfortable homes west of the Mississippi, are lessening. Other tribes are going and getting their choice of the country. Let these be encouraged to remove speedily; provide funds for their removal, for their comfortable support for a season. Furnish them a permanent home; guarantee it by all the solemnities which can be deemed necessary, and then faithfully observe this guarantee. Upon these points, if additional legislation is found to be proper, I am willing to go to any extent which may be deemed necessary, and which is not inconsistent with what is due to the interests of the great body of our community.

In a letter to J. A. Whiteside, Esq., dated Sept. 17, 1835, Judge White furnishes a valuable statement of his views on the Indian question. In a portion of that letter he says:

I most heartily approve the policy of the present Administration in removing the Indians settled within the States and territories, to the western side of the Mississippi; and then settling them beyond the limits of any State or organized territory, and have given such aid as was in my power to effect that object.

During the session of 1829–30, the plan was submitted to Congress, and after a most laborious examination and discussion, was sanctioned by that body. In that examination and discussion, it was my lot to take no inconsiderable part, and at that day, those with whom I was associated were pleased to think my exertions were of no inconsiderable value. Public opinion was much divided; it has now settled down in an approval of the plan then adopted. Many treaties have been formed with the various tribes of Indians, and numbers of them have been actually removed. Those residing east of the Mississippi, to wit: the Chickasaws, Choctaws, Creeks, Cherokees, and Seminole Indians, were the hardest to convince that their interest would be promoted by a removal. All of these, except the Cherokees, have at length become convinced, ceded their country, and have either actually removed, or agreed to do so. The Cherokees yet remain, and parts of their country are in Tennessee, N. Carolina, Georgia, and Alabama. To each of these States, it is a matter of peculiar interest that their claim should be extinguished, and they removed. In repeated instances, the United States have made treaties with the Cherokees from the year 1785 up to the year 1819, and solemnly bound themselves to guarantee to them the country where they now reside. As early as the year 1802, the United States made a compact with the State of Georgia, in which they bound themselves for a valuable consideration to extinguish the Indian tribe within her limits, so soon as it could be done on reasonable terms. On the one hand, Georgia has been pressing for a compliance with this stipulation; on the other, the Cherokees have been urging a compliance with the guarantee contained in the treaties. These inconsistent obligations have occasioned much embarrassment. I have mentioned the doctrine, that if no other government were concerned but the United States, they were bound to make good their treaty stipulations, by securing to the Indians the enjoyment of the country guarantied; but that Georgia was completely sovereign and independent within her own acknowledged limits, except so far as she had *expressly* surrendered her sovereignty to the United States; that she never had granted the power to the Federal government, by treaty or otherwise, to dispose of any portion of her territory; and therefore these guarantees to the Indians could not be complied with specifically, but must be compensated by paying to the Indians the full value of their country whenever the state chose to assert her rights within her own limits.

This subject I had occasion to discuss at length, in the early part of the year 1830, and have maintained this doctrine, at all times, and in all places, when it was spoken of in my presence, from that day to this.

On all occasions I have used every *fair* means in my power to produce a disposition on the part of the Indians, to sell out their claim to the United States, and remove, and he who asserts to the contrary does himself great injustice, because he asserts that which is untrue.

By those who have latterly been disposed to find fault, it has been alleged, that winter before last, the United States negotiated a treaty with the Cherokees, which, if ratified by the Senate, would have put this question at rest, and that I was opposed to its ratification.

It is true, at the time mentioned, Andrew Ross, James Starr, and some others, came on to Washington, and there made what was called a treaty; and it is also true, that instrument was submitted to the Senate for ratification, and that the whole committee, of which I was *one* member, reported against its ratification, on the ground that it was not a treaty.

A treaty is a contract or agreement between two or more nations or countries. To give it any validity, it must have the assent of *both* parties. This instrument, if ratified, was intended to bind the United States on one part, and the Cherokee Indians on the other.

Andrew Ross and his party were not *chiefs* of the nation; they did not pretend to represent the nation; they were not authorized by the nation to make the treaty, *nor did they pretend they had any such authority;* and there was a *protest signed*, or pretended to be signed, by almost the *whole nation*, against *any attempt of theirs to make a treaty.*

Under these circumstances, I could find no principle or precedent which would justify me in calling that a treaty, which not only had not the assent of the Indians, but was made against their express wishes; therefore I held myself bound not to recommend its ratification. I sought information from the Secretary of War and others, and could find no one man who could furnish me with either principle or precedent for a course different from that which I pursued. It will be recollected, that during a prior administration, by some inadvertence, a treaty had been made and ratified with the Creek Indians, which, upon examination, was found to be *without authority from the Indians*, and what were the consequences? A civil war; the principal Indian negotiators put to death, and the treaty annulled by the President and Senate.

With a full knowledge of all this, I could not recommend the ratification of this instrument *as a treaty*, when, in my best judgment, it wanted the *essential requisites* to make it binding upon the parties.

It has also been objected to me, that during the same winter, I introduced and urged the Senate to adopt a resolution, requesting the President to negotiate with the State of Georgia, for a *portion of her territory for the Cherokees.* It is true, such a resolution was recommended by the unanimous consent of the Committee on Indian Affairs, of which I was chairman, and the Senate did not adopt it. I was induced to give my support to that resolution for the following reasons:—Georgia had extended her laws over the Indians. She had parcelled out among her citizens the Indian territory, *reserving to the Indians the tracts of land upon which they actually resided.* Ross and the other chiefs petitioned Congress to make good the guaranties contained in the treaties. Georgia was pressing to have the Indian title extinguished according to the compact, and one of the senators had introduced a bill, the first section of which provided that the United States should *purchase out from the Indians* those settlements which had been *reserved* by the Georgian laws, if they were willing to sell; and the second section provided, if the Indians would *not* sell, that then the United States should purchase out from the *individual citizens* their *jus simplex* in those reservations, and vest the same in the Indian occupants.

These various matters were all before the committee at the same time, and in addition to this, Ross and his party communicated to the committee a wish, if nothing more could be done, that the Federal Government should endeavour to procure from Georgia a small portion of her territory, upon which the Indians might reside a *few years*, until they could be *better qualified for the civil government* of the State of Georgia, and alleged that some influential men in Georgia had assured them that the State would be willing to make such an arrangement, and if she would not when applied to by the Federal Government, that then the Indians would sell out their whole country and remove.

In this state of things, and under these circumstances, I gave my sanction to the resolutions, without much expectation that Georgia would yield to the wishes of the Indians; but with a settled conviction that if Georgia *refused, that then the Indians could have no pretext for longer delaying a treaty;* and I yet believe, if the Senate had adopted the resolution, and Georgia had refused, that before this time we should have had a treaty with the Cherokees. In this I may be mistaken, therefore find no fault with that part of the Senate who thought differently.

During the last session of Congress, there were two parties of Cherokees in Washington, the one headed by John Ross, and supposed to represent the whole of the Cherokees, the other by Ridge, and said to represent a small portion only. Memorials from both these parties had been presented to the Senate, the first, praying Congress to make good their treaty stipulations, and the last, praying provision to be made for their removal west of the Mississippi. These memorials were referred to the committee, of which I was chairman. Near the close of the session, I was informed by the Secretary of War that the executive had been negotiating with Ross and his party for the extinguishment of their title to the whole country now occupied by them, and that they had disagreed as to the price to be given, and that Ross had proposed to accept any sum which the Senate would say was reasonable, and therefore it was wished the Senate should give its advice as to the price.

The difficulty at once presented itself, what mode could be adopted to bring the subject before the Senate, so as to enable that body to express its opinion. I took the liberty of suggesting that the President ought to send a confidential message, asking the advice of the Senate, and then, without doubt, it would be given, as this had been the course pursued by President Washington and the Senate, prior to the treaty of 1791, with this same nation of Indians. The Secretary afterwards informed me he had conferred with the President, who declined sending any message asking advice from the Senate, and thus it appeared the negotiation must fall through, as at that time no other regular mode of bringing the subject before that body occurred to me, or was suggested by any other person. Much solicitude was felt by several members with whom I conversed, as well as by myself, that the opportunity of settling amicably a controversy which had occasioned much trouble often, and serious apprehensions, should be lost, and in reflecting upon the subject, a mode of bringing the matter before the Senate presented itself to my mind, which was satisfactory. I stated it to the committee; they concurred in it; we brought the case before the Senate, and it aided in the adoption of a resolution which you have seen published.

Any statement or suggestion which has been made, that either publicly or privately I have said or done anything since being a member of the Senate, with a view, in any respect, to delay or defeat a treaty with the Cherokees, is entirely erroneous; my best exertions have, at all times, been used to effect that object, and when the resolution, just alluded to, was adopted, I felt that my task was finished, and that a treaty would be the immediate consequence. If it fails, the fault ought not to be placed to my account.

In 1826, soon after his entrance into political life, Judge White, in common with the whole party of which Gen. Jackson became the head, and in conformity to the declarations of that leader, was an avowed enemy to the existing system of executive patronage, and the class of measures naturally resulting from it. In 1833, upon the receipt of Mr. Calhoun's report (from the select committee appointed at his instance) to inquire into the extent and operation of the constantly increasing patronage of the executive of the United States, Judge White spoke in support of this bill, although by so doing he incurred much displeasure from his friends of the party in power. He avowed the same principles that he had avowed before, in 1826, and afterwards in 1830. He was consistent in action and in speech; but his friends of the Democratic host, who were now using for their own purposes the machinery whose use had afforded them so fine a subject for invective when in the hands of their opponents, could not patiently listen to a speech which, while it was strictly and entirely a repeated statement and a support of Judge White's own views, was indirectly though clearly a thorough exhibition of their own inconsistency. Judge White's remarks on this subject are of lasting interest; and that not the least at the present day. We subjoin the essential portions of this forcible and valuable speech. February 16th, 1835, Mr. White said:

Mr. President: It was my fortune to be placed on the committee of nine, in the year 1826, whose proceedings have been spoken of in this debate. I am one of the committee who concurred in reporting the bill said to be similar to the one under consideration. I am now as ready to carry out the opinions then entertained as I was at that time, unless it can be shown that Congress has no power to make the enactments, or that they would be injurious to society.

The number of officers employed in handling public money was necessarily very much increased during the war which terminated in 1814–15. Although the President had the power to remove all the officers mentioned in this bill, yet it was believed, in the year 1820, it had not been exercised as frequently as the public interest required; officers who had collected money which they ought to have paid into the treasury, and officers who drew money out of the treasury, which it was their duty to disburse according to the requirement of acts of Congress, had in many instances failed in the performance of their duty; losses had been sustained, and more were feared, unless additional provisions were made; these circumstances gave rise to the act of 1820.

By this statute, at the end of every four years each of these officers is to be out of office as a matter of course, without the exercise of any executive power whatever; and during four years, the President, if he chooses to do so, has the power of removing all or any of them from office. In carrying into effect the provisions of this act, it was expected that when the term of an officer expired, the President would inform himself through the proper department, whether the officer had discharged his duty with fidelity; and if he was informed he had, that he would then renominate him for the same office for another term. I believe that the benefits expected from this law have been realized by the practice under it. Ever since I have had the honor of a seat on this floor, I affirm that, both under the past and the present Administration, I have witnessed the strictest scrutiny into the conduct of these officers, whenever renominated; and I do not remember a single case in which there was a disposition manifested to continue any one of them who had been faithless in his trust. But in 1826, the committee believed, that although much good had resulted from this law, yet, in the struggles for place and for power between parties, very great evils which had not been foreseen, would in all probability be experienced. The whole of these officers, amounting to a vast number, all going out at the end of each four years, and being entirely dependent upon the will of the President, for the renewal of their commissions, many of them would be induced to look more to their own situation and interest than to the welfare of the country; and, with a view to secure themselves, they would be most likely to conform their opinions to the wishes of the President, whoever he might happen to be. If he was a candidate for re-election himself, they would most likely vote for him; or if one of his friends was a candidate, they would vote for him, although they might not conscientiously believe the best interests of the country would be promoted by the interests of his opponent. It is no answer to this argument to say it casts reproach upon these officers to suppose they would surrender their opinions to those in power. Mr. President, is it a reproach to say they are men? Is it a stigma upon their character to say that while they live in this world, that while they have families to provide for, they must have the means of living? We all know that we are too apt to conclude that our neighbors will be pretty well provided for when we are very well provided for ourselves. Experience convinces us that when a man who is dependent on his own exertions for a living, obtains one of these offices, he and his family manage well if they keep their expenditures within their salary. They become dependent upon the quarter's salary for food and clothing. If deprived of the office, the man knows not what to turn his hand to, to earn a dollar to subsist upon. To be deprived of the office is to be deprived of the only means of obtaining a livelihood by honest means. Under such circumstances, it is most likely the officer will not give his judgment fair play; he will conform his opinions to the opinion of the man who has his all in his power; or if he has manliness enough to form an impartial opinion of the merits of the respective candidates, he will too seldom have the fortitude to express it, either in conversation or by his vote. The probability is that he will soon lose all that manly independence so essential to the preservation of a free government.

But, Mr. President, this evil does not stop with the head of the family; the same tone of servile feeling is communicated to his whole family. It stops not with his wife and his children; it is communicated to his family connections. They know the situation of the officer; he and they talk it over in their family circle; they sympathize with him and all know the feelings of the executive will be the more kind towards him in proportion to his influence among his friends; and the result will be that in most cases they will all settle down in the conviction that it is most wise to think and vote as the President wishes. Very little reflection, I think, must satisfy us of the alarming extent of this influence in our elections. All district attorneys, all custom-house officers, all paymasters, all receivers of public moneys at your land offices, and all surveyors of your public lands, with their clerks, and all their family connections, placed in a situation to do as the President of the United States may wish; add to this the further consideration that these men, from their official stations, each has vastly more influence among his acquaintances than he would have if he were a private man. Society, from the very situation of the officer, will suppose him a better judge of the fitness of a man for the presidential chair than he would be if he were a private man: besides that, many will know that the officer will have it in his power to do them good turns in his office if they can secure his good opinion.

Now, let us suppose a President in office, possessed of the mass of influence thus collected, wishing to be elected for a second term, when it was the interest of society to leave him out and put some other person in: or let us suppose a President in for the last time, and wishing to designate some individual as his successor, who would not be the choice of a majority, if left free to act according to their unbiased judgment. What then would most probably happen? We might some time find that the President would not, in such a case, be contented with all these people simply thinking with him and voting with him; they must do more on pain of not being renominated; they must each man do his best to influence as many to think, to speak, and to act with them, as they can procure. Where could you find a man able to make a stand in opposition to this demand? Nowhere; and you would seldom find one willing to make the experiment. Every one must believe he would have no chance of success against such fearful odds. These officers and their friends would act in concert from one end of the Union to the other. They will have it in their power to pour out at once through the whole body politic, a flood that would sweep from the purest man that lives, every particle of reputation he had acquired by a long life of virtue and usefulness. In 1826, as one member of the committee, I came to the conclusion that it was dangerous to leave such a power in the hands of the executive, and through our chairman expressed that opinion to the world. I entertain the same opinion now, and am prepared to re-affirm, and to act upon it. Then I was in opposition to the Administration; now, I am a friend to the Administration. This can make no change in my course. When we have a pure and virtuous man for our Chief Magistrate he will thank Congress to take from him every discretionary power which it can take with propriety. It will ease him of a labor and responsibility most unpleasant to a good man, and he will still have as many discretionary powers as he will know how to exercise for the public good. If ever it should be our misfortune to have one of an opposite character, disposed to use all his powers for the benefit of himself and his friends, and for the purpose of perpetuating power in his and their hands, then society at large ought to thank us for stripping the executive of this influence.

My opinions upon this subject are not founded upon the petty consideration of who is in power, whether he is a political friend or a political opponent; they rest upon the eternal principles of what I think is right and wrong between those who are in and those who are out of power. They are founded upon principle deep as the foundations of government itself; upon principles the disregard of which will poison the very fountain from which all the blessings of our free and happy government flow. The elective franchise—corrupt that; place our citizens in such a situation that they will not freely form opinions for themselves and fearlessly act upon them; and we shall have little left worth preserving.

When called on to act my part, it is matter not to be considered by me, whether my friends are in or out. In 1826, when called on for an opinion, my friends and myself were at the bottom of the political wheel. I then entertained and expressed an opinion. Now it has turned; my friends and myself are at the top; our opponents are at the bottom; where we may be with the next whirl, no man can tell. As wise men, what ought we to do? We ought to act justly to all men, honestly carry out our own old opinions, and secure the people, as far as we can, in the free, uninfluenced exercise of their own opinions at elections. My principles are to limit power, if we can, so as to make every man secure in voting for whom he pleases, as he is in matters of religion; in worshipping his Maker according to the dictates of his own conscience. When power is so limited that no man can so use it as to injure his opponents, then, and then only, do I consider myself safe.

The question recurs, how can Congress secure the citizen in office against an arbitrary exercise of this power, in cases where the public good does not require it? The committee have attempted to give this security by providing that whenever a nomination is made to the Senate to fill a vacancy occasioned by a removal, the President shall state the reasons for such removal. This it has been contended Congress has no power to do, because all executive power is vested in the President by the Constitution, and removal from office is an exercise of executive power.

The arguments upon this point are far from being satisfactory to my mind, and I must crave the indulgence of the Senate while I present as briefly as possible my own views upon it.

Is any gentleman prepared to state it as his opinion that under our form of government, executive power is unlimited and undefined? I hold no such doctrine; and it would appear to me a most wild and mis chievous opinion.

The executive power, in our government, in the President, is that vested in him by express grants in the Constitution, or by acts of Congress passed in pursuance of the Constitution, and no more. By the Constitution, "all legislative power herein granted is vested in Congress." By the same instrument the executive power is vested in a President. In this latter clause, the words "herein granted," used in the former are dropped. The reason for dropping them is to my mind very obvious. If they had been used as to the President, he would have but a small portion of the powers necessary to be vested in him to enable him to carry on the affairs of the government. The framers of that instrument foresaw that he must have many more powers than they could specify in the Constitution, and therefore they say the executive power shall be vested in a President, intending that he should have and exercise all the power they themselves afterwards might vest in him, and also all others which Congress might from time to time vest in him by laws passed in pursuance of the Constitution. And afterwards they sum up his duties by saying that he shall see that the laws are faithfully executed.

Under these several clauses the executive powers are easily ascertained. We first look into the Constitution, and there see what powers are expressly given to him. Next we look at the acts of Congress, and there find what powers Congress has invested him with; and thus we ascertain his whole powers, and then we see that his duties are to see that all these powers are faithfully executed. Whatever powers are vested by the Constitution, Congress has no power to change: whatever powers they vest by statute, they may change and modify at pleasure. Any other notion of executive powers vested in the President, it seems to me, cannot be maintained under our frame of government. By the Constitution two classes of officers are evidently intended. One of these, Congress is bound to create; and when created, the tenure of their office is fixed by the Constitution, and can never be changed by act of Congress. As relates to the other class, Congress may create the office or not, as they please. In creating it, they may fix the tenure as they please; for life, for years, or at will; they prescribe what duties they please, and fix the compensation to suit their own pleasure; and they may point out the mode in which the officer is to be removed or displaced.

Ours is emphatically a government of laws. We are a free people because it is so. Whenever the will of the people is expressed, either in the Constitution or in a law passed in pursuance thereof, it must be complied with, because, according to the theory of our government, the people are sovereign. No person doubts, or can doubt, the power of the President to remove in such cases; but the manner in which he acquires this power is a different question. Gentlemen who argue against this section say, he has it from the Constitution, because it is an executive power. I deny this, and say it is an executive power because it is made so by statute, and he performs a constitutional duty when he removes, because he is as much bound to perform executive duties pointed out by statute as he is to perform those specified by the Constitution. It is an executive power, because it was the will of the people, through Congress, as their agent, to make it so; and the same power, through the same agent, could have made it a judicial duty, if it had been deemed wise so to provide.

Mr. President, these are the principles upon which I was prepared to act in 1826. They are those upon which I wished to bring into power the present Chief Magistrate. I speak only for myself; but I believed they were the principles of the party with which I acted, and that we were to give effect to those principles, so far as we might have the power. For one, I have seen no sufficient reason to change them, and am prepared to act them out. It is in vain to tell me that this is a party question. It is a question of fundamental principles, and I am on that side of it in which I have been educated, on which I have heretofore acted, as well as my humble abilities have enabled me; it is one I cannot abandon for any earthly consideration, because in its maintenance I believe the prosperity, happiness and security of the present and succeeding generations have a deep and abiding interest. It is asked by the opponents of this bill, what benefit its friends expect from a statement of the reasons of the removal when the nomination of a successor is presented to the Senate? I answer for myself, I wish to cut up by the roots the demoralizing tendencies of office-hunting. I wish to make such provisions by law as will shield the Chief Magistrate from impositions practised upon him to induce him to remove men from office. I wish to shield him from being imposed upon as to the character of those who apply for office. As the law now stands, whenever a man may take a fancy to an office filled by his neighbor, all he has to do is to poison the mind of the executive against the incumbent, and to make a favorable impression as to the fitness of him who desires to be the successor. These objects can be accomplished by making characters in secret upon paper. Before the officer is aware of it, his reputation is blasted by secret and confidential communications made by some of those he had esteemed his friends; they are lodged with the executive, where it is expected they will remain secret; and upon the strength of these representations the officer is removed. When this is accomplished, the scuffle commences for a successor, and paper characters are procured for perhaps half a dozen applicants; and very frequently, the individual having, in point of fact, the worst character of any in the group is so dressed up and supported by certificates as to convince the executive that the public interest will be promoted by selecting him as the successor, and he is nominated to the Senate. The business does not end here. All the disappointed applicants then go to work with senators to defeat a confirmation of the nomination, each hoping that if that is done, he stands next best with the executive, and will secure the office.

Under the present state of things, society will become demoralized; men will be constantly coveting that possessed by their neighbors; and for the sake of procuring what they covet, they will themselves bear, and will procure others to bear false witness. Under the laws, as they now stand, the business of office-hunting will become a science. Men will be selected and furnished with funds to defray the expense of coming to Washington, for the purpose of having one set turned out and another set put in, by means of artful tales, secretly gotten up and reduced to writing, which, it is supposed, will never see the light. This officer and representative of office-hunters will come on with one pocket full of bad characters with which to turn out incumbents, and the other full of good characters with which to provide for his constituents.

Pass this bill, and a wholesome check will be given to this whole system. Require the reasons for removal to be stated, and no man will dare to make a statement which he does not believe to be true, because exposure and disgrace will certainly be the consequence. You will take out of the hand of the cowardly assassin, the poisoned dagger heretofore used in the dark. You will shield the executive from mistakes founded on false representations. No executive can be personally acquainted with the characters of all men in office, nor with the characters of all those who desire office; he must act upon information derived from others; he ought, and I feel persuaded the present Chief Magistrate will, thank Congress for any plan by which he may be the better enabled to discharge his official duties to the enhancement of the welfare of society.

Another advantage to be derived from this bill is, that it will check the thirst for office, and restore harmony to society. When a man is removed for want of capacity, for want of integrity, for intemperance, or for lack of business habits, why not put down the reason? Who is harmed by it? Nobody. Now a man's reputation is stabbed in the dark; by whom, or in what manner, he is unable to find out. Pass this bill, and if a man is injured, he will know by whom, and in what manner; and can wipe out the stain, not by a controversy with the President, but by a controversy with the man whose falsehoods mislead the President.

Again; we shall in all time to come secure honest officers in the enjoyment of honest political opinions. No President will ever remove an officer, simply because he will not think and act with him in politics, when he knows this reason is to be of record, and to remain through all time. For myself, now above all others is the time when I wish to see this security furnished to honest men in office. I wish the credit of it for this Administration, for this executive. His anxious wish has been to secure to the States and to individuals what, in his judgment, they had been improperly deprived of by federal power; and I wish to see in his day a surrender of all means which an unprincipled Chief Magistrate might use to influence the political opinions of men. I know him too well not to believe it would meet his hearty approbation; and in time to come, when the historian shall record the beneficial acts of our illustrious men, I feel persuaded that this act will not escape his attention.

The sentiments expressed in this speech are alluded to in a letter to J. A. Whiteside, Esq., Sept. 17, 1835. Judge White says to that gentleman:

When this subject was before the Senate, I took occasion to state the reasons for my course so fully, as to render it unnecessary now to say much on that subject. It was a subject which had excited much interest, while Mr. Adams was President of the United States; I formed the same opinions then which I expressed last winter. The subject was again before the Senate in 1830, and at that time my opinions were the *same* they had been in 1826, and yet are. I firmly believed they were the same opinions entertained by Mr. Jefferson, and by the political party to which I belonged. I not only believed they were the principles of the present Chief Magistrate, but thought one great object of the struggle to bring him into power, was to maintain, and to carry out by legislative enactments, and by his practice, these very principles.

I would have held myself dishonored as a man, and felt as if bringing disgrace upon the Republican party, and more especially upon the Chief Magistrate, if I had maintained one set of principles *to acquire place and power*, and then, for the purpose of retaining them, attempted to practise upon another.

No matter who is President of the United States, I firmly believe executive power ought to be limited within the *narrowest* limits compatible with an administration of the government; otherwise all *efficient agency of the people*, in their own affairs, will soon be lost. If the executive power and patronage be left as they now are, and we should ever have a popular Chief Magistrate willing, from any motive, to lend his influence, and to use his patronage for the purpose of designating and electing his successor, then will this tremendous power be felt, and if it does not end in the destruction of those rights secured to the people, and substituting in their place the will of one man, then shall I think the people of the United States a peculiar race, and more highly favored of heaven than any who have preceded them.

I was born under a king, but raised and educated in a Republic. To secure to our posterity the same freedom for which our fathers toiled, it is essential that executive favor and patronage should be limited by law; otherwise the day may not be remote when we will have in fact a monarchy, and it the more odious because a deceptive form of a republic may be continued.

Mr. Benton, of Missouri, whose rugged instinctive honesty was in full sympathy with Judge White on this point, alone of all the administration phalanx in the Senate, voted with him for the passage of the bill.

In March of the year 1835, Judge White had occasion to state his views upon the much contested question of the Expunging Resolutions, so widely known and so exciting in their day; and which were introduced by Hon. Thomas H. Benton of Missouri. It may not be entirely superfluous to mention that these resolutions contemplated the actual expunging—the wiping out, or erasure—from the journals of the Senate, of a certain vote of censure upon General Jackson, for his conduct in removing the deposits from the United States Bank, which vote was there recorded March 28th, 1834. Judge White contended that the Senate had no right thus to destroy the records of their doings. Upon offering an amendment which would call for the "rescinding, repealing, reversing and declaring null and void" of the resolution censuring General Jackson, instead of the expunging it, he said:

Mr. President: The object of my amendment is, to enable each senator to express the opinion he really entertains of the resolution formerly passed by this body.

To vote for the resolution of the senator from Missouri in its present shape, I cannot. He proposes to "expunge" from our journals one of our resolutions, which was adopted when our votes were taken and recorded by yeas and nays. The Constitution requires that "each House *shall keep a journal of its proceedings, and that at the decision of one-fifth of its members, the yeas and nays shall be taken on any question.*" This Constitution each member has solemnly sworn to support. When we speak of the journal of our proceedings, we speak of a book kept here, *under our own inspection*, in which is faithfully recorded, under its *appropriate date*, every transaction of the body. This book is the *original* and all others are only copies of it. Now, what is proposed by the resolution? It is to expunge one of the resolutions which we all admit we actually adopted, upon yeas and nays, on the 28th of March, 1834. Now if we adopt this resolution, we solemnly order that our former resolution shall be erased, rubbed out, blotted, obliterated, or so corrected that it cannot be read. Suppose this order carried into effect, and any man to read our record, our journal, under date of the 28th March, and he would have no knowledge that such a resolution as that complained of had ever existed.

The answer given to this argument by the honorable senator is not satisfactory. He says in his resolution now under consideration, "It is preserved, because it is set out word for word." But it is not under its true date; and upon that principle, if we wish to ascertain what was done 28th March, 1834, we must look not to the journal of that year, but to the journal of 1835. This would not be a diary or journal of our proceedings according with the facts.

Again, what would become of our yeas and nays? Are we to deprive ourselves, those of our own day, and posterity, of all means of knowing how we voted? The gentleman does not propose preserving our yeas and nays. I do not wish to lose mine, nor do I suppose any other member wishes to give up this record evidence of his opinion.

It appears to me plain that we cannot vote for expunging the journal, because it is contrary to the positive injunction of the Constitution, which we are bound to observe. Adopt my amendment, and then pass the resolution, and we accomplish everything desirable. We "rescind" and declare "null and void" the original resolution. This is all that can be wished by any person; we reverse our decision because we now think it was *wrong;* and we declare it *null* and *void*, because it was always wrong, and ought never to have been adopted.

This is the effect of my amendment as first proposed by me; and now at the instance of the honorable senator, from Pennsylvania (Mr. McKean), I have modified, so as to incorporate into it the additional words "repealed and reversed." It now reads that the resolution of 28th March is "rescinded, repealed, reversed and declared to be null and void." This, it appears to me, is as strong an opinion as we can give, that the original resolution shall not stand as the judgment of the Senate, and that it ought never to have found a place upon our journals.

Thus far I am willing to go, because it conforms to the opinion I now entertain, and to the opinion I entertained when the original resolution was adopted.

If time permitted, I would gladly say more on this subject; but it does not, and I must content myself with expressing a hope that my amendment may be adopted, so that I can vote for the resolution without a violation of one of my most solemn obligations.

The question was quieted for that session by means of a motion to lay it on the table. Next year however, under the indomitable lead of Benton, it was started again; and Judge White defined his position upon it more at length, in a speech delivered June 28th, 1836, as follows:

The following preamble and resolution offered by Mr. White being under consideration:

Whereas, on the 28th day of March, 1834, the Senate of the United States adopted a resolution in the words following, to wit:

"*Resolved*, That the President, in the late executive proceedings in relation to the public revenue, has assumed upon himself authority and powers not conferred by the Constitution and laws, but in derogation of both:"

And whereas, upon the question whether said resolution should be adopted, it was decided by one-fifth of the senators present that the same should be taken by yeas and nays; and the votes of the several members now stand recorded on the journal of the Senate:

And whereas the said resolution still remains on the journal of the Senate in full force, not rescinded, reversed, repealed, or annulled; and cannot now be expunged, cancelled, or in any way obliterated or defaced without violating that clause of the Constitution of the United States which is in the following words, to wit: "Each house shall keep a journal of its proceedings, and from time to time publish the same, excepting such part as may in their judgment require secrecy; and the yeas and nays of either house on any question shall, at the desire of one-fifth of those present, be entered on the journal:"

And whereas each senator, before taking his seat, was bound to take, and did take, an oath to support said Constitution:

And whereas the President of the United States, in the late executive proceedings in relation to the public revenue, alluded to in said resolution, did not, in the opinion of the Senate assume upon himself authority and powers not conferred upon him by the Constitution and laws: Therefore, it is

Resolved, That the said resolution, and the opinion therein expressed, be, and the same hereby are, rescinded, reversed, and annulled; and it is hereby declared that the said resolution ought not to be considered as having had, or as now or hereafter having any force or effect whatever.

Mr. White addressed the Senate as follows:

Mr. President: By means not within my control, I have become so far connected with this subject as to consider it a duty to submit the resolution now under consideration, and to urge its adoption by such reasons as are satisfactory to my own mind. During our last session, the honorable senator from Missouri offered a resolution, proposing that we should order the resolution of the 28th March, 1834, to be expunged from the journal. When it was taken up for consideration, entertaining the opinion that the Senate had not the power to make such an order, I moved to amend the resolution, by striking out the order to expunge, and all which followed it, and inserting that the resolution should be rescinded, reversed, repealed, and declared to be null and void. The senator from Alabama moved that the question be first taken on striking out the word "expunge," and, after a very short debate, it was stricken out, by almost a unanimous vote; and then, upon the motion of one of the senators from Massachusetts, the subject was laid on the table. At this session we have a proposition, which is now on the table, for a qualified or limited expunging. Still believing my first impressions on the subject were correct, I have ventured to submit my resolution, and upon it will desire the decision of the Senate.

The first position assumed in the preamble to my resolution liable to doubt is, that we have not the power to expunge from our journal the resolution of the 28th March, 1834.

Our government is republican, and, by the Constitution, it was intended that all agents in the different departments of it should be responsible for their public conduct. With a view to secure this accountability, so far as the two Houses of Congress are concerned, and also for the purpose of perpetuating a knowledge of what should be done by them, it is provided by the Constitution of the United States, 5th section of the 1st article, that "each house shall keep a journal of its proceedings, and from *time to time* publish the same, excepting such parts as may, in their judgment, require secrecy; and the yeas and nays of the members of either House, on any question, shall, at the desire of one-fifth of those present, be entered on the journal." Generally, that interpretation of the Constitution, or of a statute, is the true one, which would be put upon it by a common man.

It appears to me very clear that were a common man asked what did the framers of the Constitution mean should be done, when they used the language just quoted, he would answer, that each house should have faithfully *recorded* the proceedings of each day, and *carefully preserve the book* in which they were recorded. To determine the meaning of this word "*keep*," we are not to look into a glossary to see how many different definitions we can find, but to the *context* and to the *object* the framers of the Constitution wished to attain. Each house is directed to keep a journal of its proceedings, and *from time to time* to publish the same. The object evidently is, that the body itself may at all times know what it and its predecessors have done, and that the constituent may also know what has been done, and by whom.—[*Bayard's Exposition of the Constitution*, p. 58.]

If, as soon as we have recorded our daily proceedings, we have performed the whole duty required by this clause, and may then burn, tear up, obliterate, or *expunge* the journal, the whole object will be defeated. The convention were aware that neither house would be always in session, and that when in session the members themselves could not in *person*, keep the journal; provision is therefore made in article 1, sections

2 and 3, that each house shall have power to appoint the necessary officers. Through officers thus appointed the journal is kept and preserved, as the records of courts are kept and preserved by their clerks.

We are not only to keep the journal, but *from time to time to publish* the same. The journal which is kept is the one which is to be published; not *once only*, but from *time to time.* If we admit that after our proceedings have been *once published*, then we may expunge, how shall we comply with the injunction to publish from *time to time?* Those to whom the printed copies have been delivered are under no constitutional obligation *to preserve their copies.* They may be destroyed at pleasure Upon their care we must depend to enable us to publish a *second* or *third* edition; yet we have been directed to *keep* and, from *time to time*, publish. Again, if we do publish a second or third edition from our own journal, having expunged some of our proceedings immediately after the first publication, then the first edition and the subsequent ones will *not agree*, because the expunged proceedings will not appear in the last publications, no matter whether the expunging is considered literal or figurative. And what will make the matter worse is, there will be no record in charge of our own *officer*, by which to prove which edition is a true copy.

The provisions in the 7th section of the same article strongly support the construction for which I contend:

"Every bill which shall have passed the House of Representatives and the Senate, shall, before it become a law, be presented to the President of the United States; if he approve, he shall sign it; but if not, he shall return it, with his objections, to that house in which it shall have originated, who shall 'enter the objections at large on their journal,' and proceed to reconsider it. If, after such reconsideration, two-thirds of that house shall agree to pass the bill, it shall be sent, together with the objections, to the other house, by which it shall likewise be reconsidered; and, if approved by two-thirds of that house, it shall become a law. But in all such cases, the 'votes of both houses shall be determined by yeas and nays, and the names of the persons voting for and against the bill shall be entered on the journal of each house, respectively.' If any bill shall not be returned by the President within ten days (Sundays excepted) after it shall have been presented to him, the same shall be a law, in like manner as if he had signed it, unless the Congress, by their adjournment, prevent its return; in which case, it shall not be a law."

The like ceremonies are to be gone through in relation to order, resolutions, or votes, in which the concurrence of both Houses is necessary.

Now, sir, is any gentleman prepared to say, that in any case arising under this section, we have the power to expunge the journal? If we cannot, how can we in any other case? The language requiring us to *keep a journal* of our proceedings is as strong and imperative as the language in this section, requiring the President's objections to be entered on the journal, and the names of the voters to be recorded. The same solemn guards are thrown around both: and if we now have the power to expunge the journal of March, 1834, we also have the power to go back and expunge from the journal the proceedings in relation to any veto sent to us by any President.

To keep a journal of our proceedings must mean that we shall have them faithfully recorded, and then the *record carefully preserved*; otherwise, the whole context is disregarded, and the great object of responsibility of legislative agents defeated. Let us, for a moment, consider some of the familiar cases put by the other side.

We employ a man "to *keep the door*." After he has opened it, and let some person in or out of the house, surely he is not at liberty to break the door.

A man employs a person to keep his house. After the house is put in good order, the house-*keeper* is not at liberty to break or burn the furniture, or to expunge it, by making black marks around it.

A merchant employs a person to *keep* his *store* and *books*. After the day's or week's work is over, the clerk is not at liberty to tear out or expunge any of the entries, showing the goods sold, or the cash received; yet all these things might lawfully be done by these different persons, if the arguments in favor of expunging our journal are correct.

It has been sometimes urged that each house has a *discretion* as to the matter that shall be put on its journal. This, to some extent, is true, but cannot affect my argument. Each house is for ever bound to put enough *matter* on the journal to show on what *subjects* it acted, and the *decision* of the body on *each subject*.

To prove this discretionary power, it is said we may select for publication such parts of the journal as we please, and keep the rest secret.

It is true, by the clause under consideration, each house is bound to keep a journal of *all* its proceedings, but may refrain from having published such parts as the public interest requires should be *kept secret*.

This power to refrain from publishing is *expressly* given, and therefore may be *legally* exercised. It is, with me, conclusive to show that we are bound always to *preserve the journal*. Parts of it we need *not publish*. Now, if we are not bound to preserve the record of our proceedings, there would be no evidence in existence of what had been done upon those subjects in relation to which the journal had not been published.

Again: we have the *express* power given *not to publish* some parts of *our proceedings*; if, in addition to this, we *assume* the power which is not given to expunge what we please, we may, and probably will, some time choose not to publish some proceeding which would not be acceptable to our constituents; and then, after it had performed what we intended, we could expunge it, and thus evade all that responsibility intended to be secured.

It is said the journal is nothing but inducement to some other matter more important. This opinion I do not think is well founded. The journals, so far from being considered as merely introductory, or inducement to something more important, and therefore in our power to dispose of as we please, ought to viewed as *sacred*, because they contain the *only evidence* of the judgment of the representatives of the people upon the different subjects acted on; they are the very essence, or, as the lawyers term it, the *gist* of the whole matter.

In our free and happy country our laws are binding, because they contain the *will* of the *people themselves*, expressed by their representatives, in the mode pointed out in the Constitution. The journal is the only evidence of this will. An act is not binding because it is signed by the presiding officers of the two houses, but because it is the expressed will of a majority in each house; and the journal is the highest evidence of this will. At the last session, by some mistake, a bill, which our journal shows was *indefinitely postponed*, was signed by the presiding officers and by the President. It was *no law*, although it had the form of one. It wanted the *essence*, the *will* of a majority of one of the houses, and the *journal* of that house is the highest and only evidence of the defect. I, therefore, deny that we have any power to expunge, on the ground that the journal is mere inducement to something more important. But, again: even if it were only inducement, I deny, on that account, we have any power to disobey a *command* of the Constitution. It says we *shall* keep a journal of our proceedings. We call Heaven to witness we will obey this command. In consequence of this solemn promise, we are intrusted with matters of the highest interest. We have faithfully recorded one of our proceedings, but afterwards tear or blot it out, or expunge it—that is, prick it out—and are called upon for the reason, and answer, it was of no consequence, because it was mere inducement to something else. The excuse ought never to be admitted; if it is in one case, it may be in every case. We may obliterate, expunge, or burn the whole.

It is further urged, if the whole record is destroyed, after the journal has been published, it makes no difference, because each *printed copy* is the journal.

This I think an entire mistake; the printed journal is only a copy of the original, and, although it may be admitted as evidence in court, it is only because it is supposed to be a *true copy of the original*, as it has been printed by public authority; and because you cannot procure the original, it being the duty of the secretary to keep it in his *own possession*.

The original is the best evidence; and the party is only excused from producing it because he cannot procure it. Suppose the copy offered not a true one, the error is always corrected by having recourse to the original.

Again: if all these printed copies are *originals*, and we order the journal to be expunged, we must make our secretary apply the process to each copy; if he does to one, and not to all, they will vary from each other; and if we apply the process to the original, and not to the printed copies, every copy will vary from the original.

The journal of 1834 has been published—many copies of it—the obnoxious resolution with the rest. Suppose we now expunge it, actually or figuratively, and then publish another edition, the resolution would not appear in the last edition, and thus it would vary from that now in existence.

If we decide that the printed copies are to be considered as the originals, and not *copies merely*, it appears to me we endanger the purity of our whole proceedings. It will be very easy for those who are ingenious in villany to print with our mark and impose on the world spurious copies, and *insert as our proceedings* matters which never occurred.

It is thought we err in giving the same sanctity to our journal which is properly given to the records of courts of justice, which, it is admitted, cannot be expunged, or altered after the term.

In my opinion, our journal ought to be considered the most sacred of the two. The records of the courts only affect the private rights of individuals; our records affect all society. Records of courts are only required to be kept by *legislative* enactments; the records of each house of Congress were not left to statutory enactments, but are required to be *kept* by the *Constitution* itself.

Those who insist that we have the power to expunge seek support from precedents; and it has been said that in the sixth year of the reign of Henry VIII. it was enacted that a record should be kept of the *leaves of absence granted to different members* of the Parliament. And from this it is argued that Parliament was bound by *law after that time* to keep a journal; and if they expunged any of their proceedings, so may we. To this I answer, that the expunging of any entry made on the journal after that time, on any *other subject* than that of giving *leave of absence* to a member, is of no more weight than if such a statute had never been enacted; and gentlemen have not produced, and I do not believe they can produce, a case in which either House expunged any such entry.

The statute did not require a record to be made of anything except *leave of absence*, and if any other proceeding was recorded in the same book, it was by some *order* of the house; and the *same* power could, at any time, order it to be expunged, just as well as if it had been recorded in any other book.

Our constitution requires that we shall keep a journal of *all* our proceedings; and we ought to preserve the *whole* with as much care as the Parliament did their leaves of absence.

By the articles of confederation, Congress was required to publish every month the journal of their proceedings; and from this it is inferred they were bound to keep a journal of all their proceedings. In the first place, I think this inference very far from imposing the same obligation upon the old Congress that is imposed on us by the present consideration, in language too plain to be misunderstood. In the next place, if it did, what cases have gentlemen shown of any matter being expunged from their journals? None.

It were a useless consumption of time in me to notice in detail the different cases cited, to show that the journals have been expunged by both Houses in Great Britain, under the Colonial Government in Virginia, and in the State of Massachusetts, because the same general answer may be given to all. The legislature was not required by either a constitution or a law to keep a journal. The journal was only kept by virtue of the order or usage of each house, and could be changed at any time, to any extent either house might think right.

But a precedent has been referred to in my own State, and there the Constitution *does require* that each house shall *keep a journal.*

Gentlemen who rely upon this precedent have been misinformed. They have not named the case, but I can be at no loss as to what the reference is made. It must be the case of Judge Williams, who was impeached, and tried; and to convict, the Constitution required *two-thirds* of the members. When opinions were expressed, there were two-thirds for conviction, if *absent* members were *not* counted; if they were, there were not two-thirds. Upon this point there was a great variety of opinion, and ultimately the presiding member *discharged* the judge as *acquitted.* On the next morning, when the journal was read, a member moved to correct it, because the court had authorized *no such order.* This motion, it will be perceived, was in a court, therefore, no precedent for us.

Next, it was not to expunge anything which the Senate had *done*, but to strike from the journal that which had been put there by mistake, and which the body never had ordered.

Now, sir, if a man were set to search a case unlike the one before us, he could not do better than take the Tennessee case.

Two precedents have been referred to in the proceedings of Congress, upon which I will make one or two remarks.

On the last day of the session of 1806, two petitions were presented by a member of the Senate, complaining of the conduct of one of our courts; they were received by the body and disposed of. During the same day a member moved to return the petitions, and to expunge the order for their reception from the journal, which was done accordingly.

The first observation I make is, that we are to keep a journal of our proceedings. In other words, at the end of *each day* our record ought to show the *result of our judgment* upon each subject before us.

The journal of that day does show this precisely. After the entry was expunged, the subject of those memorials was placed precisely where, in the judgment of that body, it ought to rest, and that was, that Congress should have nothing to do with it.

I will illustrate my meaning by a familiar case. A merchant, in the forenoon, sells a bale of cloth to a customer, who pays him one hundred dollars for it. He enters the transaction on his journal. In the afternoon, of the same day, the customer returns, and asks the merchant to take back the cloth and return him his money; with which request he complies, and, instead of incumbering his journal with another useless entry, he scratches out, or, in other words, *expunges* the entry he made when he sold the cloth. After this expunging, his journal will show the exact truth relative to this bale of cloth; that is, it will give no account whatever of the transaction, because the cloth was his in the morning, and it is still his the next morning.

If we expunge the resolution of 28th March, 1834, by an order now made, our journal of that day will be so altered as not to show the result of the Senate's judgment on *that day* upon that subject; therefore, there is no likeness in the two cases.

Again, if they were similar, the precedent ought to have no weight whatever. There was no time for either discussion or deliberation. Besides, this was done in high party times—related to an exciting topic—Burr's conspiracy, and the expunging was ordered by a strictly party vote.

The second case is that which occurred in the House of Representatives in 1822.

Mr. Randolph announced the death of Mr. Pinkney, who was not dead, and for that *reason* moved an adjournment. The adjournment took place, and the next day he moved that the *reason assigned* for the adjournment should be expunged, because it was not true, and it was accordingly expunged. In this case, what the House did was *not expunged.* It had *in fact adjourned*, and so the journal *still shows ;* but the *reason* why they came to a decision to adjourn, being founded in mistake, was expunged.

Now, sir, the journal at this moment shows, as well as it did when the entry was made, the *proceedings* of the House on that day; and all the alteration produced is, that the *reason* for one of their acts cannot be known, as it is expunged.

But in the case under consideration, to expunge would be to destroy all evidence of a *decision itself*, for which I insist we have no precedent in the case relied on.

The truth must be, the members of the convention were well aware of all the precedents in Great Britain, and in our own country, which existed when they framed the Constitution, and intended to leave nothing to the discretion of either house. They intended effectually to secure a just accountability from the representative to the constituent; therefore they used the Constitution itself the imperative language, "each house shall keep a journal," &c. Let us not, then, be misled by precedents which we fancy may bear us out. At best they are nothing, but "crutches on which weak minds sustain themselves"; and if we are sustained by these precedents in expunging the resolution of 1834, the precedent which we will now make may sustain those who come after us in expunging important principles from the Constitution itself.

It is urged that the mere act of expunging the journal is not a matter of any importance; it is the effect or *moral* of the resolution which it is desired to remove.

Why not adopt my resolution, then? No man can doubt our power to rescind, repeal, and reverse the resolution.

The bad *moral* taught by the resolution will be removed by the subsequent decision pronouncing the former one to be erroneous. But it is thought best to use the word "expunge," as, by the use of that word in parliamentary proceedings, the principles of civil liberty have been maintained in other countries.

If it has been always used for wise and good purposes elsewhere, let us be cautious that *we* do not so use it as eventually to produce mischief in this, the most free and favored country in the world.

It appears to me, however, that this word, like everything else over which we have control, has been sometimes used when correct principles were asserted, and, in other instances, when the reverse was the case.

When King James entered one of the houses of the British Parliament, and with his *own hand expunged* the journal; when the House of Lords expunged the recognizance entered into before the Lord Mayor of London, and when the journals of the Virginia Legislature were expunged, or attempted to be expunged, during the Colonial government, it was not the watchword of the friends of liberty. I am not aware that it ever has been used, and I fear it never will be used, in aid of civil liberty, or the rights of man, when the process is resorted to to gratify the feelings of *those in power*, who are generally too prone to believe liberty is attacked whenever any portion of their conduct is disapproved, or there is any attempt to impose restraints on their liberty to do as they imagine is most for the public good.

Mr. President, I propose in the next place to examine the soundness of the reason assigned why we may, and ought, to expunge.

It is briefly this: that, as the Senate is the tribunal established by the Constitution to try the President when impeached, it is unconstitutional to pass a resolution which charges him with a crime for which he might be impeached, and that this resolution not only charges, but convicts him of a *crime*. I do not concur in this opinion, and beg leave to assign my reasons for dissenting from it.

Under the Constitution, the powers of the Senate are judicial, executive, or legislative; judicial, when trying impeachments; executive, when advising the President in relation to treaties, or as to the persons to be appointed to office; legislative, in making laws, and in everything connected with making, amending, or repealing them. (Constitution U. S. art. 1, sect. 1.)

The power of the Senate in all legislative matters is equal to that of the House of Representatives in all respects, with the single exception that bills to *raise* revenue must originate in the House. In the discharge of any legislative or executive duty, any individual member may say in his place that the President, or any other civil officer, has assumed powers not conferred upon him by the Constitution or laws.

What any one may lawfully say, every other may say with equal propriety. What any one or all may say, individually, all, or a majority, may with propriety express by way of resolution, which is nothing but an expression of the opinion of a majority on a given subject.

The objection to this resolution is, that it charges the President with, and convicts him of, a crime, for which he may be impeached by the House; and in that case it would be the duty of the Senate to try him; therefore, it was unconstitutional to adopt the resolution.

To this I answer, first, if it were an unconstitutional act to pass the resolution, it furnishes no reason why it should be expunged. If it did, we might go back and expunge from the journal everything which had been done by political opponents, from the adoption of the Constitution, which we chose to say was unconstitutional—all entries, relative to the alien and sedition laws, chartering the banks, &c. These entries, which we deem violations of the Constitution, of all others, are the ones we ought to desire should stand. By them, the disgrace of political opponents would be perpetuated. Were I one of a majority who voted for such unconstitutional proceedings, I would feel very grateful to opponents who would wipe out, or *expunge*, the evidence of my disgrace so soon as they obtained the power.

But again: we find in the Constitution, 1st art. 3d sect. these words:

"Judgment in cases of impeachment shall not extend further than to removal from office, and to disqualification to hold and enjoy any office of honor, trust, or profit, under the United States; but the party convicted shall, nevertheless, be liable and subject to indictment, trial, judgment, and punishment, according to law."

And, in art. 2, sect. 4, the language following:

"The President, Vice-President, and all civil officers of the United States, shall be removed from office on impeachment for, and conviction of, treason, bribery, or other high crimes and misdemeanors."

To my mind it is very clear that neither the President, nor any other civil officer, can be impeached, unless he is charged with some *crime*.

The question then is, does the resolution of the 28th of March, 1834, charge the President with the commission of a *crime?* It is in these words:

> "*Resolved*, That the President, in the late executive proceedings in relation to the public revenue, has assumed upon himself authority and powers not conferred by the Constitution and laws, but in derogation of both."

It is with this resolution, and this *only*, we have to deal. As to what the bank or its agents had said or done, or as to the arguments or speeches of gentlemen, the Senate has given no opinion; and upon the question now pending, we have nothing to do with them.

I affirm that this resolution does not impute to the President any *crime* or *misdemeanor* whatever. There can be no such thing as a crime, without a *bad* motive. The resolution is entirely silent as to the *motives* by which the Chief Magistrate was governed. It therefore charges nothing but mere *error of judgment.* It alleges he assumed powers not conferred by the Constitution or laws; but whether the motives which induced him to assume these powers were virtuous, or the reverse, is not stated. If they were to promote the public good, and he honestly believed the powers he assumed had been conferred, although he might be mistaken, yet he ought to be applauded as a patriot, instead of being censured as a criminal.

Intention to do wrong—*bad* motives—are the *essence* of crime; and without them there can be no such thing. In this very case, if, in every act the President did, he mistook his powers, but still acted from high and pure motives, no honest tribunal upon earth could convict him of *crime.*

This new doctrine of crime without *evil intent* has no sanction in morals, in reason, or in any adjudged case. The only cases referred to for its support are the impeachments against Judges Chase and Pickering. In the first of these, it is true, some of the articles of impeachment did not charge bad motives, but upon those he was *acquitted without a dissenting voice.*

In Pickering's case, the question was whether he was sane or not. He had been a highly respectable man, but acted badly on the bench, and it was alleged he was deranged. It was answered, if he was deranged, it was from *intemperance*, and therefore an aggravation of the offence; and on that ground he was convicted.

God forbid that a doctrine so unreasonable, so inconsistent with our imperfect condition, as that of crime without *evil design*, should ever be sanctioned anywhere, especially here. You and I are obliged to act in this very question; it is our public duty to form opinions, and act upon them; we disagree; must one of us be guilty of a crime? Look at the situation of courts. A cause is tried before two judges in an inferior court, and they disagree; must one be a criminal? A writ of error is taken from an inferior to a higher tribunal, and the judgment reversed; are the judges of the court to be viewed and treated as criminals? If they are, suppose there to be a still higher tribunal, to which the same cause is carried, and the last decision reversed, and the first established; what are you to do then—punish the second set of judges?

In the federal circuit courts, a judge of the Supreme Court and the district judge decide a cause; a writ of error is taken to the Supreme Court, where the same judge forms one of the court, and he concurs with his brethren in reversing his own decision. What is to be done with him? According to this strange doctrine, he is obliged to be guilty of a crime, because he has decided against himself. Away with such doctrine, it is absurd. Error and crime are as distinct as the motives by which angels and devils are governed.

The great error in the argument on the other side is occasioned by not attending to the distinction between the acts of *private citizens* and of *public officers.* A private individual does an unlawful act; the law *presumes* he did it from bad motives; because, so far from being compelled to act, it was his duty not to act. In the case of a public officer, he is *compelled to* act; *he is sworn to do so;* and whenever he does an official act, the *presumption* is, that his *motives were good*, although the act may have been *contrary to law.* If the law were not so, no honest man, conscious of his defects, would ever fill an office. He is bound to act—*sworn to do so;* and when he uses all the means within his reach to inform himself, and exercises his best judgment, he is *innocent*, whether his acts are *lawful* or the *reverse.* This distinction between the acts of individuals and of public officers runs through all the cases which can be found in our books. The acts spoken of in the resolution as assumptions of power in derogation of the Constitution and law, were acts done by the President in his official capacity; therefore, the resolution imputes to him no criminality whatever.

The Senate unanimously adopted a resolution against the late Postmaster-General, condemning some of his acts as unlawful; but it charges him with no crime. If error is hereafter to constitute crime in our public officers, I should like to know who is to be judge. Who feels that he has the infallible standard? If any one will say "I have it," my word for it, if you will cultivate his acquaintance, you will soon find he wants the common requisites, *integrity and talents*, essential to constitute a tolerable judge.

If we expunge the journal, then we will have established the doctrine that, in every case, a President, or any other civil officer, may assume authority and powers not conferred by the Constitution and laws but in derogation of both, and we dare not say that is our opinion. Against such a doctrine I enter my protest. We not only have the power, but it is our duty to exercise it whenever such a case occurs. Suppose the

President to nominate for some office a man who already holds the office of governor or judge, I surely would have a right to say I will not vote for him, because I think he has, in the office he now holds, assumed powers he did not possess, and therefore I will not trust him farther.

After having said so, if he is impeached, I cannot be challenged and excluded from sitting as one of his triers. I have charged him with no crime; and, having given an opinion that his conduct was unlawful, does not disqualify me. If this were so, we must reverse the whole order of things; and whenever a judge is called on to decide a cause similar to one he had before decided, we must exclude him, and appoint some other; whereas the common impression has ever been, that the judge is the better qualified for having examined and previously decided the same or a similar question.

In England a peer cannot be challenged because he has previously given an opinion; nor can a Senator here. They are judges, having a right to decide the law as well as the facts of the case.

But the Senate heretofore attempted to exercise this very power in the case of the Panama nominations. Mr. Adams (I beg pardon, the late President), in his message, told us he had the power to have sent ministers without consulting the Senate; but, as they were soon to be in session, he thought it best to delay the appointments, and consult them. A resolution was submitted denying this claimed power, and a long discussion ensued. If we contested this claimed but unexerted power, can any one doubt but, if it had been exercised, we would have denied it by a resolution if we could? For one, I never doubted but the President honestly entertained the opinion expressed.

The subject of removing the deposits had been regularly brought before the Senate by the report of the Secretary of the Treasury. It was one on which we had a right to legislate. We had a right to know why it was done, and how it was done, to either approve or disapprove; to legislate upon it: to direct the money to be returned, or to be kept anywhere else; in short, to approve or disapprove what had been done.

We could have thanked the executive for his prompt attention to the public interest; for his efficiency in displacing one Secretary, who would not remove the money, and appointing another who would. Why, then, had the Senate no power to say that, in doing these things, he transcended his power? To me it appears they had constitutionally the power to pass the resolution. But it then was, and yet is, my opinion that, in exercising this power, the Senate themselves erred when they resolved that he had assumed powers not conferred. I believed he had the power to remove the Secretary, and to do every other act then attributed to him, if he believed a proper case was made out for its exercise. Am I to be told by Senators who voted for the resolution that I committed a *crime* when I voted against them? I hope not. Nor am I at liberty to say they committed a crime when they disagreed in opinion with me. This is everything the resolution charges the President with. He thought he had the power which he exercised; a majority of the Senate thought he had not, and so expressed themselves in the resolution, not questioning the purity of the motives from which he acted. By doing so they did not assume any power not conferred on them by the Constitution.

In Great Britain the House of Lords acts as a court. A writ of errors lies there to remove a cause from the Court of King's Bench. Suppose a cause thus removed, and the judgment reversed, because the judges had *assumed* powers they did *not* possess; if they were afterwards impeached for so deciding, because they were bribed, could not the peers try the impeachment? Undoubtedly they could. I cannot vote to *expunge or deface* our journal, because I think the Constitution forbids it. I cannot assign as a reason for either expunging or rescinding the resolution that the Senate had no power to adopt it, because I do not think so; and because I think it of the last importance we should retain with the Senate those powers vested in it for high and important purposes, and which are, or may be, essential to preserve the liberty of the people; but most willingly can I vote to rescind, reverse, and repeal the resolution; because I think that the Senate erred in adopting it. To say the least, there are *doubts* of our power to expunge: and no one, I think, ought to be certain the Senate had no power to adopt the resolution. Why, then, shall we cling to the word "expunge," and to this *reason*, when there is a plain course to pursue, in which what is due to the Chief Magistrate and to ourselves can be accomplished. To me, the reason is obvious. To expunge has become an *executive measure*. It is now the watchword of a party; and, by its use, those are to be hunted down who will not conform to the will of the party. In March, 1834, when the resolution was adopted, a *majority* of the Senate was *opposed* to the Chief Magistrate. His long and valuable services have *endeared* him to the American people. They are sensitive as to everything which can affect his reputation as a man or as an officer.

My opinion had been expressed, and was well known; I believe it conforms to the opinion of my State and its legislature; and I hold myself especially bound to endeavor to have it effected by the adoption of the resolution which I have submitted. Those who believe that either I or the people of my State are opponents of the Administration, mistake our character. Our politics are as they have been; we now stand on the *same ground*, advocate the *same principles* we did in 1828, when sustaining General Jackson to bring him into power. But we are the slave of no man; and when it is attempted to ingraft on our principles a system which does not belong to them, I will not yield my assent, be the consequences what they may. My wish is to rescind, reverse, and repeal the resolution of 1834, because, in my judgment, it is *erroneous*, and because

I believe such is the judgment of my State. To vote to expunge it, I cannot; because, in my opinion, the Constitution forbids it; and, anxious as my constituents are to vindicate the character of the Chief Magistrate, they will never require me to do so at the expense of that sacred instrument, which we are all under the most high and most solemn obligations to maintain inviolate.

The objections thus made were ultimately evaded by so wording the resolution as to make it define the mode of performing the proposed operation; and after a desperate resistance by the opposition, which at last, in the words of Mr. Webster, as recorded by Mr. Benton in his "Thirty Years' View," had "degenerated into a question of nerves and muscles," the expunging resolution was passed, March 16th 1837. Upon that day the secretary, in the presence of the Senate, produced the original journal, and (in the words of the resolution) "having drawn a square of broad, black lines around the 'obnoxious censuring resolution,' wrote across its face in strong letters these words: 'Expunged by order of the Senate, this 16th day of March, 1837.'"

CHAPTER XI.

SENATORIAL CAREER—ABOLITION—PUBLIC LAND DISTRIBUTION—SUB-TREASURY—TARIFF—DEMEANOR—BUSINESS HABITS—SURNAME.

UPON the disturbing question of slavery, which has since grown so portentously in importance, Judge White's sentiments were loyal to those of his native State, and were characterized by the solidity and prudence which were such important elements in his character. These sentiments he expressed March 2d, 1836, upon occasion of the presentation of one of the petitions then so frequently presented by some northern members for the abolition of slavery within the District of Columbia. Upon that occasion he spoke as follows:

Mr. President: I address you under the solemn conviction that if this government is to continue to accomplish the great purposes for which it was established, it can only be, by administering it in the same spirit in which it was created.

When the Constitution was framed, the great and leading interests of the whole country were considered, and in the spirit of liberality and compromise were adjusted and settled.

They were settled upon principles that ought to remain undisturbed so long as the Constitution lasts, which I hope will be for ever; for although liberty may be preferable to the Union, yet I think the Union is indispensable to the security of liberty. At the formation of the Constitution, slavery existed in many of the States; it was one of the prominent interests that was then settled. It, in all its domestic bearings, was left, exclusively to the respective States, to do with, as they might think best, without any interference on the part of the federal government. This, it is admitted, by every gentleman who has addressed you, is now the case, in every slaveholding State; therefore, it is only urged that Congress has the power to abolish slavery in the District of Columbia. It should never be forgotten that when the Constitution was formed and adopted, what is now the District of Columbia, was then comprehended within two of the slaveholding States, Maryland and Virginia.

Suppose when all the details of the Constitution had been adjusted, it had been foreseen, that the District of Columbia would be formed out of a tract of country ceded by those States, and situated in the centre between them, it had been asked of the members of the convention, what do you intend as to the district? You have placed the question of slavery in the States, entirely under their control within their respective limits, do you intend that Congress shall have the power to abolish slavery in the district? Would not every man have answered in the negative?

It has been said that when petitions to abolish slavery are presented to either House of Congress, those who demand the question whether they shall be received, and thus produce discussion, are *agitators*, and produce excitement on this delicate subject. To me it seems this is unfair. Let us for a moment consider the circumstances of the country, and the situation in which we are all placed.

There are twenty-four States, several Territories, and this District. Thirteen of these States have no slaves, the other eleven have slaves; in fact, their slaves constitute a large item of all the property they own. During the past year, it has so happened, that many newspapers, pamphlets, and pictorial representations made their appearance, and through the mail, and by other means, extensively circulated in the slaveholding States. By these means, a spirit of discontent was created, which occasioned much excitement and disorder in various places, and rendered it necessary, in a summary manner, to put to death several white persons, and a number of slaves. In various quarters of the Union there were assemblages of people, who expressed their opinions with great freedom. In the course of the fall and winter, many of the State Legislatures have been in session—they have been addressed on this subject by their respective governors. They have expressed publicly their opinions—the President, in his message, has invited the attention of Congress to it—the Senate has referred that part of the message to a special committee, which has made a lengthy report, accompanied by a bill, which is now upon our docket, and must, in due course, be discussed, and either passed or rejected. Are all these to be called *agitators*, and charged with unnecessarily producing excitement? If not, how is it that members of Congress are to be thus charged when petitions are presented that we must in some mode dispose of? Each of us must suggest such mode as we think most correct, and none can justly be liable to any such charge. If there is any wrong, it is found in those, who, in such a state of public feeling, will press their petitions upon us. The petitions are forwarded to members who feel it their duty to present them; when presented, others think it their duty to demand the question whether they shall be received. Is it true that on this delicate subject, every officer of the federal or State government, can express his opinion, as to what it is best to do, and that a senator dare not express his opinion without being liable to censure? I hope not.

This is a delicate subject: would to God it had not been pressed upon us; but as it is placed here by the petitioners, we must dispose of it. To enable us to do so, we must think upon it, and we may tell each other what we think, and our reasons for so thinking.

It is not by speaking upon it we will be likely to do mischief. Everything depends upon the *temper* with which we express our opinions, and the *sentiments* we advance. My wish and aim is, if I can do no good, to do no harm, and if I believed in what I propose to say, I would utter a sentiment from which mischief would be produced, I would close my lips, take my seat, and content myself with yea or nay, to every question proposed by others, leaving every person at liberty to conjecture the reasons for my votes; but entertaining no fear of that kind, I must ask permission to state, as briefly as I can, some of the reasons for the course I shall pursue.

In doing this, I shall not address myself to senators coming from either the East, or the West, the North, or the South, in particular, but to the Senate, the whole Senate, because if it is desired, as I believe it is, that we should remain together as *one people*, secure, prosperous, happy and contented, the whole country, every section of it has a deep interest in this matter, this agitation and excitement must cease.

What then ought we to do, as most likely to put an end to those angry feelings which now prevail.

In my opinion, we should refuse to receive these petitions. It is a mere question of expediency what disposition we shall make of them. All who have yet spoken admit that Congress has *no power* whatever over slavery in the respective *States*. *It is settled.* Whether slavery is right or wrong, we have now *no power* to consider or discuss. Suppose, then, a petition were presented, to abolish slavery in the States, would we receive it? Assuredly we ought not, because it would be asking us to act upon a subject over which we have *no power*.

But these are petitions asking Congress to abolish slavery in this district. Have we the power? *I think not.* I consider the argument of the honorable senator from Virginia (Mr. Leigh), upon that point, conclusive. It has not beeen answered, and I do not believe it can be. Slaves are property in this *district*—Congress cannot take *private* property, even for *public use*, without making just compensation to the owner. No fund is provided by the Constitution to pay for slaves which may be liberated, and the Constitution never gives Congress the power to act upon any subject, without, at the same time, furnishing the *means* for its accomplishment. To liberate slaves is not taking them for public use. It is declaring that neither individuals nor the public shall use them. I will not weaken the honorable member's argument by going over it.

This district was intended as the place where the great business of the nation should be transacted for the good of the whole. Congress, under the Constitution, is placed here to legislate upon those subjects enumerated and specified in the Constitution, that we might be able to protect ourselves, and the officers residing here, and be out of the reach of the laws of any State. It was never intended that we should have any local legislation, except such as would meet the wants and the wishes of the people residing within the ten miles square. We should never permit this place to be converted into a political workshop, where plans would be devised, or carried into operation, that will have the effect of destroying the interest of any of the States.

Members of Congress, executive, and judicial officers, were to come from any, and every section of the Union. From the slaveholding, and the non-slaveholding States; and their property was to be as secure here, in this ten miles square, as it was in the States from which they respectively came. They would bring their habits and their domestic servants with them. Those from the non-slaveholding States their hired servants, and those from the slaveholding States their slaves; and who can believe it was intended to vest the power in Congress to liberate them if brought within the district.

Again, the right of property in slaves in the States is sacred, and beyond the power of Congress to interfere with, in any respect; yet, if it be conceded that we have the power to liberate them in the district, we can as effectually ruin the owners as if we had the power to liberate slaves in the States. By abolishing slavery here, we not only make a place of refuge for runaways, but we produce a spirit of discontent and rebellion in the minds of slaves in the neighboring States, which will soon spread over all, and which cannot fail to compel owners to *destroy* their own slaves, to preserve their own lives, and those of their wives and children. I beseech gentlemen to look at this matter as it is. Take for illustration the case of a small planter in Mississippi, living on his own land, with thirty slaves to cultivate it. Suddenly it is discovered that one half of them is concerned in a plot to destroy the lives of their master, his family, and neighbors, with a view to produce their freedom, and immediately with or without law they are tucked up and hanged. The man is thus deprived of his property without any chance for an indemnity, besides the disquiet and anxiety of mind occasioned by a loss of confidence in his remaining slaves. It cannot have been intended that Congress by acting on this subject, should have a power thus to occasion a destruction of slave property.

To me it seems that we ought to treat these petitions precisely as we would do, if they prayed us to abolish slavery in *one of the States.* We have no more power to abolish it here than we have there.

I think in either case we ought to refuse to receive them. I hold that if the petitioners ask us to do that which we have no power to do, or to do that which will be productive of a great and lasting mischief, we not only have the *right*, but that it is our *duty* to refuse to receive them.

By the Constitution no man can be held to answer for a criminal charge but by presentment, or indictment. Suppose a petition presented here, alleging that some citizen in the district had been guilty of a crime, and that he was so influential that he could not be reached by the ordinary forms of law in court, and therefore we are asked to pass a bill of attainder. Ought we to receive the petition? Suppose a petition to ask us to pass a law to prohibit any member of this body from making a speech against the prayer of the petitioners, would we receive it? Suppose a petition to be offered asking us to establish a particular religion in this district, or to prohibit any publication in a newspaper on the subject of abolishing slavery, unless it was previously approved of by a committee; would we, ought we, to receive any such petition? I think, most certainly, we ought not. But suppose we have the power, is there any senator who believes we ought exercise it. I trust not. Those who urge the reception of this petition, which is from the Society of Friends, have spoken most highly of the petitioners and the class of citizens to which they belong. In all this I cheerfully concur. These particular persons are strangers to me. I doubt not the purity of their motives; the sect to which they belong is worthy of all the encomiums passed upon it. I respect and esteem them most highly, and do not feel that in my composition there is a particle of unkindness towards them; but I think they would have us do that which we have no power to do, and if we had the power, by exercising it, we should do infinite mischief. This, *these* petitioners do not desire. They have discharged what they think is their duty by having their petitions presented; I only discharge mine when I say, consistently with what I feel to be my duty, I cannot receive them.

But it is further insisted, that the right of petition is a sacred one, that belongs to the nature of free government, and existed before the formation of our Constitution, and that instrument did not *give* the *right* to petition, but intended only to secure it. This is sound doctrine, and has my hearty assent.

The people are sovereign; members are their agents, or servants; they have a right to make known their grievances, real or imaginary. We can *pass no law*, we can make no rule to abridge or destroy that right.

But what do gentlemen mean when they speak of the *right* of petition? Do they mean that when the petition is presented we must receive it, and do that which is prayed for? No. Not one member contended for this; so far from it, they say, that if the language of the petitioner is *disrespectful to the body*, or *any member of it*, we may, and ought to *refuse to receive it*.

How is this? I beg that we may reflect seriously upon this matter. We are about to establish a doctrine to which I can never yield my assent.

Are we to be exalted above our employers? Is our dignity to be of higher consideration than the property and lives of those who send us here? If a petition contains matter charging disgraceful conduct on the Senate, or any of its members, we *may not receive it;* but if it contains matter which is to *destroy* the slave property in this *district*, and in *eleven States* of this Union, and also to endanger the *lives*, and *dwellings of every citizen within their limits*, we are bound to receive it?

This is the doctrine contained in the arguments. I deny that there is any such distinction to be found in a single feature of our political institutions. The truth is, we have the power *in both instances* to refuse to receive the petitions, but in exercising it when we *ourselves* only are assailed, we ought always to act *most liberally* in receiving, but where the safety, the lives and the property of our *masters* are concerned, we have no right to exercise the same liberality.

With great deference for the opinions of others, I think the force of their whole argument rests on a plain mistake.

They argue as if we never became *acquainted* with the contents of a petition, or could *consider* and *decide* upon *its merits* until after it is received.

This is most clearly not correct. What we have been doing for the last few weeks is full proof of it. These petitions have been publicly read, their merits and tendency, and our powers to abolish slavery have been long under discussion—has any man denied our right to do so? Not one. The only doubt suggested is, whether it was prudent to adopt this course.

By our 24th rule, when a petition is presented the member must briefly state its contents, and what the petitioners wish should be done. He then *asks that the petition may be received*, and specifies what he wishes to be done with it after it is received. If no member objects, for the purpose of saving time, it is received and disposed of without formally propounding the question of reception; but if any member objects, he may call for the reading, and then urge his reasons why it should not be received.

This rule establishes no new doctrine, it is founded in good sense, is perfectly consistent with the right of petition, and is laid down as the correct practice by Mr. Jefferson in his Manual at page 140.

What is the right of the petitioner? It consists in his having free permission to make known to Congress what he esteems a grievance, and to ask them to provide a remedy. When his petition is presented, the duty of Congress commences. That consists in the members making themselves acquainted with the contents of the petition, and granting its prayer if it be just and consistent with the public interest, or in refusing to receive the petition, or making some other disposition of it, which in their judgment will more conduce to the good of the community.

When we refuse to receive a petition, we no more destroy or impair the right of petition, than we do when we receive the petition and lay it upon the table, or reject the prayer of it, or refer it to a committee who report that it is unreasonable, and ought not to be granted.

In each of these cases, the complaint of the petitioner has been *heard*, *considered* and *decided on*. In neither instance has he obtained a redress for what he supposed a grievance, but each leaves him equally at liberty to renew his petition at any subsequent period.

Four modes have been suggested by which to dispose of this and all others on the same subject.

The first we have been considering, and is to refuse to receive it.

The second is to receive them, lay them on the table, and there let them lie.

The third is to receive them, and then instantly reject the prayer of the petitioners.

The fourth is to receive them, refer them to a committee, and let that committee make a report upon them.

I prefer the first, because, when we refuse to receive the petitions, they are returned to those who sent them, and it will most strongly discountenance all hope that Congress ever can, or ever ought, to pass any law upon the subject to which they refer.

In each of the other three, we retain the petitions, place them on our files in the custody of our officer, and at any subsequent session they are here, and it will be competent for any member to move their reference to a committee; whereas, if returned to the petitioner, if they ever again make their appearance, it must be by their being re-sent and re-presented.

I think that plan is the most advisable, and will be most likely to calm the disturbance in the slave States, which will most strongly manifest to all, in every quarter, that Congress will not interfere with slavery as it exists in the States and in this district.

If these petitions are received, I then think the disposition of them proposed by the senator from Pennsylvania the next best—that is, immediately to reject their prayer. This would be far preferable to laying them silently on the table without expressing any opinion whatever.

There is another aspect in which this question may be viewed that has had great influence on my own mind.

Congress sits here as the legislature of the whole Union, and also as the *only legislature for the local concerns of the District of Columbia.* These petitions do not ask us to make a general law, operating *throughout the whole Union*, but a law, the operations of which are to be spent entirely upon property within the ten miles square. Now if we were in *form*, as well as in substance, a local legislature when acting on this question, which gentlemen say is to affect slavery in the district, and no where else, would we be bound to receive these petitions? No more than we are bound to receive petitions from France or Germany. Would gentlemen, if sitting as members of the legislature of Alabama, feel bound to receive petitions from citizens of Maine or Pennsylvania to emancipate slaves within their own State? Assuredly not. If that be so, is it not most reasonable, when we are called upon to pass an act confined exclusively to this district, that we should conduct towards the people here, as if in this matter they were our constituents?

Will it not be time enough to *receive petitions* on this subject when they are presented on behalf of those upon *whose property alone*, it is said the law would operate?

Honorable senators have told us there are two classes of abolitionists, and that public opinion will soon put down the mischievous class, which is small in number. Gentlemen, I doubt not, think as they say. All we know is, that our peace has been very much disturbed by them, whether few or many.

Their newspapers, their pamphlets and pictorial representations have been plentiful. They have come to us through the mail, and by other means, in great abundance, and if we are to live together as one people, they must stop. It is vain to reason with people about the liberty of speech, and of the press, when their lives are put at hazard. When the domestic circle is invaded, when a man is afraid to eat his provisions, lest his cook has been prevailed on to mix poison with his food, or dare not go to sleep, lest the servants will cut the throats of himself, his wife and children before he awakes, he will not endure it; and, when he can lay hands upon those who prompt to such deeds of mischief, he will not wait for the ordinary form of law to redress him. He takes the laws into his own hands, and everything which accustoms us to violate the law, is a serious evil in a country as free as ours, where the laws should govern.

The honorable senator from Mississippi has shown us something of the feelings of his State, which has suffered much. In mine, when we first heard of punishing persons in Mississippi, without legal trial, we thought it all wrong, and some of our leading newspapers courteously found fault with it. Their columns were not long dry until one of these distributers of abolition pamphlets was found in our most populous and respectable city, and an assemblage of our most orderly and discreet citizens immediately resorted for address to the same summary process which had been used in our sister State.

Public opinion may have done something on this subject. I know of only one attempt to establish a press for such publications in any slaveholding State. The neighbors of the gentleman informed him that his press would be productive of mischief, and he must not establish it in their town—he answered that he held it a high duty which he could not dispense with, to proceed, and he would do so. They replied if he did they would consider it their duty to demolish his building, and sow his types broad-cast in the streets. This manifestation of public opinion he respected. He knew that those with whom he had to deal would keep their word. He desisted, retired to a neighboring State, where, as I have understood, he is now publishing his paper.

I beg gentlemen to consider that it is of no consequence to us whether the abolitionists, in their States, are many or few; their publications are numerous; they have already produced much mischief, and if persisted in, must end in consequences to be for ever regretted by us all.

For myself, on the subject of the disposition we may make of these petitions, I can have no other wish than that it may be such, as will most tend to allay excitement, and restore that harmony, which is so essential to the common interest of our whole country.

When Mr. Clay's bill for the distribution of the proceeds of the Public Lands was first presented, Judge White voted against it, for the plain reason that the treasury was comparatively empty, and the nation in debt. When it was subsequently presented, the treasury was full to overflowing, and he voted for it; sustaining it in a speech worthy of his reputation, in which he maintained that the surplus in the treasury had been gathered by taxation from the people, and that it was but just that it should now be distributed for their benefit. He also forcibly exhibited the vices of the various other plans for the use of the same funds; and took occasion to urge the adoption of measures substantially identical with those at present urged for facilitating the purchase of land by actual settlers upon it. This well-considered and valuable speech, delivered April 26, 1836, is as follows:

Mr. President: The subject under consideration is not new, but the circumstances connected with it are both novel and important.

Formerly we were in debt, and had no money in the treasury, which we could not conveniently use. Now we owe nothing, and have an overflowing treasury. The common wants for an economical administration of the government, will require but a small portion of our vast and accumulating treasure; and the question is, what disposition shall we make of the surplus.

Several projects have been presented. An increase of the Army, of the Navy, additional fortifications, and munitions of War, is one plan. Another is to put the funds in the power of the Commissioners of the Sinking Fund, and let them vest them in stocks, which will add to our wealth. A third is, to form contracts with incorporated railroad companies, for transporting the mail, your warlike stores, and your armies. And the fourth is that presented by this bill, which is to distribute the proceeds of the public lands among the several States.

In forming an opinion upon this subject I find myself compelled to form some opinion on each of the others also, that I may be able to decide which ought be preferred.

But the first question to be settled is one of *power*.

If we have *no power* to dispose of this money, as this bill proposes, it is only a waste of time to pursue the subject any farther.

Some of our enlightened public men, years past, foresaw difficulties, which would, in time, originate from surpluses accumulating in the treasury, and suggested this very plan for disposing of them. Some doubted the power under the Constitution, and suggested an amendment to remove the doubt; others felt no doubts, therefore did not deem any amendment necessary. All, however, seem to have concurred in the *fairness* and *justice* of this disposition of such funds, as might not be needed, for the uses of the federal government.

If I mistake not, Mr. Jefferson, while President, made a suggestion to Congress on this subject.

Ten years ago an honorable senator, from New Jersey, now Secretary of the Navy, and I do him the justice to add, then, as well as now, a zealous friend of the present Chief Magistrate, moved in this body on this subject, had a committee created, made an able, detailed report, accompanied by a bill, which was not finally acted on during the session.

To do that gentleman justice I must recur to this report, and read such parts of it as are material, that we may have the benefit of his opinion as enforced by himself. It is found in the 4th vol. of the Senate Documents at the session 1825 and 1826: doc. 95, page 1; and is in these words:

The Committee, from as careful an examination of the subject, as a due attention to their other duties would permit them to make, have come to the conclusion that great advantages would result to the United States from an annual distribution among them, by some equitable ratio, of a portion of our national revenue, for the purposes of education and internal improvement, or for such other purposes as the State governments may respectively deem most to their advantage. Whether the United States shall divide the whole of their revenues, beyond what are required for the usual expenditures of the government, domestic and foreign, civil, military, and naval, to the reduction of our public debt, until the whole of it shall be extinguished; or whether they shall apply a portion of those revenues, as proposed for the most important purposes, and thereby cause a more gradual reduction of the public debt, resolves itself into a question of expediency.

It remains for Congress to determine which of these courses will most effectually promote the present, as well as the future, prosperity of the country. There can be no doubt, that money distributed among the States as proposed, would be invested in a way to give much greater profit, than the interest on such money would yield at three, four and a half, or even five per cent, which are the rates of interest now paid on the greater part of our public debt.

As a large portion of this debt is payable to persons in Europe, to discharge it as fast as our means would permit, would be to send from the country sooner than necessary, funds that are wanted at home; the inconvenience of which would be sensibly felt in the present embarrassed state of our money market, and most probably, for several years to come.

Money distributed as proposed, would give new ***activity to industry and enterprise*** in ***all*** the States; and that ***equally*** and ***simultaneously***.

It would create a vigilance on the part of the State governments, over the expenditures of the general government, and thereby prevent the waste of money, and the adoption of extravagant measures, that might diminish the amount of the annual dividends.

It would secure *impartial justice to all the States* in the distribution of the expenditures of our revenue, a failure in which at present is a subject of loud and just complaint.

It would relieve the general government of the serious inconvenience of an overflowing treasury, which, if not provided for in the manner proposed, or by a reduction of our revenue, will impair the most important principles of our Constitution.

It would relieve the two Houses of Congress of a large portion of legislation, now devoted to the disposal of our surplus funds—legislation of the worst kind, calculated to produce combinations, sectional feelings, injustice and waste of the public treasure.

It would transfer to the States, the regulation of expenditures for internal improvements by roads and canals, which if retained and exercised by the general government, contrary, as is believed by many, to the letter and spirit of our Constitution, will, in time, so far decrease the powers of the State governments, and increase those of the United States government, as to destroy the federative principle of our Union, and convert our system of confederated republics into a consolidated government.

It would remove the cause of the great and increasing difficulties arising from an objection, on constitutional grounds, to the exercise of the right claimed on the part of the United States, of making roads and canals through the different States of the Union. It would enable the general government to keep in operation an efficient system of finance and revenue with advantage to the States. And should the exigencies of the country require the application of all our means to some object connected with our national peace and prosperity, those means could soon be brought into operation, by suspending, for a time, the dividends to the States. By this our treasury would be filled without a sudden resort to new taxes, which might be oppressive to agriculture, and which might create much inconvenience by interrupting the pursuits and industry of our citizens.

Money collected from the sources which now give us our revenues and distributed among the States as proposed, would produce a rapid and profitable circulation of our funds, from the centre to the extremities of the Union, and thus add to the force of the moneyed capital of the country.

It will here be remarked, no doubt was felt or expressed, as to *power* to distribute every portion of the revenue, which could be spared, and a plan was recommended for adoption immediately, although we then owed a large debt, bearing various rates of interest from three up to six per centum.

Next in the order of time, is the message of the present Chief Magistrate at the commencement of the session of Congress in 1829, found in the Senate Journal, pages 13 and 14. That part of it which is material, is in these words:

After the extinction of the public debt it is not probable that any adjustment of the tariff, upon principles satisfactory to the people of the Union, will, until a remote period, if ever, leave the government without a considerable surplus in the treasury, beyond what may be necessary for its current service. As then the period approaches when the application of the revenue to the payment of debt will cease, the disposition of the surplus will present a subject for the serious deliberation of Congress, and it may be fortunate for the country that it is yet to be decided. Considered in connection with the difficulties which have heretofore attended appropriations for purposes of internal improvement, and with those which this experience tells us will certainly arise, whenever power over such subjects may be exercised by the general government, it is hoped that it may lead to the adoption of some plan, which will reconcile the diversified interests of the States, and strengthen the bonds which unite them. Every member of the Union, in peace and in war, will be benefited by the improvement of inland navigation, and the construction of *highways* in the several States. Let us then endeavor to attain this benefit in a mode which will be satisfactory to all. That hitherto adopted has, by many of our fellow-citizens, been deprecated as an infraction of the Constitution; while, by others, it has been avowed inexpedient. All feel that it has been employed at the expense of harmony in the legislative councils.

To avoid these evils, it appears to me that the most safe, just and federal disposition, which could be made of the surplus revenue, would be its apportionment among the several States according to their ratio of representation—and should this measure not be found warranted by the Constitution, that it would be expedient to propose to the States an amendment authorizing it. I regard an appeal to the source of power, in cases of real doubt, and when its exercise is deemed indispensable to the general welfare, as among the most sacred of all our obligations. Upon this country, more than any other, has, in the providence of God, been cast the special guardianship of the great principle of adherence to written Constitutions. If it fail here, all hope in regard to it will be extinguished. That this was intended to be a government of limited and specific, and not general, powers, must be admitted by all; and it is our duty to preserve for it the character intended by its framers. If experience points out the necessity for an enlargement of these powers, let us apply for it to those for whose benefit it is to be exercised; and not undermine the whole system by a resort to overstrained constructions.

It will be perceived that in these two short paragraphs, the justice and utility of distributing these surplus funds, are presented to the mind, in language as clear, distinct, and forcible, as can well be employed.

It was not necessary to his purpose, and therefore he did not examine the question whether the powers of Congress over the moneys arising from the *public lands*, were as limited as those possessed over moneys derived from *taxes*, and he contents himself with the expression of a general doubt on the question of power, and recommends an amendment of the Constitution to remove it.

At the session of 1831 and 1832, this subject is introduced into the report of Mr. McLane, then Secretary of the Treasury, and afterwards Secretary of State. What he says will be found in the Senate Documents, vol. 1, doc. 3, page 12—and is in these words:

The sources from which the revenue has hitherto been derived, are the imports, public lands, and bank dividends. With the sales of the bank stock the latter will cease; and as the imports, according to any scale of duties which it will be expedient and practicable to adopt, will be "amply sufficient" to meet all the expenditures, that portion of the revenue heretofore drawn from the sale of the public lands may be dispensed with, should Congress see fit to do so.

On this point, the undersigned deems it proper to observe, that the creation of numerous States throughout the Western country, now forming a most important part of the Union, and the relative powers claimed and exercised by Congress and the respective States over the public lands, have been gradually accumulating causes of inquietude and difficulty, if not of complaint. It may well deserve consideration, therefore, whether, at a period demanding an amicable and permanent adjustment of the various subjects which now agitate the public mind, these may not be advantageously disposed of, in common with the others, and upon principles just and satisfactory to all parts of the Union.

It must be admitted that the public lands were ceded by the States, or subsequently acquired by the United States, for the common benefit, and that "each State has an interest in their proceeds, of which it cannot justly be deprived." Over this part of the public property, the powers of the general government have been uniformly supposed to have a peculiarly extensive scope, and have been construed to authorize their application to purposes of education and improvement, to which other branches of revenue were not deemed applicable. It is not practicable to keep the public lands out of the market, and the present mode of disposing of them is not the most profitable, either to the general government, or to the States, and must be expected, when the proceeds shall be no longer required for the public debt, to give rise to new and more serious objections.

Under these circumstances, it is submitted to the wisdom of Congress, to decide upon the propriety of all the public lands in the aggregate, to those States within whose territorial limits they lie, at a fair price, to be settled in such manner as might be satisfactory to all. The aggregate price of the whole "may then be apportioned among the several States of the Union," according to such equitable ratio as may be consistent with the objects of the original session, and the proportion of each paid.

The vigorous and discriminating mind of this highly gifted and useful man, at once recognizes as sound, a distinction in the powers of Congress over moneys derived from a disposition of the public lands, and those powers which that body may be supposed to possess over moneys derived from other sources, and he strongly urges the necessity and propriety of a distribution among the States.

It is fortunate that we are not yet placed in circumstances which make it essential to decide whether we have a power to divide *all* surplus revenue, no matter from what source derived.

I profess to be what is called a strict constructionist of the Constitution, and that our power to *appropriate* money is necessarily confined to appropriations, *to effect some object upon which Congress is expressly empowered to legislate*, or some necessary and appropriate means to effect such enumerated objects. Still I never have been *satisfied* we do *not* possess the power to distribute surplus revenue, if it is believed wise to do so.

No just government will take, either by direct or indirect taxes, more money than is necessary to defray all the *reasonable expenses* of the government. When taxes are imposed either directly, or by an assessment of duties, it cannot be foretold precisely how much will be wanted, or how much will be received, in the treasury. We must necessarily act upon estimates. To some extent, we shall be mistaken. Foreseeing this, and for the sake of collecting what will be certainly sufficient, we shall almost invariably collect more than is necessary. In a series of years, these accumulating balances will amount to a sum too large to remain locked up and entirely useless. What then is to be done? We surely are not at liberty to devise some wasteful and mischievous project, merely to use the money.

It came into the treasury by mistake—mistakes which, in the nature of things, could not be avoided. Have we no power to correct them when discovered? Is not the power to refund the money a *necessary result* from *the power to assess and collect it?*

Is not this a power which Congress has always exercised, and must exercise, as to individuals?

By mistake, our officers collect and place in the treasury, money which ought not to have been collected; the mistake is discovered, and the individual calls on Congress for redress. We pass a law to refund the money. Where do we get power to do this? There is no express grant of any such power; but it results from the very nature of the relation which exists between the *payer* and *receiver*. The latter must always have power to act *justly*, to act *honestly*, and whenever he finds he has money through *mistake*, he would seem to have power to return it. But I do not intend to express any opinion on this point, or to prolong a discussion, by introducing important topics, not necessary to our action on this bill. All I intended, was to state, for myself, that should it ever become necessary to discuss the general subject of our power to distribute the *whole surplus*, no matter from *what source* derived, for one, I think it well worth a careful and deliberate consideration, before it is either *affirmed* or *denied;* and I most heartily concur in the sound doctrine of the President, that we ought *not to act*, when there is a reasonable doubt of our power.

The question which we must now decide is, whether we have power to do that, which all admit, it is perfectly *just* we should do, if we have the *power*—distribute the proceeds of the sales of the public lands.

The following considerations have satisfied my own mind, and they are respectfully submitted for the reflection of others. Our public lands were acquired by the United States, by deeds of cessions from several *individual* States, and by the purchase of Louisiana and Florida, which were *paid* for by moneys derived from the *lands which had been ceded by individual States.*

The most important cession was made by the State of Virginia, in the year 1784, and that part of the cession material to our present purpose, is in the following words:

> That all the lands within the territory so ceded to the United States, and not reserved for, or appropriated to any of the before-mentioned purposes, or disposed of in bounties to the officers and soldiers of the American army, shall be considered as a "common fund" for the use and benefit of such of the United States as have become, or "shall" become, members of the confederation, or federal alliance of the said States, "Virginia inclusive, according to their usual respective proportions in the general charge and expenditure," and shall be "faithfully and bona fide disposed of for that purpose, and for no other use or purpose whatsoever." —*Laws U S. vol. i.*, p. 474.

This language creates an *express trust* between the United States and each individual State.

By it the United States stand pledged to hold these lands in *trust*, that they shall be *faithfully managed*, and their avails applied for the *joint benefit of all.*

So far as it has been applied to the payment of debts due by all, the trust has been complied with; but now the debts are paid, and there is a surplus, have we the power to give this surplus to those for whose use the trust was created?

I might ask who can doubt it?

Suppose the States still bound together only by the articles of confederation, out of money raised in its own way, and out of its own means, each State had paid, when called on, its regular quota for the expenses of the federal government, and for the payment of the national debt, and there was a surplus of twenty or thirty millions of dollars, for which the federal government had no use, would we not be bound to distribute it? I say we would not only have the power to do so, but if we did not exert it, a court of chancery *would compel us*, if we could be sued.

The very terms of the cession look to *distribution.* If this were not so, why say in the deed, that when used for the benefit of all, "*Virginia*" *shall be included?* Why fix the "*ratio*" in which payments shall be made to each? If we only have power to *pay debts*, and bear *common expenses of government*, with these moneys, and can do nothing else with them, both these regulations would have been useless.

I take it, therefore, as too clear for a doubt, that if now connected by the articles of confederation only, we would have the power to distribute.

The next question is, did the adoption of the *present Constitution* alter the rights of the parties, *or take from Congress* the power to comply with their *engagement?* I answer, unhesitatingly, no.

In the 6th article of the Constitution, the first paragraph runs thus:

All debts contracted, "and engagements entered into," before the adoption of this Constitution, shall be as valid against the United States under this Constitution "as under the confederation."

In the third section of the fourth article of the same instrument, this language is found:

The Congress shall have power to dispose of, and make all needful rules and regulations, respecting the territory or other property of the United States, and nothing in this Constitution shall be construed to prejudice any claims of the United States, or of any "particular State."

Thus we find all debts contracted, and *engagements* entered into, *before*, were to remain unchanged, and the *respective rights* of the United States and of each *individual State*, were to *remain precisely as if the form of government had not been altered*, and express power is conferred to dispose of the public lands, and to make all needful rules and regulations respecting the territory or other property of the United States.

With these different provisions before him, who can doubt the power of the United States, to do that which, by accepting this trust, they expressly agree to do?

Cessions from the other States are made substantially on the same conditions, and liable to the same dispositions by Congress. Louisiana and Florida were purchased with the *avails* of those ceded lands, *the trustee is the same*, and that trustee holds these lands *loaded with exactly the same burden*, and is bound, if those for whose use they are holden desire it, to dispose of them and their proceeds in the same manner.

I hold, therefore, that, be the general question of power to distribute the *whole revenue* settled as it may, there ought to be no question as to the *power* to divide moneys *arising from the sales of lands.*

But it has been argued that if we have the power there is no money to divide. That when the amount is settled, the net gain will not exceed $400,000.

To this I can never agree. The United States took this *trust fund*, and with it purchased *Louisiana* and *Florida*, and now we are told they have had the use of the money for nothing, and will only account for the *principal.*

This is not the rule. If the trustee takes the trust fund and trades upon it, he must account to the *cestuy que use*, for all the profits made.

The question in chancery would be, not what these countries cost, but what they are worth.

You cannot fix a price. Louisiana and Florida! The sovereignty and jurisdiction over them *alone*, is worth more to this Union, than all the national debt we ever owed.

How much duties have we collected from their ports? How much have we avoided paying, by making them our own, instead of letting them remain foreign ports? How many wars have we avoided by their purchase? In short, what would you take for them? No sum! They are beyond price to the rest of the Union.

On this part of the subject, the question with me is, not what sum we now have in the treasury, which was received for the *sale of lands*, but whether we have a sum in the treasury equal to that proposed to be distributed, over and above all that is necessary to be appropriated to take care of the great *interests of the country*, and without debiting the States with the sums paid for Louisiana and Florida, because I am sure, upon a fair settlement, the sum due from the Union is at least equal to the sum which it is proposed now to distribute.

What sum have we, and what shall we probably receive, in the course of the year?

I will take round sums, disregarding fractions.

We now have in the treasury	$32,000,000
Of this sum, the quarter ending 31st March, produced $11,000,000. Suppose the remaining three quarters to average the like sum, and we will have on the 31st December, more by	33,000,000
Add the value of our bank stock	7,500,000
Estimated amount	$72,500,000
Deduct for falling off and deficiencies	5,500,000
	$67,000,000

After this liberal deduction we shall have sixty-seven millions at the end of the year.

Now for expenditures:

The ordinary wants of the government ought not to exceed $15,000,000. Mr. McLane, in the report of 1831, to which I have adverted, fixes upon that as a sum *amply sufficient*, and it appears to me in all conscience it must be enough, unless our prosperity is to drive us into most mad excesses.

Let us then take this as the sum necessary for our ordinary expenses in the course of the year	$15,000,000
Add to this, to be distributed among the States . .	27,000,000
These two sums amount to	$42,000,000

Take forty-two millions from sixty-seven, and we still have in the treasury *twenty-five* millions of dollars, to apply to any extraordinary expenditures for the army, the navy, for fortifications, or for any other purpose whatever.

The army ought to be increased so much as to render secure our frontiers. The increase of our navy may be hastened to some extent; we ought ultimately to have a naval force, more than able to chastise and drive off any *foreign fleet* sent to *blockade*, or seriously to infest our coast. Larger than that we do not need, and ought not to have, if it were given to us.

Fortifications are only wanted for important points, at which an enemy might do much mischief to public or to private property, by a sudden incursion. The whole coast we never can, and should never attempt to defend by fortifications.

If we do, we must have a large standing army to defend them; otherwise they will be applied to the protection of our enemies.

We are told by the Secretary of War, in a document before me, that Old Point Comfort covers sixty-three acres of ground, and to protect it by an adequate force, would require *several thousand men.*

We never can, we never ought to attempt to defend our whole coast, by so many fortifications, as will require any considerable increase of our army.

If we do, in time of peace, these troops will come on days of *election*, and as they are hired to do our *fighting* they will do our *voting* likewise, and in a short time leave us nothing worth fortifying.

Such defences are contrary to the spirit and genius of our government, and ought never to be *countenanced, or tolerated* to the unreasonable extent, which some appear now to desire. In the same document at pages 21, 22, from the War Department, the Secretary says, no new fortification ought to be commenced until all the proposed sites are re-surveyed and plans devised upon a suitable scale, and recommends a board for that purpose, which will require a small appropriation of thirty thousand dollars.

He also recommends experiments to be made in relation to steam, or movable batteries, which will require an appropriation of one hundred thousand dollars.

Well then, if we concur with the Secretary, we want at present no appropriation for new fortifications, but these two sums equal to one hundred and thirty thousand dollars to defray the expenses of a board, and the experiments of which I have spoken.

As to the fortifications, *now in progress*, let such increase be made in the appropriations, as can reasonably be used in the course of the year.

As to the suggestion made that we ought, at once, to appropriate a sum large enough to *complete the work*, although it may be five or ten years before it can be completed, I do not think it ought to be sanctioned. It is unnecessarily, and for a long time, putting at hazard in the hands of agents, who may prove faithless, large sums of money. From year to year let the appropriations be made, and thus avoid all unnecessary risk.

According to this same document, the expense necessary for ordnance must be comparatively trifling. We can be much more readily supplied than I had imagined.

Upon the whole I think all the reasonable demands for the army, for the navy, for fortifications, ordnance, and other munitions of war, can be supplied without making any serious impression upon that large fund left in the treasury, after providing for the distribution, as proposed in this bill.

Allusion has been made to matters pending before us, when not acting as a legislature, which, if perfected, may occasion a considerable increase of expenditure.

That may be so; yet we must remember that not much of this expenditure will, or can be this year, or the next, and that these very measures will increase our resources, if not entirely equal to our increased expenditures, very nearly so. These matters, therefore, may be laid aside.

Another project for ridding the treasury of its surplus, is that of placing it in the hands of Commissioners of the Sinking Fund, and authorizing them to vest it in some secure stock, yielding a reasonable profit. This might do, and is probably intended as an expedient to save the money from loss; but as to a mode of lessening the fund, it would be making bad worse, it would be devising a plan to *increase* our store, because we should expect a return of the principal and the *interest* produced by it.

But for myself, I have no idea of sending our money among stock-jobbers, into the market, to be higgling for bargains, which in one way may be very good, and in some other, very bad. Far rather would I prefer they should remain where they now are.

The last scheme for adoption is, that from the Post Office Committee with the aid of steam. With the aid of this machinery, I have very little doubt the whole can be accomplished in a very short time.

The whole of this, which, without intending disrespect to the Committee, I must call artful contrivance, is neither more nor less, than the *old system of internal improvement, with federal means, and by federal power*, revived, and the more odious, because of the attempt at concealment. The old system has the merit of manliness. Its friends think the federal government has the power, and openly avow that they will exercise it, because, in doing so, they promote the public interest. This seeks to violate the Constitution by stealth, and the contrivers of it must think the device is so artfully concealed, that the public can never find out the design.

Now, sir, I think it perfectly proper, that where a railroad can be had, the Postmaster General ought to have the *power to contract with the company*, to carry his mail, and I understand he *has this power already;* therefore, as to existing roads, the bill will be of no use. He can make just as good a contract without, as with, this bill.

It can only operate on roads commenced and unfinished, or ones being commenced. How then will it operate? Say the road is to be one hundred miles long, and ten or twenty miles only finished, and the company to need funds, they make a contract to carry the mail, and receive at once out of the treasury, a sum of money, the interest on which, yearly, will be equal to the sum paid yearly in time past, for carrying the mail; with this money the company are to progress, and make another part of the road, then the contract will be enlarged on the same principles, an additional sum paid, and thus the road completed. Can this be anything but an *enlarged, masked* system of internal improvement? and if the charter of the company is for fifty or an hundred years, or for ever, your contracts are to be in the same way. To carry out this system, what sum would it probably cost? No man dares to offer a conjecture.

To enable us to have a glimpse of it, let us suppose one case. Upon a given route the sum paid for carrying the mail was twenty thousand dollars per annum. We are now to give to the company presently, and to be retained as long as the charter lasts, a sum which, at an interest of six per cent., will produce twenty thousand dollars yearly.

What sum would that be? No less than three hundred and thirty-three thousand three hundred and thirty-three dollars and one-third.

This would be but one route, and I presume of the middling class, and pray what sum would it not require, to spread this system over the United States?

Suppose one of those companies, directly after receiving your money, to fail, and decline business, what then? We must lose the money, or take the road. We take the road and employ managers, and hands enough, to carry on business, *on our own account.* We should then have a little army of our own, moving to and fro by steam. Under such a system, we would be steamed out of all our money, all our character, and everything but a handsome addition to federal patronage.

Adopt this plan, and my word for it, we will never have another argument on the subject of disposing of our surplus revenue: it will be scattered to the four winds.

As this project is brought forward by a friend of the Administration, it is supposed to be an Administration measure; by this I mean, a measure approved by the President. How this fact may be, I do not profess to know, but I have seen enough in my day here, to satisfy me, that it is very unfair, that every measure brought forward, and advocated by members professing to be friends of the Administration, should be considered as having the sanction of the President. I know not what his opinions on such subjects are now; I know what they *have been*, and until informed in some authentic mode, they have been changed, I esteem it fair to suppose they remain unchanged.

Let us hear him speak for himself, in two of his communications. In his annual message, 1830, the President says:

In speaking of direct appropriations, I mean to include a practice, which has obtained to some extent, and to which I have in one instance, in a different capacity, given my assent—that of subscribing to the stock of private associations. Positive experience, and a more thorough consideration of the subject, have convinced me of the impropriety, as well as inexpediency, of such investments. All improvements effected by the funds of the nation, for general use, should be open to the enjoyment of all our fellow-citizens, except from the payment of tolls, or any imposition of that character.

Same message, he says farther:

That such improvements, on account of particular circumstances, may be more advantageously and beneficially made in some States than in others, is doubtless true; but that they are of a character which should prevent an equitable distribution of the public funds amongst the several States, is not to be concluded.

We have it constantly before our eyes, that professions of superior zeal in the cause of internal improvement, and a disposition to lavish the public funds upon objects of that character, are daily and earnestly put forth by aspirants to power, as constituting the highest claims to the confidence of the people. Would it be strange, under such circumstances, and in times of great excitement, that grants of this description should find their motives in objects which may not accord with the public good. Those who have not had occasion to see, and regret, the indication of a sinister influence, in these matters, in time past, have been more fortunate than myself, in their observation of the cause of human affairs.

In his message of 1832, he says:

I recommend that provision be made to dispose of all stocks, now held by it (the government), in corporations, whether created by the general or State governments, and placing the proceeds in the treasury. As a source of profit, these stock are of little, or no, value; as a means of influence among the States, *they are adverse to the purity of our institutions.* The whole principle on which they are based, is deemed by many unconstitutional, and to persist in the policy which they indicate, is considered wholly inexpedient."

Are we to infer, after this, that he would approve of this plan? I think not. To me, it appears much more probable, were we to pass such a bill as this, that it would be vetoed by him, than that he should negative the distribution bill, when he would reflect upon the altered state of things, since that subject was acted on by him.

Such a system as this would be one of internal improvement, with the moneys, and under the patronage of the federal government. It would be for the benefit of companies, some of whose charters may be for long periods, as without limit as to time, they would still continue to receive toll from the people.

It would operate partially and unjust to the different sections of the country. Some would receive plenty; others none.

Instead of trying to rid the government of *all connection* with *stock companies*, we would be forming more extensive and dangerous connections than have ever been thought of in time past. I therefore conclude, such a scheme, however plausible at first view, can never ultimately find favor from any majority in Congress.

I will now advert to some of the strongest objections which I have heard, to the policy of distribution.

It is thought a system of distribution will make the States feel *dependent on the federal government*, and induce them to engage in enterprises not necessary, and beyond their fair means.

Ought we not to remember that it is the same people, who are represented, both in the State and federal legislatures? That they are competent to understand their own rights, and have the power to compel obedience to their will, by their representatives at home as well as here?

Will they not know that the money distributed is their *own money*, not a boon from Congress? How then will they feel dependent upon those who have done them *no favor*, but the simple act of justice, *of paying them their own money*, in place of keeping it locked up, or having it wasted by others.

If the people are capable of self-government, they must be capable of understanding their *own rights*, and pursuing their *own interests*. They will not view this as a *boon*, but as a delivery to them of that which is their *own*. They will never look to distribution as a *regular* and *certain* resource for State purposes, but as an incidental addition to their other means, which will enable them to carry on with more vigor, any plan, which in their wisdom may be devised, for improving their country, or increasing the means of education.

Again. It is said the *new States* may justly fear that distribution will induce the old States to keep the price of lands high, and thereby check settlements in them.

It appears to me there can be no real foundation for any alarm on this account. The new States now form a very respectable minority. That minority will soon be increased to the number of ten or eleven. If we are fit to live together under one general government, there never can, there never will, come a time, when so large a minority cannot prevail upon enough to make up a majority, to do that which is not only just, but liberal to them.

Nothing can be so likely to prevent this, as a contracted and illiberal policy on their part. If they prevent distribution, and thus prevent others from attaining any participation in a common fund, and this with a view to benefit themselves, may they not destroy all disposition to meliorate their condition? Will it not be more wise in them, to let that, which can well be spared from the proceeds of the public lands, be distributed, and with their fair proportion of it, in common with other States, go on and make such internal improvements as the interest of their people demands, and rely upon the justice of Congress, from time to time, to make such reductions in the price of the public lands, in favor of *actual settlers*, as the interests of the new States may require?

For one, having been raised, and having lived in a new State, and knowing the difficulties they have to encounter, my feelings have been with them, and, since honored with a place here, I have ever been disposed by my votes to favor their wishes and interests, so far as it could consistently be done. I hope still to do so, let them pursue what course they may.

Either now, or at any subsequent time, I am ready to vote a reduction of the price of the public lands, in favor of the *actual settler*, the cultivator of the soil; but not to favor the *speculator*—he who would buy largely at a *small price*, to sell to the *settler* in *small quantities* at a *high price.*

Of all the evils which can befall a new State, none is greater, than to reduce the price so low as to encourage individuals or companies to purchase large quantities of the public domain. They will be *held up* for *increased prices*, and effectually check the growth, the prosperity, and wealth of any State, where such policy is pursued.

But the *actual settler* may well be favored by procuring a home of his own, at a *low price*, where he can cultivate his own soil, and independently of all others, maintain his family.

I voted yesterday against the amendment of the senator from Mississippi, because it did not provide for *actual settlers*, only for those who *represented that they wished to become settlers.* Let lands be entered upon such statements, and those who entered them would, in many cases, soon change their minds, and *some speculator* would be found to be the *true owner*, at the *reduced price.*

Whenever the lands have been so long in market, at a reasonable price, as to show that they are not of value to the general government, let them be transferred upon some fair terms to the States in which they respectively lie.

In the State which I have the honor in part to represent, the United States now own some lands, which never have been, and never can be, brought into market by them, so as to produce any benefit whatever; to the State they would be worth something; there is now a bill pending in the other house, which has for its object their transfer to the State, and if it reaches the Senate, which I hope it soon will, it is believed we shall be able to show the propriety of passing it.

Let us now reflect a little on some of the advantages which will flow from the passage of this bill.

In the first place we shall do that which is an act of justice to the individual States. Several of them, my own among the rest, have never received a dollar from the federal government, while others have received large donations in lands, or in money.

In some States, opposed to internal improvements by the federal government, no contributions have been made for either roads or canals, while in others large sums have been expended. This inequality has produced heart-burnings and discontents. Give to each its own proportion of this fund, to use as it pleases, and this cause of discontent will be removed.

Each State is the proper judge what ought to be done with its own money. I am, therefore, opposed to giving any direction as to the objects to which it shall be applied: but I have no doubt, in most instances, it will be expended either in internal improvements, or in the business of education.

I have been one of those, who do not believe the federal government has the *power to carry on a system of internal improvements within the States;* and I shall now think it peculiarly hard, when we find a large sum of money, which we have the power to distribute, if it should be taken, and wasted upon remote and distant objects, and my State receive nothing. I should consider myself criminally negligent, if I did not urge the necessity of giving that, which I think is justly our due.

By making this distribution we shall withdraw from the deposit banks a large sum of money, now locked up from the common and beneficial pursuits of life, and put it in circulation, not in one State or place in particular, but in every State in the Union, so that its beneficial effects will be felt by all.

Now, if this money is loaned by the banks, it is evident to my mind, the loans are not made to commercial men, accustomed to bank accommodations, but to companies, engaged in speculations in our most valuable public lands; by means of these loans, the honest settler is driven off from your public sales, or is forced to join some company, for the sake of enabling himself to procure, at a fair price, the small piece of land on which he has settled.

Formerly, we sold the public lands upon credit; while that was the case, companies were formed, and speculations carried to a great extent. I attended one of those sales, and saw enough to satisfy me, Mr. President, that if you and I could unite our capacity for business, we would not then be able to purchase, at its value, a section of land. The speculators would force us to join them, or drive us out of the market. They would tell us the land we desired to purchase was worth ten dollars per acre, and if we would give them the difference between the sum we had to give at sale, and ten dollars, then we might buy, otherwise they would run it up to twenty dollars per acre; and they would keep their word, if we did not come to terms; if we did, then we could bid off the land at a dollar and a quarter, which we would pay to the *government*, and in addition we would pay the *company eight and three quarter dollars per acre.*

The Congress determined to break up these speculations, by requiring cash payments. It worked very well till lately. Within the last year, the land speculations are revived to a fearful extent. Now what is probably the cause? These large sums, *so long on deposit*, enable the banks to make to these companies *large loans on long credits*, and with the money thus *borrowed*, your best lands are sacrificed. This is nothing but the *credit system revived in a new shape.* Formerly, the government itself, openly gave credit—now the banks give the credit, but the *government furnishes the funds which enable them to do so.* This is a growing evil. It is like rolling a snow-ball; every turn makes it larger, and if not checked, we shall soon have this matter carried to an extent, which will make the mischief incurable. *Divide this money*, and we take from the banks the *power* of making these loans, and your lands will be purchased in *fact*, as well as in *form*, for *money*.

Beside these considerations, we shall prevent our deposit banks from overtrading to an unreasonable extent. If these speculations are to be persisted in, a day of reckoning will come. If a run is made on your banks, which they cannot stand, we not only lose our money on deposit, but what is infinitely worse, we bring upon the country the evils of a *depreciated currency*, which always fall most heavily upon those least able to bear the loss.

Pass this bill, and we not only avoid these evils, but we furnish each State with the strongest inducements to aid your banks, in maintaining a *sound* and *wholesome* currency; with their proper proportions of which, when received, I have no doubt, all will make judicious *internal improvements*, and take care to have the business of education suitably encouraged.

When the leading measure of Mr. Van Buren's administration, the Sub-Treasury bill, was before the Senate in 1838, and was discussed by some of the ablest men in that body, he again avowed himself an enemy to "*federal incorporated banks*," and "*federal bills of credit.*" He opposed this measure principally upon the ground that it was putting the control of the whole moneyed capital of the country into the hands of the executive; and that, especially in view of the unwillingness of the executive to have the powers and patronage of the government curtailed, such a control was hazardous to the prosperity of our free institutions. On this subject he spoke as follows, March 24th, 1838:

Mr. President: I address you under circumstances of peculiar disadvantage. The subject is one of the greatest importance. It has been long discussed, ably discussed, by those of most distinguished talents. Their highest efforts have been made on both sides to present its advantages and disadvantages in every view the human mind can take of it.

The crowded audience has become wearied, and even many senators themselves can hardly give respectful attention to our most interesting debates.

Up to the termination of the last address of the distinguished senator from Massachusetts who sits nearest to me (Mr. Webster), I was not satisfied whether it would be my duty to do more than listen respectfully to others, and then say yea or nay to the different questions presented to the Senate.

At the close of his animated, able, and interesting speech, he recurred to a *scrap* of the history of my *own* State, fifty years ago. Instantly my mind settled down in the conviction that my constituents had a right to expect more of a son of one of the actors in that scene than a bare vote.

I promise those who may favor me with their attention, that if what I say should not be interesting, it shall not be tedious.

The advocates of this bill expect to accomplish two objects by its passage:

1st. To designate the only species of funds which shall be received in payment of any dues to the government.

2d. To designate the persons by whom, and the places where, those moneys shall be kept, between the time of their collection and disbursement.

The provisions, as to the first, are, that after the lapse of six years nothing shall be received but gold and silver, and such *paper* as shall be issued by or under the authority of the federal government; and, in the mean time, that certain proportions may be received in the notes of specie-paying banks.

1st. My first objection to this plan is, that it sets out with a distinction in favor of those who are in the employment of the federal government, or have any money to receive from it, and those who are in the employ of the State governments, as well as the mass of the people. The distinction is odious, and ought not to be sanctioned.

Senators who support this bill say these are mere catch-words (one kind of money for the government, and another for the people), of which all have become ashamed, and that latterly they have been driven out of the Senate.

To this, I reply, the gentlemen are mistaken; this distinction is made on the very face of the bill, in terms too plain to be misunderstood.

If all the money mentioned is of equal value, why mention gold and silver, treasury notes, notes of specie-paying banks, &c.? The whole argument in favor of the bill rests on the supposition that gold and silver are the best, and *that*, as far as it goes, is to be used for federal officers and those who have federal contracts, leaving to others to get what they can and how they can.

2d. The bill itself contemplates a paper medium emanating from the federal government. To this I object, because we have no power to issue it. As a currency, they are bills of credit, unconstitutional; more clearly so than to incorporate a bank; and because, if we can issue such a medium, we ought never to do it. It will lead to the most wasteful and extravagant expenditures. It will be used moderately at first, until the people become reconciled to it, and then gradually extended in place of borrowing money, so as to meet all the calls of an extravagant administration, and must end in a large national debt, or depreciate like your continental money.

Many, with great reason, have believed that no government can long be economical upon even a system of indirect taxation. That under such a system the people generally are not conscious of the burden they bear. They pay their taxes when they buy their clothes, or other articles, on which duties are imposed, without reflecting that any part of the money they thus expend comes into the treasury; they therefore cease to be watchful over the manner in which the public moneys are expended; and, whenever they cease to keep strict watch, their agents commence useless and wasteful expenditures. But when the taxes are direct, every man knows how much he pays, and when he pays, and will carefully watch how the moneys are expended; and if the expenditures are wasteful or extravagant, a suitable corrective will be immediately applied. Our whole system of federal taxation is in the general indirect; and, if we once commence a system of supplying *deficiencies* in the treasury by an issue of paper to be used as *currency*, the country may be ruined.

At the special session we were obliged to add ten millions of dollars to our means. This we did not do by a direct *loan*, which every man could understand, but by authorizing an *issue of treasury notes*. When that bill was before the Senate, the senator from Missouri, and, if I mistake not, the senator from Pennsylvania, both friends of the Administration, placed these notes on the ground of making a loan; that they, as they were to bear an interest not exceeding five *per cent.* would be disposed of for money, and with the money thus procured, our creditors could be paid; and in this view I voted for the bill. In the House the amount of the notes was reduced one-half, and I soon perceived that the Administration intended to use them, *not* to procure a loan, but as a currency; and when the bill was returned to us, I took the earliest opportunity to record my vote against it. The notes issued under that bill have in fact been *used as a currency*, and at various rates of interest, some as low as one mill per year.

This year our revenue is again to be deficient; we will need, in addition to our means in the treasury, ten, fifteen, or twenty millions of dollars; and this addition will be made by new issues. This paper currency seems to *cost nothing;* and, as our wants *increase*, the *issues* will be *increased*, until the paper *depreciates;* and then, for the first time, the people will seriously look into the manner in which not only their *money*, but their *credit* has been squandered.

The provisons of this bill for treasury notes, bills, or other *securities*, *issued by the federal government*, or under its authority, if sanctioned by Congress, will settle a principle which, if carried into practice, must seal the fate of this nation. Office-holders and office-hunters can all be accommodated by the executive at the public expense, and the people will not be aware of it until too late. In short, it will take off almost the only restraint which yet remains to our extravagant expenditures.

This view of the subject has alarmed me. Do we not all see and know that those in office are pressing to have their salaries increased? That those who are not, desire the number of offices increased that they may get in? We are teased to increase the number of land districts; and if we do, offices are multiplied. When all the offices among the whites are filled, then we have among our red brethren exploring parties, visiting parties, commissioners and agents, by construction, at executive disscretion, and compensated as he pleases.

With the facilities of paper money to be created for the trouble of making, importunities for offices, jobs, contracts and increase of salary, will be multiplied, and the President will not have the heart to resist them when artfully pressed by noisy and worthless partisans. I have been forcibly struck with some of the remarks made upon the subject of this government paper currency. The honorable senator from South Carolina (Mr. Calhoun) thinks it will not depreciate, and if it does, it will not make any difference, as the government must always receive it at par, and therefore sustain the whole loss.

Mr. President, if the honorable senator will take a moment to think upon this subject, I am convinced he will perceive the error. No paper currency, *not convertible into specie at the will of the holder*, ever did or ever will long retain its nominal value.

If a man has a note of any kind, and has confidence that he can get the amount of it in specie at any time he pleases, most generally he would rather have the note than specie, because more convenient; but the moment he doubts, then he wants the specie presently. In the issue of treasury notes, that moment the amount issued much exceeds the revenue to be paid into the treasury, and the purchase of public lands, they must and will depreciate, unless provision is made that they shall be paid when presented at the treasury. When they do depreciate, the whole loss will not fall on the treasury, but will fall likewise on those through whose hands they have passed. The very case put by the senator proves it. A treasury note issues for fifteen dollars. It depreciates until it can be purchased in market for ten. Some person who owes the treasury fifteen dollars, goes and purchases it at ten, and pays his debt of fifteen dollars. Now does not every one perceive that the profit of five dollars, made by the man who paid the note to the treasury, must have been a loss of the same amount to the man from whom he purchased, or to some other person through whose hands it has passed? In all such cases, profit and loss are correllative terms, and that which is one man's gain must have been a loss to some other.

As you increase expenditures you increase executive power, already too great. The President or those acting under his orders, must necessarily select the recipients, who, it will always be understood, can only be those who conform to his wishes in elections. These objections are independent of the consideration whether this bill will establish a bank or not. It will certainly sanction the issuing a paper medium of circulation. Those who advocate this provision certainly think as I do, that the country must and always will have bank credits, or paper of some kind, to use as a substitute for the precious metals. The business of the country can never be done without it. A support of the State banks is the only shield which can be presented against federal bills of credit, and a *federal incorporated bank.*

I hold both these last unconstitutional, and the first of them infinitely the most dangerous to the liberties of the people. In 1834, I heard of this plan of separating government from all *banks as depositories*, and thought well of it. Indeed, I would then have gone for it, if political friends had agreed upon it. Then there was no idea of issuing *paper money* by government. Then *State banks were paying specie*, and their notes would have continued a circulating medium. Then I had confidence in the Administration, and believed that none would ever dare to interfere with the elective franchise, or to refuse to have the executive patronage limited and curtailed by law. Now all these things are changed. The Administration want paper money issued by government, substituted for loans. The State banks are not paying specie, and this bill forbids the receipt of their notes.

The executive is disposed to hunt down any and every man who wishes to limit his power. He openly interferes in elections, both State and federal, and uses all his powers to have them carried according to his will. Under these circumstances, in my judgment, I would be a traitor to civil liberty were I to sanction the idea that we will make federal paper the circulating medium.

What has become of our bills, five or six in number, to limit executive patronage, reported in the days of the younger Adams? They sleep the sleep of death. The honorable chairman of the committee, who originally reported them, felt it his duty to endeavor to revive them under the administration of the late President, and received so little countenance from *old friends* that he ceased his struggle with them.

The honorable senator from South Carolina, who never thinks any load too heavy, took up one of them, and made one of his most powerful efforts, and it passed this body. But how many old friends voted for it? Sir, all had been whistled or ordered off, except the senator from Missouri, and one or two others.

I have been honored with a seat here for the thirteen or fourteen last sessions, and believe I have never once recurred to the journals to see how any gentleman had voted; but there are some things I find it impossible to forget.

When that bill was before the Senate, believing that I could give the senator from South Carolina something more than my vote, I made a speech in its favor; and that speech sealed my fate with the great democratic party. I respectfully ask the senator from Missouri, whether any of the former friends of that measure, the Jackson democrats, voted for it, except he and myself?

It went to the other house, and as they were more fresh from the people than we, better understood what is meant by *modern* democracy, they put this aristocratic bantling to sleep; and we have never heard a cry or even a whimper from it since. Since then, executive power and patronage have put forth their branches in every direction, and no man dare raise his voice against them on pain of political death.

Shall we then put this rich bed of manure to the root of this dangerous power, that the crops of executive influence may be increased in our elections? Nay; God forbid!

I have been zealous for putting down the Bank of the United States, and for maintaining a sound metallic currency, and, to do this, believed we ought to sustain, as far as we could, State banks; prevailing on them, by all incidental means in our power, to cease the use of small notes and had hoped we could have succeeded: but specie payments have been suspended, and the advocates of this bill say we must try some other experiment.

Divorce, divorce, *a vinculo matrimonii* is the watchword whenever you find a modern democrat.

That there is a divorce *a mensa et thoro* existing, I admit, but am of opinion that it has been produced by *violent temper*, and want of *due care* on the part of the *federal head*, and too yielding and complying a disposition on the part of the banks, and that the whole might yet be reconciled, at all events to the advantage of the family.

I have heard of cases where a dashing libertine married a wife, attached to, and every way worthy of him; that he, upon looking farther into the world, concluded that if he were freed from his first love, he could be better suited on a second experiment; and, with a view to obtain a divorce, threw temptations in his wife's way which she had not stern virtue enough to resist; she sinned, and then he applied for a divorce. And what have courts of conscience said in such cases? Depart hence! you have contributed to your wife's transgression, and shall not profit by your own iniquity.

Apply these principles to this case. When the executive wooed and won the State banks, they were pure and unsullied. Their utmost exertions were necessary to aid in prostrating the Bank of the United States; they were coaxed, almost commanded, to extend their loans. They did so, to imprudent lengths. The executive saw and knew this. Were they admonished to diminish their discounts? Never! So far as I know, on the contrary, they were eulogized up to July, 1836; then came the executive denunciations, and they have never since ceased.

The executive is to blame, so are the banks; but on account of their quarrel, the great American family ought not to be sacrificed.

If none were to be injured but themselves, I certainly should feel no inclination to interfere; but I do think it nothing but just that both parties should bear their due proportion of blame, and that a separation ought not to be permitted under circumstances by which *an unoffending community* must be the sufferers.

But again; I think if it is even proper to establish this system, and to have this divorce, now is not the proper time.

The banks are State institutions; society have a deep interest in their maintaining a sound currency; this can only be done by resuming specie payments; this they never can do until their credit is reëstablished; while the whole weight of a popular Administration is against them, they never can resume with a hope of continuing specie payments. You separate now, and why? Because, say the whole Administration and its friends—and if we pass this bill we join in the cry—they are unworthy of credit! Every man who believes this statement, and has a claim against them, would apply for his money, and they would be compelled immediately to stop again.

Take the weight of the federal government off them. It is now pressing them into the dust, and while it is upon them, you might as well order a man, whose legs had been cut off, to jump to his feet and walk, as to require them to resume, with a hope that they can do so. Let their credit be again restored, and if we must separate, they could better then, than now, sustain the shock.

The federal government obtained the use of them when their credit was good; it should be restored, and then, if ever, they ought to be returned, in equally good credit, to the exclusive use of the States.

Suppose we pass this bill, and then the banks resume, five-sixths of the revenue must be taken in their notes; in a very short time, enough would be received to enable your depositories to withdraw so much of their specie as to compel them to suspend. And if they do not resume, their paper depreciates, and specie becomes an article of merchandise, and thus the federal servant will receive better money than the State officers, or the masters of both—the mass of the people.

The State banks never can resume with a hope of doing a profitable business.

Suppose the system in complete operation. Then all the revenue is received in specie, your average surplus in the treasury will be at least seven or eight millions of dollars. This, if left in the banks, would furnish a specie basis upon which safely to issue three for one. Hence, by this process, you abstract and lock up twenty or twenty-five millions of dollars of the circulating medium, which is of no more use to the government or individuals than if sunk in the ocean.

Banks go to excess occasionally, and there is temporary suffering: so of every thing else—we have nothing good but what produces evil when carried to excess. Banks issue too much paper, but that is no reason they should all be destroyed. Over-issues produce individual suffering. but even this is productive of some benefit. It makes roads and canals, and improves plantations. Although all these change owners when a curtailment takes place, yet the improvements remain for the benefit of the people at large.

What do gentlemen mean? Do they mean to put us back to the year eleven hundred, when they say banks commenced; Are we to quit our ordinary business, and commence wading branches in search of golden pebbles, to add to the stock of precious metals? Are we to give up the earnings of our families, our porringers, and our spoons to this Aaron of democracy, that he may melt them, and, with his graving tools, make us our own metallic god to worship? The more free a country is, the more prone are its people to run into *excess*, and none so much as our own. What was Great Britain before the establishment of her bank? Like other nations, who are destitute of everything but a specie circulation, poor, unthrifty, anti-commercial. And what is she now?

We need a larger circulation than any country upon earth of the same population, because we are freer than any other. The circulation ought always to bear a due proportion to all salable or exchangeable commodities. In some of the States everything is of that description. Entails are destroyed, all property, real and personal, is unfettered, and for sale whenever a man thinks he can better himself by selling in an old, and purchasing in a new State. In many States so much is land unfettered that it can be sold in fee simple upon a writ of *fieri facias.*

In our country a man's capital, in many instances, is his character for integrity, his capacity for business and his business habits. These give him credit with banks. With the aid of bank accommodations, in many instances he makes himself wealthy in a few years, and every man who adds to his own stock of wealth enriches the whole country.

Give me *wealthy* people and a *poor* treasury, and then the country is rich, and its liberty safe.

Destroy banks, and you throw every man again into the hands of capitalists, Jews, money-lenders, where few can borrow who cannot mortgage land to secure payment. Whereas banks always feel it a favor conferred on them when they can get a good customer.

Although I speak thus freely of the utility of banks, they never have been favorites of mine, but we must have them. The country cannot, and will not do without them.

We must have a *treasury bank*, *a bank incorporated by Congress*, or *State banks*. And I prefer the last. They are the least dangerous, and the States have clearly the power to incorporate them. The States, in granting charters, can, if they choose, guard generally against excesses. If they were to direct all profits over six or eight per cent. per annum to go into the treasury, as a school fund, the temptation to shave and to make excessive loans would be taken away. And if they would prohibit standing accommodations, few bad debts would be contracted.

2d. The other object of the bill is to compel our collectors and receivers to cease depositing money in banks, and to compel them to deposit all moneys in the hands of officers *appointed by the President*, and *removable* at his *pleasure*, there to be kept till needed for disbursement. I think this arrangement much worse than to deposit in the banks.

First, because the directors and officers of the banks will be more likely to be faithful than officers appointed by us. The stockholders will always intend to select those who will be most likely not to waste their moneys. Our officers for some time have been, and I consider the system is to be continued, selected more with a view to influence in elections than to any qualifications for the particular offices they are to fill. Let me not be misunderstood. I do not mean to say that every office-holder is a mere party tool. I think there are many who are not. But I do mean to state it as my opinion, that now, and for some time past, the principal qualification looked for is *political influence*; and such men, appointed from such motives, I think will generally be unsafe depositories. Supposing these officers equally faithful, they will not generally have places *as safe* as those provided by banks.

Again: this plan will occasion a great increase of expense. New officers, clerks, visitors, houses, safes, vaults, &c. There will be no effectual checks, either upon those officers or upon disbursing officers. It is said there have been, in modern times, but few losses by defalcation of disbursing officers.

One principal, if not the sole reason of this is, the check upon them, by ordering them, whenever their position will enable them to do so, to keep their moneys in banks, and every week or month an account is furnished the Secretary of the Treasury by the deposit bank showing the sums deposited, and by whom. This furnishes strong reasons against using or loaning money; immediate detection would be the consequence.

Under the proposed system this check is entirely removed, and the public money will, in many cases, be misused.

I now have in my drawer a document showing what has been done in one case by an officer in whose integrity I once had unlimited confidence. He collected a large claim from one debtor to the government, and immediately loaned the amount received to some *political friends*, not only without authority, but contrary to his instructions, and, at this moment, two suits are pending against these *new debtors*, who have refused to pay their notes as they fall due. If I mistake not, one of the parties to this very transaction has been appointed to, and now holds an office which will make him a sub-treasurer if this bill should pass.

A bank in my own State has been alluded to, in a letter read by the senator from Missouri, which he has received from the late Chief Magistrate.

A brief review of the history of that bank, and matters connected with it, may be of use to us on the subject under consideration.

The act establishing that bank was passed at a called session, in the year 1820. The charter of the United States Bank was passed in 1816, and the bank went into actual operation the 1st of January, 1817.

It was no administration measure, and when the bill was before Congress, the representative from my district sent me a copy of it, with a request that I would give him my opinion of its provisions, which I did, in a pretty lengthy letter. That opinion was very decidedly against the bill, and the opinion I then formed and expressed I have ever since entertained, and still entertain. He, alone, from Tennessee, as I believe, voted against the bill. For this vote he was attacked at home, and I felt in duty bound to maintain him as well as I could. This brought me in direct conflict with the friends of the United States Bank as early as 1816.

Soon after the bank went into operation, it established branches in Kentucky, and, before the fall of 1817, many of the loans first made had fallen due, and payment was exacted. To this the people had not been accustomed; and, as is always the case, although the bank had been popular when *making loans*, it soon became very unpopular when trying to *collect its debts.*

Stories of the ruinous operations of the bank in Kentucky soon reached us in Tennessee, and in the autumn of 1817, with a view to save Tennessee from the like oppression, her legislature passed an act, as I believe, unanimously, imposing a very heavy tax, say fifty thousand dollars, upon any persons attempting to bank in Tennessee without authority from the State.

A few years since, while the controversy was going on with the Bank of the United States, the Senate created a committee, of which Mr. Tyler, of Virginia, was a member, to examine into its proceedings, and when they made their report, for the first time, I found a letter dated in 1818, now bound up in our documents, soliciting the president of the bank to establish a branch in Nashville, notwithstanding the act of assembly, informing him that the act was passed by contracted, illiberal men, and, after furnishing a list of names for directors, assuring him that if a branch was established, and directors appointed from the list, he would see that a good account should be given of those who would attempt to enforce the State law.

Mr. Jones, the then president, answered this letter, and, very properly, refused to send a branch into the State contrary to the expressed will of the legislature.

Thus the matter rested until 1826, when this same gentleman was a leading member of the Tennessee legislature; and, not having been able to get a branch bank of the United States, he and others determined they would have a *paper bank*, founded on State funds and *the faith of the State.* They passed an act creating a bank. There was then in the State a bank in which the State had twenty thousand dollars of the stock. It was called the Bank of the State of Tennessee, and had been so conducted as to give society confidence in it; and, in baptising this new bank its authors gave it exactly the same name, and thus we had, at the same time, two banks, having the same name, in the same State. The friends of the old would not have hesitated in charging the leaders who established the new with pilfering their name, that they might derive benefit from their credit, had they been other than members of the assembly.

The plan of this new bank was not to pay specie, and to please the people, it was said it was a bank to relieve the people from pecuniary distress.

At the same session, and to force into circulation paper money not redeemable in specie, laws were passed to prevent levies of execution, unless plaintiffs would agree to receive irredeemable bank paper.

These proceedings met with very decided opposition from the supporters of a sound currency.

They denounced a depreciated paper currency as a curse to the country and the old State bank would not touch the paper of the new; and, after a long controversy between the directors, under the administration of an enlightened and worthy directory of the new State bank, it was so conducted as to be converted into a specie paying bank, and I believe it has faithfully redeemed whatever notes it put in circulation.

But, then, what became of the capital and profits? Much of them were wasted. There was a branch or agency in each county.

The cashier of the principal bank, a highly worthy, intelligent, and generous man, could not resist the temptation; he permitted importunate and needy friends to draw checks, which he paid when they had no funds in bank. This practice was detected and exposed, and he ruined.

Some of the agents, men of as much integrity as those to be found now, either used, or permitted others to use, the moneys entrusted to their care. Those moneys were in some instances lost, the agents ruined, and the State has been for several years endeavoring to save something from the wreck.

With these examples before me, I cannot, I will not, I dare not, give my sanction to a scheme so demoralizing, and fraught with so many mischiefs.

But, sir, our history stops not here. I think, about the year 1826, a Nashville bank failed, and occasioned much excitement. The legislature, then in session, repealed our act of 1817, imposing the tax of which I have spoken; a branch of the United States Bank was applied for, and established. It went down with the principal and the other branches, and from that time, until July, 1836, we were State bank men, generally: these banks having a *safe specie* basis, and always *paying specie*. During the whole of these arduous conflict, others have had an advantage over me.

They first wanted a United States Bank, that we might have a good currency *everywhere*. Next they wanted paper money, and creditors forced to receive it, or to get nothing; then United States Bank notes again; and now, when the monster is slain, and we can all venture to measure the length and breadth of its supposed deformities, nothing will do them but the pure unadulterated *hard money*.

Mr. President, these politicians ever have the advantage of me. I never can give up an old opinion, until I am sure I have found better reasons for a new one. They have the full benefit of what is called *the march of mind*. They march and countermarch so that I cannot keep pace with them. I turn slowly, awkwardly, and these politicians give me the dodge, and are sometimes out of sight before I know they intend to change. But this is of no consequence to me. Such wills-with-the-wisp or jacks-with-the-lantern I would not follow, if I could see them. They would only pilot me into some quagmire or swamp, and then leave me, although their dexterity could easily extricate themselves.

For myself, I now am, and ever have been a hard money man, to every reasonable and Constitutional extent. Nothing is with me money, within the meaning of the Constitution, but the *precious metals*, and they either coined, and their value fixed by acts of Congress, or foreign coin, whose value is declared in the same way. No government, either State or federal, can make anything else a tender in payment of debts. This kind of money, and this only, is the end of the law, where pecuniary compensation is to be made. It is not only the standard by which the value of property is to be fixed, but it is in itself *property*, which can be applied to other useful purposes. The federal government has no power to incorporate individuals, and bestow upon them banking powers and privileges, to be exercised within the States.

The federal government cannot issue, or authorize to be issued, paper to be used as currency.

The Constitution takes from the States the power to issue bills of credit.

It does not confer upon Congress any such power, and it can exercise no power except that which is expressly granted. The framers of the Constitution having taken from the States the power to issue bills of credit, and having refused or omitted to confer such a power on Congress, believed they had secured the country against the *issue* of a paper currency by *either* government, which individuals could have no means by suit to compel the payment of, and which, if tolerated, would be sure to depreciate.

Before the Constitution of the United States was framed, the State had the power to incorporate individuals, and give them banking powers and privileges; this power was never taken from them, and, therefore, they still possess it.

I have believed, and now do, that in a country so extensive as ours, so highly commercial, and so free, our business cannot be transacted without paper of some kind, which is *not money*, but *credit*, the representative of money. These credits will be highly injurious, unless regulated by law. I therefore have maintained State banks, at the same time wishing to put down, by all means in my power, small notes; to have none less than five, ten, twenty, and even higher than that, if a majority wished, so as to furnish a broad specie basis the better to maintain and support the organized credits, evinced by *bank notes or checks.*

It is all idle to tell me that the only mode to have hard money is to put down State banks. Put them down to-morrow, and then we will find it indispensable to have a United States Bank owned by individuals, or a treasury bank owned by the United States, and governed at *the will of the executive.*

Being opposed to both these, and thinking the country must have credits in some shape, I support State banks as the only means of preventing the establishment of some one of the others. I think them both unconstitutional, and the treasury bank infinitely the most dangerous.

We might as well at once put the whole moneys of the government at the disposition of the executive as to pass this bill; because, although some of the officers who are to have charge of it must have the sanction of the Senate in their appointment, yet the President can remove, or have removed at his pleasure, every man of them.

This bill, in truth and in fact, *creates a bank* with *vast powers* and extensive *capacity*.

Suppose Congress to incorporate a number of individuals, and confer upon them powers to do exactly the same thing which the officers named in this bill are empowered and required to do, what would gentlemen call their institution? It must and would be a bank; they would have all the usual powers of a bank, except to loan money by discounting notes.

The only use of an act of incorporation is to empower a number of individuals, or some one man, to transact certain business under particular restrictions. Now if we give to our own officers exactly the same powers which, if given to one or more individuals, would denominate the establishment a bank, it is equally so in both cases.

This bill provides places where our whole treasure, hard money notes of specie-paying banks, treasury notes, or other paper issued under the authority of the government, are to be kept.

It authorizes the transfers and re-transfers of those moneys from point to point, at the discretion of the Secretary. There is now a bill before the other house authorizing an issue of ten millions of treasury notes; it will certainly pass for that or a larger sum.

Now let us consider how these powers will be made to operate.

1st. The capital is the whole treasure of the nation, say any sum we please not less than twenty-five, nor more than fifty millions of dollars.

This sum can be concentrated at one place, or dispersed to different places, as the Secretary chooses. A merchant of New York owes fifty thousand dollars for duties, and this sum he is to pay to the collector there, who is to deposit it in his vault. He borrows the amount from a specie-paying bank in the notes of the State bank, and pays the debt. Instantly the collector goes to the bank, draws the specie, and returns its notes, and locks the specie up in the vault, where he is to keep it till needed for disbursement; and by pursuing this plan the whole specie may be withdrawn from the banks, or so much of it as to compel the banks to wind up.

Again: a merchant in Nashville owes fifty thousand dollars for goods purchased in New York; he gets that amount in notes of the Nashville banks by borrowing or otherwise, but they will not answer to pay his debt in New York; he therefore goes to the sub-treasurer, who has his proportion of these treasury notes, and gives him his fifty thousand dollars, and receives a treasury note, or notes, and perhaps allows one per cent. as the difference of exchange, and the sub-treasurer immediately goes to the State bank, returns its notes, takes the specie and locks it up in the vaults. When a creditor of the government applies for payment of his salary, or other dues, he may be paid in treasury notes, and thus we find this is a bank of *issues*.

It is useless to pursue this subject farther. Every practical man must see this is in substance a treasury bank, with immense funds as a capital, with unlimited power to draw and redraw, and that it is a bank to *issue* not *hard money alone*, but *paper money*, *issued by or under the authority of the United States*. That it confers powers and capacities which will enable it to *prostratė the State banks*, *any and everywhere at its pleasure*.

It will not only *control* the State banks, and make them *subservient to its will*, but will also *influence all men engaged in commerce*, *which requires the use of funds at distant places*.

Pass this bill, and we put it in the *power of the President*, *through his Secretary of the Treasury*, *to control* the whole *pecuniary active capital* of the country. We are to add this tremendous power to a patronage already dangerous in the extreme, and this at a time when we have a Chief Magistrate who is not only *unwilling* to have his *power* and *patronage curtailed* and limited, but is desirous to add to them, even to the extent of encouraging armed voluntary associations to stand ready to carry out his views by force of arms.

In the early and pure days of the Republic, in 1789, the republican doctrine was, that no President would ever dare to remove an officer who held office at the will of the President, simply on account of his politics; and, if he did, *Mr. Madison* said it would be a crime for which he should be impeached.

Mr. Jefferson, upon assuming the reins of government, prohibited all inferior officers from interfering in elections, further than to vote, on pain of dismissal.

In the canvass, which brought the late President into office, we all thought the same way, and that this was the sound democratic or repubcan doctrine.

Do we not all remember the outcry against Mr. Adams, because we thought, through a Mr. Slade, a clerk in some of the departments, he had signified to the Vermont legislature that he preferred the old senator, Mr. Seymour, to Mr. Van Ness? The newspapers rung with this charge, and if Mr. Adams or his cabinet had avowed that they had a right to endeavor to influence people in elections, it is doubtful how he would have got through even the four years to which he had been elected.

Now the whole course of thinking and acting is changed.

During the last Administration it was not only maintained that the

President and all under him had a right to interfere, but, for the sake of securing a democratic Administration, it was a duty to aid in electing his successor, members to both houses of Congress, Governors of States, &c.

The present incumbent improves upon this, and countenances what may be called legions of honor, to maintain him by force in carrying out modern democracy.

I have been surprised that in none of our discussions has any gentleman alluded to a correspondence between an association in Philadelphia and the Chief Magistrate during the past year.

They informed him that they had voluntarily associated together, had armed and equipped themselves, and made a tender of their services to carry out the laws.

In a country as free as ours, where the laws themselves are nothing but the will of a majority of the people, constitutionally expressed, every thing which tends to weaken or diminish our respect for the laws is highly reprehensible. Now what would we reasonably expect as an answer from our Chief Magistrate to such a tender of services?

I looked for grateful acknowledgments for their good feelings towards him, and a request that, as they regarded him and his fame, they would immediately lay aside their warlike implements and dissolve the association; because, if the country was to remain free, such voluntary associations could never be necessary. Public opinion, and forces, when indispensable, called out under the *authority of law*, would always be sufficient in the hands of the executive to give effect to the will of the people, expressed through their acts of Congress.

But I was sorry to find no such sentiments; on the contrary, sincere thanks, and a manifest willingness to countenance the use of such forces if emergency should require their services.

The good sense of society must check this course of thinking, or there is reason to fear that, at no distant day, we may have, through the agency of such means, *anarchy first*, and then *despotism*.

The senator from Massachusetts (Mr. Webster), at the close of his reply to the senator from South Carolina, "for his special benefit," in very good temper, and in a most happy manner, referred to the early history of that portion of my State, now called East Tennessee, once known as the *State of Franklin*. He read us a part of one of her acts of assembly, which fixed the salaries of some of her officers, and directed the *species of currency* in which they were to be paid.

I always feel gratified when I know, or hear, that my State has done anything which benefits any portion of my fellow-men.

"Blessed are the peace-makers," is the language of Holy Writ. On this occasion the two honorable and distinguished senators had assumed an attitude so belligerent, that I really feared it might end in something worse than words. But no sooner were the labors of my State fifty years ago brought to the notice of this grave body, than we all forgot that any of us had ever been out of temper, and so soon as we could recover composure enough to adjourn, we separated like a band of brothers—no two leaving the chamber in better temper with each other than the two honorable senators.

But, sir, the senator knew nothing of the practice under the State law, therefore we have not the full benefit which we ought to derive from his reminiscence. He could have related the whole incidents so much better than I can, that I regret he did not mention this subject to me before he addressed the Senate; if he had I would have given him the additional facts, that the whole might have been detailed in the Senate in his good tempered and felicitous manner.

It will be remembered that the governor, chief justices, and some other officers, were to be paid in deer-skins, other inferior officers were to be paid in raccoon-skins. Now, at that day, we were all good whigs, although we had some of the notions of the democrats of the present day.

We thought these taxes might safely remain in the hands of the collectors as sub-treasuries until wanted for disbursement. The taxes were, therefore, fairly collected in the skins and peltry pointed out in the law. But the collectors, as report says, knew that although raccoon-skins were plenty, opossum-skins were more so, and that they could be procured for little or nothing. They, therefore, procured the requisite numbers of opossum-skins, cut the tails off the raccoon-skins, sewed them to the opossum-skins, paid them into the general or *principal* treasury, and sold the raccoon-skins to the hatters.

The treasurer had been an unlucky appointment, although a worthy man; he was a foreigner, knew nothing of skins or peltry, and was, therefore, easily deceived by his sub-treasurers. When this imposition was discovered, the whole system went down, and we never have had a great fancy for leaving the taxes in the hands of the sub-treasurers or collectors from that day to this.

But, sir, these old proceedings more clearly developed the true character of my State than almost anything of the present day.

The territory or tract of country called Franklin, was composed of four counties of North Carolina, and separated from the body of the State by the great ledge of mountains, called at different places by different names, and from what is now West Tennessee by the Cumberland Mountains, and a wilderness of two hundred miles.

The Revolutionary War had terminated with Great Britain in 1783, but it continued with the powerful tribes of Indians who had been in alliance with her. The depredations of these Indians were so serious that aid to arrest their ravages was desired from North Carolina; that State was not in a situation to furnish protection, and instead thereof, from good motives, no doubt, but without due consideration, passed an act ceding us to the United States. When the news was received the leading men, who were *King's mountain men*—Sevier, the companion of the gallant Campbell and Shelby, at their head, took fire; the discontent ended in a declaration of independence, and the formation of the State called, to perpetuate our whig principles, "*Franklin.*"

North Carolina discovered her error, and, before Congress could act on the subject, repealed her act of cession. But it was *too late.* We had been disposed of without our consent. Though but a handful, with a powerful savage enemy infesting our whole frontier, and without a dollar to begin with, we set up for ourselves. We would not brook the indignity; we had begun the fight for liberty, and liberty or death we would have. We continued the controversy till 1789, when an accommodation with our parent State took place; and with our own consent, and upon terms thought just, we, with other portions of territory, were ceded, in 1789, to the United States.

In 1796, we became the State of Tennessee, and how we have since conducted, I willingly leave to the judgment of our sister States.

I confess, instead of feeling humbled by, I am proud of, this ancient reminiscence. I feel proud that my ancestor was one of that unyielding band; that I now find myself associated here with a Sevier and a Tipton; and although I sometimes think two generations back those of their name would not have worked so tamely in party gear, yet every once in a while the *blood shows itself*, and you can see, that if their home concerns are not attended to here, according to what is just, they *break party bandages*, and walk abroad in that freedom for which their fathers perilled every thing.

It is true we are neither whigs, tories, nor democrats by inheritance, but there is much in blood, much in education. Early lessons from mothers are apt to have an influence upon us through life. What the father says when he first sends his boy to school is hardly ever forgotten.

When that law was passed, and for years afterward, the first morning the son was to start for school, he was sure to receive the father's advice, in emphatic terms, calculated to make a lasting impression, in language like the following: My son, you are now going to school, you must render a willing obedience to your master; he is in my place, obey him, if you love me. Be kind to all your school-fellows, do nothing offensive or unjust to them. Be careful in all you say, and do not give any of them cause of offence, and, if they will quarrel with and abuse you, take care you never come home *whipped* by any one of them, if you have the power to prevent it.

Children were taught from infancy the doctrine of equality, that no distinction ought to exist except that which was produced by vice or virtue.

And as to a circulating medium, this old act contains a volume of instruction for me. At that day, the medium of our exchanges was skins and peltry, or furs. They were the the currency in which the people were obliged to transact their business, and my father, when voting for that law, thought it just that our officers, from the governor to the constable, should be paid in the same kind of currency which the people were compelled to use in their dealings with each other, and so think I now as to our federal officers. Such, I think, have been the opinions of a majority of my constituents from my youth to this day.

My wish is to carry into effect their *will*. If I had fortitude enough to venture into an unknown world, I would rather do so *now*, and upon this *spot*, than knowingly to give a vote upon a subject so important, which would disappoint the wishes of the companions of my youth, the associates of my maturer years, and those who have ever *sustained* me against all attacks, at every stage of life.

What I believe to be their will, corresponds with my own judgment on this subject; and, however much I may and do regret a difference of opinion with enlightened men from other States, yet I acknowledge no responsibility to any human power except to the citizens of my own State who have so long honored me with their confidence.

Judge White's opposition to the tariff was always firm but judicious. He never doubted the power of the federal government to give protection, to a certain extent, to home manufactures by imposing taxes on foreign merchandise; but *that*, he thought, like every other power, ought to be exercised for the good of the whole, and under that impression he never would vote to impose a tax upon a *foreign* article, which *as a nation* we could conveniently dispense with, when he saw, or had reason to believe, it would increase the price of the article throughout any large portion of the country, and none were to be benefited by it but a few capitalists, who would be thereby levying a tax upon a considerable portion of the community for their individual benefit. He liked to see domestic manufactures flourish, but never wished to see them brought into existence, or nourished, in one section of the country, at the expense and to the positive detriment of another. He therefore uniformly opposed a protective tariff both by his votes and speeches.

In 1835, there approached one of the most momentous periods of our national history, namely, that session of Congress during which was originated and conducted with such talent and fiery zeal on either side, that discussion of the Tariff question, which had well-nigh rent the Union, and filled the land with civil war and bloodshed. Just before this memorable session, Mr. Calhoun resigned the Vice Presidency—which resignation called Judge White to occupy a position still more responsible and conspicuous than any he had hitherto filled. How fully he met the expectations of the body that promoted him, and of the nation at large, in this season of impending danger, is now a matter of history. The firmness, impartiality, decision, and dignity with which he presided over these stormy debates, were commended by the Hon. Henry A. Wise, during the debate in Congress on the Treasury note bill.

I should have remembered (says Mr. Wise) another model of wisdom, and virtue, and patriotism whom I have seen, and seen in all situations of life—long and intimately did I know him—well did I love him, and sacredly do I cherish his memory. He is no more. I wish I could imitate his virtuous and hallowed example in life. I mean the lamented Hugh Lawson White, a servant of Tennessee, a son of North Carolina, without whose aid the compromise act never could have become a law—without whose patriotism and firmness there would have been a civil war upon a sovereign State, and upon the Union. South Carolina ought to be told of this, who, in 1836, threw her vote from him, her best defender against a tyrant. When this act was before the Senate, he was president pro tem. of that honorable body. He was in the chair, and had the appointment of the committee which had to consider the report upon the plan of adjusting the tariff difficulties. In this high place, with this power, he was warned—I will not say by whom*—*not to put a certain gentleman* (John M. Clayton, of Delaware) on the committee. The reason was, that there were rival plans, one proposed by the Senator from Kentucky, of whom, and whose measures that gentleman was the friend; and the other plan was that of the Administration then in power. That Administration was governed by one of two motives, perhaps by both, in wishing to defeat this act. They wished, certainly, to give preference to their own plan, and to deprive the authors of this of the honor of the compromise; and, perhaps, the head and chief wished nothing so much as the opportunity to apply "*the second section*" to the leaders of resistance whom he charged more with treason to *him* personally than to the country. The president pro tem. of the Senate knew well the danger of defeating this act, but when orders were issued to him not to appoint its friend and advocate on the committee, what was his reply? The reply of that sage, and patriot, and hero—hero he was, for he had, like his chief, been in the wars—his reply was a

* By Gen. Jackson, or by a message from him.

plea to the jurisdiction of any power to dictate the manner of discharging his duty. He told the man who assumed this authority: "You are too late. Mr. Clayton is appointed; and, if he was not, he should be. I voted for the Force bill *as a decision merely that the Government had the power to execute its laws.* I never intended it should operate or actually be put in force against any of my countrymen who happened to differ from me in opinion, and who are as honest and conscientious in their opinions as I am in mine. And, having voted for it, I will afford every opportunity to legislation in my power, to prevent its effect." And this, sir, produced the first cause of difference between him and Gen. Jackson. He muzzled the blood-hounds, disappointed his chief of his prey, aided the compromise, and gave peace to a distracted people.

Judge White's punctuality and devotion to business, as we have remarked, were most exemplary.* "His deportment in the Senate," says a senatorial contemporary, "was quiet and dignified. He spoke but little, but when he did it was to the purpose. He was very attentive to what was going on; and I have often seen him in his seat, almost the only listener to a dull speech. I once remarked to him that I thought him the best listener to speakers of all the Senate. His reply was to this effect: 'Well, it is my duty to be here; and when a member is speaking, nothing else can be done, so I keep my seat and listen to him. I find that I can learn something from even the poorest speech that is made here.'" The writer adds, with great truth, "This was a just remark; for however incompetent a speaker may be to discuss the question which is the subject of his speech, and however deficient in general intelligence, he will usually suggest some facts, and make some remarks worthy the attention of those better informed and more able."

Judge White's regularity in attendance was extreme and remarkable. He was always in his place. "I know of no man," said a distinguished member of Congress, "except Judge Marshall, who rides about the city so little in carriages." It was his habit to repair to the capitol every morning immediately after breakfast, and to spend the time in the committee-room until the regular hour of convening Congress. So universally was this the case that he became proverbial for being the first man in the Senate, and the last to leave it. Col. E. H. Foster, his colleague during his last term, one day remarked to his companions that he was determined to have it said that

* Hon. John M. Niles, lately deceased.

he had beaten Judge White at the capitol at least once. Accordingly, he departed one morning in great haste, and upon reaching the Senate chamber found it vacant. Quite delighted at having accomplished what he considered so great a feat, he exclaimed: "I am satisfied, I have beaten the 'skeleton' once in my life." But upon entering the committee-room he there found the Judge, standing in the middle of the floor, and holding a bundle of papers. He had a hearty laugh at the disappointment of Col. Foster, who, seating himself, remarked, "It is useless to try any further, Judge; you are entitled to the palm."

Judge White was not less strict in the observance of all arrangements necessary for his seasonable arrival at Washington, than in the performance of his official duties when there. No ordinary circumstances prevented him from setting out upon his journey at the appointed time. The valley of Virginia being the nearest and most frequently travelled route, his colleagues, journeying on horseback, would frequently stop and rest a few days with him. In the fall of 1832, Hon. Felix Grundy, with another member, paid the Judge a visit of this kind. He had fixed upon the next Monday morning to commence his journey. Sunday night a deep snow fell. The visitors did not relish the idea of turning out in such weather. Perceiving this, their host said, "Gentlemen, here are my house and servants at your service. Order what you want, and make yourselves perfectly at home. The time has come for *me* to leave; and I must go." The others made some pleasant remark in reply about his "old fashioned habits," but on the whole, thought it not best to separate themselves from such good company; and the three legislators accordingly, upon the Monday morning, set out together.

On another occasion, he had allowed himself time to make a visit to friends in Philadelphia. The family invited certain of their acquaintances to meet at their home and pass the evening with him. Judge White, however, without knowing this circumstance, had fixed upon that day to leave the city, and no importunities could induce him to remain. He had allowed himself just time enough to reach Washington in season for the meeting of Congress; and would not permit himself to be tardy even for a day. On but one occasion was he ever absent from his seat when Congress convened; and this was in 1838, when he was suffering under severe bodily infirmity. And on that occasion, so conscientious was he, that he intended to resign in time for the Governor to make a *pro tempore* appointment; and actually sent in the resignation, which, however, the Governor refused to accept.

While in the pay of the country, he was accustomed to consider his time, strength, and talents the property of his constituents. He suffered neither his private interests, his personal gratification, nor (as in the case of his speech on the Indian question) even the keenest and deepest afflictions, to interfere with their claims. He not only performed the public duties of his station, but was accustomed to adjust private claims for individuals, without compensation. During his early residence in Washington, an old Revolutionary soldier, living in Claiborne County, East Tennessee, applied to him for the purpose of having his name placed on the pension list. His claims proved valid; and the Judge presented to the worn veteran his pension certificate, together with all his back pay, which amounted to a sum more considerable than the old man had ever had at one time. Said he, with deep gratitude, "Judge White, how much do I owe you?" "Not one cent, sir," replied the Judge; "when I was a whistling ploughboy, you were fighting for the liberty of our country. I then knew, or, indeed, cared but little about it; but, my old friend, I have since learned to estimate the value of those efforts; and to all who fought our battles in those 'times that tried men's souls' I owe a debt of gratitude I can never repay."

As an instance of the like scrupulousness in fulfilling prescribed duty we may present an extract from a letter written to a friend in Knoxville, in 1833, in relation to his becoming a candidate for the convention which was to meet in the next May, at Nashville, for the purpose of amending the Constitution of Tennessee. He says:

I have reason to think that Congress will be in session on the third Monday in May, when the Convention is to sit in Nashville, 750 miles distant. To reach that point in season, I must leave this the first of May, the most important business of the session probably still unfinished. The General Assembly elected me to the Senate. The same body, though not the same men, fixed the time for the meeting of the Convention; when it must have been expected that the Senate would then be in session. Under these circumstances, were I to abandon my post here, for the one proposed, I feel that I could not assign any reason for so doing, which ought to be satisfactory.

I hope, my friends, upon reflection, will see the propriety of my declining to consent that my name be used as a member of Convention. I would rather serve my friends and neighbors than any equal number of people; but it ought to be remembered the whole people of the State sent me here, and that a small number of the same people cannot give me leave of absence.

Although his other public duties prevented his co-operating with his friends in this important movement, yet he felt the greatest solicitude on this subject, and his anxiety that the power should rest where it belonged, *with the people*, will be seen from an extract of another letter to this same friend:

I have great fears that the alterations which may be made in the Constitution will not really be *amendments*. The idea ought to be constantly impressed upon the public mind, that no alteration will be part of the Constitution, until approved by a vote of the people. In the proposed amendments the Convention should insert a provision, that the Constitution shall remain as it now is, unless the people, by their vote shall sanction the proposed amendments.

When Judge White entered the Senate, he was fifty-two years of age, five feet eleven inches in height, of erect form, very slender but graceful proportions, and with a firm and elastic step. His brow was broad and full, his eyes blue, and deeply set; and his firmly compressed lips bore testimony to his unwavering tenacity of purpose. His abundant gray hair was thrown back from his forehead, and curled at considerable length upon his shoulders; its silvery waves adding to his venerable and remarkable appearance. The usual expression of his face in repose was sad. When thought deepened, this sadness gave way to a look of sternness. But both these were dissipated under the influence of his social feelings; and at such times his whole countenance became illuminated with a bright expression of kindness.

By the talents and virtues, the strength and integrity of character displayed in this eminent station, by zeal for the promotion of the public good, by uniform moderation and love of justice, by jealous watchfulness over the public wealth, by that indifference to public honors which prevented him from ever canvassing for any office, or from any other demonstration than the mere expression of his willingness to fill such places as might render him useful, Judge White acquired his high rank among the first men of the nation, and his extended and firmly based influence among its masses; and likewise the expressive and appropriate surname of "The Cato of the Republic."

CHAPTER XII.

HIS FIRST POLITICAL POSITION—ITS SUBSEQUENT CHANGE.

WHEN Judge White entered the Senate in 1825, Mr. Adams was the occupant of the Presidential chair. Supposing that the General Assembly expected him not to array himself in the party ranks either of the Administration, or of its opponents, but to act simply as the servant of his country, and to vote as in his judgment would best promote its interests; he was ready to give to the measures of the Administration his prompt and efficient aid, so far as those measures coincided with republican principles.

He believed that those who denied to the federal government all power except that which is granted in *express* terms, or which is necessary to carry into effect some power expressly granted, expounded the Constitution more correctly than those who contended for the exercise of implied powers. Being here associated with men, who espoused different sides of all the doubtful political questions then agitating the country, and who were in every way well qualified to discuss them, his mind settled down, before the election of Gen. Jackson to the Presidency, in favor of all those great political principles, which were adopted by that President, in the outset of an administration, undoubtedly one of the most marked and eventful in the political history of the country. We have every evidence, that Judge White was something more than a mere *supporter* of this party, which a friend of General Jackson says was "more perfect in its organization, and more lasting in its duration, than any before established, giving its own line of statesmen and its own course of policy to the country; a party which was to exert a stronger influence upon the world, and to cause a greater increase of the wealth, territory, and population of the republic, than any had yet caused or exerted.

As an evidence of General Jackson's regard for Judge White, and of his appreciation of the aid rendered him by the latter in founding his political system, we shall here give a few extracts from unpublished letters, showing that he may in fact be considered the author of many of the leading measures of General Jackson's Administration. The first two are from General Jackson, and were written immediately after his elevation to the Presidency. The first is dated Hermitage, Oct. 17, 1828:

I thank you kindly for the suggestions you have made, and will always thank you for your friendly counsel. We have grown up together, have passed to the top and over the hill of life together, and permit me to assure you there is *no one* in whom I have greater confidence, in their honor, integrity, and judgment than in yours.

The second letter bears date Judge Overton's, Dec. 31, 1828.

It will give me pleasure at all times to receive your views upon all and every subject; you have my confidence and friendship, and to you and Major Eaton I look as my confidential friends.

After General Jackson went to Washington—Mr. Tazewell, who was a warm friend of Judge White's, and a firm supporter of General Jackson's Administration says:

Judge White was one and I believe the most confidential of all his advisers, as well before as after his inauguration, while the Senate continued in session. I have good reason to justify the opinion, that many of the most important measures, adopted by the President during that period were the result of the sound advice given to him by Judge White, in whom the President then reposed the most unlimited confidence—a confidence zealously reciprocated by the Judge, whose personal attachment to General Jackson was most ardent and devoted.

When the Senate adjourned in 1829, Judge White went home and did not return until the commencement of the next session. I was prevented from taking my place in that body until Feb. 1830. Very soon after I took my seat, I saw very plainly that new relations had sprung up between the President and some of his former friends. Judge White did not seem to have observed this; and his feelings toward General Jackson remained unchanged, although it was evident to all others, that he no longer occupied the same place in the estimation of the President which he had done. I never knew the cause of this apparent estrangement, but thought it might be easily conjectured.

The cause which led to a dissolution of General Jackson's cabinet in 1831, was General Jackson's determination to have Mr. Van Buren elected his successor, and to attain this end it was determined to dismiss such cabinet officers as were unfavorable to this purpose, and to appoint others, who could be moulded to it; those who sanctioned it having voluntarily resigned. And notwithstanding this apparent estrangement which was so obvious to all, General Jackson again tendered the war department to Judge White, and the pertinacity with which it was urged upon him will be seen from the following letters. One of these selected from among a large number, because it was written at the instance of the President; and the others, show the opinion which their authors (of whom the next chapter treats) entertained of Judge White at that day:

COLUMBIA, *May 5th*, 1831.

MY DEAR SIR: The last mail brought us the letters of resignation of Mr. Van Buren and Major Eaton, and also a rumor, which I doubt not is true, of the resignation of the other members of the cabinet. This event I cannot say surprised me much. We had reason to apprehend an explosion of some sort, but could not anticipate the manner or the time at which it would occur. I am anxious to see the letters of resignation of the other members of the cabinet, which have not yet reached us. Should all have retired in such a manner as to impress upon the public mind the idea that a part did so voluntarily, and a part by coercion, I cannot see that the party or the country is to be affected by it. That the new cabinet, profiting by a knowledge of the difficulties which their predecessors had to encounter, will act in harmony with each other, and with the President I have no doubt. Avoiding the causes which have led to the present state of things, I doubt not that their labors will prove eminently beneficial to the country, by sustaining the great principles which have marked the course of the Administration.

I need not assure you that I am highly gratified to find your name, among those whom it is said the President intends to invite into his cabinet. Upon this point but one sentiment has been expressed among our intelligent and common friends here. In the course of his Administration the President has had many difficulties to contend with, not among the least of which, has been the want of harmony, and concert of action, among his confidential and constitutional advisers. As against an organized and vindictive, and I may add, in some respects, unprincipled opposition, he never had nor has he now anything to fear. I know he has unlimited confidence in you, and in this his hour of need will I have every reason to believe be anxious to have your assistance in the Administration. Should he invite you to a place in his cabinet I trust you may reconcile it to your sense of duty and propriety to accept, and that no considerations may induce you to decline. Your friends in the

State may regret to lose your services in the Senate, but no one of them sincerely attached to our cause can, I think, or would for one moment hesitate, not only to assent to your acceptance of the new station, should it be offered to you, but to advise it. We would hazard nothing I think in supplying your place in the Senate with a man of *the right politics*, though none can be found in whom the people of the State would have so much confidence as in yourself. I trust therefore that you will duly appreciate my motives, when I insist that you will not decline if invited by the President (of which I have no doubt), to accept a place in his councils.

Very sincerely and truly,

Your friend,

JAMES K. POLK.

NASHVILLE, *May 17th*, 1831.

DEAR SIR: I hope before this time, you have accepted the office of Secretary of War. If not, I now write for the purpose of uniting my solicitations and that of my neighbors in favor of your acceptance.

There is entire confidence here in the proposed new cabinet—for myself I can say, it affords the first clear sunshiny political weather I have seen for some time. Whatever your diffidence may suggest, rely on one thing, there is no other man who under all the circumstances will unite so much public confidence—all past notions of non-acceptance of office &c., should be surrendered at this time for the public good.

Your friend,

FELIX GRUNDY.

NASHVILLE, *May 1st*, 1831.

MY DEAR SIR: When the news reached us (1st May), of the resignation of the cabinet, the same account brought the suggestions of the successors. From that time until yesterday I have been to Kentucky on a visit to my parents. That the war department has been tendered to you, I am told is true. I have been out amongst the people since the report went forth, in the south of Kentucky, and in Tennessee. For a range of 150 miles I am sure of public opinion. It is not only in favor of your accepting, but that no man could be found so likely to fill the station satisfactorily to the West and South—and all things considered it was the very best selection that could have been made—the Clay men generally said to me—"with Hugh White, we are perfectly satisfied." So I find opinion here. The desire that you should accept, is most anxious with the Jackson men, and your declining would dishearten very many, under the impression of difficulties attending the administration of the government, that deterred the most prudent, and efficient men from taking office under it. A thing the farthest imaginable from being true, under the present aspect of affairs.

I think it due to the country, and the party of our opinion politically, that you should accept the office.

I would not have written you, but our friend General Coffee, on being informed of the facts above, suggested the propriety of my writing—saying he had done so—and if it did no good—no harm could come of it.

As a Western man, I should feel disagreeable with *all* strangers in the cabinet—one *old* acquaintance of General J. ought to be there—and a man not wanting too much hereafter—one that feels as if, "in the fork of the poplar, safe from the pack." Out of Tennessee he cannot be found. If you refuse, we will feel restive, unsafe, and anxious.

The Kentucky people in the south of the State are generally for office on the Clay side—the aspirants are waiting until they are wearing out with age—are becoming doubtful that a union of N. Light Federalists with Kentucky republicans, if possible, cannot last—are dropping off, and if the government is successfully administered, will not long seriously oppose it. Such are the symptoms at present.

For your health and happiness accept my best wishes.

J. N. CATRON.

WASHINGTON CITY, 1st *May*, 1831.

DEAR JUDGE: I have just parted from the President. He informs me, confidentially, that you have declined the office of Secretary of War. The old man said he wrote you yesterday, urging you still to accept.

I know your friendship for the President, and I know, too, Judge, the sacrifices you have ever been willing to make for the love of your country. I write this at the request of the old General, because he says I have been present here, and can describe plainly to you the situation of things as they are. The old man says, that all his plans will be defeated unless you agree to come; should it be but for a period short of the continuance of his Administration. The public have settled down on you, Judge, as the man. The wishes and confidence of every one seem to require your acceptance. Nothing that you can offer will satisfy your friends; because, as the old man says—this is a crisis in which he wishes his best friends to be with him—and you well know that you are the nearest; so he declares, Judge--now for my own views. The good of the country—the honor of your best friend—the character of the State—and, lastly, it must not be said, that aid is refused the old chief from Tennessee, and that, too, by Judge White.

Judge, pardon me for attempting to influence you. I write because I know you will do one thing, and that is, believe what I say. Could you but witness the anxiety of the General, and the distress that follows, under the supposition that you will not join him, I know you would yield.

Yours truly,

F. W. ARMSTRONG.

The importunities of these mutual friends did not succeed in effecting their object, and it was determined to make another attempt to operate upon Judge White from another quarter. For this purpose General Jackson, accompanied by Judge White's brother-in-law, Judge Overton, visited Virginia, and conferred with Mr. Tazewell; as it was well known that the relations existing between Mr. Tazewell and Judge White were of the most intimate and friendly character. Mr. Tazewell, in speaking of the alienation of General Jackson from Judge White, says:

Under this impression, I was somewhat astonished at an incident which I will now relate. During the summer or fall of 1831, General Jackson, accompanied by Judge Overton, of Tennessee, paid a visit to Old Point Comfort, a watering place not very far from here. So soon as I was able, after I was informed of their arrival there, I called to see them. Upon this occasion, I was told by Judge Overton, that the office of Secretary of War, then vacant, either had been or would be offered to our friend Judge White; and I was asked my opinion as to his qualifications to fill it, and as to the probability of his accepting it. To these inquiries I replied promptly, that the war department, during several years past, had been getting into much confusion, as I thought, and that none of my acquaintance was so well calculated to restore it to order as Judge White, of whose unwearied industry and sound judgment I had had the best opportunity to form a correct opinion. But that from my knowledge of him, I did not believe that he would accept such an appointment. Judge Overton concurred in the opinions I had expressed; and as I believe communicated them to the President. For in a very short time, similar inquiries were addressed to me by the President himself, to which I returned the same answers. He too expressed his apprehensions that Judge White might not accept; and requested that I would write to him, advising him to do so. With this request I declined to comply, stating to Gen. Jackson as my reason for doing so, that I thought it would be indelicate on my part to give such advice to any one situated as Judge White then was. I had just heard of the sad domestic bereavement with which he had been afflicted.

When we met in Washington, at the commencement of the next session of the Senate, I communicated to Judge White the substance of what had occurred. He then informed me, that the war department had been offered to him, which he had promptly declined; and thanked me, with much feeling, for the part I had taken in the subject, of which Judge Overton had informed him.

His utter refusal to accept this position under Gen. Jackson, and thereby to aid in the elevation of Mr. Van Buren, to the Presidency; his firmness and impartiality in favoring Mr. Clay's compromise in 1832; his endeavors to check the constantly increasing patronage of the executive, by voting against large appropriations, to be expended as the President might choose; and above all, his permission to his friends to use his name as a candidate for the Presidency, in opposition to Mr. Van Buren, gradually alienated Gen. Jackson from him, and at last widened the breach between them, until they became totally separated in their feelings and principles.

Judge White's position in the Senate now became singular. If there was any one of his own political sect whose judgment coincided with his, the moral courage was wanting to stand by the side of one looked upon as a victim marked for destruction. But this isolation had no terrors for Judge White. Although his course was necessarily solitary, yet it was marked with a fixed determination at any hazard "to maintain what he believed *sound principles* and *sound practices*, under the supposition that his constituents, when they re-elected him to office in 1835, intended *he should resist every attempt of the executive through his patronage to influence public opinion;*" and but few public men ever received such decided marks of approbation, or were so fully sustained in their course, as he by the people of his own State.

When the subject of the Presidency was agitated in 1838, and Mr. Clay and Mr. Van Buren seemed likely to be the favorite candidates of the two parties, Judge White, who had opposed the ruinous policy pursued by the latter, in his administration of the government, did not stand aloof because he could not find a candidate to suit his own views in every particular. Had it been his province to nominate one, he would not have selected either of these gentlemen, as he differed from them both upon important questions; but as this was not his prerogative, and he felt no disposition to occupy a neutral position, he deemed it expedient to support the one whose policy would best promote the interests of the country. With these views his choice was fixed upon Mr. Clay, and he avowed his determination as a private citizen to sustain him for the Presidency—but at the same time declared his purpose to resist in the Senate, any measure which in his judgment might be adverse to the prosperity of the nation. Instead of Mr. Clay, Gen. Harrison was the nominee of the Harrisburg Convention, and although Judge White would have preferred the former, he announced his determination to support the new candidate. This he would doubtless have done in good faith had his life been spared.

CHAPTER XIII.

RELATIONS TO MESSRS. GRUNDY, POLK, JOHNSON AND CATRON.

The peculiar relations which these gentlemen sustained to Judge White, and the prominent position they occupied as politicians, render it necessary to take special notice of their course. Judge Grundy was for a number of years Judge White's colleague in the Senate. They all belonged to the same political party. Although not on terms of particular intimacy, they labored together harmoniously up to 1834, on most points of importance. Judge White had the kindest feelings towards his colleague, and never doubted the sincerity of his professions, until certain developments connected with a meeting at Washington, which was designed to test Judge White's strength in the Tennessee delegation, proved that his friendship was not to be relied upon. About this juncture, affairs connected with Judge Grundy's course in regard to the U. S. Bank, proved that the suspicions awakened as to his fidelity were not without foundation.

To Mr. Polk, Judge White was very much attached. During the session of 1833–34, when he and Col. Bell were both run for speaker of the House of Representatives, Judge White wrote to the editor of the Knoxville Register—"Polk and Bell were both run for speaker; the latter is elected. I fear a want of kind feelings between them may grow out of the canvass, and be the means of dividing, at home, those who now pass for friends. Both are to me like children; therefore I took no part in the contest.

"Justice to these gentlemen, as well as sound policy, requires that nothing should be said, or done, which can have the effect of wounding the feelings of either."

Some months after this, during the summer of 1834, Judge White's name was freely used in connection with the Presidency. Upon hearing of some threats from Gen. Jackson of what he would do, in such an event—Judge White addressed a letter to his friend Mr. Polk, and received the following answer:—

COLUMBIA, *Sept. 2d*, 1834.

MY DEAR SIR: I received your letter of the 26th ult. on yesterday. I am surprised and astonished at the information which has been communicated to you—*that one of your oldest and most valued friends*,* *now high in office*, has said that "*he will denounce you as soon as it is ascertained that you are willing to be a candidate*," &c. There must be some mistake about it. It certainly cannot be so; and unless your information comes in a most unquestionable shape I should be slow to believe it, but should much sooner suspect that the communication came from an interested source, or from one having some object to effect, by separating in feeling at least, old and long tried personal and political friends. It has not been a great while since the person to whom I presume you must allude, gave public evidence of the estimate in which he held your private and public character; as well as of your capacity for high office, by his willingness to have you associated with him in highly confidential and responsible public relations. This opinion of you was, *I know*, long since that time unchanged, and I have never had any reason to believe, for one moment, that his former confidence in you was in the slightest degree impaired. I would much sooner suspect the accuracy of my information therefore, than yield for an instant to the impression which the information itself is calculated to make upon your mind. Nothing could pain mutual firiends more, than the idea, that anything could occur, to break up, or in the least disturb the intimate relation of private friendships which have existed for more than forty years, or to separate those now in the evening of life, who for so many years have acted together upon public affairs, and who have always agreed—with perhaps unimportant exceptions—upon all measures of public policy, and especially those which have engaged the public attention, during the present and pending Administration.

I am very sincerely,

Your friend and obt. servt.,

JAMES K. POLK.

It would appear from the contents of the above letter that Mr. Polk was at that time not well informed as to the sentiments of Gen. Jackson in regard to his successor; but so soon as he became fully satisfied on this subject, a certificate which we will insert presently, will show, that his determination was taken, to shape his course according to the President's wishes, although motives of personal

* Gen. Jackson.

policy, and the watchful eye he ever kept in the direction of his own political aggrandizement, decided him not to define his position until after his re-election the ensuing August.

It was already understood that the party would support the nominee of the Baltimore Convention. Judge White's friends determined that at the meeting which was organized to test his strength, his claims should be presented without respect to this convention. No one better knew than Messrs. Grundy, Polk, and Johnson, what would be the result of the Baltimore Convention, and none better understood the object of this meeting, and yet in the face of all this they made slight excuses for absenting themselves from the meeting —but at the same time, avowed that they were in favor of Judge White, and privately pledged themselves to his support, as the certificate above referred to, shows.

The following letter written a few weeks after this meeting by Judge White to E. Alexander, Esq., shows the course these gentlemen were pursuing towards him.

WASHINGTON, *Jan.* 12, 1835.

MY DEAR SIR: I have avoided, during the present session, writing to any person when I have not been compelled to answer letters, for reasons obvious to you.

While society is employed in scrutinizing my character with a view to know whether they will wish to employ me in a public station different from that which I now occupy, I hold that I ought so to conduct myself, as to give no reason to suspect that I am saying or doing anything with a view to influence the public judgment.

Three of my colleagues, Grundy, Polk, and Johnson, think the use of my name as a candidate for the highest office known to our government, may be the means of breaking up the democratic party, that it will be disapproved by my own State, and that by not stopping the use of it, I am placing myself in a situation that must destroy me at home, as well as abroad. In this view of things they are zealously and cordially supported by Judge Catron, who has been here some time. Mr. Laughlin from Nashville, arrived here on the 8th inst., and it is said comes here to aid these gentlemen by his services as a letter writer.

All the other representatives from Tennessee think differently, and urge, in conversation, my pretensions, and represent the wishes of my State as being different from what is urged by Mr. Grundy and those who act with him. Which of them is right, I do not profess to know. All I have said, and all I will say is that *I have had no agency in causing my name to be used and I will not prohibit the use of it.* My political friends at home and abroad I hope and believe have not used it, and will not use it for any purpose other than the interest of the country; and whenever they are satisfied the country will be injured, not benefited, by its use, they will give me sincere pleasure by withdrawing it.

Neither Mr. Grundy, Colonel Polk, Colonel Johnson, nor Judge Catron has ever alluded to the subject in conversation with me, and I cannot but feel it personally unkind, that any of them should be injuring me in the judgment of strangers without knowing *from myself* whether I deserve their condemnation or not.

The honorable judge is, I think, treating me with great unkindness to give every body else the benefit of the information he has acquired in his extensive travels, and withhold it all from me.

He is viewed by some of my friends as a political commissary, sent out to receive just such news as he has brought, and in consideration of his endeavors to detract from my standing here, and destroy me at home, he hopes to fill the first vacancy on the bench of the Supreme Court of the United States, which can with propriety be given to him. In all this matter I feel no personal interest; a greater personal favor could not well be bestowed on me, than by leaving me at home after the 4th of March next.

These people are preparing for a great effort in Tennessee next summer. They think they can send to the legislature such materials as will supersede me in the Senate. Thus dropped, my pretensions to anything else are at an end.

I put up no pretensions to anything, and therefore can never be disappointed.

Subsequent events showed Judge White's surmises to be correct. A correspondence in February, 1835, may demonstrate that Polk and Johnson, at least, had determined to pick a quarrel with Judge White if possible. He had made certain inquiries of them as to a nomination for the district attorneyship of West Tennessee. The note containing the inquiries was answered by the following sour epistle, in Mr. Polk's handwriting:

WASHINGTON CITY, *Feb.* 25, 1835.

DEAR SIR: We have received your letter of yesterday, in relation to the nomination of Mr. Brown, of Nashville, to be District Attorney of West Tennessee, which you inform us is now pending before the Senate. You express your surprise at this nomination, as you "had not heard of Mr. Collingsworth's resignation, and knew that Mr. Brown had come to this place as an applicant for the office of Judge in Arkansas." You state that we "are the only members of the Tennessee delegation who have recommended Mr. Brown," and you "therefore presume" that we "are the only ones here acquainted with the circumstances," and you "therefore ask" us "to inform" you "whether the profession in Nashville and the other parts of West Tennessee were apprised of Mr. Collingsworth's resignation, so that recommendations for others might have been furnished before the nomination of Mr. Brown." In answer to this inquiry we have to state, that it is known to you, that we left town early in November. At that time we had not heard the resignation of Mr. Collingsworth spoken of, and whether and to what extent his intention to resign had subsequently to that time attained publicity, you as well as other members of the delegation have the same means of knowing that we have. * * * We have to regret the opinion which you seem to have formed that "the case as it stands is calculated to make the impression that there has been a secret contrivance to have Mr. Brown appointed, before his brother lawyer could be apprised that the office was vacant." We are not aware of any such "secret contrivance." We do not believe that any such exists; but if there be the slightest grounds for such an opinion, we are wholly ignorant of it. If it is intended by you to convey the idea that we could be capable of lending ourselves to any such "secret contrivance," we feel ourselves called upon to repel an insinuation which, your own sense of justice must satisfy you, nothing in our conduct, public or private, has ever justified. You must know that the President of the United States, who made the nomination, is equally incapable of lending himself to any such "secret contrivances," for the advancement of any such purposes as those indicated in your letter. You must know further, that the President of the United States was intimately acquainted with the members of the bar at Nashville, as much so as any representative of the State could be, and from his knowledge of their qualifications and character was in possession of information to enable him to make the nomination without any recommendation whatever. Although this was the case, and was known to us, still we did not hesitate, at the request of Mr. Brown, to address the letter in his behalf to the President, which we infer from your letter, has been communicated to the Senate, and read by you. In recommending Mr. Brown, we have done nothing more than we have often done for other citizens of the State, who have desired letters to be addressed to the executive for appointments within his gift. We think it probable that you and others of the delegation have often addressed such letters to the President. * * It is proper that we should add that we have understood that a recommendation had been signed by some members of the bar at Nashville, (though we have never seen it), in favor of the appointment of another person. The President, with a personal knowledge of both gentlemen, as well as of the other members of the bar at that place, possessed information altogether sufficient to enable him to select a person qualified for the office. He has chosen to nominate Mr. Brown.

Your obedient servants,

JAMES K. POLK,
C. JOHNSON.

To this prickly effusion Judge White answered immediately and temperately, but with all needed plainness, as follows:

GENTLEMEN: Your favor of this date, in answer to mine of yesterday, was handed me a few minutes since.

During the last session of Congress an idea was somehow taken up in West Tennessee, that Mr. Collingsworth would not be re-appointed; and several members of the bar were applicants for the office in case it should be vacant. Mr. Collingsworth was, however, appointed and continued in office until 25th of January, when he resigned. His resignation was received at the State department on the 2d February, and on the 4th Mr. Brown was nominated, and until some days after the nomination, I had no knowledge that Mr. Collingsworth had resigned. I had been informed that Mr. Brown's business here was to procure the office of judge in Arkansas.

Under these circumstances I really did think, as I had heard of no application on behalf of any other gentleman, and as there did not appear among the papers any recommendation this winter from the profession, that it was my duty to the profession to make some inquiry to know whether they had been fairly treated. I found no recommendation from any of my colleagues except you, and very naturally concluded you could give me the information I desired; and I was the more inclined to apply for it, having always had a good opinion of Mr. Collingsworth, with whom I was acquainted, and having received a very high character of Mr. Brown, from friends in whom I had confidence.

I regret to see the spirit in which this inquiry is met in your letter; and that you feel yourselves called upon to "repel" what you are pleased to fancy an imputation upon yourselves, and upon the President of the United States. Neither of you believes for one moment that I intended to insinuate anything to his disadvantage, nor can you believe from the style of my letter that I intended any imputation upon Mr. Brown. I sincerely wish that if ever the President should be attacked, when he has *few* friends, he may find as many zealous advocates as he now has when he has more friends than he can provide for.

I have too long known the President to insinuate aught to his disadvantage, or that he is capable of sanctioning a secret contrivance to do anything incorrect if he knew it; but, I tell you in candor, that I have not the same exalted opinions of all other. Many of those who beset him with professions of friendship, I think every way capable of making every cent out of him they can, either by telling what they know to be untrue, or by suppressing what they know to be true.

It will be time enough for you to repel insinuations against yourselves when you have reason to think they are made. When *I* make them, they shall be in language not to be misunderstood, and supported by facts which will remain, any efforts to repel them to the contrary notwithstanding.

I am, with great respect, your obedient servant,

HU. L. WHITE.

Despite these bold assertions by Messrs. Polk and Johnson, there can be no doubt of the duplicity of their conduct regarding Judge White; and of Mr. Grundy's participation in the same, the following correspondence respecting him and Mr. Polk appears to furnish sufficient evidence.

You, sir, must remember, that as soon as the subject of the meeting was taken up, it was mentioned, as a matter of regret, that all the members of the delegation friendly to the Administration were not present, as it was very desirable that the views of all should be known, and, that whatever course should be resolved upon, should be done by the unanimous voice of the delegation. To this it was replied by one of the undersigned that although a part of the delegation were not present, the absent gentlemen had been consulted upon the subject of the meeting, and that their views had been expressed, and were known to one or more present. Whereupon one of the undersigned (Luke Lea) stated that he had requested Col. Polk to attend the meeting, and that he said he did not think he could do so, owing to the personal relations in which he stood to some of the delegation, and asked the relator's advice upon the subject, but although he declined attending, he stated he was for Judge White in preference to any other man for the Presidency—that the people of his district were for him, and that he would go as far as any of the delegation, in support of his election under any circumstances that he, Judge White, would permit his name to be used. Another one of the undersigned (James Standifer) stated that he had conversed with Mr. Grundy upon the subject of Judge White's being a candidate, and had requested him to attend this meeting; that Mr. Grundy said that he did not know that it would be altogether proper for him to attend the meeting, but if Judge White was brought out, he would show by his actions that he was as much his friend as any other man, and would support him in any way in which he would permit his name to be run. The same member stated, that he had seen Mr. Blair, who was out of the city that evening, and that Mr. Blair had told him, that Judge White was his choice; that he would be found as earnest in his support as any other man; and that he would co-operate with the delegation in whatever course they should adopt, to bring Judge White out.

This was the substance, and as near the language as we can recollect, of the report made in your hearing, of the views of those gentlemen who were absent, and whose co-operation was sought. When they had finished, you remarked that, as to Mr. Grundy and Col. Polk, you could state, that they stated to you last summer, at Nashville, that they should support Judge White, if he was a candidate. One of the undersigned inquired whether Mr. Grundy and Col. Polk mentioned in that conversation whether they expected Judge White to be nominated by a national convention before they would give him their support. You replied, that nothing was said about a convention, and that you understood them to mean they would support Judge White, if he was run as a candidate, in any way he would suffer his name to be used. The undersigned clearly understand from what you said, not only that those gentlemen were anxious to run Judge White, but that you, as their friend, were putting in their claim to be considered original White men. They further considered this disclosure as an evidence of the zeal and sincerity with which you espoused the cause of Judge White.

[Signed] JAMES STANDIFER,
BALIE PEYTON,
WILLIAM M. INGE,
JOHN BELL,
JOHN B. FORRESTER,
LUKE LEA,
DAVID W. DICKINSON.

To the Hon. CAVE JOHNSON.
January 1, 1835.

P. S. In making a report to the meeting of what my colleague Mr. Blair said when applied to to attend the meeting, I omitted to state that Mr. Blair objected to any formal nomination of Judge White for the Presidency by the delegation. I did not understand that any member of the delegation proposed to nominate Judge White under their names.

JAMES STANDIFER.

I do not recollect the particulars of the conversation which Mr. Johnson said took place between him and Mr. Grundy and Col. Polk, at Nashville, last summer, but the impression I have is, that they expressed themselves favorable to the pretensions of Judge White for the Presidency.

WM. M. INGE.

The meeting of a part of the Tennessee delegation in Congress, in December last, for the purpose of consulting together as to the propriety of running Judge White as the successor of Gen. Jackson to the Presidency, was a project of my own without being prompted by any one. My reasons for asking my colleagues to meet was, that when talking to the delegation they all, with whom I spoke on the subject, said they were in favor of Judge White, but I was occasionally told that Judge Grundy and Col. Polk were opposed to him, which I did not believe. Being on the strictest terms of friendship with Grundy and Polk, I mentioned to them the reports I had heard, informing Col. Polk I had heard that when he passed through Pennsylvania a short time before the meeting of Congress, he had been speaking in opposition to Judge White; he denied the truth of the report, and appeared angry; and to convince me of his attachment to White he spoke in the highest terms of him—saying he boarded with him, and complained that he should be so badly belied. Col. Polk inquired of me if Col. Bell was for White; I told him I did not know, I understood he was; he said he had understood that Bell had written letters, which could be produced, to some of Mr. Van Buren's friends, inducing them to think he was for Van Buren. I informed Judge Grundy that I had heard he was opposed to White, and was throwing difficulties in the way of his election, which he denied, and said no man could say so and tell the truth. He then inquired how Col. Bell was going, I told him I did not know, not being in the habit of conversing with him on those subjects, but had understood he would support White. Judge Grundy observed that Bell was playing a double game, to which I replied, if he was playing a double game I was too old a politician not to catch him. I then determined to ask a meeting of my colleagues for the purpose of consulting as to the propriety of running Judge White; but another object with me, which I did not disclose, was to ascertain who was playing the double game.

The first or second person I spoke to in relation to the meeting, was Col. Bell, on the morning of the day before the meeting, on Pennsylvania Avenue, on our way to the Capitol. When I mentioned the object of the meeting, and requested his attendance, he hesitated, and spoke with caution, and seemed to measure his words. He was well apprised that I had voted for Col. Polk against him for Speaker, which I supposed was the reason of his hesitation when I mentioned the subject of the meeting to him. I insisted we ought to meet and consult together, and ascertain whether we were all for supporting Judge White, or what other course we had better pursue. He at last said, if the members of his own State met to consult together, he did not know that he could refuse. About the time of the House's meeting that morning, I mentioned the intended meeting to such of my colleagues as I saw. I saw Col. Polk in his committee-room, and mentioned to him the contemplated meeting, and requested him to attend. He inquired if Col. Bell would attend; I told him what Bell had said to me, and that I supposed he would. Col. Polk then declined, remarking that he and Bell were not on speaking terms, and that his constituents would not approve of his consulting with a man he would not speak to. I then told Col. Polk I would ask Mr. Lea to call and see him on the subject; he replied he would be glad to see Mr. Lea at any time. When Judge Grundy was requested to attend, he made use of the expressions reported to the meeting.

[Signed.] JAMES STANDIFER.

Mount Airy, August 15, 1853.

Polk, Grundy, Johnson, and Catron, all became fierce opponents of Judge White, and denounced him as a deserter from the Republican ranks. Whether Judge Catron was working for pay or not, must perhaps remain uncertain. But it is not uncertain that he filled the first vacancy that occurred afterwards on the Supreme Bench.

As had been predicted, every means was used by these gentlemen to induce the legislature of 1835 not to re-elect Judge White to the Senate; but the people of Tennessee too well understood their course to be influenced by them. Mr. Polk, however, was steady to his purpose. From this time forward, everything that could be done was done by him, both publicly and privately, to injure Judge White. He misrepresented his course, by giving, in his "Address to the people," garbled extracts from his speeches; took the stump against him; and undoubtedly furnished his organ at Nashville with materials which he had every reason to know were untrue. During the session of 1839, when the Instructing Resolutions were before the legislature, it was currently reported and believed, that Governor Polk attended the caucus meetings, and was unceasing in his efforts to have them passed.

The sequel of these resolutions is before the world. They drove Judge White from the Senate. When this was accomplished, Col. Polk, with his usual diplomacy, after the death of Judge White, which soon followed, attempted to make capital of their having so long acted in concert:—and his organ avowed that Judge White had always been a "strict constructionist of the Constitution"—thereby paying him the highest compliment according to its views that could be passed upon a politician.

There had never been any special intimacy between Judge White and Col. Johnson. They were colleagues in Congress, and boarded at the same house. An inspection of MS. letters and papers, reveals a coincidence, which is noticed here more with a view to show the nature of the charges that were made against Judge White, as well as the character of the men who made them, than as of any great importance in itself. In Mr. Johnson's stump speeches in 1835 he says, "When General Jackson was surrounded with difficulties, and when it was necessary for him to have by his side some of his old and well-tried friends—he called upon Judge White and offered him the appointment of Secretary of State. Judge White declined to accept the offer. He then offered it to Mr. Van Buren. He stepped forward, and accepted. Since then he has been the main pillar of the Administration."

It would seem that the leading Jackson men must have known, that Mr. Van Buren received his appointment upon General Jackson's going into power, and not, as Col. Johnson supposes, when he was surrounded with difficulties. Instead of Mr. Van Buren's extricating General Jackson from these difficulties, he was their very cause. But it is a little strange that this charge should be in substance the very same that was made against Mr. Johnson himself in 1833; and that he should, as the following correspondence proves, have called on Judge White for, and actually procured, his certificate to prove that to the best of his knowledge he had on a former occasion, sustained General Jackson's Administration.

CLARKSVILLE, *April 20th.* 1833.

DEAR SIR: I find upon my arrival in my district such a variety of stories in circulation as to the course pursued by me, as a member from Tennessee, that I feel myself somewhat under the necessity of calling on my friends for the expression of an opinion as to the course pursued by me at Washington, as the most ready means of putting an end to the various stories circulated here. It is said here, that I have been, and am, unfriendly to the President and his Administration. Such general and undefined charges are scarcely worth notice; but as I have two of the strongest men in the district to contend with, it is a matter of some importance to me, to suppress if possible all such accusations. I know they have had their origin from Major Eaton, and W. B. L. in consequence of the course pursued by me in relation to the Chickasaw treaty, but that is never urged as an evidence against me. If therefore you feel no delicacy in the expression of an opinion upon my course, you would greatly oblige me by stating whether I have not uniformly sustained the Administration, and whether I have not been always so esteemed among members. I am not aware of having separated from my political friends upon any important question, except the Force Bill, which I thought unnecessary after the passage of the Tariff Bill. I shall be a good deal pressed by my opponents but do not fear the result.

Very respectfully,

Your friend,

C. JOHNSON.

KNOXVILLE, *May 16th*, 1833.

DEAR SIR: Your letter under date of the 20th ult. was received a few days ago. You state that in your district a story is circulated that you are unfriendly to the present Administration and wish upon that subject a statement from me.

In answer to this point I can only say, that so far as has come to my knowledge you have always in Washington and elsewhere avowed yourself friendly to President Jackson and his Administration, and I have never doubted the sincerity of your declarations. Entertaining no doubt that you were a sincere supporter of the Administration, I state in candor that I was surprised when I heard of your vote against the bill to enforce the collection of the revenue.

My recollection of the passage of that bill, and the one to modify the tariff, is different from yours. You think the bill to modify the tariff was *first* passed, and thereby the other rendered unnecessary.

My impression is that the bill to enforce the collection of the revenue was first passed in the Senate and sent to the House of Representatives. Then Mr. Clay's bill to modify the tariff was passed by the Senate and also sent to the House. The House then took up the Tariff Bill reported by the Committee of Ways and Means, and amended it by striking the whole of it out and inserting the bill which had been sent by the Senate, and thus amended the House passed the Tariff Bill and sent it to the Senate, not having finally acted on the bill to enforce the collection of the revenue which had been first sent. The Senate took up the Tariff Bill which had been sent from the House and passed it twice and let it lie for a third reading until it was informed the House had finally passed the bill to enforce the collection of the revenue. Upon receiving this information the Senate took up and finally passed the Tariff Bill. So that according to my recollection the Force Bill, as it is called, finally passed the House before, and not after, as you suppose, the bill to modify the tariff.

But as to myself, I repeat I never doubted the sincerity of your attachment to the Administration, nor do I now, although I differ with you in opinion as to the propriety and necessity of passing a bill to enforce the collection of duties.

With sincere esteem,

Your obedt. servt.,

HU. L. WHITE.

CHAPTER XIV.

HIS RELATIONS TO GEN. JACKSON.

THE first recorded account of the association of Gen. Jackson and Judge White, is at the bar of Tennessee. They were both of Scotch-Irish descent. Both were Carolinians by birth. Both were Tennesseans by adoption. Gen. Jackson being six years the senior, was on the supreme bench of the State, while Judge White was a practising lawyer. Here a personal friendship sprang up between them, which lasted many years. The latter, who was never a man of words, but of deeds, exhibited the warm attachment he felt for his friend, on many trying occasions. The first manifestation we have of it, is in the severe trials he encountered in his trip to the Creek nation, and the important services he there rendered him.

Next, when Gen. Jackson was on a trial before the Senate of the United States, and his destruction was sought by his enemies, in the highest tribunal in the nation; when the committee reported unfavorably, concerning the manner in which the Seminole war was conducted, Judge White boldly espoused his cause, and avowed the opinion that Gen. Jackson deserved praise rather than censure; incurring by so doing the displeasure of some of the most prominent members of the government.

In 1824, when Gen. Jackson was first a candidate for the Presidency, a majority of the legislature of his State wished to send him to the Senate. Judge White was in Murfreesboro' (then the seat of government), and remonstrated against such a movement as impolitic, for the reason that his election to the Senate must necessarily diminish his chances for the Presidency. A majority however differed with him, and chose to run Gen. Jackson for the Senate. Judge White found no fault with them for so doing, but uniformly urged the propriety of acquiescence by the voters of East Tennessee in the decision. He steadfastly believed in Gen. Jackson's honesty; considering that he possessed qualities which would make him highly useful to the country, when associated with honest, honorable, and well-informed men; and on all occasions and at all places, unfalteringly supported the General's claims to the Presidency, both in 1824 and in 1828. Of the estimation in which Gen. Jackson held Judge White, before, at, and even after the time of the elevation of the former to the Presidency, abundant evidence is extant in the General's own handwriting, and in that of his well-known confidential friends. In truth, as a well-informed friend of both parties has said, "the entire policy of the Jackson administration was directed by Judge White, so far as currency and Indian emigration West were concerned—which embraced two-thirds of the Jackson policy now memorable."

Major J. H. Eaton writes him as follows, February 23d, 1829, while arrangements were being made for the organization of the cabinet and for the determination of the course of the Administration:

DEAR SIR: A letter received some time ago from Gen. Jackson, stated he desired *you*, or *me*, to be near him. In a recent conversation with him, he remarked that he had had a full and free conversation with you; and at the close remarked that he desired to have me with him. I presumed, without inquiring, that he had probably talked with you on the subject, and that you had declined accepting any situation, as you before had told me would be your feelings. Nothing definite has taken place on this matter between General Jackson and myself, and I hope you know me well enough, and my regard and friendship for you, to know this, that I should never permit myself to stand in competition with any desire you may entertain. If you have any desire, say so to me *in confidence*, and it shall so be received. If you have none, then in reference to every and all considerations I should consent to any such appointment. Think of this, and give me your opinion frankly.

Your friend

J. H. EATON.

Gen. Jackson's wish to have him in his cabinet, upon his first accession to power, and the anxiety manifested by both him, and his friends, in 1831, that Judge White should take charge of the War Department (though, from Mr. Tazewell's account, he seems not to have been in full communion with the party at *that* time), prove the President's unlimited confidence in his integrity and his capacity for business. These honors were not tendered to Judge White in compensation for any favors he had shown the Administration, or its members. Both General Jackson and his friends expressly stated that it was for the benefit of the Administration and of the country that they urged him to accept; knowing full well, that such motives only would govern him. Judge White, however, declined to accept in the first instance, for reasons best known to himself. The cause which led to the dissolution of the cabinet in 1831, and which he relates in his "Address to the Freemen of Tennessee," was a scheme, which he would not have sanctioned for a moment, under any circumstances, and was doubtless one cause of his refusing to go into the cabinet at that time.

He earnestly desired to retire from the Senate in 1829–30 and 31; but, to please Gen. Jackson, and his friends, who assured him they could not dispense with his services in that body, he remained; and while there gave Gen. Jackson his hearty support on all measures, which were not at variance with his professed principles.

The following quaint letter from General Jackson will exemplify the terms in which the continuance of Judge White's services in the Senate, or his acceptance of higher office, was sought, or acknowledged by the President:

WASHINGTON, *Oct'r 12th* 1829.

MY DEAR SIR:—

I have rec'd your letter from Nashville, 26th ult., and am pleased to learn from it your determination to remain in the Senate a little longer. Your services there, for the present, is* all-important to your country, and your continuance in the Senate very gratifying to me. The severe affliction by the loss of so many of your children, I was aware, made public life a burden to you; still, I knew the high estimation in which your public services were held by your country, and that you would find it difficult to obtain the consent of your constituents to retire; am truly happy that you have consented to continue, for I had a hope that I would have your aid in the Senate so long as I remained in the executive. Both of us, I do suppose, would be more contented and happy in private life; but the lord† hath willed it, and we must submit.

How grateful I feel to you for your kind and friendly visit to the Hermitage, where lies all that made life desirable to me, and whose loss I can never cease to mourn, and over whose tomb I would like to spend the remnant of my days in solitude, preparing to meet her in a happier and a better world.

Be pleased to present me kindly to every branch of your family, and believe me your friend,

ANDREW JACKSON.

* So written in the original. † So written in the original.

Judge Overton, a confidential friend of the President, writes in a similar strain :—

NASHVILLE, *Oct. 5th*, 1830.

* * * * I pray God that you may be able to get along amidst your accumulated misfortunes, without resigning your seat in the Senate. The Gen'l* and myself are sensible of your value to the country at all times and under any circumstances; but now, my friend, your presence in the Senate, is all-important * * * The times, especially as respects the Senate are peculiarly delicate and hazardous.

One staunch, undeviating and intelligent friend there now, is a jewel of the first water, and without its compeer. I have always, and so does the Gen'l, viewed you as such. But if there be any other, I do not know him. * * *

Your friend as usual,

J. OVERTON.

The following letter, of later date, refers to the Secretaryship offered to Judge White when General Jackson was reorganizing his cabinet, with reference to the support of Mr Van Buren as his successor in the Presidency.

NASHVILLE, 3*d May*, 1831.

DEAR SIR: We have just received in handbills the account of a general dissolution of the cabinet at Washington, by resignation of all the principal secretaries. I suppose you have seen the same, and probably more, as rumor says the new cabinet has been designated, and that you are one of them. The friends of the President here are highly pleased with the arrangement, and more particularly that you will be with him. My dear sir, I know, that you are not desirous to be placed in such a situation. We all know that you have ever refused to accept of appointments to leave home. But at this particular crisis, when all seems to be at stake, and nothing but a firm steady course, to be well marked out, and steadily pursued, by the Administration, will or can support us, and prevent division in the republican ranks, I hope you will make the sacrifice of feelings, and accept of appointment if called on by the President; and I feel assured that in his present situation, his attention would first and very naturally turn toward you, in whom he can confide. You and he have grown up together, and have passed from youth to mature and somewhat advanced age; your friendship has been uninterrupted: you understand each other, and I believe your political views are the same;

* Jackson; with whom Judge Overton was very intimate.

and from these circumstances and facts, there is no one so well fitted to be with him as one of his counsellors and advisers, as you are; and therefore it is the earnest wish of your friends here that you will yield to the call. * * *

I beg you, my dear sir, to accept my best wishes for your health and happiness.

JNO. COFFEE.

In such terms was the support and co-operation of Judge White acknowledged, and the continuance or special use of the same solicited by General Jackson and his confidential friends during his first Presidential term.

There is little doubt that the uncompromising and inaccessible independence displayed by Judge White was profoundly displeasing and disappointing to the President and his especial co-laborers in political schemes for the future. That this was the case, and that Judge White saw it and coolly and unfalteringly recognized it, and as coolly and unhesitatingly disregarded both the anger and its consequences, when principles and consistency required it, the following extract from a letter to a confidential friend* is sufficient evidence.

SENATE CHAMBER, May 18, 1832.

* * * The true reason why nothing I have said is noticed in the Globe, I have no doubt is, because I have never assured any man that as soon as Gen. Jackson's terms of service are at an end, I will use all my endeavors *to elect the favorite of those who direct the operations of that paper*. I am for Gen. Jackson; but am not either a Calhoun Jackson man, or a Van Buren Jackson man, and therefore it is pleasing to the Globe and Telegraph not to notice favorably anything I can say or do; and as I am opposed to Mr. Clay, his papers will of course speak disrespectfully of me. Notwithstanding all these difficulties, I will go on exactly as I have done, making myself as useful as I can; determined to leave myself at liberty, when Gen. Jackson is off the stage, to exercise my own judgment on the question of a *successor*.

I cannot attend the Baltimore Convention, from which I expect nothing of benefit. My duties in the Senate preclude the possibility of my being absent.

Your friend,

HU. L. WHITE.

* F. S. Heiskell, Esq., editor of the Knoxville Register; a true and able friend of Judge White, and to whom were written many of the letters used in this volume.

Even at an earlier date, there is reason to believe that advisers of the Administration, if not the President himself, had begun to harbor secret dislikings against Judge White. The cause, in all probability, was apprehended opposition, or at least failure of hearty support from him, in their scheme of a re-election of General Jackson: a plan which flew directly in the face of their previous noisy advocacy of the one term principle, and which was justified only on the ground of its being necessary to keep "the party" together; although its secret motives were the doubts of Calhoun and Van Buren respectively whether an election as Jackson's successor was at so early a day in their power. There seems no other interpretation for the allusion in this extract from a letter, of date April 28, 1830.

* * * The Bill to provide for a removal of the Indians west of the Mississippi has finally passed the Senate by a vote of 28 to 19. This has taken off my mind a burthen which has been oppressive from the commencement of the session. I hope it may pass the other house.

Cold as the notice taken of our exertions in the Telegraph* is, no Georgian nor Tennessean will ever be mortified by hearing the debate spoken of, if truth be told. We had, I think, in the estimation of all intelligent men, at least as much ascendency in the argument as we had in the vote. As good fortune would have it, Judge Overton, Collingsworth, district attorney of West Tennessee, Major Armstrong, and many others from different quarters, were present, and know that our side was sustained in a style which gratified our friends, and mortified our opponents.

I have not, nor will I, commit myself to support any particular pretender after Jackson is off the stage. Of course I shall never have my exertions applauded in the Telegraph, nor in any other paper published here, while things remain as at present.

I have as much of the kind feelings of all as I can expect, unless I become the partisan of some one, which I do not intend to do prematurely.

Your friend,

HU. L. WHITE.

We here insert a correspondence between Judge White and Francis P. Blair, editor of the Globe. This also may be interpreted by the supposition of positive or negative unfairness in that print; which must be supposed to originate from an apprehension similar to

* Conducted by Duff Green, and in the interest of Calhoun.

that alluded to in Judge White's letter of May 18th. It presents evidence of the high valuation set upon his services, that such elaborate efforts were made to keep on good terms with him; and his terse replies indicate consciousness that his offences against the friends of the Globe, being such adherences to principle as would necessarily exhibit by contrast their dereliction from it, could not in fact be atoned for except by some means which he would not stoop to use. The first overture is from Mr. Blair, dated June 2d, 1832, as follows:

Dear Sir: Doctor Jones and Major Lewis have both informed me within a day or two past, that some person (whose name they did not give me) is using to my disadvantage, a *displeasure* which it is said you have conceived at my course in relation to yourself.

I am confident there must be some mistake in this matter. Entertaining as I do the highest consideration for your character, and having as I trust, manifested the respect I bear you, as far as opportunities have permitted me, I feel the most perfect consciousness that I can have done nothing to offend you, *certainly not intentionally.* I am equally certain that your elevated sense of propriety would not conceive an offence unless you had some reason to believe one was intended.

Do me the favor to inform me frankly whether anything has occurred which could authorize the assertion made by others that I have given you cause of dissatisfaction. I assure you that it will give me gratification to explain any accidental omission or inadvertence on my part, which may have excited a feeling to authorize the report to which I have alluded.

Your most obedient servant,

F. P. Blair.

To this Judge White replies, on the next day but one:

Dear Sir: Your favor under date of the 2d was handed me yesterday afternoon. In answer to its contents permit me to say, that as I am ignorant of what Dr. Jones or Major Lewis may have reported to you, as proceeding from me, I am, of course, unable to make any statement.

I have been a pretty attentive observer of the course of the Globe and on some occasions expressed the opinion I entertain, not only of it, but of the motives of those who influence it.

For myself, I have no inducement to trouble the editor to explain any part of his conduct. It is sufficiently explicit to enable me to form opinions upon every point, in relation to *him*, and *the patrons* of his paper, where it may become my duty as a public man, to act. Most respectfully, I am

Your obt. servt,

HU. L. WHITE.

June 8th, Mr. Blair makes a still more elaborate effort, thus:

DEAR SIR: On the first perusal of your note of the 4th instant, it seemed to preclude any further correspondence between us. Upon a further consideration of it, I am led to believe it may not have been so intended.

It is proper that I should inform you that Major Lewis and Dr. Jones *reported nothing to me as proceeding from you.* They merely stated generally that they had understood that I had in some way occasioned a dissatisfaction in your mind, and that this feeling on your part was used to my injury. From respect to you, and a wish to prevent any mischief to me, from what originated in misunderstanding on your part, as they supposed, or misrepresentation on that of others, they were desirous that I should communicate with you on the subject. Their motives were *honorable and charitable.*

Supposing that the cause of dissatisfaction (of which I am still entirely ignorant), related personally to yourself, I was desirous to ascertain the fault imputed, that I might dissipate it by an explanation. I felt confident that I should have no difficulty in this, because my own heart assured me that if I had a conscience void of offence towards any human being, it was so in relation to you.

From your note I am left to infer that the course of the Globe has not met your approbation. I am sensible of the difficulties and of the responsibilities I encounter as the editor of this print, and of my inadequacy to meet them; and you certainly have a right to animadvert on the manner in which I conduct it, because of the deep interest you have in the Administration, with which it is in some sort connected. But does not this circumstance give me some claim to ask of you in what particular, according to your judgment, I have offended? As the disinterested, long-tried, and most trusted friend of the President, I should take advice from you as a kindness, and receive even censure with respect. If I have erred from want of judgment, information, or experience; if, as you hint, I am operated on by any sinister influence, may I not hope, seeing, as you do, the mischiefs I may draw down upon myself, if not upon the cause with which I am connected, that you will apprise me of the danger in which I stand?

"Plain and round dealing is the honor of every man's nature," and if there be any man living from whose character I could expect this, it is from yours. I ask it from you on the present occasion. I should be glad to have a private and, if you please, a confidential interview, that the mystery (with me) which has led to the present correspondence may be solved.

With high respect, I am, sir,
Your most obedient servant,
F. P. BLAIR

To this Judge White answers, next day, still more decidedly:

DEAR SIR: Your note of yesterday has been this moment handed to me. You are certainly right in coming to the conclusion that my answer to your former communication was not intended to change our relations towards each other in any respect.

Should you believe an interview necessary, I assure you it would at all times give me pleasure to converse with you; but for the purpose of any explanation, no such thing is necessary. I have no desire to be on unfriendly terms with any man living, and cannot possibly have any motive for a controversy with you.

If I have had any causes of complaint, they have been upon points in relation to which I can never ask or expect redress. The time for either explanation or remedy has gone by. They must remain as they are; but, rest assured, I know too well what is due to myself as well as the public, to permit myself to take any course by way of redress, which is calculated to injure the political party to which I belong.

Most respectfully, your obedient servant,
HU. L. WHITE.

Here Mr. Blair gave it up.

Secret dissatisfaction at the evident impracticability of harnessing Judge White into the traces in which certain politicians were drawing, or indeed into any man's harness, began thus and henceforth to sap the friendship of the President for him. The first circumstance, however, which gave opportunity for open objection on the part of Gen. Jackson and his friends, was Judge White's vote in the Senate upon the Three Millions Appropriation, so called; which was appended to the Fortification Bill on short notice, at the close of the night session, March, 1835. Early in the succeeding session, Col. Benton in the Senate, and Mr. Adams in the House, charged the senators who voted against this appropriation, with having caused the loss of all the appropriations contained in the Fortification Bill. These accusations were met by firm and fearless denials. During the discussion, which was conducted with great acrimony, Judge White (the only Administration member who voted against this bill) made a personal defence in his speech on the Surplus Revenue, which could not fail to carry the conviction to every impartial mind, that instead of being governed by unkind personal feelings, he was just to the President, and true to his country. He showed that the bill was lost in the House instead of the Senate.

That portion of this speech which refers to Judge White's vote is as follows:

"I am one of those who voted against that appropriation, and against whom the charge is made. Against the accusation I might well plead a former acquittal, by the only tribunal competent to try me. This accusation was made in my own State, those to whom only I am accountable for my conduct here, have passed upon it, and their unanimous verdict of acquittal I presented the other day, and it now remains on the files of the Senate. But I scorn to rely on that plea; I have a right to a separate trial, to plead not guilty, and give the special matter in evidence.

"I do not feel that I, or any of those with whom I voted, are answerable for the loss of that bill. The vote I then gave was the result of my best judgment. I then approved of it, have done so ever since, and probably ever shall, so long as I am capable of reflecting on the affairs of this world.

"It will be no part of my plan, to attach censure to any one for his vote; all may have been governed by motives as worthy as I feel my own were. The time will soon come when we must all appear before that tribunal, where there can be no mistake either in the evidence or the judgment which ought to be pronounced. To that tribunal, then, where my motives and conduct must be submitted, I cheerfully leave the decision of the *motives* of all others; but it is due to the country and to myself, that I shake from my own skirts that blame which others seek to attach to me.

"A few very plain views of this matter will, I think, satisfy every honest mind that the Senate are in no fault whatever.

"The bill was originated in the House of Representatives, passed that body in the month of January, and was sent to the Senate. It then contained the whole sum esteemed by the Executive and the House necessary for fortifications and ordnance. This sum amounted to about four hundred and thirty-nine thousand dollars. The Senate might have given its consent to the bill without any alteration. If it had done so, there would have been a grant of the sum just mentioned, and no more, to these objects.

"The Senate, from the best information it possessed, believed the defence of the country required much larger appropriations, and as it had a right to do, increased some of the items of appropriation, and added others to the amount of about four hundred and thirty thousand dollars, thus increasing the grant from $439,000 to $869,000, and on the 24th day of February, returned the bill to the House, for the purpose of ascertaining whether the Representatives would agree to the increased grant made by the Senate. If the House had simply agreed to these amendments, the bill would have become a law, and there would have been an appropriation for fortifications, &c., equal to $869,000. The House did not do this, but retained the bill from the 24th of February, till 8 o'clock in the night of the 3d of March, and then returned it to the Senate with a new section as an amendment to the amendment of the Senate.

"This new section has been read so often, that every member, I presume, has it by memory. It is in these words: 'That the sum of three millions of dollars be, and the same is hereby appropriated out of any money in the Treasury not otherwise appropriated, to be expended in whole or in part, under the direction of the President of the United States, for the military and naval service. including fortifications and ordnance, and increase of the Navy: *Provided* such expenditures shall be rendered necessary for the defence of the country prior to the next meeting of Congress.'

"For one, I declare, when this new section was read, I was as much surprised as I could have been if it had been dropped through the sky-light above our heads into the bill. The chairman of the Committee of Finance moved that the Senate *disagree* to the amendment, and after some discussion, in which I took no part, the vote was taken, and stood 29 to 19, mine among those in the affirmative.

"At that time I knew not who had proposed this amendment in the House. The President had not asked, as far as I knew, for any such appropriation; there was no estimate sent from any department on which to found it. My belief was the President did not wish it. I supposed it had been offered by some member opposed to the administration, who wished a free disbursement of money about our seaport towns, not caring what embarrassment was occasioned by such a loose appropriation, and that in the hurry and confusion of a night session, it had been permitted to pass without any particular examination, and fancied that, so soon as their attention was particularly called to it, the House would recede from it, and the bill be passed as originally sent from the Senate.

"In these conjectures I soon found I had been mistaken, for presently the bill was returned to the Senate with a message stating that the House insisted on the amendment. A motion was made that the Senate adhere to its disagreement. Before voting on that question I took the liberty of stating very briefly the reasons upon which my first vote was given and upon which the second would be founded.

"The President had sent no message asking such an appropriation, no estimates had been sent on which to found it. I believed it would have been the duty of the Executive to have sent such a message and estimates, and I farther believed he would faithfully discharge his duty, and therefore concluded that he did not think the interest of the country required this additional grant. Beside this, the question was then pending and undecided before the French Chamber relative to the appropriation to comply with their treaty. I believed the strong probability was that it would pass, either then, or at the next session, and that with a little patience and good sense we should receive the money without any warlike preparation. This was not only my own opinion, but the declared opinion of all with whom I had conversed.

"I was what I professed to be, and ever had been, a friend to the administration; I had received no information that the President desired the appropriation, and I saw the section was so worded as to throw upon him a responsibility which he ought not to bear. The proviso left it discretionary with him whether the money *should be used or not.* I thought all the interest of the army, the navy, the large cities, and those who had ordnance to dispose of, would be brought to bear on him, to induce him to use the money: if he did order it to be used, and there should be no war, as I hoped and believed would be the case, he would be censured for wasting this large sum. If he resisted all importunities and did not use the money, and war did come, he would be censured for not providing for the defences of the country.

"Again, suppose the money to be drawn, what was to be done with it? How much to the army, to the navy, to fortifications, and to ordnance? The section does not say; all is indefinite, vague, loose, and left to Executive discretion.

"These reasons were satisfactory to my own mind—I voted upon them. From the time the three millions was first mentioned in the Senate until we adjourned, I did not converse, as I believe, with a single member of the House upon this or any other subject — nor did I converse with any member of the Senate except my colleague, who joined me in the lobby behind the colonnade, after our last vote. He was kind enough to speak favorably of my humble effort, and to express his regret that I had not made my argument before the first vote; but neither he nor any other member of either House ever intimated that the President wished such an appropriation.

"I sincerely believed he did not; but in that it seems I was mistaken, and the first notice I had of my mistake was in his answer to a company of gentlemen in New York, who, after the rise of Congress, made him a tender of their service to defend the country. Whether I would have voted for the amendment in this loose shape, if I had known it comported with the views of the President, I do not pretend to say. I think I ought not, but am willing to state, because such is the truth, that if, upon reviewing my whole votes since honored with a seat in this Chamber, any votes could be found which I would wish had not been given, the error is more attributable to my unbounded confidence in the Executive, and anxious desire to sustain him as far as I conscientiously could, than to any other cause whatever.

"But it has been urged by the honorable Senator from New Hampshire, Mr. Hubbard, that on the 28th February the Chairman of the Committee of Foreign Relations of the House had given notice that when this bill should be taken up he would move an amendment appropriating one million of dollars for *fortifications*, and two millions *for the navy*, and that this accorded with the views of the Executive, and the gentleman adds, the members of the House no doubt made this the subject of conversation, and that Senators would probably secure the information; and also that in the Globe newspaper of 2d March, this notice is published and has passed into the history of the country.

"To all this I answer, I did not hear of this notice. If any members with whom I associated heard this notice, they never mentioned it in my presence. So far from it, one of my colleagues of the other House, probably as attentive as any member there, assures me he did not hear any such notice; and when the amendment was under consideration he had a curiosity to know whether the President desired the appropriation or not, that he conversed with a colleague sitting near him, and neither of them knowing, he asked another of his colleagues, then Chairman of the Committee of Ways and Means, who told him the President did wish it, and added *that he must say nothing about it.* He did say nothing about it till since this discussion commenced during the present session. With the motives for this request to conceal I am not acquainted, therefore can say nothing.

"The other source of information, The Globe, I did not apply to, I never read it till since I heard the gentleman's argument. If I had wished to read the newspaper for information I had no leisure, my place was here, my duty here, and I had quite as much as I could attend to without reading the Globe. If I had wished information to guide my judgment, and felt bound to look into newspapers for facts, the Globe is the last place upon earth I should look into for *the truth.*

"Again, if I had seen this notice, I am yet to learn that the President has any member of this House to act as his substitute, and to give that information to the Senate which we have a right, by the Constitution, to receive from the Chief Magistrate himself.

"Lastly, if I had seen that notice, I would not have supposed this section was what was intended by it. The notice was specific—one million for *Fortifications*, and two millions for *the Navy*. The amendment is for every thing relating to either sea or land, *in a general mass*, for the Executive to divide out, as well as he could, according to his discretion.

"If the amendment had pursued the notice, it would have been well expressed; but in the shape presented in the bill, I doubt whether the combined talents of the members of both Houses can frame a section on such subjects more loose, more general, and more indefinite than it is.

"It has been insisted by the Senator from New Hampshire, that this section did make a specific appropriation of this three millions of dollars, and was justified by precedents in the days of General Washington, President Jefferson, and of President Madison.

"By the term specific appropriation, I understand that we mean *the direction of the law to apply a given sum of money to the accomplishment of a particular object, in exclusion of all others.*

"If this idea be correct, this section has no claims whatever to the appellation of specific. The object of it was to place every thing at the *discretion* of the Executive. 1st, Whether the money should be used at all. 2d, If used, to apply it to any object he pleased, connected with the land or naval service, or defence.

"The precedents referred to, do not bear out the arguments. The first is an appropriation of $116,000 to pay the civil list. Here the sum must all be applied to the discharge of the civil list, and nothing else.

"The next is $70,500 for fortifications. Although it is not said what sum should be applied to this or that fortification, yet the whole must be applied to fortifications, and to no other object. The third and last precedent rests on the same principles.

"In the case, now under consideration, every thing is vague, indefinite, and left to Executive *discretion*, and without any communication from the President, or any estimate whatever. I venture another remark, founded on what I heard said by a gentleman of much experience, not now among us, that during the period of a *popular* Administration, was the very time we must expect *bad precedents to be set.*

"These precedents, incautiously set, when we have *unbounded confidence* in the Executive, are sure to be relied on, in after times, by those who may wish to use power without regard to the public welfare.

"This section, if adopted, would in after times have furnished a precedent, by which any grant of the public money might be made, to be used at *Executive discretion.*

"I now put it to gentlemen with whom, on former occasions I had generally acted, to say, whether if such a grant had been proposed during the late Administration, a single man of them would have voted for it? No. It would have been said this money would be drawn and used, not for the public interest, but in jobs to control and regulate public opinion.

"Upon this matter, for one, I am perfectly satisfied that I, and those who voted with me, were right in not agreeing to this amendment; but the matter did not end with the vote of the Senate, the bill did not necessarily fall thereby. Let us pursue the subject, and see when, how, and where the bill was finally lost.

"The Senate returned the bill to the House, accompanied by a message, informing them that the Senate adhered to their disagreement to the amendment as to these three millions. Upon receiving this message, it was competent to the House to have receded from their amendment, and then the bill would have passed, appropriating the $869,000 proposed by the Senate; but instead of that they took a vote, and determined they *would not recede.* House Journal, page 518. After this, page 519, a motion was made that the House do ask a conference on the disagreeing votes. This motion was agreed to, and a committee of three appointed, and a message sent to the Senate, asking it to appoint a committee to confer on the subject. This message is found in the Senate Journal, page 236. As soon as it was received, the Senate agreed to the conference, and appointed a committee on their part, page 237. In the course of a short time, the committee on the part of the Senate returned, and reported that the conferees had agreed to recommend to their respective Houses as a substitute for the $3,000,000, an appropriation of *three hundred thousand dollars* for arming the fortifications, and an additional appropriation of *five hundred thousand dollars* for the repair and equipment of ships of war. Senate Journal, page 237.

"If each House had agreed to this report, then there would have been the appropriation of $869,000 contained in the bill as sent from the Senate, and an addition of $800,000, making in all, instead of $439,000 which the Executive had asked, $1,669,000. Here the question recurs, whose fault is it that this was not done? Unquestionably not that of the Senate. Its conferees had acted promptly, and promptly made their report. The Senate could go no further; *it could take no vote, as the bill and other papers had been carried to the House* by the conferees on the part of the House. This was entirely wrong. When the conference ended, it was the duty of the conferees on part of the House to have delivered the bill and papers to the conferees on the part of the Senate, who would have presented them when they made their report; the Senate could then have sanctioned the report by a vote, which I have no doubt would have been unanimous, immediately sent the bill to the House, which could have given its sanction, and the bill become a law. Instead of this, the House conferees kept the bill and papers, and by so doing defeated the whole bill.

"The rule upon this subject is so perfectly plain it cannot be mistaken. It is this: in all cases where a conference is asked before a vote of disagreement, the conferees of the House asking the conference, when it is over, must take the papers back with them, because their House is entitled to the next vote; but in every case where a conference is asked *after a vote of disagreement*, then when the conference is over, the conferees of the House asking the conference must deliver over the bill and papers to the conferees of the other House, because that other House is entitled to the next vote.

"In this case the Senate had voted to adhere to their disagreement to the amendment. The House had *after this*, voted that they would not recede, and then proposed the conference, therefore, as the House had given the last vote, the Senate was entitled to the next, and to enable them to give it, it was the duty of the conferees of the House to have given the papers to the conferees of the Senate, and if they would not receive them, they might have been left in the committee room.

"This doctrine, so reasonable in itself, is laid down in Jefferson's Manual, at 187, title Conference, in language too plain to be misunderstood, and it has been practised on by Congress in the cases with which I am acquainted, see the case of the bill for the relief of Mr. Monroe, in Senate Journal, page 374, of the session 1825 and 1826, and House Journal of the same session, pages 616 and 628.

"Let it not be supposed that the conferees of the two Houses were equally to blame for permitting the papers to remain with the conferees not entitled to them after the conference ended; because the conferees of the Senate did *not* know, and had *no means of knowing* that the House had voted not to recede *after the Senate had voted to adhere*. Strange as the fact may seem, the truth is, that the House, in its message to the Senate proposing the conference, *omitted to state the fact* that a vote, not to recede, had been taken after the House last received the bill. See the message, Senate Journal, page 236.

"The conferees on the part of the House knew the fact, because their Journal shows they were *present, and voted*, see the House Journal, page 518, 519.

"The conferees of the House having improperly taken the bill and papers, and thereby put it out of the power of the Senate to take any step whatever, are answerable for all the consequences.

"I do not state this omission in the message by way of censure on the Clerk for any intentional wrong. All these matters relative to this bill took place in the night, in the confusion which occurred at the end of the session, and it is very seldom that the most temperate and prudent are as well qualified to do business or have their wits as well about them after a comfortable dinner as they have in the early part of the day.

"Mr. President, let us now see what the conferees of the House did with these papers after taking them from the conference room. They returned to the House and the chairman made no report whatever, the Senate waited from one to two hours, and being able to hear nothing, sent a respectful message calling the attention of the House to this subject, see House Journal, page 530. Then the chairman stated that the committee had returned at the time a vote was taken on a resolution providing for the payment of Mr. Letcher, by which it was ascertained there was not a quorum, and that the constitutional term had expired, and that for these reasons he had declined making a report. Mr. Lewis, another member of the committee, then took the papers and made the report, which was never acted on, and thus the matter ended.

"The first reason assigned for not having made the report was the want of a quorum, this it is said was ascertained by the vote on the resolution just mentioned.

"The chairman ought to have put the House in possession of the report as he found the House in session. Had he done so, no doubt it would have been acted on. The Journal shows that much business was done afterwards, and a resolution reported by Mr. Wm. Cost Johnson was adopted by the House, see House Journal, from page 524 to 530.

"Now, if there was a quorum to do other business, to adopt other resolutions, how is it that there was not a quorum to receive and act on this report?

"The remaining reason assigned is, that the constitutional term for which the members were elected had expired. In other words, it was after 12 o'clock on the night of the third of March.

"How can this be? There must have been some mistake on this point. If it was not too late to do the other business I have mentioned, how did it happen to be too late to make this report.

"Again, the most certain information we have as to time is derived from the statement of the honorable Senator from Virginia. He tells us he looked at his watch when the conferees left the Senate chamber, and it then wanted fifteen minutes of eleven. When they returned and made their report, he was not in, but returned shortly afterwards, and it was then twenty minutes after eleven. We may, therefore, suppose the conferees had returned about one quarter of an hour after eleven, leaving *three-quarters of an hour to have disposed of this bill before the hour of twelve o'clock arrived.*

"There was, therefore, ample time, if the report had been made, to have disposed of this before our constitutional term expired according to the strictest construction.

"Mr. President, this is the eleventh session I have been here, and until last session never knew of an important measure having failed because 12 o'clock had arrived.

"So far as I know, the universal course has been, if the business necessary to be done could not be finished before twelve o'clock, to go on and accomplish it if it took till daylight.

"I well remember on one occasion, at a short session, we sat all night, and before I got to my lodging place, it was broad daylight.

"There always have been some members who had conscientious scruples about sitting after 12 o'clock. I always have, and always shall, respect men who act on such scruples, although I may differ with them in opinion.

"For myself, I have never felt any hesitation about voting after 12 o'clock, when the business required it.

"By the Constitution, members of the House are elected for two years. The President and Vice President for four, and the Senators for six. The only difficulty is to ascertain when the term commences. The Constitution does not fix it, but authorized the old Congress to do so. That Congress fixed the first Wednesday in March, 1789. That happened to be the 4th day of the month. Now, if we believe the first Congress met in the night at 12 o'clock, the 3d of March, 1789, then our constitutional term will expire in the night at 12 o'clock of the 3d of March, every second year, and the terms of the President and Vice President at the same hour every fourth year. But if we suppose Congress did not assemble earlier than 12 o'clock on the 4th of March, 1789, then, in truth, our constitutional two years, &c., do not expire till the same hour of the 4th of March, and we have our constitutional day, as it was, when light and darkness were first separated, and it was said the evening and the morning should be the first day.

"I submit to gentlemen who have these scruples, whether it is not worth while to reflect maturely on this subject. If the term of Congress expires the night of the 3d of March, so must that of the President and Vice President. This will always leave an interval of several hours, when we will have no President or Vice President. It appears to me those who framed the Constitution did not so intend. It is easy to think of cases which would be very hard upon such a construction. Suppose shortly before the expiration of a Presidential term, a man to be sentenced to be hanged in a federal court. Afterwards it should be ascertained to a certainty that the person was innocent, and a messenger is sent for a pardon, but cannot reach the President till after 12 o'clock on the night of the 3d of March, is the man to be hanged because there is no President until his successor is sworn in? This ought not to be the construction.

"I apprehend the whole difficulty originates from our perplexing our minds with a legal fiction that there can be no fraction of a day. This, like every other fiction, must yield to *fact* when justice requires it.

"A man sells a tract of land for a full consideration in the morning of the 4th of March, and conveys it. In the afternoon he sells and conveys the same land to another person; both vendees cannot hold, and yet, according to the idea produced by this fiction, both deeds were executed the first minute of the day, and are of equal date; but every man knows that this fiction would yield to fact, and that the first vendee would hold the land.

"Whether these reflections be altogether accurate or not, they have always satisfied me that I did not act unconscientiously, or assume powers I did not possess, when I voted in the night of the 3d of March after 12 o'clock.

"The honorable member from New Hampshire will perceive that the resolution he has read, which was adopted in the year 1790, does not remove the difficulty. That resolution only says the term expires on the 3d of March; but still the question recurs, when does the 3d of March end according to the meaning of the Constitution.

"To Senators on all sides, I submit, whether this crimination and recrimination for past acts, or omissions, is likely to produce dispositions now to act together harmoniously, and to endeavor to devise and perfect such measures as will most promote the interest and welfare of the country.

"Mr. President: In every view I have been enabled to take of this whole subject, it has appeared to me that this bill was lost in the House, not in the Senate; that the Senate were right in the votes which a majority gave as to this sum of three millions. I was satisfied with my votes when I gave them, and am yet satisfied, more, I am proud of them. I feel that the Author of my existence will approve of them, and to use the language of a distinguished man, now no more, 'I wish they were recorded in the centre of Heaven, in characters as bright as the sun, that the whole world might read them.'"

The statements in this speech were corroborated by Mr. Webster and others. Mr. Peyton says: "It was party spirit in the House which defeated the measure, many of the Van Buren members refusing to answer to their names when called, although present; thus depriving the House of a quorum, and defeating the bill."

Mr. Wise said, in his speech on the causes of the loss of the Fortification Bill, "Neither the House nor the Senate were chargeable with the act." But he affirmed that "it was certain Van Buren members, C. C. Cambreleng, and those with whom he acted, who defeated the measure, for the purpose of affecting Judge White's interest." He charged it against Speaker Polk, (and proved the charge by a written statement given to him by the Hon. Luke Lea, and corroborated by the Hon. Samuel Bunch, and admitted by Mr. Polk himself, who was, at the time, chairman of the Committee of Ways and Means,) that "he knew the fact that the President wished the appropriation, but did not communicate it to his committee or the House; but only to a few individual members in their seats, requesting them to say nothing about it." No estimate had been sent to the House by the President. Judge White did not know that he wished the appropriation, and therefore voted against it.

So great was his devotion to the Administration, and so effectively did he sustain it, as to call forth such testimony as that borne by the Hon. Mr. Clayton, of Delaware, who, in his speech on Mr. Benton's fortification resolutions, used the following descriptive language to prove the motive of the ill-timed and unprovoked assault upon the Senate. The thoughts expressed in the extract occurred to him while Judge White addressed that body in vindication of his vote against the Three Millions Appropriation, and he was led by them to form his conclusions as to the real object entertained by the Administration upon that vote. Judge White plead his acquittal by the legislature of Tennessee, which had unanimously re-elected him, after he gave that vote. Mr. Clayton said:

It may be considered necessary to make the most of this, the only offence he has committed against the Administration. The difference in the votes of the honorable senators from Tennessee (Mr. White and Mr. Grundy), on the amendment to the Fortification Bill, has called up some reminiscences of bygone events, exhibiting some other differences between them. When I first came into Congress, they were both considered so true to the Administration, and so effective in its aid, that, out of sheer compliment among their friends here, they were called "Jackson's Tennessee Rifles." They both proved true for a time, and told, with unerring certainty, in every conflict with those who opposed the executive. But although both were good rifles, there was an allowed difference between them. One missed the mark altogether, during that famous contest which was carried on here about the time of Mr. Foote's resolutions. It was believed to have been near bursting, in consequence of being overcharged with nullification powder. There was also another failure. This same rifle was assigned to the defence of the post-office, and was charged to the muzzle for keeping and maintaining that position; but the post was carried by its assailants, and the defence was censured by those who directed it, because the enemy entered in despite of the garrison, and exposed most piratical depredations which had been committed on the people. For my own part, I have always inclined to attribute this failure to the indefensible condition of the post. But, said Mr. Clayton, pointing to the seat of Mr. White, the old Tennessee rifle which has stood against that desk ever since I knew it, was a rare piece, and always has attracted my especial admiration. Although fighting on the other side, I never like to see it come into action. For six years, although it was almost every day engaged, it never snapped, missed, or hung fire; nor was it ever said to have failed to hit the mark, until about midnight of the 3d of March last. The people of Tennessee, who are said to be excellent judges of a good shot or a gallant blow, have since decided that this was a most "palpable hit," and that, however others, who are ignorant of the qualities of a first-rate weapon, may have foolishly desired to break the old rifle of the West, *they* still hold it entitled to the first rank when engaged for their defence; and will never consent that it shall either be injured by abuse, or left out of service. Even those who have condemned it, because, as they think, it has once missed the mark, may relent, when they reflect that it has been clearly shown in this debate that, on the occasion alluded to, the President himself did neither charge nor pull the trigger.

When Mr. Clay's resolution, censuring General Jackson's removal of the deposits, "upon the ground that he had assumed to himself authority and powers not conferred by the Constitution and laws, but in derogation of both," was before the Senate, Judge White not only voted against it, but argued that the President had the *Constitutional right to remove the public moneys whenever he had reason to believe them unsafe.* But the resolutions were adopted and entered upon the journals. The President protested against the stigma that had been attached to his name by the proceeding. Mr. Benton, in his devotion to General Jackson, afterwards brought forward his Expunging Resolutions, the object of which was to remove this reproach. Judge White voted against them. He had done all he could to prevent this unpleasant procedure: but the work had been done, and he maintained that it was unconstitutional and a dangerous expedient to obliterate the journals. In lieu, however, of these resolutions, he offered one, ordering Mr. Clay's to be "rescinded, reversed, repealed, and declared null and void." He wished to do justice to the Chief Magistrate, but at the same time, to do justice to the public and to the Senate. And in this opinion he was joined by most of the Administration members, only six or seven of whom voted to retain the word "expunge."

That General Jackson had received favors from Judge White, without any obligation on the part of Judge White to confer them, except that induced by friendship, both he and his friends admit. How were they returned?

The time came when General Jackson could have shown his gratitude by simply remaining silent; instead of which, because Judge White did not choose to acquiesce in all his views with regard to the succession, he entered personally and warmly into the presidential contest of 1836, denouncing all the friends of the latter who differed with him in opinion as "Federalists," "Nullifiers," and "New-born Whigs." Not only was this done, but he permitted and even encouraged office-holders to use their time and talents in the same cause. An instance is noticed in the remarks of Judge White, on a resolution submitted by him to the Senate, on the subject of Benjamin F. Curry's employment—and in his correspondence with the Secretary of War, in reference to a letter written by Mr. Curry, and published in the "Nashville Union." It is due to Judge White, to publish here his remarks and the correspondence. January 12, 1836, Judge White addressed the Senate as follows:

Mr. President: I rise to offer the resolution which I hold in my hand; but to enable the Senate to understand why it is offered, and the object I wish to accomplish, it is a duty incumbent on me, to accompany it with some explanation; I will therefore read and then pass it to your table:

Resolved, That the Secretary of War be, and he hereby is, requested to inform the Senate what office Benjamin F. Curry holds in the Cherokee nation, under what law he was appointed and at what time; what salary he receives, and whether he has at any time received any allowance, in addition to his salary, and how much; stating particularly the whole amount he has received each year.

This Mr. Curry went into the nation some time after the election of the present Chief Magistrate, and I believe until about twelve months ago, he had been employed as an inferior agent to superintend the enrollment of Cherokees for emigration, to have their improvements valued, &c.

During the last winter he was here, and when I returned home last spring, I understood he was making some figure as a politician; that out of his own head, or by the instigation of some person more wicked than himself, he had, while here, written some letters for publication to a small newspaper in my own State, which had engaged in the business of traducing me. In the course of the summer, we had, in some of our Congressional districts, animated contests between candidates for Congress. This gentleman, I understood, took an active part. He sometimes travelled out of the nation, and even out of his Congressional district, was zealous in propagating his opinions, and as I am informed and believe, either wrote himself, or furnished the materials for one or more pieces for the same vehicle of slander, to which he had written while in Washington.

In the district including the Cherokee agency he was zealous in opposing the election of the former member, and with the view to enable him to act efficiently, was in the habit of reading and showing confidentially, a letter said to be written by the President himself, finding fault with the former member by name, and using general expressions which Mr Curry said were intended for me. I have likewise been informed, that still farther to succeed in his plans of defamation, he confidentially used a letter, said to be written to him by my honorable colleague, in which my name was used, not much to my advantage; and I now take this occasion, in the Senate, in presence of our brother senators, in the presence of this audience, in the face of the world, to ask my colleague to say, whether at any time, he wrote any letter to Mr. Curry, in which my name was used.

[Mr. Grundy answered—"That he was taken by surprise with the question; but he did not remember he had ever written a letter on any subject to Mr. Curry, and he felt certain if he had, he had never used his colleague's name in other terms than those of respect."]

Mr. White proceeded—I am then satisfied with the answer given for the present, and this artifice must have been used by Mr. Curry, the more effectually to mislead and deceive those to whom he made such statements.

All this conduct I disregarded, and did not think it worthy to be made matter of conversation. Our elections terminated, the former member was reëlected; and when the legislature met, I was again honored with a seat here by a unanimous vote.

Some time ago, a friend brought me a Georgia newspaper, and pointed out to me a letter *under the signature of Mr. Curry*, dated 1st December, 1835, and addressed to the editor of a newspaper called the Federal Union. In that paper it had been published, and from it copied into various other papers, and finally into one in my own State called the Nashville Union, gotten up by funds furnished here, expressly for the purpose of distributing, in my own State and elsewhere, all the dirty filth and slanders which could be collected, with a view to detract from my humble standing.

The time at which this letter was published, as well as the place where and the matter of it, struck me with some force. The legislatures of Georgia, of Alabama, of Tennessee, of North Carolina, Virginia, and several other States were then in session, if I mistake not, and if I do I hope gentlemen will correct me, and that of Mississippi was soon to meet. Four of these States had a deep stake in the Indian question, because the Indians were residing, and yet reside, in portions of them.

I saw that the most gross and base falsehoods were contained in it as to myself. This I did not so much regard, but I saw further, that with a view to reach me, a statement was made respecting Mr. M'Connell, one of my constituents, a humble and inoffensive citizen, which would, in all probability, cost him his life. I felt hurt by this, as I had been the medium through which the Secretary of War had induced him to undertake this delicate, confidential and hazardous agency.

The falsehoods were so glaring, and the mischievous tendency of the letter so obvious, that I at first hoped, as soon as it met the eye of the Administration, the matter would be set right without any application from any quarter. After waiting some time without any step having been taken, and having good reason to believe the letter had been seen by at least one member of the Administration, I addressed a letter to the Secretary of War under date of the 2d inst. a copy of which I will now read.

WASHINGTON, *Jan.* 2, 1836.

DEAR SIR: I must take the liberty of inviting your attention to a letter under the signature of Benjamin F. Curry, published in a newspaper called the Federal Union, and bearing date, "Cherokee Agency, Dec. 1, 1835."

In it you will see in speaking of Samuel McConnell, Mr. Curry uses this language—"He has for some years past, under the procurement of Judge White of Tennessee, been receiving pay from the United States Government, as a secret and confidential agent, while all his visible efforts have been to defeat the measures of the ostensible agents in bringing about a treaty."

I feel assured your own sense of justice will at once pronounce that this statement, so far as I am concerned, is entirely unfounded.

The name of Mr. McConnell was not brought to your notice by me; I never asked or procured the department to appoint him. Any agency I had in the matter was at the instance of the department, and to carry into effect its wishes, as is fully disclosed in the letter from the acting

Secretary of War to me, and my answer, with its enclosure to him, to which I beg leave to refer you.

In that, as in everything else, I was willing to do all in my power to aid in carrying into effect the wishes of the department in relation to the Indians, and must think I am treated with great injustice, if your agents, attached to your department, are thus to misrepresent and calumniate me. From all the information I possess, I must think that in the charges against McConnell there is a great disregard of truth. I had once believed, and yet do, that he acted with great fidelity, and that from his services much benefit resulted.

But, sir, if Mr. McConnell was a secret agent, appointed by your department, does he merit that his life should be endangered by this statement of your agent? If he was not a secret agent, is it right that he should be endangered by the statement of such a falsehood?

In another part of Mr. Curry's letter he states that shortly before the council, Lewis Ross came to Knoxville, and after his return, rumors were put afloat connected with my name.

The inference which Mr. Curry wishes should be drawn from this statement no doubt was, that Lewis Ross came to Knoxville to consult me. I assure you, if Mr. Ross was at Knoxville, from the time I left Washington in March till my return this fall, I never heard of it until I read Mr. Curry's letter, and have had no communication whatever with him.

The whole tenor of this letter, so far as I am concerned, is a tissue of misrepresentations, intended to place my conduct in a false view before the world.

I am well aware that those who know Mr. Curry would not excuse me for taking any notice of his slanders generally, but from the particular nature of his charge, and the circumstance of his being connected with your department, his statement may be thought entitled to some credit, should it pass without rebuke.

He is your officer, you are the witness who knows the gross injustice done me, and to you I confidently appeal for such steps as will do that which is just to the country, to Mr. Curry and to myself.

I beg to be informed what course you will pursue in this matter.

I have the honor to be, most respectfully,

Your obedient servant,

HU. L. WHITE.

Hon. LEWIS CASS.

On the night of the 15th I received his answer dated the 14th, inclosing a copy of one written to Mr. Curry on the 9th.

DEPARTMENT OF WAR, *Jan.* 14*th*, 1836.

DEAR SIR: I must ask your indulgence for not having answered your letter of the 29th inst., which was received here on the 15th. The delay has been owing to the great press of business, and to the propriety of laying the matter before the President.

I have now the honor to send the copy of a letter addressed to Major Curry, and in which the President's disapprobation is conveyed to him. The statement that Mr. McConnell was employed at your suggestion is altogether erroneous, and I have put the matter right by giving the true facts of the case. I consider the department under obligations to you, for the trouble you took on the subject of the employment and proceedings of Mr. McConnell, and I have endeavored to do justice to his services, so far as these are known to me. If Major Curry intended to intimate, as you suppose, that there was a communication between yourself and Mr. Ross, such an intimation was highly improper. Independent of the entire want of proof of such a course, your word is quite sufficient to satisfy me that there was no just ground for the suggestion.

I am, dear sir, very respectfully,

Your obedient servant,

LEWIS CASS.

HON. HUGH L. WHITE.

WAR DEPARTMENT *Jan. 9th*, 1836

SIR: The attention of this department has been drawn to a letter from you to the editor of the Federal Union, and which was published in the Augusta Centinel of the 22d ult.

I am instructed by the President, if that letter was written by you, to convey to you his disapprobation of a part of it. There certainly can be no impropriety in an officer's communicating to the public proper information, when circumstances require it, and the general proceedings relating to the prospects and progress of the Cherokee emigration, are of this nature. But it is with regret the President observes, in this communication, allusions to persons and parties, which do not seem to be necessary, and are calculated to produce an injurious effect. There is one error of fact, which it becomes the special duty of this department to correct, as the requisite information is upon its files. You state that Mr. McConnell "has for some years past, under the procurement of Judge White of Tennessee, been receiving pay from the United States' Government, as a secret and confidential agent," &c. You have been led into a mistake on this subject. Mr. McConnell was not employed under the procurement of Judge White. The suggestion that Mr. McConnell's services might be useful, as well to the United States as to the Cherokee Indians, was made to this department from another and very respectable quarter. As all the necessary circumstances were not fully known at the department, proper instructions were given to Mr McConnell and enclosed to Judge White, to be delivered, if he thought the arrangement would be useful. Judge White had no agency whatever in the matter, until he was requested, by the express direction of the President, to serve as a medium of communication between Mr. McConnell and this department.

Mr. McConnell transmitted various reports, containing information respecting the state of things in the Cherokee country. But there is nothing in these, going in the slightest degree to show that he did not act with due fidelity, as well to the United States as to the Cherokee Indians.

It is also a matter of regret, that you should have alluded at all to the employment of Mr. McConnell. From the relation in which he stands to the Cherokees, and the suspicious disposition of Indians, the disclosure may even put his life at hazard. It is therefore the more imperative upon me, to state explicitly, as I have done, that there was nothing in the report of Mr. McConnell which could give just offence to the Indians.

The President has directed me to say, that he has read and approves this letter, and that while he appreciates the zeal you have displayed in the execution of your duties, he deems it incumbent upon him to recommend to you great discretion, and particularly to convey to you his disapprobation of the allusion you have made to the employment of Mr. McConnell.

Very respectfully,

Your most obedient servant,

[Signed] LEWIS CASS.

MAJOR B. F. CURRY, *New Echota*, *Georgia*.

To this, on the 16th, I wrote a very short reply:—

WASHINGTON, *Jan.* 16*th* 1836.

DEAR SIR: I have the honor to acknowledge that I received last night, your favor under date of the 14th, with its enclosure, in answer to mine of the 2d inst.

The result is so different from what, I think, I had a right to anticipate, that I refrain from any remarks on the contents of the letter written to Mr. Curry, by direction of the President.

I have the honor to be, most respectfully,

Your obedient servant,

HU. L. WHITE.

I had applied in the only friendly mode I could devise, for the interposition of the executive power. I remembered well the great principle for which the party had struggled to elevate the President to his present station. I remembered his recognition of it in his inaugural address, which thousands of the citizens of the United States, as well as most of those now in the reach of my voice, heard him deliver, as containing the principles upon which he would administer the government. The paragraph is in the following words:—

"The recent demonstration of public sentiment inscribed on the list of executive duties, in characters too legible to be overlooked, the task of reform; which will require *particularly* the *correction of those abuses* that have brought the *patronage of the federal government into conflict with the freedom of elections*, and the counteraction of those causes which have disturbed the rightful course of appointment, and have placed, or continued power in unfaithful or incompetent hands."

This short paragraph shows the main ground on which the contest rested, when ended in the election of the present Chief Magistrate. It contains the sentiments avowed by him in presence of nearly twenty thousand freemen. It contains the sentiments which, as one of his advocates, I honestly entertained. It contains the sentiments on the maintenance of which I believe our freedom and liberty especially depend. I felt hurt and mortified upon reading the Secretary's letter; I could not reply without using expressions not fit to address to a member of the President's Cabinet. In place of Mr. Curry's receiving such a rebuke as would deter him from committing a similar offence in future, it appeared to me that he was complimented. Although his conduct was not approved as to Mr. McConnell, as to me it was very well, that instead of an inferior agent he was to be viewed as an electioneering political diplomatist, and that hereafter, if the Gardiner spoke of by the senator from Massachusetts, the other day, is to wear his diplomatic button, Mr. Curry ought to figure in his political electioneering star and garter.

But, sir, what was I to do next? The falsehood has gone forth to answer the meditated mischief. In some of the States it is probable it has accomplished its object; how is it to be contradicted? I have been furnished with a document proving the falsehood. Is it supposed that I would sneak to a printing office to beg a publication of its contradiction? No, I cannot descend to such an act of meanness. If I could, I dare not. The proud, high-minded honorable men who sent me here would, for such an act of degradation, recall me from a station among honorable men, and thus gratify some high in office who seek to displace me.

My course is here; my place is here: from my stand on this floor I contradict the falsehood and expose the injustice. If my opponent will deny my statement, or justify this outrage, I meet him here openly, face to face, eye to eye, and maintain and assert what is due to my constituents and myself, by all honorable means in my power.

But the Nashville Union—this vehicle of slanders and falsehoods, gotten up in this city, as I have understood for just such purposes. The editor came here last winter, upon his own mere notion, or by the solicitation of some other person, with, as I have understood and believe, not more money than would bear his expenses; he lived in the house with my honorable colleague, and while here, was furnished with some five or six thousand dollars, to establish his press in Nashville, and, without relying upon subscribers, to be enabled to throw his paper into the hands of every man who would condescend to read it. Even this very number, containing this letter, I have no doubt, has been innocently sent under the frank of senators from this floor, to many of the States in the Union.

If there is any person within my hearing who can contradict my statement as to the manner in which this paper was established, I wish to hear him do so.

[Mr. Grundy rose and stated:—"That the editor had come here last winter, not at his instance; that how the money was raised, or by whom, he had no knowledge; that the paper had taken its side, and was maintaining it as well as it could; that he had not noticed this letter in it, and that he knew there was great scuffling to get subscribers for it at home. Mr. McConnell he knew, and thought him a clever man, of good sense, and he believed he had recommended him for this office."]

To which Mr. White replied—Yes, Mr. President, there *was* a great scuffling to get subscribers for it. So great, that our old acquaintance, Samuel Gwin, the land officer, from Mississippi, was called into service, and when procuring subscribers at Gallatin, in April last, wrote to Mr. Ritchie, of the "Enquirer," the celebrated letter as to Tennessee politics, intended unjustly to influence the Virginia elections, and which no doubt had the desired effect. Mr. President, I have made these disclosures with great pain and the most deep mortification; but I deemed it my duty to do so. The answer to my resolution will show whether it will be in my power, and whether it will be my duty to attempt anything further on the unpleasant subject.

The following is an extract from Mr. Curry's letter, alluded to in the above remarks:

At the October council, there attended a certain Mr. Payne, and one Samuel McConnell, of Tennessee; Payne hails from New York, but came through Georgia. He is of the whig party, and rumor makes him an abolitionist. He, it is said, formed an alliance with Mr. Longstreet, of Augusta, and other editors, by which he was to furnish matter, and they were to print it for political effect. McConnell is the same who instigated the arrest of the Georgia surveyor, and had him carried to Athens, Tennessee, for a violation of the intercourse laws some three years ago for making lines within the limits of your State. He has large claims for reservations made to Indians under the treaties of 1817–19; and has for some years past, under the procurement of Judge White, of Tennessee, been receiving pay from the United States government, as a secret and confidential agent, while all his visible efforts have been to defeat the measures of the ostensible agents in bringing about a treaty.

Lewis Ross, one of John Ross's executive counsellors, visited Knoxville about the commencement of this council, and, while absent, much concern was manifested by John, to know where his brother Lewis could be. Lewis at length arrived.

Rumor was put afloat that Judge White, if made President, would do much for this people.

So constant and glaring did infringements on the rights of the people, similar to those exhibited above, become, that they were a constant theme of remark on the floor of Congress. Many members of the opposition made assertions which were never answered from the other side. In 1836, a special committee was appointed by the House of Representatives, of which Mr. Wise was chairman, to inquire into the condition of the public funds. At the instance of General Jackson and Mr. Van Buren, Judge White was summoned to appear before this committee, which he did in January, 1837, and gave evidence upon oath, of many instances in which officers of the government and those in their employment, had attempted to influence public opinion in elections; and made a statement of the part the President himself had taken in the late presidential canvass, as well as his attempt to influence him in his public duties, both while he was President of the Senate and subsequently. General Jackson answered these charges in a publication some months afterwards, in which he complained of Judge White's deposition, and flatly contradicted his statements. This drew forth Judge White's "Address to the Freemen of Tennessee." This was the last intercourse, either of a public or private nature, that ever took place between them.

Judge White's testimony before the committee, and also his answer to General Jackson's circular, are here subjoined, that all who desire may read and decide for themselves.

TESTIMONY OF THE HON. HUGH L. WHITE

Before the committee appointed to inquire into the executive departments, &c.

Monday, Jan. 30, 1837.

Hon. Hugh L. White, a senator of the United States, summoned as a witness, appeared before the committee, and read a paper of the following import:

Declaration of the Hon. Hugh L. White.

SIR: On Saturday evening last, I was summoned to attend before the committee of which you are chairman, and give evidence touching the matters submitted to your investigation. I now appear before your committee, at the time specified in the subpœna, *but not in obedience to its mandate.*

I am a member of the Senate of the United States, now in session, and in the daily discharge of my duties as a senator, and, while I am thus engaged, *do deny* that any committee of the House of Representatives has the power, by its mandate, to compel me to absent myself from the body of which I am a member. I do, therefore, protest against the power assumed by your committee, in the issuance and service of said subpœna.

But, at the same time that I feel it my duty thus to protest against the exercise of a power which I believe is not vested in your committee, I assure them that I will at all times, when my duties as a senator do not compel me to be elsewhere, voluntarily attend and give them upon oath, all the information I possess in relation to any of the matters which may come within the range of their investigation.

I respectfully ask that this protest may be entered on the journal of your proceedings, lest hereafter, it may be thought I have sanctioned the exercise of a power which, it is easy to foresee, may be so used as to destroy that body of which I am an humble member.

I have the honor to be, most respectfully,

Your obedient servant,

HU. L. WHITE.

To the Hon. HENRY A. WISE, *Chairman of the Special Committee of the House of Representatives.*

The Hon. Mr. White then read to the committee another paper of the following import:

Reasons of the Hon. Hugh L. White for consenting to testify.

"Mr. Chairman: Before being sworn, it is due to the committee, as well as myself, that I should make a very short statement, to show the situation in which I am about to be placed, without any agency of mine.

"For many years I have been on the most intimate and confidential terms with the Chief Magistrate. We have conversed with, and written to, each other, perhaps with as much freedom as if we had been brothers; much that has passed was, of course, highly confidential.

"I should hold myself disgraced by designedly bringing any matters of this kind before the public.

"If sworn I must tell what I know or believe to be true; and I consider myself called upon to testify, *at the instance* of the present Chief Magistrate, and of the distinguished citizen who has been chosen to succeed him; and that, if any disclosure I may make would seem to be of matters which, as a man of honor, I ought not to make public, I do so in consequence of the necessity they have imposed on me; and that the injunction of secrecy has been removed by them, and not by me.

"With this statement, I am now ready to be sworn, if the committee desire it."

Testimony of the Hon. Hugh L. White.

Monday, *Feb.* 13, 1837.

A communication in writing, in answer to the interrogatory put to the Hon. Hugh L. White, was received through the chairman, and read to the committee, as follows:

The oath administered to me was, "to tell the truth; the whole truth, and nothing but the truth," &c.

After being thus sworn, the interrogatory put to me is in the words following:

Question. "Do you, of your own knowledge, know of any act by either of the heads of the executive departments, which is either corrupt, or a violation of their official duties?"

"From the manner in which this question is worded, it is somewhat difficult for me to determine to what extent I ought to proceed in my answer. I presume it could not be the meaning of the committee to constitute me the judge of what shall be considered corruption, or a violation of official duty, by any of the heads of the executive departments. If so, I might believe facts within my knowledge did not amount to either corruption, or a violation of official duty, and on that account omit any statement whatever; or, on the other hand, state facts which I believe prove one or the other, when the whole committee might disagree with me in opinion, and consider the disclosures entirely useless, as not tending to prove any impropriety whatever. In this situation, I presume I shall best discharge my duty by telling what I may know falling within the range of either of the executive departments, and such circumstances as may tend to show the motive with which the act was done or omitted, leaving it to the committee to determine whether any statements I may make will be of use or not in their investigation.

Of my own knowledge I do not know of any frauds actually practised either as to the sale of public lands, or in the purchase of Indian reservations; yet, from information I have received, in which I confide, I do believe great frauds have been practised, and are yet going on, as to both; and that in some of these, our own officers or agents have been, and now are, concerned or interested; and that if the committee will call upon persons who were and yet are in the vicinity of the places where those transactions have taken place, to disclose what they know, these frauds, and those concerned in them, can be ascertained. Whether the heads of either of the departments are liable to be censured for any of these acts, the committee will of course decide for themselves, when they shall have ascertained all the facts.

In the year 1830 the system now going on for removing the Indians, with their consent, out of the limits of the States and territories, and settling them west of the Mississippi, was sanctioned by Congress It has been progressing as rapidly as possible ever since. The duties relating to this branch of business pertained to the War Department.

At the session of Congress for the years 1831 and 1832, and near the time when a short session would have terminated, the Secretary of War came to me, as chairman of the Committee on Indian Affairs, and stated that his duties were becoming so onerous that he could not discharge them without an alteration in the Indian Department; that the gentleman who was then at the head of the Indian bureau, and who was then receiving a salary of fourteen or sixteen hundred dollars, although a very amiable man, was entirely incapable of discharging his duties in such a manner as to give that aid which the public interest required; that he had drafted a bill to create the office of Commissioner of Indian Affairs, with a salary of three thousand dollars per annum, which he wished me to introduce, and endeavor to have passed into a law. I informed him that the session had then so far advanced, and the opposition to the Indian system was so strong, that I doubted it would be out of my power; besides, that some of the appointments which had been made, were, in my opinion, injudicious, and that if this office were created and filled by a person as incompetent as he represented the person then at the head of the Indian bureau to be, the public business would be no better done, and there would be necessarily a considerable increase of expense, and that I was unwilling to move on the subject, unless I could be assured, if the office were created, *it should be well filled.* This he assured me should be done. I then requested him to speak with the chairman of the Committee of Indian Affairs of the House, and if his co-operation could be procured, I would on my part, do all in my power to give effect to his wishes.

The bill was introduced, and, owing to the strong representation made of the necessity for its passage, the opposition in the Senate was withdrawn and the law was passed. Congress adjourned, and no appointment of commissioner was made until the next session; and then the same gentleman whose supposed incompetency at the head of the Indian bureau, with a small salary, had given rise to this law, was nominated to fill the office of commissioner, to which was attached the salary of three thousand dollars per annum. The nomination was referred to the Committee on Indian Affairs, and they reported recommending that the nomination should be confirmed. At that session I happened to be in the chair; and when I heard the report, withdrew from the chair, and spoke to the gentleman who made the report; told him what had passed between the secretary and myself, and that I felt it due to the Senate and to the country that the facts should be disclosed, so that the nomination might be acted on with a full understanding of the facts. He told me he would have the nomination laid on the table, until he could see the secretary, and have his explanation on the subject. He did so, and afterwards informed me that he had seen and conversed with the secretary, and communicated to him my statement; and that the secretary admitted my statement to be true, as to what passed between us, but that after the passage of the law Mr. Herring had devoted himself to acquiring a knowledge of the duties pertaining to the office, and was then well qualified to discharge them. Under this statement I said nothing further, and the nomination was confirmed; and it so did happen that, although I never heard Mr. Herring's integrity called in question, yet his want of capacity was admitted by all with whom I conversed before he quit the office.

During the last session he was appointed pay-master, and Mr. C. Harris appointed commissioner, who, so far as I can judge, is a most faithful, competent and efficient officer.

I think the public interest suffered much from the incompetency of Mr. Herring while he was in office; and that it will take some time still to come before his successor, with all his zeal, watchfulness and industry, will be enabled to make those reforms which the public interest requires.

I feel that I should do the late secretary injustice, were I to stop here. I do not believe he intended to deceive me, or to injure the public, when he promised me that if the office was created it should be well filled; but that after it was created, *as it connected itself with all the ramifications of the Indian Department, and the officer might have a very extensive influence*, it was esteemed a matter of importance to have it filled with a decided friend to the gentleman who was then looked to by the President and many others as the person who ought to succeed the present Chief Magistrate; and that the secretary was constrained to yield to an influence which he believed he had not the power successfully to resist. I am the more inclined to adopt this opinion, because, from a very extensive intercourse with the secretary relative to the Indian affairs, I was impressed with the belief that in all cases where he was left free to pursue his own judgment, he was disposed to act with the utmost fairness, and with a strict regard to public interest; and because I know, in a manner most satisfactory to myself, that, as early as 1831 (if not sooner), when the first cabinet was dissolved, and a new one to be created, the President had fixed his mind upon the present President elect as the most suitable person to succeed him; and that, with a view to procure harmony among the members of his political family, it was considered important to remove from the old cabinet three gentlemen, who, it was believed, did not coincide in opinion with him upon that subject, and form a new cabinet which would be a *unit;* that is, each member of it concurring with the President as to the person most proper to succeed him when his eight years of service should terminate.

When the old cabinet was broken up, it was not wished to have the services of Major Eaton; the intention and wish was, to put me in his place, and with my aid in Tennessee, to have him elected to succeed me in the Senate.

This opinion as to the motive for the appointment of Mr. Herring is still further fortified and confirmed in my mind, from the belief that a very large portion of all the officers appointed from that time to this have been selected upon the same principles, and with a view to the same object.

Connected with this subject, and tending to show that I am most probably correct in the view which I take of it, there are many circumstances which I have become acquainted with, which show that the President watched with care, and uniformly endeavored to prevent, everything which would have the effect of enabling any other citizen to compete, successfully, with the gentleman who was his favorite. During the same session of 1832 or 1833, when Mr. Herring was appointed, it will be remembered, the United States seemed to be on the eve of a civil war with South Carolina, on account of the tariff; and that a bill was sent to the House of Representatives from the Treasury Department, proposing a modification and a reduction of it; that the provisions of that bill were so changed in the House, that it became very unacceptable to a large majority, and had no prospect of finally passing; that, in this state of things, and after what was called the Force Bill had been considerably discussed in the Senate, Mr. Clay introduced what is commonly called the Compromise Bill, and, upon its second reading, it had been referred to a select committee, composed of seven members. This committee, it was my duty, as presiding officer, to appoint. Before the members of it were named, I received a note from the President, requesting me to go to his house, as he wished to see me. I returned for answer, that while the Senate was in session it was out of my power to go, but that as soon as it adjourned I would call on him. I felt the high responsibility which rested on me in appointing the committee; the fate of the bill, in a good degree, depended on it; and if the bill failed, we would probably be involved in a most painful conflict. I endeavored to make the best selection I could, by taking some tariff men, some anti-tariff, one nullifier and

Mr. Clay himself—hoping that if a majority of a committee, in which all interests and views were represented, could agree on anything, it was likely it would pass. Taking these principles for my guide, I wrote down the names of seven members, Mr. Clayton, of Delaware, being one; and immediately before we adjourned, handed the names to the secretary, with directions to put them on the journal, and in the course of the evening waited on the President. Soon after we met, he mentioned that he had wished to see me on the subject of appointing a committee on Mr. Clay's bill, to ask that Mr. Clayton might not be put on it; as he was hostile to the Administration, and unfriendly to Mr. McLane, he feared he would use his endeavor to have a preference given to Mr. Clay's bill over that of the Secretary of the Treasury, or words to that effect. I observed, in answer, that it would always give me great pleasure to conform to the wishes of my political friends, whenever I could do so with propriety; but that the treasury bill had been so altered and mangled, and that, as I understood, in a good degree by the votes of his own party, that it had but few friends; that we seemed to be on the eve of a civil war, and that for the sake of averting such a calamity, I would further all in my power any measure, come from whom it might, which would give peace to the country, and that any bill, having that for its object, was esteemed by me a measure *above party*, and any man who was the author of it was welcome to all the credit he could gain by it. But, at all events, it was too late to talk on the subject, as I had handed the names of the committee to the secretary before we adjourned; and that as I had a very high opinion of Mr. Clayton's talents and liberal feelings, I had put him on the committee, without knowing he was personally unkind to the Secretary of the Treasury. He then asked me if I could not see the secretary of the Senate that evening, and substitute some other name for Mr. Clayton, before the journal was made up; I told him I could not—in my judgment it would be wrong; and then the interview terminated.

An incident occurred relative to an appointment, falling in with the business of the State Department, which I feel it my duty to state, but do not know that the Secretary of State had any participation in it.

At the session of 1833 and 1834, if my memory serves me, Mr. Stevenson, of Virginia, was nominated as Minister to Great Britain, and his nomination rejected. At the session of 1834 and 1835, on the Sunday immediately preceding the close of the session, a gentleman called at my lodgings to see me, and informed me that he had called, at the instance of the President, to consult me on the subject of again nominating Mr. Stevenson as Minister to Great Britain; and to say, that if I believed a majority in the Senate could be procured to confirm the nomination, the name of Mr. Stevenson would be sent in; if not, no nomination would be made during the session. I observed to the gentleman, I could not give any answer, as I had heard nothing on the subject, and had not reflected on it; and further said, from what I could hear, I was at a loss to know whether I myself was viewed as friendly, or the reverse. The gentleman replied, there was a mistake on that subject; that it was commonly thought Mr. Stevenson and Mr. Ritchie, of the Enquirer, were friendly to Mr. Van Buren, but that was not so; they were soured with him, believing it was his wish to make Mr. Rives the great man of Virginia. After some further conversation, I told him I would think of it until next morning, and would then tell him what I thought. He did call the next morning, when I requested him to say to the President, that I had no means of knowing how other senators would vote, and that the only advice I could give was, for the President to do what he believed to be his duty, leaving the senators to discharge theirs.

The nomination was not sent in till the next session; and, in the mean time, Mr. Stevenson had been presiding officer at the Baltimore convention, and an active partisan in aiding to carry out the views and wishes of the President as to his successor.

As the time of the election of his successor approached nearer and nearer, the Chief Magistrate became more and more open and undisguised in his interference to influence and control public opinion. I am well acquainted with his signature, and have seen many newspapers and other publications sent under his frank to individuals, and to members of assembly, calculated and intended to injure, in public estimation, those who were unwilling to act in accordance with his wishes as to his successor; have seen a toast given by him at a public dinner; have seen letters published from him in newspapers, and have heard of many others and now have copies of some never published; and all this after he had endeavored to induce me, and the State in which I reside, to accede to his wishes, under the promise of his influence to have my name used in the first instance as Vice-President, and afterwards for the Presidency, as I have been informed, and verily believe. And to satisfy the committee that I do not speak unguardedly, and from unkind feelings upon this subject, I subjoin to this answer the extract of a letter dated 23d August, 1836, from Mr. Orville Bradley, of Hawkins county, Tennessee. He is a man of high character for intelligence and veracity, and I have not the shade of a doubt that everything he there states on the subject of his conversation with the President is strictly true.

In the course of last summer, the President made a visit to his home in Tennessee; and, as I have been informed, and verily believe, almost as soon as he entered the State, denounced me and several of my colleagues, who are my political friends, publicly, and in strong terms; charging some of them, and especially Col. Peyton, with having given a vote relative to an appropriation on the Cherokee treaty, directly contrary to what the journal, the newspapers, and members who had been present, at the passage of the bill, showed, and stated to be the fact; and, as to another of them, Mr. Huntsman, in answer to a question from him, he alleged *he was on the fence*, and it was *doubtful* which side he would *fall;* and afterwards, when written to by Mr. Huntsman, would appear to have forgotten that he ever used such expressions: all which will appear by a copy of Mr. Huntsman's letter to him; and a copy of his answer, and my reply, hereto attached; and the committee will readily perceive, by an extract of a letter from Col. O'Brien, and a certificate of Mr. Carriger, both highly respectable men, that his memory is so much impaired, as not to be relied on, even for a few months, for what he has said relative to the character and conduct of a representative in Congress.

Under all these circumstances, although I feel I, and the Senate through me, were misled, in the creation of the office of Commissioner of Indian Affairs, and in the appointment of Mr. Herring to fill said office; and believe that, upon investigation, it will be found that frauds, in this branch of the administration of the War Department, have been committed; and that some of the officers or agents of the government have participated in, and derived pecuniary benefits from them; yet I do not believe the Secretary of War intended to do wrong, but was constrained to act in accordance with the wishes of others.

Amidst the variety of daily duties claiming attention, and without anything but a general question pointing to a particular transaction, it is very probable that some facts and circumstances, within my knowledge, are omitted, which more direct and specific questions would bring to my recollection. It has been my wish to make my answer as full as I reasonably could, that I might save the committee the trouble of a protracted examination.

Extract from Mr. Bradley's Letter.

HAWKINS COUNTY, EAST TENNESSEE, *Aug.* 23, 1836.

In the fall of 1834, on his return from the West, General Jackson called at my father's; I was with him then, and travelled some distance with him along the road in this county (Hawkins). In the course of the time we were together, the subject of succession was freely discussed. Your claims were mentioned, and the feeling of the State to have opposition to Van Buren. I spoke of the attempt which had been made in the assembly of 1833, of which I was a member, to nominate Judge White, which I told him I thought I had been mainly instrumental in defeating, by virtue of an authority you had given me before you left Nashville, to say you desired it should not be done. I told General Jackson that I thought, after having had considerable opportunities of forming a correct estimate, that I felt satisfied that two-thirds of the members of that assembly were indisposed to support Van Buren, and would not do it, if they could get any other respectable man of their own principles to vote for; that the assembly was only restrained from nominating Judge White, by his own disinclination to such nomination, and by an apprehension that in the condition of the public feeling in the United States (it was just after the removal of the deposits), that his nomination might throw such a firebrand into the ranks of the Administration as might break down Judge White, and prostrate the whole party, and throw the power of the government into the hands of the bank party, and by the further consideration, that as Tennessee had the incumbent of the Presidency, that it might be considered arrogant in them to be the first to nominate another of her citizens for that high office. I also stated to General Jackson my opinion, that if Judge White should receive a respectable nomination anywhere out of the State, that it would be immediately and generally followed up in Tennessee. I told the President that immediately after the rise of the assembly, and before I left Nashville, I had written to Judge White a full account of the state of things at Nashville, all that had occurred, the part that I had taken, and the reasons that had influenced me, and that Judge White had immediately answered me, approving of my course, and stating that if he had been nominated, that under the state of things that then existed at Washington, he should have felt bound to put down the movement under his own hand and signature.

I further told General Jackson, that I thought there was a decided indisposition in Tennessee to support Van Buren, and intimated to him, that although, under the circumstances that then existed, I had felt it my duty to oppose, among the members, any attempt by the assembly to bring out Judge White, that I did not like to support Van Buren, if I could please myself any better. General Jackson entered warmly into a vindication of Van Buren; spoke of him in the highest terms, said that he was the man to whom the party, generally, out of Tennessee, was looking to be his successor; that White could hardly get a vote out of Tennessee, and that Tennessee must not separate from the rest of his friends; that he found there was a strong disposition in this State to press the claims of Judge White, but that it would not receive any countenance or support elsewhere. But further, said he, this matter must be compromised. Judge White and the State of Tennessee ought to be satisfied to have the name of Judge White on the ticket with Mr. Van Buren as Vice President. Judge White is yet young enough to come in after Mr. Van Buren, and such an arrangement will make all right now, and secure the certain elevation of Judge White, after Mr. Van Buren. I do not know, said he, with a smile, what we shall do with Richard M. Johnson, but I suppose we can arrange the matter with him some other way. General Jackson requested me to come on to Washington at the commencement of the session of Congress; and when I told him I could not, he requested me to write to him during the winter what was going on in Tennessee.

I told General Jackson, when he proposed that Judge White should be put on the ticket as Vice President, that if Judge White should be run on the same ticket with Van Buren, that I would support it, and I thought a majority of those who were desirous of bringing out Judge White in Tennessee would do the same, but that it would not satisfy all.

I told the substance of this conversation to Judge Powell, and John Kennedy, Esq., shortly after it occurred; I think, also, to John Young, of this county, and S. D. Mitchell, and, perhaps, to some others.

When you came on afterwards, the same fall, on your way to Washington, I told it to you at Rogersville. Your reply, after listening till I got through, was, that the office of Vice President of the United States was a place not unworthy of the ambition of any man, when properly obtained; that it was, perhaps, greatly superior to your merits, but that you would not accept that or any other office, when your name was to be used as a lure to draw men into the support of a ticket they would not otherwise vote for. We had other and further conversation on the matter of the same tenor, which it is not necessary now to recapitulate. Immediately after my leaving your room, I was accosted by several of those to whom I had told General Jackson's proposition of your being put on the ticket as Vice President, and asked if you would accede to that proposition. I gave them your reply, as above set forth. They then said you would [not] run; for in the conversations they had heard upon the subject of your nomination, it had been maintained by many—perhaps, a majority—that you would not allow your name to be run at all. General Jackson had expressed that opinion in the conversation we had. He had also stated, he had no objection to a nomination of Judge White, if he was only recommended to the American people, and to the favorable consideration of a general convention of the party; but that any attempt to procure an absolute nomination must be put down by his friends.

The foregoing is the substance of my conversation with General Jackson, in relation to your nomination and being run for the Presidency to the best of my recollection. At this late period, I have, for the first time, attempted to reduce it to writing, and, of course, cannot pretend to be absolutely and certainly right in every particular. But I think I have committed no essential errors.

You are at liberty to use this letter as you please. I do not wish it to go into the newspapers without some strong necessity. But if such should exist, I will not shrink from the responsibility.

Your friend,

ORVILLE BRADLEY.

The Hon. HUGH L. WHITE.

WASHINGTON CITY, *Jan.* 1, 1836, (7.)

DEAR SIR: In a speech which was made by Judge White at Jonesboro, Tennessee, and which has been published in the papers of that State and elsewhere, he stated in substance (I have not the speech before me), that you were asked how I stood in relation to the Administration, and the coming election for President; and that your reply was, I DO NOT KNOW HOW HE STANDS; I BELIEVE HE IS UPON THE FENCE, AND IT IS UNCERTAIN WHICH SIDE HE WILL DROP. The first time I saw Judge White after the publication of his speech, I requested to know who was his author in regard to the expression you were said to have made. He gave the name of Mr. O'Brien, of Washington county, Tennessee (if I remember right), as the person who heard you make the expression. It seems that one of my colleagues, and an honorable member from Virginia, have thought proper to reiterate this charge upon the floor of Congress, in the discussion of a question now pending and undeterminated in the House of Representatives.

Not having any acquaintance with Mr. O'Brien, and having some doubts in regard to the accuracy of his statements, I hope you will not deem it disrespectful in me to ask from you a *refutation* or a *confirmation* of it.

I know, sir, that the weighty affairs of government, which draw so largely upon your time and attention, leave you but little time to attend to small matters like this; yet it has become one of considerable importance to me, or it is made so through the agency of others.

As I do not consider that I occupied the doubtful position assigned me, and having no reason to believe that you would knowingly do me the least injustice, I ask with the more confidence your answer as early as my be convenient.

With sentiments of respect, I have the honor to be,

Your most obedient servant,

ADAM HUNTSMAN.

The President of the United States.

WASHINGTON, *January* 2, 1836, (7.)

SIR: Your letter of the 1st instant is before me. I have not the slightest recollection of having made the remarks in reference to you, which, it seems from your note of yesterday's date, was imputed by Judge White to me, in a speech at Jonesboro, Tennessee. I do not know, nor have I any recollection of the witness to whom Judge White refers you. I have no acquaintance with the O'Brien family. And it is scarcely possible that I should have entered into the familiar discourse described by Judge White with a perfect stranger, without retaining some trace on my memory of the man, or of the extraordinary questioning to which it would seem he subjected me. If I had been interrogated about you, by one whom I thought entitled to take such liberty, I should have said to him that I esteemed you, from your votes and course in Congress, as a friend to the Administration; that in regard to the then pending election for President, you were the avowed friend of Judge White for President, but willing to give effect to the wishes of your constituents, if they preferred Mr. Van Buren, in case the election came into the House of Representatives.

It is, however, superfluous labor to contradict the fabrications put forth by Judge White and his speech-makers, who, it seems from your note, are repeating the stories made up for their electioneering harangues in the House of Representatives. The public know how to estimate their assertions. If it were worth the trouble, there is not one of their narratives with which they have connected my name, so far as I have heard, that could not be proven as mere fiction by all the persons whom they represent as bearing a part in what they pretend to describe.

But I do not blame these subalterns. Judge White himself, in his Knoxville speech, did not hesitate to lead the way in this sort of traduction. To distinguish his own purity, and claim credit for disinterested moderation in declining the Vice Presidency (and at the same moment when he was seeking the Presidency itself, and electioneering for it by boasting of his incomparable modesty), he gave the people of Tennessee to understand that I had attempted to purchase his support of Mr. Van Buren by an offer of the Vice Presidency as the first consideration, with the Presidency itself in reversion. There never was a grosser libel than this. There is about as much truth in it, as there was sincerity in that lame apology in the Judge's letter to Mr. Prior Lea, wherein Judge White pretends he was desirous to prevent my election to the Senate of the United States, and send my bitterest enemy to that body, giving him a high station whence to scatter calumnies against me, merely for my good —namely to advance my pretensions to the Chief Magistracy, by saving me from the suspicions of accepting the senatorial office as a means of electioneering for myself! An office which he lately accepted precisely under the circumstances which subjected him to the identical imputation from which he was so anxious to screen me! This, and many recent developments of character, show that Judge White, under strong temptation, has a lax code of morals for himself; and his remarkable readiness to invent pretexts to cover the naked and palpable selfishness of his late tergiversations and multiplied inconsistencies, shows that he need not tax the invention of his subordinate instruments for falsehoods to suit his exigencies. Whether, then, he has fabricated himself the improbable story to which you refer, in addition to the other shameful imputations with which he has associated my name, or is indebted for them to some of the numerous family of the O'Briens, is matter of but little moment to me. They all now stand in equal credit with the country.

I am, sir, your most obedient servant.

ANDREW JACKSON.

The Hon. ADAM HUNTSMAN, in Congress.

P. S. As Judge White has been the subject of your letter and this reply to it, you will please show him this my answer.

A. J.

Copy of a letter to the Hon. Adam Huntsman, from the Hon. Hugh L. White.

WASHINGTON *Jan. 4th*, 1837.

DEAR SIR: Herewith I return the correspondence between you and the President, dated the 1st and 2d instant, which you handed me this afternoon. As you requested, I have not shown it to any person, nor have I mentioned to any one that I have seen it.

I feel called on, when returning it, to say something in relation to its contents.

In the President's answer, he says he has no recollection of Mr. O'Brien, and thinks it not likely he would have been catechised by an entire stranger, &c.

I never said that Mr. O'Brien had conversed with, or asked him a question, but that he heard him make the statement in answer to questions put by others in Jonesboro. All I know is, that Mr. O'Brien gave me the information. He is a respectable man. I believe what he told me to be true; and the circumstance that the President does not recollect anything on the subject is only additional proof that the best of us cannot always recollect what we have said. Our colleague, General Carter, was present, and heard my conversation with Mr. O'Brien, and to him I refer you for the accuracy of my statement.

As to the other parts of the President's letter, I regret to find the temper in which it is written. It indulges in statements and suspicions not only erroneous, but unfounded and unjust.

Everything in the speech stated as of my own knowledge was true, and everything derived from the information of others I then believed, and yet believe, to be true.

I hope you will not deem me unreasonable, when I ask a copy of this correspondence.

I do not complain of the injunction imposed, *not to show it to any person;* but if you have allowed others to see it, and make its contents the foundation of accusations against me, I would think I was unfairly treated, and that you ought to remove that injunction.

Most sincerely and truly yours,

HU. L. WHITE.

Copy of a letter from John O'Brien, Esq. to the Hon. W. B. Carter.

PURLIEU IRON WORKS, *Jan.* 19*th*, 1837.

DEAR SIR: Yours of the 5th instant was received on yesterday evening, requesting me to state the particulars respecting an expression I heard General Jackson make while in Jonesboro. On the evening of the day of General Jackson's arrival in Jonesboro, I accidentally happened at the place, and after night, was invited by the Hon. John Blair, to walk with him to Nathan Gammon's, Esq., to see the President. I accompanied him, and was introduced by him to the President. Immediately after my introduction, I took a seat but a short distance from the President, near Mr. Donelson and G. Gammon, Esq. I was so near the President, that I could distinctly hear every word he said. He was asked by some gentleman in the room (for there were several present), what he thought of several of the Tennessee delegation in Congress; to all of which questions he replied. Amongst the rest he was asked what he thought of Mr. Huntsman. He replied: "He is on the fence, sir, and I do not know on which side he may fall." I remained in the room a short time after the General had made the foregoing expression, and left the room with the Hon. John Blair.

Enclosed is a certificate from under the hand of Christian E. Carriger, Esq., who accompanied the Hon. John Blair and myself from Mr. Blair's to Mr. Gammon's. I will go to Jonesboro this evening, and endeavor to obtain the statements of some gentlemen there, who were present at the time, which I will enclose to you so soon as I obtain them.

With high consideration, I remain your friend,

JOHN O'BRIEN.

Gen. W. B. CARTER.

Certificate of Christian E. Carriger, Esq.

January 19, 1837.

I do hereby certify, that on General Jackson's last visit to Jonesboro, on his way to the Hermitage, at the request of the Hon. John Blair, I went in company with him and John O'Brien, Esq., to see the General, at Nathan Gammon's, Esq. That at Mr. Gammon's, in presence of Mr. O'Brien and several other gentlemen, I heard some gentleman ask the General several questions respecting the Tennessee delegation; among other questions, what he thought of the Hon. Adam Huntsman? "He is on the fence, sir, and I do not know on which side he will fall;" was the General's reply, (as near as I can remember) verbatim.

Given under my hand,

CHRISTIAN E. CARRIGER.

*Reply of Judge White to General Jackson.**

TO THE FREEMEN OF TENNESSEE:

FELLOW CITIZENS: A recent production, over the name of the late Chief Magistrate of the United States, now going the rounds in our newspapers, imposes on me the duty of addressing you. We live in strange times. At peace with all the world, a handful of savages excepted; a few months ago, apparently prosperous to an extent almost unexampled, with funds in the treasury so far beyond the economical wants of the federal government, that statesmen were perplexed to know how to dispose of them. Now, our commerce destroyed, our merchants in every direction ruined and breaking; the crops of our planters without a market, and they in debt, without any means with which to make payment; specie payments suspended by our banks, and their notes depreciated, and the government itself placed in such a situation, as to its moneyed concerns, that it cannot move; hardly a dollar can be collected or paid without a violation of our acts of Congress. What has caused these misfortunes, is a question of grave and solemn import. It is one, in relation to which, every man is called on to form an opinion, and a free expression of opinions sincerely entertained, may, it is to be hoped, lead to some suitable remedy.

For myself, I cannot doubt but the specie circular, as it is called, which issued in July last, and the mode adopted to transfer to the respective States their proportions of our surplus treasure, were the immediate causes.

I have ever believed *that* circular less justifiable than any act of our federal executive. It undertakes to *legislate* for the people of the United States by the *sole* power of the *President*. It makes distinctions between *different classes* of our citizens, which I doubt whether Congress, with the aid of the President would have the power to make; and I feel confident, if they had the power they *dare not exercise it.*

Independently of the President having no power to cause such an order to be issued, its provisions were unwise, unjust, and calculated to produce the very state of things which now exists. From the time I first read it, I have ever most firmly believed the true reasons which gave rise to it were not avowed by its authors. It bears date in July, a few days after the rise of a Congress at which an act had passed directing a portion of the surplus revenue to be deposited with the States. This act was very offensive to the President, although he gave it his signature. One object then, of this circular was, to lessen the sales of the public lands, so that there might be little or nothing to divide on the first day of January and afterwards.

A Presidential election was then pending and the incumbent was using his influence in favor of one of the candidates, and it was believed the

*From the Knoxville Register of July 12, 1837.

permission to the people of the *new* States to pay for *their* lands in *bank notes* till after the Presidential election, would influence their votes in favor of his candidate, and a still more important object was, to produce such a run upon all banks as would compel them to suspend specie payment. Every holder of a bank note is told in substance, that it is doubtful whether his note is good, that the banks had overtraded themselves and would probably be unable to pay their debts. This idea is advanced by the President of the United States, in whom the people had unbounded confidence, and who from his official station had a right to *know* the *funds* and *condition* of each of the *deposit* banks. Nothing could have been better calculated to produce a run upon the banks than such a statement from such a source. In addition to this destruction of their *credit*, all those who held notes and did not reside in the State where they might wish to purchase lands must necessarily call for specie from the banks, as nothing else would be received at the land offices.

This attack on the credit of the banks and the runs either made or expected, compelled them not only to withhold the usual accommodations from merchants, but to exact payment for debts already contracted. Thus merchants must probably fail *first* and then the banks must surely follow, shortly afterwards.

But if the circular itself was not sufficient to destroy the credit of the banks, the mode proposed for transferring the funds to the respective States was well calculated to give it the final blow. The specie was to be drawn from the deposit banks, to be placed in the State treasury. Could any plan have been devised better calculated to alarm the banks and society? Beside, no conceivable benefit could result to the States from such an operation. If each State had been furnished with drafts upon banks in proper sections of the Union, upon these drafts they could have received their moneys at home, and the trade and commerce of the country been essentially benefited, without incommoding in any degree any of the banks.

I have no doubt the banks had extended their discounts too far in many instances, and it may likewise be true that merchants had overtraded; but I have no doubt the great error in some of the banks consisted in making extravagant loans, to companies of *land purchasers*, at our public sales, and of Indian reservations. This prevented in many instances the usual accommodations to merchants, and enabled the friends and favorites of the Administration to monopolize immense bodies of our most valuable lands, at the minimum price. No attempt that we know of was made to *check* the deposit banks in this course, until the desired purchases were completed, and the political views of the party were accomplished. They were *lauded*, and society was *taught* to believe the wise measures of the executive would presently give us all wealth to our hearts' content. Thus then the banks were first *encouraged* in their imprudence, and when the proper time arrived, those who had used them for pecuniary and electioneering purposes, *caused* the treasury order to be issued, and followed up by the worse than useless mode of transferring the public moneys, and by these means have caused the disasters to the merchants, and the suspension of specie payments, to the great discredit of the banks and loss of every portion of the community.

It will be asked why I believe the Administration wished to compel the banks to suspend specie payments.

I will answer the question in all sincerity; because I believe General Jackson *now wishes* a *bank* of the United States founded *upon the moneys of the United States*, and attached to the treasury department.

We all know that in more than one of his messages he recommended such a bank, and I know that in 1829 he wished Mr. Grundy elected to the Senate, in preference to Judge W. E. Anderson, because he believed Mr. Grundy could better aid in making up a party in Congress to establish such a bank.

His object when he came into the Presidency was to have such a bank; nothing was said by him recommending it after Mr. McDuffie's report. In common with others, I believed he had despaired of it after that report, until I read the treasury circular, and from that time I have believed it was an object that he had never lost sight of, and that he and his advisers have put into operation a series of measures, disastrous to the country at large, and ruinous to many individuals, in order to prepare the public mind for such a bank.

The President has repeatedly said, that unless the successor designated by himself was elected, the great measures of his Administration would not be carried out, and if they were not carried out, the great value of all he had done would be lost.

What great measure is yet to be carried out? I answer *the making a treasury bank.* How was the public mind to be prepared for such an institution? *By the very means he has employed.* The United States Bank must first be put down, because while it lasted there could be no use for a treasury bank, and in the second place, it must be proved by actual experiment, that the State banks cannot do the fiscal business of the government, and give society a sound currency. Now, whenever the banks refuse to pay in specie the government deposits, and decline paying specie generally, what is the argument? It is, that we have tried a bank of the United States by incorporating *individuals*, and find that it will not answer, because it will soon have so much power that it will control the government itself. We have made an experiment with the State banks, and find they cannot do our fiscal business, nor can they give us a sound currency; therefore, there is no alternative, but to create *a bank of our own*, upon *our funds*, and which will always be subject to *our control.*

Every circumstance which is now transpiring, connected with this subject, confirms me in the opinion which I have expressed.

1. The tenacity with which any deposit with the States is resisted.

2. The manner in which the illegal treasury circular is adhered to, although the decisive opinion of Congress and of society is known to be opposed to it.

3. Mr. Cambreleng's letter in New York, in which he is opposed to giving the banks any indulgence.

4. The loyalists in this State and others, candidates for Congress, are said to be advocating it.

5. The Globe has ventured to broach the subject likewise.

6. A pamphlet, purporting to be written in Great Britain, which is now in circulation, recommending such a bank.

While the people at large are lamenting the serious misfortunes which have befallen the country, the President is, as I believe, felicitating himself that the time is rapidly approaching, when one of his great, unfinished measures, is to be accomplished under the management of his successor.

In all this he may be very honest; he may conscientiously believe, that our highest interests will be promoted by it—that we can be secured in a sound currency—have our fiscal concerns well managad—and above all, that the great democratic party will thus be enabled always to retain the political power it now possesses. Those engaged in speculations in public lands, who are debtors of the banks, must be delighted with the present state of things. Specie payments are suspended; this will enable the banks to give them longer indulgence; the notes have depreciated, and will continue to depreciate, and they will presently be able to purchase, at a *great discount*, notes enough to discharge their debts, and thus realize the speculations which they anticipated.

But General Jackson says, in substance, that I advised the removal of the deposits from the Bank of the United States, and that my only complaint against his conduct was, that the removal was not made soon enough, &c. He has expressed himself too loosely upon this subject, to give to the public a correct idea of the part I took in this matter.

He never had a personal conversation with me on the subject of removing the deposits from the Bank of the United States. He *never* consulted me by *letter*, or *otherwise*, but once, and that was by letter bearing date the 24th of March, 1833. In answer to which I gave him my opinion in the following words, under date of April 11th, 1833:

"To this inquiry I answer, we ought not only to do that which is for the public interest, but we should do it under circumstances which will enable us to satisfy the people whose business we transact, that the change was necessary to promote their interest.

"When the Bank of the United States failed to obey the directions of the government in paying off its debt and negotiated with the creditors for indulgence, I think the deposits ought to have been immediately withdrawn, and every federal officer instructed not to receive any of those small drafts or checks, now used as substitutes of five, ten and twenty dollar notes. Public opinion I have no doubt would then have sustained the executive in such a course; but the government, from motives which all ought to approve, wished to be certain of the insolvency of the bank before it withdrew the public deposits, therefore appointed an agent to examine and report its condition. That report is before the world, and is as flattering as the bank could wish, as to its insolvency. Since then the matter has been brought to the notice of Congress, a committee has been created by the House of Representatives, and a majority of that committee has made a report most favorable to the bank. The minority of the committee has also submitted its view of the solvency and management of the bank, in such terms as, if it stood alone, would create a well-founded belief, that the public money was unsafe where now deposited. But the question occurs, what opinion will society form from these documents, taking them altogether? The opinion of the confidential agent of the treasury, and that of a majority of the committee one way, and that of the minority of the committee the other, places the question of the solvency of the bank in such an attitude before the public, that I do not believe the executive would act wisely in ordering a withdrawal of the deposits from the Bank of the United States, and placing them in State banks at this time. Public opinion will, in my judgment, best sustain the executive in permitting them to remain with the Bank of the United States until its charter expires, or some future development shall show that the bank is so managing its concerns as to make it necessary to the public interest that the public money should be withdrawn from the power and control of the bank."

During the session of Congress next succeeding the removal, upon a question whether a bill might be introduced to prolong the charter of the Bank of the United States, I took occasion to express my opinions as to the *power* of the President to cause the removal, and against the *restoration* of the deposits to the bank; but as to the wisdom or policy of the removal at the time it took place, the preceding autumn, I explicitly stated that, as a question upon which the best friends of the President might well *differ* in opinion.

I was then, as I ever had been, and yet am, of opinion that Congress had *no power* to grant the charter, or to *renew* it, and that if they possessed the power it would be bad policy to exercise it, and as the deposits had been removed, and constituted a fund upon which State banks were doing business, that it would be unwise to restore them to a bank, the charter of which must soon expire, and which I did not believe ought ever to be renewed.

These were my opinions, freely expressed and acted on. They may have been erroneous, but were honestly entertained, and if the President intends to communicate to the public the idea that I ever gave any other opinion, or advice, as to the propriety of the removal, than those I have now adverted to, he is doing himself, as well as me, injustice, because he is communicating to the public information which is not in conformity with the fact.

At the time the deposits were removed, before that time, and ever since, I have been of opinion the fiscal concerns of the government could be managed through the agency of State banks, and that they could at the same time furnish the country a sound currency, and I had the most unbounded confidence in the integrity of the Chief Magistrate, and believed he would cause a fair experiment to be made. Had I then foreseen what I now believe to be true, that the real design was to obtain a control over the public moneys, that they and the State banks might be used for electioneering purposes, and as a means by which favorites could monopolize our public lands, and that then the banks were to be compelled to suspend specie payments to prepare the public mind for a treasury bank, such a course for such purposes could have had no countenance from me.

I consider the experiment which has been made with the State banks an experiment to ascertain whether our public deposits will enable an executive to obtain so much control over the State banks as to enable him to induce them to overtrade themselves, and after the political and pecuniary purposes of himself and friends have been accomplished, then to compel them to suspend specie payments, and *that that experiment has been successful.*

It is in vain to expect benefits to society from this or that system of laws, upon any subject, unless the system is to be carried into effect by men of *integrity* and *capacity*. The best system which can be devised by the wisdom of man will terminate in ruin and distress to society, if its administration is placed in the hands of *dishonest* and *incompetent* men. No man can shut his eyes so close as not to see that many of our offices have been filled during the late Administration with the very worst material the country furnished; and this is the inevitable effect of party excess. The great democratic party must be kept up, and how? By the Administration making a democrat whenever one becomes necessary to control an election, and this is speedily done by taking a *rancorous old federalist* or monarchist, getting him to promise allegiance to the party, for which he must be given, or promised, an office for which he is unfit, or favored with the purchase of public land, or an Indian reservation; he then becomes *ipso facto* a democrat, and is sent forth "*to shoot as a deserter*" any honest man who does not choose, to every extent, to give up his principles and become associated with a party, which has no fixed principles, save the one "*that to the victors belong the spoils.*"

I have felt it my duty to make these remarks to prevent, if possible, my constituents from being incautiously led into a trap, which I think has been set for the people of the United States; I mean the support of a *treasury bank*. Should such an one be established, and placed as it must be, under the control of the federal executive, the power thus conferred, when added to that already possessed, will give us to every substantial purpose, as complete a monarchy as exists anywhere, and one which will equal, if it does not excel, in its means of corruption, any government known to the civilized world.

According to what we see in the public prints, Congress is to convene on the first Monday in September next, for what purpose we are not told, but all presume, to aid in some plan to relieve the country and the government from the existing embarrassments. Should it be my fortune to make one of that honorabe body, I will most heartily concur in any measure which may conform to the Constitution and be calculated to promote the welfare of the country; but I use this occasion to say, explicitly, that I will be asked in vain, as now advised, to concur in the establishment of a *treasury bank*, because I believe it would destroy the last hope, that your children and mine could enjoy that liberty which is their birthright.

I now proceed to make some remarks on the comments General Jackson has seen fit to make on my deposition before the committee of investigation, of which Mr. Wise is the chairman:

In the card which preceded, by several weeks, the extensive commentary, we had a foretaste of what might be expected.

It commenced with a statement that his (the General's) attention had a few days before been called by a friend to my deposition. As much as to say in plain language, that until his attention was thus called to it, he was ignorant of its contents.

This statement is not such an one as ought to have been expected from so distinguished a man. In Washington it was repeatedly said, and I have no doubt truly, that some of the members of that committee daily submitted to the labor of making a copy of whatever was deposed to, and furnished the President with it, before he retired to take his night's repose. When the circumstances under which I was called before that committee, what occurred before I was sworn, and the President's letter to the committee, are considered, it is hardly within the range of probability that he should be indifferent to the matter which the deposition contains as not to have immediately procured a copy of it. Indeed the dates of the very certificates he publishes to counteract its contents, and what is stated in that from Mr. Randolph, prove that he was familiar with it long prior to the time indicated in his publication. His real object, no doubt, was to so time his publication, as to have the most effect upon our approaching elections; some apology for delay was necessary, and the one made is, as I think, not consistent with the high character a retired President ought ever to maintain.

His next object seems to be, to show that I acted incorrectly in saying anything on the subject of privilege, and then submitting to be sworn as a witness.

In endeavoring to do this, his advice, his quotations, and his statements are so lengthy, that it is with some difficulty we can keep pace with him. It may be that I erred in suffering myself to be sworn as a witness; but as I had to act according to my own feeble judgment without the benefit of his advice, I took that course which I believed to be the most correct. The investigation of the committee had developed some facts not pleasant to those concerned; if a fair examination was persisted in, farther disclosures would add to the unpleasantness of their situation. To avoid this, I have no doubt, the expedient was resorted to, of having several members of Congress, myself among the number, summoned as witnesses. I was *not* summoned at the instance of any one who *wished* to pursue the investigation to ascertain whether frauds had been committed or not. The application for the summons was made by Mr. Mann, of New York, and it was distinctly understood that he made this application at the instance of the *President.* The committee had no right to issue any such subpœna for me, and this must have been well known to gentlemen as well informed as the President, and the majority of the committee, and I had no doubt, they expected and hoped that I would disobey the subpœna and refuse to be sworn; then the cry would have been raised that the charges were all groundless; I knew it, and had refused to testify; but all these calculations were defeated when I voluntarily appeared, protested against the legality of the proceedings and showed a willingness to be sworn, and at the same time distinctly stated that I understood I was summoned *at the instance* of the *then President and his successor*, and that if sworn must tell what I knew, confidential or otherwise. Mr. Mann was then present, did not contradict one word that I said, and it was evident the party was brought to a pause. After some time I was told by the committee I could then retire, and when they wanted me I should be notified. This gave rise to the President's letter to the committee, which has been published, and it must be seen he had so entangled himself he could take no other course but that which his letter indicated. I was afterwards notified to attend, did so and made the deposition of which the President complains.

In all this it appears to me I was right. I had stated nothing either in the Senate or elsewhere, which I did not either know or believe to be true. On my own account, I had nothing to conceal—and, if those who had made confidential communications would have me sworn, what must I do? Nothing but that which I did do, tell the truth and nothing but the truth.

He next proceeds to that part of the deposition relative to the creation of the office of Commissioner of Indian Affairs, and the appointment of Mr. Herring.

The deposition affirms that the Secretary of War induced me to introduce the bill and have it passed, upon a representation that Mr. Herring, then at the head of the Indian bureau, with a salary of sixteen hundred dollars, was so illy qualified for the office, that the public interest was likely to suffer—and that after the law had passed, this same individual was appointed to the new office with the salary of three thousand dollars, and that he was really not qualified, and that the public interest has suffered, and then offers as matter of excuse for the secretary, that he was probably induced to acquiesce in this appointment, by others for electioneering purposes, &c. Now, what material part of this statement is contradicted? Not one word of it, by either the President, or any of his witnesses.

No man has said, or can with truth say, the secretary did not represent him as incompetent. Nor has any one pretended he was competent.

Why did not Major Donelson or Mr. Harris testify to one or both these points? Mr. Harris *knows he was incompetent*, and that in consequence of it, the public interest has suffered, and if asked, cannot say otherwise.

In what situation then does the President's comments and testimony place his secretary? Why, in the situation of a man who has practised a gross fraud upon Congress to obtain the creation of a new office, and increased salary for Mr. Herring, and had made the two chairmen of the committees on Indian affairs his dupes to carrry such unworthy views into effect.

I did not believe the secretary capable of such conduct, nor do I now think so. I made such apology for him as I believed to be true, and in that belief am not in the least shaken.

If the Indian department was intended to be used for electioneering purposes, an incompetent man of all others was best suited for the office.

It appears to be thought as Mr. H. was a Clintonian in New York he must have been an enemy to Mr. Van Buren's election as President. Strange conclusion. Clinton is dead, and since his death Mr. Van Buren is himself his friend, and pronounced to his colleagues in Congress a high-wrought eulogy upon his worth and character.

Mr. Herring in his manners and deportment is a gentleman; I never have heard his integrity questioned, and regret that I have been compelled to speak of him, as I have done; but truth is truth, and if any one can conscientiously say his appointment, under the circumstances, "was with a single eye to the public interest," then I can only say I entertain a very different opinion.

The President states that after the law passed he had intended to nominate another individual for the office, had made out the nomination, and was prevailed on by his secretary not to send it to the Senate, *and that in conversation with me he had told me so.*

To this statement, so far as it relates to any communication of such a fact to me, I can only say the President is undoubtedly mistaken. *Neither at the time spoken of by him, nor at any other time*, did he ever communicate any such fact, nor did I ever hear of it until I read his publication.

In time past when the President has made statements of facts, which I knew or believed to be erroneous, I was ready to find an apology for them in what I supposed his decayed memory; but in this publication his statements of some facts and contradiction of others are so extraordinary that I must leave it to others to find out the cause. I hope it will not be considered as disrespectful when I add, there is reason to believe the loss of memory is not the only mental loss he has sustained within the last few years.

The attempt to get clear of the effects which he fears may be produced by that part of the deposition relative to the dissolution of the first cabinet in 1831, is both in the matter and manner of it well calculated to mortify every sincere friend he ever had. *It discloses the want of memory and mind*, to an extent of which I was not aware. Formerly, although his style was rough and generally not very good English, yet it was nervous and perspicuous. In this effort he appears bewildered, and to have lost all distinct recollection of what occurred in the first years of his own Administration. It is confused as to the dates of different facts and transactions, and huddles together a confused mass of matter, much of which can have no bearing on the subject.

The deposition affirms, that when the cabinet was dissolved, the President had made up his mind that Mr. Van Buren should succeed him—that he wished to get clear of the old cabinet, and create a new one that would be a unit towards accomplishing that object—that he did not wish to lose sight of Major Eaton's services, and therefore desired me to be Secretary of War, and Major Eaton to succeed me in the Senate, &c.

Now, this is all true, before God, as I religiously believe, and General Jackson can never forget that I know it, in a mode which ought to leave no doubt on my mind; and he certainly cannot have forgotten that he was told by me, that if even my seat in the Senate were vacant, it would be very difficult to procure Major Eaton's election, on account of some of his votes while he had been a member of that body. He now states, that at that time Mr. Van Buren had not been thought of as his successor. He is entirely in error, and can perhaps correct himself, if he will recur to *Mr. Van Buren's letter of resignation, and other written evidence, which either is, or ought to be, in his own possession at this time.*

The old cabinet was composed of Messrs. Van Buren, Eaton, Barry, Berrien, Branch, and Ingham. The three first were friendly to Mr. Van

Buren's elevation, the three last were supposed not to be so, and therefore produced a want of harmony. The real desire was to get clear of these gentlemen. It was supposed that if the two first resigned, the three last would follow their example, and supersede the necessity of their dismissal. The experiment was made and failed, and the President was driven to their dismissal, although he admitted their duties had been faithfully performed.

Now, if the truth were not as I assert, why was not Barry dismissed also? The President did not wish to lose him, and if dismissed there was no chance of his coming in from Kentucky.

Unfortunately for the President, but fortunately for the development of truth, he has gone into some of the secret history of the early part of his Administration; and among other things, states, that he had reduced to writing the principles upon which his Administration should be conducted —and one of these was, that *no member of his cabinet should be a candidate to succeed him; that this paper was shown to me, and I approved of it, &c.*

Now, is not this admission proof as clear "as evidence from Holy Writ," that my statement is correct? Mr. Van Buren, from March 1829, to 1831, was a member of the cabinet; then it was determined that he should be the candidate to succeed General Jackson, and as it was an article in the Jacksonian creed, reduced to writing and shown to the members of the party, and approved of by them, it became essential that he should cease to be a member of the cabinet, and he resigned accordingly.

If General Jackson's mind is so enfeebled that he cannot comprehend this, I feel confident the public will understand it very fully.

These ancient reminiscences give rise to very unpleasant reflections.

Some former Administrations have been suspected of using the patronage and influence of the federal government to control public opinion in the Presidential elections, simply because members of the cabinets had been candidates. General Jackson and his whole party had warred against this abuse, had represented it as a high moral and political offence, and when he came into office he came in solemnly pledged to reform this most gross, demoralizing, and alarming abuse of power; and to assure his friends he would carry out this principle in practice, his creed containing *this article* was reduced to writing, and shown to myself and others, *and I approved of it.*

True as gospel, I approved it then, ever since, and never saw the necessity for it so strongly as now.

How has this solemn pledge been kept? To the ear only, but to the sense most shamefully, openly and notoriously violated.

If Mr. Van Buren had continued in the cabinet, and been a candidate to succeed General Jackson, it would have been suspected that the patronage and influence of the government was used to elect him. To avoid this suspicion he must resign, and then openly and notoriously this very patronage and influence is brought to bear with its whole force upon public opinion, and through this means he is elected; and I and all others who will not say this is right, and in conformity with the Jackson democratic creed, are to be excommunicated, and, to use the New York phraseology, "shot as deserters;" that is, calumniated out of all the character we ever had.

But the General says, that my statement of his using the appointing power to bring in Mr. Van Buren is unfounded, because after that time he appointed my step-son, at my instance, to an office, and that he also appointed many other of my friends.

This statement is calculated to deceive if unexplained. It is true that at my instance he appointed Mr. Frost secretary to the French commission, and about the same time may have appointed other officers upon my recommendation, and I have the gratification of believing that Mr. Frost discharged all the duties pertaining to the office with integrity and ability.

At the time this appointment was made I was in full communion with the church, as the President supposed, my name had never been thought of as a candidate, so far as I was informed; and he no doubt believed that whenever he and those he could control changed their creed, I would change my creed likewise, and he never was convinced to the contrary, until after his attempt upon me through Mr. Bradley, which was in the autumn of 1834.

If the President or any of his new party will give me the name of any avowed friend of mine having been appointed to office *after it was known I had consented that my name might be used as a candidate*, other than some one whose opinion was changed, or expected to be changed, by virtue of such appointment, I will thank them for it.

I too well know the names of some, who professed to be my friends, having received offices *immediately preceding the election, and that they changed their opinions and became loyal members of the democratic party*, whose whole creed is comprised in the few words, "*to the victors belong the spoils.*"

This political simony is the very thing of which I and my friends complain, and if either the white people or the Indians, or both, do not in the end, find that they have a hard bargain of some of these "patent democrats," I shall be very much and agreeably disappointed.

It is admitted in the commentary upon the deposition that a conversation was held with me in relation to appointing Mr. Clayton upon a committee, but it is alleged this conversation was at another time and related to some other committee.

This allegation is founded in error. The conversation was at the time, and related to his appointment upon the committee, mentioned in the deposition, *and to no other*, and the substance of that conversation is correctly stated in the deposition. If it had been at another time, and in relation to another committee, why was not the other time and committee mentioned?

It is asked why I did not give the names of the other members of the committee? The answer is so ready that I am surprised it should be asked; it is, because no request was made of me as to any other members of the Senate, and the very reason I placed Mr. Clayton on the committee was, that it is in conformity with parliamentary law, to so constitute a committee as to give the proposed measure the fairest chance to be put in such a shape as that it will pass. From Mr. Clayton's talents, his liberality of sentiment, the position of his State in the Union, and his known influence with his political friends, I believed his course would have a most decided influence on the fate of the bill, and in this belief I was not disappointed. I very naturally concluded the President, and all others as attentive as he was to what was constantly passing, would form the like opinion.

My wish was to give upon the committee a fair representation of *every interest and party* in the Union, under the hope that they would agree upon some compromise, and if they did, and the law should pass, it would most likely be acceptable to the nation.

Mr. Clay was a tariff man, had introduced the bill, was from the West, and was placed as chairman; Mr. Webster from the East, a tariff man; Mr. Clayton from a Middle State, and friendly to the tariff; and these three were national republicans; Mr. Calhoun from the South, a nullifier and anti-tariff; Mr. Grundy from the West, a nullifier and anti-tariff likewise; Mr. Dallas from a Middle State, and a tariff man, and Mr. Rives from a Southern State, and anti-tariff. The four first named of these gentlemen were opposed to the Administration and the three last friendly to it.

The bill was a measure proposed by an opposition member, who in my judgment was entitled to be chairman, and to have a majority who would probable be inclined to favor his measure.

Thus, a view is given of the whole committee, their politics and a summary of the reasons for their selection, and who can say it was wrong? No one except some person who thinks a presiding officer, in party times, should be a mere party hack, who would disregard the parliamentary law, the interest of the country, and pack a committee who would stifle a measure lest his party might lose some influence by its adoption.

The venerable ex-president thinks that all who know him will believe if I had stated to him what the deposition imports, he would have given a suitable reply, &c.

My own opinion is, he did conduct, in the only manner which was suitable, and it ought to be remembered if he had made what he would insinuate would have been a suitable reply, it could have received a suitable rejoinder.

This idle vaunt is all lost upon me. There is no man who knows the ex-president has more confidence in his chivalry and readiness to resent an insult, than I have—but at the same time, the history of his life will show, that whenever he intends to make such a reply as might provoke controversy, he has always timed it so prudently, that there should be a sufficient number of persons present to prevent ill temper from producing bad consequences. There were none present but he and I; no insult was either offered or intended; but I did mean, as I hope I always shall, to state my sentiments precisely as they were, without stopping to consider whether they would be acceptable or not.

The statement in the deposition relative to Mr. Stevenson, it is said, is a fabrication. This is a very simple mode of getting clear of an unpleasant point. The General is mistaken, the facts occurred as detailed, and the gentleman who was the bearer of the message, must have strange and unpleasant sensations, when he reads the charge made by the general, that the story is a fabrication. He may make new friends by such charges, but by them, he must *stagger the faith of old ones.* Had the committee asked the name of the gentleman, I should have felt bound to have given it, and he could have been examined, but they did not, and I am sure the General can have no need of the name, as he must well remember it, and far be it from me uselessly to drag any individual before the public.

The General next proceeds to controvert the statements made by Mr. Bradley in his letter, a copy of which was attached to my deposition.

That Mr. Bradley's statement is strictly true, I have no more doubt than I would have had, if I had been present and heard the conversation between him and the President, and I do not believe, among the whole circle of his numerous acquaintances, one man can be found who, in his heart, believes him capable of making such a statement, if it were not strictly true. The General has, at least, brought nothing to counteract it, but the statements of his two travelling companions: and according to their own account of the matter the whole conversation and propositions might have been repeated ten times over, while Mr, Bradley and the President were together, and those two gentlemen not have heard one word of it.

The relation in which Mr. Bradley stood to me, our known intimacy, the part he has acted in the legislature of 1833, at my instance, in relation to my nomination, his detailing to several gentlemen, whose names are *given by him*, *this very conversation* with the President, *immediately after it took place*, the support it derives from the testimony of Mr. Peyton and Col. Standifer, place the statement beyond the reach of doubt in any mind desirous to ascertain truth.

The fact, no doubt, is, that the General has determined that in his biography his character shall appear to posterity, to have been *a perfect one*—he thinks *this proposition*, and several other disclosures which have been made, will not well bear examination, when the heat of the moment shall have passed away, and wishes to get clear of the effects to be produced by them: Let me assure him he will never mend the matter by *his flat contradictions of every man*, who does not testify to suit his wishes. His biographer, if he be honest, in enumerating the many excellent and striking traits in his character, will not put it down, that in his *latter days*, he was a correct narrator of matters of fact.

He next passes to the statement respecting Mr. Huntsman, and produces a number of certificates to disprove the statement made by Col. O'Brien and Mr. Carriger. With an enlightened public, such certificates can have no effect. O'Brien and Carriger are men of excellent character, could have no inducement to fabricate such a statement; they positively assert, they did hear the President make the statement respecting Mr. Huntsman; his certifiers only say, that they did not hear it. Had he obtained an hundred such certficates, the facts would still remain *proved to be true.*

But on this part of the subject, the ex-president is peculiarly unfortunate; he has taken some pains to prove that he did not reach Jonesborough for some days *after* I had passed that place, and had made my speech, in which I should have stated, that he had said Mr. Huntsman was on the fence, &c. He therefore argues, that it is absurd to suppose I could know what he would say *three days after I had made* that speech.

Now, the facts are, that I was in Jonesborough about the 20th July, 1836--dined there, and made a very short speech, in which Mr. Huntsman's name was never mentioned, and which never was published. The President reached that place about the 22d July, *and then made* the statement respecting Mr. Huntsman. Some days afterwards, Col. O'Brien came to Knoxville, and while there, repeated to me what the President had said, and on *the 31st August*, 1836, I made a speech at *Knoxville*, which was published; *in which I stated the liberty which* had been taken with Mr. Huntsman's name. In addressing the President, Mr. Huntsman, in his letter, *by mistake*, says my speech was made in *Jonesborough* when he ought to have said *Knoxville.* As soon as Mr. Huntsman showed me his correspondence with the President, *I addressed him a note, which was appended to my deposition.* This note of mine to Mr. Huntsman, no doubt was perused, when the other parts of the deposition were under examination, and I leave it to the public to judge, from what motive it has been suppressed, and a miserable quibble resorted to, which I must think, could not be creditable to a pettifogger.

It must be painful to any sincere friend of the ex-president, to see the infatuation under which he seems to act, owing, no doubt, to the influence artful and designing men have obtained over him. In almost every paragraph he writes, something can be found to take from the high character we were generally disposed to ascribe to him. Look at his statement, *even now*, in relation to Col. Peyton's conduct relative to the Cherokee treaty. He set out in the first instance, by asserting that Col. Peyton both *spoke* and *voted* against an appropriation to carry it into effect. He was told by those who knew better, and in whom he ought to have confided, that he was misinformed, that Col. Peyton had not only voted for, but had made an excellent speech in favor of the appropriation. He still persisted in a repetition of his assertions, and even now, after he, and every other intelligent man, ought to be possessed of the most authentic information, *proving his error*; he *persists* in asserting to the world that although Mr. Peyton voted for the appropriation, he had made an argument against it. If any member of Congress has practised upon his credulity, and caused him to be the retailer of such a *glaring mistake*, his name ought to be known, that he might be shunned by every honorable man.

The General supposes that Mr. Wise and Colonel Peyton, who were my messmates and friends, were stimulated and advised by me to pursue the course which they did in Congress. I do not think hard of this suspicion, although it is unfounded in fact, and both these gentlemen know it, yet we were messmates for the two last winters, and I am proud to believe I had their most sincere friendship. They certainly had mine. The General ought, in charity to the country, to believe that there are yet some few men, who would not be dictated to in the discharge of their public duties, by either him or myself. Wise and Peyton are two of them; talented, well-informed, honest, bold, and men who fearlessly discharged their whole duty, in defiance of all the calumnies of degraded and hired presses, the frowns of those who sat in high places, and even the statements of the Chief Magistrate himself, that they ought to be "Houstonized."

Their names will be hailed as the dauntless friends and champions of civil liberty, in after times, when the political course of some of their revilers will be spoken of, as the severest affliction with which our beloved country has ever been visited. To have obtained the friendship of such men, is one of the most prized achievements of my whole life. Their course relative to the investigations spoken of, was the dictate of their own judgment. Their country ought to thank them for it. They have elicited enough to show fuller investigations are necessary, that something is probably wrong, otherwise so many obstructions would not have been thrown in the way of ascertaining truth; and when we shall have a Chief Magistrate who will lend his aid to a fair and faithful investigation, I firmly believe it will be found the public has been deceived and injured to an extent of which not one citizen in one thousand has any conception.

For myself, I most solemnly declare, I have not either in the Senate, or elsewhere, uttered one sentence relative to the supposed abuses which I did not know or believe to be true; and if after a thorough investigation, by an impartial, *not a packed* committee, it can be shown that my suspicions are unfounded—I would consider it one of my first duties, publicly to acknowledge my error.

The General at the close of his address intimates that he has attained an advanced age, has infirm health and desires repose. Why, then, the statements before leaving Washington, that he intended to feast this summer upon John Bell and myself—that Tennessee should stand erect, in her politics, in less than six months?

As I believe, he has come home determined to destroy every man who dared to differ with him in opinon as to his successor, and *that is the experiment* he is now making. If it be his will, let him proceed. Angry discussion can never add to my comfort, it may to his. Our temperament and aim are, as I believe, a little different. I endeavor to take facts as I know or believe them to exist, and meet all the responsibility they justly throw upon me. In the temper he now is, and with enfeebled faculties, he views everything as an *enemy* that stands in the road of his ambition. He *personifies* truth, justice and everything else which obstructs his course, and attacks them with all that gallantry, with which he assails political or personal opponents. He has determined he will die *having* the character of a *great* man. While my highest ambition is to die conscious that I *deserve* the reputation of an *honest* one.

Your fellow citizen,

Hugh L. White.

July 12, 1837.

Jackson, *July* 1*st*, 1837.

Dear Sir: Upon reading Gen. Jackson's review of your testimony, I discovered that it seems to be considered a matter of importance in regard to the *place* where you made the speech, in which you alluded to the statement of O'Brien. I had not your speech before me at Washington city, when I addressed Gen. Jackson upon that subject, consequently I had to depend upon recollection only as to the place. Since I came home I have had reference to your speech, and find it was delivered at Knoxville, instead of Jonesboro', as I had first supposed, when my letter to the General was written. This may serve to correct the mistake by me in this particular.

With much respect, yours,

A. Huntsman

Hon. Hu. L. White

This reply, addressed to the freemen of Tennessee, was reckoned a satisfactory disposal of the charges mentioned in it. We add a letter addressed to its author in reference to it, shortly after its publication:

* * * "I hope to meet you at the opening of the special session of Congress; but I cannot without violence to my feelings permit the occasion to pass, without thanking you most sincerely for your masterly 'Address to the Freemen of Tennessee.' The ex-president has at no time, nor by any person, been so severely handled, and so fully exposed. I think he will be advised not to enter the field of controversy again with *you*, hereafter. * * * You have done no more than justice to Mr. Clayton, in the part he took in the passage of the Compromise Bill. I was advised from day to day of every important proposition that was made in the committee, and out of it; and I say without hesitation, that if Mr. Clayton had not been on the committee, the Compromise Bill would not have passed.

"His geographical residence gave him an influence over both the Northern and the Southern members; but aside from this, there was no man, in or out of Congress, within my knowledge, so well calculated to conciliate the contending parties and interests on that great and momentous occasion, involving the fate of the nation, as was Mr. Clayton.

"His intelligence, his pure intentions, his firmness, his urbane manners, his enlarged national views, and his talents, rarely equalled, qualified him for that occasion. All the faculties of his mind were brought into exercise; for on the fate of the compromise depended, in his judgment, the fate of the Union.

* * * "Gen. Jackson did not wish any compromise of the question. He had no personal objection to Mr. Clayton, as a member of the committee, and in sending to you, he was influenced by a third person, who was hostile to Mr. Clayton.

"The President wished an opportunity to subdue the disaffected in South Carolina, and then it was his intention to propitiate the South by reducing the Tariff at once. The bill gained strength from a desire to defeat his intentions in both particulars mentioned.

Very sincerely and respectfully yours,

E. WHITTLESEY."

CHAPTER XV.

CANVASS WITH MR. VAN BUREN.

The estimate placed upon Judge White's character and services by his State and his country is evidenced by the movement in favor of his election to the Presidency; for he did not become a candidate voluntarily.

There was a strong wish on the part of the Tennessee legislature, in 1833, to nominate him for that high office, but he withheld his assent, and took pains to discourage the movement, and even went so far as to leave it in charge with some of his friends in that body to prevent such a nomination, if attempted in his absence. After his name had been freely used in other parts of the country, the meeting of the Tennessee delegates took place in Washington city. This was not a movement exclusively on the part of his Tennessee friends. At the time, they supposed, and had a right to believe, that he could and would be successfully sustained, and that his Presidency would be the inauguration of a new era in the government. At the time they moved in his behalf, they had assurances of many, not to say of all the leading Jackson men, in every Southern State, that he would be supported. Some of them were a little coy, but still they were relied on, and encouraged the movement.

Judge White was known to have been opposed to all the leading measures and policy of the whigs of the Northern States. He was the friend of Gen. Jackson, had supported all his leading measures, and it was not natural to suppose that he would detach himself from his fortunes. This point was fully discussed between them and his friends, and was an obstacle to their support; but it was conceded by all that he was a *safe* man, without intrigue or management, and as his course had always been dignified and liberal towards them, they were resolved to overlook this objection to him, as they greatly preferred him to Mr. Van Buren. The main reliance, however, was upon the South, which there was every reason to calculate would be united. A few States at the North, or even one large State there would thus have secured his election. That many in that section were casting their eyes hopefully toward Judge White as a pure and available candidate, may be inferred from various letters received by him about this period. One from Condy Raguet, has already been given. Below follows an extract from another, which may be considered at its date (whatever artificial direction may afterwards have been given to popular feeling), to have represented the sentiments of no small number of true and honest men.

DORCHESTER, *Apr.* 27, 1834.

Will you permit me to add, sir, that your opinions and sentiments in reference to the topics of these pamphlets [sent with the letter] will be received with great respect by all who are interested in them; and that a personal visit to Massachusetts by you, would afford the highest gratification to some of her citizens. There are some, if not many, who are seeking for an individual on whom to bestow their suffrages, whose moral and political character will furnish a guaranty of the perpetuation of what still remains of the patrimony of liberty, and who will firmly resist those intrigues and blandishments which have sometimes seduced those we had confided in, from the paths of Constitutional Republicanism.

With great respect, &c.,

SAMUEL WHITCOMB, JR.

Of Judge White's answer to this letter—an answer containing no reference to the suggestions just given, but discussing some remarks on Labor, Capital and Society in a former portion of it—we give a portion, valuable for clear views and strong good sense.

* * * We need but one distinction in our society, and that ought never to be lost sight of. It is the distinction between vice and virtue. If a man's occupation is lawful, useful to himself and his fellow-men, honestly and diligently followed, he ought to be esteemed respectable; every one ought to be pleased with his prosperity; and the road to trust and honor ought always be open to him. We know, however, in fact, that those who own capital are always seeking profitable investments for it; that the owners have acted, and will act in concert, and that by doing so, they have more *actual* influence in directing all the operations of gov-

ernment, than ten, nay, twenty times their number, without spare capital, and compelled to pursue some honest and useful occupation for a living. This is not just, but I know of no corrective for the evil so likely to be effectual as by all means to enable and encourage this latter class to better their condition, and increase their information, as to the political concerns of the country.

In our government there is a thirst for office that is alarming. If this originated in a wish to be useful to the country generally, or in the wish to gratify personal pride by occupying places of distinction, it might be well; but there is reason to fear that in too many instances it has its origin in a wish to make the operations of the government subservient to the pecuniary interest of those in public life, their friends and connections. If this latter be the motive, a mere reduction of salary would not correct the evil, because an unworthy occupant will always make sufficient individual gain, by sacrificing whatever public property or interest may be committed to his charge.

Everything which tends to the dissemination of useful information among that class of individuals who have to labor for a living, and to make it convenient for them to act in concert, when their peculiar interests are likely to be assailed or sacrificed, would in my opinion be an improvement in the condition of our society; and in no instance ought any man to be placed in office who is not honest, capable and *habitually attentive to his business.*

Sound morals, as well as sound politics, and permanent truth, are most eminently in point at the present day.

Judge White signified his willingness to be nominated for the Presidency on the 20th December, 1834. The Tennessee delegation in Congress had requested his decision in the following letter :—

WASHINGTON, *Dec.* 29, 1834.

DEAR SIR :—You cannot be unapprised that for some time past your name has been frequently mentioned as a desirable person to succeed the present Chief Magistrate of the United States.

Being your colleagues in Congress since the commencement of the present session, we have been repeatedly asked what were the sentiments of our own State upon that subject, and more frequently, what were your own wishes, and what would likely to be your course, should public opinion seem to require the use of your name as a candidate, and fears are often expressed that you would not give your consent.

Upon this latter point we are at some loss what answer to give.

It is our wish not to deceive ourselves, or to be the means of deceiving others. We will therefore esteem it a favor if you will put us in possession of your wishes and determinations.

Very respectfully, sir,

We are your oot. servts.

WM. M. INGE,
BALIE PEYTON,
JAMES STANDIFER,
JOHN BLAIR,
W. C. DUNLAP,
SAML. BUNCH,
JNO. BELL,
DAVID CROCKETT,
JOHN B. FORRESTER,
LUKE LEA,
DAVID W. DICKENSON.

Judge White's answer was this, dated next day:

GENTLEMEN:—Your note dated yesterday was handed me a few minutes since.

I am aware that for some time past my name has been occasionally mentioned in our own State and elsewhere, for the office you mention. I had never supposed it would be so far acceptable to the public, as to render an application to me necessary to ascertain my wishes or determination.

Not having taken any pains to ascertain public opinion upon that subject, I am, perhaps, less acquainted with the sentiments even of our own State than any of my colleagues. As to my own wishes and determination, I can have no difficulty in giving you an answer.

I am not conscious that at any moment of my life, I have ever wished to be President of the United States. I have never knowingly uttered a sentence, or done an act, for the purpose of inducing any person to think of me for that distinguished station. When the duties and responsibilities of the office are considered, in my opinion it is an object more to be avoided than desired. I shall certainly never seek it while I have so little confidence in my own capacity to discharge the duties of it, as I now have.

Those for whose benefit it was created, have a right to fill it with any citizen they may prefer, provided he is eligible by the Constitution; and the person who would refuse to accept such an office, if offered by the people of the United States, ought to have a much stronger hold upon public opinion, than I can ever hope to possess.

My most anxious wish is, that in any use you may think proper to make of my name, you may lose sight of every consideration except the public interest. I have not had any agency in causing it to be used, and I do not feel that I would be justified in directing the use of it to be discontinued. I can, however, with truth say, that if those political friends who have used it thus far, shall have reason to believe that a further use of it will be an injury, instead of a benefit to the country, and may choose to withdraw it, they will have my hearty concurrence.

I am, most respectfully,
Your obedient servant,
HU. L. WHITE.

This permission having been given, Judge White was formally nominated for the Presidency of the United States by the Legislature of Tennessee, on the 16th and 17th of October, 1835, by the adoption of the following preamble and resolutions :

WHEREAS, the people of the State of Tennessee in 1822, in 1825, and again in 1827, animated by a sincere determination to support those cardinal doctrines and principles which had distinguished the true republican party from the commencement of the federal government, up to that period, and also to correct and reform those practices which appeared to be erroneous, and to constitute abuses in the policy and administration of the government, brought forward General Andrew Jackson, our present distinguished Chief Magistrate, as a person qualified by his principles, energy, and great popularity, to effect these objects. And *whereas*, among the most important of these objects were: 1st. To secure to the people the exercise of the right of suffrage in the election of the President of the United States, independent of the influence and dictation of caucus nominations. 2d. To resist the establishment of the practice of electing the President of the United States according to any plan of regular succession among the great functionaries of the government. 3d. The limitation and control of executive patronage within such safe and expedient bounds as to secure the freedom and purity of the elective franchise against all undue official influences. And *whereas*, we are firmly persuaded that the principles upon which General Jackson was originally nominated and supported for the Presidency, by the people of the State of Tennessee, have lost nothing of their truth or importance by the lapse of time, and change of circumstances, we feel impelled by a proper regard for consistency, now, when again called upon to reconsider them in reference to the choice of a successor, or to re-affirm them by a renewed and solemn declaration.

In the organization and proceedings of the late Baltimore Convention we perceive the same violation of the spirit of the Constitution, the same tendency to a usurpation of the rights and powers of the people in the election of President, the same spirit of intrigue, the same liability in the members to be corrupted and influenced in their course by the promise and expectation of office, which we saw in the organization and proceedings of the Congressional caucus in 1823, and then condemned in the most public and solemn manner.

And *whereas*, no individual has been presented to the consideration of the American people as a candidate for the next Presidency, whose character and political opinions afford the same guarantee for the maintenance of those principles which brought General Jackson into office, and for carrying out the principal measures of his administration, and which so well accord with the political sentiments of the people of Tennessee, as set forth in this preamble, as our fellow citizen, HUGH LAWSON WHITE—therefore,

Resolved, That HUGH LAWSON WHITE be recommended to the people of the United States as a man eminently qualified to fill the office of President.

Resolved, That we approve generally of the principles and policy, both foreign and domestic, of the administration of the federal government during the term of service of our present distinguished Chief Magistrate, General Andrew Jackson.

EPHRAIM H. FOSTER,
Speaker of the House of Representatives.
JONATHAN WEBSTER,
Speaker of the Senate.

Adopted in the House on the 16*th, and concurred in by the Senate on the* 17*th of October*, 1835.

These proceedings were communicated to Judge White in the following letter, dated Nashville, Oct. 22, 1833:

TO THE HON. HUGH L. WHITE:

SIR: The undersigned have been appointed a joint committee of both houses of the General Assembly, to inform you that the people of the State of Tennessee have by their representatives nominated you to their fellow-citizens of the United States, for the office of Chief Magistrate.

This duty, we conceive, will be best discharged by communicating to you the preamble and resolutions adopted by both houses of the General Assembly. From them you will learn the principles on which the nomination was made. These, as also the attending circumstances, we take leave to say, appear to us no less honorable to the people of the State than to yourself. By this act, they have shown a discrimination and devotion to principle, worthy the imitation of posterity.

We avail ourselves of this occasion to tender to you the assurances of our esteem and veneration for your character, and our ardent wishes for your personal happiness.

WM. LEDBETTER, ROBT. H. HYNDS, TERRY H. CAHAL.	*Committee on the part of the Senate.*
ADDISON A. ANDERSON, WM. MCCLAIN, GRANVILLE D. SEARCY, LION ROGERS, G. W. CHURCHWELL, HARVEY M. WATTERSON, WM. B. CAMPBELL, J. A. MABRY, CHARLES READY, ROBERTSON TOPP.	*Committee on the part of the House.*

To this communication Judge White responded in the following dignified letter, dated Nashville, Oct. 23, 1835:

GENTLEMEN: I have the honor to acknowledge the receipt of your communication under date of yesterday, inclosing a copy of a preamble and resolutions of the General Assembly of the State of Tennesee, recommending me as a suitable person to succeed the present Chief Magistrate of the United States.

To receive evidence at any time that the representatives of the people of my own State continue to repose confidence in me would be highly gratifying; but at this particular time, and after such multiplied efforts have been unceasingly made from various quarters to destroy my reputation, to receive such testimony of increased confidence is matter calculated to call forth my most profound acknowledgments.

Some of those who are members of the present General Assembly, and who were members of the same body two years ago, can bear testimony to the fact that I earnestly endeavored to prevent my name from being submitted to the American people for the highest office within their gift, but my efforts have been unavailing. A state of things has been produced which induces a portion of my political friends to believe the interest of the country would be promoted by the use of my name as a candidate, and when applied to on various occasions, I have given my consent, and I now take this opportunity to state that this consent will not be withdrawn.

In common with a large majority of the citizens of Tennessee, I was an humble advocate of the principles set forth in the preamble to your resolutions. Time and increased experience have tended to confirm me in the opinion that on the maintenance of these principles the liberties of the people of the United States essentially depend.

From the formation of the Federal Constitution, up to this time, there have been parties in the United States. Where they are separated upon principle the members of each may honestly believe the permanent welfare of the country depends upon having the government administered upon the principles which they advocate, and may honorably use every fair effort to elevate their own party, and put down their opponents. But when an attempt is made to create a party not founded upon any settled political principles, composed of men belonging to every political sect, having no common bond of unity save that of a wish to place one of themselves in the highest office known to the Constitution, for the purpose of having all the honors, offices, and emoluments of the government distributed by him among his followers, I consider such an association, whether composed of many or of few, a mere *faction*, which ought to be resisted by every man who loves his country, and wishes to perpetuate its liberty.

To conciliate the favor, or procure the support, of any man or set of men, belonging to any party, I have not changed, nor agreed to change, any one political principle I ever avowed. Those upon which I have heretofore practised shall continue to be my guide in whatever situation I may be placed, so long as I believe them to be correct; disdaining, as I hope I ever shall, an attempt to win my way to power upon one set of principles, and then to practice upon another.

Through you I beg leave to tender to the General Assembly my unfeigned and heartfelt thanks for this additional evidence of their continued and unbroken confidence, and for yourselves be pleased to accept the assurance that I am, with sentiments of the highest respect,

Your most obedt. servt.,

Hu. L. White.

The President, upon finding that he had been foiled in his efforts to influence Judge White to become a candidate on the Van Buren ticket for Vice-President, or to accept a seat on the Supreme bench, now began to use the patronage of the government to seduce from Judge White's interest some of the leading men in the Southern States. The plea urged by them for withdrawing from Judge White's support was, that, by running more than one man, the great republican party would be divided, and that unless Judge White obtained the nomination of the Baltimore Convention, they could not sustain him. Had General Jackson's election depended upon a caucus nomination, he would never have been President; but he entertained different views at that time; and when first presented by the people of Tennessee and Pennsylvania did not prohibit the use of his name, although there were no less than three other candidates in the field, besides himself; Mr. Clay, Mr. Crawford, and Mr. Adams.

General Jackson having decided upon his course, his confidential friends, the Editor of the Globe, and Major Donelson, his private secretary, circulated a statement that the contest in this canvass would really be between him and Judge White. The Van Buren papers spoke confidently of Judge White's defeat even in Tennessee. This prediction, as they affirmed, was based upon General Jackson's preference for Mr. Van Buren. Neither Judge White nor his friends gave any attention to these movements; and General Jackson, in the confidence of his power over the minds of the people of Tennessee, took occasion fully to define his position through a letter to the Rev. Samuel Gwinn, in which he advocated the Baltimore Convention. It was then said in Washington (alluding to this letter), that a document had been sent to Tennessee, which would settle the matter there.

This Convention—which assembled at Baltimore on the 20th May—had been gotten up for the express purpose of nominating Mr. Van Buren, who very naturally received its unanimous vote. The three States of Alabama, Illinois, and South Carolina, were not represented in the Convention. As the President had recommended this Convention to his Tennessee friends, a failure on their part to appoint delegates, created such a universal regret in that assembly, as to induce a Mr. Rucker, a gentleman from Tennessee then accidentally present, and invited to act as delegate, to cast fifteen votes for the State, and thereby to secure Col. R. M. Johnson's nomination for the Vice-Presidency. To show the invalidity of this vote, it is only necessary to insert Mr. Rucker's own letter to the Editors of the Nashville Union, explanatory of his conduct on this occasion.

You will discover my name introduced into the proceedings of the Baltimore Convention. To prevent all misunderstanding, I make the following statement: I was not delegated to act in that convention. I happened in Baltimore at the time of its sitting, and after the delegates from the different States had their credentials examined by the committee appointed for that purpose, there appeared to be no one present representing Tennessee. This circumstance seemed to be deeply regretted by many, and upon its being mentioned that I was there, and a Tennessean, it was suggested by some that I might vote, which I accordingly did.

E. Rucker.

This latitudinarian proceeding gave rise to the phrase "Ruckerize," which was then and afterwards used to describe that and other similar contrivances.

It was supposed that the decision of the Baltimore Convention, and the Gwinn letter, would have the effect of causing Judge White's friends to make the issue between him and Gen. Jackson, which was so desirable to the friends of Mr. Van Buren. Charges of cowardice, and want of chivalry, in not assailing the President at once, with various taunts and epithets of abuse, such as "disorganizers, intriguers, anti-republicans," were heaped upon that portion of the community which could not perceive the justice, or acknowledge the truth of the accusation that Judge White had lost his claim to the names of a good republican and a virtuous citizen, by consenting to become a candidate for the Presidency. It now seemed that all their efforts were about to prove abortive. The Gwinn letter had failed—the hoped-for issue had not been secured—and other means must be resorted to—the work *must be accomplished.*

The public mails were soon flooded with "Globes" and extras, containing most virulent attacks upon Judge White, with specific charges, of "bargain, intrigue and corruption," between Judge White and Mr. Bell, and Judge White and the opposition. These papers bore the President's frank. The dishonorable course of the Administration, in this franking privilege, became necessarily subject to the animadversions of the public press. Even then, Judge White's friends were willing to believe, and to avow their belief, that Gen. Jackson's confidence had been abused and his name used in this illegal way by designing men. Investigation proved this supposition to be correct, to some extent. However, when suspicion settled upon Major Donelson, the President's private secretary, Gen. J. wrote a second Gwinn letter, asserting that he had never franked any packages for Major Donelson, without a perfect knowledge of their contents, and contending, that the packages contained public documents, though it was notorious and has been fully proven that they were those malicious assaults upon Judge White, which have just been mentioned.

These things transpired a little before the State elections; and one object evidently was, to influence those elections in such a manner, as to secure a legislature, subject to the will of the party in power—and who would relieve it of Judge White's opposition in the Senate, by passing resolutions instructing him to vote for Mr. Benton's expunging resolutions. To insure success in this experiment, the copies of the

Globe, containing Col. Benton's speech on these resolutions, were franked by the President to many members of the legislature, and letters were written by him to Mr. Brown, and A. O. P. Nicholson, complaining that "Judge White had not only failed to take part in his defence, but had moved to strike out the word 'expunge,' and all the reasons on which Mr. Benton's motion rested."

In his course on this subject, Judge White was sustained by many distinguished members of the Jackson party, viz., King of Ala., King of Ga., Cuthbert, Buchanan, McKeever, Tipton and Hendricks. What was a virtue in them was a crime in him. His political enemies were not yet fully aware of the materials of which the Tennessee legislature was composed, and their great desire to expel Judge White only made his friends more resolved to sustain him. They had elected him a few months before, with a full knowledge of this objection, and could not be induced to instruct him to act differently. So, instead of holding his seat by the President's endorsement, he unexpectedly held it in defiance of his protest.

Col. E. H. Foster, writing to Judge White, date Nashville, Feb. 26, 1836, gives the following graphic account of the struggle in the legislature of Tennessee, to manœuvre through the instructions to vote for expunging, and the resolutions to withdraw Judge White's nomination:

In other matters, a very large majority of that legislature who elected you, sir, *with one voice*, have proudly distinguished this noble State before the whole American Republic. They have withstood alike the persuasions and the threats of the strongest arm in the nation, and that mighty arm laid bare and unblushingly held up to the gaze of all, that nothing of its overwhelming effects on popular love and veneration might be lost—that arm, hitherto and perhaps still invincible, was laid upon you and your friends. Thank God, here we have thus far withstood its withering, destructive, paralyzing force, and we stand proudly erect after the storm has spent its violence and wasted its strength. How happy I am in the reflection I leave your own patriotic feelings to paint. * * * The "expunging resolutions" had been suffered to sleep in quiet for the space of near a five-month. Meanwhile, as you have no doubt heard, no means were left untried to gain friends indoors and without. The people were invoked, and Gen. Jackson's reputation, like Cæsar's pierced and bloody mantle, was held up before them. Public meetings were called, and private memorials circulated. They sought to seduce the ignorant by misrepresentation, and to allure others by promises and flatteries. Gen, Jackson, as you may have seen, did not think it out of the way to address himself personally, and by strong appeals, to many members of the legislature, and among them to some who must have been designated by some shrewd friend at Washington (the Speaker of the House, we suppose here), for they had never had the honor to see or be seen by the President, and were surprised—not flattered off by the distinction. Well, the session was fast drawing to a close, and the Van Buren leaders (not bad tacticians, I assure you), determined on an effort. Friday, the 12th instant, they [the expunging resolutions, *Ed.*] were called for, and notwithstanding many of your friends, anxious for the fight, voted with the enemy to bring them up, the call failed. Not to be out-done, or disappointed in all hopes of making something by a discussion that might bring your name into angry collision with the President's, they then called for Col. Johnson's "*Te laudamus*" resolutions. The call succeeded, and the forgotten and long-neglected paper, almost covered with dust and cobweb, was dragged to light. The question was on the amendment in lieu of the whole, offered by Mr. Whiteside, when the paper came from the Senate last October. Mr. Ridley obtained the floor, and moved to amend Mr. Whiteside's amendment, by engrafting on it most of the *servile* matter contained in the original resolutions. Mr. Martin, of Madison, inquired if a motion to amend the *original* would take precedence of a motion to amend the amendment? Being answered from the chair in the affirmative, he proposed an additional resolution approving "both generally and specially," the President's proclamation against South Carolina nullification; "not" as he observes, "that he approved of the reasoning or the doctrine contained in that paper, either in whole or in part; for he had made, and still made open-day war against the instrument, its logic and its conclusions, and his arm would never be grounded; but he felt a desire to try the stomachs of some of his over-righteous, whole-hog Jackson friends, and as the occasion fitted so well, he could not forego the pleasure, or the malice, as gentlemen might choose to call it, of making the experiment." If a whizzing little bomb had fallen on the floor, it would not have produced more amazement in certain quarters, than this villainous amendment did. Mr. Humphreys, Mr. Overton, and Mr. Allen, of Perry, all "good men and true" to the cause of Mr. Van Buren, sprang on the nullifier. It seemed as if they really intended to devour him. I cast a longing eye towards Martin, for I felt for him. One glance convinced me that I might save my compassion. There he sat, like a huge bull-dog, casting a calm and indifferent eye, now on this side and now on that, at the whole pack that bayed him, conscious no doubt of his own strength, and knowing that he could crush them whenever they ventured too far. On the question, the amendment was ordered by a large vote, Mr. Humphreys and Mr. Allen voting with the minority, and doubtless cursing the artificer and the artifice that forced them to so unmannerly an exposure. Not contented with this experiment, but resolved to try their "faith" by the most horrible and at the same time indisputable test, Martin again reached the floor, and moved an amendment, that the President's course, in attempting by his influence to secure the election of a successor of his own choice, by his franks and his letters, so far as any member had knowledge of such letters and franks, met the hearty approbation of the General Assembly. This, indeed, was the "unkindest cut of all." Old Job himself, patience personified, could not stand it longer. But necessity is the mother of invention; and the Van Buren men, thus chased and caught in their own toils, immediately took shelter under the "expunging resolutions." Col. Guild moved a substitute in lieu of Mr. Martin's amendment. It was a new and improved edition of the "expunging resolutions," just from Washington, dispatched by Col. Benton, as was publicly charged in debate and not denied; and defined "expunging" to consist in drawing black lines around and making notes across, and not in blotting out or erasing an offensive entry. And then by a war of ingenuities, a debate not anticipated originated in the House. It presented, I assure you, an animated scene. The lobby was soon thronged to overflowing, and many went away who could not crowd in. In justice to all, I must say, the discussion was ably, adroitly and at times eloquently conducted, on both sides. It continued Friday, Friday night, Saturday all day, and until 12 at night, and despite all my exertions, was received at times with loud applause in the lobby and on the floor. As you will readily imagine, yourself and Mr. Van Buren both got some hard knocks, and among hands the "old hero" himself now and then received an unlucky blow, only, however, when the stroke was aimed at Mr. Van Buren ensconced behind his mighty buckler. As I told you, the House continued the debate until 12 o'clock, and then adjourned without taking the question. On Monday, and perhaps the next or a succeeding day, several ineffectual attempts were made to bring up the subject. On Saturday morning last, and when but few anticipated the movement, Mr. Topp, the talented, eloquent and spirited member from Shelby, having being deprived of an opportunity to address the House when the debate was in progress before, and resolved not to be cut off from delivering his sentiments, rose in his place, and offered a preamble and resolutions highly complimentary to you, and approving your course on Mr. Benton's expunging resolutions. He followed up his motion by one of the most pungent, forcible, and interesting speeches I have yet heard. He cut all round with a two-edged sword, and being about to close, mentioned that it was not his intention at that late period to lay the resolutions before the House--that he had simply introduced them to enable him to give his honest sentiments against the odious proposition to expunge, and that he would now withdraw them as he had a right to do by the rules. * * * And thus the "expunging" and the "laudatory" resolutions descend for the present to the "tomb of the Capulets;" the former, I trust in God, never to rise again, nor the latter, while they come to us in strains of adulation more suited to the attributes of his Maker than of man.

Judge White's correspondence at and about this period bears sufficient testimony to the equanimity with which he bore the assaults and manœuvres of his enemies, although a proper regard for his own character and for the friends who were upholding him rendered it a right, that he should now be interested in his own success, and at least do whatever was necessary to a proper appreciation and acknowledgment of their endeavors. These letters show likewise that he was well aware of the corrupt means used by his opponents, who descended even to the unlawful examination of private mailed letters.

A personal friend writes to him, to Washington, from home, date January 7, 1836:

I have this moment had a conversation with Mr. James Jackson, who is directly from Nashville, and who says that the members of our Legislature have very lately received communications from the President, urging them to adopt the resolution instructing you to vote for Benton's expunging resolution, and very abusive of yourself.

Believing it the duty of a friend to advise you of such proceedings, I do so, and in addition that you may not be deceived, I here state to you that *Andrew Jackson's* frank is very frequent on papers abusive of yourself and Col Bell, sent to this office. I think (though you did not as early as myself make the discovery) you will be satisfied that he is not the man we at one time took him to be.

At one time I was a very clever fellow, and so were you and Bell; but we have become great scoundrels in the estimation of the tyrant who wields the executive department (indeed all) of the government.

A short statement made by Judge White in the Senate, June 28, 1836, furnishes a summary of the various underhanded engineerings to which his opponents were stooping:

At the last session, the member from Missouri (I doubt not from a conviction of the correctness of the procedure) submitted his proposition to expunge. The Chief Magistrate had made up his mind who should be his successor, and had determined to use all his personal influence and official patronage to secure his election. Whilst there was a majority of the

Senate opposed to him, this patronage could not be brought to operate with full effect. Upon discussing the expunging resolution, the opinions of every senator were expressed. The times of some were then expiring—the very day of voting. The venerable Chief Magistrate at once saw the use which could be made of this instrument, and he has given it his full influence ever since, under the hope that, through its use, the Senate could be expurgated, members whom he deemed unworthy of the station excluded, and their places supplied by others, in his opinion, more worthy. He seized the weapon, and has wielded it with all the effect he could. The cry "expunge" was raised, and has been continued.

I shall speak of what I know, and what I believe to be true. The time of one of the senators in my own State had expired. Members of the legislature and to the House of Representatives were to be elected in August. The Chief Magistrate interfered, through the agency of others, in the elections to be made by the people, and in the election to be made by the legislature.

Does any one who hears me doubt this statement? He need not. The following facts will show, incontestably, that he interfered in the election to be made by the people:

1st. His two letters addressed to the Rev. Mr. Gwin, which all who look into newspapers must have read. They were intended for publication, and were actually published.

2d. Besides the number of copies of the Globe itself, hundreds of which he has sent to Tennessee under his frank, he franked many copies of the prospectus for the extra Globe, which contains very little except misrepresentations and insinuations utterly unfounded and untrue. There can be no pretence that this was sent because it contained any speech, or any public document. There is no such thing in it. I hold one that he sent to Tennessee, frank and all, in my hand, just as received by the gentleman to whom it was addressed; and many others were scattered through the country under his frank.

3d. He wrote a letter to Mr. Curry, which was used in Col. Standifer's district, with a view to influence public opinion.

4th. He wrote a letter to my colleague, a copy of which was furnished to Mr. Johnson, who used it in his canvass upon the stump with a view to aid his election; and it must have been intended for such use when written, otherwise we must suppose my colleague abused the confidence of the Chief Magistrate, in permitting his letter to be applied to a purpose not intended by the writer.

These few facts, independent of many others which might be stated, satisfy me that he did interfere, and use his influence with the people to regulate their opinions in the elections.

Secondly. He interfered with the legislature.

1. On the next day after they assembled, under his frank, each member

received *three* numbers of the extra Globe, amounting to three hundred. Here is one of them, frank and all. Some of these Globes contain matter of the lowest kind, intended, no doubt, to disgust the members with their former senator, and to prevent his re-election.

2. He wrote a letter to Mr. Nicholson, one of the members, which we have seen published in the newspaper, in which he complains of the former senator for not defending him on the expunging resolution at the last session, and justifying the use made of his franking privileges.

3. He wrote a similar letter to Mr. Brown, another member, a copy of which I now hold in my hand.

4. He wrote to Mr. Guild, one of the leading members, a letter containing an argument to prove the propriety of instructing the senators to vote for expunging the resolution of March, 1834, and urging the propriety of giving such instructions, and authorized Mr Guild to submit it to the perusal of other members; which he did; and

5. *From this place was sent to this same Mr. Guild* a copy of the form of expunging, which the senators were to be instructed to use; and this form corresponds, as I have understood, with that used in the resolution proposed at this session by the senator from Missouri.

All these facts prove that the first object was to defeat the re-election of a senator, who, at the last session, had shown he would not conform his conduct to the will of the Chief Magistrate; and, when that failed, to cause *such instructions* to be given as it was known that that senator *could not obey*, and thereby force him to resign. Both these objects failed. The senator was re-elected, and the legislature would *not give* any instructions.

Mr. President, I have not stated these facts by way of complaint against the executive. I perhaps am, least of all others, competent to judge whether such a course was in conformity with his station or his peculiar situation; but I state them that justice may be done to the independence of the legislature, and to their determination not to be persuaded or forced from what they thought the path of duty. Their course is the more commendable, when it is remembered they sat within a few miles of his residence; were surrounded by his personal friends; and that they themselves can furnish from their own body many of his earliest, firmest, and most undeviating *political* and *personal* friends. Let it be remembered, also, that they then were, and now are, the firm and unflinching *supporters* of his Administration, upon every point where his measures *conform* to the principles *avowed* to *bring him into power*. Yet they would not, and did not, give their senators any instructions upon this question. They were willing to trust them without instructions upon this as well as other points; and on this account it is that I feel myself under higher obligations to endeavor to carry out the will of my State upon this subject, than I should have been if formally instructed.

Writing to Hon. Geo. W. Churchwell, date Washington, January 3, 1836, he says:

My Dear Sir: I ought to, as I do, sincerely thank you for your two letters. They are the only ones received from any member since I reached Washington. Your last letter had evidently been opened and very clumsily closed again.

Every effort has been making here to influence public opinion. B was beaten for no other reason than because he would not go against me. It was urged by the faithful, that by the election of Polk, the vote of Tennessee would be changed. The course of Alabama, it is now said, will be followed by the legislature of Tennessee, and that in a very short time my name will be dropped everywhere.

I have never had a word from Mr. Clay, but understand from others that he says without hesitation, that he will not be a candidate. Webster, it would seem, having lost the nomination in Pennsylvania and Maryland, will either be dropped soon, or if his name is continued, it will be thought to be done to benefit Mr. Van Buren.

I have not heard that Mr. Webster himself has said one word on the subject. Gen. Harrison, from every indication, will continue a candidate, and my friends do not believe my prospects are to be materially changed by it.

Everything which can be done to my injury, within their power, is done by Grundy and Johnson, from my own State, and probably by Polk, also.

By the faithful, it is confidently supposed, that you will pass the resolutions, ordering us to expunge.

Those who can be seduced by hopes of power and benefits are operated on in that way; others are denounced in the coarsest terms.

As to myself, I await my fate with the most perfect indifference on my own account. For others, I have much feeling; but for nothing so much as the reputation of my State. She now has the proudest name in the Union, and upon her firmness in this crisis, her future fame essentially depends.

Her citizens, in primary assemblies first, and her legislature afterwards, have brought my name before the world. Torrents of unmerited abuse have been poured on my devoted head, for not prohibiting them from doing so, and if now it is withdrawn by the mandate or management of any earthly power, then, indeed, will I admit I knew nothing of the character of the people among whom I have been raised.

I wish the expunging resolutions were disposed of, if they are to pass, the public interest would require I should know it in time to apprise the legislature of my course before they adjourn. Write me frequently; even if our letters are read, it makes no difference, provided they would even then forward them.

What will be the fate of any nomination before the Senate, I know not. My course must be an individual one, as I am not in the confidence of any party. I shall, so far as my vote will go, carry out the great principle of checking executive patronage, being employed to influence the right of suffrage.

With the most sincere esteem and regard,

Your obedient servant,

HU. L. WHITE.

Hon. GEORGE W. CHURCHWELL.

And again, a little later:

SENATE CHAMBER, *February* 23, 1836.

MY DEAR SIR: Your favor under date of the 8th instant, was received, apparently safe, on yesterday. We have had, almost constantly, a state of very high excitement in Congress, and have, as yet, done but little, except talk.

The Globe has become more and more abusive. It is now plainly seen that I will neither be coaxed, nor driven from the position, in which I have been placed by my political friends. The only alternative, therefore, is to destroy me if possible. I am charged with insincerity, duplicity, falsehood, suppressing the truth &c., without stint. In addition, it is obvious the whole power and patronage of the executive is brought to bear. For all this, I care not. My leading friends here, stand firm, and fearlessly do their duty. How many of them may do so elsewhere, time alone will show.

I shall calmly, coolly, and without faltering, as well as I am able, discharge what I think the duty assigned me, without stopping to consider whether it will elevate or depress me in public opinion.

The policy is to whistle off as many of my friends as possible, and to sacrifice the rest.

When the contest is over, even if left a private citizen, I would not exchange either feelings or character, with the venerable Chief Magistrate. I intend to act, as far as God may enable me, upon the principles which I have ever avowed, which I believe are sound and correct. I will, therefore, have my own approbation: whereas, my old friend is in open disregard of the leading measures he professed to entertain when he sought power, and is saying, and countenancing others in saying, things against me, which he has the strongest reasons to believe are unjust and unfounded.

Our French war is happily ended. Should the instructing, *expunging* resolutions have passed, I shall leave for home as soon as I can make the necessary preparations.

If permitted to remain here, I have no doubt we shall have the names of some of *Our Flying Squad* in Tennessee before the Senate for their pay. My health continues very good.

Most sincerely and truly,

HU. L. WHITE.

HON. G. W. CHURCHWELL.

WASHINGTON, *June 18th*, 1836.

MY DEAR SIR: I thank you most sincerely for your letter enclosed to Mr. Lea, and which he handed me on yesterday.

I see no reason to conclude that anything which has occurred here during the session can have the effect of doing us harm; on the contrary I think we may well flatter ourselves that progress has been made in giving to the people some useful information.

Everything in the power of the executive to do for the purpose of injuring me has been done, and I doubt not the same course will be continued.

In conformity with my own judgment, as well as what I believed the wishes of my constituents I have in every instance sustained the executive, excepting only in such measures as I believed inconsistent with the great principles for which we all struggled when the present President came into power.

Strange as it may seem, I have no doubt the truth is, the President is exceedingly anxious that it should be known that his successor will have been elected by his means and influence; and I am perfectly convinced he intends to put down every man who dares to throw any obstacles in his way.

That the timid and calculating will yield to his wishes is according to the common course of things; as to myself I am content to await the result without anxiety. I will never yield to the dictation of any one man living, but will willingly abide the expressed will of a majority, be that what it may. That the patronage of the government has been used, is now being used, and will continue to be used to influence public opinion, I firmly believe. After the 4th March, 1837, the opinion and influence of General Jackson will be regulated entirely by the manner in which his whole public conduct shall be estimated by the community at large.

I venture one prediction, and that is that if he ever after that period should need friends he will find very few among those he is now serving most zealously.

Why should we try to prove our letters were broken? Who cares? Those who are profited by such villainy will only be the better pleased. All we can do in such cases is to state the truth as it is, whenever and wherever we please, and let others believe or disbelieve us as best suits them.

You must expect and so you will find the truth to be, that you will have the opposition and enmity of all those who believe you are, or will be, in their way; and you will have better luck than I, if you do not find those most bitter whom you have treated best.

Patience and good temper under injustice is always the best policy. When people lie, live them down by exemplary conduct.

Your letter at the close of the session was received and answered. As you did not receive the answer some one else received the benefit of it.

If ill usage could disgust any one with the world I ought to be disgusted: but I am not. When those who ought to treat me well, ill use me, I am more than compensated by the friendship and support of those who are under no obligation to me.

Most sincerely and truly, yours,

HU. L. WHITE.

GEORGE W. CHURCHWELL, Esq.

A speech made by Judge White at a dinner given him by his constituents at Knoxville, in August of the same year, contains a clear exposition of the principles upon which he was and had been acting, of the gross violation and desertion of them by the party who were now seeking Mr. Van Buren's election, and of the methods and motives by which the opposition to himself was conducted by the Administration. The sentiment introducing him was the following:

Our distinguished guest and neighbor the Hon. Hugh Lawson White.—His public career has been no less conspicuous for its consistency, independence, and usefulness, than his private life for its propriety, purity, and uprightness. Malevolence and persecution cannot prostrate him. Tennessee will sustain him firmly and fearlessly against the slanders of malice and the magic of the most influential name.

After the loud and reiterated bursts of applause with which this sentiment was received, had subsided, Judge White rose and said:

GENTLEMEN: The sentiment just given, and the feelings with which it has been received, encourage me to do something more than make my acknowledgments for your undeviating support, and continued confidence.

After an absence of almost nine months, seven of which were devoted to my duties in Congress, upon my return home, to find my neighbors, the people of my own county, ready to greet me as a friend, and to declare in the face of the world, that my character as a private citizen does not deserve reproach, and that my conduct as a public man meets their approbation, is a source of the highest gratification. More especially when I reflect how incessantly I have been assailed, and with how much industry the vilest slanders have been circulated, under the sanction of names, some of which I know are, and long have been, very dear to you, as well as to the great majority of my fellow-citizens.

For eleven years I have, in part, represented Tennessee in the Senate of the United States. Until the two last, my services, humble as they were, appeared to be acceptable to the great body of the people. Any complaints against me were made, comparatively, by a few, and they were of those decidedly opposed to the present Chief Magistrate and his Administration.

Now the matter has changed, and I have been violently assailed by some of those with whom I have formerly acted, and several of those who were my bitter opponents on account of my attachment to the Chief Magistrate, have become his zealous friends, while they still continue their hostility to me. Having resided in the State from my boyhood, and having, from the time I attained the years of discretion, been busy among the people in some capacity or other, I believed a large and overwhelming majority of our fellow-citizens were decidedly *Jeffersonian Republicans*, and belonging to that school of politicians myself, when honored with a seat in the Senate, I flattered myself that on all important questions, when I honestly carried out, in practice, my own political opinions, I would also faithfully represent the opinions of my constituents. I have neither solicited nor desired the berth, and could not have been induced to accept it, if a sacrifice of any of my principles had been required. At one period, domestic afflictions visited me in such rapid succession, and with such weight, that I had made up my mind to withdraw, and let my place be supplied by some one, whose mind would not be doomed to brood so much over his own misfortunes; but abandoned the idea at the earnest solicitation of some, whom I, childishly, then thought my friends, and who are now under the hypocritical pretence of continued friendship, my most deadly enemies.

In the great struggle to bring the present Chief Magistrate into office, it became necessary that *his friends* should proclaim and enforce, by all the arguments they could advance, their political principles; and what were they?

1st. All useless expenditures of the public moneys should be discontinued.

2d. All offices should be filled by men who were honest, capable, faithful to the Constitution, and of business habits.

3d. That neither Congress nor any department of the federal government had any power, except that which was *expressly granted* by the Constitution, or was necessary and proper to carry into effect some power which was expressly granted.

4th. That the Executive power should be so *limited* and *regulated* by *law*, that neither the *President* nor any officer appointed by, or dependent upon him, *could use his influence or power to control or guide public opinion in elections.*

5th. That the Constitution should be so amended as to *secure* to the *people* the *right of choosing* the Chief Magistrate *themselves.* That the same person should not be elected for a second term, and that offices should not be filled with members of Congress.

6. That all surplus moneys which might accumulate in the treasury, beyond the *reasonable* wants of the federal government, should be divided among the States by some fair ratio, to the end that the people, to whom it rightfully belonged, might have the benefit of it for internal improvements, education, &c.

7th. That all *caucuses* or *combinations* of men, whose object it was to create or control *public opinion* in the election of President and Vice-President should be discountenanced and put down.

These were the great and leading principles for which we, in common with *others*, contended. The public voice sanctioned them by the election of the Chief Magistrate in 1828. In his inaugural address in 1829, and in his subsequent addresses, he has avowed and proclaimed several of them.

They are the very *doctrines* on which *I have practised* from that day to this, so far as my humble capacity enabled me; and I now challenge my persecutors to put their fingers on the cases in which I have departed from them.

How then has it happened, that for the last eighteen months, or two years, my humble name has, in a certain set of newspapers, and among a certain clan of politicians, been constantly coupled with some degrading charge?

Upon this subject, I can, perhaps, give you some facts not heretofore generally known, and this I shall do, not for the purpose of injuring any one, but for the sake of making a just defence of myself.

The General Assembly of this State sat in Nashville in the fall of 1833. At the commencement of its session, as is my habit, I was there. While there, the news reached us that the deposits of the public moneys had been removed by the order of the President, from the bank of the United States. I immediately foresaw that this would produce a violent effort in Congress to put down the Administration. I ascertained that there was a wish among the members, before the session closed, to present my humble name to the people of the United States, as a suitable person to succeed the present Chief Magistrate. To every member with whom I conversed, and to every other person who addressed me on the subject, I used all the arguments in my power to prevent them from doing so; and with some that I could take most liberty with, when coming away, left it in charge, that should a nomination be attempted in my absence, to have it prevented.

At the close of the session one of those gentlemen wrote me, that he was censured as unfriendly, for not concurring in the plan of a nomination. I immediately answered his letter, assuring him he had not only acted in conformity with my wishes, but in accordance with my request —and that so sure was I that such a nomination would have weakened the President in Congress, that if it had been made, I would have held myself bound to withhold my assent.

In the spring of 1834, I received communications from different quarters upon the same subject, proposing that if it met my approbation, there would be meetings of the people to nominate me. To this course I gave no encouragement. During that year the President visited Tennessee, our convention was in session, and after their rise, I was informed, that some of the members had wished to nominate me, but had abandoned the attempt after they had ascertained it would incur his displeasure. On his journey to Washington, he conversed freely with some of my friends, and remonstrated against any attempt to nominate me as President—said that there must be a national convention, that Mr. Van Buren ought to be nominated as President, I, as Vice President, *and when his eight years were expired I was young enough then to be taken up as President.* All this was communicated to me, and the only answer that I could make was, that either office was beyond my merits, but that I could not enter into any arrangement, which would operate as a *lure* to induce any person to vote for myself, or for any other person contrary to his judgment. Thus the matter stood when the session of Congress commenced in December 1834. During that winter, many county meetings were held, at which my name was brought before the public, as well as by the legislature of Alabama.

Under a full belief that a system was about being put in operation, which would destroy the freedom of election, which was intended to transfer all federal power into certain hands, who, by the like process, would transfer it into the hands of others at their pleasure, and that the effect of this would be to give the operations of the government such a direction as would favor the interests of one class of citizens, at an entire sacrifice of the interests of all others, I consented that my political friends might use my name, or not, as they believed would most promote the public interest.

In this I might have erred; but if I did it was an honest error.

After giving this consent, and before the Baltimore Convention, I was repeatedly forewarned what I might expect if my name was not withdrawn. These threats carried no terrors to me. Whatever of character I have, was given to me by my country, and whenever it becomes necessary to *risk the whole of it,* in defence of those principles which I think *essential* to the preservation of liberty, I willingly stake it all. I feel that I was not intended to be the *slave* of any man or set of men--that I have some mind, and that the author of my existence intended that I should exercise it—that I should form opinions as to *politics and religion*, and freely and fearlessly act upon them, without being intimidated by what either man or devils can do. Could I have hesitated for one moment in my course, I would have fancied that I heard myself addressed from the tombs in yonder church-yard (pointing to the place where his father and mother are buried), in language like this: my son, remember that the same principles are now involved, which were proclaimed in July, 1776. That to maintain them, I risked my life, and everything dear to man—that after struggling through a seven years' war, with my compatriots in arms, we succeeded in the establishment of a free government —under it I lived happy, prosperous, and died without leaving a spot upon my name—that good name, and that free government, I left my children as an invaluable inheritance; and is it possible that, for the lack of *moral courage*, you will deprive yourself and your children of those blessings for which I toiled so long, and risked so much? If I still doubted, a voice still more endearing, if that be possible, would salute my ears in accents like these: can you for an instant forget the lessons taught by your mother?—remember you have not only your father's name in charge, but that you have also that of my family. Do you not recollect how I used to encourage you, and your brother to discharge your duty, as my only sentinels to watch and warn me when the tories would approach our dwelling for plunder, in your father's absence in the tented field? That I would then inform you, that my family were among the first to hoist the *pole of liberty* in the South, and among the most firm and fearless in defending it! And will you, who have not a drop of any but whig blood in your. veins. hesitate as to the course you ought to pursue? To these questions I could give but one answer—Fear not for me. The same good name you have transmitted, and the same rich inheritance, shall be left unstained, and transmitted unimpaired to your grand children.

But to proceed—the Baltimore Convention met, and in due form nominated a candidate for the Presidency and Vice-Presidency, against whom no man has heard me say one word. They have accepted the nominations, and I have no doubt, in doing so, acted on those principles which they think it right to maintain. As to myself, I solemnly declare that with the knowledge I have of the manner in which that convention was brought about, the object it was intended to accomplish, and the consequences expected to flow from it, had I been nominated by it for either office, such nomination would have been almost the *only contingency* upon which I would have *prohibited* the use of my name.

Let me not be misunderstood—I am very far from intimating it as my opinion, that the whole of that assemblage, or a majority of them, were either dishonest, or dishonorable men. Many of them are strangers to me, and I hope were governed by worthy motives, and I doubt not believed great good would result from their labors. I, on the contrary, think nothing but evil can result from a nomination by a set of men collected under the auspices of the executive, with a view to nominate an individual designated by him.

Notwithstanding this nomination, my name has been permitted to remain where it was before placed, and the threatened vengeance has been pouring out upon my devoted head ever since. "Tray, Blanche, and Sweetheart, little dogs and all," have been let loose upon me. I have heeded them not. It has been my aim to bear any and everything I have uniformly conformed my *public conduct* to my *avowed principles*, and what I believed the politics of my State. So far as the Administration has acted on the *principles which brought the Chief Magistrate into power*, I have been, as I think, a uniform and steady, though very humble, supporter. If on any point *he has changed his principles*, it is unreasonable to expect me to change with him, unless I can be furnished with sufficient reasons for such change.

Humble as my pretensions are represented to be, we all now see, and know, that my venerable friend, the Chief Magistrate himself, in his own proper person, has openly, and in the view of the sovereign people themselves, undertaken to control and regulate public opinion. This is a trouble which I am very sorry he had to take on my account. His acts are to live after him. He occupies the most dignified station upon earth. If any man living did more towards elevating him to that station than I did, it was because he had more influence. He has the efficient control of the whole fund of the nation—the disposal of our invaluable public domain—the appointment of all officers at home and abroad—the power to remove tens of thousands of officers, who have no means to procure subsistence for a day if he chooses to remove them; they must do as he directs, or be turned loose to starve. All this power I zealously strove to give him, and I did so under a thorough conviction that he would only use it in accordance with the spirit of the Constitution. That he would follow the wise example of Washington, of Jefferson, of Madison, and Monroe. That so far from openly interfering in the election of his successor, or encouraging any executive officer to do so, he would sternly prohibit it in others, and think it a high political and moral duty in himself to be perfectly "*neutral*," and lest he should disclose his preference would "*avoid conversing on the subject with his most intimate friends.*" In this I have been disappointed. I have been apprised that for twelve months past he has neither been sparing nor backward in his censures of me. It gave me no uneasiness—I was willing to bear it all without complaint. My only wish was that he might so conduct as to take nothing from the high charactor which in common with others, I had for years endeavored to give him. Not content with this he comes to our own State, among my own constituents, those in whose employ I now am, took a circuitous route through East Tennessee, so as to be in many villages, and is still on his tour through West Tennessee into North Alabama, openly denouncing me as a "*red hot Federalist*," *having abandoned his Administration, and being as far from him as the poles are asunder*, &c. Now with great deference to the opinion of that highly esteemed and venerable man I must be allowed to say he is entirely mistaken. I am not now and never was a Federalist, in any sense of that term recognized by or known to the American people. I am now and ever have been, a Republican of Mr. Jefferson's school, so far as I have been able to comprehend the doctrines taught by him. The true way to test this matter is for each of us to put down the articles of his political creed, and see in what we disagree. I have given you mine; you and the American people, who have taken the trouble to read what I have said, or to notice my recorded votes, know that I have practised on my professions. It is not with me to say whether the Chief Magistrate has practised on his or not. If we now disagree in anything, I aver that I agree with the Republican creed, and that he will be found on that side which leads directly to monarchy, although I hope he does not so intend it.

It is undoubtedly true that upon one point he and I are antipodes, as far apart as the poles are from each other. He thinks it an important point of *his Administration* before his time expires, to select his successor, and through the medium of a Convention, got up under his own auspices, to have the person thus selected, recommended as a suitable candidate, to use all his influence and patronage to procure the election of the person thus recommended, and *he denounces every man as a Federalist, and as opposed to his Administration, who will not vote for and support such person.*

I disagree with this whole doctrine, and insist, it is no part of his duty to *select* his successor, to have him recommended by a convention, or to use his influence or patronage to induce or coerce persons to vote for him. This is obviously the *point of disagreement*, and I willingly leave to the present generation, and to those who are to succeed us, *to say which of us holds the Republican side.*

Suppose Mr. Adams to be now President, and his term about to expire, and he had *designated* Mr. Clay as his successor, and was using all his patronage to induce persons to vote for him, and was actually travelling through Massachusetts and elsewhere, haranguing the people and denouncing General Jackson as a red-hot federalist, because he would not withdraw his name and vote for Mr. Clay. What would be said by our venerable friend in such case?

With a view to bring this doctrine home to the comprehension of every man; suppose there were now a proposition to amend the Constitution, and make it the duty of every President before his term expired to select the man in his judgment best qualified to succeed him—to have a convention called to recommend such person, and then to use all his patronage and influence to have him elected. Is there any one man in America so stupid as not to see, it would be taking from the people all choice, all power in electing their Chief Magistrate, and vesting it in the hands of one man? If such an amendment were to prevail, so far as the election of President was concerned, we would have to all intents and purposes a Monarchy. Well; if we can be prevailed on to think this practice ought to be pursued, without such an amendment, practically the government is a monarchy, because the people will have given up their right of choice and transferred it to one man. It is not me alone that is denounced, but every friend I have in Congress from the State. They are taken up one by one by name and denounced by the President as federalists, and opponents of his Administration. In what have they opposed his Administration? Did they vote against his three millions session before last? Did they vote against expunging the journals? Not they. Not one of them. Yet they are opposed to his Administration, because they will not vote for the person he has selected as his successor. It is true as to one of them, Mr. Huntsman, when the President was asked how he was, he said he did not know, he was hanging on the fence, and it was doubtful which side he would fall.

In justice to that gentleman I must be permitted to state, if there be any sincerity in man, he is as much on the Tennessee side of the fence, as any of his colleagues. I have thought it right on this occasion to bring this point plainly and distinctly to your view that you might every one see the reason why I and my friends are denounced as Federalists, opposed to the Administration and the antipodes of our esteemed and venerable Chief Magistrate.

The real offence which I have committed is not the abandonment of my principles, but that I would *not abandon* them. Not because I became the *tool* of the *opposition:* but because I would not unite with an old and valued friend in doing that, under evil and mischievous advisers, which before God I believe, would rob the people of that freedom for which our fathers "perilled their lives, their fortune and their sacred honor," and bring reproach upon our memory when we are numbered with the dead.

I have no controversy with the Chief Magistrate. I aspire to nothing which he wants. If there is any controversy it is between my countrymen, who solicited the use of my name, and him. They have solicited me to let my name be used as his successor, and I have consented. This is my whole offence. If there be anything wrong in it, who is the cause of it? It is not I who am to be put down and disgraced in this controversy, if Tennessee is either coaxed or coerced to surrender her choice. It is the people, who have placed me in the position I now occupy. The Saviour of the World, when upon earth, found among the small number of his disciples, one Judas, who not only sold, but betrayed him for his thirty pieces of silver. It were vain for one of my humble attainments, who has nothing to offer but his best efforts to promote the public welfare, to hope that all who professed to be his friends would continue to act up to that character. Already have I found more than one Judas, who by parting with their interest in me have received or expect to receive more than twice their thirty pieces. I doubt not there may be more who will yet do so; but if it is the will of Providence that the use of my name shall be of service to my fellow-men, it will be so ordered that in place of such hollow-hearted and false friends, I shall receive the aid and support of many honest men, who will desire nothing but that the government may be preserved in its purity: and if there lives the man, who can induce a majority of the people of Tennessee to abandon their own principles, and sacrifice an individual, whose name they had placed before the public to gratify his wishes, then will I admit that I never understood the character of the people among whom I have lived for almost fifty-two years.

My enemies have made a mistake. They imagine that as I have determined not to advocate my own pretensions for the most dignified station upon earth, that they may charge me with what misconduct they please, in my present station as senator, and that I must remain silent, or lay myself liable to the charge of indecency in electioneering. I cannot and will not act on any such false delicacy. If I am unjustly accused—if I am charged with entertaining principles, which do not belong to me, and these charges are made to my own constituents, by a person of the highest standing, it is due to you, it is due to the country and it is just to myself, that I not only repel the charges, but disclose the motives of those who make them.

My political friends who have placed my name before the public, are *Jeffersonian Jackson Republicans*, professing and practising now, the same creed they professed in 1828. Our motto is "*not words but deeds.*" We determine to prove our "faith in our creed by our practices." If for this we are to be denominated "new-born Whigs," we are content. Instead of being placed in the company of aliens and strangers we will still be in the embraces and arms of our long-cherished principles. "Names are nothing," said our venerable Chief Magistrate, in his letter to Mr. Monroe. Dress a tory in the garment of a whig and he will be a tory still. As well might we expect to conceal the wolf by putting on the covering of the lamb, as to suppose that we conceal the conspirator who seeks to deprive the people of their right of suffrage, by throwing over him the name of a "good old Jeffersonian democratic republican."

All political power is vested originally, in the great body of the people. It all resides there yet, except such portions of it, as they have vested in their different agents, to be used for their benefit. They have reserved to themselves the right freely to choose the two highest officers, known to the Constitution, in that mode pointed out by it.

This right is the sure rock, upon which the whole superstructure rests. Upon it I have planted myself—"The rains of slander may descend, the floods of calumny may come, the winds, the storms, and the tempests of denunciation may beat upon me," but there will I remain unmoved, until some political earthquake shall shiver both it and me to atoms.

In conclusion, permit me to add, that as to our venerable and esteemed Chief Magistrate, if in anything I have said there is the appearance of unkindness, or want of respect, it was certainly not intended. He has assailed me openly for my conduct, while in your employ. One of the first laws of our nature is self-defence. I obey that law as a freeman, whose rights and reputation are dear to him. We disagree in opinion on a most important subject. At our age, and every circumstance considered, it becomes us both to disagree, in opinion, in good temper. In times past he has had his troubles, and in them, he never was without a friend to justify or excuse his conduct when I was present. He has decreed that we shall separate, or I surrender that freedom for which my father fought. The first is the only alternative for a man determined to preserve his self-respect. He and I are poorly employed, if we lose our temper about human governments. In the course of nature they must soon cease to have any operation upon either of us. We must soon appear before a tribunal where the Judge himself will be the only witness. He cannot be *misled* as to our *acts* or our *motives;* and my prayer is, that instead of applying the rules of strict justice to either, our errors, vices and infirmities may find forgiveness in his mercy.

If thanks from the fullness of a grateful heart would avail you anything for your unshaken confidence and steady support under every change and vicissitude of life, I would pour them out as long as my strength would permit; but I feel that I have detained you already too long. I offer you the following sentiment, in which I know you will cheerfully unite.

Practices, not professions:—The Republicans of Tennessee are now what they were in 1828, *Jacksonians, following the creed of that Apostle of Liberty, Thomas Jefferson.* Should this entitle them to a "New-born" name, they care not; provided they are left in the *full enjoyment* of their inalienable right of suffrage. They would rather have even a *bad* name with good principles, than bad principles *concealed under a good name.*

The President now determined to make the issue boldly and publicly between Judge White and himself; and for that purpose, when Congress rose in 1836, he made a second visit to Tennessee. As he passed through East Tennessee, he appeared in the character of an open electioneerer. His conversations at Blountville, Jonesboro', Greenville, and Newport proved that the object of this tour was to aid Mr. Van Buren. Judge White was denounced by him as a federalist; and Mr. Van Buren was eulogized as one of the purest democrats that ever lived. He remarked to Mr. Sewell of Lebanon, that no one could be his friend, who was Judge White's; that they were as far apart as the East from the West. The same remark in substance he made in the presence of Mr. Gillespie of Nashville, a strong Jackson and Van Buren man. But he ascertained, that as his former interference, through the agency of others, could effect no change in favor of his candidate, so neither could his presence now. The freemen of Tennessee claimed the right of thinking and acting for themselves, and by their independent course, did more honor to their State than any other could have secured.

The result of this contest is known to all. Judge White lost the election, but received the handsome majority of 10,000 votes in his own State, notwithstanding the whole power of the press, the patronage of the government, and the personal popularity of General Jackson were used to prevent it. The vote in the Hermitage district was forty-three for White, eighteen for Van Buren. Besides Judge White and Mr. Van Buren, there were three other candidates in the field; Mr. Webster, Mr. Mangum, and General Harrison. The last mentioned was the third person presented, and his introduction into the canvass was supposed to have been a movement on the part of Mr. Clay. To this opinion Judge White subscribed, and avowed it to his constituents in a speech at Knoxville, 1st August, 1838. This speech follows. It is another proof of the inflexible honesty with which the speaker clung to his principles, and of the easy versatility with which his opponents held or dropped them, as the case might demand.

Fellow Citizens: I accept your invitation, not so much to partake of your hospitality, as to thank you, in great sincerity, for your continued confidence and support. You have been to me an impenetrable shield against calumniators and enemies.

After an absence of twelve months, with but little intermission, I am again among my constituents.

Thanks to a kind Providence, and to my enemies, I am in good health, ready and willing to converse with you, on all that has passed, and is likely to happen.

My political enemies sought to destroy me; they fancied it an easy task;

more of life was left than they or I supposed; their unjust attacks revived energies which I myself believed were extinct, and to all appearances they have renewed my life's lease for some ten or twenty years.

I am not only here, but in good health; and although the two last sessions of Congress were among the most laborious I have ever served, I have no want of health to plead, for any deficiency you may find in the performance of my official duties.

I am grateful to Providence, and proud before you, in the belief that I have not been that simple automaton which, by the official organ, I was represented to be, capable only of saying yea or nay to the different questions presented to the Senate for decision.

The labors of Congress, both at the called and regular sessions, have been arduous; and although but few laws of a general nature have been passed, yet it has not been from inattention to the great interests of the country. There was a continued struggle between the executive and Congress; the first wishing to obtain an unlimited discretionary power and control over the moneys belonging to the public; the latter anxiously endeavoring so to provide as to have them safely kept and secured, in such manner as to make them applicable at all times, to the wants of the public. To the opposition in the House of Representatives, the credit is due, of preventing the moneyed power from being, in due form, added to the other powers of the executive.

Shortly after I entered your service in the Senate, the great controversy commenced, which ended in *ousting* the then incumbent, and placing the late Chief Magistrate in the executive chair. The principles for which you and I contended, and which we successfully maintained, ought never be forgotten, and cannot be too often recurred to.

We contended that the powers of the executive were too great, and ought to be reduced, and limited by law.

That the expenditures of the government were extravagant, and ought to be reduced.

That it was a crime in the President, or any officer under him, to use his official station to influence the people in elections.

That all moneys which came into the treasury, beyond those which were necessary to defray the economical expenses of the government, ought to be returned to the people, who were the true and legitimate owners.

And we solemnly pledged ourselves in the face of the civilized world, that if we could obtain place and power, retrenchment and reform should be the order of the day. That the Augean stable should be thoroughly swept out and cleansed.

Emblematic of what we intended to accomplish, we chose for our motto the broom, not one of the common material, but the Hickory broom.

Hickory, when young, is of all descriptions of wood the most *tough*, *strong*, and *durable*, but when old and *worm-eaten*, the most brittle and *worthless*.

Confiding in the sincerity of our professions, the sovereign people, through the ballot box, placed our political friends in power, and after a most solemn and formal renewal of our pledges, we commenced our operations, and for the first four years I believed we were making some headway. We had checked internal improvements within the States, by mere federal power, by vetoing the Maysville Road Bill, the Rockville Road Bill, and by vetoing a bill to re-charter the Bank of the United States; but when the second four years of our terms commenced, then commenced also a controversy upon the question, who should succeed the then Chief Magistrate.

For one, I kept on, endeavoring to accomplish the task we had undertaken, but the more we swept the dirtier the stable became, and eventually we found our *broom* would not perform its office; the political moths and worms had got into it, and had eaten the splits so badly, that the moment we attempted to sweep, they broke off, and finally, when the second four years ended, and we come to look into the Augean stable, we found it ten times as full of litter and filth as it was when we commenced our operations.

In the Senate we made an effort to pass, and did actually pass, a bill to limit the power of the executive in removals from office. This bill was precisely similar to one reported by a committee of which I was a member, while Mr. Adams was in office. So far as I know, it was then approved by the whole political party to which I belonged; I therefore gave it all the support in my power, and made in favor of it, what I thought the best speech I had ever made in Congress. But alas! when we came to take the vote, had it not been for Col. Benton, who with difficulty voted for it, of all my old *Democratic friends*, I would have been found "solitary and alone" in its support.

For this vote and this speech, I have never been forgiven by these in power. I was excommunicated; that which was *sound democracy* when Mr. Adams was in power, was, in their opinion, rank federalism in the days of his successor.

They did right to excommunicate me. It was a mistake to suppose I ever belonged to such a set of *changelings*. I had been in earnest in my professions, and wished to carry them out in practice. You know what sort of a democrat I am. I claim to be a republican of the Jefferson school, such an one as my God and my education have made me. Modern democrats are a different sect entirely. They are made at any time the federal executive needs them. He makes a modern democrat out of an old federalist, or any other worse material. You and I both know some, that not many years since were made out of anti-war federalists, so rank, that during the late war the young men had thoughts of soaking them in the tanvats, on account of their tory sentiments. The process is a very simple one; the President has a political jar ready filled with a yellow metal, and by rubbing well the candidate for democracy, with this metal, his views and principles are entirely changed, and he immediately becomes a fit communicant of this modern church. Away with such democrats; they cannot, and will not long deceive the people. Ere long it will be found by all, that while this sect have democracy on their lips, at heart they are tyrants and despots.

For what did you and I toil and labor to displace Mr. Adams? It was that we might bring back the practice of the government to sound Jeffersonian principles; to an economical expenditure of the public money.

Before the second term of his successor had expired, some of my political friends believed my humble name ought to be presented to the people as a candidate for the high station he filled. Some in this assemblage well know I remonstrated against this use of my name, and foretold that with my limited capacity and humble pretensions, no hope of success ought to be entertained. They thought differently; I did not, and would not yield my assent until informed that the federal executive had threatened that if I did permit the use of my name, I should be rendered *odious to society*. This threat answered a purpose that the persuasion of friends could not. *Despotic power* never has governed and never shall govern me. My name was given to the public, and should have been, if the act had lost me the good opinion of every political friend I had upon earth, and I might almost add if it had even endangered the good opinion of my wife and children. The result is known to us all. The Administration did its worst. Its thousand presses were opened upon me and my friends, and here I am, in better health, and I think entitled to more character than when they commenced upon me. Still, let no man scorn the power of the press. To withstand its influence is a perilous effort. I have made the experiment, and now assure you, that I should feel less risk in to-morrow shouldering my musket and knapsack, and marching to the swamps of Florida for a six months' campaign against the Seminoles, than in encountering such incessant discharges of calumny and slander from all the presses which an American executive has the power to bring into action.

In this conflict you, the freemen of Tennessee, were my shield. The poisoned arrows of my enemies have fallen harmless at my feet. I have sustained no injury, and your firmness has given a brilliancy to the star which glitters over the name of Tennessee, of which we may all be proud.

For one, I am quite satisfied with the result. Let none suppose I am either disappointed or mortified. Still more, all may be assured, that with my consent my name will never again be used for any office whatever. If I ever had any aspirations for high office, time has put an end to them. I am not so old yet, as to have the childish belief, that my vigor of body and mind are to last always. In all the stations I have yet occupied I have been enabled so to acquit myself, as never to mortify my friends. Humble as my pretensions are, I have sometimes been placed in high office, as the associate of some, who have had much character among men; many of you were witnesses of the manner in which our official duties were discharged, and I am proud in the belief that my reputation has never suffered by any comparison. My hope and prayer is, that I may have discretion enough to surrender even my present station, before I am so enfeebled, either in body or mind, as to make it necessary for the interest of Tennessee to hiss me from the stage.

The late executive, then, has had his will carried into effect by the vote of the American people. They have listened to his statements "that the whole value of his Administration would be lost, unless Mr. Van Buren was elected to carry out his unfinished measures." The appointee of the late President has been elected to "finish his unfinished business."

My friends, is he not getting through it with a rapidity which you did not anticipate? From the height of prosperity, in about six months from the day of his inauguration, the country was brought to a state of unexampled embarrassment. Should he keep on in his ill-advised course, he will have performed his allotted task, long before the lapse of his four years. The great interests of the country will be all sacrificed, and by an addition of the moneyed power of the government, in an organized form, to the powers already possessed by the federal executive, the liberty of the people will be near its termination.

Do not deceive yourselves by thinking that the executive project for uniting the purse with the sword, is to be abandoned.

No such thing. It will be renewed, again and again, so long as the most distant hope of success continues. The present executive knows full well he has no distinctive character of his own. That he must conform to the will and wish of those who placed him in his present high station. He knows the means by which he acquired it, and must act out his part.

Remember that the miserable lizard can reach the pinnacle of the same spire on which the eagle proudly perches himself; but the process by which he reaches it, is very different. The latter trusting to his native strength and his own good wings, fearlessly soars aloft, and proudly perches himself on the summit, in view of all beholders. While the other, degraded reptile, stealthily and cautiously creeps up, clinging to, and ascending, that side of the column which will but screen him from observation until he reaches the pinnacle, and then slily peeps over, ready to shrink back when he finds himself discovered.

Do you ask what then is to be done, when a political lizard has taken possession of the station which ought alone to be occupied by the eagle? My answer is ready. Through the ballot-boxes, keep steadily switching him, until he descends to that level which it is the interest of mankind he should occupy.

It is useless to deny the fact, it is undeniably true, that notwithstanding all the promises, professions, and pledges of the late Administration, the executive branch of the government has become a piece of mere party machinery, operating in all elections, both State and federal. Some few years since, on the centenary birth-day of General Washington, it was beautifully said, by one of our most distinguished men, "that wherever our government became a party machine, the liberty of the country could not be preserved; that the government could, by law, protect men against murder, but not against suicide." There is great force in the remark, yet I hope it is not true. There is, however, but one remedy in either case. Take from the individual the razor with which he is about to cut his throat, and he is, for the present, safe against suicide. In the same way, when you find those in possession of executive power using it as the machine of political suicide, take away the means of mischief, and you prevent political suicide. Take from them their offices, and place them in hands more worthy, and the Republic may yet be saved.

The late Administration came in on the question of reform, and a retrenchment of expenditures. Pray, what abuse has been corrected? Not one! What retrenchment has taken place? None. Abuses have been multiplied and expenditures have been increased.

Mr. Adams was turned out because he was expending from twelve to thirteen millions of dollars per year, and now we are expending from thirty-five to forty millions per annum.

Can any man be so stupid as not to see this is all wrong? Can the babble of democracy sanctify such a course?

Partisans may sing democracy until, like the locusts, their backs are split, but it will not satisfy the people. We must be taught two things, and that speedily. We must have *sound currency*, and the government must expend less money.

There is a constant press to increase offices, and to increase salaries. Can any friend of the Administration put his finger upon any message, specifying the office to be abolished, or the salary to be decreased? Yet they prate of democracy.

A short time since, we had a great struggle to know what should be done with surplus money in the treasury. Now the struggle is to know how to raise enough to keep the government in motion.

That which we had, is all gone. Onr currency is destroyed, and with it the commerce of the country. Our sources of revenue are the sales of public lands, and duties upon importations of goods.

While the currency is deranged, both these sources of revenue are drying up, and we are without revenue to supply actual wants, and what have we resorted to? To making paper money; to issuing treasury notes.

A short time since, we and our families were to be made glad, by peeping at our Benton yellow jackets, that were peeping through our purses at us: but what now have we? Nothing but yellow-backed treasury notes, intended to supply the double purpose of a deficit in the treasury, and a circulating medium.

Since the first of September last, we have authorized the issuing of twice ten millions of treasury notes, and why? Because we needed money, and had it not.

The credit of the United States is good, and we have an express power to borrow money; but if we borrow, the public will see that a national debt is contracting, and will inquire into the expenditures; therefore, the Administration prefer a resort to treasury notes. They appear to cost nothing, and if tolerated, extravagant expenditures may be continued without alarm to the public. This contrivance ought to be nipped in the bud.

Treasury notes are unconstitutional, except used as a means to procure a loan. Bills of credit cannot be used as a currency, by either federal or State authority. If tolerated, we will soon have an extravagant government, and a depreciated paper currency. Whenever an amount of treasury notes is issued as a currency, beyond the duties and sales of the public lands, they must and will depreciate, and the mass of the people are to be the sufferers.

Against these issues I have raised my voice, and recorded my votes, and shall continue to do so.

You are ready to ask me what is a remedy for the evils under which the country labors? I tell you plainly. The remedy must be found in a firm and manly exercise of the elective franchise. Vote for no man, who will not firmly and fearlessly exert himself to prevent these now in power from accomplishing the purposes they have in view, and when the time arrives, let us exert ourselves to displace the present Chief Magistrate.

I may ask, who will you put in his place? Is he not one of your own original party and will you go against a man of your own principles?

In all sincerity I will answer these questions. In the first place then I say, at present, I do not know whom we ought to endeavor to put in the place of the present incumbent. Two years and more are to elapse before the election. Previous to that time every man whose name has been mentioned as a probable candidate, may be removed from the stage of action, as matters may be disclosed in relation to him, which may change entirely our opinions of his character and qualifications. There is only one thing on this subject upon which my mind is at rest, and that is that for the present incumbent I will never vote, while I entertain the same opinion of him which I now do.

I have now the same politics, and the same political objects to accomplish, which I had in 1828, when you and I successfully exerted ourselves to elect the late Chief Magistrate.

Towards the accomplishment of this object, we have made no progress whatever. We have been deceived and disappointed, and in my opinion the present incumbent has been the chief instrument in effecting this deception and disappointment. To continue him longer in office would therefore be giving up all wish for those improvements in our public affairs, which I believe the interests of the country pressingly require.

Before the time of election arrives, some man, not now thought of as a candidate, holding political opinions similar to my own, may be brought before the public with a reasonable prospect of success. In that event he should have my cordial support.

Although much has been said during the last session of Congress on the subject of the next election ; yet I have taken no part in it, either directly or indirectly, and to no one of those spoken of as candidates have I in any degree committed myself. I am now as free to make my choice as any of you can be.

I have however reflected on this subject, in all its bearings and contingencies, and am free to state, that from present indications, I think it most probable Mr. Van Buren will be a candidate for re-election, and that he will be opposed by some one, only, of the old opposition. Very probably Mr. Clay. In that event I have asked myself the question, what course ought I to pursue?

For Mr. Van Buren I have already said I never can and never will vote, if he pursues the course pursued for the last few years. My motto is "not words, but deeds." I judge of him by what he has done, and caused to be done, and not by what he has professed.

It is true he has professed, at times, to belong to the same political party to which I have ever adhered; but his practice has on no one point corresponded with that profession.

He is a tariff man and voted for that most odious of all our tariffs, that of 1828. I am against all tariffs for protection merely.

He is for internal improvements by the federal government where the object is what he calls national, and actually voted for the erection of toll gates on the Cumberland Road.

I deny that the federal government possesses any such power within the State.

He is against a national bank, and so am I, but then he goes for a treasury bank, which I think is worse than a national bank, by incorporating stockholders.

He is for increasing executive power and patronage. I am for diminishing and limiting them.

He is in favor of the federal executive, and officers under him using their power to influence public opinion in elections; I am decidedly opposed to any such practices.

He is in favor of the Chief Magistrate, in office, selecting his successor, and using all his influence to have him elected.

I think such a practice calculated to convert our Republic into a Monarchy, and therefore believe no man ought to be President who holds such doctrine.

It is useless now to pursue this contrast any further, You will readily perceive it is an entire mistake to suppose we ever belonged to the same party; yet it is true we once nominally did. He came into it, and gave his support at rather a late day, when possibly he believed he would succeed whether he joined us or not.

To him I have still another objection. He did not come into office upon any character of his own, and no man is fit for the station he now occupies unless he attains it upon the strength of his own principles and character. He is nothing but a mere tuft of political misletoes, having no root of his own, adhering to and supported by, the limb of a distinct trunk altogether, and must as infallibly perish whenever that trunk ceases to nourish him, as the tuft on yonder oak, whenever that oak shall have decayed and fallen.

The question then recurs, should Mr. Clay be the opposing candidate, what ought I to do?

I answer I ought to exercise my right of suffrage, so as most to promote the public welfare. I am entirely opposed to following the exam ple of throwing away my vote, because the community will neither select me nor the man of my choice. It is my duty deliberately and impartially to compare the principles and characters of those between whom the choice is to be made, and to vote according to my best judgment. Permit me, then, for a few moments, to draw your attention to a contrast between these two gentlemen.

Mr. Van Buren is in favor of a protective tariff, and voted for that of of 1828.

Mr. Clay is also in favor of a protective tariff, but did not vote for that of 1828. He is the author of the Compromise Act of 1832, which settles the question to the satisfaction of the country at large, and which he believes ought not to be disturbed.

Mr. Clay thinks the federal government has the power to make internal improvements within the States, but ought not to exercise the power except upon an object of general or national utility, and that now, as the States have taken up the business of internal improvements, the federal government ought not to meddle with it, but rather aid the States with means by distributing, when our funds will permit us, the proceeds of our public lands.

Mr. Van Buren thinks the federal government can and ought to make internal improvements when the object is national; but has no such power where the object is local.

This opinion I think more exceptional than that of Mr. Clay, because under it, the President has a discretionary power to make improvements where he pleases, by calling the objects national, and refusing them at pleasure, by calling the objects local.

Mr. Clay thinks we have the power to charter a national bank, and that we ought to exercise it.

Mr. Van Buren is against a national bank, but is in favor of a treasury bank.

The last is in my judgment the most dangerous opinion.

One great objection to incorporating a national bank is a fear that the directors and president might co-operate in elections, and if they did, that the moneyed power united with executive patronage would be an overmatch for any power in the hands of the people.

Now in case of a national bank owned by stockholders, this Union might, or might not take place; but in case of a treasury bank the Union is certain, and everything is in due form of law put into the power of the President.

Even upon these great leading points, I think Mr. Clay greatly preferable to Mr. Van Buren; but the contrast ought not to stop here.

Mr. Van Buren is in favor of executive power and patronage in its very worst forms and ramifications. Mr. Clay is in favor of reducing and limiting them by law.

In a few words I must state, that I think the great difference between the two men is, that Mr. Van Buren will *profess* any opinions which will gain him most votes in an election, and that when elected, he will practice on whatever principles will give to himself and his partisans the most money, without any regard to the great interest of the country.

That Mr. Clay is a bold, ambitious, frank, and talented man. That in office he would be ambitious so to administer the government as to make for himself the reputation of a great man, in the estimation of enlightened men in his own day, and of posterity in all time to come.

I have thus frankly stated to you my opinion in relation to these men. I have done so the more willingly, because I am under no obligation to either, nor have I anything to hope from them.

It has been the fashion with you and with me, to endeavor to put down and keep down Mr. Clay in time past. In turn he has helped to put and keep me down. His third candidate for the Presidency furnished the only argument which enabled the late Chief Magistrate to transfer the Southern States to his candidate. For all this I care not. I had no claims on Mr. Clay. On several great questions we had ever disagreed and still do. Should I support him in the coming contest, it will not be because I have changed or intend to change my principles; but because I like his better than those of Mr. Van Buren, and because should he be elected I expect much benefit to the country; but not all I would expect by electing a candidate with whom I accorded in opinion, upon all great questions.

Be it therefore remembered, that if I sustain Mr. Clay, neither he nor his friends are to believe for a moment that I surrender any one of my political principles. Far otherwise; I will retain them all, and should I still be in the Senate, if he were elected, and attempted to carry out any principle in which I have disagreed with him, he would find in me the same opposition I have ever manifested.

In voting in elections, as in the discharge of every other duty to society, it is my business to do all the good I can, and if I cannot get a candi date to vote for, who comes up to my political standard, to select that one who comes nearest to it.

Fellow-citizens: I thank you for your continued confidence and good opinion; I thank you for the patient manner in which you have given me your attention. Had I the voice now, which I had, when, forty-two years ago I first addressed my countrymen on yonder hill (pointing to the court-house), you would have been enabled to hear me without crowding together in so small a compass: but your kindness can always remedy my imperfections. I ask you to join me in the sentiment which I will read, and pass to your president to be proposed as one nearest to my heart:—

"*Tennessee.*"—May she ever adhere to her own principles—remain too honest to be purchased, too well informed to be mislead, and too unyielding to be subdued. In every struggle between parties may her sons rally as a body-guard to protect the Constitution.

In reply to this avowal of Judge White's sentiments respecting Mr. Clay, the latter gentleman addressed to him the following letter; which is published in justice to that distinguished statesman, and as proof that the charge of a coalition between Judge White and the opposition was unfounded.

ASHLAND, *Aug.* 27, 1838.

DEAR SIR: I am indebted to you, or to some other friend, for a copy of the speech which you delivered on the late occasion of a public dinner with which you and Mr. Bell were complimented on your return from Washington. I have attentively perused it, and with much satisfaction; and I cannot deny myself the pleasure of saying to you that it is candid, independent, and in perfect consistency with your own principles, character, and course. I might not be willing to admit the ambition which you ascribe to me; but I do not mean to insist upon that observation of yours as detracting from the general fairness of the speech. My chief object, however, in now addressing you, is to correct an error into which you have fallen, in respect to the last Presidential election. You appear to be under the impression that Gen. Harrison was a candidate brought out by me, and brought out to avenge injuries which I had previously experienced from you. Now, I assure you, sir, that I had no more agency in presenting the General as a candidate than you had. It was done without any prompting of mine, and without any prior consultation with me, Nor did I, during the whole of the canvass, take any active part in it. I felt the difficulty of supporting the General, on account of the military basis of his pretensions: and I felt the difficulty of supporting you, on account of the difference which existed between us on some leading points. But I never forgot that it was due to my own character to avoid becoming an active partisan. Towards the close of the canvass, in October of 1836, a great barbecue was gotten up in sight of my house, connected with the presidential election, and I was invited to it. I could not decline going; and very much against my wishes, I was drawn out to say a few words on the subject of the approaching election. The main idea which I expressed was, that it was the duty of the people, in my opinion, to make the most determined opposition to Mr. Van Buren; and for one, I declared my hearty preference for either of the other candidates. I spoke of you in terms of high respect, and avowed my preference of you to Mr. Van Buren. Finally, I stated to the meeting that I should vote for Gen. Harrison, because I thought that he combined the greatest prospects of defeating Mr. Van Buren. Most certainly the General was not my first choice. I should have preferred Mr. Webster to him, and so stated.

The condition of the opposition to Mr. Van Buren at the last election, was unfortunate. No mode was devised, and none seemed practicable, to present a single candidate in opposition to him. The Southern, and Southwestern States would not unite in the election of Gen. Harrison or Mr. Webster, and their friends would not unite in your election. Under these circumstances it was thought to be the best that could be done, by those who took an active part in those matters, that all three of you should be run. On a review of the past, I think you must admit that the disappointment was greatest in those States which were supposed to be friendly to you. That may have been in consequence of the number of candidates in the field; but that cause did not prevent Gen. Harrison from obtaining quite as many votes as were ever expected. And I am sure you will regard it only as matter of history when I express the opinion that if the General had been out of the way, I do not think that you could have obtained the votes which he received. They would have gone to Mr. Webster, or, which is more probable, have been divided between him and Mr. Van Buren. In the course of a long conversation with Mr. Webster, months before the election, I expressed to him the opinion of the expediency of his retirement from the contest, but he did not retire.

If, as by this time I hope, you will believe that I had no agency in putting forward Gen. Harrison, and certainly no purpose of injuring you, you will do me no more than justice in believing the assurance that I now make; that I felt no injury from *you*, which required to be avenged. I certainly felt no obligation to the party of the late President to which you were once attached; but I had never understood that you had been distinguished by any peculiar enmity towards me. And at the period of the late election I regarded you with feelings far different from those of a political enemy or opponent.

I thought these explanations due. I hope they will be received in the same frank and friendly spirit in which they are made.

I hope you have recovered from the fatigue of our late exhausting session of Congress. Although I have not been five miles from home since my return, I feel the want of further repose.

Mrs. Clay desires her respects to be presented to Mrs. White, and I beg leave to add mine also, and for yourself, assurances of the most cordial esteem and regard of

Your faithful and ob't servant,

H. Clay.

The Hon. Hugh L. White.

CHAPTER XVI.

RETIREMENT FROM PUBLIC LIFE.

In the fall of 1838, Judge White's health became much impaired, in consequence of an attack of congestive fever, which had prevailed to an alarming extent in Knoxville. Under the belief that he should be unable to reach Washington in time for the meeting of Congress, he sent in his resignation, which Governor Cannon refused to accept.

As soon as it was ascertained that the legislature of 1839 contained a majority of Administration members, it was at once determined by them, to instruct him out of the seat which he had so repeatedly desired to resign, but had retained to gratify the leading men of their own party. To effect this object as speedily as possible, and at the same time to avoid, if it might be, the odium that must attach to them in consequence of such a course, they, in the first place, endeavored to make his resignation, which had been tendered the preceding fall, take effect then; and a resolution was passed by the Senate, calling upon the governor for the correspondence which had passed between them.

In answer to which resolution his excellency sent in reply the following communication :—

Gentlemen of the Senate : In compliance with your resolution of the 11th instant, I have the honor to state that there is not in my possession, or in the executive department, or ever has been, a copy of the correspondence between the Hon. Hugh L. White and myself, touching his resignation as senator. No copy of the same has ever been taken, nor is his letter to me on that subject in my possession, or in the executive department, it having been returned to him, by his request, a short time after it was received. I have kept no memorandum of this communication, nor do I now remember its precise date. I am under the impression, however, that it was in the early part of November last, that I received a communication from this honorable senator informing me of the severe affliction he had suffered and the very feeble state of his health at that time; also expressing his belief that he would not be able to reach

Congress by the ensuing session. And in consequence of his inability he proposed resigning his seat in the Senate of the United States in order that a *pro tem.* appointment might be made by me in due time. On the reception of this letter, I determined to suspend my official action on the resignation thus tendered for a reasonable length of time, for the restoration of the health of our senator, sufficiently to enable him to proceed to the discharge of his duties; which determination was communicated to him with such reasons and suggestions as at that time were deemed appropriate, and resulted in an acquiescence of the withdrawal of his letter containing the proposition to resign, which was returned to him by his request, without my acceptance of his resignation or my official action on it in any way whatever.

This is, according to the best of my recollection, the substance of the correspondence which took place between the honorable senator and myself, during the time and on the subject referred to in your resolution. His praiseworthy course on this occasion afforded to my mind strong additional evidence (to a long course of the most faithful public services) of the most exalted and refined sense of honor and honesty, by which he has been influenced, and few examples of which have been set before us, by the public men of our times. It has seldom happened that those occupying similar situations, whether in reference to the general or State governments, have shown, under such circumstances, equal patriotism and devotion to the public interests, and in the assumption of authority on my part, which has been exercised in this case by me as executive of the State, I am conscious of having been influenced by honest views of the interests of the people for whom I have acted, together with what was due under the circumstances, to a well tried and faithful public servant; and in assuming the responsibility which belongs to the station I have occupied, in the discharge of this part of my duty, I cannot for a moment believe that I have misconstrued the just and generous character of the people of our State or that of their senators in the legislature, with regard to the kind and indulgent feelings which animate them towards those faithful public servants who have rendered faithful and important services to our country, to every citizen of which, as well as to your honorable body, I feel equally responsible for every official act.

"Very respectfully,

"NEWTON CANNON.

"*Executive office, Nashville, Oct. 12th.*"

Resolutions to the following effect were shortly introduced by Mr. Levin H. Coe, instructing their senators, and requesting their representatives to vote for them—

1. Against a national bank.
2. In favor of the sub-treasury.

3. Against Mr. Crittenden's Bill to secure the freedom of elections, or any similar bill.

4. Against the distribution of the proceeds of the public lands.

5. In favor of a bill repealing all duties on imported salt.

6. To support in good faith the leading measures and policy of the present Administration.

While these resolutions were under discussion in the House of Representatives, previous to their passage in that body, the representative from Knox county, Gen. Jacobs, by reading the following letter gave the House full assurance of the course which Judge White would pursue in the event of his receiving such instructions.

Sept. 5th, 1839.

Dear Sir: Your note of this date has been handed me a few hours since. By it you request me to inform you what course I will feel it my duty to pursue, in case the General Assembly should pass resolutions instructing their senators to vote for the bill, denominated the Sub-Treasury Bill, or resolutions simply expressing the opinion that such bill ought to pass, without any *express instructions* to the senators to vote for it.

I have long been an advocate for the doctrine of instructions, and am of opinion that when a senator receives instructions from the legislature of his State, upon any subject, when no constitutional question is involved, he ought to conform his conduct to, and vote according to such instructions, or resign; and I have never been able to see any good reason why the expression of an opinion by the legislature should not be considered as instructions, although no express instructions accompany such expression of opinion, unless the legislature say they do not intend an expression of their opinion to control the conduct or votes of their senators.

I have considered a senator as the agent or trustee of the *people* of his State, and that he ought to carry into effect, so far as is in his power, the sentiments of a majority of the people he represents upon all subjects, when he can do so, without violating the Constitution. He ought to suppose the legislature, who are his immediate constituents, express no opinion, or give no instructions which do not accord with the sentiments of a majority of the people, and if he does not conform his conduct to the expressed opinion of the people, through the agency of the legislature, he is guilty of a breach of trust, and does not faithfully represent his State.

The Sub-Treasury Bill, so far as I am advised, does not involve any constitutional question; therefore, if the General Assembly deem it proper to instruct their senators to vote for its passage, or consider it wise to express the opinion that it ought to pass, in either of these cases I should consider myself bound, either to give it the support of my vote, or to resign; and I should certainly adopt the latter branch of the alternative. No consideration could induce me knowingly to misrepresent the people of Tennessee, especially upon a subject so important, and by my vote, no bill productive of so many ill consequences, as I think this would be, shall ever be passed. Consistently, therefore, with my principles, no course would be left me but to resign.

I have heretofore opposed the sub-treasury, and voted against it, under a firm conviction, that if passed, it would be productive of much mischief; I believed a large majority of the people of Tennessee entertained the same opinion. At the last session our General Assembly instructed me to pursue this course; with much pleasure I conformed to those instructions, and I cannot now act so inconsistent a part as to support a measure, in my judgment fraught with such ruinous consequences to society. I still believe a majority of the people of this State accord with me in opinion upon this subject, but *as a senator*, do not consider myself at liberty to go behind the legislature in search of public opinion. I will act as if I believed they correctly expressed the opinion of my State, and if they do not, they are accountable, not to me, but to the people who are our common constituents or masters.

It is true, as I have heretofore said, that in 1834, when the sub-treasury was first spoken of, I thought favorably of it, and would have supported it, provided my political friends had agreed with me in opinion, but the matter is now entirely changed in my view of this subject. Then my idea was that the details should be such as to lessen, not to increase, the power of the executive over the public moneys. Now the project is to give, in my opinion, almost unlimited control over them.

Then it was very doubtful whether safe banks could be induced to take charge of the public moneys upon reasonable and fair terms. Now, no such doubts are entertained.

Then, I had entire confidence in the executive; now, that confidence does not exist.

Then, we had not the benefit of experience on this subject. The sub-treasury has now been in actual operation for several years, and I consider that this experience ought to have taught us all, that, under its operations, the public money will be unsafe, and society will be demoralized by the illegal use of it, and that the power of the federal executive will be increased to an extent inconsistent with our liberties.

It was my intention not to obtrude my opinions upon this, or any other subject, upon any of the members of the General Assembly, but at the same time, I can have no inducement to conceal them. I have, therefore, endeavored very briefly to answer all the points embraced in your note, and have no difficulty in giving the permission you ask, to use my answer in any way you may think proper.

With sentiments of the most sincere regard, I am

Your ob't servant,

HUGH L. WHITE.

Gen. SOLOMON D. JACOBS.

Completely frustrated in their previous attempt, the political opponents of Judge White now determined to effect what seemed to be their sole object without regard to consequences. After the disposal of a long and tedious series of obstructing amendments offered by whig senators, Mr. Gillespie, at the end of a month's hard labor, moved the previous question, and succeeded in carrying through the resolutions at midnight, November 8th, by a strict party vote.

These proceedings brought upon their contrivers the reprobation of the country, as is shown by the tone of the public journals of the day.

The "Madisonian" thus treats the subject :—

Since the destructives carried the State of Tennessee by political turpitude and chicanery, they have been unceasing in their efforts to push Judge White from his seat. We do not wonder at it—there is a daily beauty in the presence of that pure and exalted patriot, which makes this hideous; hence the ghost of the blood-stained Banquo was not a more unwelcome visitor to the tyrant at his feast, than would be Judge White to the ruling party in the Senate. We most sincerely trust he will not resign. At this particular juncture, the nation at large, as well as the State of Tennessee in particular, has a deep interest in his retaining his seat. We cannot bear the idea that a station held with honor to himself and usefulness to the nation, should be yielded to make room for some of those suppliant tools that have been engendered through the base degeneracy of the times. Although in some instances, the private station may be the post of honor, yet in others it becomes the duty of the statesman to yield his individual views to the wishes of the country. We feel persuaded that however much Judge White may have desired repose, their base attempts at intimidation will nerve him to a proper resistance of their nefarious schemes.

The "N. Y. Times," in speaking of the movement of the ruling party in Tennessee, says :—

We are sorry to say that the manner in which these gentlemen were "instructed" out of their seats, was grossly rude and insulting. More disgusting samples of low-bred abuse than are to be found in the speeches made by some of the locofoco members *at* Judge White during the debate on the instructing resolutions, never disgraced a parliamentary body. This portion of the picture is, however, somewhat relieved by a contemplation of the beautiful dilemma in which the locofocos were involved by their acute and eloquent opponents. So completely were the former entangled in a web of contradictions, so ludicrous were their perplexed efforts to steer between the *Charybdis* of giving the *lie* to Gen. Jackson, by voting against resolutions embodying his very words, and the yet more awful *Scylla* of repudiating the sub-treasury by endorsing them, that we suppose we must find some palliation for the overflow of their malignity in the agony of their annoyance.

The "Louisville Journal" thus commented upon the subject: —

The speaker of the lower branch decided that an amendment could not be laid on the table without carrying with it the main question. This decision was clearly correct; it was in accordance with all parliamentary usage. Some members, however, in order to test the sense of the House, took an appeal to that body; and the decision was almost unanimously confirmed, the locofocos going for it in a mass. Well, only two or three days afterwards, while the instructing resolutions were up for consideration, the whigs began to torment the locofocos by proposing certain troublesome amendments, which the locos did not dare to vote either for or against. The only way they saw of getting rid of them, was to *lay them on the table;* and so in direct defiance of the previous decision, the *speaker* decided and all the party except three sustained him in it, that *an amendment* might be laid on the table without carrying with it the main proposition.

The following is from the "Hamilton Gazette," a neutral paper, published in Tennessee:—

Well might the venerable White exclaim against his own State, as did the noble Cæsar against his fellow and friend Brutus when he too stabbed him in the Roman Senate. Judge White is an old public servant; he has won a good name from every dispassionate man. We are told that in Washington City his unbending morality and inflexible patriotism, manifested by every action public and private—his lofty demeanor and talents of the first order—his attention to business, and whole general bearing is so much assimilated to that of the "father of his country," that he stands pre-eminent, even among the Clays, Calhouns, Websters and Adamses. Yet this man, for no other reason than because his views and sentiments do not exactly tally with the majority of the legislature, has been requested to resign his seat in the Senate of the United States. It is not often that we permit our feelings to lead us into a censorious notice of either party. But we confess, that when we think of the disgrace that has been brought upon our State, by the reckless mendacity and total disregard of every principle of right, to foster the pretensions of a party, our "gorge rises," and we are almost disposed to think that a worse curse is coming upon us through the management of our rulers, than rested upon France in her most bloody era. If it were possible for a more judicious choice than Judge White to be made in Tennessee, the case would not be so bad. But every man in the majority, knows full well, that if half a dozen of their leaders were thrown into a crucible, purified, and cast into one man, that he would fall short of the merits of Judge White."

The party being now anxious to precipitate measures at Washington, on the 13th January, Mr. Wright called up the Sub-Treasury Bill in the Senate, and pressed its consideration on that body. Thereupon, Judge White rose and said, that "he held in his hand a number of resolutions adopted by the legislature of his State, one of which instructed him to vote in favor of the bill, proposed for the consideration of the Senate to-day."

He requested permission to read to the Senate his reply to the legislature, which was granted.

Mr. White then addressed the Senate to the following effect:

Mr. President: I have a duty to perform this morning, before we proceed to any regular order of the day. Presuming that the business of presenting petitions is now over, I proceed to discharge it with as little delay as possible.

When I reached this place on the 29th of November last. I was furnished by one of our officers with a letter, which contained several resolutions adopted by the legislature of Tennessee, condemning one of the votes given by the senators from that State, at the last session, and instructing them how to act in future, on many subjects. I believed my duty to my State, and to the public, would be best discharged by remaining in my seat and continuing to attend to the business of the Senate, in the manner I had been accustomed to do, until some of the subjects *specifically* mentioned in the resolutions should be placed before the body for discussion. On this day of the last week, the honorable chairman of the committee of finance reported a bill, commonly called the Sub-Treasury Bill, and gave notice that on this day he would ask for its consideration. This being one of the subjects mentioned in the resolutions, the time has arrived when, in my opinion, it is respectful to the legislature of my State, that I should present them to this body, to the end that the members of it, as well as the community at large, may be made acquainted with what the General Assembly has chosen to express as public opinion in Tennessee. I move that the preamble and resolutions, which I now send to the secretary, may be read, printed, and laid on the table.

After the resolutions had been read, Mr. White proceeded and said,

Mr. President—As I am now a member of this body, and my instructions have been read and ordered to be printed, I consider it proper that I should follow the example set by others, and make equally public the conclusions to which I have come in relation to them.

The subjects of which they treat are of vital interest to the country, and I am anxious that the opinions I entertain and express upon them should neither be *misunderstood* nor *misrepresented*; I will, therefore, take the liberty of deviating from my usual course of delivering my sentiments (which has been not even to use notes), and will now read the answer which I have prepared, and intend, without delay, to forward to the same body which adopted the resolutions.

Mr. White then read his answer in the following words

To the Honorable the General Assembly of the State of Tennessee.

Gentlemen: On the 29th of November last, in the city of Washington, I received a copy of sundry preambles and six resolutions, which appear to have been adopted by you on the 14th of that month, instructing your senators, and requesting the representatives in the Congress of the United States how to act on a variety of subjects.

An answer to the resolutions would have been immediately given had I not believed it my duty to remain at the post assigned me by your predecessors, until some of the matters specified in them should be presented to the Senate for its action. Although I might entertain an opinion different from that employed by your honorable body, and might be unwilling to surrender that opinion; yet if no case should be presented for the action of the Senate, in relation to which such difference of opinion existed, I could perceive no good reason why I should state what course I would pursue, upon a subject, which might never be presented for consideration. Now, however, bills are presented to the Senate upon some of the subjects embraced in your resolutions, and I deem it my duty, without further delay, to inform you, that I cannot obey the instructions contained in some of those resolutions, and respectfully to assign some of the reasons which influence my conduct.

That I may be the better understood, I will notice each of the resolutions in the order in which they were adopted.

First. As one of your senators, I am instructed "to vote against the chartering by Congress of a national bank."

This instruction corresponds with the opinion I have repeatedly expressed and acted on, and I could now feel no difficulty in conforming my vote to your wishes on this subject.

Secondly. I am instructed "to vote for, and use all fair and proper exertions to procure the passage of the measure brought forward in the

Congress of the United States, commonly called the Sub-Treasury Bill, or Independent Treasury Bill," &c., &c.

The following, with many other reasons, induced me to believe I ought not to comply with the instructions contained in this resolution.

It has often happened, and will generally be the case, that a considerable time must elapse between the receipt of public money from the debtor to the United States, and its disbursement to their creditors; during this interval the money will be much more safe in the custody of well selected banks than it can be in the hands of individuals, supposing them to be faithful.

Supposing any one of your honorable body had one hundred thousand dollars of his own money, which he did not intend to use for six or nine months, and lived in the vicinity of a bank of respectable standing, would he keep the money in his own house, under his own care, or would he deposit it in bank for safe-keeping until he wished to use it? If he was a prudent man, regarding his own interest, he certainly would deposit it.

Are we then justified in taking less care of the people's money than a prudent man would take of his own? With great deference to your better judgment, I think not.

It often happens that the receiving officers have on hand much larger sums than that named in the supposed case, and as the sum is increased and the time it is to be kept between its receipt and disbursement enlarged, the danger of loss, when in the hands of an individual, is increased likewise.

Again. All experience teaches us that large sums of public money left in the hands of individuals will be misused and squandered. It will either be used by the individual himself for his own purposes, or loaned to importunate friends whom he may wish to accommodate, and who are sure not to be able to return it when called for.

It is said banks are irresponsible, therefore not to be trusted. In my opinion, generally, they are more responsible than individuals. They have more means with which to pay, and if they fail to make payments when required, they are as much amenable to the process of a court of justice as individuals are; and in addition, they are to be found with much more certainty, as a corporation aggregate can very seldom abscond, or leave the country, which an individual easily can, and often does do when he misuses the public money.

We need all the checks which can reasonably be imposed on our collecting and disbursing officers. Banks have been found to furnish one highly beneficial upon both of these classes. By a regulation between the treasury department and each deposit bank, the latter has been required at short periods to furnish its account current with the treasurer, and on the face of it to show all sums deposited to his credit, when such deposits were made, and by whom. By comparing this account with the accounts furnished by the respective officers themselves, it can readily be discovered whether they are misusing the public money or not. By the proposed change, and allowing the collector or receiver to be himself the *keeper*, until the money is wanted for use, you have no check whatever, and the whole money received by an officer may be squandered before it is wanted for disbursement, without any means of detection.

I, therefore, conclude the Sub-Treasury Bill ought not to be passed, if there were no other objections to it save that of the public money being less secure. But there are other weighty objections.

The only plausible reason which can be assigned why we should discard banks entirely and appoint sub-treasurers, keepers of the public funds, must be, that the banks are unworthy of confidence.

If that be so, does it not necessarily follow that you ought either not to receive any bank notes in discharge of dues to the government, or if received, that you should order the officer with whom they are deposited for safe-keeping, immediately to call upon the banks for specie to their amount. It is absurd to say we will not deposit with the bank, because we have no confidence in it, and at the same time to allow our officers to receive bank notes, and retain *them* in the hands of our officer, up to the time we wish to pay the money away. There is less probability that the banks would redeem their notes in specie when called on, than that they would deny the payment in specie for money received on deposit.

The practice, then, of receiving nothing but specie from debtors, or of immediately converting the notes received into specie, and locking that up until the time of disbursement arrives, must be resorted to, in order to carry out your wishes.

This, I apprehend, would be ruinous to society. A large portion of the specie that might otherwise circulate, would be withdrawn from the use of every person a considerable portion of each year. This would affect the prices of property, of labor, and of everything else, and would render it next to impossible for even a prudent man, who happened to be in debt, ever to extricate himself.

Beside this, the heavy draws for specie upon banks, would compel them, in a short time, either to wind up or to do a very precarious business. Whenever a suspension of specie payments would take place, we would have a depreciated paper currency, on which to do the business of the country, and specie would become an article of merchandise. The man in office, or who had a job or contract with the government, would receive his salary or his pay in specie, which he would immediately sell for bank paper, receiving a premium of some ten or fifteen per centum, and with that paper pay his debts or purchase such property as he might wish. This practice is at this moment in operation. For every hundred dollars paid me as a member of Congress, I can receive one hundred and eight or nine dollars in bank notes, and with them pay the landlord who feeds, or the tailor who clothes me.

It has appeared to me, if we commence this entire operation which your resolution contemplates, and go into this thorough hard money system, we shall presently, in Tennessee especially, be in a deplorable condition. Look at its effects: all debts and taxes are to be paid to the federal government in hard money, or in bank notes, for which the specie will be immediately received, and the specie thus received is to be locked up securely, until it is paid out in discharge of some debt due by the government. Suppose our first year's taxes paid, in all the States, amounting to some twenty-five or thirty millions of dollars. That is only to be returned into circulation when the federal government pays the debts which it owes. What chance will Tennessee have to receive, by federal disbursement, any portion of what she may have paid? We have no forts, no foundries, no arsenals, no fortifications, no army, no navy, navy-yards, or dry-docks. In short, we have next to no objects upon which the federal government expends money; therefore none of it would be returned to us. We must pay up our full proportion of all indirect taxes in hard money, with a certainty that little or none of it would be returned to us by federal expenditures, and in the course of a very few years, we must be drained of every hard dollar we now have.

There is another class of objections against this measure, entitled, I think, to still more grave considerations.

The addition it will make to the powers of the federal executive. Every officer with which the money is to be deposited, or left for safe-keeping, will be *appointed* by the President, and *removable* at his pleasure. We might as well give it to the President himself, as entrust it to those whom he can and will control.

This plan will multiply officers and increase considerably our expenses at its commencement, and in the end, no man can foresee the swarms of dependents it may generate, and the additions it may occasion to our expenditures of the public money.

By the use of the patronage already belonging to that officer, we all know and feel that a large portion of the power vested in the legislative department exists only in name; it is in substance vested in, and expressed by, the President as he wills; shall we, then, give him a controlling power over all the pecuniary resources of the federal government? For one, I cannot consent to it.

Lastly, this sub-treasury is nothing but a stepping-stone to a bank created by the federal government, bottomed on its own funds, attached to the treasury department, and all placed at the control of the President, or of those who will never have any will which does not correspond with his.

It appears to me, no reasonable man can think if we commence this system we are to stop short of such a bank.

Let one year only pass with all your revenue in specie, and that locked up, your State banks and paper currency deranged, and what then? Those who may wish to carry out this system will then recur to the sound doctrine advanced by the late President Jackson, "that the money of the country ought not to be kept locked up by the government, any more than the arms belonging to the citizens—both will be sure to be misused." And it will be urged that society is suffering for a sound circulating medium; we must pass a law authorizing this money to be loaned, the interest will ease us of the payment of much taxes, and by circulating treasury notes, or drafts drawn by one of these treasurers upon another, we will have a sound paper currency, good everywhere, and bottomed on a metallic basis. This doctrine will become the *democratic* doctrine, and every man who opposes it will be denounced as a bank-bought federalist; the law will pass, and in due form we shall have the *Treasury Bank;* and what then?

The purse and the sword will be united, and a power to *increase the purse*, as need may require, not by adding eagles and hard dollars to our funds, but by issues of paper, in such sums as may be deemed necessary and proper. This bank, with its pecuniary means, and the credit and resources it will possess, can either destroy or render subservient to the views of the executive any State banks which may be in existence. The whole moneyed power, not only of the federal government, but of all State banks, being thus placed in the hands of the President, he will be able to control the destinies of the country.

His *will* becomes the law of the land. He will never again have to appeal to "*the sober second thought of the people*" to carry any favorite measure. His first recommendation will always secure its speedy enactment into a law.

In the views which I take of this subject, I may be in error; but they are sincerely entertained. In the first instance, I placed my vote against it, under the belief that such were the sentiments of the people I represented. Afterwards, I was instructed by the legislature to continue my opposition. I did so, from a conviction that I was right; and nothing would give me more pleasure than to conform my vote to your wishes, if the measure were an ordinary one, or if I believed the error of sanctioning it could be corrected; but believing, as I do, that the power once granted to the executive can never be recalled, and that its exercise will take from the people that freedom of thought and of action which alone entitles our government to be considered free, I most respectfully, but decidedly state, that I *cannot* and *will not obey the instruction* contained in your second resolution.

Your third resolution unqualifiedly condemns the provisions of a bill of the last session, entitled, a bill to prevent the interference of certain federal officers in elections, declares the same to be a violation of the Constitution of the United States, unqualifiedly condemns the vote given in favor of said bill by my colleague and myself, and instructs your Senators to vote against, and to use all fair and proper exertions to prevent the passage of the same, or any similar bill.

When my colleague and myself gave our votes in favor of that bill, we acted under the same solemn sanction of an oath to support the Constitution of the United States, that the members of your honorable body did when they voted in favor of this condemnatory resolution. We had the benefit of very able arguments both for and against the bill. We examined it with all the care we could, and came to the conclusion that it was not unconstitutional, and believing that the prevailing practice of the President interfering in elections, both State and federal, through the instrumentality of officers, who hold their places during his pleasure, called loudly for a remedy; we voted in favor of its passage.

If your decision was final, I would not be so childish as to ask of you to reconsider the constitutional question.

To men of ordinary capacity, or equivocal moral character, I might make such a request, from a belief that the decision was a *hasty one*, produced by some *extraneous influence*, and that a more deliberate investigation of the subject might lead to a different conclusion; but when I reflect that the *leading* members of that *majority* which passed the resolution are men as much distinguished by their *moral* character as by their *intellectual* attainments and *deep research* on subjects connected with constitutional law, and see that my vote is not only "*condemned*," but "*unqualifiedly* condemned," I cannot hope that one of my humble pretensions could urge anything which would occasion even a doubt in your minds of the correctness of your decision.

But there is a higher earthly tribunal than your honorable body, that will judge both *your* vote and *mine*, and pass sentence dispassionately, without any predisposition to *unqualifiedly* condemn either of us, but in charity hoping that each believed, when giving his vote, he was acting correctly. To that tribunal, then, *our common constituents*, through you, their immediate representatives, I beg leave respectfully and briefly to assign some of the reasons which influenced the vote complained of.

Every officer named in that bill holds his office at the *will* of the President, and is liable to be dismissed whenever it is the *pleasure* of the President to dismiss him. Each and every one of the offices is created by act of Congress. The qualification for the office, the *tenure* of it, and the duties to be performed by the officers are, and were, matters of legislative enactment.

The President has no power to dismiss or control one of these officers, merely because he is President, but because Congress, *by law*, gave him that power. The bill itself expressly provided that all these officers should be secure in the *right to vote on all elections, according to their own judgment*, and only forbid their interference to control and influence the votes of others.

I affirm that Congress had the power to create these offices, or not, at its pleasure. That, when they were created, Congress could prescribe the duties of the officers. That, if it had been deemed necessary, Congress could have enacted that the officers should hold the office *during good behavior;* but that, if any one of the officers interfered to influence *the votes of others*, in any election, either State or federal, it should be a *misdemeanor in office, for which he should be dismissed.*

When the bill complained of was under consideration, Congress had exactly the same power over the subject that it had when the offices were *first creating.* They might have repealed the law entirely, and thus have turned out every one of these officers.

Suppose, instead of the bill complained of, a bill had been introduced and passed, stating that, whereas these officers were in the habit of interfering to influence the votes of the citizens in elections, therefore, Be it enacted, that the law creating their offices should be repealed, &c., would your honorable body venture the opinion that such law would have been unconstitutional, and that these officers would still have remained in office? I think not.

On the question of constitutional power, there can be no distinction between the case supposed and the bill complained of. If the one would have been constitutional, so is the other.

Prior to the year 1820, these officers held their office during *pleasure.* Congress then believed many of them had misdemeaned themselves, were defaulters, &c.; and, with a view to provide a remedy, on the 15th of May, in that year, an act was passed *changing their tenure*, and limiting each of them to the term of *four years*, and made them removable at pleasure within these four years. Has it ever been thought that act was unconstitutional? Not at all. Yet such an objection might have been urged with much more force in that case than in this.

The only reason assigned in your resolution why this bill was unconstitutional is, that it took from these officers the liberty of speech, and the Constitution provides that "Congress shall pass no law abridging the freedom of speech and of the press."

This provision in the Constitution was intended for the safety and protection of the common citizen who holds no office. It was foreseen that those *in office* might *abuse their trust*, and to protect themselves against exposure, might pass laws restraining the citizens from censuring them, either in speeches or through the press. Now, in your resolution, you exactly reverse the matter, and suppose it was intended to protect the instruments of the President, who hold office at his will, in their endeavors to influence and mislead the people in elections. During the administration of the elder Mr. Adams, many complaints were made and charges urged, both in speeches and through the press, *by the citizens*, against him, and those in office under him. With a view to silence the *citizens*, and to *maintain and shield those in office*, the sedition law was passed. The Republicans, one and all, condemned it as unconstitutional and unjust, and they were right in such condemnation.

Your resolution maintains now, exactly the same doctrines then advanced by the federalists. They wished to silence the people, that they might retain their places and power, and your resolution seeks to allow the officeholders to go forth with all their power and influence, to *mislead* and *corrupt* the people—obtain their votes in elections, and thus *retain* their offices with all their *emoluments*.

Does your honorable body intend to affirm that Congress has no power to regulate the conduct of this class of officers?

Are they to be allowed to go forth on days of election, and with a view to procure votes for the President or his favorites, *promise money* or *offices*, *jobs* or *contracts*, by which much money may be made with but little labor? The officeholder, in making these *promises* to *influence* voters, would be using his *powers of speech*, which the resolution affirms Congress cannot *abridge* or lessen. If the proposition can be maintained, then Congress had better go home, and yield up everything to the President, and the *corps who hold office at his pleasure*.

We will, after a little reflection, perceive that this resolution not only unqualifiedly condemns your senators for their vote, but necessarily the conduct and opinions of others whom the country has most delighted to honor.

The only reason assigned in your resolution why this bill was unconstitutional is, that it *abridged the freedom of speech*.

If you are correct, how dare Mr. Jefferson, "the Apostle of Liberty," in his letter to Governor McKean, use the language he did on this subject? Still more, when he came into office as President, why did he dare to issue his circular letter, prohibiting this class of officers, on pain of dismissal, from interfering in elections farther than to give their own votes?

He was *sworn* to support the Constitution, and if Congress abridges the freedom of speech, secured by the Constitution, by the enactments proposed in this bill, it follows clearly that the *President in his circular violated the same provision*, by pronouncing the *like penalty* for the *like offence?*

I defy any person to condemn the one without condemning the other; unless, indeed, we suppose there is a class of politicians who believe the Constitution does not and ought not to impose any restraint upon the President.

I fear such a sect has lately sprung up, and is increasing. It cannot be too speedily suppressed.

The late President, General Jackson, in his inaugural address, when "he was fresh from the people," inculcated the same doctrine with Mr. Jefferson. "To prevent the patronage of the government from being brought into conflict with the freedom of elections, was a duty inscribed in characters too legible to be misunderstood," &c., was the strong language he then used. How was the duty to be discharged? Did we not one and all, believe he would discharge it as Mr. Jefferson had done? If, then, these Presidents could, *without violating the Constitution, prohibit these officers from interfering in elections*, why could not Congress by its enactments prohibit them likewise?

No satisfactory answer can be given to this question.

The President already had the power vested in him to dismiss these officers at his *pleasure*; and Congress unquestionably had the power to *limit his discretion*, by specifying the cases in which he should exercise it. If, then, my colleague and I erred on this question of power, with great deference I submit that, the company with which our opinions were associated ought, at least, to have softened the asperity of the language in which our condemnation was pronounced. If there was any one subject above all others, upon which I believed my colleague and I could not mistake the sentiment of our constituents, it was that embraced in that bill.

To prevent the President, through those officers, from interfering in elections, was a theme upon which the friends of the late President (Jackson) had dwelt most, both in and out of Congress. In 1826, a committee of the Senate, of which I was a very humble member, through their chairman had made a most able report, the principles of which were applauded by the whole party, and *by our State in particular*. Upon them, mainly, General Jackson came into power; he gave them his solemn sanction in his inaugural address, in presence of thousands of witnesses. I had been twice elected after my opinions were well known upon this subject, and now, when I endeavor faithfully to carry them out, to be *unqualifiedly condemned* for doing so, and that by those who then *professed* to think as I sincerely did, was what I did not anticipate. I am sure that, upon this subject, my practice has corresponded with my professions. Still, I should feel degraded if I were to pronounce any old associate a traitor, or liken him to Benedict Arnold, because at this time he disagrees with me in opinion.

They are greatly mistaken who suppose the object of this bill was to take from this class of officers any right whatever. Precisely the reverse was the intention. It was to *emancipate them from the slavish bondage* in which they were held. It was to enable every man of them to vote according to the dictates of his own judgment, and to absolve them from the painful alternative of being compelled to not only vote, but to electioneer for candidates not of their choice, but of the President, on pain of dismissal from office.

The great object was, to prevent the President from *controlling the people* in the choice of their officers, State and federal. This class of officers, whose daily bread for their families, depended on executive favor.

were constrained, as a part of their *official duty*, not only to vote *as the President wished*, but to endeavor to influence others to do so likewise. If they did not perform this duty they were dismissed, and with their families left to starve. An enlightened statesman once called them the "enlisted soldiers of the President."

A politician who knows as well as any other man the motives by which men are influenced in relation to elections, says:—"*Whenever he sees an officeholder interfering in elections, he concludes he is thinking of his salary and his bread, and is a very unfit adviser of the people.*" By the passage of this bill it was hoped the instruments for misleading the people would be taken from the President, that these "enlisted soldiers" would be discharged from electioneering duties, and yet receive their pay; and that if they performed the duties of their offices faithfully, they might safely vote according to the dictates of their own judgment, and yet be secure in their "salaries and their daily bread."

By your fourth resolution, as one of your senators, I am instructed to "vote against the measure heretofore brought before Congress, which had for its object, the distribution among the States of the proceeds of the sales of the public lands."

In justice to myself, as well as to my constituents, I must be permitted to state the manner in which my mind has operated on this subject at different times and under different circumstances.

When a bill was first introduced, having such distribution as that spoken of for its object, I voted against its passage, and in favor of the veto of the Chief Magistrate, on the ground that no such distribution ought to be made *until the public debt was all paid.*

Upon looking into the deeds, by which those lands were ceded to the United States, by the respective States, I found that they were conveyed in trust to pay out of the proceeds of their sales, our public debt then owing by the United States, and that the residue should be for the joint benefit of each of the several States, including those making the cessions.

At that time a portion of the public debt was *unpaid*, and I deemed it improper to distribute any part of this fund until the debt was fully discharged, that being the primary object of the donor.

When a like bill was afterwards introduced, I not only voted for it, but gave it such support as my feeble abilities enabled me.

By this time the public debt had been fully paid, and we had a very large sum in the treasury, beyond the necessary wants of the federal government.

I could not doubt the power of Congress to make the distribution. because there was an express trust that this fund should be for the use of the respective States; we had a large sum on hand which I thought, in honesty, belonged to the States, and the portion belonging to Tennessee, I believed, would be highly useful in enabling her to make internal improvements, and in providing a system for the education of those who might be unable to bear the expenses of educating themselves. In addition to these considerations, I perceived if this large sum was not distributed, it would encourage a system of extravagant expenditure inconsistent with the welfare of the country.

I still believe these views were sound, and that if I committed any error, it was not giving my support to the first bill as well as the last. I believe it would be unwise, perhaps unconstitutional, for the federal government to impose taxes for the purposes of collecting more money than is necessary to carry out its affairs, to the end that it might have a surplus to distribute among the States: but this fund stands on a different ground; it is a trust fund which belongs not to the federal, but to the State government.

The ordinary duties necessary and proper for the regulation of our commerce with foreign nations, ought to be sufficient to bring into the treasury, as much money as would defray the economical expenses of the federal government, and each of the States ought to receive its fair proportion of the proceeds of the sales of the public lands.

I consider Tennessee as honestly entitled to her proportion of this fund, as any of your honorable body is to a tract of land devised to him by his father.

It appears to me, even at this time, our State very much needs her proportion of this fund, and that in a short time we shall be much more in want of it.

Your honorable body may be satisfied that a majority of our citizens are willing to relinquish their interest in this fund, but I am not so satisfied, and as a senator in Congress, I will not do any act by which such an idea is to be sanctioned.

It may be in the course of a very short time, that this fund will be indispensably necessary to save our citizens from *heavy taxation*, and I should never forgive myself, if by yielding to your instructions, I did an act which produced a serious injury to the people, who have so long honored me with their confidence.

By the last clauses in your fourth resolution, I am instructed to vote for graduating the price of the public lands, and for granting pre-emption rights to occupants.

These instructions correspond with the opinions I have maintained and acted on, therefore, I should find no difficulty in conforming to your wishes in relation to them.

In the fifth resolution, your instructions are "to vote for and use all fair and proper exertions to procure the passage of a law repealing the duties on imported salt."

This subject has been before the Senate on several occasions since I have been a member, and my votes have ever been in favor of removing this duty, and I should still conform my conduct to my settled conviction, that my past course on this subject has been correct.

In your sixth resolution you state, that you "heartily approve the leading measures and policy of the Administrations of Andrew Jackson and Martin Van Buren, and" instruct "your senators to support in good faith, the leading measures and policy, as brought forward and advocated by the present President of the United States, and to use all fair and proper exertions to carry out, sustain, and accomplish the same."

The phraseology of this resolution is so general and indefinite, that I am not sure I comprehend the meaning of your honorable body; but believe you intend that I shall support all the leading measures of the Chief Magistrate, as well those hereafter to be brought forward as those heretofore recommended.

To instructions of this description, I could not with propriety, pay any attention whatever.

Our fathers and statesmen believed they had done much towards the security of civil liberty, when, by the Constitution, they divided the great powers conferred into *three departments*, each, in its sphere, independent of the other two. These were the legislative, the executive, and the judicial.

If the powers of any two of these departments should be placed in the same hands, the whole machinery of the government is destroyed, and the checks interposed are removed.

You instruct your senators to conform their votes on all the leading measures, to the will of the President, who is at the head of the executive department. If you have a right to give such instructions, and your senators are bound to obey, every other legislature in the Union has the same right, and their senators would be equally bound to yield obedience.

Why not let the President at once make the law, and then execute it? If we are bound to vote as he recommends, it is a solemn mockery to consult us at all. The law would not be the will of the Senate, but the will of the President. By this process the whole legislative power would be yielded up and surrendered to the executive.

I have been educated to believe, that continued watchfulness, and constant jealousy of those in power, are essential to the preservation of liberty.

Your honorable body would now teach me a different lesson, and instead of being a sentinel on the watch-tower, to guard the liberty of my constituents, I am to betake myself to slumber, examine nothing, but vote on all leading measures as the President may recommend.

If this be the kind of service to which your senators are to be applied, I never can perform it, and feel myself unsuited to a station, which I have heretofore considered most honorable as well as confidential.

After your resolutions shall have performed their *wonted office* and *my resignation shall have been received*, *before electing my successor*, I hope in your wisdom you will either *rescind* or *expunge* this sixth resolution. Our common constituents, the free and chivalrous citizens of Tennessee, I hope will ever be represented in the Senate by those whose principles and feelings are in accordance with their own; and while this resolution is suffered to remain, no man can accept that high station but one who is himself *enslaved*, and fit only to represent those *in the like condition with himself*.

I have now troubled you with all the remarks I deem it necessary to make upon your six resolutions, taken separately, but do not feel that I will have discharged my whole duty until I have shown the deduction to be drawn from them when connectedly considered.

They contain the political creed of the present Chief Magistrate of the United States, as expressed through his friends in the Tennessee legislature; and what is it?

By the 2d resolution it is proved he wishes the whole moneyed power of the United States vested in him, and subject to his control.

By the 3d it is proved he will not agree that the patronage and power he now exercises shall be either lessened or regulated by law.

By the 4th, it is proved that in order to have full coffers, he wishes the States to surrender their right to the moneys arising from the sales of the public lands, and

By the 6th, it is proved that he wishes Congress compelled to vote for every leading measure he may recommend, and I am instructed in good faith to give my aid to maintain this creed.

These instructions I cannot and will not obey. So far from it, my creed upon these points is:

1st. That the power over the public purse ought to be constantly kept under the control of the legislature.

2d. That the patronage as well as the expenditures of the executive are already too large, and ought to be reduced.

3d. That instead of surrendering the rights of the States to any portion of the public moneys, they ought to adhere to those rights, and in due season provide for a fair distribution of the land funds; and

Lastly, for no consideration ought we to agree that any other portion of the legislative power shall be vested, either directly or indirectly, in the President, save that which is already vested in him by the Constitution of the United States.

At last, no person can help seeing that the difference between your honorable body and myself is, that you wish to add to the power and patronage of the executive, I wish to lessen his power and patronage.

On the decision of this contest by the American people, in my opinion, the liberty of the country depends. Should your creed prevail, ere long the whole legislative power, vested in Congress by the Constitution, will be transferred, substantially, to the President, and the only use of Congress will be to *stand between the President and public odium*, when laws are enacted which are disapproved by the people.

In addition to this, the election of State officers, and State legislation, will be regulated according to the will of the executive of the Union. Should mine prevail, the States will retain the powers they now possess; the powers of the federal government will remain divided into different departments in substance as well as form.

Which of these creeds will best secure the liberty, the happiness and prosperity of the people, I cheerfully submit for decision to the *Freemen of Tennessee.*

In England, this would be the common contest between the *prerogative of the crown* and the *privileges of the people.* Those maintaining your side would be called *tories*, those maintaining mine would be called *whigs.*

Here it is a contest between the *patronage of the President* and the *right of suffrage of the people.* I will not at present give those who maintain your creed any name—you may give those who maintain mine any one you choose.

"Names are nothing with me." My motto is, "Principles in preference to men;" while I sometimes think that of some of my opponents ought to be, "Men without principles;" though I would be sorry to intimate that such a motto would suit your honorable body.

I shall trouble you with no further observations on these important topics. It has been my aim to state my opinions with candor, and to maintain them with firmness; but, at the same time, to treat your honorable body with the most perfect respect.

I was called to the service of my State, fifteen years ago, without any solicitation on my part. With reluctance I accepted the high station I now occupy. I have been continued in it, perhaps, too long for the interest of the country. I have been thrice elected, by the unanimous vote of your predecessors. My services have been rendered in times of high party excitement—sometimes threatening to *burst asunder the bonds of this Union*—and your resolutions contain the *high compliment* that bitter political opponents can find only a *solitary vote* worthy, in their judgment, of "*unqualified condemnation.*"

I hope it will be in your power to select a successor who can bring into the service of the State more talents—I feel a proud consciousness, that more purity of intention, or more unremitting industry, *he never can.*

For the sake of place, I will never cringe to power. You have instructed me to do those things which, entertaining the opinions I do, I fear I would not be *forgiven for, either in this world or in the next;* and practising upon the creed I have long professed, I hereby tender to you my resignation of the trust confided to me, as one of the senators from the State of Tennessee to the Congress of the United States.

Allow me to add my sincere prayer that the Governor of the Universe may so over-rule *our dissensions as to secure the liberty and promote the prosperity of our common constituents.*

I have the honor to be, gentlemen,

Your obedient servant,

HU. L. WHITE.

Senate Chamber, Jan. 11, 1840.

After which he proceeded and said:

Mr. President—I have now finished my task; henceforth, I am to cease being a member of this body. I cannot share with former associates, the *honors*, the *privileges*, or the *emoluments* of a senator in the Congress of the United States. At the same time, I will be relieved from my portion of the *labors*, and from sharing with you the *high responsibilities* which necessarily pertain to the station.

In taking my leave of you, in the utmost sincerity my prayers are, that collectively and individually you may be enabled to pursue a course, which will afford you the highest comforts in this life; and that your labors may be so blessed as to secure you the grateful remembrance of the present and all succeeding generations.

His retirement from the Senate is thus described by the correspondent of the "Knoxville Times:"

WASHINGTON, *Jan.* 13*th.*

The Hon. Hugh L. White resigned his seat in the Senate to-day. The Senate chamber was crowded with members of the House, and the galleries thronged with citizens and strangers attending to see this veteran Statesman quit the field in which he had so long and so faithfully toiled.

Speaking of his letter to the legislature, the writer says:

It is a most able paper, giving at its conclusion a short review of his political life. It was received in the most profound silence, and created deep feeling. His remarks on the resolutions of the legislature instructing him to vote for and sustain the leading measures of the Administration were very severe. He then bade adieu to the senators, tendering them, individually and collectively, his best wishes for their happiness, and remarking he had now no share in the honors of that body, and was excused from any participation in its labors. Judge White's old friends went up and shook him cordially by the hand, as he stood by the *fire-*

place, in view of every one, and expressed their regret at parting with an "old soldier," who had so faithfully served his country. Messrs. Clay, Southard, and Preston were among the rest. It was a proud day in the history of Hugh L. White. He has left the Senate with the pleasant consciousness of having never failed in his duty to the people. His hands are not soiled with the public plunder, nor his heart stained with either treason or hypocrisy. Had the old farmers of Knox--had the people of Tennessee witnessed the scene, how would their eyes have flashed with virtuous indignation, and their lips muttered of future revenge!

The "National Intelligencer" thus notices Judge White's retirement:

The Senate chamber has rarely presented a scene of more solemn interest than that exhibited yesterday by the resignation of Judge White. The universal estimation in which this venerable citizen was held by men of all parties—his long services—the unquestionable honor of his character, and his antique sternness of virtue, combined to make him, at such a moment, the object of great and just interest. And well was this interest sustained by the able, eloquent, and dignified document, which he read to the profoundly attentive Senate. There has rarely been a more solemn sacrifice upon the altar of party.

A correspondent of the "Cincinnati Gazette," writing as a retired citizen of Campbell county, thus speaks of Judge White's letter of resignation:

Mr. Editor: Although an obscure individual, of a remote spot in Campbell County, Ky., there occasionally falls into my hands a newspaper, by private conveyance. Some days since a gentleman of Newport, Ky., handed me your paper of the 6th inst., in which was published the Hon. Hugh L. White's letter of resignation to the legislature of Tennessee.

This letter of Judge White's is a strong document. It is couched in terms which show the great depth of his intellect, and the incorruptibility of his heart. As an *exposé* of the great political heresies of the day, it is pre-eminent. His strictures upon the spirit of the Tennessee resolutions are so palpable, that the absurdities are made manifest even to "the wayfaring man."

What does the language of the Tennessee resolutions convey, but the precise doctrines of passive obedience and non-resistance, which came into repute immediately after the abdication of Richard Cromwell, and upon the accession of Charles II. to the throne of England. This vasalage was opposed, indeed, by the enemies of the crown, and here (1360) we date the origin of the distinction of whig and tory; the whigs opposing the crown, the tories advocating it. But in Judge White we had a senator who was not that pliant sycophant, that, "for the sake of place," would yield his principles and become the mere tool of the President. Beholding the corrupt and dangerous tendency of the resolutions, he spurned, with indignation, their propositions, and by his resignation has given Tennessee the opportunity to fill his place with some one more flexible and temporizing. But in his response, he has exhibited facts which deserve the deep contemplation of every *American citizen.* He has shown that submissiveness to the President's will on the part of our legislators, or their constituents, would but presage the *wreck* of our boasted republic. Yea! it would but augur the speedy destruction of all that renders us happy and free.

When Judge White's letter of resignation was read before the House of Representatives of the General Assembly on the 28th Jan., General Jacobs moved that the letter be entered at large upon the journals, which motion was accompanied by the following remarks:

Mr. SPEAKER: I request the indulgence of the House for a single moment, while I make a few remarks in relation to the individual who is the subject of the resolution which I have just had the honor of submitting; to the adoption of which I trust there will not be a single dissenting voice.

I wish not, I intend not, sir, on this occasion to arouse a single party feeling, or to add a solitary splinter to the political flame which is already burning with too intense a heat among us. I should do injustice to the distinguished author of the communication which has just been read, as well as to my own feelings, were I to attempt to do so. With the act of the majority of the legislature of Tennessee, which has compelled him to retire from the Senate of the United States, I have nothing, at this time, to do; it is before the tribunal of the people whom we represent, and it is their province to pass judgment upon it.

In my boyhood, Mr. Speaker, I was taught to reverence the name of Hugh L. White, and I have lived to witness the reality of all that my youthful imagination had pictured of this truly good and great man. I have known him intimately for more than twenty years: I have seen him at the bar, on the bench of the Supreme Court of the State, and on the floor of Congress: I have known him in the domestic and social circle, and in the heat and turmoil of political agitations, and can bear testimony to his claims to the character of a profound lawyer, an able and impartial judge, a consistent politician, a pure patriot, and an honest man. I have seen him under circumstances the most trying, and amid afflictions the most severe, when one after another of a numerous, most interesting and amiable family were cut off in the prime of youth, and yet has he never been absent from his post, or swerved from the path of duty and rectitude. Bold, firm, manly and independent, both in his private and political department; possessing an intellect, clear, powerful and discriminating; pure, spotless and uncontaminated by the pollutions of party, and unawed by the strong arm of power, this venerable statesman has kept "the even tenor of his way," regardful only of his country and his country's good. He has never cringed for favor, or shrunk from responsibility; he has never feared anything but dishonor, or loved anything better than his country.

Nor, sir, is his private character less pure and unexceptionable, than his political career has been consistent and patriotic. The record of his private life does not exhibit a single spot or blemish. No violation of promise; no sin of ingratitude; no act of extortion; nothing illiberal, unmanly, immoral, or dishonest, from his infancy to the present moment, can rise up in judgment against him. His friends, his neighbors, his acquaintances, all, all revere him; around him are entwined the strong cords of their affection, and nothing but the hand of death can unloose them.

By the deliberate act of the majority of this legislature this incorruptible citizen, this venerable patriot has been compelled to retire to private life. His political race is run; and in the course of human events his earthly pilgrimage, in a very few years, will also be terminated; and when the waves of oblivion shall have swept over the present, and the party feelings and political excitements of the times shall have become hushed into a calm; when the prejudices consequent on this state of things shall have been consigned to the "Tomb of the Capulets," and sober, dispassionate judgment and reflection resume their sway, full and ample justice will be done his character. He has served his country forty years and, in the name of this venerable statesman, and incorruptible patriot, and on account of his long and faithful services, I do most respectfully ask that this House will spread upon its journals the communication which has just been read, that they will admit to record this last will and testament of his political existence.

"The motion was carried by 47 to 26 votes. In the Senate a similar motion was made and rejected by a vote of 13 to 11."

To show that the people did not sanction the course of their representatives towards their senators, we have but to read the preamble and resolutions adopted by a whig convention which met at Knoxville on the 10th Feb. 1840. This convention was composed of delegates from the various counties of East Tennessee convened for the purpose of nominating electors for the districts of East Tennessee and the State at large. Judge White's name was placed upon the latter ticket; and that, together with the other proceedings, certainly may be considered an indication of the sentiments of the people whom he had so long and faithfully served.

Whereas, we have recently seen with mingled feelings of regret and indignation, an old, faithful and well-tried public servant, the greater portion of whose life has been spent in the councils of his country, proscribed by the blind, infuriate zeal of faction—therefore,

Resolved, That the Hon. Hugh L. White be invited to meet his East Tennessee friends in Knoxville, at such time as may suit his convenience, and partake with them of a barbecue, to be prepared for the occasion.

Resolved, That the president of the convention express to Judge White the kind feelings and grateful recollections of the members of this convention, and tender to him the invitation to the contemplated festival.

Resolved, That a committee of thirty be appointed by the president, to superintend the necessary arrangements for the proposed barbecue.

The preamble and resolutions were adopted, but Judge White's health was too feeble on his return home to accept the flattering and kind invitation and receive the gratulations of his many warm friends. But he placed the highest estimate upon their attentions.

CHAPTER XVII.

WASHINGTON DINNER: SPEECHES OF JUDGE WHITE AND OTHERS.

A FEW days after Judge White's resignation a dinner was given him in Washington City, as a last mark of affectionate respect from those with whom he had been so long privately and politically associated. To give an adequate idea of this deeply interesting scene, a sketch of some of the speeches made on the occasion by distinguished men, as well as of that of Judge White himself is here inserted. Mr. A. R. Humes, at the expense of some time and much trouble, collected copies of these proceedings and transmitted them to the "Knoxville Times" for publication. Below is an extract from his communication on this occasion.

WASHINGTON, *Jan.* 18th, 1840.

The public dinner, given yesterday in honor of Judge White, was attended by many of the most illustrious and distinguished men of whom our nation can boast. It was one of the grandest exhibitions of varied talent ever witnessed on a like occasion. The several *impromptu* speeches abounded in sallies of wit, the keenest satire, and the richest classical allusions.

About one hundred and fifty were present, principally members of Congress.

At 8 o'clock, the company was ushered into the splendid hall at Brown's hotel, and when Messrs. Clay and Preston entered with their distinguished guest, the "National Band" struck up the inspiring air of "Hail Columbia."

It was indeed a scene of melancholy and imposing grandeur. By the patriotic Tennesseean, it would have been witnessed with the most contradictory emotions. To see the father of his State dishonored in his old age, by the blind infuriate zeal of party! To see the man who had achieved for Tennessee a just and honorable fame!—"the noblest Roman of them all"—a willing victim upon the altar—preferring banishment from office, to the desertion of principle—he would have most deeply felt that the true glory of his State was indeed eclipsed for the moment.

The Hon. William C. Preston presided; at his right and left were seated Hugh L. White and Henry Clay. One might easily have believed that he lived in times equalled only by the best days of the republic of Rome for *here* were senators of more than Roman virtue. There stood the aged Cato with the crown of martyrdom on his head—banished from the councils of his country, yet firm to his faith, and inflexible in truth.

Messrs. Davis of Massachusetts, Biddle of Pennsylvania, Gen. Walter Jones, Col. George Washington of Maryland, and Mr. Corwin of Ohio, acted as vice-presidents on the occasion.

It was indeed a brilliant scene. The rich chandeliers threw a blaze of light over the extensive room, which was tastefully decorated with evergreens, and wine gushed forth from the bottle, and mirth from the heart.

But there was yet higher banquetting.

Mr. Preston, the president, said:—

"I rise to perform a very agreeable duty. We are here to do honor to a man whose private worth has commended him to our affections, and whose public services challenge our approbation and gratitude. The vicissitudes of public life have removed him from a high station, which he has long filled in such a way as to honor it, as much as it had honored him. He ascended to it through various gradations of public service, both in his own State, and in this government—at each step displaying an assemblage of high and useful qualities—of virtues and of talents, which showed him capable of a still more extended sphere.

His life has been a pattern to statesmen of an honest and unflinching adherence to principle. He came here to Washington, the loved and honored favorite of a great and dominant party, who had the power, and the inclination to gratify all that his ambition might have aspired to; but when their policy no longer conformed to his judgment, he surrendered at once the smiles of power for the duties of patriotism.

The purity of his motives is vindicated by the fact, that he left the strong for the weaker side. The vigor of his patriotism is shown, by his willingness to incur for the sake of his country, the displeasure of a friend in the moment of his power, to whom, in every variety of his fortune, through a long life he had adhered with a romantic fidelity. He quitted the palace for his principles, he gave up the court for his country. He did not believe that a palace sanctifies what without its walls was reprehensible. He was of sterner stuff than to 'crook the pregnant hinges of the knee,' where 'thrift might follow fawning.' With a noble self-sacrifice he pursued the steady tenor of his principles wherever they led him, and has permitted me to present his name to you. I doubt not it will so stand in after times:—

"HUGH L. WHITE.—The man and the statesman, without fear and without reproach."

These remarks were delivered in the most finished style of oratory. and when Mr. Preston pronounced the above sentiment, its reception was hailed with loud and continued "huzzas." But when the venerable form of that veteran statesman, to whom it was addressed, was seen rising from his seat, the welkin rung with "yet a louder, and a louder strain."

Mr. White rose and said:

"Gentlemen: The most eloquent response I could make to the sentiments contained in your toast, would be to remain entirely silent. No language of which I am master, can convey an adequate idea of the emotions produced by the expression of such sentiments, and the manner in which they have been received by this large and respectable assembly. At a time when I am *banished from the service of my country*, without any hope that I can be longer useful to any man, to find myself surrounded by so many men, whose friendship and countenance, any man in any age or country, in possession of the most extensive power, would justly feel proud of, overwhelms me. Thanks, from my heart, I return you, and it is probably the only return I can ever make, for your kindness and attention.

"Were I to go alone from the service of the public, I could find but little to regret. My country would be more ably served by some one who has seen *fewer years*. [Cries of 'never! never!'] Now in my sixty-seventh year, the last thirty-eight almost wholly spent in some public employment, little more could be expected of me; but, for the sake of reaching me, my late colleague must be made a victim likewise. [Cries of 'shame! shame!'] He had served his State but one session in the Senate, and I think all now present, who are acquainted with him, will agree with me in opinion that no man who has entered that body in our day, made more friends in the same length of time. ['No! none.'] A man of the strictest integrity, with a mind highly endowed and well cultivated, aided by manners pleasing to all with whom he associated, of untiring industry, and in the vigor of life; had he been spared, his State and the country at large, had much to hope from his labors. For myself, I am proud that my State can, *in my person*, produce yet one man willing to be *made a sacrifice rather than sacrifice his principles*." [Nine cheers!]

Mr. White continued—"One thing may yet be permitted to me, and that is to beseech my State that when, hereafter, that "monster, party spirit," shall call upon her to furnish a victim for the altar, she may spare her younger sons, and let loose her blood-hounds upon some man already worn out in her service, who may be found willing to be offered up as a sacrifice, rather than stamp as hypocritical his former professions."

He next alluded to his separation from the late Administration, and said—"When my countrymen asked the use of my name, as a candidate for the Presidency, and I gave my consent, my destruction was decreed, and how was it to be effected? In no way but by driving me from the Administration; and how was this to be accomplished? I would *not* and *did not abandon* any one political principle, I had ever professed. The separation, therefore, could only be brought about by the Administration *changing its practice* in relation to every great subject, except that of removing the Indians. It did so, wheeled to the right about, and I kept on, directly in its former course."

[Mr. White was here interrupted by loud bursts of applause and confirmations of his statement.]

He continued—"That branch of the public service in which I labored most, related to the Indian affairs. In that I, and the late Administration, had stuck together to the last, and the Indians are mostly removed from Georgia, North Carolina, Tennessee, Alabama, Mississippi, Louisiana, Missouri, Illinois, Indiana, Ohio, and Michigan." And he asked, with boldness and emphasis—"Who dare charge me with failing to give my best support both to the late and present Administration, on that great and interesting subject? Upon this subject, I willingly leave my character, to be settled by the testimony of my colleagues, upon the committee." [A voice from a senator—'I am a witness.']

"I am thankful to my State, that she permitted me to remain here, until her Indians were removed, and our lands brought into market, so that the State is now receiving into her treasury the proceeds of their sales."

[It is well known that Mr. White has long been the able chairman of the committee on Indian affairs.]

"There is yet a most important part of the great plan to be accomplished, and that is establishing a plan for their government, by which they can be made secure among themselves, and the neighboring whites rendered safe from any of their depredations, and one upon which they can be civilized and christianized.

"This latter object the committee have endeavored to accomplish. They have for several sessions, reported a bill, and had it passed in the Senate. They at first had the aid and sanction of the Administration for the measure. Now, however, it has got off the Jackson track, (laughter) and is discountenancing the measure, and what the President wishes done, the Lord only knows. (Loud laughter.) *I* do not know, and he has not deemed it necessary, in his labored message, to give us a useful hint upon the subject.

"A high responsibility rests upon the executive, and to my old associates I say, if this subject be not faithfully attended to, and delicately, as well as ably managed, we will, I fear, ere long witness the blaze of war, from one end of our southern frontier to the other.

"Before the year closes a Chief Magistrate is to be elected for four years, succeeding the 4th March, 1841. Since the respective parties have agreed upon their candidates, I have amongst you, said nothing as to whom I should prefer.

"Upon this subject I do not wish to be non-committal. Neither of the gentlemen named would have been my choice. I would greatly have preferred the distinguished gentleman from Kentucky, now near me. (Mr. Clay bowed—the whole company rose as by one impulse, and gave three deafening cheers at the mention of this great man.)

"Upon some subjects, he and I did not agree; but upon the same points, I disagree with the present Chief Magistrate also. Most of these have now ceased to be practical. Upon the great subjects now practical, I coincide heartily with that gentleman, and disagree with the present incumbent. Had he continued a candidate, I would have given him a cordial support. His talents, integrity, and past services, in trying times, at home and abroad, entitle him to it. His qualifications are of that order which would have made me feel my country safe, under his administration. He would have been as great, if not a greater man, than any one called to his aid, and therefore could not have been misled by any pretended friend, in or out of his cabinet.

"I once exerted myself in favor of an intimate acquaintance, in whose honesty, decision, and knowledge of human character, I had unbounded confidence. I believed a defective knowledge of what was in books, could be supplied by calling in the aid of enlightened and honest men, and thus the well-being of the community secured.

"I was disappointed, and determined never again to make such an experiment.

"General Harrison is by birth a Virginian; his father was a patriot, and signer of the Declaration of Independence. At an early age he joined the army, and was distinguished under the gallant Wayne. Preceding and during the last war, we find him battling with the savage foe at Tippecanoe; then with the combined British and Indians at Fort Meigs, and finishing in a blaze of glory at the river Thames.

"These important services, no man can doubt. Real and documentary testimony establish them beyond contradiction.

"In the civil department, his services have been still more useful. He was governor, and superintendent of Indian affairs, north west of the river Ohio, over a tract of country of immense extent. Look at your Indian treaty book, and you will find him the able negotiator of many Indian treaties. He was a delegate in Congress, a member of the House of Representatives, and afterwards, a member of the Senate, and finally a minister, to represent us in Spanish America.

"In each of those stations, he was useful and conspicuous. He probably had control of millions of dollars of public money, and not one dollar did he squander or misuse. He gives the highest evidence of honest integrity. Although frugal, he is poor—with not more ready money than his necessities require." [Mr. White here said, he had detained the company long enough. Cries of "No! no! go on! go on!"]

He continued—"What are the services of his opponent, in military or civil life? He has been long a public man, and I wish I could find one of his friends, who could point me to any one, great measure, beneficial to his country, of which he was the author. *In, and of himself* he is entitled to less standing than almost any one of his party who is at all distinguished.

"Take from him the importance he has acquired, by glueing himself to General Jackson, and there is nothing of public character left, which any man need envy. He is a feeble glimmering rushlight, which when the *sconce* of General Jackson, from which we have a bright reflection, is withdrawn [roars of laughter] nothing is left, by which anything useful can be discovered.

"When we are to choose men for office, we commonly judge of what they *will do* by what thay *have done*. As General Harrison has been found honest and capable heretofore, I am willing to trust him again. As he has often *risked his life* for the country, I am willing to *risk my vote* for him. ["So are we! so are we, *all!*"]

"With a heart full of gratitude for all past kindness, I have one last favor to ask—that you join me in the sentiment with which I close:—

"*Our country*—May every whig stand prepared to be offered up, as a sacrifice for the welfare of the republic, in preference to witnessing the sacrifice of the public interest, to the aggrandizement of selfish individuals."

This is but a faint outline—an imperfect sketch—of the eloquent remarks of Judge White. They were received with marked interest and the most enthusiastic applause.

Having taken his seat, his friends and fellow statesmen thronged around him once more, to shake the hand of him whom they loved to honor, and whose public services, if denied him by his own State, demand the gratitude of our common country.

Vice President Davis was then called upon, and Massachusetts was ably represented. After a few brief and appropriate remarks, he said—"that the old Bay State, had gotten *drunk* on fifteen gallons, but was just getting *sober*." He alluded, in a glowing strain, to the mists that shrouded Bunker Hill—but they were soon dispersed. It is true, that clouds now overshadow Massachusetts, but they too would soon be dissipated, and *the whigs* again would triumph.

He concluded by offering the following sentiment:—

"*The great West*—She has unfurled her banner in the Great Whig Cause; as *she* goes, so goes *the Country*."

Loud and repeated calls were here made for Mr. Clay from every quarter of the room, and when he arose, he was greeted with thunders of applause.

He spoke, with deep feeling, of the occasion which had called them together, and delivered a most eloquent and appropriate eulogium on the character and virtues of the late venerable senator. He denounced with an unsparing hand, the ruinous policy of the past and present Administration, and briefly alluded to General Jackson as "the distinguished person of the Hermitage." He referred to the Harrisburg convention, and said that the result of the deliberations of that enlightened body, met his most hearty and cordial approbation. In conclusion, he gave a sentiment:—

"May Tennessee yet learn to honor and do justice to her distinguished son, whom by her mistaken course, she has compelled to quit the councils of his country."

Mr. Clay's remarks, though few, were received with great and universal acclamation. They were worthy of him and of the occasion.

Mr. Preston was here called upon, and in addition to his introductory speech, made some eloquent remarks, which I regret for the present I am unable to furnish you.

Vice-president Corwin of Ohio, being called on by the president, rose and said:—

He responded to the call with feelings of mingled triumph and regret. He had listened to the noble and patriotic sentiments which an honored guest (Judge White) expressed with no common interest. Mr. President, said Mr. Corwin, a great ethical writer of integrity, has said that the noblest sight ever exhibited to the eye of man, is that of a great patriot struggling and falling with the falling institutions of his country. We see before us, one of the oldest, most beloved, and faithful of the American patriots of our times, nobly sacrificing station, and power, and the means of serving his country in its public councils, to his own stern regard for a great principle. We see him driven by his old associates, either to forsake *his* and *their* former principles, or himself to surrender the station he holds in the public service. He has not hesitated, sir! if he had, he would have proved false to his own history, false to his country, false to himself. It is melancholy to see selfish faction, combined with executive power thus even temporarily successful, in their most unhallowed purposes. Still, as I have said, sentiments of triumph are inspired, when we behold such martyrs falling in our cause. If human nature is not changed, if past history has not ceased to instruct in the future, then such a cause as ours, so sanctified by principle, so consecrated by sacrifice, so illustrated by the men who sustain and adhere to it, *must triumph.* Sir, I only rose to express in a few words, my hearty and sincere concurrence in the sentiments of high regard for our venerable friend (whose retirement has called us together), which have echoed from every quarter of this crowded hall. A gentleman from Massachusetts has to-night alluded to the banner of our party lately unfurled in the "great West." As a citizen of the West, I cannot but feel some pride that the standard-bearer of that host of battle for constitutional liberty, is taken from amongst the citizens of my own State, and let me assure you, Mr. President, let partisans from any quarter say what they will, throughout the whole extent of that great West, victory, *proud* and *complete victory* awaits that flag. Mr. President, we have met here to do honor and homage to one who has nobly sacrificed self to duty, who has turned away from old friends and clung only to his country. Sir, I see before me others, who in a sphere less conspicuous, but with a courage not less unyielding and steady, have fought the same battle, and conquered. Men, who, in opposition to great names, and what was thought overwhelming influence, did not hesitate, when their country called, to defy names however great, influence however powerful, and old associates however strong. Sir, when I look around this hall, and over this country, I see in our cause, and those who sustain it, the sure indications of future and speedy triumph. I remember, sir, when a boy, to have listened with strong interest to the narrative of one who had been present at the battle of the Rapids, where Gen. Wayne finally vanquished the Indian forces in the North-West, and gave peace to a widely extended frontier settlement. The old soldier said, that whilst the battle was raging hottest, many in that wing of the army where he was, were beginning to falter and think of a retreat. Just at the moment when this feeling began to be prevalent, a young lieutenant, who was known as the confidential aid of old Mad Anthony, galloped up to the line and called to the men, with a voice that was heard above the roar of battle: "Onward! my brave fellows! the enemy is flying, one fire more and the day is ours." Sir, that young lieutenant was William Henry Harrison, now, the bearer of that glorious banner under which we wage war against usurping power, crafty peculation and blind hostility to the good old maxims of our fathers. There are our foes—there are our country's foes; let me exhort you in the language of the young lieutenant—"*One fire* more, and the day is ours!"

Mr. Evans of Maine being called upon, said:—

He appeared there in a representative capacity, and although he was not generally much in favor of the doctrine of instructions, especially practised, as it has been, to drive from the service of the country, at a critical period of its affairs, one of the most venerable, distinguished, and useful of its public servants, yet he acknowledged and would obey the instructions, which he (Mr. E.) had received on the present occasion.

It happened, Mr. Evans said, that although he was anxious to unite in this testimonial to the worth of the honored guest of this evening, he, accidentally, had expressed his determination in the hearing of a fair friend, just before coming to the hall, not to obtrude any remarks or sentiments of his own, upon the attention of the meeting. To this, the lady to whom he referred made decided objection, and finally laid commands on him, in her behalf, to express the sentiments, which according with his own she entertained for the public character and private worth of the distinguished guest, in whose honor we are assembled. The friend in whose behalf he spoke, was a lady of great classical and historical attainments, of varied learning, of accurate taste, and just perception of the appositeness of comparisons—and her first thought was to propose a sentiment, alluding to the ostracism of the Just, from the city he had served so long, and faithfully. Yet a moment's reflection suggested the thought, that the allusion was so obvious, that doubtless it would occur to many others also, and would be frequently made during the evening. We, therefore, acknowledging the great propriety of the comparison, concluded to abandon the idea of designating the honorable senator as the Aristides of the Republic. The event has proved the accuracy of her observations, for the allusion has been made more than once already, and all of us perceive its propriety.

It then occurred to her, to apply to our venerable friend, the cognomen of the Cincinnatus of our Commonwealth. To which I objected, as we had already appropriated the title to another, whom, by the blessing of God, the people of these United States designed to call, not many months hence, from his farm, on the banks of the beautiful Ohio, to the executive mansion, and the executive duties, here. My objection was deemed valid.

My learned friend then suggested that in the ingratitude of the Republic toward this eminent servant, he bore resemblance to Belisarius, among the last and most distinguished sons of the Ancient Mistress of the world; but we could not bring ourselves to confess, even so remotely, that our country was yet in its last days of degeneracy and corruption. We looked forward to the day, now dawning, when the pristine virtues of our country would again be restored and illustrated—a day which our aged guest, we trust, will be spared to see and rejoice in.

Coming down to later days, and regarding the purity of the character of our friend—knowing that he was without fear, and without reproach, and if he is now to fall, he falls with his face to the enemy, it was suggested to me, that allusion might very appropriately be made to the celebrated chevalier of the sixteenth century, the Chevalier Bayard, and this was the sentiment I was *instructed* to offer. Anticipating, however, from the manifest fitness of the allusion, that some other gentleman might propose it, before I should have the opportunity, as has in fact happened, and to guard against being unprepared, in such an event, various other references were suggested. In recalling to mind the history of eminent patriots, statesmen, and philanthropists of other days, wherever worth, public and private, integrity without blemish, patriotism pure and unalloyed, had appeared among men, or many points of resemblance existed, to which reference could be made, so much of all that was glorious and valuable, and praiseworthy in human character, and conduct, had been displayed and developed in the life of the eminent statesman who is about to leave us, that the great difficulty was from which to select.

We thought of Pericles, of Themistocles and Cato, and of the wise and good of later days, but circumstances in the life of each, rendered the allusion not, in every particular, literally correct, without some alteration.

Finally, not to be tedious, I was reminded of the expression of the mother of Brasidas, over his dead body, which had been brought home from the battle, where he so gloriously fell. It was the answer of a *Spartan* mother. Tennessee may, in some respects, in the coming contest be our Sparta, and although I see around me distinguished men of that State, and others I know to be in the field not now here, they will excuse me, I know, in the sentiment I was charged to offer, for altering somewhat the expression of the mother of the Spartan hero.

Our Honored Guest.—"**Sparta hath ne'er a worthier son, than he.**"

A sentiment from General Thompson, of South Carolina, elicited the following remarks from Mr. Habersham:

Mr. President: The honor which has just been conferred upon me, was so wholly unexpected, that I feel myself entirely unprepared to make a suitable acknowledgment. I feel, however, that *that* compliment was rather extended for the State which I here in part represent, than for any merit of my own. It is a fact which may have been forgotten by many, perhaps by most of the gentlemen at this table, that in the great contest for the Presidency some three or four years ago, Georgia was almost the only State which cast her vote in favor of the venerable and distinguished man whom we have met here to honor. Sir, I took part in that contest in behalf of that venerable man, and battled in the ranks of his friends. Sir, as I have said, Georgia stood almost alone in her vote for that individual. She stood so, in support of that great principle which she has so often carried out into practice—the great principle of nullification. I mean nullification in its only true and legitimate meaning: the principle of sustaining the Constitution and *the law, as passed in pursuance thereof.* Yes, sir, she stood in his support to maintain that principle, as far as circumstances would permit. 'Tis true, that this venerable guest had opposed that principle as acted out in South Carolina; but of the candidates then presented to our choice, he was in our opinion, the man most likely to stem the torrent of corruption, to maintain the rights of the South, and the integrity of our beloved Constitution. *He had not promised " to follow in the footsteps."*

Sir, on this principle I and my friends had dared also to stand forth in maintenance of Carolina, in her great struggle for Constitutional rights—in that struggle, we had fallen into a minority in our own State, and the victory obtained in behalf of Judge White, was the first which graced our banner, after a long series of defeats.

In maintenance of that principle Mr. President, once so dear to your own beloved State of South Carolina, I was sent here—and to maintain it, I have *come* here. Yes, sir, I and my colleagues have maintained it in an assembly here, more noisy and boisterous than this, composed of the representatives of twenty-five States and the sixth of a State. We maintained New Jersey, by our vote, in her struggle for those Constitutional rights of which she has been robbed. We maintained the principle in our vote in behalf of the Constitution and the laws passed in pursuance thereof.

I little dreamed, sir, when I came here, of the scenes I was about to witness. In the *one* hall I saw, as it seems to me, a majority of the representatives of the people, trampling under foot the sacred compact of our Union. From that hall, I passed into the other, at the further end of the Capitol, and there again, I witnessed a scene, which was enough to make the heart of any man bleed, who respected the sacred institutions of his country. I know not that I have ever had my feelings so deeply excited, as in witnessing the retirement of our venerable guest from his seat in the Senate, which he had so long honored. Sir, he was at that moment obeying the mandate of his legislature; and, however I may differ with him on the right of a legislature to instruct, I could but commend him, for he was acting honestly, and carrying out the principle which he himself had always maintained. Sir, in my humble opinion, this doctrine of instruction, as now insisted upon and practised, is destructive of that permanence and independence which the Constitution intended to secure in the Senate; I maintain the *right of the people to instruct*—but it belongs *solely to the people in their sovereign capacity when met in Convention.* The legislature is the mere agent provided by the Constitution to elect a senator—he is elected for *six* years—the legislature for but *one.* He represents the *sovereignty* of the State in the *Councils* of the *Union*—they, the sovereignty of the people, to make laws for the States; they are both agents for the people of the State—neither the *Constitution* nor the *people* have given to the legislature the right to *dictate* to, or to *control the senator. That right the people have reserved to themselves, to be exercised in Convention;* and the *attempt to instruct a senator* is an *usurpation* by the legislature, of the *right reserved to the people.* The senator is *not the agent of the legislature.* The legislature is but *itself an agent of the people for certain purposes specified in the Constitution of the State.* The senator is the *agent*, and *representative* of the *sovereignty of the State* in the Senate of the Union, and is *only bound* by instruction from *that* sovereign body, *the people of the State*, to whom *alone the right belongs, and by whom alone it can be exercised.*

But, sir, that venerable man, that honest man, felt himself bound to obey the instructions, and there, in that Senate Hall, I saw him standing—his grey locks streaming over his shoulders—a tear, not of weakness, but of deep and manly feeling, trembling in his eye—there he stood, while in tremulous tones of the deepest feeling, he took, perhaps, a last leave of the associates with whom he had so long acted. It almost seemed to me as if that tear was about to fall upon the very ashes of the Constitution. It seemed to me as if the last pillar of the Constitution was about to crumble into dust—I almost imagined, that I saw "the hand-writing on the wall." But God in his mercy has given us time for repentance—He still spares us from the wrath of his mighty indignation.

Thus, at both ends of the Capitol, in that self-same hour did I witness what seemed to me, the utter destruction of the great compact of our Union. I have done—I did not expect to make a speech at this board, and was utterly unprepared to do so. I do trust that our honored guest may live long enough to allow his State to do him justice by sending him back to his old seat in the Senate. I give you, sir,

The Hon. John Bell of Tennessee.—The man who had the courage to grapple with the lion in his den.

Mr. Biddle, on a call from the president, alluded to the terms in which that honorable gentleman had himself deprecated, and for some time eluded, a similar call on the plea of shrinking from an attempt to follow the eloquent addresses that had been heard.

It looked a little like mockery, after a noble addition to the formidable list, to turn round and make the present requisition. Yet he (Mr. B.) was willing to believe that the feeblest echo of the prevailing sentiment might prove acceptable to the enthusiasm around us. He must, in candor, admit that he had no other sentiment about him—absolutely none—but the absorbing one of the evening—profound respect, and he might add affection—for him whom they had assembled to honor.

It is not known, perhaps, said Mr B., even to that gentleman himself, that he and I, sixteen years ago, were fellow-laborers in the same political struggle, Yes, sir, in 1824, I was amongst the ardent supporters in Pennsylvania, of Gen. Jackson for the Presidency. We were not led away merely by military renown. Who has forgotten the lofty and noble principles of action announced in the memorable letters to Mr. Monroe? These letters were surreptitiously obtained and published to do him prejudice, yet, what a trumpet-note of hope to the young and the sanguine!—What blessings, in the perspective, upon our beloved country, when party, with all its vileness, its profligacy, its fraud, its idolatry, its proscription, was to be trampled into dust with an iron heel!

It is not a little curious to look back and recollect who, at that period, were the most bitter and vindictive in their opposition to Gen. Jackson. Whose ridicule was most pungent at his pretensions? Who loudest to declare that his election would be a curse to the country? Sir, they were the mere party hacks, the professional politicians, who found matter for alarm in the very freshness, purity, and ingenuousness which seemed to breath in every line of those letters. He was not a safe President for them. Can it be denied that the men who thus reasoned, and with whom, in Pennsylvania, we had to struggle, were afterwards rallied to the contest by Mr. Ritchie in the South, Mr. Van Buren in the North, and Mr. Benton in the West? His supposed virtues were a terror, and it was not then ascertained that his foibles and his passions could be turned to profitable account!

Sir, I well remember how often, in those days, the name of Hugh L. White was upon our lips. When Gen. Jackson was denounced as a man of violence and outrage, we pointed to those who were known to be his closest friends, his most confidential advisers, and whose characters afforded a guarantee for the manner in which public affairs would be conducted. Need I say that foremost on the list was Judge White? All had heard of, and revered, a name identified with profound wisdom, lofty honor, and ardent patriotism. The severe and fixed simplicity of his life was believed to furnish the best security that human frailty affords against mutability amidst the temptations and blandishments of prosperity As a commissioner under the Florida Treaty, his reputation had, of late, been more widely diffused, for indefatigable industry, unerring judgment, and spotless integrity. It was known too, that his high spirit (of which some flashes had been seen to-night) would for ever prevent his becoming a tool of power, or being approached by grovelling and sinister influences.

At the end of sixteen years, I am in the presence of this man! And how crowded with great events are these memorable years! Who are now to be found in the pride of power and place, under the protection of the name of Jackson? The very spoilers who trembled at the lofty aspiration of his outset; but who found, at length, with the cunning of their tribe, that by ministering to his passions he could be made to minister to their interest and advancement. And where is our guest? The same as in 1824, unchanged, unchangeable; faithful amongst the perfidious; pure amongst the sordid; the victim of his virtues, with the crown of martyrdom upon his brow!

Sir, it cannot be that such triumphs over integrity and moral worth are to be perpetual. In those days of the revolution, to which our venerable friend has so touchingly alluded, the prospect often seemed darker and more appalling. At Brandywine, our fathers had to give way before Howe—backed as he was by the corps of Hessians, under Kniphausen, and Count Donop. The Capital was taken. And may we not take it as an omen, that he who in after years became the guest of the nation, was on that occasion trodden upon under foot by mercenaries, and desperately wounded, yet lived to take part in the great triumph at Yorktown?

Mr. President, it is not for us, as I very well know, to read lessons to the gallant State of Tennessee. Her spirit would take fire. She will permit no interference with her domestic differences. It is for *her* and her *only* to say, how she will regard this attempt to stigmatize her venerable statesman in the high presence of this whole Union. Denunciation from us would but wound the ear of our honored guest, who kindles at even a sarcasm against Tennessee, from the lips of strangers. He has told us that he goes home with no rankling in his bosom, but to seek repose and a final resting-place:—

> "An old man broken with the storms of State,
> Is come to lay his weary bones among ye;
> Give him a little earth for charity."

Yes, he asks but for a little earth—yet it must, in charity, be the earth of Tennessee. He would fain take his last sleep amidst those hills and streams and valleys that he loves so dearly; where each inanimate object may often times cast back the glow of other days upon the chillness of age; and where stands, in sacred privacy, the domestic altar at which his heart has ministered from youth upwards! No, sir, no! this is not the place for invective. Yet may we not hope that a better and a kinder feeling will spring up? Can it be that this savage cry of exultation over prostrate integrity, is to be for ever heard? Can it be that, while the hearts, even of strangers, weep at this spectacle of degradation, it shall be gloated over in triumph by those who are the friends, the neighbors, the daily companions of the victim? I will not believe it.

Our excellent guest is about to leave us. Let him on his return, appeal, I will not say from Philip drunk to Philip sober, but from the Jacksonism of 1839, to the Jacksonism of 1824! Can we doubt that on such an appeal, justice, good faith, consistency, fidelity to principle, may be triumphantly rallied? Sir, I will not despair; and, in view of such a resurrection (if you will pardon the term) I propose to you

"The *Future* State of Tennessee."

CHAPTER XVIII.

JOURNEY HOME.

Soon after the scene just described, Judge White set out for home. At almost every step, he was greeted with spontaneous and hearty applause. At Lexington, Va., a public dinner was tendered him, the acceptance of which, however, in consequence of the uncertain state of his health and the long journey before him, he was compelled to decline.

As he drew near his own State, he met a deputation of citizens from Sullivan County, inviting him to attend a public dinner, at Kingsport. Similar manifestations of respect were shown him at every town from the Tennessee line to Knoxville. He invariably declined these invitations; but, when he reached these several places, he was forced to accept their hospitalities, everything being in readiness for his entertainment. These manifestations bore a superabounding testimony to the high appreciation that the people placed upon his eminent public virtues and private worth. This was peculiarly grateful to the heart of him against whom the storms of political injustice had beaten with such violence, because it was an affectionate emanation from the hearts of the dwellers around his own fireside; of those who knew him best, and best understood the motives that governed all his actions. These testimonials were especially grateful from their entire disinterestedness and sincerity. For the people of his own State well knew, that the days of his political power had passed away, and that he would never again have public favors to bestow.

The malevolence of his enemies, however, kept pace with the affections of his friends, and this spirit determined them not to permit him to pass on his way without insult. At Rogersville, a number of the leaders of the party hung over the principal street by which the town was entered, a cloth upon which was written in large letters, "Van Buren and Polk," declaring, that Judge White should, by passing under this, acknowledge himself the victim of the President of the United States, and of the Governor of Tennessee. Several of the most respectable citizens of Rogersville requested, as a special favor, that this inscription should be removed. Instead of granting this request, a band of ruffians rallied around it, to defend it and prevent its removal by force when Judge White should reach the place. Upon being informed of the affair, with his usual disinterested consideration for his friends he requested to be conducted on his way by a more unfrequented route, declaring that "no one, capable of such disgraceful conduct, had the power to insult him." His enemies were thus denied the gratification of accomplishing their malignant purpose. Escorts of citizens accompanied him along the whole route from the Virginia line; and even in the country, and by the road-side, as he pursued his way, his fellow-citizens greeted him with smiles of affection, approbation and hearty acclamations of applause. A gentleman of Rogersville, Mr. Wales, voluntarily preceded Judge White, having under his charge a piece of artillery, whose frequent discharges sent the reverberating echo through hill and valley, announcing the coming of "the man who esteemed honor dearer than office." The banner that floated above the gun, was surmounted by a wreath of evergreen presented by the ladies of Rogersville, and bore this inscription:

HUGH L. WHITE,

WORTHY OF ALL HONOR

BOTH AS

A MAN AND A STATESMAN.

He now entered Knoxville, the place where he had been reared from his boyhood, where he was greeted by the firing of cannon, the ringing of bells, and the earnest gaze of old and young, who thronged the streets to look upon him. Accompanied by a large procession of persons on horseback, with his aged head nncovered, he passed on to his own residence, through a multitude, who testified in various ways the high estimation in which they held him. The following extract from the "Richmond Whig," written by a distinguished Virginian, is evidence of the high reputation he sustained abroad, as well as at home:—

The name of this gentleman demands a passing note. If there be truth in the adage, "*nemo felix ante mortem*," then is he more to be envied than any man on earth. His political life was more than half his existence, and he has rendered it up and rendered up an account of his deeds, and received while he yet lives, that judgment in which even his enemies concur, and which, therefore, posterity must ratify. He lives to read his own epitaph, and its language is that of praise. He lives to hear the voice of lamentation at his untimely fall, arising from all the land. He hears himself mourned as a father by his children. He walks among us as though his disembodied spirit had returned to earth, and we turn aside with awe, and look upon him as a thing not of this world. Men gaze upon him, as he passes, and the question "Which is he?" is asked, not because he is a distributor of honors and emoluments, but because he has secured to himself an honor which the world gave not, and cannot take away—an honor greater than any the world can give. We have God's word for it, that his gray hairs, worn, as they have been, in the "paths of righteousness," are indeed "a crown of glory." May God's peace rest and abide with him.

An appropriate requiem is found in the following lines addressed by an English poet to an old oak, uprooted by a tempest:—

"Thou who unmoved hast heard the tempest chide,
  Full many a winter round thy craggy bed;
  And, like an earth-born giant hast out-spread
Thy hundred arms, and heaven's own bolt defied;
Now liest along thy native mountain's side
  Uptorn; yet deem not that I come to shed
  The idle drops of pity o'er thy head,
Or basely to insult thy blasted pride.
No! still 'tis thine, tho' fallen, imperial oak,
  To teach this lesson to the wise and brave:
That 'tis far better, overthrown and broke,
  In freedom's cause to sink into the grave,
Than, in submission to a tyrant's yoke,
  Like the vile reed, to bow and be a slave."

He came back among his old friends worn down by severe illness; having performed a trying journey of thirty-three days, in a state of such extreme debility, that his friends watched each day, with trembling, lest it should be his last. Yet, throughout all this suffering, the public welfare continued to excite his deepest interest. The subjoined letter, one of the last which he ever wrote, shows that his country, her institutions, and her prosperity, inspired him with the profoundest solicitude.

My Friend:—If towards any man I ought to use that term, I know of no one to whom I can apply it with a deeper conviction it is merited. You have stuck to me through good and evil report, without ever faltering or making a false or foolish move. The object of this letter is to give you all now in an old man's power, and one who feels on the verge of the grave—my most heartfelt thanks for your kind, able, and efficient care of me and my reputation. I am now through. On the 13th Jan. my political life was terminated by my enemies. I have no faith in the political resurrection of old men; but think not I am either mortified or depressed. Although I may be placed *hors de combat*, I hope that some seeds have dropped even from the last limbs of my decayed trunk, which, if watered and cherished, may yet bring forth fruit for the good of the country.

Late letters from some of my colleagues in Washington, assure me that from every quarter the news in relation to General Harrison's prospects are most encouraging.

I like your electoral ticket with the exception of my name. That I think unfortunate, considering the state of my health; but time will show what ought to be done, and my rule is never to act in haste.

Would to God I could be with you a day or two. I write now to show that there is yet something of me left, although you will see there is very little of either mental or physical strength.

Sincerely

Hugh L. While.

A. A. Ball, Esq.

His last prayer was answered. His country was redeemed from the reproach which had been thrown upon it. Although the grave closed over him, before he was permitted to witness that redemption, yet the foul stain, which had been cast upon his own fair fame, was wiped out by an overwhelming majority in the Presidential contest of 1840, a result to which the influence of his speeches and actions largely contributed.

CHAPTER XIX.

HIS FAMILY—HIS AFFLICTIONS.

JUDGE WHITE's social and domestic affections were remarkably strong; and so far as his political career withdrew him from the sphere of their attractions, it was far from delightful to him. He loved home as such, and seldom left it except when business rendered it necessary.

In 1798 he married Miss Elizabeth Moore, daughter of his early friend and instructor, the Rev. Samuel Carrick. She was born in Rockbridge county, Virginia, and possessed all the warmth, frankness, and generosity characteristic of the people of her native State. Her father was one of the early settlers of Tennessee. He was the first Presbyterian minister who ever had charge of a congregation in Knoxville, and was afterwards the founder and first President of Blount College

His daughter was but just verging upon her fifteenth year at the period of her marriage; and although her personal beauty was the first cause of attraction, yet, even at that early age, her capacity for fulfilling the important responsibilities of the position then assumed soon developed itself and proved to be of no ordinary grade. She was early distinguished for her many domestic virtues. As a wife she was preëminently faithful to all the interests of her husband, kindly caring for his personal comfort, and in his absence zealously watching over his pecuniary interests. Nor was her usefulness confined within the limits of her household.

She seldom lost an opportunity of alleviating the distresses of the miserable and destitute.

It was the will of Providence to continue this conjugal relation, which was productive of so much domestic happiness, for thirty-three years. They soon found themselves surrounded by a large family of children. Four sons and eight daughters cemented this union—

of whom two died in infancy, and the remainder reached years of maturity.

For twenty-five years they lived in the full enjoyment of all the social pleasures the little world of home could bestow; and the happiness they themselves enjoyed was imparted to others. "Their house was the abode of every delight and virtue." * The fond attachment of the husband was manifested by the regard and acts of kindness which he showed to all who were objects of interest to her, and on her part was reciprocated by cheerfully gratifying the wants and promoting the welfare of all his friends.

As parents they labored assiduously to "impress the minds and imbue the hearts" of their children with all those graces which would alone fit them for time and eternity. He was peculiarly gifted in awakening and encouraging their most confiding affection, and at the same time commanding their most profound respect, while she as a mother, was eminently qualified to keep alive and growing these important principles; and the result was, they were happy in seeing these objects of their warmest solicitude, grow up around them models of gentleness and truth.

But the scene changed. Death entered their quiet and happy home, in that insidious but most fatal of all forms of disease, pulmonary consumption; and the first born was the first victim of the relentless tyrant. Carrick, their eldest son, died in 1826, in the 27th year of his age—when, says a cotemporary, "the attainments of his mind were but just developing themselves, and yet already in his profession of the law, his brethren of the bar, and the public were ready justly as well as generously, to award him the praise of almost unrivalled acuteness and promise, and his clients the most unbounded confidence in the strictness of his integrity and the fidelity of his course."

The following letter to his friend James Park, Esq., the father-in-law of his son, shows that notwithstanding the sad news was not altogether unlooked for, yet his sensibilities were completely overwhelmed when it reached him.

WASHINGTON, *Jan. 31st*, 1826.

MY DEAR SIR.—Be pleased to deliver the inclosed letter to Nancy. Letters from James and Doctor Watkins had taught me expect the sad news, which this morning's mail brought me. That my beloved son is

* Dr. Foot's funeral sermon upon Judge White.

no more. Yes, that Carrick is gone, gone forever, and that without the farewell of his father. Dreadful, heart-rending, and life embittering thought!

I am incapable of offering any advice about anything. I should be glad to hear from you, who are capable of deriving consolation in the midst of all misfortunes, from sources of which I have no right to draw.

Most sincerely yours,

HU. L. WHITE

JAMES PARK, ESQ.

From this time his domestic life became a scene of constant trial. The destroyer severed in rapid succession the ties of affection. From time to time he was doomed to drink still more deeply of the bitter cup of sorrow, which only a parent's heart can know as he sees the objects of his fondest hopes, in the full prime of manhood, and in the full blush of womanhood sinking one after another into premature decay. Early in the year 1827, another daughter and daughter-in-law passed away.

In anticipation of the calamity, he again writes to the same friend.

SENATE CHAMBER, *Feb. 6th*, 1827.

DEAR SIR:—Your favor of the 22d January is this moment received. Your previous letter loitered long by the way. I answered it immediately after it was received.

I have for some time been desirous to write to Nancy and to Lucinda; but cannot bring myself to write to either.

For some weeks I have been under the belief that even the painful satisfaction of ever seeing either of them in this life is not to be afforded me.

I already feel as though they were lost to me; the affliction you realise I know: But "shall we receive good and not be prepared to submit to affliction from the hand of the Lord?"

I have no news.

Your friend,

HU. L. WHITE.

JAMES PARK, ESQ.

On this occasion his fears were not fully realised. He arrived at home on the morning of the 20th March, and his daughter Lucinda, of whom he writes in this letter, died on the evening of the same day. So that she died not, without giving a parting look of recognition to the father she loved so tenderly.

The year 1828 was more fatal to him than any which had preceded it.

In this year his second daughter, Mrs. Mary L. Swan, who had been married but eight months, died. The following July his eldest daughter, Betsey, relict of Newton Scott, died. "She was early taught by the death of her husband, but a few months after their marriage, the entire instability of all earthly expectations, and she had the happiness to profit in the school of adversity." In November of the same year he was deprived of his second son, James, under circumstances, if possible still more distressing. Soon after obtaining a license to practise law, he removed to Huntsville, Ala., and commenced his professional career. He had remained there but a few years, when his course was arrested by disease. He then returned with his family to Knoxville, in the hope of recovering his health. At the approach of winter he sought a milder climate, presuming it would be more congenial to his constitution, and assist in the restoration of his strength; but he was unable to proceed farther than Tuscaloosa, where he died, without the affectionate care of wife, mother or sister, to watch over his helpless hours of sickness, to soothe his pains, or minister to his infirmities.

Says a friend, in writing of this son: "In his profession, though young, he was conspicuous; though his career was short, it was brilliant. He was argumentative and eloquent, ingenious and profound, and had a fair prospect of obtaining a preëminent reputation."

Although Judge White's heart was filled with profound sorrow at these untimely losses, yet there was no murmuring or repining. His entire submission to the Divine will in these bereavements will be seen from the following letter to Dr. Coffin, President of East Tennessee College, and former preceptor of his sons.

WASHINGTON, *Dec. 6th* 1828.

DEAR SIR.—By the mail which arrived this morning I received a letter from Tuscaloosa, which gave the sorrowful information that James is no more. Believing, when I parted with him, that we would never meet again in time, I had been striving to reconcile my mind to such a separation, and hoped that I could hear of his death with composure, but while there was life there was also hope, and I found the news had an effect I did not anticipate. In and by my children I expected to obtain my distinction while I lived, and by the same medium to be known to posterity. My leading object was to deserve the reputation of integrity, to acquire funds equal to a comfortable support, and to the giving them a good education. Providence favored these endeavors to every desirable extent. With my elder children, good dispositions and an aptitude to learn, it appeared to me, were found united. My assiduous attention was given to inculcate, in the first place, the value of good morals, and in the next, to create a strong desire for the improvement of their minds. I was flattered in the belief that I had succeeded, and they had become my most intimate companions. I was proud of them, they were just as I had desired they should be. Now, where are they? Of twelve, only five younger ones remain. Seven have had their state of probation, and have passed to their everlasting home. Good God! I am forced to realize the solemn thought, that they and I never can see each other in time. This is a heart-rending reflection, which I can hardly summon up fortitude enough to bear. So it is, and I must submit to it.

In the midst of all these bereavements I have had, and continue to have, some sources of high consolation. Of the five who were grown, no one was addicted to any one vice, so far as I know. If not entitled to the appellation of pious, each of them was at least moral. It pleased God so far to restrain them, that each of them lived esteemed, and died without having done any act disgraceful, in the estimation of society. They were so far favored that each died of a slow, and lingering complaint, seldom, if ever deprived of the full exercise of their reason. They were thus enabled solemnly to review their short lives, to repent of all departures from the Will of their Maker, and to pray for forgiveness to that Being who alone has the power to pardon.

While spared to me I had all the satisfaction with them, and believe they had with me, which can reasonably be expected between a father and his children. Enabled by the blessing of Providence to supply all their temporal wants, and having done so with the most heart-felt satisfaction, and they in return having given me not only their gratitude but their fondest filial love, I see not why I ought to grieve. "The Lord gave them" to me, He made them a blessing to me while here, "He hath taken them away," and surely I ought to add, "blessed be the name of the Lord." He knew best when to give them, how long to permit them to remain, and when and how to remove them to that place, as I hope, "where the wicked cease from troubling and the weary are at rest."

If, according to my blind wishes, he had permitted either of them to have lived in health, a week, or even one day longer, they might have committed some act more distressing than their death. I will then try to be satisfied. He who removed them hence knows all things, and orders everything for the best. Therefore His will, not mine be done.

Present me in terms of kindness to your good lady and your children, and believe that,

I am, with the highest regard and esteem,

Your most ob't servant,

HU. L. WHITE.

Doctor CHARLES COFFIN.

Two other daughters soon followed. In January 1829, his fifth daughter, Cynthia, died at the age of seventeen; and Melinda, his sixth daughter, in April 1830, at the age of fifteen.

Though the recital of so many similar events has made the scene familiar, yet we have now to record one, if possible, of more melancholy importance. The malady which had carried away the children, demanded also the mother. In the autumn of 1830, she was attacked with illness, and to avoid a separation, accompanied her husband to Washington, where she lingered through the winter. All hopes being abandoned of her restoration to health, her only wish now seemed to be, to reach home, and see those of her family who remained behind. She and her husband left Washington on the 5th March and travelled at the rate of ten or twelve miles a day.

She continued to decline, and died on the 25th March 1831, at a public house near the Natural Bridge in Virginia, in the same county in which she was born. Her remains were placed in a coffin, and brought to Knoxville, three hundred and twenty miles, and deposited in their ancestral burying place.

Although there were friends with him, who would have done him any act of kindness, yet lest the carriage should be rudely driven, the mourning husband undertook the sad task, and carefully conducted her lifeless form to its last resting-place.

The day preceding his arrival at home, he was met by a number of his friends and neighbors, who remained with him all night, and by many acts of personal kindness, softened the private afflictions he had been doomed to suffer, and enabled him to remain at his post, and fearlessly and unfalteringly to discharge his duty to them and his country.

His fourth daughter, Margaret W. Alexander, upon learning her mother's real situation, requested to be taken to her. Her friends, knowing the difficulties and dangers which must attend a trip through the valley of Virginia, at that inclement season, attempted to dissuade her from it. For a while she acquiesced and endeavored to comply with her father's injunction to remain at home. But finally, upon hearing of the low condition of her mother, she could not be dissuaded from her purpose. She left home in company with her husband, and reached the Natural Bridge on the morning of the 26th, too late to receive the parting blessing of her parent. From exposure consequent upon this trip, she contracted the same disease, and died the following September.

But few men have ever been so severely chastened. Death was so continually and so suddenly destroying all around him, that in the short space of six years he was called to resign the companion of his youth and eight grown children, and so rapidly that four were consigned to the tomb in the short space of nine months. The duties of his position were such, that he had the privilege of being with only three out of the number in their last hours. Even his wife, whose fortitude never forsook her, amidst those multiplied trials, was denied the comfort of his presence.

These afflictive dispensations produced their legitimate results. Under the first bereavements he turned tremulously away from God, as one who felt he had no claims upon His promise of sustaining grace; but as renewed strokes of chastening from a kind Father's hand were laid upon him, he bowed submissively, not only acknowledging the power, but the goodness of God.

He now found himself alone with "the recollection of what they were;" and still so strong were his attachments for home, that he preferred remaining by his now desolate hearthstone to seeking enjoyment elsewhere. It was at this period that he was more than ever resolved upon retiring from public life, but was induced to sacrifice his personal feelings to the interests of his friends and the public.

Out of twelve, two children were all that were left him; a son aged six years, and a daughter aged nine.

His grandchildren now shared with his children his paternal solicitude. His sons left four children, and his eldest daughter one; the latter was reared in his own house—and the education of all was his peculiar care. But while engaged in discharging his duty to the living, he did not forget the sacred debt he owed to those who were no more. Upon leaving and returning home his first and last visits were to their quiet resting-place. This habit continued with him throughout life, and proved that their virtues were embalmed in his memory.

In November, 1832, Judge White formed a second marriage with Mrs. Ann E. Peyton, of Washington City, a lady of fine mind and polished address, with whom he lived eight years, in great happiness, and from whom he was seldom separated. She proved herself an affectionate and devoted wife, and shared a large portion of his last thoughts. She survived her husband seven years, and died at his residence near Knoxville, in April, 1847. Her remains were taken by her request to Washington, and interred by the side of her daughter

CHAPTER XX.

HIS DEATH.

JUDGE WHITE's health was somewhat impaired, in consequence of an attack of pneumonia, which he had before leaving Washington. The fatigue and exposure of travelling at so inclement a season of the year, caused his disease to terminate in pulmonary consumption. As soon as he found himself upon the soil of his own State, the very air of Tennessee seemed to exert a reviving and invigorating influence upon his health. After he reached home, he so far improved, that he was able to take an interest in everything around him ; and his mind was constantly employed in devising plans for the future comfort of his family. He made a contract for building on his farm (two miles distant from his residence) where, as he frequently expressed himself, he would pass the remainder of his life with his wife and children.

His physical strength did not entirely forsake him to the very last. He was able to take his accustomed rides of one or two miles, almost daily, either on horseback or in a carriage, which gave his friends cause to hope his life might yet be prolonged. On the 8th of April he rode four miles in a carriage, but was unable to sit up all the way. This was the last exercise he took. On the 9th, the day previous to his death, he did not leave home, but sat up the greater part of the day and until a late hour at night, and was unusually cheerful. He slept as comfortably as usual until two o'clock, A. M., when it was discovered that his cough was changed. The abscess on his lungs had broken, and being too feeble to discharge it, he lived about six hours, suffering apparently little pain, and died at half-past eight o'clock, on the morning of the 10th of April, 1840. To the last hour of his life the vigor of his intellect remained unabated. Although unable to talk much, he was perfectly conscious, and occasionally expressed great concern about his family.

He never made any public profession of religion; but, from the pious precepts and examples placed before him in early life, he imbibed a veneration for all its institutions. He believed that religion consisted more in doing right, from a sense of obligation to the Supreme Being, than in forms and ceremonies. His resignation to the Divine will, and confidence in his acceptance with God, was full and perfect. A few days before his death he was visited by the Rev. Dr. Foot, president elect of Washington College, who conversed with him fully and freely upon the subject of his approaching change. Judge White was a firm believer in Christianity as revealed in the Bible, and as expounded by orthodox Christians. He had entire faith in the plan of atonement. He affirmed in his last hours, that "having made it a point through life, to do all the good in his power, and as little harm as possible, and placing a firm reliance on the merits of Christ to supply all the deficiencies incident to human frailty, he now had no more fear of appearing in the presence of his Heavenly Father, than he would in that of a kind, earthly parent.

When the intelligence of his death reached the town, all business was immediately suspended. The Chancery Court, which was in session, adjourned over to the ensuing day.

His body was interred in the burial ground of the First Presbyterian Church on Sunday, at two o'clock, P. M., and was followed to the grave by an immense concourse of citizens. The procession left his late residence in the following order:—Clergy—members of the medical profession—judges and members of the bar—pall-bearers—the body—relatives of the deceased—trustees of East Tennessee University—president and professors of East Tennessee University—students of the University—principal and students of Hampden Sydney Academy—citizens. Immediately behind the body of the deceased, followed his riding horse, Rienzi, with saddle and bridle, but without rider; whose slow and measured tread seemed to betoken that he, too, sadly felt the loss of his master, and called forth a fresh burst of grief from his friends and fellow citizens.

Appropriate services were held at both the house and grave. After which the assembly dispersed; and all classes of the community seemed to feel that they had been called to mourn a heavy calamity.

A plain tomb-stone marks the spot where rest the ashes of this good and great man, with the following simple inscription:—

To

THE MEMORY OF

HUGH LAWSON WHITE,

"The Just,"

Who was born Oct. 29th, 1773, and departed this life April 10th, 1840.

Composed in suffering, and in joy sedate,
Good without noise, without pretension great,
True to his word, in every thought sincere,
He knew no wish but what the world might hear.

This humble tribute of devoted affection and deep regret is deposited by his bereaved wife.

In different parts of the country, numerous public discourses were delivered on the occasion of his death, and frequent testimonials of respect appeared in the public journals of the day. One is selected from those published in each division of his State, because of the treatment he had received from a small portion of its citizens. An account of the meeting at Washington is also given in consequence of his long residence and services in that city. These addresses were delivered by men who had known the deceased intimately for many years both in his public and private capacity; and therefore their testimony is entitled to confidence.

On the 26th April, 1840 a funeral sermon was expected to have been delivered in the Presbyterian church at Knoxville, by the Rev. J. I. Foot, D. D., who was killed by a fall from his horse on the 20th of the same month, within a few miles of Rogersville, while on his way to Washington College. A part of the sermon was, however, prepared, from Isaiah xl. 6. "The voice said, Cry. And he said, What shall I cry? All flesh is grass, and all the goodliness thereof is as the flower of the field: The grass withereth, the flower fadeth."

At a meeting of the members of the Bar, at Knoxville, Hon. Thomas L. Williams was called to the chair, and John H. Crozier, Esq., appointed secretary.

The Hon. Edward Scott presented the following preamble and resolutions, which were unanimously adopted.

A GREAT MAN HAS FALLEN IN ISRAEL!

This day, about the hour of nine o'clock, at his residence near this place, the Hon. Hugh L. White ceased to exist. Henceforth he will live only in the memory of his friends and his countrymen. He was certainly a great and worthy man; a friend to truth, virtue, liberty, and the Constitution. His was a life of labor and activity—a life of usefulness, moderation, regular conduct, and inflexible integrity. The law was his profession. By his fair, open, and manly conduct, he won the sincere affection and approbation of all his contemporaries. He was an agreeable and eloquent speaker. In him were happily blended a profound judgment, and accomplished address. In him the unfortunate and the honest ever found a protector, while the guilty were marked for punishment. Raised to the highest office in his profession, he did honor to the station, and was among the greatest, and ablest magistrates that ever lived among us. Elevated to a seat in the United State Senate, he maintained hat purity of character which marked his private life. He loved the Constitution, nor would he consent to a forced construction of that instrument for the oppression of the people. The future historian will not fail to record his virtues. We all know that his private character was without blemish; he was an affectionate husband, a kind parent and a steadfast friend. In short, he died as he lived, a true republican, an ardent advocate of the rights of man, and an enemy to arbitrary power.

Resolved, That in token of our high respect and esteem for the private virtues, and public character of the deceased, we will wear the usual badge of mourning for thirty days.

On motion of John H. Crozier, it was

Resolved, That the foregoing preamble and resolutions be presented by the Hon. Edward Scott, on to-morrow morning, to the Chancery Court now in session in this place, with the request that the same be entered on the record of the Court.

Resolved, That we tender to the family and relatives of the deceased our sincere condolence on their late distressing bereavement, and that the Secretary furnish them with a copy of these proceedings.

THOMAS L. WILLIAMS, *Chairman*.

JOHN H. CROZIER, *Secretary*.

At a meeting of the citizens of Nashville, Thursday, the 6th of April, Col. George Wilson was called to the chair, and Edwin H. Ewing, Esq., appointed secretary.

The chairman having stated the object of the meeting, Allen A. Hall offered the following preamble and resolutions:—

THE BEAUTY OF ISRAEL IS SLAIN UPON THY HIGH PLACES.

Hugh Lawson White has passed off the stage of the great theatre of life! Well and nobly has he sustained the high character for which he was cast. Would that the curtain of mortality had not fallen, till the *epilogue* to his eventful life had all been acted out and spoken, in the surely vindicating future. *Quod scriptum scriptum est!* "What is written, is written." Yes! in the court above, the decree—how truly irreversible!—has been entered up: and the name, and virtues and services of Judge White are become the priceless inheritance of his country. Conspicuous among those of his day, to whom it has happened to have lived, acted and spoken under the scrutinizing eye of history, he has labored for the benefit of his country, as truly as ever a man toiled for his family.

Illustrious by the eminence of his virtues, the usefulness of his talents, the importance of his functions, his character needs no indeterminate commendations, no accumulated epithets—no didactic reflections. His merits require no exaggeration. He had nothing to dissemble. His history, written with faithfulness, will be his best eulogium. "He hath so planted his honors in our eyes, and his actions in our hearts, that for our tongues to be silent, and not confess so much, were an ungrateful injury: to report otherwise, were a malice, that giving itself the lie, would pluck reproof and rebuke from every ear that heard it."

The spontaneous feeling of unaffected sorrow, which has here convened the friends of the deceased, can find but imperfect expression in these extemporaneous and preliminary proceedings. We pause at the threshold till, some orator, worthy of his subject, shall bid us enter, with becoming awe, the temple of his fame.

From the age of thirteen, roughly disciplined in the border life of Tennessee; at nineteen, acting a manly part in savage warfare; a judge, at the early age of twenty-eight, and for twelve years giving universal satisfaction by able, and in many instances important decisions; twelve years president of the Bank of Tennessee, it was always prosperous by his prudent and wise counsels; a senator in the State legislature; district attorney of the United States; commissioner between Virginia and Kentucky in the settlement of important land claims, and again, under the Spanish treaty. In all these varied trusts, equally honest and capable, he was the exact, efficient man of business; twice was he elected without opposition to the Senate of the United States, and on a memorable occasion, when in the conflict of great principles, an arbiter was needed to control giant minds, he was chosen to preside over that body.

As self-poised and magnanimous in declining honors, as in accepting office; he refused a seat on the Bench of the Supreme Court of the United States, and more than once a place in the cabinet of the federal executive. In a public career of forty years, of spotless integrity, with a rare disinterestedness, he twice refused compensation, to a large amount, for most valuable public services.

Nor is the reverse of the medal less beautifully defined. His private life exhibited the perfect harmony of his whole character; and so attractive has it ever been, that his numerous friends have regarded him more with the sentiments of paternal affection, and the tenderness of a near relationship, than with the ordinary feelings which attach a public man to his constituents. Accordingly they have rejoiced at his well deserved success, or have been indignant at the ungrateful returns, which the best benefactors often receive, and in all vicissitudes, they have felt his reputation dear to them as their own personal concern, and they still

> "Wear him
> In their heart's core; ay, in their heart of hearts."

Ungrateful returns! They were the vouchers of his uncompromising integrity and consistency; they were the evidences of his greatness

When attacked, he defended himself beyond all ordinary powers of endurance, with the weapons of truth, and the bravery of conscious uprightness. That reputation which grows, as the oak, through all changing seasons amidst alternate storms, and sunshines, shall still be firmly rooted and majestic, when the rude tempests of party strife are all blown over. The subject of our eulogy has been in *this* triumphant, that his last days were the best witnesses of his worth. Death only could subdue him. "Without fear and without reproach," he had a right to demand an honorable discharge; but his self sacrificing, generous love of country, brought him to the foremost place in that hot fight, in which we are now engaged. He has died in his armor, covered with glory. "His end lamented by the good, by none more than by us."

> "Dear let his memory be, and proud his grave!
> And this his epitaph: "He lived, he fought
> For truth and wisdom, foremost of the brave,
> Him glory's idle fancies dazzled not,
> 'Twas his ambition, generous and great,
> A life to life's great end to consecrate!"

"He came to his grave in full age, like as a shock of corn cometh in, in his season." Full of years, and of just honors full, the venerable White "rests from his labors, and his works do follow him."

Resolved, That we lament the death of the Hon. Hugh L. White, as a great calamity; in which our sense of loss to that cause to which he was more especially pledged, in the present posture of public affairs, is merged in condolence with the good, the enlightened, and the liberal of all parties.

Resolved, That it be suggested to the whig electors to wear the usual badge of mourning ninety days.

Resolved, That we deeply sympathize with the immediate family of the deceased, and that a copy of these proceedings be transmitted to them, as an expression of our condolence.

Resolved, That the record of these proceedings, signed by the Chairman and Secretary, be published in the newspapers at Nashville.

Ephraim H. Foster, Esq., having seconded the adoption of the foregoing preamble and resolutions in a few appropriate remarks, they were adopted without a dissenting voice. Whereupon the meeting, on motion of Henry Hollingsworth, Esq., adjourned.

GEORGE WILSON, *Chairman.*

EDWIN H. EWING, *Secretary.*

The Supreme Court of the State of Tennessee, in session at Jackson, on receiving the melancholy intelligence of the death of the Hon. Hugh L. White, immediately adjourned; after which the members of the Bar of West Tennessee, in attendance on the Supreme Court, convened at the court-house for the purpose of paying a tribute of respect to the memory of the deceased.

Whereupon, on motion of Adam Huntsman, Esq., P. M. Miller Esq., was called to the chair, and Micajah Bullock, Esq. and Austin Miller, Esq., were appointed secretaries.

Henry G. Smith, Esq., then offered the following preamble and resolutions, which were unanimously adopted:

Information having been this day received of the death of the Hon. Hugh L. White, of Knoxville, formerly a judge of the Supreme Court of this State, and long a distinguished member of our profession; as a testimonial of respect to his memory, due alike for his eminent public services, for his great private worth, to the purity, propriety, and dignity, of his long and active life, the members of the Bar of West Tennessee in attendance upon the Supreme Court at Jackson, assembled for the purpose of declaring their sentiments:—

Resolved, That in his death the Bar of this State has sustained the loss of a most distinguished member and ornament; the people of Tennessee, of a long tried and faithful servant; society, of a good and useful citizen; his family, of a kind father and affectionate husband; mankind, of one of the noblest of the race.

And, therefore, that we are penetrated with feelings of an unfeigned sorrow and regret upon the occasion of his death; and that the members of the Bar of West Tennessee, assembled at this meeting, respectfully and affectionately tender their condolence and sympathy to his bereaved family.

Resolved, That a copy of the proceedings of this meeting be presented to the Supreme Court at this place, with the request that the same may be entered on the minutes of the court; and that a copy be addressed to the family of the deceased;

And that a copy be furnished for the press, with a request that the proceedings may be published;

And that the same be signed by the Chairman and Secretaries.

Whereupon the meeting adjourned.

P. M. MILLER, *Chairman.*

M. BULLOCK, A. MILLER, } *Secretaries.*

JACKSON, *April*, 18, 1840.

And afterwards, on Monday, the 20th day of April, the resolutions above were presented to the court at its opening in the morning, with the request that they might be entered on the minutes of the court. The request was promptly complied with, and the following response to the motion was made by his honor Judge Reese, presiding on behalf of the court:—

We have been requested to cause to be spread upon the records of this court, a copy of the proceedings of a meeting of the members of the bar of West Tennessee, in attendance at the present term, intended by them as a testimonial of their regret for the death, and their respect for the memory of the Hon. Hugh L. White. We promptly and cordially assent to this request.

We received with the liveliest sensibility and profoundest regret, the melancholy intelligence that one so long and so eminently distinguished, as a member of our profession, and as a judge of this court, is no more to be numbered among the living. The individual upon whom has devolved the duty of responding to the request of the gentlemen of the bar, has known the deceased intimately for the last twenty years. The traits of his character were strongly marked. His intellect was unusually active, acute, clear, and vigorous. He had great firmness of purpose and energy of will, and if his temper was ardent, and his emotions sometimes intense, he had a prudence, discretion and fairness which directed his efforts to right ends by the use of proper means. His professional career commenced about the time when this State became a member of the Union, and he rose at once to honorable distinction. Although his preparation, scholastic and professional, as might be expected from the character of the country and the times, was rather accurate and useful, than extensive; still, such were the endowments of his mind, and the strength of his character, that for forty-five years, and to the last, he kept up with the improvements of society and the development of our institutions, and never lost that position in the very first rank of his profession with which he set out. As a lawyer, he was ever at his post and always prepared. As a speaker at the bar, he was animated, argumentative and eminently impressive; force and perspicuity were his striking attributes. As a judge, he was courteous, dignified, impartial and able. This elevated station he reached at an early age, and he largely contributed by the purity of his personal character and the energy, wisdom and justice of his official actions, to impress upon a new community that respect for, and submission to, an enlightened administration of the law, which has in all times and under all circumstances since, so honorably distinguished them.

The moral qualities of Hugh L. White were of the first order. Truth, that basis upon which must rest all the virtues he strongly loved, and scrupulously practised. His integrity was inflexible; no example of others, no fashion of the times could tempt him, for a moment, into any transaction, questionable in the motives, or equivocal in the tendency. He was an honest man, and ever kept his escutcheon stainless; and this he himself regarded as the highest and most honorable point in personal character. As a husband, a father and neighbor, he was all that a man, such as we have described him, could be expected to be. His long and active life brought him in contact with society at points which we mean not here to discuss. He was much in the political service of his country: even here we may be permitted to express the individual conviction that the period is not distant, when the turmoils of the present moment having passed by, few, if any, of his countrymen will be found to question the motives of his public conduct, or to deny that, in all the solid and essential qualities of a virtuous patriot and an enlightened statesman, he was eminently distinguished among the men of his time.

Upon Judge White's death being announced in the Senate by his successor, Mr. Alexander Anderson, the motion for the customary honors to be paid to his memory was seconded by Mr. Preston of South Carolina, who at the same time pronounced the following brief and merited eulogy upon the virtues of the deceased:

"I do not know, Mr. President, whether I am entitled to the honor I am about to assume in seconding the resolutions which have just been offered by the Senator from Tennessee, in honor of his late predecessor; and yet, sir, I am not aware that any one present is more entitled to this melancholy honor, if it belongs to long acquaintance, to sincere admiration, and to intimate intercourse. If these circumstances do not entitle me to speak, I am sure every senator will feel, in the emotions which swell his own bosom, an apology for my desire to relieve my own, by bearing testimony to the virtues and talents, the long services and great usefulness, of Judge White.

"My infancy and youth were spent in a region contiguous to the sphere of his earlier fame and usefulness. As long as I can remember anything, I remember the deep confidence he had inspired as a wise and upright judge, in which station no man ever enjoyed a purer reputation, or established a more implicit reliance in his abilities and honesty. There was an antique sternness and justness in his character. By a general consent he was called Cato. Subsequently, at a period of our public affairs very analogous to the present, he occupied a position which placed him at the head of the financial institutions of East Tennessee. He sustained them by his individual character. The name of Hugh L. White was a guarantee that never failed to attract confidence. Institutions were sustained by the credit of an individual, and the only wealth of that individual was his character. From this more limited sphere of usefulness and reputation, he was first brought to this more conspicuous stage as the member of an important commission on the Spanish treaty, in which he was associated with Mr. Tazewell and Mr. King. His learning, his ability, his firmness and industry, immediately extended the sphere of his reputation to the boundaries of the country. Upon the completion of that duty, he came into this Senate. Of his career here I need not speak. His grave and venerable form is even now before us—that air of patient attention, of grave deliberation, of unrelaxed firmness. Here his position was of the highest—beloved, respected, honored; always in his place — always prepared for the business in hand—always bringing to it the treasured reflections of a sedate and vigorous understanding. Over one department of our deliberations he exercised a very peculiar control. In the management of our complex and difficult relations with the Indians, we all deferred to him, and to this he addressed himself with unsparing labor, and with a wisdom, a patient benevolence, that justified and vindicated the confidence of the Senate.

"In private life he was amiable and ardent. The current of his feelings was warm and strong. His long familiarity with public affairs had not damaged the natural ardor of his temperament. We all remember the deep feeling with which he so recently took leave of this body, and how profoundly that feeling was reciprocated. The good-will, the love, the respect which we bestowed upon him then, now give depth and energy to the mournful feelings with which we offer a solemn tribute to his memory."

At a meeting, in the Capitol at Washington of the personal friends and admirers among the members of the House of Representatives in Congress, of the late Hugh L. White of Tennessee, called on the 21st instant, for the purpose of paying a tribute of respect to his memory;

The Hon. Thomas W. Chinn, of Louisiana, was called to the Chair, and the Hon. William K. Bond, of Ohio, was appointed secretary.

The Hon. John Bell, of the Tennessee delegation, rose and introduced the object of the meeting, with the following remarks:—

As the senior member of the Tennessee delegation, now present, it may be expected that I should state the object of this meeting, which is simply to make some suitable manifestation of our sorrow for the death of the late Judge White, and to pay such tribute of respect to the excel lence of his character, as I am sure will be equally grateful to our own feelings, and to his numerous relatives and friends, wherever they may be.

Not having been a member of the House of Representatives, the precedents do not authorize the annunciation of his name in that body, nor admit the customary proceedings in honor of departed fellow members. The deep and unaffected concern with which the melancholy intelligence of his death was received by every member who had formed a personal acquaintance with him in the course of his public service, and the anxious solicitude they expressed that some mode should be adopted, by which they could testify their feelings to the world, will, perhaps, after all, be regarded as a higher testimonial of his worth than any we can now offer.

Many were of opinion that his long and useful public services, the venerable age at which he had arrived, and above all, the unblemished purity of his whole life, were sufficient to set aside all precedents, and to justify an extraordinary proceeding in the House. But on reflection, it was concluded that nothing should be attempted, which under the excitement of the times, could be attributed to any possible motive except the desire of doing sincere homage to the virtues of the deceased. I must confess, however, there is something very unsatisfactory to the feelings, in the customary proceedings of the two Houses, upon the occasion of the decease of a member. They are, for the most part, indiscriminate; there is the same routine in every case; oftentimes the duty of speaking the eulogy is devolved upon one who has neither the heart to appreciate, nor perhaps, the inclination to do justice to his memory. I, therefore, on every account, prefer the mode of our present meeting. Here, there is no involuntary or exacted homage; none give their attendance, but those whose feelings would not allow them to be absent. Here, too, we can give full scope to our friendship and admiration, unrestrained by the fear of giving offence to the taste of the cold and indifferent; and besides, it is not the member of Congress whose death we now deplore, to whose memory we offer the tribute of our sorrow and our tears. It is to the man, the public officer, the statesman, who was an honor, and a bright and shining one, not only to the State in which he lived, to the country he served so long, so ably, and so faithfully, but to human nature itself. For if there be truth in the proposition, that the noblest work of Deity is an "honest man," then was the late Hugh Lawson White, of Tennessee, one of the noblest specimens of divine workmanship. Altogether, he formed a character of rare perfection. Though determined in his own purposes of ardent and decided attachments, though engaging freely and actively in all the concerns of life, there was nothing in his whole career, no infirmity, no act, public or private, over which his friends need draw a veil in charity. The history of his last days we all know. Retiring from the Senate, in obedience to his principles and that inexorable sense of duty which had influenced his whole life, though suffering from indisposition at the time, he resolved to set out immediately for his residence in Tennessee. Incapable, from long habits of self denial, of personal indulgence, the entreaties and warnings of his friends, who had but too clearly foreseen the perils of so long a travel, in a season of such uncommon severity, were unavailing. The exposure and privations of his journey were fatal to his health. Disease fastened on a vital part of his system, and he finally sunk under it, with signal composure and fortitude.

Thus terminated a life of uncommon usefulness, and one which, I trust, when it shall become more generally known, will leave a salutary impress upon the whole country. Judge White was, indeed, in many respects, a man of most rare and felicitous endowments, some of which may have passed unobserved even by many of those who enjoyed his friendship during the latter years of his existence. His manly patience and fortitude under the severest afflictions, are known to but few. Though tender and affectionate to the last degree, in his domestic relations, yet his patient endurance under the greatest and most overwhelming domestic bereavements, was almost superhuman. By calling to his aid the *will*, that faculty, which, with him, when once summoned into action, was absolute and invincible, he could appear among his friends with serenity upon his brow, while his heart was pierced with the keenest anguish.

It may not be generally known, that this venerable patriot was, late in life, destined to the affliction of beholding the objects of his early paternal care, the pride, and joy, and hope of his affections fall, stricken by the "insatiate archer," one by one, in succession, until two only of a lovely and cherished group of ten remained; and what seemed yet a harder, and more relentless fate, all these sank into the tomb at full maturity—his sons in the vigor of manhood, and giving high promise of all their father was—the more tender and lovely members of his family in the full bloom of youthful beauty. Yet so stern was the sense of public duty, which always governed this eminent citizen, that, at its bidding, I have known him to allow himself but a single hour in which to weep the early doom of still another "daughter dear."

By a singular and unfortunate coincidence, a measure of great importance in the Senate of which he had charge, and which he alone, from his intimate acquaintance with the subject, was able to explain and enforce, was set for the very day on which he received the melancholy tidings of this new bereavement. The measure was urgent, and admitted no postponement. One moment I saw him with his heart wrung by inexpressible anguish—the next, he appeared in the Senate, composed and resolute, and a moment afterwards he entered upon one of the ablest and most effective speeches ever delivered by him in that body.

One other illustration of these less conspicuous, and perhaps, less useful qualities, yet still so characteristic of the man, I cannot forbear to give. I would speak of his gratitude—a virtue which he highly prized in himself, and the violation of which in others, he was less able to bear than any man I have known. Yet this cup, bitter as it is, he was, near the close of his valuable life, compelled to drain to the dregs.

It gives me great pleasure to see in this assembly so many of those who assisted upon another, but very different occasion, to consecrate, and canonize the last public act of this distinguished public servant. The generous sympathy, the just measure of approbation and applause you bestowed upon his public course, and upon the principles and sentiments he avowed in that, his last intellectual effort in this capitol—in this world—contributed to make the close of his public career the proudest and most glorious event of his life. I am sure it will long be a subject of pleasing reflection to each of you, to be informed that the recollection of the friendship and admiration so kindly manifested by you on that occasion, continued to animate and console him during the remaining, but too short, period of his life. It supported him in his painful journey home, as the letters which now lie before me fully evince. It continued to be the frequent theme of his conversation and of his pen in the last days of his affliction, and it afforded a gleam of light to illumine the darkness of his last hour. This will not appear extraordinary, when we know that next to the approval of his own conscience, he valued and coveted, above all things, the good opinion of his friends and countrymen. His great ambition through life was to live without reproach, to be esteemed in private life, an honest man, and in public, a useful and faithful servant. This was his passion, and surely no man in our times, through so long a life, and filling so many important stations, has lived so well and so successfully up to the standard his ambition had prescribed for the regulation of his conduct.

It is no common-place or unmeaning eulogy to say, that Aristides was not more just. He was in truth a model to two generations, for the moral conformation of the youth of the country around him—a mirror in which to dress themselves out in all the moral excellences of our nature —in all those qualities which make up the eminently useful and distinguished citizen.

When we reflect upon the keen sensibility of our lamented friend, his leading passion, the moderate though noble measure of his ambition, judge ye what must have been the intensity of his emotions when—after a life of nearly forty years spent in the public service, filling with the unanimous approbation of the whole people, for so long a period, the highest and most responsible stations, without censure or reproach, or question of his fidelity, and at a time, too, when, in the course of nature, he verged towards the close of his public labors—he was abruptly driven from the public councils, dismissed that public service he had so long adorned, not only with indifference, but with personal indignity and invective superadded. We can better imagine than embody in words the effect of such treatment upon a man constituted as he was. In truth, it

28

came near riving his noble heart. For a moment it quite vanquished him; for one moment his inflexible spirit seemed to give way, but it was only for a moment. The consciousness of having discharged every duty faithfully to the last, and a strong sense of the unmerited censure which had been cast upon him, soon came to his relief, and restored him to the exercise of his accustomed fortitude and power of endurance.

My feelings will allow me to proceed no further. I offer to the meeting, for their adoption, the resolutions which I hold in my hand:

Resolved, That the present meeting, composed of the personal friends and admirers of the late Hugh Lawson White, of Tennessee, have received the information of his death with the deepest emotion and regret.

Resolved, That, in testimony of those feelings, and as some small tribute of respect for the rare virtues, the distinguished ability and usefulness of a man who, in his whole life, was an example fit for the study and imitation of the present and future generations of his countrymen, we will wear the customary badge of mourning during thirty days.

After the reading of the above resolutions, Mr. Wise, of Virginia, rose and paid an eloquent tribute to the character of the deceased, and when he had concluded his remarks, the above resolutions were unanimously adopted.

Whereupon, on motion of Mr. Wise,

Resolved, That the chairman of this meeting forward a copy of these proceedings to the family of the deceased.

Resolved, That copies of these proceedings be sent to the editors of the "National Intelligencer" and the "Knoxville Times," with a request that the same be published in their respective papers.

THOMAS W. CHINN, *Chairman*.

WILLIAM R. BOND, *Secretary*.

At the Young Men's Whig Convention assembled in Baltimore, May, 1841, Mr. A. R. Humes of Tennessee being called upon for a report from that State, alluded in the following touching strain to Judge White. The "Madisonian" says, one of the most striking incidents of the day was the manner in which the immense assemblage received his reference to the good and great Hugh L. White. He said:—

"Fellow Citizens: In the midst of this 'army of banners,' borne aloft by the stout arms of freemen, there is *one* robed in the sable weeds of mourning. Tennessee deplores the death, and this day honors the memory of Hugh L. White."

The very moment the name of the departed patriot was mentioned, the thousands who surrounded the rostrum simultaneously took off their hats, and bent their heads in mournful homage to his memory. The effect was instantaneous—was sublime—was electric.

Mr. Humes continued :—

You, my countrymen! by your uncovered heads, at the mention of his great name, and by the holy and virtuous indignation you feel, written in legible characters, upon every face in this vast assembly, pay a just tribute to the worth of this parted patriot. He now sleeps with "the illustrious dead." His heart no longer throbs with the pulsations of freedom; his voice no longer eloquent in the councils of the nation, is hushed for ever, in the unbroken silence of the grave.

Mr. Humes, in alluding to the universal proscription of the party in power, said :—

"Among the many victims, who have bled upon the altar of this modern Moloch, this fierce, relentless despotism, was that man, who has been justly termed "the Cato of the Republic." He forsook a past Administration in the noon-day of its power in defence of the Constitution and the laws—he renounced adherence to men, for the sake of principle. He "passed the Rubicon" and the decree went forth. He was *banished* from office—and with a heart full of deep, unutterable feeling, and a venerable form, trembling beneath the palsying hand of age, he returned, once more, to the peaceful abodes of private life. But the storms of winter, and the baseness of ingratitude, "more strong than traitor's arm, quite vanquished him." Disease and calumny completed their work—he returned to his final home—a dishonored soil received the ashes of her injured exile. There we might hope, he would rest in undisturbed repose. But no! with fiendish malignity, do his defamers pursue him. Like fierce hyenas, they prowl around his grave, and insult his injured manes. But, fellow citizens! there is a day of terrible retribution. The blades of twenty thousand freemen are leaping from their scabbards to revenge his wrongs. A voice, from his fresh sodden grave, speaks in tones of thunder to you, this day. The foul stain upon the brightness of gallant Tennessee, will soon be wiped off—her glory is eclipsed, but not departed—the dark spot upon her broad disk, will soon pass away, and the year 1841 will dawn upon the young Switzerland of America regenerate and redeemed."

These eloquent tributes to the memory of Judge White, emanating from such high sources, were, certainly, grateful to his many friends. They were no less gratified by the many other marks of the same deep respect for his character and of the same unaffected and sincere sorrow manifested at his loss by the people.

A battalion of militia mustered in Roane County, Tennessee, when Judge White died. When the news of his death was carried to the place, by request of the commanding officer, the event was announced to the battalion, by Thomas J. Campbell Esq., who was present, and who added appropriate remarks touching his public and private character. The whole battalion evinced the deepest interest on the occasion, and unanimously determined on their return march from the field, to proceed with muffled drums, shrouded in black, which was accordingly done.

Another incident shows the affection with which he was regarded by the people. At the great whig convention held in Knoxville, in August, 1840, a gentleman who was present, and heard Col. David W. Dickenson's speech, says that, "when he (the orator) came to speak of Judge White, almost every man in that vast assembly was in tears."

CONCLUSION.

Having given the leading incidents in the life of Judge White, and shown him firm in his adherence to all his duties both of a public and private nature, in defiance of all denunciation, or seductive influences, the subject might well be left, in the confident belief that posterity will not fail to render that award of lofty merit which his character so eminently deserves. Testimonials to his worth have been inserted from so many and such high authorities, that it is scarcely necessary to say much in conclusion. But for the more perfect completion of the task a few observations may not improperly be added, descriptive of his appearance, or illustrative of his character.

His health, naturally delicate, had given him much trouble from the year 1819 until his death. His lungs were the seat of his disease, and although he was never so ill as to render it necessary for him to absent himself from his public duties, yet his hemorrhages were so frequent as to keep him in a constant state of apprehension.

His personal appearance changed but little towards the close of his life; he retained his erect form, and elastic step, almost to the last. He had an acute sense of the ludicrous, and was a lover of wit, although his appearance indicated a want of mirthfulness.

Assiduity in him was combined with great mental activity. He was distinguished for his ability to apply his mind intensely and protractedly, and for an unusual power of concentrating his thoughts upon a single subject. Accustomed from the beginning to consider seriously the impediments in the way of his attaining an object, he attentedly weighed them, and when he had undertaken to execute his purpose, his perseverance overcame every obstacle. Additional obstructions awakened additional strength, new and unforeseen difficulties led to the device of new and unforeseen expedients, until he, who might, in a sense, have appeared to be weak, and unable to maintain his own position, was changed into an intellectual giant, divesting his adversary of his armor, destroying his strong-hold, and leading him captive at his will. His mind was not of that brilliant order, whose only use is to astound the multitude. It delighted not to indulge in flights of the imagination, nor in sallies of wit. It did not chiefly rely on circumstances for its operation. What it had accomplished at one time, and in one class of circumstances, it could also accomplish in others of a widely different nature. Those mental efforts which depended on external and occasional excitements in other men, were by industry and perseverance easily and habitually performed by him. It was this reliable and ready power which made him equal to the exigencies of every cause which he undertook, and the duties of every office which he was called to fill. The vigor, which in some other men of equal, and perhaps superior, genius was fluctuating and doubtful, was with him more uniform.

He was a deep thinker, and remarkable for his power of comparison and of discovering inconsistencies, and of clothing his ideas in suitable language.

He examined thoroughly the arguments of others, his mind grasped and retained the leading points of a subject with great vigor, and his reasoning was so clear, that he made his ideas intelligible to the understanding of all. His style was forcible, perspicuous and concise. His sentences were commonly short and so selected and arranged that whatever he said could readily be followed. His style was often figurative, for purposes of illustration ; never for the sake of ornament. He addressed himself to the understanding and moral sensibilities and not to the passions—and when speaking, either in popular assemblies, or in parliamentary debate, his manner was marked by the most impassioned earnestness and he seldom failed to fix the attention of his hearers.

The operations of his mind were rapid ; his feelings were quick and intense and susceptible of exquisite enjoyment or extreme pain. His mental activity grew out of an ardent temperament. He used to say that he was naturally one of the most irritable and passionate of men, but he governed his temper well, and that was one secret of the influence which he exercised over the minds and conduct of others.

His own purity of motive rendered him slow to suspect or to censure the doings of others. Yet he was not deficient in the power of resisting ; and he never allowed his character to be trifled with, his rights invaded, or his friends imposed upon. This trait was more frequently exercised and clearly exemplified, by means of circumstances occurring during the last years of his life.

His incorruptible integrity was, however, the most prominent feature in his whole character. He abhorred the subtlety with which some advocates are accustomed to plead, and to seek to obtain an unjust verdict, and every course where success depended upon management and intrigue he regarded as unsound. Neither personal friendships, nor personal dislikes or animosities, ever colored his decisions; and the accuracy of his opinions and his uncompromising honesty secured for him universal respect.

In private life he was remarkable for the dignity and simplicity of his manners. In all his transactions the same honorable frankness of heart manifested itself. No instance is known in which his probity was ever suspected. His domestic habits were simple. He was an early riser, and when he had no particular business to transact, he spent his time in reading or in some other useful occupation. He was an excellent marksman, and rode much on horseback. Many of his journeys to Washington were performed in that way, and so particular was he in his attention to his horse, that he was never known to take his meals without first seeing that it received attention. Although his family were provided liberally with domestics, his habit was to wait upon himself, and he seldom called upon them for attentions; he required his children to imitate this example. He was systematic and orderly in all his habits; he had a place for *everything* and kept everything in its place. He particularly disliked any disturbance in the arrangement of his room; and was quick to detect it.

He was not insensible to praise or censure. He valued much the good opinion of his fellow-men--but highly as he prized the approbation of the public in regard to his public conduct, he valued far more the testimony of his companions and competitors in the same profession, and of his neighbors and friends, who had been witnesses of his conduct from his entrance upon the busy scenes of life. His reputation in distant parts of the land, was not greater than that he enjoyed in his own State and town. By his long and constant attention to the interest of his friends, he had become so endeared to them, that they never withheld an expression of their warmest approbation, or lost an opportunity of bestowing their renewed confidence and honors upon him. In all the domestic relations his character was without a stain. He was a devoted husband, an affectionate father, a kind neighbor, and a good master. His servants loved, yet feared to offend him. He rarely passed one of them, however small, without speaking a kind word.

One or two anecdotes will exemplify this trait. Judge White owned a number of slaves, and had a manager to see that they discharged their duty. It so happened that the family were unprovided with fuel at a time when the weather became extremely cold and unpleasant, and probably neither the manager nor servants were apprised of the fact, or if they were, considered that no one in his senses would think of turning out in such weather. The negroes were collected around a log-heap fire in their cabins, and the manager, a man of by no means slight figure, or delicate constitution, in his own comfortable quarters, all in full view of Judge White's dwelling. Upon being notified that there was no wood, the Judge, without saying a word to any one on the subject, protected himself as well as he could against the weather, went to the stable, harnessed the horses and hitched them to the wagon before it was known what he was doing. As soon as the news reached the cabins he was immediately waited on to know what were his wishes. He very mildly and calmly requested the manager and servants all to return to their homes, and make themselves comfortable; that he could, without the least inconvenience, endure the cold. Of course he was not left alone, however, but made it a point to drive the horses himself.

In relating this, the manager said, as long as he was with Judge White, after this, he never found the weather too bad to do whatever was necessary to be done.

A little domestic occurrence may indicate his careful oversight of the moral training of his family.

One Saturday in August, a grand-daughter and two nieces of Judge White went out to make their grandfather and uncle a visit. The Judge was then living in the suburbs of the town, and near him resided a Presbyterian clergyman. Soon after their arrival, it was announced by one of the company that the Rev. Mr. M—— had a peach tree loaded with ripe fruit, the first that had been seen that season. It was at once agreed by the whole party, including the Judge's daughter and a grand-daughter, residing with him, to visit the parson's garden some time during the day, and, if possible, procure some of the fruit. The day passed away pleasantly enough until dinner was over, when the little party assembled themselves together, and began to speculate as to the best means of accomplishing their object. After some consultation, one of the number, rather more expert than the rest, proposed that the daughter apply to the father for permission for the party to take a walk. The unseasonableness of the hour (for it was mid-day of mid-summer) struck the Judge's mind as rather odd for such recreation, and he at once began to interrogate as to the object, and direction, and extent of the ramble. All questions were promptly answered, that but a short walk was contemplated, not beyond the confines of an enclosure, containing some eighteen acres, which lay immediately in front of the house. Finally, consent was obtained, but it was expressly enjoined upon the young people that they should not transcend the bounds agreed upon. Bonnets were put on, and all hands started off in high spirits; some of them, perhaps, fearing that they were engaged in a rather hazardous expedition, but still not sufficiently impressed with the idea to induce them to abandon it. The guilty company sauntered along leisurely for some time, every now and then one of them turning round to see that no one was near who could or would report them. After making an almost entire circle, they reached at length that part of the lot which lay nearest the parson's. It was now determined that three of them should remain on watch, while the other two crossed the fence, went to the house and obtained permission to gather the fruit. However, upon reaching the place, they found the house closed, and the whole family absent. So, not liking the idea of being disappointed, they resolved, as circumstances did not seem to favor their obtaining the fruit by leave, that it would do no harm to help themselves to a few without leave. Aprons were filled, and a return made to join their former comrades. Now all was glee, each one feeling perfectly satisfied that they had not been discovered. Seats were procured under a large oak tree, the fruit disposed of, and the seeds scattered, and the little folks began to retrace their steps. They had got about half way when they met the Judge, who accosted them with "Well, children, you did not go outside?" "No, sir," responded all, save the daughter, who was silent, and feeling some misgivings about deceiving her father, returned and communicated all that had taken place, though remonstrated with by her friends, and urged not to expose them. This conduct, of course, drew upon them the displeasure of the Judge. He directed them to proceed to the house, and not to leave until his return. In the course of an hour, the whole five were summoned to appeared in his presence. There being no alternative, they obeyed — all the time feeling that they would rather face the world than the Judge, under the circumstances. After hearing that the Judge had witnessed the whole affair from a window on the second floor, and hearing a lecture of some twenty or thirty minutes' length, many promises of better conduct in future were given, and those of them not belonging to the family began to make arrangements for home. To this Judge White objected, assuring them that they should have tea in time to return before night. Here again the guilty trio were compelled to face him at table. Scarce a word was spoken. Now they were suffered to depart, and it became the Judge's time to take a stroll. He returned with his hands full of peach-seed, and presenting them to his children, said, he had always heard that stolen fruit was the best, and requested them to plant the seed, and thereby be saved the necessity of robbing a clergyman's orchard in future. There stand the trees now, a monument of disobedience, and other juvenile peccadilloes. The lesson was never forgotten.

The elevated moral qualities and the lofty mental powers, which are essential to the character of a perfect statesman were united in Judge White. Intrepidity and determination were combined with freedom from prejudice, and from excesses of every kind; and firmness of purpose, which seemed to calculate the consequences of doing his duty, with prudence in counsel, and energy in action. At the time of his death he had nearly completed his 68th year, and had been engaged uninterruptedly almost forty years in laborious public duties, and at the close of his political life, he exhibited the same purity of intention, and earnestness and ardor in the promotion of the public welfare, which were manifested in his earlier days.

He was strictly just in his dealings with all men, whether of business or friendly intercourse. He loathed anything like duplicity. His desire was, to be to all men in truth, what he appeared to them to be. His great purity of character placed him above the intrigues of politics, and, consequently, he was seldom or never cognizant even of those of his own party.

Upon this trait Dr. Ramsey remarks:

I can recollect well when he was last a candidate for the State Senate. He was too honest to act the demagogue, and had too high regard for the constituency to try to deceive or flatter them. He addressed only their cool and dispassionate judgment — neither laughing himself nor exciting laughter in others; I remember that he spoke of his competitor rarely, and that then he used the adjective *worthy* when he did mention him. He never spoke to *Buncombe* (excuse the vulgarism), and his high eulogy is that he never courted the people, nor sought to be their favorite. He tried to *deserve* applause rather than to receive it.

In relation to other points of Judge White's character, Dr. Ramsay says:

Another instance of benevolence, more private, but not less honorable to his memory, I may not omit to mention; as it was not heralded abroad, and, indeed, was known only to a few intimate friends. Rev. T. H. Nelson, pastor of the Old Presbyterian Church in Knoxville, was, as is well known, a poor man, and inadequately supported. In the erection of his humble residence he had not only exhausted his private means, but had contracted considerable debt, which he had no means of liquidating, and which hung like an incubus upon his drooping spirits. For some reason, too, a portion of his salary had not been paid; and these accumulated discouragements led him almost to despair. Judge White, though not a member of his church, hearing of the embarrassed condition of Mr. Nelson, called upon Captain Crozier, an elder in his church, and proposed to be one of eight, six, or even four, to assume Mr Nelson's debt, and take up his note, then in bank, for the amount. In the captain he found a congenial spirit. Four men were found who paid the bank debt; the note was sent to the minister cancelled, and his mind set at ease."

The judge was present once when an effort was being made to get up a dancing school. He favored the object by remarking, "that young men should learn to dance, for if they were unable to participate in that amusement, they would at parties resort to *cards*, which would lead to *gambling*. He was a great student; if he was not always reading, what was still better, he was always thinking. Earnest and profound thinking was a (perhaps the) prominent feature of his intellect. He thought quickly, yet deeply and accurately. What others found by a pains-taking search and tedious investigation, he obtained intuitively. To look at a subject at all was to penetrate it with an eagle's glance, to touch was to dissect, to handle was to unravel and analyze. He wrote well, yet his productions possessed few of the embellishments of art, and none of the ornaments of style, though always enlivened and brilliant from the flashes of a true and innate eloquence.

Like other truly great men, Judge White's manners were simple and unpretending. He rarely, out of the private circle, jested, and though an impressive and instructive talker, he never was loquacious. In large assemblies he was rather retiring and taciturn; and yet when he did speak, the attention of every hearer was arrested with the good sense, the originality, and the profundity of his remarks. Where he chose to use them as weapons of defence, he resorted effectually to irony, ridicule and sarcasm, and woe to the antagonist on whom he turned these instruments of torture, accompanied by the significant pointing of his finger, and the withering glance of his piercing eye—"I would rather be in hell," exclaimed a profane juror, "than to have been in ——'s shoes to-day, in the court-house." And yet to his friends he was habitually kind and benignant, and faithful. None were more so—he was grave without being haughty, and dignified without being arrogant. He had a lofty reserve and a consequential bearing, which belong to, and are inseparable from, superior mental endowments, and superior moral principle, and a severe public and private virtue; but nothing of the superciliousness that belongs to, or is affected, by the weak pretender or the pedagogue. *Mens conscia recti* did elevate him in his own, as well as in the esteem of others, and no one man than he better deserved the proud epitaph,

"Integer vitæ scelerisque purus."

On his first election to the United States Senate, he remarked to a number of young men around him, when the news arrived from Nashville, "Young gentlemen, never seek office—let office seek you."

He was exceedingly industrious, punctual, and methodical. An early riser, he was generally in town, and in his office, before the citizens had eaten their breakfast—though his residence was for many years two miles in the country. He was very domestic, and though qualified to figure in the public counsels, he was always fond of home and retirement. I mention a single other trait of character—his filial piety. He not only venerated his father, but he bowed before and idolized his mother. From her he inherited his genius, and his intellect—his quickness, and his originality, and her he never ceased to admire and reverence.

I have thus thrown together some of my recollections of the subject of your volume—some of my remarks are condensed from my manuscript of a future volume of my History of Tennessee. Take them for what they are worth. Your theme is an interesting one, and will, I doubt not, be a valuable contribution to Tennessee Literature, and Tennessee Biography. I am already impatient to see it.

Very respectfully, your obedient servant,

J. G. M. Ramsey.

Mecklenburg, Tenn., Dec. 18*th*, 1855.

But honest and benevolent as were all his intentions throughout life, his character would have been greatly defective without that confidence and serenity which he displayed amidst his many vexations and disappointments. Friends became estranged from him — he was called to surrender up parents, brothers, sisters, children, and wife—and to follow their cold bodies to "the home appointed for all the living." Yet in all afflictions he acknowledged the hand of God—and by them his heart was brought into a holy conformity to the divine will.

When through the machinations of his political opponents he was not only driven from an honorable station, but abused and insulted even along the highway, his patience and gentleness, and his noble saying that he could have no other feeling than pity for those who thus assailed him, showed that he lived in a continual sense of the presence of God; and committed his cause into the hands of Him unto whom reward and punishment belong.

A single characteristic anecdote of Judge White, extracted from Rev. James Gallagher's "Western Sketch Book," is here added:

From his youth, Judge White was characterized by profound reverence for the ordinances of the gospel. He was a regular attendant at the house of worship. And while he was a Presbyterian, that being the church of his fathers, and the church of his choice, he was benevolent and liberal towards other branches of the great Christian family. He gave to the Methodist church, at Knoxville, the ground on which their house of worship was built; and occasionally he would appear in the congregation and join them at their worship.

Now in those days there was a notable "presiding elder" in that region, called Father Axley; a pious, laborious, uncompromising preacher of the gospel, who considered it his duty to rebuke sin wherever it should presume to lift its deformed head within the limits of his district. And while Father Axley was a man of respectable talents, undoubted piety, and great ministerial fidelity, he had moreover a spice of humor, oddity, and drollery about him, that rarely failed to impart a characteristic tinge to his performances. The consequence was, that amusing anecdotes of the sayings and doings of Father Axley abounded throughout the country.

On a certain day, a number of lawyers and literary men were together in the town of Knoxville, and the conversation turned on the subject of preaching and preachers. One and another had expressed his opinion of the performances of this and that pulpit orator. At length Judge White spoke up: "Well, gentlemen, on this subject each man is, of course, entitled to his own opinion; but I must confess, that Father Axley brought me to a sense of my evil deeds, at least a portion of them, more effectually than any preacher I have ever heard." At this, every eye and ear was turned; for Judge White was never known to speak lightly on religious subjects, and, moreover, he was habitually cautious and respectful in his remarks concerning religious men. The company now expressed the most urgent desire that the Judge would give the particulars, and expectation stood on tiptoe.

"I went up," said the Judge, "one evening to the Methodist church. A sermon was preached by a clergyman with whom I was not acquainted; but Father Axley was in the pulpit. At the close of the sermon he arose, and said to the congregation: 'I am not going to detain you by delivering an exhortation. I have risen simply to administer a rebuke for improper conduct which I have observed here to-night.' This, of course, waked up the entire assembly; and the stillness was most profound, while Axley stood and looked for two or three seconds over the congregation. Then stretching out his large, long arm, and pointing with his finger steadily in one direction, 'now,' said he, 'I calculate that those two young men who were talking and laughing in that corner of the house, while the brother was preaching, think that I am going to talk about them. Well, it is true, that it looks very bad, when well-dressed young men, who you would suppose, from their appearance, belonged to some genteel, respectable family, come to the house of God, and instead of reverencing the majesty of Him that dwelleth therein, or attending to the message of everlasting love, get together in one corner of the house (the finger all this while pointing straight and steady as the aim of a rifleman), and there, through the whole solemn service, keep a talking, tittering, giggling, laughing, and annoying the minister, disturbing the congregation, and sinning against God. I'm sorry for the young men. I'm sorry for their parents. I'm sorry they've done so to-night. I hope they'll never do so again. But, however, that's not the thing I was going to talk about. It is another matter, and so important that I thought it would be wrong to suffer the congregation to depart without administering a suitable rebuke. Now,' said he, stretching his huge arm and pointing in another direction, 'perhaps that man who was asleep on the bench out there, while the brother was preaching, thinks I am going to talk about him. Well, I must confess, it looks very bad for a man to come into a worshipping assembly, and, instead of taking his seat like others and listening to the blessed gospel, carelessly stretch himself out on a bench and go to sleep! It is not only a proof of great insensibility with regard to the obligations which we owe to our Creator and Redeemer, but it shows a want of genteel breeding. It shows that the poor man has been so unfortunate in his bringing up, as not to have been taught good manners. He doesn't know what is polite and respectable in a worshipping assembly, among whom he comes to mingle. I'm sorry for the poor man. I'm sorry for the family to which he belongs.

I'm sorry he did not know better; I hope he will never do so again. But, however, that is not what I was going to talk about.' Thus Father Axley went on for some time; 'boxing the compass,' and hitting a number of persons and things that he was 'not going to talk about,' and hitting them *hard*, till the attention and curiosity of the audience were raised to the highest pitch, when finally he remarked: 'The thing of which I *was* going to talk, is *chewing tobacco*. Now, I do hope, when any gentleman comes here to church who can't keep from chewing tobacco during the hours of public worship, that he will just take his hat and put it before him, and spit in his hat. You know we are Methodists. You all know that our custom is to kneel when we pray. Now, any gentleman may see in a moment how exceedingly inconvenient it must be for a well-dressed Methodist lady to be compelled to kneel down in a great puddle of tobacco spit!'

"Now," said Judge White, "at this very time I had in my mouth an uncommonly large quid of tobacco. Axley's singular manner, and train of remark had strongly arrested my attention. While he was striking to the right and left, hitting those things that he was not going to talk about, my curiosity was roused, and conjecture was busy to find out what he could be aiming at. I was chewing my huge quid with uncommon rapidity, and spitting, and looking up at the preacher, to catch every word and every gesture, and when at last he pounced on the tobacco, behold, there I had a *great puddle* of tobacco spit! I quietly slipped the quid out of my mouth, and dashed it as far as I could under the seats, resolving never again to be found chewing tobacco in a Methodist church."

APPENDIX.

It was not until after the printing of the foregoing pages that there appeared, in Chapter L. of Vol. II. of Senator Benton's "Thirty Years' View," certain unfortunate misrepresentations respecting passages in Judge White's life. The evident fairness of intention with which Mr. Benton has written, and the value and authority of the opinions of one so able, generally reliable and experienced, render it the more requisite that these errors should here meet a suitable correction.

Mr. Benton, after having spoken of Judge White's life, services and character, so worthily and nobly as even by his own words to seem inconsistent in what follows, proceeds to state his reasons, why Judge White, although "so favored by his State during a long life, should have lost that favor in his last days, received censure from those who had always given praise, and gone to his grave under a cloud, after having lived in sunshine." He accounts for this version of Judge White's non-election, and for what he represents as disappointment and grief arising from it, as follows: "The reason is briefly told. In his advanced age he did the act which, with all old men, is an experiment, and with most of them, an unlucky one. He married again; and this new wife, having made an immense stride [!] from the head of a boarding-house table to the head of a Senator's table, could see no reason why she should not take one step more, and that comparatively short, and arrive at the head of the Presidential table." And lastly; he says that the various opponents of Mr. Van Buren, with intent to use Judge White in defeating Mr. Van Buren, "combined and worked in concert; and their line of operations was through the vanity of the victim's wife. They excited her vain hopes. And this modest, unambitious man, who had spent all his life in resisting office pressed upon him by his real friends, lost his power of resistance in his old age, and became a victim to the combinations against him—

which all saw and deplored, except himself." Mr. Benton further quotes as corroborating authority an extract from a letter, written not in the most delicate manner, by a member of Congress from Kentucky, Hon. R. P. Letcher, and published by his correspondent, after a fashion still less gentlemanly, as follows: "Judge White is on the track, running gaily, and won't come off; and if he would, *his wife won't let* him."

Some of these expressions are somewhat deficient in point of decorum; but they are liable to the much graver objection of unreasonable error.

To consider these points in the order of time, Mr. Benton says, in substance, that Mrs. White was vain and ambitious even to folly; that Judge White exhibited equal weakness by permitting her to govern his public conduct; and that the opponents of Mr. Van Buren made her the instrument of deceiving him with unfounded hopes of the Presidency, merely to further their own intrigues.

It will hardly be claimed that there was anything wrong or foolish, in a desire or aspiration on the part of Mrs. White, to see her husband President, and herself at the head of his table; for unless some privileges of some aristocratic order are to be set up, it is difficult to see on what principle *any* lady in the United States is to be blamed for the same; and much more then, was the desire a right one, when the circumstances of the case rendered its fulfilment so honorably probable.

But there is improbability in this imputation against Mrs. White. She was of a respectable and influential family; the daughter of Colonel Craven Payton, of Loudon County, Virginia, who lost his life in the war of 1812. Educated most thoroughly, and possessed of uncommon force of character, as well as great talent, she was one of the most attractive women in the Union. She had been unhappily married; and having been divorced, and nobly resolving not to be a burden upon her friends, she deliberately undertook to maintain herself and her two children by her own exertions. Having failed in an attempt to establish a school at Alexandria, she opened a boarding-house at Washington, and by financial tact, skill and perseverance, not only extricated herself from the pecuniary embarrassments which her first failure had brought upon her, but also accumulated a considerable property. Her house was well known as the resort of the most respectable class of visitors to Washington; and after Judge White had resided there while in that city, from 1820 to 1832, she became his wife. She was abundantly qualified for her new position, and she filled it with credit, attracting much attention, and giving great pleasure to her husband, who loved her and was proud of her.

But that he suffered himself to be governed by her desires in determining his official or public course, and especially that he was led away into a vain and foolish ambition by her, is a gratuitous assumption, totally irreconcilable with the main body of Mr. Benton's own statements respecting his character, and with the truth. He would doubtless do all that was possible to comply with her wishes; but there is not one action or word in all his life, which does not aid in demonstrating that in regard to the ordination especially of his public and official acts, he proceeded according to the principles of right and duty, without swerving aside in deference, either to his own comfort or pleasure, or to that of others, however near and dear.

It is not a little surprising that Mr. Benton should have reproduced, even with the modified form of expression which he has substituted, so vulgar a piece of slang and scandal as the remark about Judge White's being now "on the track," &c., and that even if he should desire to come off, "his wife won't let him." Mr. Letcher's conduct in relation to the nomination of Judge White, and his motives as indicated in this letter, were discreditable enough to have justified entire silence about the transaction; but since Mr. Benton has chosen to endorse the idle tale, it is best to answer it. Mr. Letcher was sharply reproved for his conduct and his words, and that by men not suspected of unduly favoring Judge White. Mr. Blair, of the Globe, says, in an editorial, Nov. 30, 1835, "With regard to Mr. Letcher's introduction of Judge White's wife into his political epistle, we think no reprehension too severe. Enjoying as he did last winter, the confidence and intimacy of Judge White and his friends, and the portion of his family then in this city living in social intercourse with that of the Judge, we cannot conceive a more ungrateful return than the ridicule he attempts to cast on the victim of his political intrigues, through his dearest domestic relation."

Whatever Mr. Blair's personal relations with Judge White may latterly have been, his words in this relation are entitled to great weight. And he more than once repeated the reproof.

But Mr. Benton represents Judge White as having been a mere tool in the hands of his wife; and the intelligent and passive victim through her means, of the deceitful machinations of Whigs, Calhoun men and disaffected Democrats, working together to defeat Mr.

Van Buren at any sacrifice. This has always been the representation of the partisans of Jackson and his successors, who of course were interested to maintain the reputation of their own managers. Mr. Blair, in the same articles which administered to Mr. Letcher a deserved castigation, gave, as his version of the facts, precisely the substance of Mr. Benton's representations.

It is true, as Mr. Benton himself states, that Judge White did not, like most political men, seek office, but merely consented to accept it, often refusing. As of other nominations, so was this true of the Presidential nomination. It was repeatedly pressed upon him before he consented to accept it; and when he did accept it, it was in answer to the calls of duty, not of ambition. His nomination, instead of being a contrived scheme of Calhoun, Clay, and other opponents of Van Buren, working together, was the spontaneous voice of his own and other States; and the ultimate partial abandonment of it was not the result of the further efforts of those same schemers, but of the machinations of those pretended friends of Judge White, within his own political party, who, along with General Jackson, were determined to continue what might be called a dynasty of Jacksonian Presidents, by the election of Van Buren. The abandonment of his nomination by the Legislature of Alabama, was one success for this combination; but the rebuke which they received in Tennessee, has been stated. That this is the real state of the case, satisfactory evidence has been adduced in the preceding chapters; especially in the twelfth, and the five next succeeding.

Mr. Benton also states very positively, and as a thing undisputed, another old partisan story, viz., that Judge White's alienation from the "Democratic" organization, and his opposition to Mr. Van Buren's administration, brought upon him the censure of his own State. Now it is very true that this alienation and opposition brought upon Judge White the bitter and unscrupulous enmity of the leading "Democrats," who, even then, both at Washington and in Tennessee, had degenerated from statesmen into mere managers and place hunters; and that the machinations of these men prevailed to carry, in the Tennessee Legislature, those instructions in response to which Judge White resigned his seat in the Senate of the United States. But it certainly is altogether incorrect to represent this vote as the voice of the State of Tennessee. The hearts of the mass of citizens in that State were steadily with Judge White, as well after his difference with Jackson and the other schemers for Van Buren, as before.

Was it a sign of departed confidence and a mark of reprobation, that in Jackson's own State, and against the whole immense weight of his official and personal influence, strenuously used and *abused*, Judge White had a majority of ten thousand, forty-three to Van Buren's eighteen in the Hermitage district itself? And although the administration members of the Tennessee Legislature did afterwards contrive to pass the instructing resolutions which it was well known would oblige Judge White to resign, yet the work was only done after a desperate struggle, and by the stringent operation of party and parliamentary machinery. It certainly was not done in obedience to any call from the people of Tennessee, for the subject was not passed upon or even alluded to during the election which constituted that Legislature. It was not the deliberate demand of a dissatisfied constituency; it was a sly contrivance, sprung and engendered by a few angry and unprincipled enemies. The indignation meetings which afterwards took place in various parts of Tennessee, the triumphal progress of Judge White's final journey from Washington to his home, were much truer indications of his place in the esteem of the voters whom he had so long and so faithfully represented.

Judge White never swerved from consistent practice accordant with the principles which governed his conduct. These principles were perhaps too pure and lofty to harmonize with the views of most of those who then led the "Democratic" hosts. At any rate, it was Judge White who *did not* deviate from pure and consistent Democratic principles, and from upright political conduct, but Jackson and the remaining friends of Mr. Van Buren who *did* so deviate; and thus it was, according to all experience, that the delinquents expended all their anger, and strove to cast all the blame of the difference in opinion, upon him whose unstained honor and undeviating consistency was a standing monument of their own duplicity and shame.

As Mr. Benton says, Judge White, although of measured and quiet deportment, was a man of strong feelings. He was peculiarly alive to anything savoring of ingratitude, meanness, or deceit. Such being the case, it would not be strange if the proceedings of these men in the Jackson and Van Buren interest, who had formerly been his own personal friends, had received so many kindnesses from him, and had made so many professions, not only of general good feeling, but of efficient advocacy and support in that very nomination — it would not be strange if these evidences of foul play touched him deeply. They did; but that either they, or the ignoble mortification of a disappointed office-seeker, were causes sufficient to shorten a life so pure, self-sustained and noble, so unstained by passion, and so uninfluenced by selfish interests, is a proposition absurd on its face. It is, moreover, directly in conflict with the uniform assertions of Judge White himself, before, during, and after the election; and whatever distrust is usually felt of such professions from men in public life, probably no man will impugn the absolute and perfect truthfulness of Judge White, even in a matter so immediately concerning himself.

These misrepresentations, in short, are neither even presumptively reasonable, nor based upon correct statements of actual fact. It is as absurd as it is untrue to assert that after a long life of honor and usefulness, passed, before the sight of all men, upon an eminence so lofty as that to which Judge White's integrity and abilities lifted him, and under the searching gaze which always scrutinizes such men, without a single stain or shadow of folly or wrong doing—it is as absurd as it is untrue to assert that the patriot grown old in the practice of wisdom and in disinterested toil, closed the long succession of his honorable and honored actions, with the exhibition of superannuated folly and imbecile grief charged upon him by his former opponents, and yet reproduced even by the best of their survivers.

It remains to suggest adequate reasons for these erroneous imputations of passive folly, of weak ambition, and of weaker lamentation. They are not wanting.

First. That which is described as having been the unresisting submission of a weak old man, was singly perseverance in a long life rule "never to seek office, but to let office seek him." Such were Judge White's own words; and as always before, so did he now quickly prepare to respond to the call of his fellow-countrymen, if it should be uttered. It was a thing of course, that his unmoved and dignified conduct should, in the eyes of the greedy, grasping and intriguing class of selfish politicians, who at that period descended like a cloud of locusts upon the land, seem to be foolishness and imbecility. Nor were they the first shrewd men who have been "wiser in their own generation" than the loftier and more far-sighted, whose principles of action and views of *true* expediency they could neither practice nor comprehend.

But—with due respect be it said—it is, secondly, to be observed, that this verdict from Mr. Benton seems easily to be accounted for by his very general habit of attributing all the actions of his prominent political cotemporaries of opposite belief, to motives purely selfish and personal. He has given, for Judge White's conduct, such reasons as it is his habit to give for the conduct of many other eminent men; although, indeed, he has not attributed such to Gen. Jackson, or to any others of those with whom his own political communion has been undisturbed. The "Panama Mission" is said to have been contrived and used, only as an Administration measure, in the behalf of President Adams and Mr. Clay; vol. I., p. 65. The Tariff of 1828 was advocated by Mr. Clay and the Administration, with reference to the election of 1828, as a means of beating Jackson, not for the good of the country; vol. I., p. 95, *et seq.* Clay and Calhoun desired the Tariff question to be withdrawn from politics, because they could not use it to become Presidents with; vol. I., p. 314. Calhoun attempts to become President by Nullification; p. 340. Both these gentlemen, Chap. LXXXV., arranged the "Compromise of 1833" with sole reference to their own Presidential aspirations. Clay, Calhoun, and Webster, join to aid the United States Bank in procuring a re-charter, that they may overthrow Jackson and rise by his fall; Chap. XCVIII. Indeed, assertions and implications to similar effect are too numerously sprinkled throughout Mr. Benton's work, to permit more than a very few of them to be referred to. It need not be supposed that that honest and upright statesman has consciously wronged any man. Such a conviction has not improbably been the legitimate result of his observations. His error in this single case is simply failure to recognise an exception to a rule unhappily generally correct.

THE END.